D1135189

The First Mn . . .
Second To None

THE AUTHOR

Richard Krom, a Great Grandson of Edward H. Bassett, developed an interest in history at a young age. Perhaps it was the book on Andrew Jackson from the bedroom shelf or the classic tales his mother read the family in the evening that sparked his curiosity. It could have been the large photographic history of World War 2 or the days sitting beside Grandma Bassett as she read her husband's diaries from the Spanish American War that kindled the flame.

After many years spent reading about the Civil War and motivated by the revelation that his Great Grandfather's letters may still exist, he began the long search to find them. Nearly nine years elapsed before this historian finally acquired copies of Edward's letters.

This work is the culmination of his desire to tell the heroic tale and preserve these treasured documents for the future.

The 1st MN...
Second to None

A narrative of the life and death
struggles of the soldier in the Civil
War, including 218 letters by
Edward H. Bassett

Richard G. Krom

COVER ART BY: JAMES M. KROM
Jameskromnaturalimages.com

Published by Richard Krom
Rochester, Minnesota

FirstMNPatriot@aol.com

First Printing 750 copies
June 2010

Library of Congress Control Number:

ISBN: 978-0-9827562-4-9

Published by: Richard G. Krom

Printed in U.S.A. by:
Bang Printing
Brainerd, Minnesota

Includes bibliography and index.

TABLE OF CONTENTS

ACKNOWLEDGEMENTS

Over the course of the years that have elapsed since the idea to write this book first formed in my mind, many people have provided assistance, needed advise, information and most of all encouragement. To all of these I owe a deep debt of gratitude for helping me fulfill my purpose of preserving the letters of my Great Grandfather Edward H. Bassett, written while he served his country in the Civil War.

To Johnnie Rice, a delightful lady, who kindly provided me with copies of the transcribed letters, I shall ever be indebted.

Without the tireless research efforts of my wife Sharon, I never could have told the story with as much interest, detail and illustration.

A sincere thanks is also in order for the kind assistance provided by the staff and volunteers at both the Nobles County Genealogical & History Group and The Minnesota State History Center.

The illustrations and photos in this book were chosen primarily from sources of the time. Harper's Weekly and Frank Leslie's Illustrated Weekly were two of the primary sources of information for Edward Bassett and his fellow soldiers and the papers Edward often sent home to his family. The drawings of numerous illustrators that were present in the field, lend an authenticity untainted by time. Numerous stationery illustrations taken from the letters and envelopes reveal the depth of patriotic fervor that covered the land.

Most of the photographs were taken by Mathew Brady or his assistants and have been reproduced from the collections of The Library of Congress.

Richard G. Krom

PREFACE

The First Minnesota Volunteer Infantry Regiment served with honor, valor and distinction unsurpassed in the annals of American Military History. From its beginning as the first unit to come to the aid of the nation, to its last battle at Mine Run, the men of this outstanding regiment never yielded or retired before the enemy unless ordered to do so. Even then, they did so only under protest and always in good order. Perhaps the quality that permeated this exceptional unit, formed from hardy men of all occupations and persuasions and gathered from the small towns and frontiers of Minnesota, has already been best conveyed by the words of one of its members. Lieutenant William Lochren, in his "Narrative of the First Regiment," published in 1890 in the book Minnesota in the Civil and Indian Wars, wrote:

> ".....this regiment, which took part in every battle of the Army of the Potomac during the first three years of the war, achieving a reputation certainly **second to no regiment** in the service, and which, on the memorable field of Gettysburg, performed such an act of successful heroism as has no parallel in history.". . . . . "this regiment, whose perfection in discipline and in the execution of every movement of company and battalion tactics and care for personal appearance, made it a favorite and model regiment in camp or on review, and whose espirit du corps, pride in its reputation as a regiment, and the chivalric, soldierly feeling pervading all ranks would never brook thought of defeat or disgrace, and never permitted it to

hesitate or falter on any occasion". ..... "The fame and glory of the regiment need not be dwelt on, it is known throughout the country and especially to all the people of this state (Minnesota)"...... "Every member justly regards his own connection with the regiment as the highest honor of his life, - the one thing respecting himself to which his own posterity will always refer with greatest pride. May our state always send forth such regiments whenever its safety, or the safety or honor of our beloved country, shall call its sons to arms."

The First Minnesota Volunteer Infantry Regiment was mustered into service at Fort Snelling on April 29, 1861. In the three years following, the regiment would be involved in 61 engagements, including 34 battles, and numerous skirmishes that decimated the battle lines of this proud regiment and left only a large handful to be mustered out on April 29, 1864.

This chronicle is not a treatise on military tactics, rather, it is the story of the struggles in the everyday lives of these American Heroes. Based on the personal letters of Edward H. Bassett, its purpose is to relate their story of valor, glory, deprivation, hardship and unquestioning devotion duty.

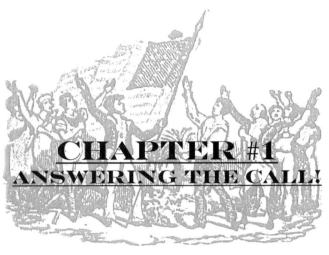

CHAPTER #1
ANSWERING THE CALL!

THREE CHEERS FOR
THE RED WHITE AND BLUE

Following the fall of Fort Sumter, April 13, 1861, President Lincoln called for 75,000 men to serve for three months. Minnesota Governor Alexander Ramsey, in Washington at the time, met the next morning with Secretary Simon Cameron at the War Department. Governor Ramsey, who had come to offer 1,000 men to support the government, was asked to put the offer in writing, as the Secretary was on his way to see President Lincoln. This offer became the earliest tender[1] of troops in the war. The proposal was accepted and the next day Governor Ramsey telegraphed Lieutenant Governor Ignatius Donnelly requesting that he issue an immediate call for volunteers. The first volunteer to sign was Josias R. King, who would later become Captain of Company G, of the First Minnesota Regiment. He became the first volunteer to serve in the war. By April 29th, ten regiments had reported to Fort Snelling, on the Mississippi River, at St. Paul, Minnesota. Edward H. Bassett, Private in The First Minnesota Volunteer Infantry was mustered into service on April 29, 1861.

---

[1] Tender in this instance means "an unconditional offer."

EDWARD H. BASSETT [2]

Edward H. Bassett was a young man 19 years of age, working on his father's farm near Morristown, Minnesota when the call went out for volunteers. He stood 5'-7 3/4" tall and weighed 150 lbs. He was a fine looking lad with black hair and steel grey eyes. His dedication and sense of duty to his country reflected the proud heritage of many generations

[2] This photo of Edward has often appeared in publications. It has always been printed in reverse, the US on the belt buckle showing backwards. This is the correct version.

of his family who landed in America with some of the earliest immigrants from Scotland and who came to America's aid in many wars and battles in the past. Like most of the young men with whom he enlisted and served, he was a quiet man and one that accepted conditions as they were, without complaining. He liked army life and as his letters testify he took an interest in the places he went and people he met. He had an innate sense of curiosity, an inquisitive mind and a spirit of adventure. He also manifests a bent for invention or at least innovation as illustrated by "D", a correspondent from his company for the Faribault Central Republican:

"We slept under the canopy of heaven, or one of leaves as we chose, we generally chose the former as being better ventilated! And the soft sand was our bed, unless like Ed Bassett, we constructed a hammock of grape vines, suspended between two trees."

There was another similar incident reported by one of the officers in his writings when he said:

"We are exhausted from the march in the rain and the men are sleeping tonight in the mud except Ed Bassett, who has fashioned himself a hammock of vines and is sleeping comfortably high and dry."

As his unit's service wore on and the ranks thinned with each battle, the toll on his morale is only slightly perceptible in his writings. In most instances, it appears in his longing to be home with his family and all they enjoyed doing together. The fatigue that broke many men is sometimes apparent in his letters where his beautiful script writing degrades to scribbling. But then, he had marched for days in the heat, slept only a few hours at night and ran the last few miles to join a battle where he fought for hours and, then, marched another 25 miles before joining another battle. The demands made on these men would seem to go beyond the endurance of mere mortals.

Edward volunteered, on April 25th as a private. He was one of a handful of men in the company who endured the full three years of its enlistment. The strong love of family that was so much a part of him is manifest by his frequent correspondence throughout his service. His 218 letters to his family are presented here largely as written with only very minor changes or corrections to the grammar, punctuation and spelling in hope of presenting them with all of their original flavor. Some editing has been done to minimize repetition as well as to maintain continuity to the purpose of this writing. Fifty of these letters were transcribed by the author from copies of the originals. The remainder were taken from transcriptions done by family members in the 1960's and graciously made available so that this tale could be told.

So begins the chronicle of the young farm lad from the frontier of Minnesota, who like so many others, is ....

Going to war..........

Faribault, Rice Co.
Apr. 25, 1861.

Dear Parents

The news has come from St. Paul. We are to start there at noon today. The boys are in good spirits. We will stay in Northfield tonight. I have got my money from Mr. Thaxter and can get all I want from the boys. Our company numbers 87. I will leave my things at Mr. Messick's.

I will write at every opportunity and let you know how we are getting along.

My love to all,

E. H. Bassett

FORT SNELLING MINNESOTA
Courtesy of Minnesota Historical Society
Artwork by John Casper Wild 1844

Fort Snelling
April 30, 1861

Dear Friends,

Once more for the news. We arrived here yesterday and are now guarding the fort. It is situated on the Minnesota river about one mile from its mouth. There is a splendid country around here. We will most likely stay here about 30 days and drill. We had a fine time coming up the river. We came on the Ocean Wave up to St. Paul on Saturday and stayed at the Snelling house over Sunday. We have received our arms and are now going to drill for some time. We got our blankets, shirts and socks. We have plenty of room and a pretty good time generally. We are going to get our mail at St. Paul. I am in good health and like the country pretty well. The fort is old and crumbling in some places but the houses are warm and large. We had a good time coming up here and plenty to eat, drink and sleep on.

Our Captain has been promoted to another office. We hope Lieutennant McKune to Captain; Mr. Messick to 1st Lieutennant; and Wm. Smith 2nd Lieutennant Governor Gorman has been appointed to command the Regiment.

E. H. Bassett

Fort Snelling
May 12th, 1861.

Dear Parents

Up to this date I have not heard from you but have written three letters & sent two or three papers but I think it is on account of the mail not being very regular between Faribault & Morristown. I am well and hope that this will find you the same. The steam packet [3] Northern Bell came up here from St. Paul yesterday with a pleasure party. They had a fine time, there was a dress parade & a good time in general. The Steamer Northerner is going to come up here from St. Paul this P.M. & the Rt. Rev. Bishop Whipple is going to preach at four this P.M. This morning's paper says that there has been a vesel fired upon at St. Louis but it may not be so. There is some sickness among the soldiers but there is but one dangerous case - there is one of our company in the hospital & he is getting better. There has been considerable excitement in camp for two or three days on account of the Gov. request that all the soldiers enlisted at the present time should enlist for three years or during the war. The Gov. has offered as a reward $100 to be distributed among the first Company so enlisted. I do not know what to do but am strongly inclined to enlist if I do I shall come home in a few weeks, the officers of the Faribault Guards will all enlist.

---

[3] A passenger boat carrying cargo and mail on a regular schedule.

I went up to the Minnehaha falls the other day it is about two miles from here   the picture in Life Illustrated is as perfect a representation of them as could be taken you can go in behind them and see through the water as it falls about 20 or 25 feet down a perpendicular rock. It is the most magnificent thing that I ever saw.

Period Photo – Unattributed

We have received our hats and pants and are going to have a coat and pair of draws pretty soon. I have not received any money yet but will most likely before long. If I enlist for three years I will draw double pay from the time of the second enlistment to the time that the first enlistment is up. I do not like to enlist again untill I have heard from you. I have plenty of time to write letters & the government furnishes paper in abundance but the postage & envelops we have to furnish ourselve which can be done very easyly at present.

I was calculating to write a short letter when I began but have got a long one before I thought what I was about. I shall wate with patience for an answer from some of you. I do not like camp life as well as I might but am not sorry that I enlisted yet nor have I been. If I should enlist again I would be discharged in one year at most as I do not think that the war will last longer.

Please write soon and let me know how you are getting along and all about the folks in general.

We have a mail every day.

From your unworthy son

Edward H. Bassett

Fort Snelling
May 15th, 1861

Dear Brothers[4]

I received a letter on the 19th ins.(instant) And was glad to hear that you were all well & had got done sowing. (planting wheat) I do not have much to do and have a pretty good time we have to be out on parade about 3 hours in the fore & 3 in the afternoon. The roll is called at six in the morning and at sundown & at nine at night. There has 5 companies gone to St. Paul this morning they are going to have a kind of a picnic I believe. There was a splendid war horse presented to Colonel Gorman yesterday he is a very large chestnut and very smart. I came across two of our old schoolmates yesterday one of them was Henry Dresden & the other one of the Rice boys. They live in Wabashaw County and belong to the Wabashaw Volunteers. They knew me at the first sight but I would not know either of them from Adam. Captain McKune & Lieutenant Messick & Charles Parker have gone back to Rice Co. to get recruits for the three year service. I do not know whether I will enlist for three years or not & shall wate untill I hear from home but I would advise you to stay at home and help the folks get

---

[4] Edward had two brothers, George and Elford, and two sisters, Ella and Anna.

along. There are about sixty of our company going for three years or during the war which I do not think will last three years. If I do enlist for three years I shall come home and stay eight or ten days. We have a pretty good band of music there is three of the Rice Co. Volunteers in it. I see by the morning paper that there has been another riot in St. Louis. The US troops have taken the St. Louis arsenal and are now occupying Camp Jackson. We intend to go up to St. Anthony tomorrow and see the falls & suspension bridge it's about seven miles.

They speak of Anna & Elford missing me tell them that I miss them to & that they will most likely see me again in a few months at most.

Tell mother that I would like to have some of them pies & would like to know how she came to know that we had coffee made of beans. Our coffee is store coffee of the right sort with plenty of sugar. We have bread that is good enough for any body and plenty of apples once a day.

1st PS,, tell father that he may send my rifle by telegraph as soon as practicable if he can get along without it.

2nd PS,, write soon

3rd PS,, give my best respects to the girls in Morristown.

From Your Brother in Company G,

Edward H. Bassett

Fort Snelling, Minnesota

Dear parents & friends at home,

I received your letter of the 15th yesterday and was glad to hear that you were all well. I am well & have enlisted for three years or during the war & was glad that you were willing that I should do it. There is between sixty & seventy five in the company now that are going for that length of time and I do not know where I could do better at the present time. We will be clothed & fed & taken good care of when sick & receive eleven dollars per month in cash and one dollar contingent expenses. We expect to go up to Fort Ridgley before long but we do not know exactly when. Major Dike told me that we were going up there & stay with him for a month or two this summer which would suit me first rate as it will be very healthy there and we will have a good place to drill. I was intending to go home this week but I do not care about it now if we go up there it will be just as near if not nearer when up there than we are now to home and I would rather be home a month from now than now as I think that things will look a great deal nicer then, than now. I suppose that you have seen Capt. McKune & Leut. Messick before now we expect them back about Wednesday with enough men to fill out our company. There will be some company go up to the fort with us but I do not know what one. We will have better quarters there than we have here but we have pretty good quarters here, they are plastered and are warmed by a fireplace. There was no parading here yesterday it rained all the day before and part of the night. I took Cyrus Aldriches place on guard the night before last. He got his discharge and wanted to go home and I took his place and let him go. We have to stand as sentry once in about two weeks when the company is full we stand in two hours then can sleep four and so on for (xzx)* twenty four. (at the point shown by the asterisk Edward had crossed out an error and noted after it, "so much for pretty."

We are going up to St. Anthony tomorrow to a kind of picknic if it is pleasant & expect to have a good time. It is a very pleasant morning and the soldiers are all in good spirits. We are expecting our shoes and coats this week and we will most likely move as soon as we get our uniforms.

I do not think that we shall leave the state this summer. There is an Ambrotype gallery just out of the fort. They took the Faribault Company on the field with the guns at the shoulder. I shall have my likeness taken this summer to suit myself when we get our pay.[5] It is quite cold here but things are beginning to look green. I am glad that the girls are going to school and suppose that Elford will go to. What has become of the school house on the hill. What kind of fish does George catch? I sent word by Cyrus Aldrich that I would be home in a few days but I do not expect to start as soon now for I can get off better after we move than now but I will come home during the summer. I suppose that wages will be pretty high in the harvest but I think that the grain will fetch a good price.

I thank you for those stamps but had a supply on hand for the present. I have plenty of time and paper and ink and spend considerable of my time writing. There are some books among the boys and papers every morning and so I get along pretty fair. This is a long letter & I must quit.

So good bye

PS. Tell George to write and I will answer him. I suppose that you have got the corn planted

(The following insert is a copy of Edward's hand written closing from this letter)

---

[5] The picture of Edward shown earlier was likely not taken at Fort Snelling as has been reported in some works, as the men did not receive regulation uniforms for several months after leaving the fort.

Fort Snelling
May 23, 1861

Dear Parents,

As there is an opportunity to send a word to you and let you know that I am well. The new recruits arrived here last night and have been mustered into the service and the three months men discharged. We have a full company of 101 men all in good spirits. Captain McKune brought a letter from you. I was glad to hear from you. I shall come home some time between now and the 4th of July. We are going to go up to Fort Ridgley before long. It will be nearer there then it is from here. We have had a very pleasent time since we came here and I hope to keep up our spirits. We have not received any money yet but will before long, I expect. We were up to St. Anthony the day before yesterday to a fine dinner. We were well treated and had a good time in general. There are several of the boys that I know in the recruits. Among them is Wm Ramsey, Johnathan Goodrich, Sam Lilly, Joseph Bemis, A.C. Strickland and Jim Beophy. The crops look pretty well between here and St. Anthony. I hope that you will have a good crop this year. I will mail a paper for you this afternoon. Mr. Mckune is very much pleased with his company. I would send my best respects to all the home guards and would hope that they will keep up their organization. Tell George to write whether there is anything to write about or not. I will answer.

Good bye for this time,

E. H. Bassett

Fort Snelling
May 30, 1861

Dear Brother,

I am now in quarters with the regiment of Volunteers at this Fort. We number about one thousand men. We have to drill twice every day. Govener Gorman is the head officer. There was a grand muster yesterday but I was not out on account of not being very well. I was out on guard the night before six hours. I have got a bad cold but it is getting better now. I put a paper in the office this morning for you. There is a news boy along every morning with papers for sale at five cents each. On the morning that we left Faribault, Mr. McKune gave me some money from you. I thank you very much for it and will return it the first opportunity. We are to get our uniforms this week and there is some talk of our leaving this Fort for another company, but I do not know when we will leave nor where we shall go. There is a fine view from the Ft. walls of the Mississippi River and the Minnesota. The town of Mendota is about one-half mile Southeast of here. It is a little larger than Morristown. The Minnesota River runs between Mendota and Ft. Snelling and there is a ferry across the Mississippi here it runs by current.[6] Some of the boys went up to the Minnehaha Falls yesterday and had a good time. The boys have just come in from drilling and are pretty jolly. We have a daily mail here from St. Paul. The boats run up the Minnesota River every day. There are no boats running above here on the Mississippi now. Our Captain, Wm. H. Dike has been appointed Major and we have appointed Lt. McKune-Captain, N.S. Messick–first lieutenant, and Wm. Smith second of Faribault. We will most likely stay here until about the 20th or 30th of this month. You must write to me and let me know how you are getting along.

P.S.) Direct letters to Fort Snelling, Faribault Guards.

From,   *Edward H. Bassett*

On May 28, The First Minnesota Volunteer Regiment, Company G, of which Edward H. Bassett was a member, and Company B were ordered to Fort Ridgley, where they relieved two companies of regular army infantry.

---

[6] Ferry boats of this time were often propelled by the current of the river.

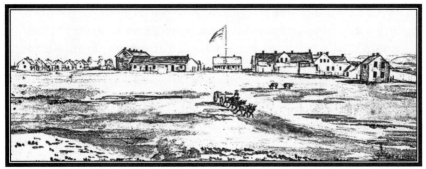

Drawing of Fort Ridgley dated 1855–Artist Unknown
Probably by Alfred M. Sully

Fort Ridgley Minnesota
June 2, 1861.

Dear Mother and Father

We have been moved out here by order of the Sec. of War to releave the regulars that are stationed here. We left Snelling on Tuesday last on the Franklin Steel, a river packet, and came up here in two days and one night. We have better quarters here. The fort is not walled but the walls of the buildings are of stone. It is situated about one-half mile from the Minnesota River. I am well and hearty and hope you are the same. I like the country around here very much. The prairie is very nice and the country nice in general. I am in hopes of coming home before long but cannot tell when. It will take about two days to walk home. It is about 40 or 45 miles from St. Peter. The Stillwater guards are here with us now.

I am one of the company cooks. There are four of us. We have to cook for 10 days. We are getting so that we get along very well now but don't have much spare time. I am in hopes that there will be a chance for me to come home this month. The Major has promised me a furlough of 20 days and I intend to get it as soon as possible.

I expect that we will go up to Redwood in July to

the Indian agency. We are having a good time and enjoying ourselves first rate. Have plenty to eat and drink and not much work which suits us well. It is late and I must quit this time for tonight.

Tell George to write and I will answer. I suppose that he is busy, but that is no excuse.

From the Volunteer

E. H. Bassett

Fort Ridgely, Minnesota

P.S There will be eleven one minute guns fired tomorrow in honor of Captain Ellsworth

Fort Ridgley
June 6, 1861

Dear Brother,

I take this opportunity to write to you. I am well. We are now stationed at Fort Ridgely on the Minnesota River about 45 miles from St. Peter. We came up on the Frank Steele, a La Crosse and St. Paul railroad packet. We were on the river two days and one night. It is about 150 or 200 miles by land, I believe and about twice that distance by the river. It is the most crooked river that I ever saw. We left Snelllng at 10 minutes past 11 on the 25th of May and passed St. Peter at one at night, Mankato at sunrise the next morn and arrived at Ridgley a little after sundown. I like the country very well around here as far as I have seen it. It is prairie on the East side of the river and timber on the West. The fort is on the East side. There was a company of regulars stationed here when we came. They have gone now to Pittsburg Penn. We expect to go up to Redwood this month to the Indian settlement and have some fun. There is 6 pieces of artilery here and we will take them along with us most likely. There is two 6 pound, 1 twelve, one 24, and two howitsers all brass and in perfect order. Maj. Sherman who is now in Baltimore went from here there. There is a boat just landed here I can hear it whistle. I have not drilled any since I came here. I was appointed one of the cooks but my time will be up day after tomorrow, having served ten days. There are three of us. One is John Goodrich and the other is a fellow from Faribault. We get along first rate. I suppose that the crops look pretty nice by this time there. I have not seen many farms this spring but what I have looked pretty well. I intend to get a furlough as soon as I can and come down there and see the folks. It is about 70 miles I believe. We now have one mail per week but they are going to have it twice I believe.

The government has got some 50 mules and 5 yoke of oxen. The men that take care of them or are in performance of any extra duty get 25 cents extra pay. But I would favor keeping away from the mules in particular on account of their playful way of boxing. There was a man (Frances Gibson) got kicked and nearly killed by them but he is getting better now. You must excuse my miserable blots and crooked penmanship this time. I will try and do better next time. I'll send you a song which is pretty good for the occassion written by our 4th Sergt.

From,

E. H. Bassett.

Fort Ridgely
June 19th, 1861

Dear Friends,

I expect I shall soon be on my way to Harrisburg, Pa. and I will write you a line. The boat is here now and we are getting ready to start. The camp is all going but 24 to guard the garrison until they can be releaved

by Federal troops. I am well and glad to go, there was a company of men from Faribault came up here yesterday but they are not going to stay. They report things alright in Faribault. I did calculate to come home before leaving for the South but cannot now. Will most likely stop at Snelling and if we do I will write but if not I will write at the earliest opportunity, We are all in good health and glad to start for the scene of action. I would like to be there at the camp meeting but cannot. We were intending to go to the Indian Pow-Wow but did not go. Mr. B. H. Soule is going with us. He is well. The camp is getting ready now and I must close.
So Good By,

E. H. Bassett

CHAPTER #2
OFF TO THE WAR

On June 14, 1861, a dispatch from Washington ordered the First Minnesota to Washington by way of Harrisburg, Pennsylvania. The St. Paul Pioneer reported the impact that those orders had on the regiment:

"The news that the First Regiment was ordered to Harrisburg was transmitted to Fort Snelling about ten o'clock Friday night. Almost everybody save the sentinels was asleep. The colonel and staff had the information first, and it was received with every demonstration of delight. Our informant says the colonel fairly howled with joy. The news soon spread to the quarters of the company officers, and then to the men and such rejoicing took place as had never before occurred since the regiment was mustered in. The men did not stop to put on their clothing but rushed around, hurrahing and hugging each other, as wild as a crowd of school boys at the announcement of a vacation. There is no sham gratification at being ordered forward. The men enlisted for actual service in the field and not to garrison forts. Many of them are farmers, and would much prefer being at home this busy season than to spend the summer anywhere in the state."

During the trip to Washington, the First Minnesota passed through Baltimore, Md., where previous regiments had been molested–even attacked–and some killed on their way to Washington D.C.

1st Camp of the 1st Reg. Minnesota Vol.
Washington D.C.
June 28, 1861

Dear Parents, Brothers and Sisters,

We started for Harrisburg on the 18th of June at 3 PM and arrived at Harrisburg on the 25th at noon. We came on the boat from Ridgely to LaCrosse and then took the cars to Chicago, thence to Ft. Wayne, thence to Pittsburgh then to Harrisburg and camped one night and started for Washington. We arrived at about noon and marched through the city with loaded gun. We passed peaceable and did see but a very few white people but plenty of negro. At one place the citizens gave three cheers for the Union flag and three groans for Jeff Davis. The Stars and Stripes reign there now. The police were plenty and active in keeping peace. One man was going to cheer for Jeff and there was a policeman who collared him and commanded silence. It is said that there was a man there going to cheer for Davis and one of the Co. B. the Stillwater Guard grabbed him and said dam you, cheer for the Union or I will knock your D---d head off. He pimped up, turned around and complied with the order. There is not many non-union people there now. They have most all gone South and joined the Army. The people of Maryland between Washington and the line are nearly all for the union and nearly every house that we passed that was in sight the women and children all would come to the windows and door and waved flags, handkerchiefs and gave every sign of satisfaction that they could. There is a guard all along the R.R. between Wash, and Penn. to guard the road and the cars are not allowed to go over 7 or 8 miles per hour. I saw several bridges that were burnt but they are all repaired now. The track is laid down again. I have not seen a secession flag as yet but there is plenty of them over across the pontoon, although our troops occupy Arlington Heights and the picket guards are fired upon nearly every night. We came from Harrisburg to Baltimore in the same (train) cars that the Mass. Reg. came in. They are pretty well smashed..

We are camped in sight of the Capitol building, I have not seen Gen. Scott nor President Lincoln but some of the boys went down past the White House and they said that they saw Gen. Scott sitting on the steps. I have been told that the government does not intend to make an advance movement until after Congress sets. There are a great many troops encamped in and around Washington. We have plenty of room, good tents with eight in a tent or mess. We had a pretty hard time traveling. On our way we traveled day and night but we are now getting some rest. The crops look pretty good all along but the best corn that I saw was in Penn. except some that I saw in the city this morning in a garden. I saw some of the guards on the R.R. on the other side of Balt. (Baltimore) cutting wheat for the farmers. Their saying is that a soldier will not work but they were at work showing that the N.Y. boys will work and it is thought, that the Minnesota boys would do the same if they were wanted. Our Captain has not arrived yet but we are expecting him every train. He will be here as soon as he can after being relieved at Ridgely. Lieutennant Messick is commanding officer of Co. G. I wrote a letter when we left Ridgely and have written one since but could not get a chance to mail it. We were not allowed to leave the cars at any of the stations to go away any distance.
Washington 29, 1861

There was some sixty secessionist captured here yesterday afternoon and one killed. They came spying around the camps and were bold enough to approach one of the guards of the Vermont Reg. and succeeded in getting his gun away when the guard sprang at him, regained his gun and knocked him down. They captured some sixty and shot one through the head. They were taken into camp and a guard of 100 men placed over them. There has been an engagement down the Potomac. There was a small boat sailing down the river and it was fired into by some 500 rebels. There was about 30 soldiers on board the boat. They killed the gunner and the Captain was just sighting the gun again and a ball came over and killed him. The boat was then run back and she is marooned along the river I did not hear of this until last night.

The U.S. Senator Cyris Aldrich has offered to frank all letters for the Minnesota Reg. I send you the print of one of the bullets that we are to use they are about one inch in length.

Photo of actual 58 caliber bullet from the Civil War– one ounce of soft lead

I am well & the whole camp in fact the whole Regiment is in good health, weather is very warm & we feel pretty lazy but we will get used to it in a few weeks. We stayed in the old First Congregational Church the first night that we got here & slept in the pews. We rested pretty well not having had any chance to sleep since we left Minnesota of any account. The boys are all well pleased that they have got as near the enemy as what they have & the Colonel is trying to get a chance to be sent over into Virginia as soon as practicable but we cannot tell what we will do next. We are to wait further orders. The city of Washington is a right smart little town & if the secessionists get possession of it there will be some wool pulled on both sides. Maj. Sherman's battery is here & the West Point Battery also. They go out on the drill twice every day & are a hardy looking set of men.

Balloon View of the city of Washington DC
Harper's Weekly July 27, 1861

I have not seen any country to compare with Minnesota for soil except Wisconsin since we left. The red sand hills of Maryland nor the clay bluffs of Ohio or the clay & stone points of Pennsylvania nor even the noted prairies of Illinois & the old farms of Indiana neither have nor can have the advantage of Minnesota if she is improved as much by the hand of the pioneer population as long as they have been. As soon as this war is over there will be a large emigration to Minnesota for there are some people that do not know that there is such a place for there was a soldier the other day that asked where we came from & when told, said Minnesota where is that showing that there is some people that have not heard of it yet.

I have not heard any news of any importance today but the rebbels are retreating & falling back. It is thought to bring on a general engagement but Gen Scott is up & ready. I did expect to see Morristown before leaving the State but do not expect to see Minnesota again until discharged if ever, but I am satisfied. We are getting along well enough & a great deal better than we would if we were to let the southern states do as they please & rule themselves & us acording to their own notions of things.

I am your absent Son & Brother

Edward H. Bassett

Please Direct to

Edward H. Bassett.
Washington D.C. Co. G
1st Reg. Minnesota Volunteers.

Camp Minnesota
Washington
July 2nd, 1861

Dear Brother,

As we are about to leave here (& I do not know where but expect into Virginia) I will drop you a line. I am well and ready for anything. We have 40 rounds of cartridge in our boxes & are now waiting to hear the bugle sound & then we will strike our tents & be ready to start we know not where, perhaps in the midst of Jeff Davis's forces but this Regiment is not alone you would think if you were here & could see the camps in & all arround Washington. The city of Baltimore is under martial law & every person that is found out after nine is taken to the fort & floged. Some say that we are to go some eight miles below here but there is not any person but the commissioned officers that do know & they are not allowed to tell us but we do not care. We can go anywhere that they can. I do not know when I will get another chance to write & I thought that I would just pencil you a word. We have not received our pay yet but expect to in a few days but if we do not have it we will not spend it & the Senators & congressmen from

Minnesota frank[7] all our letters for us. The fourth of July is at hand & we expect to celebrate it in a secession state. I have not been down in the city to see anything since we have been here but have a pass in my pocket which I was intending to get the Colonel to sign today & then I could go all over the capitol building, the navy yard, the museum, patent office & in fact most anywhere for a soldier can go all over the city in any public building free of all expense if they can get a pass. We are kept pretty close on account of there being spies arround & to prevent desertion. There was a spy from the enemy in our camp one day & he got caught passing around from one camp to another & when passing a sentinel with his forged pass made a mistake & showed his pass from Jeff Davis & he was taken prisoner & confined. If we go into a fight I intend to give some of them hell for we have the guns that can do it. The balls weigh one ounce per ball. Captain McKune has not arrived yet but we expect him every train. The State of N. York sends out a Reg. every day for ten days. There is from one to ten thousand men arrive every day.

One of the officers in the southern army that is acquainted with Colonel Gorman wrote him that he would meet him with shot guns & the Colonel told him that he had a Reg. of Minnesota boys that could carry them off with their bayonets.

You must write soon for I would like to hear from you.

Your Brother *E. H. Bassett.*

Friend George

Mr. Ed has given me an opportunity I will write you a line or two. I do not know what Ed has written but I suppose he has informed you correctly of our proceedings. We are about to pull up stakes and march, the Colonel only knows where and he won't tell.

---

[7] Frank: To mark a piece of mail with an official signature or sign indicating the right of the sender to free mailing.

We have enjoyed ourselves well so far, have had good health. Our boys *all seem to be in good spirits. As Ed is waiting for this I wi*ll scratch no more. I will write again some time so Good By. My respects to those who respect me. Write yourself and tell the rest of the boys to write soon in particular,

Jonny Goodritch.[8]

****

Wednesday, July 3, the regiment left Washington D.C. and moved to "Camp Franklin" at Alexandria, Virginia.

Camp of the Minnesota 1st Reg. Volunteers
Alexandria, Virginia
Jul. 5th, 1861.

Dear Brother

I take the first opportunity after leaving Washington of leting you know where I am. We left Washington on the 30th at about nine in the morning. We marched down through the navy yard, got on board a steam boat and in a few minutes we landed at the dock in Alexandria. I saw the house in which Colonel Ellsworth[9] was shot. We are camped about three quarters of a mile from town in a very nice place, a meadow. Colonel Ellsworth's Zouaves are camped about 80 or 90 rods from us & there is a camp of Boston boys between them & us. It is pretty warm here but I do not know as it is much warmer than in Minnesota at this date. The Boys are in pretty good health & I have not

---

8   This is a Post Script note from a friend of both Ed and his younger brother George.

9   During the first days of the war Colonel Elmer Ellsworth of the New York Fire Zouaves was shot and killed while tearing down a rebel flag at the Marshall House, a hotel in Alexandria. A personal friend of Lincoln's, he was the first casualty of the war and became a martyred national hero.

seen a day that I felt sick of any account since I enlisted nor have I taken any medicine of any kind whatever. Cap. McKune has not arrived yet but we expect him every day. I was on guard yesterday & last night. We have not seen any of the enemy yet but we arrested four men yesterday whom we thought were spies, they came into camp, looked arround & finally steped out just past the guards & went to playing cards & pitching quoits[10] & seemed to be watching things pretty close when they were reported to the Colonel he had them arrested. They were dressed in civilian clothes, some of the picket guards had a little fun yesterday morning. They were out some three or four miles laying by the side of the road when there came along some 15 or 20 of the enemy's cavalry dashing along the road. One of the pickets jumped out into the road right in sight & then back without fireing. The cavalry wheeled arround & poured a whole volley into the brush without any effect, except unloading their guns. Our men then jumped up & fired into them, killing two of the devils & they captured four horses, there was not but some four or five of our men but the rebbels are easyly routed, there was an alarm beaten & it was laughable to see the boys rally. Every one of us were asleep except the guards & most of us sleeping in the open air not having time to put up our tents that evening. The rebbels retreated & have not been heard of since.

Last night everything was quiet. There was not much of a display yesterday. A national salute was fired at 12 & the troops laid under arms while they were fired & there was some fire balls & rockets thrown in Washington & some in Alexandria. We are seven or eight miles from Washington & the light from some of the balls thrown was bright enough to read by, although it was a pretty light night and there was a comet to be seen in the Northeast.

---

[10] Quoits is a game much like modern day Horseshoes involving pitching iron or rope rings at an iron stake.

I suppose that you had a good time on the fourth. I do not know how long we shall stay here but wherever we go I will write to you as soon as I can after arriving. I like the country here very well as far as seen. The crops look well but they have not got the soil that we have in the western states. There is a pretty good crop of pears, peaches & some apples. Pears & apples are ripening some. We have not received any money yet but expect to in a few days. Things are very high here such as flour &c. Flour is worth from 10 to $15 per bbl. (barrel) Butter 20 & 25 cts. Beef 7 & 8. (cents per pound) Hay from $15 to 20. (per ton)

I did not get a chance to go around any while in Washington & did not therefore see much. We marched through the Navy yard but did not break ranks. I saw some pretty large guns, plenty of shot & there was one or two gun boats lay in the harbor. I saw the Capitol building & we were camped within about 40 rods of it & could see the upper part of it, but the finest view was comeing down the River. We could see the whole broadside of it & it does look splendid.

E.H.B.

(It appears there was originally another page to this letter, now missing.)

Camp Franklin,
Alexandria, Virginia
July 6th, 1861.

Dear Parents Father and Mother,

I thought that I would write you a line. I have just come in camp from a kind of ramble about one half mile from camp. It is a pretty hot day and it is not very pleasant walking. I went down to the river. The tide is down now & it is not very nice there. I went into an orchard & got all the pears that I could eat. They are not very ripe yet but they are better than nothing. There is a large crop of pears this year & they will soon be in their prime. I also went to the poor house & saw some of the most miserable looking creatures there that I ever saw. The blacks & whites mingled together without distinction.

The whole regiment marched down into Alexandria yesterday. It was quite cool & we got along first rate. The people are not quite so enthusiastic there as in some other places but the Stars & Stripes float there continually & there was one little girl that came out on the stoops in front of a splendid residence & waved the Stars & Stripes as we passed. There are some in the city that dare not express very strong union feelings for fear that if the U.S. troops should leave here & the traitors come in they would be done for in a short time. We have had a quiet time here so far. We have taken four prisoners & one of the guards was fired upon the night before last & they fired upon somebody, but it was dark & there was not any harm done on either side. I heard to day that the Hastings Comp. while guarding the R.R. and telegraph fired upon a man & he has since died. He was a preacher & the neighbors say that he was a secessionist. He was shot in the breast.

There was divine services this forenoon by our Chaplain. He is liked very well. It seemed kind of natural to go to meeting once more today and the first time that I have been since I left home. I have been on duty every day that there has been services before now. Our Captain has not arrived yet but there has been letters received for him here & we think that he is on his way here. The boys all say that they wish Cap. would come.

I have not heard from home since the 14th of June but expect one every day as there must be some on the road & time will bring them round. We do not have to drill very hard since we came here. I saw the N.Y. Fire Zouaves yesterday. They are a fine looking Regiment. They are all dressed in red shirts, grey pants, red caps with a tassle about 7 inches long strung in the middle. The cap has no forepiece. (visor)They all wear the no. of the fire camp that they belonged to. They go just about where they please & defy their officers to stop them. If they once get loose in Alexandria they would most likely burn the city they are so indignant.

Senator Rice from Minnesota was here yesterday. He is in good health & seemed to be at home. The farmers have got done harvesting their grain. The crop is pretty good I believe. Things are pretty high here now & there was a man telling me that if the thing could be settled tomorrow that Virginia would not recover in ten years, but it takes folks longer here to do anything than it does in Minnesota. I cannot tell how long we will stay here but most likely not long. It is said that General Scott said that the fuss would be settled without any fighting, but we are ready to meet them if they want. We did not come here to play & we await orders. The Captain of the Hastings Co., Captain Adams a very fine captain, was poisoned yesterday down town. He drank poisoned Brandy it is thought, but he is better. We have to look out what we use for there are some of the scamps in our midst. We are under Maj. General McDowell. Arlington Heights is our headquarters. I shall expect a letter before long, but we are liable to be ordered away at any hour. Several regiments arrived here last night & camped by the side of the Zouaves and there are more expected tonight & I have just been told that some of the regiments start under marching orders, it is thought to Fairfax Courthouse about 8 or ten miles from here. There is considerable of a rebble force there & we will have a light brush it is thought with them.
From Your Absent Son

E.H.B.

If you get this let me know it for I do not know as our letters all get through. Some mistrust P.M. Norton, watch him.[11]

---

[11] Apparently in jest, Edward infers that the local Postmaster is suspected of being a Southern Sympathizer.

I will write as soon as I can where ever we go but it is difficult to write at all times. I wrote to George on the 2nd of July. Tell George to write.

My respects to all the folks.

Camp Franklin, Virginia
July 11th, 1861.

Dear Brother

I take this opportunity to write you a line to let you know that I am in the land of the liveing although on the soil of the old dominion camped about one half mile from Alexandria, that infernal hole of secessionist & traitors. I am well & feel at home here as much as I do anywhere. We are surrounded by government troops on all sides. The New York Fire Zouaves are on the west about 80 rods & there is a regiment of the Mass. boys between us & them & there is some 8 or 10 thousands between here & Fairfax Courthouse. The whole country arround here is under Martial law. The day before yesterday Jeff Davis sent a messenger to old Abe with a message from him. They were seen by our pickets. The messenger was accompanied by a Cavalry guard of reconissance size. Our pickets made them dismount and advance when they came along with a flag of truce trailing along. The guards were sent back to their own ranks. The messenger was then taken under guard & taken to Washington & the next morning he was allowed to deliver his message to the President, then he was escorted back to his own ranks without an answer. It is supposed that the President did not deem it worthy of his attention. His intention most likely was to get a chance to correspond with resident spies but they were come up to that time. They have old heads to deal with in Washington–General Scott &c. (etc.)

As I have not heard from home since the 4th of

June I do not know but the State of Minnesota has set up a government by its own power & will before long be drawn up in battle array to oppose us on our return, [12] but I expect a letter every day, but I intend to write from one to two every week until I receive an answer. We are haveing a pretty good time in general. It is very hot here nearly every day. We had a good rain last night & it is quite cool today. We do not drill any since we came here of any account. We lay in camp, read papers, talk, joke, sleep & pass the time the best way we can.

I go down to the Potomac River nearly every day & take a good swim. Jonathan Goodrich is the same Jonny that he allways was, in good health & seems to be at home here just as much as he was in the sugar camp on the old Cannon. I expect that we will stay here some time but cannot tell how long. We may be sent on to Fairfax in a few hours but we do not care how soon. We are willing to begin & are confident that we can do some mischief if it is nothing more than shooting those miserable scarecrows of horses on which the secession Cavalry are mounted. There is considerable of a force at Fairfax it is believed. Captain McKune has not arrived yet but we expect him every day as we have for a week or more. The farmers are cutting their oats here & have got everything of the wheat kind out of the way long ago. Corn is about waist high here & there is some that is not more than six or seven inches high. I suppose that crops in Minnesota are as good as they are anywhere. Things here have not done as well on account of it being very dry.

You must write & let me know about the crops there & how you are geting along on the farm. Tell the price of wages and everything else that you can think

---

[12] A lighthearted joke insinuating that the fact that he has not been receiving letters may be due to Minnesota having seceded from the Union.

of. How has Father got along with his saw logs & how much lumber has he cut. Did he make anything on those logs that he sawed for Dodd.
From your Brother

Edward H. Bassett.

How does old Abe get along on the farm. Has he got any colts from dem mars (mares) yet? Did you have any fun on the fourth.

****

In the following letter, written before marching to battle at Bull Run, Edward gave an explanation of their preparations for the march in "light marching order." The letter includes a most interesting account of Edward's chance meeting with a 110–year–old Negro gentleman from the local poorhouse who visited the camp.

Camp Minnesota
NearAlexandria
July 14th, 1861.

Dear Brother,

I received your letter of the 7 inst. this day & was glad to hear from you that you are all well. I expect that you have received several that I have written by this time. Our Captain arrived here last night with the rest of our company. He is well & looks a great deal better than he did when we left him. We received orders last evening to pack up our knapsacks with our coats & take our blankets & one pair of socks & put in it, then roll it up in a long roll & tie the ends together. Our knapsacks are to be sent down into Alexandria & put into a storehouse. This with 3 days of cooked rations in our haversacks is called light marching order. We do not know where we will go nor that we will leave here at all but if we do we will most likely go out to Fairfax Courthouse or Mannassas Gap & not knowing when we will start I thought that I would answer immediately. There is a reported capture of a large force of the rebels & some of the boys that were down town yesterday saw some of the N. Y. Zouaves fetch in two or three prisoners. They had taken their arms away from them & they were a cheap looking set. The doctor went out on Arlington Heights this morning & he said they had some prisoners there. He saw the brigadier general McDowel & he sayes that the General looks hearty & well fed. I was out on picket guard the day before yesterday. We had a good time. We were on the R. R. & Telegraph, the weather is not so very much hotter than in Minnesota but we do not have such a cool breeze as there. The health of the soldiers is good.

There is an old Negro here that is 110 years old the 1st of March 1861. He was the first man that beat the drum for Washington. He says that Washington brought him up & his mother before him. He says that the General allways treated him well, sent him to school & treated him like his own child. He says that he has been owned by 13 different men since the death of Washington & has been abused. He is very patriotic & when he left he took his hat & made a very polite bow & said "Success to you - God bless you". He walked from the Poorhouse down here about 1/2 mile & back. It seemed strange to hear him talk. We cannot realize where we are.

You say that Mother has allmost given up seeing me again. Away with such ideas. I will be back in less than one year, but if not, all right. What is the use in giveing up untill we have tried. One thing is sure, I am in a good company with good officers. You done wrong in not celebrating the 4th in Morristown but are excusable for once. I wrote a letter to John Russell & one to Pf. Buck last week. I expected some letters when Captain came but did not receive any. You say that there is nothing to write about. What if there is not - write about nothing as I do or at least write the every day proceedings. You will never be sorry, I know how it is.

Baultice is well & seems to enjoy himself well. What

has Father done with his oxen? How much breaking has he got done. It is thought by some that we will drive the rebels back to Richmond & there will be a general engagement but we don't care a D - - - & they will get hell if they don't whip us you may bet. The Zouaves have built quite a strong fortification within about 1/2 mile from here. They have some 40 or 50 guns mounted. I believe they call it Ft. Ellsworth. We are all ready to march now but may not leave here in a week but if we do you will hear from me again. Be patient, things are going slow but sure. You may bet time will tell. Tell Father that I would like to help him in harvest if I could but cannot. Tell him that he has not sent my rifle along yet & he need not do it. Keep it to shoot geese with. Mother speaks of the action of Congress. I have not heard anything of importance but it is said that Jeff wants to compromise the thing & he will meet with considerable opposition for he might as well fight it out now as any time.

From Edward Henry Bassett,

your brother Now & forever - amen.

(This page was added to the letter of July 14, 1861 on the following day)

Since I commenced this there has been some pretty brisk fireing of cannons down below about 2 miles & our battery threw several shell across into VA. I do not know what they were fireing at but the shells passed directly over our heads. (There were two guns above the ferry on a high point). We could hear them as they passed through the air very plain. There has been some fireing nearly every day but there has not been any attempt to cross made yet. I am in hopes that there will be a movement made as soon as it can be with any surety. We have got some good guns here and if they attempt to cross they will be used.

Wm. Coen, George Kenney & myself have just been up into a corn field and got some corn and beans for dinner and they are over the fire cooking now. We will have some flapjacks, corn, beans, pork & tea for dinner (good enough for a day).

Corn is very good here this year although many places have been neglected and have not been cultivated as much as they ought. I often think of you and almost wish that I was in Minnesota I believe that I would like to go up arround the old lake and hunt rats, (muskrats) ducks &c. but next spring in the sugar making season will be the time that I will be the most discontented. You will most likely work the camp and I expect that it will be a good season. Time passes away very fast. Weeks seem to pass like days & months like weeks. Spring will soon be here and with it I look for a change in the governmental affairs of the country. It is now about sundown and I can hear the drums of the rebels. They are haveing dress parade most likely.

I am perfectly satisfied with my situation & have not been sorry that I enlisted for I think that there is work for us to do yet. At any rate we are ready to take it as it may come & see the thing settled. They have ruled long enough & are ruining themselves & others with their cursed slavery. You may not beleive it but it is so, the farmers arround here are from 20 to 30 years behind the times in tools & houses & nearly every thing, that is to say the most of them, but there is some inteligent people here as well as elsewhere but most of them are <u>hoosiers.</u>

I have not heard from home since the 14th of June but we have been traveling nearly all the time, but you must write for the letters will be forwarded to me wherever we go & I should be glad to hear from you.

From Your Affectionate brother

Edward H. Bassett.

At present direct to Alexandria, Virginia.
Co. G. 1st Reg. M.V.

My love to all the folks & tell them to write & I will answer if I can.

Edward H. Bassett.

On July 16th army moved out on the march toward their first fight with the rebel forces. Edward was not impressed by the country they marched through on their way to meet the enemy.

In the short time between the units' arrival in Washington and the First Battle of Bull Run, the regiments of volunteers needed to be assembled into something resembling an organized fighting force. They were assigned to their brigades and divisions to form the new–Army of Northeastern Virginia. The officers, as a whole, were inexperienced, and faced with the task of establishing an entire command, control and supply system in only a few-days time. This haste, lack of experience and lack of familiarity with one another led to costly chaos in the ensuing battle. The units were clad in uniforms of all types, colors and descriptions, making it impossible to distinguish friend from foe or even one company from another within the same regiment. The First Minnesota was no exception. They were still clad in the bright red flannel shirts and black pantaloon trousers they received at Fort Snelling, except the poor fellows who were issued the flowered shirts because there were not enough red ones. The Winona Company had smart new <u>gray</u> military uniforms, given to them by their hometown.

CHAPTER #3
FIRST BLOOD

☙ The Battle of Bull Run
Sunday, July 21, 1861

Following the opening of hostilities, the fall of Fort Sumter and the secession of Virginia, both governments scrambled to raise armies—the South for the purpose of defense and the North for the purpose of conquering the rebel states and preserving the Union. With the two protagonist capitals being within 100 miles of one another, fears of attack ran rampant. By mid–June 1861, the Confederacy had amassed a force of approximately 11,000 men, led by General Johnston. This force was then positioned in the Shenandoah Valley. Another force of approximately 22,000 men, commanded by General Beauregard, was strategically placed at Manassas Junction. It was an important railroad center and a mere 25 miles from Washington. Both of these locations were ideal for launching an attack on the northern capital or intercepting an attack directed at Richmond.

Amid the clamor of a frightened and indignant public and the insistence of nervous politicians, General McDowell was ordered to submit a plan to launch an attack to subdue the rebel army and quell the rebellion. By mid-July, the Union had assembled an army of 30,000 men in and around Washington D.C. commanded by General McDowell, a former West Point classmate of Beauregard. Over his objections that the army was untrained and not ready for such an engagement, he was, nonetheless ordered to proceed. The attack occured at what was then the somewhat obscure place called Bull Run. A second Union force of 18,000, commanded by General Robert Patterson, was to engage Johnston's forces in the Shenandoah Valley to prevent them from reinforcing Beauregard. McDowell planned to form his army into three columns, two of which would attack the rebels at Bull Run. The third would move to the Rebel's right flank, cutting off the railroad line to Richmond and attacking their rear. He intended to force the rebels to abandon their well–prepared defensive fortifications and retreat to the Rappahannock River toward Richmond thereby relieving the pressure on Washington.

The Union army left Washington on Tuesday, July 16th, in sweltering heat; the lack of training and discipline soon became apparent. The units also had widely varying training in marching discipline. Their march to battle proved anything but the orderly movement of a military column. Men were left standing for hours in the hot sun and dust while other units met the column on intersecting roads. Sometimes artillery or cavalry units caused the infantry to yield the right of way while they charged through. Thirst and hunger added to the confusion. Men abandoned the column to run to nearby streams for water, or to gather wild blackberries that were plentiful along the way. The march only made 12 miles the first day and 16 miles on the second. General McDowell was greatly aggravated by the lack of discipline and said "*the men did pretty much as they pleased.*"

As the two–day march continued, and the fatigue and hot sun wore on the men, many began to lighten their loads. They threw away their knapsacks, coats, blankets and anything else they could. Some men even went so far as to throw away their ammunition boxes. The sides of the road soon became miles–long heaps of this cast-off equipment. The red, Virginia clay soil baked by the sun and pounded into dust by the tens-of-thousands of tramping feet soon became inches–thick powder. The First Minnesota was marching well back in the column and behind an artillery regiment with its horses and gun caissons. In the choking cloud of red powder, the men marched on, their faces were caked with perspiration and red mud, and their mouths dry—most of them had little or no water. The march took the men through Fairfax Court House and on to within 1 mile of Centerville, where they arrived in the evening of the 18th. At 2:30 AM, Sunday, July 21st, after being resupplied with rations and ammunition, they advanced to Bull Run where the battle began to rage.

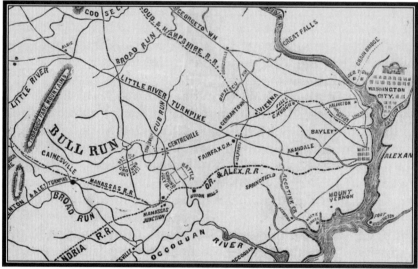

Period Map of Bull Run area–Frank Leslie's Illustrated

Bull Run is a medium–sized creek that flows southeastwardly in the vicinity of Manassas Junction and approximately five miles further downstream, empties into the Occoquan and, eventually into the Potomac River. Its course is outlined by high, steep banks lined with impenetrable brush and could only be crossed at bridges or a number of "fords" where the banks were lower and the water not too deep. As General Beauregard had been on the field for several weeks before the battle, he had gained a thorough knowledge of the area. His forces were placed in an eight–mile line along the South bank of Bull Run creek. He had fortified his position with earthworks, trenches and rifle pits and placed a strong force of artillery and a brigade of infantry at each ford. In short, he had developed a strong defensive position. Another advantage he enjoyed was the fact that he could bring reinforcements by rail in hours; whereas; McDowell's closest reinforcements were a few–day's march away at Harper's Ferry.

The Regiment was ordered to take a position on the extreme left and moved at double-quick time to an open field where they came under heavy artillery fire. After about 10 minutes, they were ordered to move a little more than one mile across the enemy's front, to the right flank. Obeying the order meant being exposed to enemy fire while running at double-quick time. Colonel Gorman wrote:

"many of the men threw away blankets, haversacks, and even their indispensible canteens in order to run with swiftness the race set before them."

Their new position put them within 60 yards of the enemy line. At first, both sides were confused and questioned who was a friend and who was an enemy. A display of flags soon resolved the matter and firing began with terrible effect. Captain Ricketts' artillery battery, which was placed at the left end of the Regiment, was almost instantly "cut to pieces"— their guns, dead horses and wreckage were abandoned. A storm of lead, iron and flame belched forth from the rebel line directly into the Minnesota ranks. Shaking off the crushing blow, they returned fire, and volley–after–volley followed. They stood in the open, taking musketry fire from a line five times their number. Despite the consequence of a barrage of grape, canister and shot from cannons on their right, they never flinched in their duty. The battle that earlier in the afternoon had appeared to be a major Union victory turned into a complete route after the rebel forces were heavily reinforced. A wild stampede of soldiers, wagons, cavalry and artillery ensued with everyone running for their lives back toward Washington. The men of the First Minnesota retreated only after Colonel Gorman, who saw that the position was too perilous and the Union forces were falling back, ordered them three times to retreat. Their retreat was carried out in good order and they formed the rear guard, standing to face a charge by the Black Horse Cavalry. They met the charge with a determination that left nearly all 500 members of the enemy cavalry dead or wounded on the field. Then the companies returned to where they had dropped their haversacks and began the march to Centerville, where they immediately fell to the ground and went to sleep. Just one-half hour later, the men were awakened by the cooks for hot coffee and then ordered to march 25 miles back to Alexandria and their camp, where they would be protected by the guns around Washington.

This engagement defined the quality of the regiment and its stalwart dedication to duty. On this day, it stood its ground under heavy fire, never turning its back on the enemy and suffered its losses with unwavering courage. Its casualties were 42 killed, 108 wounded and 30 missing—the greatest losses of any unit on the field.

Written two days after the battle, when the regiment had returned to Washington DC, to protect the capital from possible rebel attack, Edward describes the events of the battle and their engagement in the first major battle of the war.

Camp Minnesota
Washington D.C.
July 23, 1861

Dear Parents:

I suppose that you will have heard from us by telegraph before you receive this. The day before yesterday (Sunday, July 21st) was the first time that we have had a chance to try our skill in the field fighting and the boys done nobly but we lost our captain. (Captain McKune) He was shot through the heart and fell dead instantly. He stood by us giving commands and had his arms raised up encouraging the boys on. We lament his loss greatly. We all loved him and he was no coward. We lost somewhere between eight and twelve men and about that number wounded. Among the killed was one flag bearer. He was hit by three balls before he fell and after that he loaded and fired some three or four times. His name was Asa Miller from Cannon City I believe. We saved our company flag. Lieutenant Messick pulled it from the staff and wrapped it around him. We were forced to retreat for we found that we had fell in with the principal and in fact the majority of the southern army. They were somewhere between 100,000 and 150,000 strong and we were only about 53,000. The battleground was about 10 miles from Mannassas Junction. This information about the strength of the enemy and their position was received from a prisoner that was taken by Co. B. I do not know how many men were lost from the Minnesota Regiment but we suffered less than some other.[13] We were decoyed upon one of their masked batteries and they are the most treacherous people that were ever allowed to exist. They hoisted the Union flag as we advanced and would beckon their hands and show every appearance of being friendly until we got in range of them when they opened up on us. As we had special orders not to fire until ordered, we all dropped down. I did not see the boys drop at first and stood up until they had all laid down and I looked around first on one side, then on the other and could not see the enemy and as the bullets were flying about as thick as raindrops I thought that the safest place for me would be flat on the ground. We laid there about ten minutes when the order was given to retreat firing. By this time the enemy had come up in sight and the boys fired into them and killed them off pretty fast. We then retreated behind a hill covered with timber. The enemy then attempted to make a charge upon the N. Y. Zouaves and they come in range of one or two of our brass field pieces and they opened a fire

---

[13] At this point Edward is apparently unaware that in fact his regiment had the greatest total losses that day with 1 officer and 41 men killed and 8 officers and 100 men wounded.

of grape and canister upon them and it was a sight to see how quick they were driven back.[14] It was a very foolish move. When we were marched up we went up behind our cannon. The enemy were throwing[15] bombs and round shot. Our battery was then about as far off from them as Cole Bloomer's house is from ours. They threw their shot away beyond us and about 100 feet high. We were marched up on the enemy's right flank intending to give them a flank fire but they were ready for us and had the advantage of us for we had been marched at a double quick step for about one mile besides marching about 10 miles that morning starting at 2:30 in the night.

We were very weary but we gave them what they do not get everyday, although we lost our Captain. We carried him off the field and took his sword belt, pistol, hat, etc. which will be sent to his family. We did not want the rebels to rob him. We rallied several times and charged and it is pretty well known that we killed more than we lost for our boys took good aim as we retreated. Their cavalry tried to cut us off but we beat

---

[14] Grape and Canister are both artillery ammunition meant for anti-personnel purposes. Grape consisted of 1" to 1 1/2" lead balls arranged in stacked circular groups one atop another then covered with a canvas bag. Canister was constructed in the same manner but it contained cast iron balls encased in a tin jacket that looked much like a tin can, hence the name. The shells contained varying numbers of balls between 15 and 35 depending on the size of the gun. To repel enemy attack, guns were commonly loaded with two or three rounds at one time, sometimes the entire barrel was filled. When placed in battery, adjacent to one another, and fired in unison they acted like a huge shotgun. The devastation was beyond belief. It has been said that a full battery of artillery firing triple loads could knock down every man in the first rank of advancing infantry in a path 300 feet wide. The author was unable to get volunteers to prove this statement.

[15] "Throwing" here means firing from cannon and the bombs were exploding artillery shells, shot is a solid cast iron projectile.

them badly. There was not more than 5 or 6 of them escaped. Although we had to retreat we did not feel like giving up. We were on a continual move from half past two Sunday morning until Monday night, without half enough to eat but we suffered the most for the want of water. We marched from Centerville to Washington by the way of Fairfax and Alexandria, in about 9 hours, a distance of about 35 miles. We are now quartered in Washington in a huge brick building. It rained yesterday while we were on our way from Alexandria and when we arrived here we were cold and wet. The citizens brought in some hot coffee, bread, ham, eggs and whiskey and we had a dry place to sleep. This morning was the first time that I have felt sick. I did feel pretty sick for two or three hours but have got over it now and feel pretty well again. I have had good health and stood it pretty well. We left our camp at Alexandria on the 16 th of July in light marching order which consists of a gun, cartridge box with 40 rounds of ammunition, haversack with three days rations, blanket or overcoat which is rolled in a long roll and the ends tied together and put over the shoulders. I took my coat. We marched all day and camped in a thicket of pines on the ground. We heard some firing in the evening and expected an attack. I slept first rate right on the ground. We got up at sunrise, ate our breakfast and started. When we had traveled about 5 miles we came to the place where the firing had been. Some of the enemy's cavalry had been scouting and saw a man out hunting some colts. They fired on him, killed his horse, wounded him and fled to camp. This is a miserable country, thinly settled, the buildings poor and old without paint, but whitewashed. The water is poor and the people poor and ignorant; not half of them can talk anything but the Virginia tongue. We traveled on until we were about one-half mile from Centerville where we camped (a little after sundown on the 18th). We stayed there until Sunday morning at half past two. They have sent out some 100 mortars and

1000 horses and several large pieces since the battle. It is said that General Scott is mad that we were defeated and he will be apt to send on a pretty large force. It would do you good to see the earthworks around Washington. There are some very heavy pieces of cannon and they will be apt to get enough if they attempt to take Washington.

I have just come from the Smithsonian Institute. I went all through the museum and into the Indian portrait gallery and in fact all over the building. It is a grand sight. I also went up to the Patent Office. There I saw the coat that General Washington wore when he resigned his commission and also his traveling secretary. I did not have much time to look around there for they were just closing when I went. I shall go again when I get an opportunity.

John Russell says that crops do not look very well there, that the wheat is short and thin. Corn here is of all sizes, some 2 feet, some 4 and I saw some that was about 8, but it is an extra piece that will average 3 feet. You must write often and direct as before to Washington. Mr. Messick sends his respects to you. He was not hurt. Boultice Soule is also safe. We have not been paid off as yet but expect to in a few days if we stay here.

With love from your Son,

Edward H. Bassett

The following excerpt from Edward's diary also describes the battle:

"In the retreat we rallied severel times and charged to hold the Rebs back. Their Black Horse Troop of cavalry, the flower of their army, charged us several times but were beaten back and badly cut up. We were on a continual move from half past two Sunday morning until Monday night. We only had about half enough to eat but suffered most from lack of water."

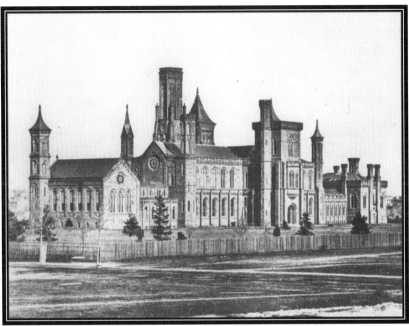

Photo of South Facade of the Smithsonian Institution, July 27, 1861,
Library of Congress

Washington City
July 26th, 1861.

Dear Brother,

I would write you a line. I am tolerable well although I have not got over our tramp to Bloody or Bull Run. I feel weak and lazy.

We had a pretty hard time on Sunday last but did not lose as many men as at first thought. There is some seven killed & missing. Among the killed, is our captain. He was killed by about the first shot of the rebels. He fell on his post encouraging his company & doing his best to make them successful. Jonathan Goodrich & several others bore him off the field & placed him beneath a large oak in the shade. His sash & sword were brought with us to Washington & will be sent to his family.

Lieutenant Messick will take his place in the Company. Messick is a brave soldier. He fought well & stuck with his men to the last. He was not hurt. Asa Miller our flag bearer was killed. He was one of the best soldiers we had. He volunteered to carry the flag. Wm. Potter was badly wounded and supposed to be killed at first but has since been heard from. Mr. A. G. Strickland was badly wounded, a ball passed through his elbow. It will most likely make his arm stiff. The loss of this Regiment in killed is some 46. There may be more but these we are pretty certain of. There are several missing in the Reg. They may have been taken prisoners & may be on their way to No. (North). It is very difficult to travel far here without a pass as the country is under martial law. There was not a ball hit me but they came very close. I have forgotten John Rhoer. He was wounded & is <u>at the hospital.</u>

I have not received a letter from home since the 10th. There is not a thing that looks better than a good long letter from home. Write all the particulars.

The troops are continually comeing in from all quarters. Send them as now is the time if there be any more send them on. We will have a quick job of it when we begin. We are resting now & will be ready to give them some of our best. Tell the girls that we are all comeing back to see them before long. It is now nearly sundown & as calm & quiet as you could wish.

Lieutenant Messick is in good health. We like him first rate. Well I must close so Good Bye

From your Brother

E. H. Bassett.

Direct to Washington as before for the country is under Martial law & it would be the safest.

Excuse such a long letter but if you read it you will do well & if you answer it you will do better.

P.S. There was two balloons sent up in Alexandria today. One was to go over Fairfax & the other I do not know where. My best respects to all the folks.

(The following is an added insert to this letter.)

When we were on the march we run short of provisions & the boys got their guns & went out into the field & shot sheep, hogs, calves & caught every chicken that they could lay their hands upon & when at camp at Centreville they drove up a lot of fat oxen that belonged to the government & got the Colonel out & made him give them permission, then they knocked them down right in the cornfield & dressed them. We took the meat & roasted it by the fire & ate it without salt. I had some pepper along & used it. This was pretty hard fare but our provision train had not come up. When it came we had enough and were treated well when we came into Washington. The citizens brought out hot coffee, bread, meat 7c. &c. (etc.) We are going to draw some clothing today & will receive our money in a few days so they say. We need it if ever anybody did for we are entirely out.

There has one more of our boys just came in. His name is Martin Healy from Waseca Co. (county) We supposed that he was killed. He laid in the woods within a few rods of the battle ground. He said that the D---d black scamps (rebels) burnt the house where our wounded were placed. If this is the case they have most likely killed all the prisoners that they took. Our two surgeons are supposed to be killed as they were with the wounded. They were excellent men both of them & understood their business. Write, write, write, write often.

From your Brother

The anticipation of going into their first battle, the sustained adrenalin rush in battle, and the long march after the battle must have caused incredible fatigue.

In a letter to his wife, Edward L. Davis wrote:

"We marched 12 miles from Centreville to the Battle grounds fought over 2 hours hard fighting & then retreated to Alexandria 42 miles doing all inside of 31 hours and only 2 hours sleep during the time & going without food for 24 hours having thrown off our rations before going into the field of action."

The men of the First Minnesota showed the "stuff" they were made of in their "Baptism of Fire." In his official report Colonel W. A. Gorman of the regiment praises them as follows:

"I regard it as an event of rare occurrence in the annals of history, that a regiment of volunteers, not over three months in the service, marched up without flinching to the mouth of batteries of cannon, supported by thousands of infantry, and opened and maintained a fire until one-fifth of the whole regiment was killed, wounded or made prisoners before retiring, except for purposes of advantage of position.

My heart is full of gratitude to my officers and men for their gallant bearing throughout the whole of this desperate engagement, and to distinguish the merits of one from another would be invidious, and injustice might be done."

During the several days when the regiment was camped in Washington the men were issued their first regulation uniforms. These replaced the bright red shirts and black pants they had received in Minnesota. The red shirts had caused nearly–fatal confusion at Bull Run when they met Confederates, who were also wearing red shirts.

Copy of the stationery artwork on this letter.
The writing on the rock in the stationery artwork illustrated above
reads: "CONSTITUTION OF OUR FATHERS"

Camp Minnesota, Washington
July 30th, 1861

Dear Parents,

I am pretty well at present but have not been so all the time since we retreated on the afternoon of the 21 & the night of same.

You are informed of all the particulars about the fight of the 21 st & the one on Wednesday at bloody run & therfore I need not repeat it. I was not in the first one but was in the second, in which our captain was killed. We have not lost as many men out of our company as we thought we had. We have since we came back heard from several of our bays & they are at Ft. Ellsworth & Washington under the care of our troops stationed at those points. Our loss in all is not more than 4 in killed I do not think. Major Dike received a letter from one of the Regimental Surgeons this week who is a prisoner in the Secession Camp. A lady that was at Mannassas on the day of the battle has since come through & she managed to secret it & fetch it through safe. I do not know the contents of the letter but he is a prisoner & not killed as some supposed.I have been down into the city all the forenoon & was on guard all the last night. I went all through the capitol & from there down to the Smithsonian then to the Patent office then by the way of the R.R. Depot back to camp. It was my second visit to the Smithsonian and also to the Patent Office & there is room for weeks more, there is neither beginning nor end. Stanley's Gallery of Indian paintings at the Institute is enough to interest any one mind one day at least. I saw at the Patent Office the printing press used by Franklin 108 years ago it looks old & somewhat worn all the better for that. The Capitol is a world of wonder but is not finished the grounds in the front & rear are most splendidly laid out truly we have something to be proud of. I have not seen the White House yet nor the gentleman that lives there (The President).

It is a very pleasant morning clear and warm. Our fourth Sergeant John J. McCallum has been promoted to the first Lieutenancy. There is some talk of our being sent to Texas to garrison some of the forts but I guess it is only talk. They have not payed us yet but promise to this afternoon. They may or may not I cannot tell for they have been promising to for a month and upwards. So far we nave not received one cents pay from the government.

We are waiting the next movement of the army. It is not known what will be done next. The rebels have a pretty strong force at Mannassas & also at Richmond. They are strongly fortified and will act on the defenceive takeing every advantage they can. The ground where they are is covered with pitch pine & the government is having large quantities of the tar balls made to throw among their works & clear the way so as to have a fair chance. The rebels will not fight in an open field if they can help it & where they have they are driven back by our troops with half their number. They have some good cavalry, but the flower of

52

Virginia, the Black Horse Cavalry composed of wealthy farmers, was very nearly all killed by our troops on the 21st in their last charge in trying to cut off our retreat. Col Gorman told the men to get behind a fence & he went to the corner of the field & stood on the top of the fence. When they came out of the woods into the open field & rushed right towards him we fired & there was not but 6 of them escaped. There would not be any trouble in conquering them if they had not had so much time to fix, but wait, General Scott is here.

I would like very much to be in Morristown this fall & help Father on the farm. I think that Minnesota is the best place to live on the west side of the Mississippi. The water, climate, soil & in fact everything is adapted to become the home of the free. I would not live in a slave state for it. They are as much behind the times in Virginia as the laws of creation will allow. I have told several persons living here in the city that when you get over out Arlington Heights way you are on the very verge of civilization & they all admit that it is so. There are some large cannon planted on Arlington. I sent a paper to Father – read what General Scott says.

C. B. Jackson has written several times. Baultice Soule has been sick for a few days but is getting better.

My love to all.

Good By for the present,
From your son

Edward H. Bassett

I went to Washington D.C.

Photo of Capitol Building under construction during 1861
Mathew Brady Photo

(Another page added to letter before it was mailed)

You speak of hearing some awful stories. That is nothing more than would be expected by the time that it gets to Morristown. Our company had not had any skirmishes with the enemy until one week ago last Sunday when we went into battle. It is true we had shot at the enemy or something else several times when on guard but there was not any damage done. We are now camped right on the edge of the city of Washington and there are troops camped all arround. We will stay here for some length of time & there will not be another fight before fall. There will have to be a heavy force raised to rout them. When I left home I weighed 150lbs. Now I weigh 144 and ½ a loss of 5-½ lbs. The health of the soldiers is generaly good. Those that were wounded are getting along fast. Our marching to Fairfax was all right but we did not go that way, we went around & the Fire Zouaves & Michigan boys went that way & routed them & took their flag. The report about one of the Hastings boys being shot is false. There has not been any person shot in our Regt. when on guard. You must not believe every report that there is in the papers. Did you ever get that coat that I sent home from Ridgley.

I am glad to hear that the crops look so well in Minnesota They will be needed. It has been quite cool here all summer so far. I have not heard of one case of sun stroke yet. There was a man here yesterday that has lived here ten years & he says this is the coolest summer he has known in that time.

Tell Anna that I would send a bundle of kisses to her for those cherries. They taste quite natural. Those flowers that Elford sent remind me of home every time I see them & I think what a good time we would have if we could get together. I hope that he will get well of the Hooping Cough soon.

E.H.B.

Lieutenant Messick is well. C.C. Parker has been complaining for a few days but is getting better fast.

CHAPTER # 4
MARCH TO THE UPPER POTOMAC

Following the battle of First Bull Run, the army encamped in Washington D.C. on Capitol Hill. It was feared after the defeat at Bull Run that the rebels would mount an attack in an endeavor to capture the Capitol. On August 2, 1861, the army began the march to Edwards' Ferry.

Camp of the 1st Reg. Minnesota
Saturday August 3d. 1861.

Dear Parents

We have left our camp in the city & are on our way to the Upper Potomac. We started about 10 A.M. yesterday. We were to start at 5 & stop at ten to rest. We stopped about noon & got some water & went out & got all the apples that I wanted. We are now encamped about 3 miles from Washington. We have to go about 5 miles farther. The intention of this movement is to cut off the provision trains of the secessionists from

Maryland. By the mail this morning we received some papers from Minnesota & also some letters. They say that the country there is in a perfect uproar & that the company of Waseca is comeing south as an independent company & that every person is ready to enlist. I suppose that the repulsion of our forces on the 21st at Bull Run has created more excitement throughout the whole United States, both north & south than anything that has occurred since the bombardment of Ft. Sumpter. It is true that the Secessionists drove us back but it was with a dreadful loss. They acknowledge a loss of 1500 & the loss on our part is known to fall short of that by several hundred. It is reported in camp this morning that our troops drove them from Fairfax yesterday but I have not learned the particulars. At any event I would not give much for Fairfax by the time that it has been taken & retaken a few more times. At present it is a pretty hard looking place of no great strength. There are several of our camp getting their discharge from service & will return to Minnesota Among them is Mr. Haely C. Hess a brother of the mail carrier. I saw it stated in the papers yesterday that since the battle of the 21st that there had been 100,000 troops offered to the government. There will be enough men offered to the Government to eat the southern confederacy up in about one week. Colonel Gorman has been appointed brigadier General & our Lieutenant Colonel Stephen Miller takes his place. The boys are pretty well. There is not many that are very sick but we all feel weak & lazy. I would not advise George to enlist if he had ever so fair a chance. There has been some talk of sending this Reg. out west but it is nothing but talk I guess.

I suppose that Abe Chake & Bassett in Co. own a reaper by this tine. How much breaking[16] have you done this summer & how much seed corn have you

---

[16] Breaking refers to plowing up virgin prairie ground.

planted & how do them bees get along. I heard that wheat was worth only 30 cts. per bushel in Minnesota Cheese is worth 16 cts. per lb. pies from one levy (12 1/2) to 8 cts. tomatoes 5 for 5 cts. Eggs 40 cts. doz. apples last night we could get a hat full for 5 cts. peaches are not ripe but are plenty. Crops are not anything extra here. There is not but little of the corn that is large enough to eat.

It is now about noon & the sunshine is too hot where I am sitting writing on a barrel of pilot bread. You must excuse the blots, dirt & mistakes & answer soon. As the south has got a large amount of postage stamps in their possession the government is going to issue another kind & I have no stamps nor frank envelopes. The Major takes the letters & franks them & the postage will have to be paid there. I will send the money as soon as I can get it.

My love to all the family & write often. Direct to Washington D.C. as before.

From your absent son,

Edward H. Bassett

P.S. We had some new potatoes for dinner today the first since we left Minnesota. They taste quite natural.

The march to Edward's Ferry got off to a rocky start due to misunderstandings about their three–month enlistments being changed to three years. Also, they had not received any pay and were only supplied with hard tack and "salt horse" (salted or pickled beef) for food—referred to as "hard grub." When ordered to break camp and prepare to march, a mild revolt occurred. The men said they wouldn't march until they were paid what was owed them. After a very unusual period of negotiations with Colonel Gorman, who promised to march four miles and set up camp in a good location until they were paid. He further promised a whiskey ration at the end of the march. Colonel Gorman was well regarded by the men; from this episode it is easy to see why. At 9 AM, the men were in line of march, and set off. They camped at Brightwood, 'a pretty place with plenty of shade'. The paymaster arrived on the second day out, but with only enough money to pay one–half of the regiment. At this point, the men agreed to march one-and-one-half miles to a woods and remain there until everyone received his pay and plenty to eat.

That night, the entire camp was aroused by a deafening noise. Assuming they were under attack, they grabbed their guns and were scampering around in the dark woods to see what the alarm was about. As it turned out, all the mules had broken loose and were stampeding through the woods and camp, knocking tents down and raising a great commotion. Most of the next day was spent rounding up the mules. Two days later, the wagons arrived bringing the paymaster, food, blankets, new clothing, shoes and, the regiment was issued new 58 caliber Springfield rifles. The men were paid $11 in treasury notes and gold for each month's service. The grumbling immediately ceased. Most of the men had more money than they had ever seen at one time. Home cooked food purchased from local farmers the only thing available they could spend their money on.

In Camp Montgomery Co. M.D.
August 6th, 1861

Dear Parents

I was glad to hear that you were well but am sorry that there should be such false reports in circulation but before this time you have heard the facts as they are. It is a fact that we had a pretty hard time but there was some things telegraphed back that never happened. We are now in the state of Maryland, Montgomery County. This is a splendid country. The farms are fixed up in good style & there seems something more enterprising in the people than there is in the old dominion[17]. We are camped about 1 mile from Rockville, the county seat of the County but we are going to march at 3 P.M. where I do not know, but I think we will get to Harpers Ferry before we stop any length of time. We left Washington on the 2nd & marched about 2 miles when we stoped in a grove of pines. We did not pitch our tents but took our knapsacks for a pillow & spread our blanket down & laid down & threw our overcoats over us. In this way I slept well. We got up about sunrise, ate some crackers & coffee for breakfast & then I took some paper & pen & set down & wrote you a letter. They paid off some of the companies that day. In the afternoon we packed up & marched about five miles when we stopped right in the road. Our wagons being delayed, we had to sleep where we could. I took two chestnut rails & laid them down just close enough so that when I laid down I would not touch on the ground & in this way I slept soundly all night.[18] That night between sundown & nine I went into a peach orchard & got what I wanted to eat. I wish that you had some of the peaches there are here. They are very plenty. The next morning I went out into another orchard & hooked all the apples I wanted besides picking all the blackberries I could eat. Well this was all we could get to eat for we have no money & the wagons did not come this was Sunday morning. We were ordered to fall in & we marched about 1 mile into a grove in the shade. There they paid us off two months & two days wages. I received $22 and 89 cts. This was in the pure quill just from the mint. After paying up my accounts for the three months of May, June & July inclusive I have $18.32 cts. left so you see that I have not spent much. I have now in my pocket a twenty dollar gold piece. I have not paid the sutler at Fort

---

[17] A common reference to Virginia.
[18] Edward's inventive approach to providing for some simple comfort.

Ridgley, his pay comes out of the next payment. I will try & send some money home for it would be a waste to spend it here. After they paid us, I went up to a farm house & tried to buy my dinner but there was others before me. I could get nothing but a few potatoes & two small pieces of bread, some molasses & some ham. The woman had been cooking untill she was entirely tired out & had cooked every thing up that there was in the house. I went back to camp & there was several wagons there from Washington loaded with pies, cakes &c. I bought some cakes & got 1/4 of a pie & ate. When I began to feel like myself our wagons had come but by this time we would not eat any of the hard bread that day. We were from Saturday night until Sunday noon without anything to eat but fruit & that we had to hook.

We had dress parade & the chaplain read a letter from Minnesota & acknowledged $1000 for the benefit of the sick & wounded, after which he read a chapter & had prayer, then he proposed to have prayer & sing a hymn after dress parade every evening. This was approved by Colonel Miller but he left it to the voice of the Regiment & there was not one dissenting voice but a loud roar for it.

We got orders to march at 5 the next morning. We got our blankets & laid down on the ground & slept well. We started the next morning. I had to go on guard & have just been relieved. We came through some fine country. The corn is all in blossom & looks very heavy. We passed through the town of Rockville. It is a very pretty place. Rockville was the head quarters of a company of secession troops but they have mostly left now. When we came through there yesterday the union flag was floating on all sides of the streets. We have camped in a field by the side of a brook of running water. There was a heavy rain yesterday afternoon.

There has three of the captains in this regiment joined the regulars. Captain Wilkins of Co. A, Captains Putnam & Acker—I do not remember the company. Captain Bromley of Co. B resigned just before we started up to Mannassas.

We all sympathise with Mrs. McKune and still mourn the loss of our Captain. Revenge is ours in time. But we did fix some of the secessionists on that very day & more are elected to the same fate. Some of the boys heard the Captain say just before we went onto the field that he would never come off alive & it proved to true. He was killed the first fire. He did not live but a short time & did not speak I believe. A. C. Strickland was shot through the elbow. He has got his discharge & is on his way home. Charles Hess was wounded in the arm near the shoulder. He has also gone home with his discharge. Martin Haely was run over by the cavalry & hurt. He is discharged. Mr. Gross, one of our company had his arm broken twice. I believe he is at the hospital in Alexandria, Walter Reid, Brother to Julia Reid, was shot through the eyelid but he has recovered. John Rhoer was shot through the hair injuring the skull. He is in Alexandria. There are several shot in the feet and hands but they will not be disabled. There was not a shot hit me although they came very close.

There was not half of the Reg. that got their uniform in Minnesota Co. G received theirs at Ridgley. We have plenty of clothes & now have plenty of money. I would send you some in this letter if I could get my piece changed. Our next pay day will be the 29 of this month but we may not receive it then. I will get my dagueriotype taken the first chance that I have.

The report that Colonel Gorman was wounded is a shameful lie. He was not hurt in the least. If I am sick I can & will get some person to write so that you need not feel alarmed about me. I am pretty well at present.

Will you please send me that dispatch containing the names of the killed & wounded in our Reg. if it would not be too such trouble. I should like to see it. I will try & answer the girls letter the first opportunity. It is the best letter that I ever saw for the first one. It is very gramatically composed & well written. They must write more.

P.S. Boultice Soule is in the hospital sick but not dangerous. I believe they have pretty good conveniences for taking care of the sick I am told. Direct to Washington.

In Love,   From Your Son

Edward H. Bassett

Envelope from letter of August 6, 1861:

Maryland, Montgomery Co.
Camp Mansfield, Aug 6th, 1861

Dear Sisters Ella & Anna,

I received your letter yesterday and was highly pleased to receive a letter written and composed by you and I must say that it was admirably done both in composition and penmanship. When I first opened it I could not think who it came from and I knew very well that it must be some new correspondent & I looked immediately for the signature. And whose should I see but Anna my sister and the second was from my sister

Ella. And then I turned the sheet over and there was Mother's Signature. We are now about to start on a march of many miles & I thought that I would answer you.

You must have a pretty nice school teacher this summer for you have learnt to write so fast. You say that you want to see me. Well if you want to see me worse than I want to see you, you must want to see me pretty bad. There is not a night that I do not think of you and wish that I could talk with you but never mind I will come back to Minnesota and see you just as soon as I can. You say that you have got some very pretty flowers. I wish that I could see them I have seen some very handsome flowers in my travels but I don't believe that they looked any prettier than yours do. We have got to start now in a few moments and I must close you must write as often as you can and I will try and answer all you will write. You say that you hope that I will keep well & not get hurt. I of course hope so & will try and take care of myself & you must not believe every report that there is in the papers for there are some men reported killed in the papers <u>that are alive and in this camp.</u> When I went into the battle I did not think that I would get hit & I did not but the bullets came very near me. They whistled like hail and killed many around me. They killed Mr. McKune and his little girls must feel very bad but he was doing his duty and was not afraid of anything.

Now we are going to camp before long I expect. I have filled this sheet & almost forgot. Tell (Toad) Elford I would like to send him some of the nice peaches and apples if I could. He must be a good boy and when I come back I will have a good time with him.

There I must quit and if you read this letter you will do well.

My love to all the family.

In haste, From your affectionate brother

Edward H. Bassett

(Direct to Washington)[19]

****

The regiment marched through the village of Rockville and to Seneca Mills where they remained until August 16. Normal intervening stops and incidents occurred as the regiment moved towards Edwards Ferry.

Seneca Mills, Maryland
August 8, 1861

Esteemed Parents,

The reason of my writing again so soon you will find within. We are camped near Seneca Mills. We were ordered here and started on the 2nd inst. and arrived here yesterday about 10 o'clock. We are about 30 miles from Washington on the Potomac River. There are camped on the other side of the river some Secession troops & the intention of placing federal troops here is to prevent the carrying of provisions and munitions of war from Maryland into Virginia. We have a pretty good camping ground, plenty of shade and water. There are two N.Y. regiments camped here with us. Some of their boys went across the River the other night and went into the rebel camp & burnt some of their tents and some other property and excaped unhurt to their own camp. The Rebels have some breastworks and batteries, it is thought, but we are out of their reach. I

---

[19] The purpose of this directive, placed at the end of many of the letters, is a notation to his parents instructing them as to where to address the letters they write him.

am not very well to day but as we are going to stop here some time I will have a chance to recuperate. I have stood all the tramps & everything that the Regiment has had to go through with so far and have not got an excuse from duty until yesterday & have not rode one step when we were on a march yet. The weather is pretty warm here now but not much more than in Minnesota in midsummer. Things sell at a pretty good price here – Potatoes are at $1.00 per bushel, Peeping chickens 25 cts. apiece, Butter 20 to 25 cts. Milk 10 cts. per qt. & everything in proportion. We are within 3 miles of a town called Darnstown. There are three stores & a few private houses there but you cannot buy much but whiskey which has been forbidden to be sold to soldiers. There are but few cases of drunkenness in the whole Reg. We are pretty temperate as a whole. The officers are very strict about such things. They have forbidden playing cards for money or anything of value & the fine for doing it is from 5 to 10 dollars. (This is nothing that will affect me and I am glad of it.)

Enclosed you will find a check for $10 to be drawn on Wm. H. Dike Bank in Faribault. The money I can spare just as well as not, for we will draw two months pay the first of September & congress has raised the wages of privates some $2.00. You will take it and spend it as you think best.

Captain Messick is well and the health of the Reg. is good considering what we have gone through.

My love to all the family,
From your son

Edward H. Bassett

Direct to Washington

The reason of my sending a check is that is safer than to send the gold in a letter and a check is just as good.

E. H. B.

Creek

CHAPTER #5
CAMP STONE MARYLAND

After two weeks on the march, the army reached their intended new campsite, located about two miles south of the village of Poolesville and two miles north of Edwards Ferry. It was in a gently sloping wheat field. The location was of strategic importance because the ferry was one of the main crossing points on the upper Potomac River which was about one-fourth mile wide there and shallow enough to pole a boat across. The Baltimore and Ohio Canal was also there, running parallel to the river about 100 yards inland on the Maryland side of the Potomac. This canal was one of the main arteries of commerce between Washington and the country's interior. Keeping it open to traffic was crucial to the trade necessary for sustaining the war effort. The banks of the Potomac were heavily wooded on both sides. Once the camp was established it was very well laid out and included rows of straight streets with ditches on both sides to carry away run-off water. The streets were marked with signs placed on poles. Evergreens were planted on some streets. The army would spend the next five months here.

View of Camp Stone, Maryland.
Photo courtesy of the Minnesota Historical Society.

The surrounding countryside was very pleasant with woodlands, fields of corn and grain and orchards and what the men considered to be "elegant" homes. This camp was the most peaceful and comfortable camp that the regiment experienced in the three years they served. The populace was primarily southern sympathizers, although many had family serving on both sides.

While at Camp Stone, the regiment's duty was to prevent the rebels from crossing the river and cutting Washington off from the rest of the country. The men spent one third of their time on picket duty or guard duty. The regiment was made up of 10 companies of approximately 100 men each, some having less due to losses suffered at Bull Run.

Camp Stone, MD.
August 17, 1861

Dear Brother

We are now camped about 1 ½ miles from what is called Edward's Ferry. I received a letter from Mother yesterday and would have answered it then if I had not been on guard. I am well. The health of the Reg. is generaly good. We have been here several days. Last Saturday & Sunday I was out on picket guard & also the Saturday & Sunday before. We had a good time. The rebels came down to the river and shot at us. They did not hit any of us but they shot pretty spiteful. We returned their compliments with equal force I bet. We do not know that there was any harm done on either side but they were seen to run pretty fast. They did not shoot at the post where I was stationed but it was only about one half mile below. It is only about six miles to Leesburg in Virginia and the rebels have got some breastworks and I suppose masked batteries. The man that kept the ferry here was forced to work on their breastworks and board himself and the only compensation they could offer was that the confederate states would be able to pay him. He is now released on parole of honor but he has told our men where their principal works are. We are now under the command of Brigadier General Stone. He is a fine looking man.

I was glad to hear that you were getting along so well with your harvesting. The reaper must work well & you must have to work very hard. (What kind of reaper[20] have you got & what teams do you work on it.)

Some think that we will not be put into another fight right away but kept here to guard Washington by keeping them out of Maryland, but we cannot tell. There is not any person except the highest officers that know what is going on. Things will not be made quite

---

[20] An early horse drawn machine for cutting and harvesting wheat.

so public as they were before the engagement at Bull Run, we are about 30 miles from Harpers Ferry. We have the river guarded all the way between there and Washington. I look for a settleing of affairs in less than one year.

Are there any berries in that marsh by our sugar camp. If there is, pick them and I will send you money to buy sugar for Mother to preserve them.

Remember your Brother

E. H. Bassett

Jonathan Goodrich is well and Jonny yet.
To George S. Bassett.

At Camp Stone, picket duty involved three companies at a time. The companies assigned would pile their knapsacks in a wagon, draw two days rations that they kept in their haversacks and then march down to the Ferry. They were stationed in groups of six or seven to a post and placed about one half-mile apart.

The ferry building served as headquarters and was manned by twenty-to-thirty men that formed the reserve. During the day most of the men slept, with the exception of those on guard duties, but at night all eyes and ears were alert to the possibility of attack. The river was about eighty rods wide, with trees and brush on both banks. The troops on both sides were able to keep concealed except when they were down by the water. Minor skirmishes occurred almost daily, although none in the regiment were killed or wounded.

Camp Stone MD.
Aug. 21<u>st</u> , 1861

Kind Parents,

I am well and enjoying myself very well considering. We are now camped in the midst of a slave holding people. Nearly every farmer has from one to one doz. Slaves. They have all their labor done by the blacks, as they call them. They are a small penurious people in general (of course there are exceptions).

There is not any particular news this morning except the reports of the different officers in command of the army. I have bought a morning paper & will send it to you. Mr. Messick is well. I was pleased with the letter from Miss Anna it was so well written & composed they both do remarkably well. I will write them again as soon as I can.

Of all the country that I have seen I do not like any so well as Minnesota & if I get out of this army alive I shall make Minnesota my home.

> *"Let me stay at my home*
> *In the beautiful west*
> *Where I roamed when a child*
> *In my age let me rest"*

I have written several letters since we left Washington. In one I sent a draft for ten dollars. You will please write and let me know how it gets along. The Maj. is in Faribault now and you will most likely see him.

Give my best respects to all the folks and write soon.

Wm. Ramsey is doing well he is an Ex-Corporal. He resigned for some private reason I believe.

My love to Elford in particular.

Excuse this poor penmanship for I am using a quill pen. I will mail the paper to you soon.

From Your Son *Edward*

Direct to Washington (plain & clear)

71

PS: I sent you a sample of wheat that was raised in the field where we are now encamped. It is a bald headed variety and I think very handsome wheat.

Black Berries are very plenty here, I never saw more. Apples are tolerable plenty but few ripe.

I have just mailed three papers.

PS. No. 87:

How much lumber did you get from your logs.

What is wheat worth.

Flour is 8 dollars per barrel here

Butter 25 cts. per lb.

Cheese 20 cts. per lb.

Potatoes $1.00 per bushel

PS. No.96

What did your reaper cost & how does the old mare work on it

The end

After the excitement of battle and the short stay in Washington where the men could go into the city and explore the many places of interest, camplife routine was quite boring. Once they had established some semblance of quarters, their only other duties were drilling once or twice a day, picket duty once or twice a week and reading and writing letters, if they had the materials. They had little in the way of entertainment. The frustration becomes apparent, at times, in the letters, especially as the stay in camp becomes extended.

In the following letter, Edward refers to having the measles. Many of the men from the western states had never been exposed to, and had no resistance to, the communicable diseases of the eastern cities. When they were placed in close proximity to the eastern men, an epidemic often swept through the camps with disastrous results. It is an often stated fact that more men died of disease than from the war.

Camp Stone, Maryland
August 30th, 1861

Dear Parents

I should have written sooner but I have been sick with the Measles. I was pretty sick for two days. I went to the hospital last Monday and just came out this morning. I feel pretty well with the exception of being pretty weak. The measles are going all through the camp but they seem to get along pretty well with them. My company is out on picket duty. They will return tomorrow. I hardly know what to write. There has not been any engagement nor do I know when there will be. I hope that before long. I wish that there would be something done pretty soon. I am tired of waiting but we have got to I suppose. Geo. B. McClellan has command of the forces in Western Va. now and the men place a great deal of confidence in him, believing that as he has been successful so far in cleaning out western Virginia that he will with the aid of more federal troops be able to drive the rebels from the Potomac if not out of the state. They seem determined to have Virginia for the battle field and we have got to fight them there. From all accounts Morristown is growing faster than ever. I hope to be able to recognize it by some landmark if ever it is my luck to get back there.

That coat was not worth much but I did not want to throw it away so I sent it home. Captain McKune had a box of clothing that he was going to send and he told me that I had better put it in with his and I did so. You talk about putting that money at interest. That would be a likely way when you need it to use. Use it and when I can I will send some more.

I have not sent any postage money yet nor do I think I will. I wrote in a little piece of paper to Elford and done up a half-dime in it but did not intend it for postage. The weather is quite cool and comfortable here now. The corn is doing well. All of the fruit in the immediate neighborhood is of an Inferior Quality I have just bought a Pie–an apple pie as they said but all it was a sesesh. I soon found out when cut there was not more than one spoonfull of apple in the whole Pie. I called the boy back and asked him who made it. He said his sister. I sent her my compliments and told her not to send any more such things into this camp. The people here are miserable cooks. They could not get up a meal of victuals that the boys in the streets of Morristown would think of eating unless starved. There are a few exceptions but few.

We will receive two months pay the first of September.

The girls wrote that the old school house frame is down on the hill. Did it blow down or are they going to finish it and have a school.

Father wants to know how many logs there was up the river. I do not know some 12 or 14. I believe they were mostly butternut. There was some basswood two pretty good ones. There was one ash. Who has removed them? I guess George will know them.

My best respects to all the folks in and around Morristown.

E. H. Bassett

Camp Stone Md.
Aug. 31st, 1861.

Dear Sisters Ella & Anna

I received a letter from Mother last evening. I was glad to hear that you were all well. It seems that you are gathering black berries. I wish that I was there and could help you gather some berries. And I would like very much to go with George and get those cranberries.

I am afraid that Elford will think that I have forgotten him but I have not. I think of him every day and you do not know how I want to see him. Tell him to be a good boy (which I suppose he is). How do his ducks get along. As it is late I suppose that your flowers are mostly getting ripe. I will try and send you some flower seeds by another spring so that you can have a greater variety. Write often and I will try and do the same.

From your brother

Edward H. Bassett

Camp Stone, Maryland
September 2, 1861

Dear Mother

Mr. Messick is well & seems quite cheerful. I would send a kiss to Anna for those flowers & would like to be there to walk in their garden & see their flowers. I will try & keep those flowers & if ever I come back will fetch them with me. I would send a kiss to Elford, yes to all of you. They must have had fine times in the black berries this summer if they are as plenty as they are in some parts of Virginia. When we were marching through there every time that we stoped where they were I would get my fill. I also got some Whortle-berries[21] but they were not so plenty.

I would say to George that he had better stay at home as it is the best place that he can find. If ever I get out of this alive I will stay out, not that I am disappointed or discouraged but it is no place for any person to spend their days. Excuse this but I cannot forbear the sight of a soldier as interesting to me. They are pretty rough.

---

[21] "Whortleberries" – an old European and New England name for blueberries.

My love to you all & write as often as you can.
From Your Affectionate Son

Edward E. Bassett.

Camp Stone, Maryland

Dear Brother George

I am well except being hoarse from a bad cold. The Measles are going the rounds in the Reg. I had them pretty hard but have got over it pretty much now. C.B. Jackson has got the ague[22] and B.K. Soule had a bilious attack the other day but they are both getting better now. Oliver Graham is down with the measles but the boys will soon be up and airing. The measles works off pretty easy although the Dr. does not give any thing for them. The boys are getting up a subscription for the purpose of replaceing the instruments that were lost at Bull Run. We had a splendid band of music before and will have a better one now if we succeed. The State of Minnesota gives $500.00 and with what we can raise I think that we will have just as good a band of music as any Reg. in the service. The boys threw in and bought a Violin and Graham plays in the evening and we have a regular tear down. There is some talk that we are going to Washington and encamp there but I do not know where we will go nor where we will spend the winter. We may spend the winter in Washington & I am sure that I would like it well enough if they say so & if not all the same. I am willing to take it as it comes. We are getting $13 per month now. I would like to be in Minnesota and help eat some of the nice melons that you raise there. I bought one yesterday for 25 cts. It would weigh about 30 lbs. and made about all eight of us could eat. It was the first that I had tasted. They were raised in the

---

[22] Ague-a fever (like malaria) marked by periods of chills, fever and sweating.

northern part of this state and brought to Washington by the cars. Everything is pretty dear here. We will have to go on picket guard tomorrow. The Secession pickets come down to the river and talk with our pickets. They promise us protection if we will cross over to them. They say that there are no more U.S. and will not be but this is their opinion not ours. I will send Father a paper containing the account of the taking of the rebble batteries off Cape Hatteras and the capture of 35 cannon without the loss of a single federal. General Butler took 800 prisoners & 1000 stand of arms. This is encourageing & something different from Bull Run.

My respects to all the folks and write soon.

As ever your Brother

E. H. Bassett.

Please direct to Washington D.C. Co. G
1 st Reg. Minnesota Vol.

Camp Stone
September 5th, 1861

Dear Parents

As it is raining & I have not much to do I thought that I would write you a letter for the sake of passing away the time if nothing more. My Company have just started out on picket. I did intend to go but the Doctor told Captain to let all those that had the measles remain in camp. I bought me a rubber overcoat this morning for $5.00. I thought that it would do me more good than the money in my pocket. It will keep me dryer at least. There are several of our Camp. sick with the Measles. B.K. Soule has got them pretty bad. Sam'l. Lilly is also comeing down with them now. They have generally worked off very easy. I had a very bad cough with them but have got about over it now. We were to go on picket yesterday but the order was countermanded and we were to hold ourselves in readiness to march at a moment's warning but where we are to go when we leave here I cannot tell. Some say to Washington, some over to Leesburg in Va. and some up toward Harpers Ferry. I feel at home any where that we are. Captain is well. The 1st Lieutennant McCallum has had an attac of the bilious fever but is about well now. I wrote George a letter the other day and sent a couple of papers. It is hard to get hold of papers or I would have sent you more.

Times are dull here now. There is nothing but the transportation of soldiers and Government supplies doing. Other business has all gone down. Crops are very good here this year with the exception of fruit which is not near as plenty as last year. Good apples sell for one ct. apiece and I have seen Peaches sold for 3 cts. but they were large as your fist. Our 2nd. Lieutenant J.R. Spencer who was the first man that enlisted in Rice County belongs to the corps of observation of the upper Potomac and is not with us. Sergeant C.C. Parker takes his place during his absence. C.E. Davison acts as orderly sergeant.

I had a drink of hard cider yesterday. It was the first that I have tasted here. It sells at 5 cts. per pint. We had religious services in a grove last Sunday and I made out to attend. It seems like a camp meeting. I have not attended the camp services but a few times I been on guard nearly every time that there has been any. The Young Men's Christian Association of N.Y. City have published a small hymn book containing all the pieces usually sung in Morristown for Volunteers and they are distributed throughout the camp gratuitously.

In haste,

E. H. Bassett.

****

There were often interesting interactions between opposing forces when they were camped on opposite sides of a river. In this letter Edward's remarks about one such exchange. Anything that broke the monotony of the day was a welcome diversion.

Camp Stone, Maryland
Sept. 8th, 1861

Dear Brother,

I am well and the Company are in usual health except the Measles. J. Goodrich is writing to you today. He is our Company cook. He does first rate. Before we had a Dutchman and two Negros and they were about as good as <u>Chance.</u> It is reported here that Minnesota has got to raise 3,000 troops and if it is so it will be a hard pull to get them. We have been expecting to move from here for several days but we may stay for a week or more yet. There was a section of one of the batteries went down to the river yesterday and fired a few shell across. It startled the rebels considerably. Their cavalry could be seen running in every direction. They undoubtedly expected an attack but they were fooled for once. It is only about six miles over to Leesburg and they have considerable of a force there. Their pickets came down to the bank of the river and talked with our pickets. They made a bargain not to shoot at one another as long as each kept on their respective grounds. I think that they have likely got sick of shooting at us for we have just as good shooting irons as they have. They call the Minnesota boys the blue bellies on account of our shooting so savage. The Tamany Reg. is just above us on the river. They have smooth bore guns and cannot shoot across the river and Mr. Sesesh shot over among them. It made <u>Paddy cry out "Och murder ah say".</u> Some of our boys went up there and shot across the river making Mr. Secesh sing the paddy's song. They soon took to their heels crying out "there are them d---n blue bellies" and got out of sight in a short time.

There was quite an accident happened in camp yesterday. A fellow by the name of Bates was drunk and fooling with his gun snapping it at one and another and snapping caps on it when he happened to think that his piece was not loaded and he loaded it and snapped it at the Negro cook. It went off and the ball passed through his side and into his arm. He died this morning and they have just buried him. The fellow that shot him was arrested and is in the guard house now. He belonged to Co. E. –the Hastings Co.

Sept. 9, 1861.

We expect the new instruments this week for the band and then for some music. Cap. Messick sends his compliments to father.

Sam'l Morris wrote me a most scandalous letter exulting in the death of our Captain McKune and I have answered him. Tell Ben to write to me, and Isaac Hand.

According to reports there are plenty of cranberries in Minnesota this year and I suppose that you will get your share of them.

I feel at home any where that I happen to be. I can lay down on the ground with nothing but my coat under me and sleep as sound as I ever did at home. I have got plenty of clothes three shirts, one pair of pants, one cap, one pair shoes, two overcoats, one dress coat, one blouse and can get all that I want such as socks, drawers, pants &c. I have no government blanket but have got an Indian blanket red, which is much better than the Government ones. We can get our washing done for 5 and 6 cts. apiece or do it ourselves. There is plenty of soap that we can get and many of us do our own washing.

C. B. Jackson is getting well & B. K. Soule is in the Hospital but is better.

Monday Sept. 9th.

It is cloudy and looks like rain. The boys are about as usual. I begin to feel like myself the first since we came from Bull Run. Boys are all in good spirits and seem to enjoy themselves. Last night on dress parade the Colonel fairly outraged the feelings of the whole Company. Chas. E. Davison whom the company had elected from the ranks to 4th Seargeant by the voice of the company was reduced to the ranks by the Colonel (Gorman). The charge was that he had violated a certain article of war (I have forgotten the number) (but it relates to talking & writing against officers). When we come to find out what the Colonel was trying to injure him for, we were ashamed for him. It simply amounts to this. Davison is the regular correspondent of the Republican. He wrote a private letter to some person in Minnesota & Colonel Gorman got it published in the paper some way and in that way seeks to wreak his vengeance on the Camp. Chas. Davison was liked by the whole company and we all feel sorry to see him used in such a way.

There is a man to be shot in the 3rd Vermont Reg. Volunteers for sleeping on his post when on picket guard near Washington. He was tried by a general court martial and sentenced to be shot to death. It is the first instance of the kind that has happened in the army this year I believe.

I remain as ever your brother and await an answer.

E. H. Bassett.

Direct to Washington

Camp Stone Md.
Sept. 15th, 1861

Dear Sisters Ella & Anna

It being Sunday and I am on guard, or rather I have to hold myself ready to go on guard, at any moment, I thought that I would write you a short letter. I am well and how I would like to be at home just long enough to go to church with you but that is impossible. I wrote a letter to Mother & Father yesterday and I do not know as I can think of anything new to write this morning. It is very hot this morning. The soldiers have all gone out into a grove to hear the chaplain preach. He is quite interesting in his discourse and it seems like a camp meeting to sit there and shut your eyes but if you should open them and look arround you would see some diference, the men all dressed in their uniforms with swords, pistols, knives &c. hanging by their sides. As for ladies, there are none hardly ever. Sometimes there will be two or three but they seldom attend. We have very good singing for nearly all the band are good singers. I would like to be there and go out with you and gather plums, grapes, hazelnuts and walnuts.

There is Elford, he would be the one that I would like to see and have an old fashioned scuffle with him. How we would make things tumble if we could get together. When you write again tell how his ducks get along and all the rest of the things that he has in his care. I wish that you could have some of the nice fruit that we have here. We have plenty of Peaches, Apples, Grapes &c. We have good times when we go out on picket guard. We can then get what we want and cook it ourselves and as we are all very good cooks we get along finely. I suppose that you will both go to school this next winter in Morristown. Sending my love to all the family and my respects to all the folks in Morristown and vicinity, I remain as ever your affectionate brother

E. H. Bassett.

Camp Stone, Maryland
Post No. 4 of the picket guard
¾ of a mile above Edwards Ferry
September 18th, 1861

Dear Brother George

I am now on picket duty. There are eight of us on this post. We came here yesterday about 11 AM & will be relieved tomorrow at eleven. Things are about as usual.

We can hear the drums of the rebels across the river. They are not more than 1½ or 2 miles distant. There was three alarm guns fired last night across the river. It caused considerable excitement. We sent up to camp and had companies A.B. & J come down to the river for a reinforcement of the pickets, not knowing what might happen. We thought best to be safe. Lieutennant McCallum came down here this morning. He says that the band have got their instruments and that the paymaster has come, all of which if so, we are very glad of. It is reported that the rebels are falling back from Washington to Manassas. They likely think that Washington is too strongly fortified. I would like to have you see the fortifications there, the guns, embankments, trenches &c. &c. They got badly whipped the other day at Chain bridge and likely think that we will not give up Washington for nothing. The day before yesterday our battery threw some shells over into one of their camps and destroyed several of their tents and they say that we killed one of their men. One shell burst when one mile or so high and a piece of it dropped on this side of the river. It fell so that it knocked a paper out of a man's hand as he sat reading it on the bank of the river. We have some guns here now that will reach over into their camps, Rifled canon about seven feet long. Our Regiment is improveing both in health and drill. There are three Reg. (regiments) camped close to us, one is the Mass. 20th. They are 1100 strong haveing one independent company of sharp shooters.

Mother wants to know if we are connected with General Banks. Tell her that we are in Brigadier General Stone's brigade and it is under General McClellan. We have been at Camp Stone over 4 weeks now and there is not any prospect of our leaving here soon although we may leave any day.

E. H. Bassett

Camp Stone Md.
Sep. 24th 1861

Dear Parents,

It has been some time since I have written home & I thought that I would improve this P.M. in so doing. I am well & the health of the Regiment is generaly good. There are a few cases of ague but none very bad. It is beginning to be quite cool nights. There was a frost last night. I believe the corn is nearly ripe. The farmers are sowing their wheat & things are progressing slowly. The war seems to be standing still as far as I know arround here. We hear of some fighting in Missouri and once in a while of some skirmishing in western Virginia. My Company is down to the river on picket. They will return tomorrow.

There was some 50 recruits from Minnesota came in last week & seven of them have joined Co. G and they are drilling and preparing to come into the ranks. We were payed two months wages last Saturday. I received $23.66. The boys are all in good spirits and want to stay and see the war ended & help do it with powder and lead. There was one of our men started for Minnesota yesterday. He has his discharge, he was shot through the arm and thigh, he will never have the use of his arm again as before. I think if the war should last long that provisions will bear a good price as everything seems to be going up. Eggs sell here for 25 cts. per doz. Honey 25 cts. per pint, Butter 25 cts. Milk 5 cts. per pint, Whiskey 25 when it can be got which is not often. Irish potatoes sell at $1.00 per bushel, Sweet Potatoes at $1.25 - $1.50. Small half grown chickens are worth 50cts. per pair. Turkeys sell at $1.00 apiece & so on everything that you can mention sells at just what they see fit to ask for it. This might all be expected where there are somewhere between seven & twelve thousand men in the immediate vicinity of Poolsville.

I often think of home and Minnesota, I would like to go to school this next winter but cannot as I see if I ever get out alive I will try and make up lost time. As there is nothing of importance to write & I am not in a writing mood I must quit.

Sending my love to all the folks,

E. H. Bassett

P.S. Enclosed find $5.00 which take & spend for the benefit of whom you please.

"Mail Call" Period Photo-Library of Congress

Camp Stone Md.
Sep. 27th, 1861

Dear Brother:

It is raining and we have nothing to do. I am well and as tough as ever. I have not heard from Minnesota for some time now but I suppose that you are all right as usual.

Yesterday was the day appointed by the President for

fasting and prayer throughout the U.S. and General Gorman had us all out to hear our chaplain. We marched out into a little grove close by where we heard a kind of historical sermon and prayers to suit the occasion, then we marched back to camp The band playing the Red, White & Blue. It all passed off in the best of order and was an interesting occasion. There is nothing particular to write about. We will have to go out on picket next Sunday.

George A. Williams, one of our Sergeants, returned yesterday from a visit to N.Y. State. He was sick and went there on a visit. He says that they are just beginning to enlist in the country now. The enlisting before has principaly been in the citys. He was glad to get back to his company having recovered his health.

The health of the camp is improveing & as it grows cool we will be as hearty as ever. I sent home $5.00 in a letter the other day, I would have sent more but I thought that I would wait untill we get another payment as I may have a chance to make something. I wish that you would write more often as I would like to hear from Minnesota every week.

One of our Surgeons who was taken prisoner at Bull Run says that our boys at Richmond are doing well. We have seven new recruits in the camp. It will be 5 months the 29th of Sept. since we enlisted. From the appearance of things now I do not think that the war will last long. I think that in about six months peace will be declared and both parties will become as one and lay down their arms, disband their troops & we will return home, after quelling the south and learning them that we are not to be bullied by them always. You must write to me as often as you can, Giveing all the news. The Captain is well. I must close this time and send my love to all.

Tell Elford that I like his idea of unfurling the flag in every state, south as well as north.

I remain as ever your brother.

E. H. Bassett.

86

Post No. 4 of the picket guard
On the Potomac above Edward's Ferry
Sunday September 29th, 1861

Dear Brother George

I now sit down to finish a letter that I began on the 27. We left camp this morning at 9 o'clock for our picket station. Things remain about as usual in camp and the Secesh are quiet I believe. I heard that they had sued for peace for 60 days. I suppose that they want a little time to prepare to meet their God (Jeff) and council with him as to the aspect of the sky in Cottondom. The river is very high and is rising fast. It is about 1 P.M. and since about 10 A.M. it has risen some 2 feet.

There was one of Co. D. died in the Hospital yesterday of the fever. His funeral takes place today at 10 A.M. It is the first death that there has been in our Reg. (except on the 21 July). Co. G is in very good health now. There is not one case in the hospital. There are some few that have the Ague but they are getting better. C. B. Jackson & Boultice Soule are getting along very well. We have got accustomed to laying around so that we do not care whether we do anything or not. We drew some clothing yesterday. I took a hat and an under shirt and a pair of socks. They are all of the best quality. We will soon have drawers & pants. Our Hats cost about $3.00 apiece and are of the very best material manufactured expressly for the Army. I now have 4 coats, 1 pair pants (am going to draw another pair soon) 3 woolen shirts, 2 pair socks, 1 shoes, a good hat and cap and one blanket. So you see that we have plenty of clothes and will keep warm here in this southern climate although I believe it is colder here than in Minnesota now. We had frost here last night. It is pretty cold here nights but we have plenty of coats and blankets and make out to sleep warm. We sleep any place that comes handy, on the ground, on the fence, on straw and sometimes we do not sleep at all.

Sept. 30th

It is clear & pleasant to day. There has been some heavy cannonading this forenoon both up and down the river.

Camp Stone, October 1st

We have just returned from picket. Things are about the same. Our men took one of the rebble posts near Washington, Munson's Hill between Washington and Fairfax. I heard it was done in the night. We took several pieces of canon. They made no stand. They fired some 75 shots at a lock in the canal yesterday but did not hit it. It is some 10 or 15 miles below here. You will think this is a queer letter perhaps but I could not mail it so I kept adding to it each day. I wish you would write often to me if you knew how glad I am to hear from Minnesota

Truly your brother,

E. H. Bassett

Direct to Washington,

Camp Stone, Md.
Oct. 2nd 1861

Dear Sisters Ella & Anna,

I now sit down to answer a letter which I received from Anna. I was very glad to receive your letter & also the one from George. It rains today and therefore we will have nothing to do "but stay in our tents and keep dry". I would like to be there and spend the day with you. I think that I would enjoy it very much.

The Governor of Minnesota (Gov. Ramsey) was here last night. He made quite a speech & said that he was very glad to see us & that there are thousands in

Minnesota that envied him his visit to our camp. He looks hearty and tough like all Minnesotans.

I am well as usual. Camp life suits me first rate and I feel at home just as much in the camp as I ever do anywhere. I would like to be there and help you to eat some of the nice mellons that you have and some of the plums would be very acceptable. Fruit is not very plenty here now. The soldiers have used it about all up. Elford takes my place does he? Well he may do it if he wants to now but he must be ready to give it up as soon as I get back. He is a good boy I know for he allways is. You say that he has not been to see Miss Ella for some time. I suppose that he has got discouraged. Tell him to be of good courage and perhaps he will get her yet. She is a fine little girl and he must not let her slip.

I would send you more papers if I could get them but they are hard to get hold of. I have received two Advocates.

Tell George to find that steer for I would not have him lost for any money. When you send another letter write how many swarms of bees you have got. Honey is worth 25 cts. per pound here. How do the steers work? Has Father got the old oxen yet?

Give my respects to all the folks, in Morristown. Tell George that I am much obliged to him for his letter and Anna also. Write as often as convenient.

I remain as ever your loveing Brother

E. H. Bassett.

Camp Stone, Md.
October 5th, 1861

Dear Parents,

Things are as quiet as usual I believe this morning. Companies G & I are down to the river. They went the night before last. I went down last night to carry the mail to them. There is an island in the river just below the Ferry some three miles long. It is thought that the rebels occupy it as a picket station. General Stone ordered two companies of our Reg. to go over onto it and try & hold it & Co. G & I were detailed to do it. They left camp the night before last. Yesterday they spent in gathering what small boats they could get & makeing paddles & last night about 10 O'clock they crossed over about 60 men. They did not see any thing, but found a fresh baked corn cake. There is a large farm on the Island. It is owned by a Mr. Young. He is a pretty good Union man now. He owns somewhere between 25 & 100 Slaves. There was no fireing last night & I have not heard any this morning. I guess the boys took it without any trouble. The Secesh threw some nine shells at us yesterday from one of their works about 5 miles distant. I should think they did not hurt any one. When they got done, Genl Stone run one of his rifled pieces up onto a hill & returned the compliment & I was told that our shell had a bad effect on a company of them that come in sight. It is generaly believed that they will not try to cross the river here & I do not know as we will.

Captain Messick started on a visit to his family yesterday. He is going to be gone 20 days I believe.

Jonathan Goodrich has just come from the river. He says that the boys took possession of the island without seeing any secesh. There are plenty of ducks & chickens on it and the boys will have a feast.

I sent Home $5.00 the latter part of Sept. Have you got it. Cal Jackson is well. B. Soule is somewhat under the weather. He is not very sick but does no duty. He is arround. C.C. Parker is well & the health of the company is good generaly. Tell George to write as often as convenient & the Girls also. I would thank them for those they have written.

We are still in Camp Stone. I do not know that we will leave here this winter. I must close wishing for a good old time with Elford & a visit with you all.

Good By for the present
Write soon. Your son,

E. H. Bassett.

P.S. My respects to all the folks.

Dear Parents

I am enjoying good health now to tell the truth I have had first rate health ever since I enlisted. I have not been sick only when I had the measles and I did not have as hard a time with them as many did. The health of the Regiment is pretty good now.

It is getting cool and it makes quite a difference in the spirits of the soldiers. I went to the little town of Poolsville this PM. As I passed along the road viewing the fields & everything else that could be seen from the highway it reminded me of old Minnesota The corn is ripe and cut up. The woods have begun to shed their foliage and every thing is tinted with the golden hue of autumn. I often think of the many happy days that I have spent in the woods in Minnesota. I cannot say that I would like to be there unless the country was enjoying peace within its own borders. As one of the lovers of freedom & justice I am willing to do what I can to restore it where it has been denied by a lawless mob and a few political aspirants who are not worthy of it. As the majority always rules in such matters the inocent always have to suffer with the guilty. This is often the case throughout the south. In nearly every paper we see accounts of the rebble soldiers entering the houses of the citizens, many of whom are good union men, and exacting the last morsel of meat, flour &c. and then because they cannot get what they want they will abuse the peaceful citizens for it. There is

91

little doubt as to the recklessness of many of the confederate soldiers but they undoubtedly have some well organized soldiery.

The boys in Company K seem to be enjoying themselves this evening, they have two violins, & triangle and & bass insturment from the band which makes good music and they are dancing. This is done considerable in the evening between sundown & 9 o'clock and at ¼ past 9 the lights are all out and everything is quiet in camp except at intervals of every 2 hours when the relief guard comes arround to relieve the camp guard when you can hear the sentry call out who goes there: halt. The corporal replies relief guard halting them at the same time, and the guard says advance corporal of the relief with the countersign. After giveing it the relief is marched up and the guard is changed for another, who stands his regular two hours.

We have pretty good discipline in camp and the laws laid down in the army regulations are pretty strictly adhered to.

My company is down to the river, they with Co. I occupy an Island just below the Ferry. I have not been down with them. They are haveing a good time I believe. I have been down to carry them the mail twice. I did not start untill after sundown and as it is some five or six miles to where they are I necesarily had to get the countersign and in passing our pickets I had to give it every little ways. This is a rather inconvenient way of traveling but when you come to think where you are you cannot help but admire the simple but efficient laws that govern the army. It is hard for a person to realize their position in the army to feel where you are & what you are doing to a person that has been in the habit of working every day and going where they please and when they please. It is apt to make them think of home and the associations arround it but you can get accustomed to it in a little time if you will only think so and when once at home here it is as any other home - there is none like it.

Wednesday morning the 9th.

It is quite cool this morning but it is all the better for that. I am going on guard this morning. The soldiers seem to feel well. They are prepareing for the various duties of the day. Three companies are going down on picket.

There was news from our two companies on the island last night that three of Co. G. and one of Co. I had been taken prisoners by the rebble pickets but whether it is so or not I cannot tell. I will try and find out and write during the day. It is hard to tell when to believe a report of any kind.

Since I commenced this morning the boys that we supposed were taken have come into camp & I have spoken with them so you see that the report was false like many others. It was generaly believed in camp last night by us here. The boys that come into camp this morning report everything quiet on the river. I will send you a Philadelphia paper to day.

We have a fine band. They have some new and valuable instruments. Genl Gorman has his appointment. The first Minnesota, the 19th & 20th Mass. and one or two N.Y. State volunteers are to be in his brigade. It is rumored that Maj. Dike is going to resign but it is not certain. Please excuse bad spelling &c. and write when convenient.

From your Son

Edward H. Bassett.

Camp Stone, Md.
Oct. 17th , 1861

Dear Parents:

We have been here long enough to get things fixed up in pretty good style. We have just got some larger tents. They were used by the 3d. Ct.. (Connecticut) in the Mexican War. Captain Messick is home on a visit. We expect him back soon. Things have been changeing arround considerable. General Gorman has his brigade, which consists of the 1st Minnesota, the 2nd N.Y. the 2nd Minnesota (which will be here this week) & one or two others. We have a new Colonel. His name is Dana, a Captain from the regular army & a West Pt. graduate. He has been living in St. Paul for some time.

Things remain about the same. We were on picket last Sabbath & will be next I think. The enemy are waiting for us to cross & we for them.

My love to all from your son

E. H. Bassett.

I see by the papers that the government has run short of blankets for the army & in many cases contracts have failed on account of the increased price of wool & the contractors would not supply because they could not make anything.

Sunday morning Oct. 20th.

It is a beautiful morning, cool & a good breese from the west which feels as if it might come from Minnesota or some place equaly as airy but in reality it is purified by passing over the mountains which are in plain sight. I am thinking how I would like to be in Minnesota this morning & as I am writing I imagine that I am in the woods on the bank of some of them silvery Lakes while the ducks & geese are swimming lazyly arround on their smooth surface. I have as fancyful a picture on my mind as I would wish to see but it is all far away in the distant Northwest where the people here think that it is so cold in the summer that it would not be profitable to keep Slaves. As far as that does go, I think they are about right. It was very still last night on the Potomac. I was up four hours. We could neither hear nor see anything across the river.

It is the intention of the rebels to make a stand at Leesburg if we should cross & if they were likely to get whiped there they would fall back to Manassas where their principal forces are in VA. It is impossible to find out the time & place of our movements, everything is kept secret & will not be publicly announced until after it has been done.

You must excuse me for this time for I expect that we will leave for Dixie before long. We expect to be relieved before long & cross the river. I close by sending my love to you all. Do not be worried about me for I think that the battles have been fought out towards Fairfax & Mannasas. I will write again before long. Write often & I will endeavor to write too.

From your affectionate Son

E. H. Bassett

Direct as before.

The boys are all well and I am as tough as a boiled Owl.

E.H.B.

We will reduce cottondom this time I guess.

CHAPTER #6
A SECOND ENCOUNTER

The presence of rebel forces on the west bank of the Potomac River posed a continual threat and annoyance. General McClellan felt the time had come to force them back from the river. The First Minnesota was involved in that effort at Edward's Ferry.

The First Minnesota and the 82nd New York regiments, under the command of General Gorman, marched the few miles to Edward's Ferry on the afternoon of the October 20 to show a display of strength to the confederates on the other side of the Potomac. Two companies poled canal boats across the river, engaged the enemy in a skirmish, and drove them back about 2 miles. After scouting the enemy side, they returned to the Maryland side of the river about sundown and marched back to their camp.

☙ BATTLE OF BALL'S BLUFF
OCTOBER 20, 21 & 22, 1861

The men were awakened at 1:30 on the cold, raw and dark morning of October 21st, ate a hastily prepared cold breakfast and in full marching order with knapsacks, marched back to Edward's Ferry where they arrived about dawn. The men immediately boarded canal and flat boats and crossed the river, two companies at a time. They formed in line-of-battle, with two companies sent ahead as skirmishers, and a detachment of Major Mix's cavalry, they began the advance on Leesburg, where the rebels were known to be in strength. The advance was driven back and a continuing skirmishing battle ensued. During this time, other forces had crossed but, due to their "worthless" guns, they were delegated to digging rifle pits and entrenchments. Gorman's command of 2,250 men remained there all that day and the following night. Additional troops were sent across the next morning using every canal boat, row boat and scow that could be found within 2 miles of the ferry. The weather had turned foul and the wind was blowing strongly from the Virginia shore, thus making crossings with men, horses and cannon an incredible task. By mid morning, approximately 4,500 men were in place on the Virginia shore, and the rain had become heavy.

Meanwhile, the main engagement of the battle had developed a couple miles up river on the high bluffs. On the same morning as the Minnesota men were struggling to bring their reinforcements across the river, General Stone had ordered Colonel Edward Baker with the 15th Massachusetts regiment to cross the river at Harrison's Island. The crossing was made in three small boats that could hold about 25 men at a time, and took a number of trips to complete. Climbing the steep 100 foot high bluff along a narrow, winding cow path and bringing along two cannons was a struggle. Arriving at the top, Colonel Baker joined a smaller force that was sent across a day earlier. They advanced to very-near Leesburg before being confronted by a large enemy force and driven back in a fierce hour's long fight. Baker was ecstatic at the prospect of getting into his first battle; a euphoria that would be short-lived. The union soldiers were forced back to an open grassland with their backs to the precipitous bluff and surrounded on three sides by brush and woods. The fight soon developed into a full-fledged massacre. Rebel sharpshooters began picking off the men from the cover of the brush and Baker set his, now three guns, to work. The overpowering fire from the woods took a terrible toll on the ever-more compact mass of men in blue. Colonel Baker was shot through the head and fell dead. The men on the guns were killed or forced from their posts. Two of the guns recoiled and cascaded over the abyss. Fear turned into panic and, rather than risk being killed or captured, the men began to jump over the edge and tumble down the jagged, rock-strewn slope. Some still held their rifles with bayonets attached, and in the wild melee, men were smashed into rocks, struck with rifles and stabbed with bayonets. The three boats that were below were soon put to use but capsized under the overload of terrified men. Those soldiers remaining on shore were being shot by the rebels looking down from the bluff. Their only escape was to swim the cold, rain-swollen river. In following days, many drowned bodies were spotted floating past Washington D.C. The total Union losses were around 900 men, with over 200 being shot and the others taken prisoner.

With the complete rout that had taken place on the Bluff, General McClellan decided, on the evening of October 22nd, that the position at Edwards Ferry was untenable and ordered a withdrawal. Acting on orders from General Stone, General Gorman ordered the boats put into the water and manned by lumbermen[23] from the First Minnesota. Knowing the steadfast dependability of the Minnesota Regiment, Gorman further ordered them to be the last to cross and to serve as rear guard. The entire withdrawal was completed in silence with good order. All 6,500 men, horses, guns, munitions and supplies were retrieved without the loss or abandonment of a single pound. During the Edwards Ferry portion of the battle, the Minnesota Regiment had bourn the brunt of the fighting, with the loss of only one man killed and one wounded.

---

[23] The men in the First Minnesota came from all parts of the state. Some companies were filled with lumbermen from the north that were very experienced in working with boats on the river.

Head Quarters
1st Reg. Minnesota Volunteers
Camp Stone Md.
Oct. 24th, 1861.

Dear Parents,

When I wrote before we were on picket on the Potomac & expecting to cross soon. Well about sundown we were relieved by three Companies of the 7th Mich. & we put on our Knapsacks & started for Edwards Ferry where Genl Gorman was crossing his forces. All of the Minnesota 1st had crossed the night & day before but the three companies that were on picket, A.B. & G. We marched up to the Ferry & made out to get accross about midnight. We crossed in a canal boat pushing it across with poles. Our men had driven the rebels back about 2 miles & we had the Star spangled banner waving o'er the sacred soil of the old Dominion & we were in posession of a corner that we were resolved to hold for a time. It was quite cool during the night but we had plenty of good old fence rails that made quite a comfortable fire where we dried our clothes & warmed ourselves. The next day it rained nearly all day & was quite disagreeable. I kept quite dry haveing a good Rubber coat. A little before sundown the rebels were met by our skirmishing party (which was from the Minnesota Reg. Comp. H & P). They opened upon us when not more than three rods distant & although they got the first fire they did not kill but one of our men. There was a company of sharp Shooters from Mass. near by & they saluted them with 5 rounds before they knew what they were about & the two <u>Howwitzers</u> that we had about 1/2 mile distant threw some few peacemakers among them they retired & let us crafty <u>Yankee Pedlars</u> have a good old cheer. While they were not much the wiser for the adventure & lost several men, we lost but one man killed. But General Lander was wounded in the leg. He rode out past our men & was taking deliberate aim at one of the Secesh when he received & ball in the leg. It is not a very serious wound & he will soon take his post again. He had command of one of the Mass. Brigades I believe. The fireing was pretty sharp for a few moments but our Minnesota men stood their ground well. Some of our boys at the time of the fireing were within shot of the rebels, getting bundles of wheat from some stacks in the field to sleep on. Some dropped their wheat & run for their guns which were nearly 1/2 a mile distant but some stuck to their wheat & brought it with them & when they came in the Reg. was in line of battle ready to march. It would be amuseing for you to see them. They did not appear to be excited in the least as to the result of the skirmish but all were ready to do their best & when the rebels began to run our lines resounded with cheers for some time, then we stacked our guns and retired for the night. The next morning it cleared off & the wind blew from the west drying the mud up very fast. It blew so hard that it was quite dificult to cross the river (which is about 80 rods wide here) & we did not get many troops across. Among them that did cross was one company of Conn. Riflemen. They were a splendid company armed with the Sword bayonet rifle muskets.

We are now in camp pretty well tired out with our running around & anxiously wait to hear the result. We did not have more than four or five thousand across all counted but there was plenty more to cross & any amount of artilery & cavalry. I do not think that we will have any fighting to do for some time yet but of course I do not know nor do I care. Genl Gorman gives us a great deal of praise & says that we are the most trusty men in his brigade. The 2nd Minnesota is not coming here as we supposed. So far the 1st Minnesota has had a good name & we will strive to maintain the same as long as we are in the service. The rebels fear us more than any other Reg. in the service at this point. We do not wish to praise ourselves but repeat what we hear them say. Gorman deserves great praise for the service in drilling & forming the Reg.

Friday morning, Oct. 25th, 1861.

It is a pleasant this morning but it was cold early. Everything was covered with a white frost. I do not see how you heard that I was in the hospital or sick. All that I have had to do with the hospital since I got over the Measles has been to go up there to see some of the sick boys. There are none of our Co. in there now. You say that you are going to use that money. I sent it for you to use & expect that you will do so. That script goes at par & I would not let any of the cutthroats have it for less. Some say that there is discount on it there. If there is, it is pure <u>stealing.</u> That Advocate that I sent I received when we were in Va. I will mail you 5 papers today. I would like to see & hear your new Preacher. Our Chaplain is on a visit to Minnesota. That dispatch that you sent I received. It is more than 1/2 wrong. The loss of our Company was little except the Captain That Chauncy Squires that Mrs. Willis inquired about we supposed was killed but he has written home from Richmond Va. being a prisoner there. He was wounded I believe through the arm. It is reported this morning that there was some 1500 of the Mass. men taken prisoners up where the 15th was so badly cut up. They surrendered themselves & their arms to some 600 of the rebels. They will not stand fire as a Reg, but there are some brave hearts in them. We knew that our men were badly whiped there (at Conrad's Ferry) but did not know the particulars until this morning.

My love to all the Family. Write when convenient.

From *Edward H. Bassett.*

I am well as usual & all the other boys.

P.S. In that other letter I was in a hurry when I sealed it for there was a man just going up to camp & I left one sheet in my Portfolio. I guess that you thought it was a queer thing but it was a mistake.

In his report of October 26, 1861, Colonel Napoleon T. Dana of the First Minnesota Regiment described the task the regiment had been asked to perform and the effectiveness with which they fulfilled their duty:

> "With great labor and in perfect silence this trying task was fully and satisfactorily accomplished. Not a pound of public property, either of provisions or ammunition or anything else was left behind, but every man, musket, knapsack, cartridge and ration which could be found was carried over by the boats; and details of men from this regiment, in addition to their own property, loaded into the boats and sent over considerable quantities of provisions and cartridges which were found to have been left behind by others. We destroyed nothing.
>
> As the first streak of dawn made its appearance, the First Minnesota again alone with General Stone, stood upon the Virginia shore, and everything else having been placed on board, the men were ordered to follow.
>
> What can I say for the men of Minnesota more than that for these few days of hardship and toil they proved themselves worthy of their state, and of the fame they have acquired for her! Patient, bold, obedient, orderly and disciplined, I claim for them the title of veterans."

CHAPTER #7
RETURN TO CAMP STONE

Following the battle of Ball's Bluff, the regiment returned to its previous camp and, once again, resumed the daily routine of camp life. The day began with a bugle blaring reveille at sunrise. Followed by policing [cleaning up] of camp, coffee and then drill at 7 AM followed by breakfast at 8 AM; drill at 10 AM, dinner at 1 PM; drill and parade at 4 PM; supper at 6 PM. The day closed with retreat, tattoo, and taps at 9 PM, when all lights were out and the camp was silent. Camp life seemed mundane and boring after the high excitement of battle. The men were kept busy with drill exercises, though they were now as capable of all the orders of march and arms as any regular army unit. Picket duty was welcomed as an opportunity to get out of camp and perhaps, to forage for fresh fruit or other foods that would supplement their usual fare. Time spent at Camp Stone was perhaps the easiest duty, with the best conditions of housing, sanitation, clothing, water and rations that the regiment experienced during its entire enlistment.

Head Quarters First Reg. Minnesota Volunteers
Camp Stone, Md. November 1st, 1861

Dear Parents,

I take the present opportunity to answer your last letters which I received one tonight & the other several evenings before. In the one that I got tonight you say that George has enlisted in the 3rd Reg. of Minnesota I am sorry that he has enlisted, but I admire his principles and his wish to do something to put down the rebellion and defend the flag of our country but I was in hopes that he would stay with you & help you to get along. But as he has enlisted now I suppose that it cannot be helped. As there are several boys in that Reg. that he is acquainted with no doubt he will find quite agreeable associates & I am in hopes that the war will not last more than one year at most. I have got a notion into my head that the national dificulties will all be settled without much more fighting. I will write to him immediately & will try & write to you more often.

There has not been any movements that I have heard of since we came from our visit to the shore of Va. a little over one week ago. The health of the camp is very good. There are a few cases of the Ague. B.K. Soule had a chill yesterday but is some better this morning. The other boys are quite well & I have not been sick on any account but once since I enlisted & I think that I have got so now that I can take care of myself pretty well & keep my health in future. In yours of the 20 & 22 you say that you are sick which I hope is not the case now. I often think of you & wonder if you are all well.

How do Mr. Buck's folks take it about Ben's re-enlisting. I did not think that he would ever do it, having been through the mill once. But I suppose that a peaceful home had no charms for him so he is (Off to the wars again). I hope that he will be successful & be an honor to his camp. You need not fear as to the morals of the camp life & when a person has once been through a campaign like the present I think that I shall know how to appreciate a life in a quiet home in the west. For all that I have seen yet I should prefer some quiet spot in Minnesota to spend my life where the continual hum of the camp will not ring in my ears.

Saturday morning Nov. 2nd

It is raining & the wind is blowing from the S.E. & it is very disagreeable to be out. However we make out to keep quite comfortable in our tents with a good fire & plenty of papers &c. We spend the day in talking, reading, writing &c. I am thinking of the way I used to spend such days when at home & unless I am badly mistaken I would enjoy a day at home now if it was raining. I was just as badly deceived in not seeing home before I left Minnesota as you were in not seeing me there. The Maj. promised me some 20 days to go home in if I would enlist for three years or during the war but he well knew that I would enlist only on such terms then for I well knew that there would be plenty of chances to enlist after visiting home for a few days & I might just as well have gone home as not. If they would only have been as good as their word but when a man gets an office in the army he is not apt to pay but little attention to their promises to privates. But as it is all past now there is no use in thinking about it but I understand them now.

I do not fear but what George will get along well enough in the army but I was in hopes that he would not enlist at present for I think that he was needed at home. I know how it would be with me if I was in Minnesota I know I would not be contented at home when all the boys were off to the wars. It is not likely that I shall see him while we are in the service for the 3rd Reg. will most likely be sent to Mo. or Kentucky. I will write to him as often as I can & get him in a notion of writing if I can.

You must excuse me for this time & write as often as you find it convenient. My love to the family. If George comes home tell him to write to me once more before he leaves & that he must let me know where he is often.

From your affectionate son,

Edward H. Bassett

When you write tell me if you get the papers I send. I sent you a map the other day. If you get it please write.

Edward's 18 year old brother, George S. Bassett, had answered the call for yet another regiment to be formed from the sparse population of Minnesota on Sept. 30, 1861. His exit from the family farm in Morristown must have put a considerable burden on his father, who was a farmer and cabinet maker. Edward had earlier advised his brother to remain at home but, apparently, the spirit of adventure was fired in his soul by his beloved older brother's example. Thus, he became a member of Company H of the Third Minnesota Volunteer Infantry Regiment. Of course, the wages and benefits offered likely played a part in his decision. Times were hard on the frontier and the fact that Edward was sending money home may have added enticement to his decision. General C. C. Andrews wrote:

"The pecuniary inducements which the Government then offered to the soldier were not slight. He was promised a bounty of one hundred dollars. The pay of a private soldier was thirteen dollars a month, as fixed by act of August 6, 1861, besides his "rations" or subsistence; and, in addition, clothing of the value of forty-two dollars per annum. The latter was always of good quality, and furnished at cost. The coat, blouse and trousers were all wool and dark blue, but after the first year of the war the trousers were light blue. The bootees or gaiter shoes, of split leather came up over the ankle, were tied with leather strings, had sewed soles, were very comfortable and durable, yet cost only one dollar and a half."[24]

---

[24] Gen. C. C. Andrews, Minnesota In The Civil War and Indian War; Vol. #1.

Head Quarters Picket Guard
Edward's Ferry Maryland
Sunday - November 10th, 1861.

Dear Parents:

I had been looking for a letter from you for several days & was very glad to hear from you. I received one from George the day before yesterday. He wrote from Snelling. He is in Co. H. 3rd Reg. M.V. He did not write many particulars, said that he supposed that I had heard of his joining the army but as he expressed it, he wrote more to find out where I was than to let me know where he was. I have not answered his letter yet haveing mailed one to him a few days before. He does not tell the name of any of the officers. He says that Withrow Sam Wyman & Hugh Donaldson are in the same company with him Co. H. He wrote that John Russell is in the 4th Reg. I am in hopes that he will improve in writing & try to give a few more particulars in the course of time. I will write to him often & keep track of him. There is but one reason why I am sorry that he has enlisted and that is because you are left alone on the farm unless you hire which will be both difficult & expensive. Although the prospects are not very encourageing at present for the speedy settlement of the difficulties of the government, yet I cannot but believe that it will come to a settlement in the course of the next 18 months & perhaps sooner.

We are getting along finely now. Co. G left camp this morning for picket duty here at Edward's Ferry. We have not been down here since the morning we left the Va. shore on the 25th of Oct. until this morning. The Potomac has been higher the last week than it has been before for years. It done considerable dammage to property along the bank in many places. It covered the

Canal & washed the banks out & the 8 mile levee between here & Seneca is drawn off now for repairs. The water is down now to its level.

Monday morning, the 11th.

It is a fine morning. There are a few of the Secesh to be seen this morning. They come down to the river on the oposite side and talk with us. They wanted us to fetch over a boat & take them accross, but as it is against orders to talk across to them we would not answer them. Our boys have crossed over to them several times & they have come over to us and talk. They think that they will whipe us out yet and seem to think that they are defending their homes & are confident that they are engaged in a good cause.

I am sorry that you feel so about my being in the army. The truth is I think it would have been a cowardly trick for *me* to have left and gone home when the three months Companies were enlisted for three years. I am sorry to hear that some of the Morristown boys should have backed out then & then enlisted again and back out again when they come to the point. I hope that they never will disgrace themselves & the town by making another attempt & a failure but I guess there is but little danger of their ever trying it again. Of all cowards such a one is the vilest. You say you think that the third Reg. will leave for the seat of war in two or three weeks. It would be a good thing for them as they will be as well off here as in. Minnesota If they are going to Soldier it they will be better satisfied to be where they will be of some service than to be in the old forts in Minnesota (I will number my letters after this and then you can tell when you miss one & if you will do the same it will be of great use in knowing when there is a letter delayed or lost. I will also number the papers as I mail them). As the winter is at hand I suppose that the mails will be somewhat irregular but I will write to you often. I am sorry that it is necessary for an army to be kept in this once happy nation to secure peace & liberty & settle the dificulty as soon as possible and that is the reason that I am here.

Remember me to Elford & the girls. Tell them to write.

As ever your Son

E. H. Bassett.

P.S. In camp Tuesday 12th all well - Just returned from picket everything quiet Weather pleasant, cool and smokey. I will mail you a paper this morning.

Edward.

THE UNION NOW & FOREVER

Mr. Henry Bassett
Morristown Rice Co
Minnesota

Envelope of letter: Postmarked Rockville, MD; Nov 20.

Head Quarters 1st Regiment Minnesota
Camp Stone, Md.
November 15, 1861

Dear Parents,

You seem to be continuously worrying about me. If you could know and believe our exact situation I am sure that you would feel different. Regarding the morals of camp life I find them to be much better than I supposed they could be. We have always had the name of being the most orderly & moral Reg. wherever we have been.

We now have one of the best of men for our Colonel. He is strictly temperate. Before he had been in the camp one week he destroyed all the whiskey that the sutler had & within two or three weeks he has spilled some $200.00 worth for the sutler in the N.Y. 2nd Reg. & is on a watch all the time to catch any that comes into camp. We all like him first rate. We are well supplied with books & papers to read. There is always plenty of papers &c &c to read in our tents. Some of the friends in Naugatuc sent me three papers this week one of the American Messenger and two copies of the Advocate & Family Guardian which is published at the house of industry N. Y. City. There was good news from our fleet last night in the Washington papers. They have captured Fort Walker on Hilton Head mounting 23 guns & Fort Beauregard on Bay Pt. mounting 19 guns. The guns were all of heavy caliber. They were completely routed & left everything behind. The fleet was not materially damaged & our men lost but few & will soon possess Beaufort the rebels had deserted. I look on this as a forerunner of a more complete victory over them. The flag is now waving in the first state that rebelled & I think that the day is not very distant when it will fill the place of the snake & cotton.

You speak of my suffering while standing on guard & of being in danger of an attac from the rebels. I have had just as hard times in Minnesota as I ever have or expect to have on guard while in the army and the danger from the enemy is so little that we scarcely think of it. In reality there is no danger from them here in MD. at all. If they should try to cross we have something that will make their eyes stick out & if we wish to cross we have the advantage of them for we can drive them back with our canons and they cannot touch us until we go some ways from the landing & then all we want is an open field to fight them on. Your fancy (imagination) makes things seem diferent from what they are. There has not been any fireing between the pickets here at Edw. Ferry for a long time but there have been several of our boys over to them & they have come over to us since the last fight.

I was on guard last night and am sleepy & it is time to mail this letter so I must close. Excuse all of it & I will try & do better next time.

Your Affectionate Son   *Edward H. Bassett*

Co. G. 1ˢᵗ Minnesota

Camp Stone, Maryland
Nov. 23ʳᵈ, 1861

Dear Parents,

I have given up all hopes of there being anything of any importance done on the Upper Potomac untill there is an important movement made below. We can easily hold our position & keep the rebels from crossing over into Maryland & raising the citizens to their aid. At present things are quiet as far as I have been able to learn. There has been some canonading in the direction of Fairfax but I guess it does not amount to anything, at least the Washington paper does not speak of any fight. I mailed you a N.Y. paper yesterday & will send you a Washington paper today.

I do not know where we will be quartered this winter but I expect that we will leave here before long. Perhaps we will go down near Washington & go into winter quarters there & we may go & occupy some of the forts taken by the fleet on the coast. At any rate we are willing to go any where even if it is to <u>Valley Forge</u>. We all like our Colonel and Brig. General & will try to give as good an account of ourselves as circumstances will permit wherever we may go.

I have not rec. but one letter from George yet but expect one every mail. I have written to him once & will write again soon.

I would like to know how you know that you have got my likeness for I never wrote you that I sent it but as you recognize it I will have to own up. It was a poor thing but the best I could get then as there are no good artists here & they are very much crowded & do not take much pains.

Ella's letter was very interesting & I shall be very much pleased to receive more of the same sort. I hope that there will be a good school in Morristown this winter. Tell Elford that he must hurry & learn to write so he can write me a line once in a while. If I should not see him for three years he will be quite a large boy by that time and I would do well if I know him.

I must close for it is time to mail this letter. Give my best respects to all the folks.

As ever your affectionate son

E. H. Bassett

Direct to Washington D.C.
Edward H. Bassett Co. G 1st Minnesota

During the winter spent in Camp Stone, Maryland, the troops had plenty of opportunity to become familiar with sticky, gooey mud. Incessant rain without freezing temperatures turned the entire camp into a sea of mud—the kind of mud that sucks your shoes off and endeavors to pull you down like a giant squid. Mud that sticks to your clothes, your equipment, your hands, your food and everything else you come in contact with. The kind of mud that is as slippery as grease, when wet, and as sticky as tar as it dries. Many a letter that was written home carried the tale of the treacherous mud.

Envelope from letter of December 1, 1861

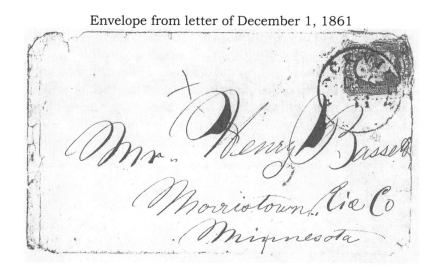

Camp Stone Md.
Sunday December 1st, 1861

Dear Parents,

There is not anything new to write. Things keep just about the same. The weather is rather cool but no snow here yet. Yesterday morning the mountains in Va. looked quite white. We have a very fine view of them from the upper end of our camp.

I was on guard last night. We had a very comfortable time. It froze just enough to stiffen the mud which is about (say from one to four inches deep). And such mud, I assure you it is none of your Minnesota mud. The soil here is about like it would be there if you were to remove about two feet from the surface of the timber soil. Charming indeed to wade through but we are armed with good heavy boots which we have bought since we were payed off last Nov. 20 th in Poolsville at a price somewhat in advance of Minnesota Prices.

We were payed two months wages on the 20, enclosed I send you $5.00 and would send more but I had to get me some boots as I thought that shoes were going to be poor things in this climate & I want a little to spend for papers, writing materials and etc.

I will mail you Harpers Weekly & Leslies Illustrated; the pictures are quite interesting I think especially the Grand review which must have been a grand sight. Last week I sent you three Leslies, Harpers & the N.Y. Illustrated & the National Republican.

Drawing from Harper's Weekly, Caption reads:
"Great Review at Bailey's Cross Roads, Virginia, on November 20, 1861"
"Sketch By Our Special Artist From The Top Of A Barn"

We have not done anything towards fixing up our quarters for the coming winter & I expect that McClellan intends to send us to invade the soil of the rebble states & winter south of here. I suppose that things are frozen up in Minnesota by this time & the ground covered with snow. I wish it was so that I could spend the next two months there but I suppose that I would be about the same as usual if I was there & wish that I was somewhere else before spring. As it is I would not take my discharge if I could get it unless the war comes to an end in the next 6 years. I intend to spend my time in the army if they don't shoot me to get me out of the way.

It is my opinion that the trouble will never be

settled as long as the cause is left, which none hesitate to say is Slavery. When the nation is restored to itself, when the North and South are at peace with each other & are governed by the same laws living under the same flag in peace then Slavery will be crushed to rise no more. But we have got to fight they are desperate there is no alternative but to fight. They know it and will fight to the last..

I must close for it is late and the bugle has just sounded for divine services. .

Captain Messick sends his respects, he is well.

My love to all the family

As ever your obedient son

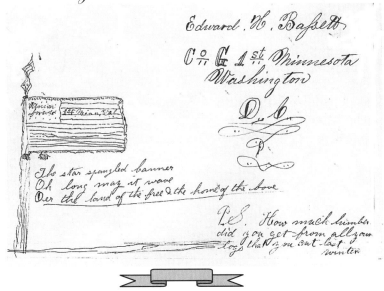

Camp Stone Md.
Sunday eve Dec. 1st.

Dear Brother Elford:

For fear that you will think that I have forgotten you entirely I thought I would write you a few lines. I would much rather see you face to face and have one of our old times but we are too far separated to talk about

115

that kind of business. I suppose that you are having a good time this evening. Perhaps you have got Charley hitched in the sleigh & takeing Miss Ella S. out. At any rate I hope that you are well & haveing a good time. I suppose that you find plenty to do helping father take care of the stock. How I often think of you & think that I would give most anything to see you & wonder when I shall see you again. I hope that it will be before long but I don't expect to until the war is ended. Now I want you to give my best respects to all the folks in Morristown. You must take good care of Ella & Anna. Help them to school & back. Try & learn all that you can. Help father & mother & do the best you can.

If the Secesh don't shoot me I will be back to see you some time.

Nov, 28 was Thanksgiving. We had no drill and had a good time generally. In the evening we had what is called an oyster supper. There are seven in the tent where I stay. We had more then we could eat. Now I have written you quite a long letter & I must close. So good bye for this time.

From your brother

Edward H. Bassett

Co. G. 1st Minnesota

Army upper Potomac Maryland

Head quarters 1st Reg M.V.
Camp Stone Md.
Sunday Dec 8th 1861

Dear Parents)

While thinking of you at home this pleasant Sabbath morning asking myself how you all are at home I thought that I would endeavor to write you a few lines.

The weather is beautiful clear & just warm enough to be comfortable. I am enjoying good health & feel as contented as I ever do after staying in one place for some four months. We went out on picket last Wednesday morning up to Conrads ferry. I was on the post just at the lower end of Harrison Island. We were in plain sight of the open field & the place where the lamented Colonel Baker was shot and where the Mass. 15th was engaged in a hand to hand contest with a foe outnumbering them three to one & the steep bank that they were driven down into the muddy waters of the Potomac. But everything is quiet now.

We have undisputed possession of the Md. Side of the Potomac and the Rebels the Va. Side and Harrison's Island which it is said that they occupy with considerable force during the night. It is only 2 ½ miles to Leesburg where they have things arranged to give us a warm reception whenever we see fit to make an attempt to plant the old flag on the sacred soil of the old dominion.[25] We had a good time while on picket.

---

[25] This location is about 20 miles Northwest of Washington D.C. on the Potomac River. This letter refers to the Battle of Balls Bluff in which the regiment participated during Oct. 20 through 23.

117

There was some slaves gathering the corn in the field where we were stationed. One has a wife & family in Leesburg. They say that they "never seed sich folks, seems like dey want to die." They did not know what to think of the Mass. Boys to see every one trying to see who could get the fairest shot, not heeding the bullets that were flying as thick as hail. It was new to them. They say they can fight with their fists but when the guns come arround they are out. They are very much in fear of being shot when they see a gun. They say that before the Union soldiers came here the inhabitants were drilling and running their horses. They say there was some union men but they did not know what union meant but as soon as the federal soldiers came they were all union.

I went down to Poolsville yesterday. There is not much but soldiers & horses, wagons & every thing pertaining to military life. There are some 4 or five stores, one or two harness shops, two or three shoe shops, Post Office, a large Catholic Church & some few tolerable decent private houses and any number of slave stables.

I received a letter from George on the 2nd of this month. It was dated Camp Bewel. (Probably Camp Buell) Louisville, Kentucky Nov. 26th. I answered it immediately, he was well. I recv'd. yours (your letter) of the 21st on the 5th of this month.

You seem to think that we are in a suffering condition and it is not strange that you should if you believe what is written to the Republican by their Regular correspondent. Now you know some men are good at begging and the more they have the more they want and would rather eat the crumbs that fall from the rich man's table than to use their own when they have plenty.

Now if there is a man in our Regiment that is so stingy & mean as to beg clothes from the Patriotic

Citizens of Minnesota when he has plenty of clothes furnished by the government besides $13.00 per month and there are plenty of everything wearable to be had for reasonable prices as handy as it is here.

"That he will be kicked from the door & sent on his way penniless. I would refer you to the Central Republican of Nov. 21." Now as to clothing, we are well supplied & as far as the suffering in our camp is concerned I hope that there never will be any thing more said about the Minnesota 1st not having things to make them as comfortable as camp life can be expected to be. So far we have not suffered any thing like what has been represented by some in writing back. I have got as many clothes as I know what to do with. I have one rubber coat, which I bought for $5.00[26], one over coat, one dress coat, one fatigue coat, one pr. pants, four shirts, 3 pr. socks, one cap, one hat, two blankets & 3pr of gloves & one pair of good heavy boots which I bought myself. Now what could be expected more for one man to wear.

There is the rubber coat which I bought for	$5.00
Two pair of gloves, one cotton-one leather	$1.20
One pair boots	$5.00
2 pair socks	$ .40
	$11.60

---

26 The raincoat shown here is an exact reproduction of those used, photo courtesy of C & D Jarnagin Company, Civil War Reenactment Outfitters, Corinth, Mississippi.

Now I could have had shoes if I had wished to but I had rather wear boots as they are better in wet weather. The socks were the only thing that there was any real necesity of my buying and that was because my feet were sore from traveling.

My rubber coat has been worth three times what I payed for it and will last some time yet. There is $11.60 out of three payments for clothing and that I could have saved & got all from Uncle Sam if I had chosen to.

I know that the people of Minnesota are ready to help the poor & those in need & are ready to make most any sacrifice for the good of the soldiers from their state but the Minnesota 1st is well provided for. Talk about suffering you might say that there is suffering among all classes of people from a Prince down to a beggar. Some people are always in distress if they cant have everything that they can think of & they will likely spend all their lives in trying to accumulate all the property that they can for fear that they will not have their share.

We are supplied with plenty of good government rations it is true some of the bread that we have had has been marked B.C. 110, and had some unmistakable signs of age but it was all very good considering their age.

****

The quartermaster was subjected a good deal of heckling about rations when some of the hardtack crackers were delivered packed in wooden crates that were marked B.C.110. The men had a field day insisting the stamp indicated the date of their manufacture.

****

You may think that I am trying to deceive you about our condition but I don't like to have you think that we are in a suffering condition & for that reason I have told you just how we are off for clothes & such things & I hope you will not worry any more about our suffering for the want of such things.

The weather is very warm today, the warmest that we have had for some time. I sent you a $5.00 note the other day in a letter. I suppose that the streams are all frozen over in Minnesota but here it seems like the early part of autumn.

Captain Messick is well and on guard duty today. The boys are all tolerable well. There are some cases of the ague. We are in hopes that the war will be brought to a close as soon as it can honorably.

I must close hopeing that this will find you all well. My love to Elford and the girls.

E. H. Bassett

Co. G, 1ˢᵗ Minnesota

P.S. I am not sure where we will stay the winter but expect some to stay here.

Please write soon and excuse poor spelling.

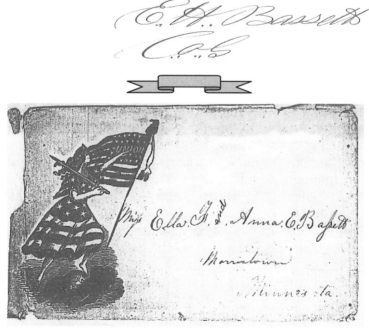

Envelope from letter of December 15, 1861

Army of the Upper Potomac
Camp Stone M.D.
Sunday morn Dec 15th, 1861

Dear sisters and brother,

Ella, & Anna .. .. ..& brother .. .. ..Elford, I received your kind letter of the 1st & 2nd last evening and I assure you that it was very welcome. It found me well & enjoying myself as well as could be expected. As today is Sunday and things are quiet we have the whole day to rest.

It is a beautiful morning clear and pleasant. There is not any snow but the ground is frozen some. I was just thinking how I would like to be there in Minnesota with you today and take a good sleigh ride but as I cannot be permitted to be there I shall try to feel contented here. But I suppose Elford will be stirring around & take you down to Sabbath school.

I am glad that you are going to school & if I was there I would try & take you to the writing school. I will send you the money now if you thought that you could go. We have preaching in camp this A.M. by our chaplain. There is not much to write about now the enemy are in quite strong force over to Leesburg but the Potomac river is between us and them.

There was a balloon went up on this side of the river yesterday for the purpose of seeing how the rebels were situated. I do not know what they saw. General Stone went up once. I believe our men threw a few shells over onto an island the other day and drove the rebels off. We have been fixing up our tents for cold weather for the last week and I expect that we will stay here for some time.

As you did not say what the name of your reader is please write next time. Do you have any spelling schools this Winter.

Give my respects to all the folks.

As ever your brother

E. H. Bassett

Co. G 1st Minn, Washington

122

Harper's Weekly Sketch By: Ed. Pietsch

Head Quarters Gormans Brigade
Camp Stone Upper Potomac   Maryland
Monday, Dec. 23rd. 1861.

Dear Parents & folks at home,

Once more I sit down to write you a few lines. It has been raining all night & is nice and slick outdoors. We have not had any rain for a long time. The weather has been beautiful. I am sorry to hear that Father is sick for I do not see how you can get along with the stock. I wish that I could be there & take care of them until he gets well. I am in hopes that the war will end soon but there is not much hope of its ending much before next fall, I don't think, although I do not look for much more fighting unless some foreign power interferes & if there should it might be settled sooner than you could think. For my part I have no fears of the English trying their hand here. They may send over forces into their Provinces to be secure of their own & prevent the colonies from annexation to the U.S. but they will never trouble us. I don't think they will make much if they do.

We are going to spend the winter here in this camp I expect. We have got two teams hauling logs to build houses today. All the companies have got cook houses built. I expect we will sleep in our tents. I hope so at least.

I rec. a letter from George dated Dec. 14th. He was well. He said that they were about 35 miles from Louisville. I answered his letter & sent him some stamps. He said that Genl Wyman has been sick but was feeling better.

There is an ambrotype gallery set up within about 30 rods from here. I am going to get my Pic. taken on cast iron or harness leather & send it to George.

How are you for hay and feed for the cattle this winter. Do you get your wood from the University this winter. How do the university setlers get along farming. How does the Prairie school get along this winter. Who teaches it? Is the school house comfortable warm? I should like to be there with you & spend Christmas & New Years but I will have to be contented here. I hope that we will be shooting the Secesh or some other game. The Sutler for the N.Y. 34th was drummed out of camp on the 10th inst. for selling whiskey. The whole Brigade was drawn up in line & he was marched the whole length with some 6 or 7 large bottles strung arround his neck & the fife & drums playing the rogues march. They took him outside the lines & warned him to not appear among us again. The boys are in as good health as could be expected. There are but two in the Hospital & they are nearly well. Our 1st Lieutennant Mac. has been sick for some time but is mending now. Captain is well. If Father does not get well soon I will try & come out there & straighten up things if I can but it will be a hard case to get a chance. It is snowing now & I guess we will have a young winter. It is about late enough.

The news in the papers is encouraging. We heard the guns at the Point of Hocks very plain.

Excuse me for this time and I hope this will find you well. *E. H. Bassett*

Co. G

Head Quarters Gormans Brigade
Upper Potomac Camp Stone Md.
Dec. 28th, 1861.

Dear Parents

It is rather cold but there is not any snow. I am well except a bad cold and my teeth trouble me some.

I rec'd a letter from George dated the 18th at Camp Dana, Ky. He was well & seems to be enjoying himself well. I have received four letters from him since he has been south. We are building some houses to live in this winter but I guess we will keep our tents and occupy them when we wish. I had rather stay in the tents than not. It is quite healthy now. There is not as many cases of the Ague as there was along in the fall. It was quite cool here Christmas but we did not have any sleigh rides nor drill. I spent my time reading & thinking of the past & future. There is some talk of England's declareing war with us but nothing official yet I believe. I wish you had some of your turkeys & chickens here. You could get a good price for them. The turkeys would fetch from 2 to 3 dollars apiece stuffed & baked & chickens 35 & 40 cts.

Captain Messick is well. Lieutennant McCallum is going home to recruit his health I believe. He has been sick for some time. I see that you still worry about my not getting along & suffering. Now I again assure you that we are just as comfortable as I could wish. It would not be reasonable to expect to have every thing as nice & comfortable as at home. That is more than I ever could expect.

Please write often & excuse me for this time.

My respects to all the folks

Edward

Happy New Year to all.

Camp Stone Md.
Jan. 14th 1862

Dear Parents

It was just 5 months ago yesterday since we came to this camp & the prospect is as fair for staying as much longer now as it was when we came for staying one week. We have anticipated moveing several times but have been deceived as often & we will not believe we are going to move until we are packed up & on the way now.

There was about three inches of snow fell last night & it looks quite wintry this morning. We were down on picket from the 4th to the 8th at Edwards Ferry the canal frozen over so that we could walk over on the ice & the morning of the 8th we could have crossed the river on the ice if we had wished. I went nearly half way across myself but it had been quite warm since & rained & the ice had about all gone.

The news in the Washington paper of yesterday was unimportant. I believe that General Burnside's expedition has sailed & there is also to be a movement made down the Miss. & we are hopeing for success. It is not likely that there will be any demonstration made here at present. We are waiting patiently for something to be done that will tell towards crushing the rebellion but we have waited so long that it seems like hopeing against hope. I think that things look just as favorable (& perhaps more so) now for a telling blow to be struck at the fiend secesh as they have since the outbreak of the rebellion, but there is a risk run and we wait the issue. I rec'd. a letter from George dated Jan. 5th he was at Camp Anderson Lebanon Junction he says that things looked quiet. They were guarding RR bridges to keep the citizens from burning them.

Have you any idea who it was that stole my logs on the river? What terms do you propose to rent the farm on and how long.

I am sorry that things should be as they are but it is too late to mourn now the only way is to hope for the best & I hope that the war will close before another year & if I am alive I will come home & try & help you straiten things up so that you can all live comfortably on the farm which I know you all would prefer to liveing in a country town like Morristown although the children would have the advantage of the town school.

We will receive our pay soon & I will send you some money. I am square with all here & intend to remain so. I do not think that I have spent more than $1.00 at the Suttler's since our last payment, there are plenty of inducements but it is a poor plan to buy much of their trash I find. It will soon be spring & then I will long to be in the woods & sugar camps. It is rather dull today here in camp. 5 months without leaving its limits but we are very well off after all when we come to think of all the army & the toils & care that are incident to the camp life of a Volunteer.

I am well as usual there are not any of our Company in the hospital now I believe. Lieutenant J.J. McCallum has gone to Minnesota on a furlough for his health & there is one of our Corpls. going out there as a recruiting officer soon.

My love to all the family and write soon

E. H. Bassett   Co. G

Camp Stone Md.
Jan. 23rd, 1862

Dear Parents

We went down on picket last Sunday & returned Tuesday evening it rained all the time while we were there & the mud was about eight inches deep. The Potomac rose some 10 feet while we were there. It beats all the streams to rise that I ever saw. The current runs as fast as a horse can trot. If we don't have some mud here I do not know where you could go to find it. We were up to Conrad's Ferry. Things were quiet we could see the secesh pickets as usual & at night I could hear guards speak very plain when they halted each other. Monday we could hear considerable stir over in Leesburg. It is reported that the rebels have left Mannassas but it is nothing more than a report I guess. There is also good news from Kentucky the rebels were whiped and routed, their stores taken & in the hands of the Federalist Gents, 3 officers killed & etc. I hope the war is fairly commenced & will be hurried up & ended soon.

I am well except a bad cold & it will not last long. I see by the Faribault paper that you have had some cold weather there on the 12th inst. That list of prisoners in the Faribault paper in the hands of the rebels from the Minnesota 1st is not correct there is but one name there that was ever in our Company & that is Chauncy Squires. The others that are assigned to Co. G never was in our company.

We expect to get our pay in a few days, it is time some of the Regiments have been payed around here. We are living first rate now we drawed a lot of fresh pork this week & we make out nicely now we have a large bakery & they bake all the bread we want. I am heartily sick of the sunny south if we have anything of a fair sample of it here this winter it is not very cold but the mud is knee deep most of the time.

I hope you can make out to read this but I fear it will be hard work excuse me for this time.

E H Bassett

Head Quarters first Regt Minn Vol

Camp Stone Maryland

Jan 23d 1862

Dear Sisters

Ella & Anna

s I was writing a letter home I thought I would write you a few lines. I got a very long & interesting one from Anna the other day.

It is very muddy here now but I hope it will dry off before long. I heard that there was about 12 inches of snow in Minnesota & sleighing must be nice. I would like to be there & have a ride with you. I want to see you all just as bad as you can think but you know I must wait. I guess the rebels are getting sick of the war there are a great many of them gone home, I believe their time being out and the Yankees not all killed.

I hope you will both write often for your letters are very interesting.

Remember me to Elford tell him that I think of him nearly every day & want to see him very much.

Edward H. Bassett

Co. G 1ˢᵗ. Minnesota Volunteer Inf.

Upper Potomac
Camp Stone Md.
Wednseday eve Feb 12ᵗʰ, 1862

Beloved Parents

Things are very quiet here as usual. We were payed off on the 31ˢᵗ of Jan. in U.S. Treasury notes. They are as good as Gold. I get letters from George quite often he is doing well I guess. The weather is quite changeable here freezing nights and thawing days sometimes snowing and sometimes raining & mud in abundance all the time. Capt Messick is off on a short furlough to recover from a hurt that he received some four weeks since. (He slipped when walking in the mud and dislocated his ankle), I hope he will recover soon for we are under command of a Lieut. from Co. A and he is a Dutch French Irishman & no count.

I suppose that you have heard of the arrest of General Stone and his confinement. I have been knowing to some of the charges that they have against him & we have long doubted his loyalty to the cause in which he was trusted we do not mourn his loss. I have allways thought that our defeat at Balls Bluff was occasioned by the traitorous conduct of the officers in command. It has turned out about as I thought it would when it was investigated by the proper authorities.

We are anticipating good news from the Burnside expedition. It is reported in camp that they have been successful & routed & captured the rebles. Colonel Dana has been appointed Brigadier General and I fear we will loose him. Lt. Colonel Miller is in command now. He looks quite feeble yet. There was several of our boys that have been off on a furlough returned lately they look fresh and hearty. There was also some fifty recruits came in lately but they all joined the other Companies being mostly from the river towns. (Towns along the Mississippi River).

It is quite healthy here now. There is not more than 6 or 7 in the Hospital, pretty good considering everything. W. W. Brown is the only one from Go. G & he was taken up this evening he is not very sick yet but as things are so much more comfortable in the Hospital than in the tents he thought he had better go there. I do not think he will be sick long.

I often think how I would enjoy a good sleigh ride this winter in Minnesota I have not seen but one sleigh this winter & that was standing by an old whitewashed house on bare ground. There has not been snow enough at once to run a sleigh in a stoney country like this.

We have the Faribault Republican of the 5th it looks quite natural we get it every week. I received an Advocate from you last week. There is a young man in my mess that receives it regularly from a friend in Mich.

Co. G. went up oposite Balls Bluff on the 5th as a reserve and returned on the 9th we had a very good time. I had to stand guard just 6 hours in the four days. We have so little to do that I fear I shall loose all the life and ambition that I ever had if I should ever get free. There is not enough to do for exercise since it has come so muddy we drill once in the morning when it freezes hard enough to stiffen the mud.

As for my becoming a correspondent for their Paper: In the first place you know I am not capable to write for any kind of correspondence. If I was there I would like to go to the writing school and also attend the Lyecum and hear the different subjects discussed that will arrise but you well know that I decline taking any active part in any thing of the kind. If I ever have a chance I intend to go to some kind of a school & learn to spell & read a little better than I now do. If I had known that we were going to stay here as long as we have I should have got some books of some kind & tried to improve some for we have been situated so that I could have studied some nearly every day. Now I shall wait until I get out of the service before I shall try to do anything of the kind.

Thursday Morning Feb. 13th. It is very pleasant this morning it froze some last night. Just such a morning as I used to like to go into the woods to work. I suppose that there will not be any sugar made on the University land this spring. (making sugar from maple syrup).

The Reg't. was presented with a fine stand of colors on the 1st inst. We have got a first rate band they play well & are improveing every day. We are heartily sick of laying here on the Potomac where we can hear & see the rebels but are not allowed to give them a single shot. We all wish that we was in Ky. or Mo. or at least where there is something doing more than straining our eyes to see as far into rebbeldom as possible and not have the privelege of wadeing into them. We would like to give them a good licking before they are surrounded and forced to surrender. It is hard for those that have not been here to realize much about the dullness of camp life in such a place as this we have been here upwards of six months & we never expected to stay that long in one camp if we should stay in the service 6 years.

We have just come in from drill. We are drilling in the bayonet exercise I like it very well although a charge would be better. The confederates are learning it and intend to make it their best holt if we ever meet them. There is some heavy firing down to the river this morning the Secesh commenced it & have thrown some 15 or 20 shells onto this side some of them burst &

132

some fell harmless. Our men are returning the compliment now they have thrown three within the last 10 minutes. I hope that there will be something done before long. We have a telegraph dispatch that says that General Burnside has beat the rebels at Roanoke Island & taken a large number of prisoners if it is so I look for the fall of Savannah & some other important places in the posession of the Rebels. We are looking for important news from Ky. & Mo. & also from the coast. The Washington papers are very hard on General Stone & it seems to be generaly believed that it is a good thing for the government. We have suspicioned him for some time & I have often heard the soldiers say that they hoped they would never be led into a fight under him & I guess they have got their wish for I think he will not be in command again for some time at least. I think the time has come where there has got to be something done on one side or the other. (We all hope for the best)

As ever

E. H. Bassett

The end

Feb 12th 62

Camp of the Minnesota 1st
Camp Stone, Maryland
Feb. 20 th, 1862

Dear Sisters and Brother --- Ella, Anna, and Elford,

As it is such a fine morning to write I thought I would try and write you a few lines. It is a very pleasant morning with the exception of the mud. But the air is almost exactly like it is in Minnesota in the spring cool and pleasant. It made me think of old Minnesota the first thing when I went out in the morning to roll call, but I suppose that you are having good sleighing there now and some very cold weather. Last Saturday there was about three inches of snow fell and Sunday morning it looked quite wintry the sun rose clear and it was as still and calm a sabbath morning as I ever saw. There was not wind enough to move the flag from its staff and it like everything else seemed to wear a solemn aspect. Everything is as quiet as usual here now. The snow has all melted and we have in its place about five inches of mud. General Gorman shells the rebels every now & then but I guess he has not injured anything except some of their earthworks that are in sight. I received the Central Republican by last nights mail dated the 12th. I have not heard from George for some time. He was well the last that I heard. Before you receive this you will hear of the recent capture of Fort Henry and Donelson and Roanoke Island the rout of Genl Price from Springfield, the evacuation of Bowling Green and it is rumored here that Savannah was captured without fireing a gun. We are still looking for more and important victories and I hope it will not be long before we will have them whipped and

the war brought to a close. The Captain is recovered and is able to do duty. I hope that we will all return to Minnesota before next winter and we undoubtedly will if things all go right. From what I hear you are having very lively times in Morristown this winter. As there is plenty of snow there I suppose you have some fine sleigh rides. Elford must have some fun in the snow and also some pretty cold fingers once in a while when he goes out to do the chores. I wish I could see him and have a good old time but I shall have to wait some time yet but we will have some fun if we ever do meet.

Good by for the present,   *Edward,* *as ever*

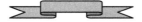

Camp Stone, Maryland
Feb. 24th, 1862

Dear Parents,

I received yours of the 13th on Sat. the 22nd. It was thankfully rec by me I tell you. It had been some ten days since I had got a letter from you. I am well and to tell the truth I never enjoyed better health than I have since I have been in the Army. There is some talk of our moving. We were ordered to pack our things yesterday and be ready to march, where I do not know and I guess we (I), have not heard anything about it this morning. Everything is as quiet as usual here. I heard some canonadeing early this morning down towards the ferry. The news from the east and the west is encourageing. The long looked for blow has at last been struck. A few more such will wind up the rebels for the present. The victory has been decisive and the rebels feel the shock. We expect to hear of more and important victories soon. It has been reported here that

Centreville and Manassas was being evacuated but I cant believe it they have built some strong works around Centreville since the 21st of July last and I do not think they are going to stand their chances in an open field. Some think we will cross here and attack Leesburg. If we do I hope we will do better than we did before when we crossed. We have a new commander now. His name is Sedgwick I believe he was one of General Heintzleman's staff. I have not spelled his name right I guess but you will know who I mean perhaps. Last Sat. being the birthday of the father of our country there was considerable of a jolifications at Washington and most of the encampments arround. Early in the morning we could hear the booming of the canon which were being fired as salutes. In the P.M. General Dana was presented with a saddle, bridle, spurs and a pair of colts revolvers by the privates of the Minnesota 1st. he was very much pleased and said it was the handsomest present he ever received. The revolvers were silver mounted ivory handles and had engraved upon them "Presented to General Dana by the enlisted men of the Minnesota 1st. The officers are going to present him with a sword as soon as they can get one suitable. General Dana has the 19th and 20th Mass and 7th Mich Regt of Vol. in his Brigade. We go on picket tomorrow at Edwards Ferry I expect we will have a good time. (Since I commenced this letter the wind has risen and is blowing a perfect gale. The tent whips around so that it is very difficult to write and you must excuse the crooks and blots). I guess it is going to be a good thing in the end for it is drying the mud up very fast. We have not had much wind this winter but in the summer it blows quite often very hard. I hope to get a letter from George tonight I have not heard from him for some time. Captain Messick is about well so that he is on duty. He says that he got a letter from his wife last week she is in better health than she had been for some time before. Lieutennant McCallum we dont expect will ever be able to return to the company. (I long for a sleigh ride but such things are only read and talked about here). We have had but very little snow here and it does not freeze nights more than half the time. That young man you speak of was our drummer his name is Louis Honnerman. The last thing I said to him the morning he left was if he saw any of you to tell you that I was all right and I guess he done it. I hope Father will rent his farm for it will be better than to hire and try to work it himself. I think by another spring the war will be over and George and myself will try to help fix it up in good shape. By the way the war is being conducted now I think it cannot last more than six months longer at most.

Well I must close. I hope the war will be vigorously prosecuted and the last vestage of secession be wiped from the continent. We are under marching orders and we may have a chance to try our hand once more before the thing is settled. W. W. Brown is getting better I guess he will be up in a few days. It is time to mail this and I must quit. My respects to all the folks and write as often as convenient.

As ever

E. H. Bassett, Co. G

P. S. I do not know who could have sent you that $2. I guess I do not know him.
Where was it mailed.

****

The letter following was originally written after February 25, of 1862; on a piece of stationery that Edward had obtained that was printed with the picture of Camp Stone, Maryland. The page had somehow been misplaced in his haversack and was sent later. Being the resourceful person he was he used it to show his family what that camp looked like and how it served their needs. The letter is placed here not in the order it was written but in the context of the time it refers to.

This camp was situated in Montgomery County Maryland about 1 ½ miles from Poolsville and about the same distance from Edwards Ferry on the Potomac. We marched up there from Seneca Mills on the 16th day of August 1861 and pitched our tents in the P.M. and remained there until the morning of the 26th day of February 1862. The day that we arrived there our pickets that had been sent up the day before and were posted along the bank of the river had quite a skirmish with the rebels across the river but in a few days everything went on quiet on the picket lines and fireing was not allowed by either side.

The country around that neighborhood had not been visited by many soldiers previous to our comeing in and consequentely the farms were in a flourishing condition the orchards were full of fruit and the fences were all standing besides several fine groves of timber that are now missing. There was a fine orchard just across the creek where we used to help ourselves until late in the fall. We used to drill every day when the weather was pleasant. There is a fine brook of water running just along the edge of the camp and there used to be a fine grove there but we cut down for wood.

This picture looks quite natural it shows nearly every tent of the camp. That grove that you see in the rear is in a field across the road. There are a number of soldiers buried under those trees. The grove used to extend farther to the right but we cut it down to build with and to burn. The log house that you see in the lower right hand corner was Co. G Cook House. The companies were camped on each side of their streets. I have lettered them so that you can see where they are. The tent on G street with a dot on it is where I stoped. The Capt's. I have marked 1 & 2. The tent to the left of the flag was the Col's.(W.A. Dana) Hd. Qtrs. Those four to the rear of the Colonel were for hospital purposes. The third tent to the left of the Col's was the post office. The log house that comes next was the Quartermasters office. The log buildings out near those four trees to the left was the guard house and just below is the sutlers shop & to the left of this was the regimental bakery which does not show. There is where we spent our first winter in the army. The rebels threw some shells over within less than one half a mile of our camp one morning from a battery near Leesburg, Va. but they could not do any damage.

E. H. Bassett

CHAPTER #8
HARPERS FERRY &
THE VALLEY CAMPAIGN

Marching orders had been anticipated for some time and on February 25th, the divisions of General Banks and General Sedgwick, which included the First Minnesota, left Camp Stone, Maryland and moved toward Harper's Ferry. This movement was known as the "Valley Campaign." During the previous several months, the Union had secured control of the Potomac River, from its mouth to Washington. Another critical supply route, the B & O Railroad from Philadelphia to Washington, had been cut in several places by the rebels and was to be recaptured and repaired. The rebels, led by Stonewall Jackson, were known to be in the town of Winchester, 30 miles southwest of Harper's Ferry. Generals Banks and Sedgwick were to move to Harpers Ferry and then, up the Shenandoah Valley to drive Jackson out.

The weather was cold and snowy and the muddy ground had become frozen and very rough but, that was better than the infernal mud. By evening, the column went into bivouac near the Monocacy River. It was a cold, restless night spent without tents or shelter. The march continued in the morning, crossing the Monocacy and reaching Adamstown. From there, the soldiers rode rail cars to Sandy Hook, a small village across the

Potomac from Harper's Ferry. That night, the regiment was quartered in some of the partially burned-out Federal Arsenal buildings. What had once been a prosperous industrial and railroad center in an idyllic valley setting, was now the deserted and heavily damaged remains of Harper's Ferry.

Of particular interest to the men was the small brick building where the abolitionist John Brown had been captured in 1859. It was here that he had tried to take the Federal Arsenal. The building was used to house a small fire engine and has (in recent years) been restored to its original condition. Brown's intention was to take the weapons from the arsenal and arm the slaves, whom he was trying to incite into rebellion against their masters. Ironically, he was captured by Robert E. Lee, who was then an officer in the U. S. Army.

The following two letters, written from Harper's Ferry on February 27, 1862, are the subject of a most intriguing anecdote that occurred 142 years after they were written.

In August of 2004 my wife, Sharon, and I were at Harpers Ferry on a trip we had taken to retrace my Great Grandfather Edward Bassett's trail during his service in the Civil War. It was a beautiful day and the grandeur of the setting in this peaceful valley between very high bluffs at the joining point of the Shenandoah and Potomac Rivers was breathtaking. We spent the day touring the remains of the old armory, the building where John Brown was captured and other buildings. We walked up the steeply inclined streets to the upper part of town and the old Catholic Church that stands much as it did during the war. Strolling back down the hill, we visited a few of the old buildings on Main Street including the General Store, which was under repair. We ventured into the National Historic Park Headquarters to look at artifacts. There on a counter, I spied an old ledger book that had been in the general store during the time of the war. The book was a chronicle of the cost of the necessities of every day life. In alphabetical order, each page contained a printed capital letter or two at the bottom margin to indicate the names of the customers. The "Y-Z" page was strangely missing ! I was sure I had seen that page somewhere before and remembered the typeface of the letters and the lines on the page. After returning home, while organizing our trip memorabilia, and while re-reading the letters of my Great Grandfather, I found the missing page! Needing paper to write a letter home, he had carefully cut that blank page from the ledger. He had also removed a blank page from the membership registry at the old Catholic Church on the hill, which he used for the last page of his letter.

Harpers Ferry as it appeared in 1865 – Period Photo

U.S. Armory Building
Harpers Ferry Virginia
Feb 27th , 1862

Dear Parents

I mentioned our being under marching orders but I did not much expect we would move.

We started from Camp Stone day before yesterday morning & marched to Adamstown Md. there we took the R.R. yesterday about 9 AM for Sandy Hook which is about ½ mile below here on the Md. Side of the Potomac & about 17 miles from Adamstown. We came across the Potomac a little before sundown last night on a Pontoon bridge.

We stayed in the U.S. Armory last night and I expect we will stay here all day it is a large brick building two stories high, slate roof & makes very comfortable quarters. I have been strolling around all over the town this morning. I was in the cell where John Brown was first confined also the house where he made his stand. The buildings are all badly torn to pieces. There is scarcely a whole window in the lower part of the town many of the buildings have been burned by our men so as to keep the rebels from shooting our pickets. It has been a beautiful place the bluffs on either side are very high and would command the whole town if guns were mounted. The federals began to cross last Monday in boats & they have the rebels driven back some nine miles now. I heard this morning that McCall had taken Leesburg & I guess it is so for he was not very far from it some time ago. There is a strong force across here now & still they are comeing. General McClellan was here yesterday & I hope he will make out as well as he used to. The time is not very far distant when Va. will be ours Manassas & all. It seems a pitty to have so much valueable property destroyed as there has been here. From the roof of this building I can see three very expensive bridges that have been burned. The railroad bridge here was a splendid structure but it is all gone now. At this end there is a locomotive laying in the river & at one place I saw something near 3,000 musket barrels that have been burned. Everything is in ruins.

I was just up to the Sons of Temperance Hall the boys have torn everything open there & their papers lay strewn over the floor, the furniture broken & every mark of destruction. This paper I tore out of a cash account book. War is to be dreaded in the mildest form but here it seems like destroying our own property if the rebels will not be sick of it by the time this one is settled they must like it better than I would. We left our tents in camp & I hope we will not go back there to stay soon. We are all glad to be on the move once more. We did not enlist to lay still & we were getting sick of doing so. I hope the time has come for a general move and a speedy settlement of the Rebelion. I wrote a letter to George last night. I hope to hear from him soon. It was raining last night but it has cleared off now & the wind is blowing quite cool. The mud has dried wonderfully within a few days & I guess the March winds will keep the roads in better condition.

Y

Z

****

The large letters, "Y and Z" are shown simply to illustrate what the original letter looked like, bearing those letters from the ledger book.

Harpers Ferry Virginia
Feb. 27, 1862

I took this (paper) from the Catholic Church in this town. Every thing is quiet here this P.M. The 1st Mich. Cavalry went out to a place called Charlestown this A.M. and captured three rebel cavalry, they went in the town & the rebels ran.

The federal soldiers are comeing in all the time. I have just been up into the uper part of the town. The houses are all empty. There are some nice houses but the windows are broken & the locks taken from the doors. We are having nice times today & I hope we will have better before long. It is a beautiful day cool & pleasant it could not be much better for an advance. The roads will soon be good as they ever are.

It is reported that the rebels are leaving Manassas & I expect it is so. The officers all say that Leesburg is taken by our men & I am very sure it is so. The rebels seem to have vented their spite on the Union by destroying their own property. The prisoners that were taken had very good horses, citizen saddles & bridles, their sabers were old fashion. They had one good carbine they were well dressed good grey overcoats & were very good looking men. I do not think we will have any fighting of any account in V.A.

The boys are all well & feel first rate. Wal Brown is in the Hospital at Poolsville but he is not very sick. I never felt better in my life it just suits me to be on the march.

Captain Messick is about well he commands his company & does very well. The Mass. 15 th, N.Y. 2nd & 34 th & Minnesota1 st are in General Gorman's Brigade.

I am getting cold & have written about all that I can this time & must close.

My love to you all
Good by for the present

In haste   *E. H. Bassett*

Direct as before
****

After spending a couple days in the town, the regiment moved uphill and quartered in more comfortable buildings on the high bluffs of Bolivar Heights.

Camped on Bolivar Heights, Virginia
March 4th, 1862.

Dear Parents,

I have just received a letter from you. It has been 17 days on the road. As I expect to be on guard tomorrow I thought I would try and answer it today. I wrote you a letter the other day telling you about our crossing the Potomac at Harpers Ferry. There is nothing like a letter from home. I got a letter from George yesterday. He has been sick with the Mumps & Measles but must have been nearly well when he wrote. (I am well).

It has been some 9 days since our men commenced crossing the Potomac at this point and they have possession of Charlestown, a place some 10 miles south of here & have a telegraph line finished. The Wis. 3rd was the first infantry that went out there. They went one day leaving all their baggage, some expecting to have a fight with the rebels but they ran leaving the boys to do as they pleased. They went into a couple of churches & stayed over night & went back the next day for their knapsacks.

Since I last wrote I have been nearly all over the town of Harpers Ferry. Nearly all the Government buildings have been burned and everything has been destroyed. We were quartered several days in some of the private houses that had been left. They took most of their furniture. We have lost one of our bravest & truest Genls. in this department. General Lander is dead. General Shields has been appointed to take command of his brigade. He just passed here on his way to Winchester which our men have just taken. It was expected that they would make a stand there but they must have left it or at least they could not made much of a stand. This is what some of the boys heard General Gorman say a few minutes ago.

Since we came over here our boys have had some fun foraging. They fetch in pigs, sheep, geese & chickens & some of the N. Y. boys took some horses & put them into their teams. There was an old farmer arround here today looking after some that he said had been taken by some of the federal soldiers. The boys had considerable fun questioning him about the rebel army. I am very well satisfied that he can be a secessionist or unionist to suit the times. The fact is the war is caused by the existence of the African slave

& is being held as property in common with other personal effects. From their way of living & the way they carry on their business, the Negro is their main dependence. The south is not very thickly settled but there are enough in proportion to the size of the country. There is a surplus of white population in the south & they want to extend slavery into the northern territories. & because they cannot get such men in office as they wish, they have armed themselves & now threaten to overrun the north & establish that cursed system throughout the whole country. I hope the war will be settled only by the emancipation of all the slaves & establish in its place white labor. The commanding Gen. issued an order yesterday forbidding the destruction of property of all kinds by the soldiers and all persons found guilty of stealing from the citizens will be severely punished.

Brig. Gen. Sedgwick has command of what was Genl Stones division. Jonathan Goodrich rec'd. a letter from George tonight dated Feb. 26. He says that he has not been returned to his company yet but felt just as well as he ever did. The boys are all well. The health of the army seems to be very good here. It has been quite cool here for 2 or three days but it is nearly spring time for things to begin to grow here. I believe the R. R. Comp.(company) are rebuilding the R.R. Bridge that was burned at Harpers ferry. I think the war will be over in Va. before long.

It is getting dark & I must quit. You will have to excuse my scribbling for I have to write laying around in the straw in the tent & I have not taken much pains. Captain Messick is well.

My respects to the folks in Morristown.

As ever you son

Edward Bassett

Wednesday morning 5th. It is quite cool this morning. I have got to go on guard. I almost wish that George and myself were up in the corner wood preparing to make sugar. I think the war will end this year. They are surrounded & they have got to give up before long.

My love to you all
E. H. Bassett

On Friday, March 7, 1862, Union General Banks, now in command of the Shenandoah Valley Campaign, with a force of 18,000 men, began a move up the Shenandoah toward Winchester. This was 30 miles southwest of Harper's Ferry. Winchester is the county seat of Frederick County, and is generally thought of as the key to the Shenandoah Valley and the origin of a direct route to Richmond, some 135 miles away. Winchester was also the current location of Stonewall Jackson with his force of about 4,000 infantry and cavalry. Taking this strategic town and destroying Jackson's forces would be of great value to the Union.

The first day's march of nine miles took the regiment to Charlestown in Jefferson County, where they remained two days. During this pause in the town where John Brown faced trial and was hung, the men were pleased to attend a worship service given by their Chaplain in a local church on Sunday, March 9th.

On the 10th, the march resumed, led by the First Minnesota. The march was on a good "macadamized" road, locally referred to as the "Stone Pike." Though the road was far better than marching in the mud, the rain fell all day and stones took a heavy tool on the men's soaked leather shoe soles. After marching 12 miles to Berryville, they arrived to find the town deserted with the exception of a company of rebel cavalry, which responded to a few rounds of artillery fire by leaving town in a hurry. The disappointment of being denied a chance to fight was somewhat lessened when they dashed into town and tore down the rebel flag. In minutes, they had the honor of hoisting the Stars and Stripes given to them by the ladies of Minnesota.

While in Berryville, several men in the regiment discovered the office of the Berryville Conservator, a local weekly newspaper. The editor, Mr. H. K. Gregg, had apparently skedaddled with the approach of the Union troops. A number of the Minnesota boys were experienced printers and, upon finding the week's edition half set in type, decided to complete the edition. They dubbed themselves "The Typographic Fraternity of the First Minnesota Regiment" and set to work. The task saw them burning the midnight oil and, by morning, they emerged with a large quantity of "The First Minnesota," a four page paper. One side of each sheet contained the original secessionist text and the other was filled with a broad mixture of humor, patriotism and the inevitable harangue focused on the absent editor. The paper was a quick sellout at 5¢ a copy.

Camped on Bolivar Heights V.A.
Sunday morning March 16th, 1862.

Dear Parents,

It has been some time since I have written to you. The last time was on the 4th inst. when we were camped here. Since then we have been out nearly to Winchester & the rebels have left all their works on the Potomac. We some expected that they would make a stand at Winchester but they left there one week ago last Friday & our men occupy the whole country arround there besides Centreville & Mannassas. We left our camp here on the 8th & marched out to Charlestown 8 miles. We camped there until Monday morning the 10th when we struck our tents & started for Berryville which the rebels were then occupying. It is situated about 10 miles from Winchester on what is called the Winchester & Leesburg turnpike. It is 12 miles from Charlestown on a good turnpike road. The Minnesota 1st was the advance of the infantry forces. Companies B & K were sent forward as skirmishers &

Co. E as Reserve. There was a company or two of Cavalry in the main road in advance of the skirmishers. They routed some of the rebel scouts about 3 miles from Berryville but they run. When our advance was within about 2 miles from town General Gorman discovered a squad of their Cavalry standing on a hill & he ordered the battery to send them our compliments in the form of a couple of shells which burst near them, when they started & run & I do not know as they have been seen or heard from since. They did not fire a shot. Our men all rushed into town & cut down their flag staff on which they had a streamer marked C.S. They also captured the mail which had just arrived from Winchester & in less than one hour Gorman had a guard stationed at nearly every house in town & would not allow any private property injured. There was some 300 rebel cavalry in the town when we came in sight but they all left for Winchester. We camped for the night just outside of town in a strip of woods. Our pickets the first were not more than 1 mile out and along towards night they had a little skirmish but no one was hurt on our side. We had a pretty hard night that night. We had a hard days march & it was raining at night. We were not allowed to have any fires the first night. Although it was quite cold & wet we all layed down & got quite a good nights rest considering.

Things were quiet all night and our tents came up the next morning. There was some of our cavalry went out into the country & had a little fun with some of the rebels. They captured 3 or 4 prisoners. The morning of the 13 we started for Winchester which was some 10 miles from camp. We marched out some 8 miles when it was found there had been some blunder made in the orders. We had marched without orders & so turned arround & went back to our camp near Berryville. Our men had taken Winchester pretty much as we had Berryville. The rebels left & we marched in without opposition. We were in hopes that we would have a sight of Winchester but we were fooled. We went about as near as we could & not see it & then turned & marched back. The next morning we started & marched to our old camp near Charlestown & stayed over night. Yesterday morning we struck our tents & packed up & marched down here where we will stay until we are ordered to Washington, Baltimore or Anapolis or some other place. The rebels are all driven out of this part of the country & we have got to march against them at some other point where that will be I can't tell nor do I care. We will finish them up in the course of the summer. I am quite well although we have had some rough times. We have got new tents & stoves & can soon fix up a pretty good place to sleep nights.

Cal Jackson was taken to the hospital in Harpers Ferry yesterday morning. He has been quite unwell for some time & I fear he will have a hard time of it. He hated to leave the Company & stuck with it as long as he could. Captain Messick is also quite unwell at present but I think he will get along with us when we leave.

There is no telling where we will go when we leave here. We will most likely take the (railroad) cars for some of the cities. For my part I don't care where we go. There are lots of the slaves leaving their masters & coming north where the colored man is free. We have two. They are very good cooks and seemed to be pleased with the prospect of gaining their freedom. One of them has a wife & he says that is all he cared about in these parts. His master is in the confederate service & will not be apt to get him soon.

The weather is quite warm & comfortable here now & it begins to look some like spring. I heard the larks singing yesterday. I hope the war will come to a close soon but there is no telling. It seems now as if they must cave soon. I rec'd. a letter from Newt Soule the other day. Tell him that I am much obliged to him & hope he will write again. The last that I heard from

George he was well. He said they were under marching orders. I do not feel much like writing I have written this in a hurry.

Give my love to all the family & write soon.

Edward

Direct as before.

On March 13, 1862, Colonel Alfred Sully joined the regiment, succeeding Colonel Dana. The men developed an almost immediate affection for Sully. He was a veteran officer in the regular army and had served at Fort Ridgely in Minnesota. If any doubt existed in anyone's mind if he was the kind of officer who would look after his men, it was soon dismissed. Sully's first order was to discontinue the camp guard, allowing the men to freely wander out of camp. He knew full well that they would not go far in enemy territory. This one simple gesture cemented a bond of mutual respect and trust that would serve the regiment well. The regiment left Charlestown, Virginia on the morning of March 14th, marching all day in the mud and cold rain. They arrived near their old camp on Bolivar Heights that evening. Their next week here would be remembered for the continual bad weather. Every day saw the men shivering in the cold rain, freezing drizzle or snow.

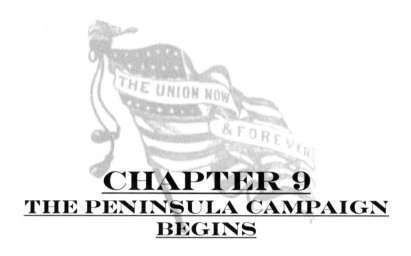

CHAPTER 9
THE PENINSULA CAMPAIGN BEGINS

Following the fiasco at Bull Run, the equally disastrous blunders at Ball's Bluff and, the inconsequential campaign in the Shenandoah Valley, the army was moved back to Washington D.C. They arrived on March 22, 1862 after midnight, and in a pouring rain. There, they received hot coffee and shelter at the Soldiers' Retreat. They remained in Washington until the night of March 26th. General McClellan was placed in full command of the army and was under considerable pressure to strike the enemy. McClellan proposed a plan to take the army down the Potomac into Chesapeake Bay and launch a full scale attack. His intent was to capture Richmond, the Confederate Capital. McClellan reasoned that this route was preferable to the only other option, from Manassas to Richmond, as it assured an open supply route by water. This water-borne supply line would be relatively immune to Rebel attack and would free up large numbers of troops usually needed to guard overland supply trains. President Lincoln and Secretary of War Stanton grudgingly approved the plan. The movement of men and mountains of material to Alexandria, Virginia began. A flotilla of about 400 vessels of every description was collected and the largest amphibious landing of the age commenced. "The Peninsula" is a 50-mile long finger of land running in a northwest-to-southeast direction, bordered on the north side by the York River from West Point to Chesapeake Bay. The south side of the peninsula is bounded by the James River which runs from Richmond to the bay.

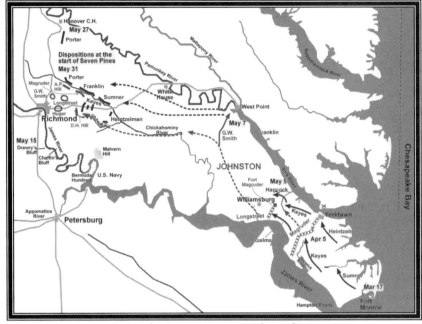

Period Map, source: Wikipedia

The Confederate army, under the command of Gen. J. B. Magruder, had prepared three extensive lines of defense across the peninsula. The first line was just in front of Yorktown to the southeast, the second in front of Williamsburg, and the last line was ten miles from Richmond.

Camped in Washington, D.C.
March 25th, 1862

Dear Father,

We are once more in the Capitol Camped just across the street from the rear grounds of the capital and within about 10 rods from the old Capital

Building, we came here Sunday morning and camped. We left our camp on Bolivar Heights Saturday morning and took the (railroad) cars for this place. We arrived here about 12 at night and were quartered in the soldiers retreat until morning. I do not know where we will go when we leave here some say that we are going down on the coast some that we will remain in the city for Provost Guard. We have a new Colonel his name is Alfred Sully he has been a Major in the regular service for a number of years we like him very well. He is very plain & seems to take considerable interest in his men. I don't care where we go. I am willing and want to go where ever we are needed. I don't believe there is one in the Regt that cares where we are sent if we are needed. There has been a large number of troops shipped to Alexandria lately for the Coast service. They are to reinforce Genl Burnside I believe. We were out near Winchester but as Genls Shields and Banks were there with their commands I suppose they thought we were not needed there and we were sent here. I see by the papers that Genl Jackson has been haveing a fight and has been driven back by Shields and Williams with a heavy loss. Our loss is heavy but that of the enemy is heavier. Genl Shields was slightly wounded in the arm by a shell fragment that burst near him. Although their numbers were twice ours we have held our ground and driven them back with a heavy loss. We have some of the right kind of boys up there and I guess Genl Jackson will have bloody work if he medels with them again. We came away too soon to have any fun up there. We have had some pretty hard times since we left Camp Stone, and some of the citizens when we came here said we were a dirty looking set and some soldiers that had just enlisted and come from the states made some remarks about our rough appearance but our dress coats came down from Poolsville and we had dress parade last night and we surprised some of them by comeing out in decent shape and some of them said that we were regulars. The Minnesota1st has a good name here now and if we should stay here a few months we will have a good time. The boys are pretty well with the exception of bad colds. W. W. Brown came back to the company last night he is nearly well. Cal Jackson was left in Bolivar Va. but I expect he will be sent to Washington he was so that he walked arround considerable when we left and I guess he will get back to the company before long. I have a letter from George dated the 13 March he writes that they are camped near Louisville he seems to be enjoying himself well.

I would like to be in Minnesota this spring and go up into the woods and make sugar, if the war was over. I often think of some of the good old times I used to have there but they are all past and I hope there are still better times comeing. I was down in the Capitol yesterday. I was in the Senate Chamber and saw the Vice President call the House to order. I did not stay there but a short time for I had no pass from Camp. They have a new painting of Genl Scott in the Capitol it is nearly as large as life and looks very fine. Genl Gorman is going to review his brigade before President Lincoln. Capt Messick is well. We are expecting Lt. Mac (McCallum) soon. The weather is quite mild here the ground has not frozen for some time. I think the war will come to a close this spring so that we will be discharged by fall. I should like to be there to help you on the farm as soon as possible not that I don't like serving Uncle Sam. I hope that you will have good luck and rent part of your farm for you can't work it all yourself. Give my respects to the folks in town and write soon.

My love to all the family, As Ever

Edward

Wednesday Morning 26th. I see by the papers that Shields and Banks have completely routed the rebels out at Winchester it is a decisive victory on our side. The fighting continued on the outposts ever since last Sat. at 10 AM.

On the move from Washington an interesting event occurred that Edward fails to mention in the following letter. It is, however, well documented by William Lochren,[27] as follows:

"until the night of the March 26th, when we marched by way of Long Bridge into Virginia, and were then conveyed by cars to Alexandria, where, through some blunder, we were left standing in the street, in a drenching rain until morning, and then taken to the ground on which we had camped before Bull Run. The men, wet and shivering, quickly resurrected the barrel of sutler's whiskey, which they had buried the year before, and its contents, fairly distributed, were probably beneficial in counteracting the effects of the exposure."

Camped near Hampton Virginia

April 1st, 1862.

We have been moveing around considerable since we left Camp Stone. We left Washington on the 26th day, the day that our review was to come off before the President. We marched across the long bridge & took the cars for Alexandria where we camped on the same ground that we did last July. We stayed there until the morning of the 29 when we packed up & went down into the town & laid around until about 2PM & then went on board the transports bound for Fortress Monroe. We have had quite a pleasant time. We came quite slow but the weather has been very good since we came into the bay. This morning when I woke up I looked out expecting that we would be out some ways from land but I was fooled. We were anchored within one mile of Fortress Monroe & the harbor was full of boats & off to our right lay the Monitor, the only thing

[27] Minnesota in the Civil and Indian War, Vol. 1, page 18.

that could have saved the Minnesota from being destroyed & no one knows what other damage the Merimac might have done if it had not been for the Yankee Cheese box on a raft. The Captain of our boat steamed up & sailed out around the Monitor & we all got a good look at her. We could see where she had been hit by the shot from the guns of the Merimac. They dented the sides of her hull a little but not enough to hurt her. The Cheese Box also had several dents in her but they failed to injure her materially.

Period photo of the Monitor showing battle damage.

I guess the rebels will not want to have another fight with her soon. We could not see much of Fortress Monroe but from what I could see I should think it was a pretty strong place. I could see some 30 odd guns this morning mounted on her. We went up to Hampton to land. The town is entirely destroyed. It is burned the cleanest of any place that I have seen. I do not know where we will go from here but some think that we will go up the James River. It is quite pleasant here. The Peach & Plum trees are in bloom & it seems quite spring like. There is something like 100,000 men here & it is reported that General Mac (McClellan) is here to command. You will hear from us during the Spring I guess. I have just received a letter from you dated Mar. 18th & also one from Cliff Davison. We have the Faribault paper of the 12th.

The troops seem to be in good spirits & health. Captain Messick is well & ready for anything. This is not much like making sugar. If I remember right last spring at this time I was some distance from here & if I have good luck next spring at this time I hope to be some little distance from here. Tell John Russell for me that I sympathise with him. I was in hopes that he would be able to go right on with the regt. as they went south. Cal Jackson was left in the Hospital but he was not very sick. I guess he will be able to join us again soon. Well I have written enough so that you will know where I am & you cannot expect to hear much news when we have been moving so often. Please excuse me this time. Please write often directing before.

As ever,

Edward

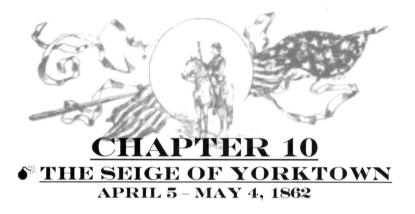

CHAPTER 10
☛ THE SEIGE OF YORKTOWN
APRIL 5 – MAY 4, 1862

General McClellan's plans for the capture of Richmond may have been doomed before they even started. When it came to security, Washington leaked like a sieve. Confederates spies and sympathizers were everywhere. They got wind of his plan soon after it was first proposed on January 1, 1862. To succeed, McClellan said he would need 156,000 men at arms and the support of large numbers of navy gun boats and warships to bombard the rebel defenses. When only a portion of the army had landed at Fort Monroe, he was notified that the navy could not assist as they were too busy protecting the Chesapeake Bay. Furthermore, he was told by the President that one third of the forces promised would be instead held in defense of Washington. Another complication arose upon his arrival on the peninsula, when he discovered that the maps he had were grossly in error. The roads that he was told were good for any weather were in fact turned into great mud hazards and the entire plains region was little more than boggy marshland.

Confederate General John Bankhead Magruder was a capable and thorough commander, though he was not known for his engineering skills. He had built a formidable array of fortifications and applied his theatrical whim to fool the enemy into believing his force was greater than it was. He marched a column of men past an opening in view of the opposition, around through a concealed route and back again.

Round and round they marched giving the appearance of a nearly endless column of troops. He had other men drag brush down dusty roads to appear like cavalry on the move. He built five dams across the Warwick River to make it unfordable at any point to create a moat in front of Yorktown.

Influenced by the aforementioned ruse, and faulty intelligence reports from the Pinkerton Agency, which he wholeheartedly trusted, McClellan was convinced by his staff that a frontal attack on Yorktown or anywhere else along the shores of the peninsula, would be a disaster. With all this in mind, he decided that, though it was likely to take longer, the best tactic was to lay siege to Yorktown to drive out its defenders. He also knew from the past that engaging the enemy without adequate preparation could lead to disaster. To this end, he brought in great quantities of large siege mortars and artillery of all kinds.

Some of the 150 heavy mortars and hundreds of artillery pieces ready to be moved to Yorktown–Matthew Brady Photo

161

The delays thus caused were interpreted by Lincoln as unwillingness to join the enemy in battle and he continually increased the pressure on McClellan. Secretary Stanton even went so far as to make it known amongst his cronies in Washington that he felt McClellan was a traitor.

The First Minnesota Regiment disembarked from the overcrowded transports at Hampton Roads on April 1st. The town lay in ruins. The voyage had been an interesting, though less than comfortable, experience. Many of the men were so cramped that they could not find room to lie down. After leaving the ships, they went into camp in a low, wet field, without shelter, wood or fresh water. They remained there in the rain and mud until 1 AM on the morning of April 5TH, when they broke camp and marched all day on muddy roads to Big Bethel. During the march, the weather suddenly changed and the march became a trying ordeal in sweltering heat. Loaded with all their equipment, the heat tired the men and the road was soon littered with discarded overcoats, blankets and anything else that could be spared to lighten their knapsacks. The march resumed the next morning at 5 AM in heavy rain and to the sound of cannonading and skirmishing ahead. The going was slow with frequent halts, followed by advances at double-quick pace when it appeared as though fighting was eminent. The army with its masses of wagons, cannons, horses and marching men struggled its way along as the roads deteriorated into deep mud. The enemy continued its contested retreat until it took up positions behind the fortifications at Yorktown and along Warwick Creek.

The First Minnesota went into camp 2 miles from Yorktown, where they remained until April 11TH. The camp was called Headquarters Camp #1; the men more appropriately dubbed it "Camp Misery." Considering they had no tents for shelter, a camp on a low muddy flat, and it rained every day, the name was appropriate.

The regiment relocated its camp about three miles south of Yorktown on April 11th, to a higher, dryer and somewhat wooded site dubbed Camp Winfield Scott. It continued to rain most of the time. Shelter tents were now issued and much appreciated, though they were not waterproof and leaked like sieves.[28] The men were engaged on alternate days either on picket duty or in building stretches of corduroy roads for supply wagon trains from Fort Monroe and Hampton.

Any event that broke the routine was widely observed and just such an event occurred on April 11; Holcombe [29] reports:

". . a balloon was sent up from York River to take a bird's–eye view of the Confederate situation. It went up in plain sight of all the camps and was an object of interest. It had lines attached to it and was to be drawn back to earth when a good view of the enemy's position had been obtained. On this occasion the lines broke and the balloon went where it pleased. It drifted over the Confederate lines and there was some anxiety lest it should go to earth there, but it finally floated back and descended at the camp of the "First". Among the occupants was General Fitz John Porter, a division commander."

The following letter is the only one Edward wrote between April 1st and May 5th. This unusual gap in communications was the apparent result of the miserable conditions the First Minnesota men endured during this period.

---

28 A shelter tent is composed of 2 pieces of canvas about 5 feet square that are buttoned together to form a simple open ended tent, supported down the center with a pole and staked to the ground. Usually occupied by 2 men.
29 Return I. Holcombe, History of the First Regiment Minnesota Volunteer Infantry, Ch. X, Page 105.

Envelope of letter of April 27, 1862

In camp near & in front of the
rebel works at Yorktown, Virginia
April 27th 1862

Dear Parents

I have just this moment rec'd. your letter of the 12th
& with which makes three that I have got in succession.
We also have the Central Republican of the 16th ...So
you will see that I have the home news to within one
week. It is cool weather it has been raining for two days.
We were down on picket the day before yesterday & had
quite a time except that we were not allowed to shoot.
The post that I was on was within 40 rods of the rebel
works & we could see them quite plainly by peaking
through the brush & timber. They appeared to be very
busy working on their fort.

Everything was quiet until about sunrise they made
an attempt to drive in some of our pickets that were
advanced to fill up some of their rifle pits. For a while
the roar of muskets & cannon was pretty loud but they
were finaly forced to go back leaving some 60 of their
men killed & wounded on the field our loss was 4 killed
we also took some 14 prisoners. (This is what the

officers told me yesterday.) During the fight I stood within about 50 rods of one of their cannon that they fired several times it appeared to be a large piece it spoke pretty loud at any rate & I could feel the ground jar under my feet. Some of our boys think they burst their gun the last shot but we could not tell for certain it made a strange report & has not been fired since. Our artillery replied with well directed shots at their barracks & the men. I could hear several of the shot as they struck the roofs of their barracks. I was out working on one of our forts last Thursday. The fort is calculated to mount 6 guns and is not more that ½ mile from the rebel works. They threw several shell at our batteries stationed on both sides of our works. There has been several of our pickets wounded in Gorman's Brigade but none from our Reg't. A Captain in the Mass. 20th who was acting as Lieut-Colonel had his leg shattered from the knee down by one of the rebel Sharp Shooters last Thursday he had it amputated.

They have made several attempts to drive our pickets in at night but have not succeeded very well so far, they can't do much where the woods are so thick at night. I would like to have O. Brown editor of the Central Republican & some few others of the blowhards arround there out here some night & take them out within about 20 rods of the rebel works & tie them up to a tree & have the rebels come down about 1,000 or 1,500 strong & open fire of musketry & about 4 pieces of artillery with grape & canister & have the balls cut ever rag of clothing off from them & peal the bark from the trees around & the flash of the guns light up the woods until it would seem as if they were all on fire.. I wonder if he could not sit down the next day and write something about the vigorous prosecution of the war. I wonder if he would not enlist in the 5 th Reg't. if they would give him the command if he would. I don't believe there are but few that would serve under him. He must be very brave in his way but it is a H--l of a way.

I recieve a letter or two from George every week. Anna speaks about them flower seeds which I had promised to send if I could get them but I have had no chance except when I was in Washington and then I had no money to buy anything and here there is nothing but pine trees & Secesh. It will be impossible for me to get any kind of seeds early enough to be of any use this year and I hope by another spring to be where I can do something in the way of farming myself. The boys are all well as usual.

I would like to have some of the Maple Sugar & Molasses this spring. I don't know when we will get our pay there will be 4 months pay due on the 29. I will try & send you some money if I can when we get our pay.

Hopeing that the war will soon end and we will all meet once more on the old farm. Give my respects to all the folks & write soon the mail starts soon I must close.

I remain as ever

Your Son in the Minnesota 1st.

Direct as before   *E H Bassett*

Yorktown Va.
May 5th, 1862.

Folks at Home,

Thinking that you would like to hear once more from the Seat of War & what is going on around Yorktown, I have seated myself in one of the rebel tents & in the same field where Cornwallace surrendered to Genl Washington. The rebels left their works last Sat. night & early on Sunday morning Genl Dana marched into their entrenchment with his brigade. He captured several prisoners & other small articles. I don't know where they have gone but I expect they have gone to

Richmond. They left most of their tents & camp equipage. In one tent I saw 15 muskets, 3000 rounds of ball cartridges &c. &c. Their fortifications were well built & they might have made a desperate stand if they had tried. Up here around Yorktown their cannon are all mounted & loaded spiked[30] & many of them fixed so if we should try to move them much they would go off & burst in a thousand pieces. All along on the parapets they have got torpedoes[31] set so that it is very dangerous to go around in the works. There was several accidents yesterday & some 5 or 6 soldiers killed. I saw one explode that blowed a man's leg off just below the knee. The foot & leg was blown some 10 or 15 rods & fell in a slough. I suppose they think they are smarter than the Yankees but if they should be here & see our engineers going around digging out the bombs they would have to say as they did about our gunboats. (They all played out). In their camps they left messages written on boards & tents. They say that they have got tired waiting for us to attac them & could wait no longer. They dare us to meet them on an open field & they will fight us 5 to 1. They say that our gun Boats are played out. They are going to retreat to the mountains & fight with knives. Our men have followed them up & there was heavy cannonadeing heard all day but it is quiet now. I was told that we have taken a large number of prisoners. If they won't stand in such works as they had around here I don't know where they can expect to make anything of a stand. The boys are well & enjoying themselves as well as they can with such weather. We left our camp yesterday morning &

---

[30] Spiked: Made unserviceable by driving a steel spike in the Primer hole so the gun cannot by made useable.
[31] The rebels had buried artillery shells in the embankments of their earthworks rigged to explode if stepped on or disturbed. This was against the rules of warfare and considered a dastardly and cowardly act not in keeping with chivalrous code of honorable men.

marched 3 miles through the rain & mud & to top off with we were out last night from dark until 3 in the morning & it was raining all the time but we have got so used to it that we don't notice it much now. Last Sat. I was out working on one of our forts & the rebels threw several shell at us & it was all good luck that they did not either kill or wound some of us. There was three shell exploded within less than 4 rods of us & the pieces flew arround rather careless.

It is reported here this morning that the rebels have evacuated Williamsburg which is about 12 miles from here & was reported to be stronger fortified than this is. There was & fight up there yesterday. I think things look as if the war was comeing to a close before midsummer. I have not heard from George for some time.

E. H. Bassett

The Confederate Generals realized from the start that they could not hold Yorktown. Making McClellan think that was their intention bought them the time needed to move more forces to the area to reinforce Richmond and build the necessary defensive works. Yorktown was under the guns of the Union gunboats on the York River as well as the massive array of siege guns McClellan now had in position. Added to this was the 85,000 man army at their "front door." General Magruder's network of observers and spies had been carefully watching McClellan's preparations and, by May 1st, were aware he was about to begin the bombardment. Saturday evening, May 3rd, the Confederates opened up with a furious artillery barrage on the Union positions. The firing lasted until midnight, with all but the old cast iron guns at the fort put into service. It was mainly a diversion to cover the retreat and did little damage. Not a single Union soldier was killed. On May 4th, the rebels abandoned Yorktown and began a hard fought rear guard action to their next prepared line of defense. Their withdrawal was verified when General Heintzleman and the noted aeronaut, Professor Lowe, went up in a balloon to observe.

The First Minnesota was on picket duty that morning and was ordered back to camp to get their equipment and prepare to march. McClellan intended to catch the retreating forces under General Joe Johnston and destroy or capture them before they could reach their next line. The march lasted only a short time when they reached the abandoned rebel works at Wynn's Mill . The Confederates had left in a hurry and the men found their breakfasts, such as they were, still on the fires. They had left behind a considerable amount of camp equipment and some stores including tents which were much appreciated.

General Headquarters Camp near Yorktown, April 1862
After relocation and arrival of tents
Harper's Weekly Sketch By: Ed Pietsch

CHAPTER 11

☀ BATTLE OF WILLIAMSBURG MAY 5 & 6, 1862

General Sumner's men fought the confederates under General Longstreet at Fort Magruder, outside of Williamsburg. The battle was directed more by circumstance and conditions than by plan or strategy. With men, horses, mules, wagons and artillery being drenched by the pouring rain and the slogging around in the deep mud, coordination of efforts was impossible. Officers and men became disoriented, the heavy wet air played tricks with the sounds of battle and, if it hadn't been so tragic, the battle could have passed for a comedy. By nightfall, Longstreet had done his job of delaying the Union pursuit of the retreating rebel army as it withdrew toward Richmond and its next prepared line of defense. The First Minnesota was being held in reserve in the abandoned rebel works at Yorktown on May 5th, when the main battle at Williamsburg commenced. The sounds of heavy cannon fire carried in the rain-filled air and were clearly heard. The men listened with anticipation all day and, as they watched troops march out, they were certain they would soon be called to join the fight. About dark, orders came and the regiment joined the march. It proved to be a very short but arduous move. The already impassible roads were now a quagmire of soupy mud and wagon wheel ruts. The pouring rain and pitch-black darkness added to the confused jumble of men, wagons, horses and cannons. Halts were frequent, leaving the men standing in the mud and pouring rain, while columns ahead tried to advance. After three hours, the regiment had moved only one mile and was ordered to return to their shelters at Yorktown–welcome orders, to be sure. The men arrived back at their captured tents about 3 AM in the morning of May 6th.

About midday on May 7th, the regiment marched once again in the rain down to the wharf and boarded the steamer, Long Branch. Early the following morning they sailed up the York River to West Point where the Mattapony and Pamunkey Rivers join to form the York River. The boat trip to shore was constantly under shelling from rebel batteries until the Union gun boats opened fire and soon silenced them.

West Point Va.
May 7th. Wednesday "P.M."

I was prevented from finishing my letter yesterday by the regt. being ordered forward. (letter of May 5th) We took a transport (The Long Branch) at Yorktown & started early this morning up the York. You will see by referring to the atlas that we are nigh unto Richmond & the rebels are trying their best to stop us. There has been a sharp skirmish today on the road leading to Richmond in which the loss was quite heavy on both sides. The forces engaged on our side were the Jersey Brigade & 42 N.Y. We have quite a heavy force here now & are protected by our Gun Boats in the York.

Richmond will be ours soon if they don't whip us. McClellan is pushing them up closely & they are still retreating. We can see thick clouds of smoke in the direction of their rear & I expect they are burning all the houses, Bridges &c. on the road. Lieutennant

McCallum returned yesterday. He looks well & resumes his duty immediately. Cal Jackson is well (him & myself chum it [32]. There is but one of our Company in the Hospital now. He is our 1st Sergeant E. W. Northrup. Give my respects to all the folks & write soon.

Edward H. Bassett

Sketch of the Gunboat U. S. S. Essex by William M. C. Philbrick; Jan. 1, 1862, U. S. Naval Historical Center, www.history.navy.mil

---

[32] Caleb B. Jackson, Corporal, Company G; Caleb and Edward were close friends and had been next door neighbors. They joined together and served through their entire enlistment as comrades and often as tent mates.

Camped on the Pamunkey River Va.
Sunday Morn. May 11, 1862

Dear Parents

It is a very pleasant morning with a good breeze from the east. Just such a morning as I would like to go strolling up arround the lakes & woods in Minnesota The boys are all well & amusing themselves as best they can, some have gone down to the river & are trying to catch some fish, some are bathing & others seem to be taking a morning walk & watching the boats as they pass up & down. The tide rises some 4 or 5 feet here & it is coming up very fast now. The river is navigable for the gun boats & small transports up as far as the R.R. bridge which is some12 miles above here. We heard some heavy cannonading last eve up in that direction which I expect was some of the gun boats shelling something. I saw the effects of some of their work the other day. I saw where two of the shell had struck the ground & went down some 4 ft. & exploded making a hole in the ground about 12 ft. long & wide and 4ft. deep, it threw the dirt up higher than the tallest trees & tore things up generaly. They were fired at a reb battery that had been stationed to oppose our landing & because we did not land just where they wanted us to they were trying to shell the boats as they lay in the river but they did not fire a shot after the gun boats opened on them but made their escape through the woods the best they could. The shell thrown by the boats weigh about 75 lbs. & are about 28 inches long & contain 5 lbs. of powder. They were fired from rifled guns.

General McClellan is crowding the Secesh pretty hard it is reported that our pickets are now within one mile of their works. I don't believe they are going to make a stand at Richmond if they can possibly get away although they may but if they do we can easily surround them on all sides & cut off all supplies from abroad & if they are so inclined they can get their heads cut off for we have got the <u>power & will be apt to use it before long.</u>

I have got to close up my things now for our Sunday morning inspection & I expect the Captain will be quite particular.

The mail has come in & brought me a letter from you dated April 28th it has taken its' time coming & seems quite fresh after so long a journey. I hope the girls mellons will do well & we shall all be there to eat some of them. It seems to me that the spring is very late here being that it is so far south of where you are. The trees are all leaved out here & the rye is up knee high but still things seem backward. The Blackberry bushes are not in blossom yet & the grass is very short. Lieutennant Mac is with us he looks first rate, Captain Is well. Our 1st Sergeant is the only one we have in the Hospital. We have very good times usualy since we have been under command of Colonel Sully. The boys all like him very much we are not confined in camp like we used to be with Gorman. It is reported in the papers that 3 of our Gun boats have gone up the James River & that the Merimac lays off Cranz island.

Well I have scribbled this sheet over & now must quit. We expect the war will be over by fall & we may get home by next winter all we have to do is to wait with patience & make the best of what we have got at present. I am enjoying myself first rate. I would like very much to see you all of course but I am quite contented to bide the appointed time if it is required.

My repects to all the folks

I remain as ever Your Son

E. H. Bassett

PS..

That yarn about the soldiers not being allowed to write was untrue. The mail was delayed at the first office a short time so that if there should happen to be anything written that would do any good to our enemys North or South they would not know it until it was too late to act.

E.H.B. Co. G

Photo of Camp on Pamunkey River, Brady Photo

On May 15th, the army, once again, was on the march and went into camp on the plantation of Dr. William Mayo, a surgeon in the confederate army. After a three-day rest, the unit was again on the move. This day, they passed the "White House," where George Washington had courted the widow, Martha Custis. The plantation now belonged, by inheritance, to Mrs. Robert E. Lee.

Gen. McClellan had made it his headquarters. Upon his arrival at the White House, McClellan found a note on the front door which read: *"Northern soldiers who profess to reverence Washington, forbear to desecrate the home of his first married life, the property of his wife, now owned by her descendants. A Grand-daughter of Mrs. Washington."*[33]

---

[33] Shelby Foote, "The Civil War – A Narrative", Vol. 1, Page 418.

McClellan honored the historic significance of this place and the request of the Southern Lady that left the note by placing a guard around the house, assuring that no one would damage or plunder it. Furthermore, he provided an escort under a flag of truce to see her safely through the lines to her husband.

Edward's letter home on May 17, 1862 gives a very good account of the conditions that the men frequently faced during their marches to new locations. With often as many as 100,000 men on the move, along with thousands of horses and mules, pulling wagons laden with supplies and heavy cannons, the roads could be reduced to long dust pits, or as we see in this letter, mud holes. The men could be found trudging through dust half way up to their knees, sometimes marching in temperatures near 100 degrees and through choking clouds of dust as fine as gunpowder. If, as on this day, it was raining, the dirt roads soon turned into knee deep seas of sticky mud. Marching in this stuff must have been extremely tiring, to say the least. Considering that the men usually wore low-cut leather shoes that would soon become waterlogged, their feet must have become blistered, bleeding and painfully sore. Conditions were often so bad that as many as 10 horses could not pull a single cannon.

The fatigue from marching while carrying a gun, knapsack, haversack with provisions, ammunition, bedroll, canteen and cooking equipment, while wearing a heavy wool uniform soaked with the pouring rain, wore the men down. When they finally reach a camp site, about 9 PM, they were anxious to lie down and rest. But, they still had to find and cut some wood for a fire to cook something to eat. Usually, their tents were somewhere in a wagon several days behind. Those that had a rubber poncho could affect some shelter, others, simply had to sleep in the mud on the ground, in the pouring rain.

Head quarters First Regt. Minnesota Vol.
Camped in the woods between
New Kent and Cumberland, Kent Co. Va.
Sat. P.M. May 17th AD 1862

Dear Parents

I am getting ashamed to write so much when there is nothing to write about but the one subject & that an old one. You speak of my not writing on account of sickness. So far I have been very fortunate there has not been a time since I have been in the service that I have been so sick that I could not write & lately I have been quite well although we have had some hard marches & some exposure. Last Thursday we left our camp on the Pamunkey at 9AM & it was raining. We marched all day through the rain & mud & camped here in the woods about sundown some 7 or 8 miles from where we started. Our regt was in the rear of Sedgwicks' Division which made it much harder on account of passing at bad places & the straglers that were in the road but at retreat there was not a man missing in our camp. It was still raining but we built large fires cooked our suppers & laid down & got one nights sleep & got up in the morning but a little worse for our march. That is about the way our marches all go (we seldom move unless it rains) but we are used to it now & don't notice it much now. There is a report in camp now that McClellan had baged some 4,000 of the rebels somewhere towards Bottoms Bridge but we have no particulars & therefore pass it for what it will fetch. (Tea is ready & you must excuse me a few minutes). *I have just partaken of the bounties of Uncle Sam's tea table & although the food was cheap & simple (consisting of hard bread & boiled beef with coffee which I use but little of). I feel encouraged to go on & finish my letter. Uncle Sam is a generous old soul I assure you & although he sets a cheap table he is free with what he has. It will be just one year tomorrow since I enlisted for three years or during the war & I feel just as much like serving two years longer if I am needed as ever. Although I know that I am needed at home & ought to be there trying to help you get along & make a living and the existing circumstances are the only ones that could keep me away.

I am sorry to hear that George is sick but I can't help thinking that he will get well soon. I thought there must be something wrong for I have not got any letters from him for some time. We heard yesterday that our orderly (1 st) sergeant had died in the Hospital, he was left below Yorktown in one of the Division Hospitals I believe. We shall miss him very much he was one of the best men in our company & loved by all. His name is I.W. Northrup[34] he was from Owatonna. I hope we will hear that he is yet alive but fear for the truth. I don't know as we will ever see the enemy again for we are in the reserve at the present we are out of both sight & hearing. The boys are all well as usual. Cal Jackson got a letter from his folks yesterday & has answered it today. Lieut McCallum brought up his trunks yesterday and distributed the things that had been sent to the boys from Minnesota I guess he had over 30 lbs of maple sugar beside numerous other articles.

Please give my respects to all the folks in favor & excuse my poorly written & composed letter.

I remain as ever your unworthy,

Edward Co. G

****

Edward's younger brother, George, left Fort Snelling in Minnesota with his regiment on November 17, 1861. George died of complications from mumps and measles in Nashville,

---

[34] Sergeant Northrup's death is erroneously reported in "Minnesota InThe Civil Wars" Muster Rolls of the First Regiment as being July 14, 1862 which of course could not be correct as his comrades in arms were informed of it in May.

Tennessee on May 16, 1862. The letter that follows was written to his parents by Sergeant Hugh W. Donaldson, a friend in Company H, it illustrates the kinship felt among these "Brothers-In-Arms":

Columbia Tenn.
May the 19ᵗʰ AD 1862

Mr. Bassett & family,

It is with much sorrow & regret that I write this melancholy news to you but I feel it my duty as a neighbor of yours & a companion of your son George to inform you that he departed this life on the 16ᵗʰ of May at 1 o'clock PM in the hospital at Nashville, Tenn. He was a tent mate of mine at the time he took sick, he was taken down very suddenly he stayed in the tent about 3 days & then was taken to the hospital at Nashville. There was two more from our com (company) sent the same time. It was impossible for any of the Morristown acquaintances of his to go to wait on him but let me tell you he was well taken care of. He will be buried at Nashville, his name, Regiment and Co. will be put on his head board of his tomb so you can find his grave if you see fit. His affairs will be promptly seen to in the company. The way I heard today that he was dead, a convalescent of Co. H is in the hospital at Nashville & wrote to his brother here & told us that poor George had gone to his eternal home. As the mail is ready to go out I must close my hasty letter please excuse this for I have written it in great haste. Anything you want to know I would gladly write to you.
Address
Nashville, Tennessee
Co. H 3ʳᵈ Reg. Minnesota Vol.
With great respect I am
Your friend

H. W. Donaldson

179

CHAPTER 12
✸ BATTLE OF FAIR OAKS
MAY 31 – JUNE 1, 1862

The land through which the army was moving was very poor. Most of the farms offered little to add to the meager subsistence of the soldiers. Even farm animals were rare and extremely few good plantations existed within miles of the low, wet flatland. General McClellan had issued strict orders, enforced by even stricter penalties that specifically forbade foraging of any kind. To make compliance a certainty, he had further ordered the Provost Guard to move in advance of the main army and to place guards at every house, farm and well.

Even the rail fences were protected.

While on the march, the men were usually reduced to what they called "hard rations." This time was no exception. Hard rations consisted primarily of hardtack, which was a cracker made of flour, water and salt that measured about 3"-by-3 1/2" and ½" thick. After baking and cooling, it becomes very hard and can be kept for very long periods of time. It was also referred to as:

Hard Bread, Worm Castles, Tooth Dullers, Jaw Breakers and numerous other derogatory names. Cheap to make and easy to store and transport, hard bread had been a mainstay of soldiers and sailors dating back to the Roman Legions and before. A day's ration was usually 9-or-10 crackers, sometimes supplemented by meat, beans or anything else available. They were occasionally infested with weevils or maggots although the men just considered them part of their rations. The crackers were often too hard to bite off and would be wrapped in a cloth and smashed with a rifle butt and then added to coffee. This procedure allowed the weevils to float to the top and be skimmed off. The demands of war meant that many thousands of suppliers were involved in the manufacture of this product. Of course, that caused the price of flour to climb dramatically and some unscrupulous bakers found inventive means to keep costs down by adding sawdust to reduce the amount of flour required.

"The Whiskey Rebellion"

Whiskey in the hands of the troops was highly frowned upon by most commanding officers. At this time, however, General Gorman issued orders for a whiskey ration to be distributed to his men. Ed Bassett noted in his journal, "Received whiskey rations for the first time." The ration was probably authorized in consideration of the extended periods of exposure and the threat of malaria so present in the low, swampy peninsula. The manner in which the order was to be carried out was the source of a minor insurrection by the men of the First Minnesota. The whiskey was to be distributed to each man at *"Brigade Commissary and consumed there, rather than to the regiment as before."* The men took the order as an insult and an inference that they could not be trusted to distribute their own whiskey ration and, therefore, promptly unanimously voted *"Gorman can keep his whiskey."* When General Gorman got word of the incident, his affection for his former regiment was manifesed when he issued a follow-up order; *"General Gorman permits the First Minnesota to draw their whiskey as formerly."*

On May 23rd, the regiment reached the north bank of the Chickahominy River. The river is more like a wide creek except when, as now, heavy rainfall spreads it out across the broad plains on either side. The stream flows in a southeasterly direction until in empties into the much larger James River and, thus, to the Chesapeake Bay. Tall banks or bluffs that bordered the flood plains on the south offered Confederate General Johnston a commanding position. From here he could defend against Union attack. Johnston had also burned all the bridges across the Chickahominy in the area, with the exception of Bottom's bridge. This one remaining bridge was used by General Keyes 4th Corps and General Heintzleman's Corps, on May 20th thru 23rd to cross in force and extend south across the peninsula to the James River. The remaining 3 corps under Porter, Sumner, and Franklin remained on the north side. The First Minnesota was under Sumner's command. McClellan's army was thus split on the two sides of a rampaging river with the force on the south side in considerable danger of overwhelming attack.

May 27th, McClellan moved to correct this situation by ordering several bridges to be built across the river. The task of building one of the bridges was assigned to the First Minnesota regiment and, was undertaken with its usual "can do" attitude. The heavily forested river banks provided plenty of logs. Grape vines, hanging in abundance, served as great lashing material. The work was carried on with determination. Hundreds of trees had to be cut down and made useable. Approaches and abutments had to be built and everything had to be done in torrents of rain. Three full companies worked up to their chest in the swirling water all day. By day's end, the bridge was completed with the exception of the corduroy work on the approaches, which was completed by other troops the next morning. All afternoon as the work progressed, the men heard the sounds of the battle raging 12 miles away at Hanover Court house. The following morning, they were marched to the front to the support of General Fitz John Porter, who was engaged in destroying two railroad bridges. They returned to camp on the 29th, after a minor engagement that left one man wounded.

On May 31, 1862, Union forces approached to within seven miles of Richmond. Confederate General Johnston moved from the fortress of the defensive works constructed around Richmond. His intention was a decisive attack against a thinly spread-out center of the Union line. To prevent yet another major defeat and the loss of nearly half of his army, which was on the west side of the Chickahominy River, General McClellan had to move fast to get reinforcements across from the east side of the now rampaging flooded river. He immediately sent orders to General Sumner to be prepared to move at a moments notice. Sumner took the order literally and moved his two divisions; Sedgwick's, which included the First Minnesota, and Richardson's, to the river where the "Grapevine Bridge" built by the First Minnesota Regiment four days earlier still stood. All the other bridges, built at the same time, had been swept away. The torrential rains of the night before and the continuing rain that had fallen all day caused the condition of the bridge to become questionable at best.

The story of the ensuing drama has been well told in the "History of the FIRST REGIMENT MINNESOTA VOLUNTEER INFANTRY".

"The rough logs forming the corduroy approaches over the swamp were mostly afloat and only kept from drifting off by the stumps of trees to which they were fastened. The portion over the body of the stream was suspended from the trunks of trees by ropes, on the strength of which depended the possibility of passage."

"The possibility of crossing was doubted by all present including General Sumner himself. As the solid column of infantry entered upon the bridge, it swayed to and fro to the angry flood below or the living freight above, settling down and grasping the solid stumps by which it was made secure as the line advanced. Once filled with men, however, it was safe until the Corps crossed; it then soon became impassible".

Report of Colonel Alexander, Engineer Corps 1864.

"It was the only bridge left intact. The rains descended and the floods came and beat upon that bridge, but it fell not because it was built by Minnesotans who knew their business. Sedgwick's three brigades crossed over it and two of Richardson's brigades followed them".

"Sedgwick's Division got the order to cross at 2:30 and almost at once obeyed it, although all conditions were forbidding. Striking the west bank of the river, the Division set out at quick time, the men walking as fast as they could pull their feet out of the mud. The First Minnesota had the post of honor. It was the regiment in the lead".

The Grapevine Bridge that Saved the Day at Fair Oaks[35]
Period Photo

---

[35] There is an ongoing discussion among historians as to whether this photo is the correct bridge.

The bridge held together long enough to get several brigades across but, finally became unusable, leaving McClellan's army still divided by the swollen river.

The Minnesota regiment had crossed its bridge at 2:30 PM and marched at quick-time toward the sound of the heaviest firing, moving as fast as they could pull their shoes from the sometimes, knee-deep mud. On the way, they were met by fleeing bands of soldiers, wounded, stragglers, skulkers and cowards, who were all spouting tales of complete and utter defeat. They arrived on the field of battle about a mile northeast of the station near the Courtney house, at 5 PM. What was left of Gen. Couch's division, which had been holding its position for four hours against vastly superior numbers, cheered wildly at the arrival of the Minnesota men. Colonel Sully, with the aid of one of Couch's staff officers, immediately placed the First Minnesota on the extreme right in a wheat field behind a picket fence belonging to Mr.Courtney. They had been positioned only a few minutes when a tremendous volley of fire spouted forth from the woods in their front.

Battle of Fair Oaks – Currier & Ives Etching (Library of Congress)

The rebel line was comprised of five full brigades, all fresh and just coming into action. Their first volley went too high and did little but tear leaves and branches from the trees and splinters from the fence. The left end of the Minnesota line extended beyond the line of advancing screaming rebels. The three left companies answered immediately with volley after volley of well-placed fire that took a terrible toll. The First Minnesota was now facing Law's brigade, the same body of troops that had bloodied them at Henry House on Bull Run. Charge after charge came and was repulsed. Three of the five twelve-pound Napoleons of Kirby's battery, which had been mired in the mud miles back, were freed and came into service about 5:30 PM, and were joined by the remaining two guns shortly thereafter. They were put to use at once and poured exploding, terrifying death into the woods. The roar of cannon and musketry from both sides was deafening and caused the ground to tremble. The rebel defensive line finally broke at dark and they left the field littered with their dead and wounded.

The night of May 31st, the rains increased and developed into a terribly violent storm. The Chickahominy River was swollen to the point of being a raging torrent. McClellan's army was still divided about equally in half by the river. Confederate General Johnston had decided to mount another attack the next morning at Seven Pines, at a point ½ mile southeast of Fair Oaks. The battle was heavily contested and is generally said to have ended in the confederate favor—a conclusion often disputed by both sides. At its end, however, the rebels withdrew in haste towards Richmond and, due to the conditions of the roads and rivers, could not be effectively pursued. For the South, the greatest impact of the battle was the severe wounding of General Johnston, the commander of the Army of Northern Virginia. At the close of the day on June 1st, he was wounded in the arm and, while reeling in the saddle from the bullet wound, he was struck in the chest by shrapnel from an exploding shell. The impact knocked him to the ground with his chest caved in. He survived, and later returned to duty minus one arm. The next day, Jefferson Davis relieved Robert E. Lee from his duties as his advisor and assigned him to replace Johnston as commander of the Army of Northern Virginia. The two days of fighting resulted in 6,134 Confederates being killed or wounded compared to 5,031 on the Federal side.

Gorman's Brigade
Camped near Fair Oaks Station Va.
7 miles from Richmond
June 5th, 1862.

Dear Father & Mother,

    Knowing your anxiety about my welfare & safety I will try & write a few lines just to let you know that I am safe & well. You most likely have heard of the battle of the 31st of May and the 1st of June in which the rebels were driven back with great loss. We were left in full possession of the field.

    We left our camp on the east side of the Chickahomony about noon on the 31st inst. & crossed it on a bridge that we had built some days before. The Minnesota 1st was in the van[36] of Sedgewick's Division. We were marched immediately to the scene of action which was around the R.R. station. [Fair Oaks Station] We arrived here just in time to prevent a flank movement of the enemy on our right. Our Regt. had just got in position & secreted ourselves in a wheat field when the enemy opened fire on our left from the woods. This was responded to by Companies H, D, L, & K. The other companies were waiting for them to come out in the open field where we could give them a deadly volley from our rifled muskets.

Photo of Model 1861, 58 caliber Springfield Rifle
Photo courtesy of C&D Jarnagin Co., Corinth, Mississippi.

---

[36] Meaning–Caravan.

The fireing commenced about 1 P.M. & lasted until nearly dark when the rebels retired leaving the dead & wounded on the field. The loss to the Minnesota 1st was one killed & 2 slightly wounded. At night we had our Company out on picket a few rods ahead of the lines & we could hear their wounded groaning & calling for water. We were under strict orders not to go near them for they had fired on us from under a white flag during the day & it was not safe to trust them any time altho it seemed heartless. It was quiet all night being no fireing. On the next morning it was found that the woods were full of the rebel dead and wounded.

About 9 o'clock Sunday the rebels made an attack to our left some 1/2 mile. They fought desperately & done their best to take the old Rickets (artillery battery) but Gen. Gorman ordered the 34th N.Y. to charge & they were driven back with great loss. Since then they have been quiet until this morning. They have been shelling our men on the right, but they have quit for a time. They fought well but were defeated with about one half their number of Yankee troops. They had no cannon the first two days that they could use. Our boys fought well & seemed as cool as if they were shooting chickens. They are all in good spirits & it would do you good if you could hear them cheer General McClellan when he rides past.

We are confident of success wherever we go. Gen. Mac says there will be but one more battle here. We are prepared for them.

The 2nd Company of Minnesota Sharpshooters is attached to our Regt. They are a fine company & have breech loading rifles.

Tell Mrs. Soule that Boult is well, also Cal Jackson's folks that he is well, if you should see them.

I don't know what you will think of me writeing on an old letter but our knapsacks are back at camp & we have to do the best we can if we write at all. I hope you will excuse me for it is the best I can do at present. I don't know how soon we will be able to get our things for the roads are so bad. I will try & write again soon. I hope the war will soon end & I shall be able to return home. I shall miss George so that I know it will never seem like home.

We have had some heavy rains lately. It rained all day yesterday & looks like rain today. You will have hard work making out but perhaps you can by sticking long enough. Our Captain is well. When you write please write how John Russel is. I wrote him a line on the 11th of May. I am well as usual and stand the rough well, altho it has been very hot.

I hope you will get this & excuse the appearance. I have plenty of paper, pens, ink &, stamps in my portfolio at camp.[37]

Believe me as ever   *Edward*

Doctor Daniel Hand, assistant regimental surgeon, relates the conditions and sights following the battle:

"By night all was quiet in front and we were tired out. All tried to get some sleep. It was late in the night before my own cares allowed me to rest, and then where should I lie down? A cold wind was blowing, and we shivered in our scanty clothing. Every foot of sheltered ground was covered with sleeping men, but near the operating table, which was under a tree in the house-yard, there lay a long row of dead soldiers. My faithful steward, Cyrus Brooks, a detailed man from the First Minnesota, suggested we make a wind-break by piling them up against the remnants of a fence. We did so, and then lying down behind them, we slept soundly until morning."

---

[37] This letter was written between the lines of a letter Edward had received from his mother. Writing supplies were usually carried in their knapsacks which had been left behind.

"Soon after sunrise I rode over the field in front of us to make sure no wounded man had been overlooked, and only those who have visited a battle-field on a hot summer day can imagine the horrors then presented. Rubens must have seen this, for he painted the colors of the dead just as I saw them that day. . . Burial-parties were clearing the field. A pit was dug some one hundred feet long by twelve feet wide about half-way between Courtney's house and the woods out of which the enemy came, and at a depth of four or five feet they came to water. Into this wet hole our dead were laid in two rows, and one above the other, until they were within a foot of the surface. Then the dirt was piled on them, and I doubt if any record can now be found of who was laid there."

Burying the dead and burning piles of dead horses at night at Fair Oaks Station, Drawing by: A. R. Waud – Harper's Weekly

Edward Bassett's diary records:

"June 2nd. We built a line of breastworks, and are busy careing for the wounded and burying the dead on both sides. June 3rd. there is still some skirmishing. Received 3 days mail. I was detailed to help butcher."

The story of being detailed to help butcher brings us back to Dr. Hand. Providing nourishing food to the wounded men was a serious problem. Hand had been instructed by the medical director as he relates:

> "to have some horses quietly killed. I acquired 2 cavalry horses and a detail of two-butcher-boys from the First Minnesota. We led the horses into a grove near the hospital and in a very short time some beautiful beef was lying on the skins with the edges carefully turned under. Another detail of men carried it to the hospitals, and the cooks were soon making soup and broth. This was served to the wounded, and no doubt helped many of them to tide over the critical time."

Camped at Fair Oak Station, Va.
AM. Saturday June 7th AD 1862

Dear Father and Mother,

Once more I have seated myself with the intention of writing to you at <u>Home.</u> Our tents and knapsacks have come up from our old camp and we are now camped on the very same ground that one week ago this P. M. was made bloody by the shooting of rebels who were trying to flank our forces. In this strip of timber there was many a rebel found a grave in trying to take us Yankees prisoners to exibit to the expectant crowd at Richmond who had been promised that if they wanted to see the Yankees in a cage to be on the streets Sunday when they would exibit some of the finest specimens of Northern vandals that had ever been captured but alas they were fooled again and had to try their luck again on Sunday when true to Genl McClellan's order and Yankee pluck they were driven back at the point of the bayonet and what were left of them have not been very troublesome since. The fight of Sat and Sunday were both very warmly contested. The Rebels were under the impression that we had but a small force here and the river was so high that they thought we could not get any reinforcements across. When they first made the attack they outnumbered our forces two or three to one but our men fought desperately and succeeded in checking them until reinforcements came across the river and came to their assistance. Our Regt had just got in position and laid down in the wheat when the rebels opened on our 3 left companies H, D, & F returned the fire doing good executions. There were two men in Co. D of our Regt. wounded slightly and one of Co. F was killed. He was shot through the head. We were waiting for them to come out in the open field where we could get a fair chance but they would not do that but came up into the woods. The firing of muskets on Sunday beat any-thing that I ever heard for about one hour it was so fast that you could not distinguish a single gun but it sounded like the roar of a large swarm of bees or a large waterfall. Our forces charged on them and drove the enemy from the field. The loss was heavy on both sides. General Dana had his horse shot from under him and one of General Gorman's orderlies had his horse shot. The weather had been very bad for the last week it has rained most of the time and when it was clear the sun was so hot that it would almost melt you. I have stood it very well. I have felt first rate until last evening I had a slight chill but I feel better this morning and I guess that I shall get along without any further trouble. There is quite a number of the boys complaining but our tents and blankets have come and I guess they will be alright in a few days. I guess it is going to clear off and we will have some pleasant weather for a time. I hope so at least. The crops here as far as I have seen are rather late the wheat is scarcely in blossom, Corn is about 3 inches high oats have just headed out. There is going to be a large crop of fruit this season. I think what few orchards there are seem to bid fair for a good supply of such as they raise in Va. I have seen some few straw berries but there are no wild ones. They sell at 25 cts. per qt. There will be a great many Whortleberries [38] and Blackberries. Our men are making a kind of reconaisance in force this morning and the regt. are under orders to march at short notice. We were out on picket yesterday but we could not see any thing of the enemy. We are expecting some thing to be done on the James river by the gunboats. The enemy are in large force this side of Richmond. In one of the Richmond papers that some of the boys got dated May 30th they seem to fear that Genl McClellan will go to using the pick and spade around Richmond as he did at Yorktown. They say that we are cowards and won't meet them in the open field. I guess they have forgotten Williamsburg and will undoubtedly forget the fight of last Sat and Sunday but we will have Richmond yet. I hope that when we do get Richmond that there will be someway fixed up to settle this for at any rate the Rebels will be about played out and I cant see what they can possibly do to in any way retake Virginia for Freemont will keep them out of the western part and there will be but a poor chance for them to make a stand in the Southeastern part of the state.

I hope I shall be there and see you next fall but I know it will seem lonely since George is gone. I know it will not seem like home to me for I shall miss him so much.

Good by for the present.

Your son E. H. Bassett

Co. G 1st Minnesota

---

[38] Whortleberry is an old European name for Blueberry.

Dear Brother Elford,

I don't know but you will think that I have forgotten you entirely but I must assure you that I have not for I often think of you and wish that I could see you but we are a great ways apart and I fear that we will not see one another for some time. Nearly every letter that I get from home there is a word in it from you and I know that you often think of me. I suppose of course that you have heard that George is dead. He died at 1 o'clock P.M. on the 16th of May in the Hospital at Nashville, Tennessee. I know that you will miss him very much. It don't seem possible that I can go home & not meet him there but I know that we can never see him again. In Mother's last letter you sent me word that the old grey has got a colt and you are going to claim it. Well I don't know as I have any claim on it. I hope it will do well and it will make a nice horse when it gets grown. I expect that you have grown so that I would scarcely know you. Are you going to school this summer. How do the girls like the school. Tell them that I wish they would write to me if they can find time. You must try to learn to write so that you can write to me. Well I must close for I have written quite a long letter and my paper is nearly full. Good by for this time.

Your brother

Edward H. Bassett
Co. G 1st Regt.
Minnesota Volunteers

Taking the Wounded to the Cars – After the Battle of Seven Pines
(Artist Unknown)
Note that these are open flatcars without shelter or comfort.

Camped at Fair Oak Station
Sunday P M, June 8th 1862

Dear Sisters Ella and Anna,

As it has been a long time since I have written to *you I thought as it is quite cool and comfortable this* afternoon I would try to write a few lines and let you know that I have not forgotten you. I often think of you and wish that I could see you both and I hope it may not be long ere we meet at home. I am enjoying very good health of late but when it is clear and still and the sun shines hot it makes me wish we had the rebels away up north where we could freeze them until they would be glad to do as they ought. It was just one week yesterday since the great battle was commenced and one week ago today there was some of the heaviest firing from muskets that I ever heard. My regiment was not in the fight on Sunday, but Saturday we had quite a time with the rebels and the bullets flew past my head saying "you" every time but they all missed their mark and went beyond. Early this morning the rebels made an attack on our pickets which are only about one half a mile from our camp in the woods they also shelled the woods but failed to drive our men in. We all thought at first that we were going to have another Sunday fight but as our forces advanced to support the pickets the rebels ceased firing and have been very quiet until within a few moments they have fired a few cannon.

It seems that you are going to school this summer I am glad of it and hope you will have a good school and learn very fast. I would like to be there and go to school with you next winter. I suppose too that you have a Sabbath school. I want you to write and let me know all about them and who goes.

We are now 7 miles from Richmond and if we have good luck it won't be long before we will have possesion of the city and then I think the war will end in a short time. How I would like to step into the room this evening where you are all sitting around the table reading and perhaps writing letters to me. Did I say you would all be there, Yes, but there is one that can never be there again and that is brother George. It does not seem possible but it is so. Oh how I shall miss him and I know you will. I do not get letters from home very often   but when they do come it is like a good meal to a starving man allways remembered. I expect that I would get more letters if it was not for our moving arround so much but it will soon be over with and when we get in a permanent camp we will get the mails more regular.

Tell Elford that I remember him but I expect that he has grown so fast that I would scarcely know him. I wrote him a note yesterday and sent it in Fathers letter.

Well I must close I hope this will find you all well and that the war will soon end so that the country can be happy as it used to.

My love to all the family

From your Brother

Edward H. Bassett

Co. G 1st Minnesota

Have you got Georges likeness in full uniform.

E. H. Bassett

The regiment remained encamped near Fair Oaks Station throughout most of June, all the while kept on relentless duty building defensive works, corduroy roads and clearing the woods away from their position. The weather was quite hot and the frequent rains continued. Wagons could not move, supplies ran short and the only way to even bring in rations was to carry them by hand until the railroad and roads were rebuilt. The only water supply was surface water and most of that ran through a swamp where the rotting corpses of men and horses were everywhere. Diarrhea and malaria were very prevalent.

The pickets were constantly under attack by infantry, cavalry and artillery and there were nightly alarms requiring the men to man the defenses. They were under orders to have their weapons with them at all times and to keep their cartridge boxes on day and night, ready to man their positions at a moments notice. On June 26th, the temperature reached 96 degrees. All the while, the men did their duty and rarely complained.

Camped near Fair Oak Station
Va. June 11th, AD 1862

Dear Parents & Brother & Sisters,

I don't know as there has been any material change

in things here since my last but I suppose the work is going on in the usual slow but certain way and as we are not very far from the last ditch I expect very soon to hear that the rebelion has been quelled and peace restored to the country. We went on picket on the evening of the 8th inst. it was quiet until toward evening 9th. The rebels threw shell in every direction but I have not heard of any one being hurt. The weather is cool and rainy, the roads are very bad but the cars run within about ½ mile of our camp and we get our provisions now quite handy. We have been hard up since we came here but the stuff is comeing along now and "we will live again" (as Davison says when the sutler arrives). [39]

There is some talk that we are going to lose Colonel Sully in the same way that we did Dana but we hope he will be with us until after things are decided arround Richmond. According to the statements in the papers the rebels are in camp this side of the city there being but very few in the city except the sick & wounded. I long for the time when McClellan will have his heavy guns in position & begin to pour in the shot & shell among them. They sent a message over to us the other day that the Yankees will have to wade in blood to get the city. They sent it by a dog tying it to him and sending him through their lines when the boys caught him & took it & read it & sent another back. They have boasted before and it is not certain what they mean.

General Prim who commanded the recent Spanish expedition against Mexico was here on Sunday he was cheered heartily by the soldiers.

We hear rumors that Fort Pillow & Memphis have fallen and the Miss. River is open the whole length. I hope it is so at any rate it will be soon if not now.

I have just received yours of the 28th containing the

---

[39] Private Charles E. Davison age 27, wounded at Bull Run; died Nov. 6, 1862, at New York

account of George's death. I heard of it on the eve of the 27th by letter from Mr. Donaldson. I have written to Hugh & will find out all that I can about George's sickness care & etc. Hugh will tell me all he knows about him. George never sent me his likeness or at least if he did I never received it. He promised to but I guess he must have forgotten it. I am going to send you the money and have one taken from one that you have if you can get one that will look natural but if you can't get one that looks natural I don't want you to send any. I would like one of those that you have that he had taken but you must not risk them by mail to me. If you can get a copy of one at the artists in Faribault I would like very much to have you send it to me. I think it can be taken on a light plate so that it would come in a letter very handy. . .I think Captain Rice shows himself a true man, he must take some interest in his men. I am glad to know that George was under a man that had some feeling for his command. George never wrote a word to me about any of their officers except to give their names. He never wrote much about whether he liked soldering or not but he seemed to be very will suited & wrote very kind and friendly letters.

Enclosed in this letter you will find a piece of poetry that was copied from an old Phonetic paper. The verses are beautiful I think and are a good illustration of a soldier on picket in a dark night.

"And then amid the lonely gloom
Beneath the tall old Chestnut trees
My silent marches I resume
And think of other times than these..."

How often have I done that very thing in the dark night when all seemed quiet save the rumbling of the water in the Potomac there would be a rat or fish or perhaps some driftwood would run against the bushes and for a moment every bush & stump would look like soldiers armed to the teeth but come to approach them you could soon find that they were harmless & perhaps you would find it was a shadow that caused the alarm.

All quiet once more pacing back and forth my mind would run back to other times. I would think of the good old times that are gone and long for the time to come when I should be sitting with Father, Mother, Brother & Sisters around the old hearth passing the (now weary hours) pleasantly.

Well I must close sending my love to all the family.

Please excuse this paper for I blotted it & then tore part of it off. I will try and write again soon.

Good by for the present

Yours in haste as ever

E. H. Bassett Co. G"

Fair Oaks / Seven Pines Camp–Leslie's Illustrated Weekly
Army of the Potomac 1862

Fair Oak Station Va.
June 14th, 1862.

Dear parents,

Knowing that you were ever anxious to hear from the seat of war I thought I would write a few lines and give

200

you what little news there is that I have chanced to pick up the past four or five days. But perhaps before this reaches you the great battle will be fought that will decide the confederate claim to a position in the old dominion if not on the continent. They are evidently waiting for us to make the attac and I don't think they will be long disappointed for little Mac will be apt to give them a trial before long if the weather is favorable. It is very hot today and I don't feel much like writing or doing anything but lay arround in the shade. There is several of the boys that are not very well & two that are quite sick but I guess they will get along well enough in a few days.

I would not give my aid to keep Virginia upon the face of the earth one moment after the federal army has been removed from the cursed wilderness. As tomorrow is Sunday we have reason to expect an attac from the God forsaken chivalry of the would be Confederacy but if they should be so foolhardy as to come out & try to carry our works by storm we will have a chance to do what we have longed to for a long time, that is to shoot their eyes out from behind works that will aford good protection. We would by that means have a chance to avenge the death of Captain McKune & others that fell on that fatal day. It is reported in camp today that the pickets on the road between here & the White House were fired upon last night & a portion of the track was torn up. It was most likely done by a party of citizens acting as Guerrillas & many of them undoubtedly have the white flag floating over their houses and the government pays them large prices for everything that is in the slightest way damaged by the army besides men that have volunteered in their country's service for the purpose of establishing the federal authority in the rebelious states & to punish all traitors to the country to the full extend of the law are posted to guard the traitors from any inconvenience that might arise from now & then a soldier calling at the house for a drink of water or perhaps a meal of victuals for which he would gladly pay for in gold & silver.

It is a common saying in Washington that the contrabands once the property of leading rebels in Va. but now in prison in Washington are treated with more respect than the Union soldiers. And I know that the prisoners both political & prisoners of war that are confined in the old Capital building get better care and have better fare than we ever got from the government when we were in the city. This may seem right to some but I am tired of treating the traitors so mildly. They deserve hanging & if we would adopt that plan the war would soon end.

Genl McClellan and staff were here yesterday & reviewed the troops. It would do your soul good to hear the boys cheer as he passed along the lines. Regiment after regiment along the line took it up as he passed and you could hear the cheering, for nearly an hour as he rode down the line. Yesterday morning the rebels opened on us with shot & shell but our guns did not answer them. The bugler of Company-I of the Minnesota 1st was killed by one of the shot striking a log in the breastwork which he was leaning his head against. His name is Ellison. A company of Mass. sharpshooters went out and crawled up to the bold Secess & a few well directed shots from their rifles forced them to cease operation for the day. The next time they open they will undoubtedly meet with warm receptions. Their shell are said to have mostly been thrown from smooth bore guns.

Sunday morning June 15th.

It is a very pleasant morning. The rebels have been quiet so far and I hope they will be all day. How I would like to be at home this morning. I believe I would enjoy a few weeks of quite life in the country away from the hum and bustle of a camp. There was a deserter from the rebels came over yesterday. He says there are many others that would gladly leave the rebel ranks if they could get a chance. The crops must begin to look nice there in Minnesota by this time. You would not know that there had ever been anything planted here. What little there has been is completely destroyed by the army. Besides there has been many hundreds of acres of timber cut to clear the way for artillery, build breastworks & forming abates [40] to check an advance of the enemy. Old Virginia is getting well payed for seceding. I wish the gun boats would run up and burn Richmond to the ground. It may look hard but it is the only way that they can be conquered. Kill, burn & destroy everything that belongs to them. When they are powerless they will give up and not until. They got a fine cleaning out at Memphis. Served them right only I wish they had drowned.

I see in the N.Y. Tribune a list of released prisoners & among them is the name of one of our Co. that bore the flag at Manassas. His name is Wm. Potter. We allways supposed that he was dead. He is the fellow that worked for Captain McKune one year ago last winter. I see by the Faribault papers that they are making preparations for a celebration on the 4th. I hope they will have a good time as they undoubtedly will if it is pleasant.

Remember me to all the friends and excuse for the present.

$\mathscr{A}$s ever $\mathscr{E}$dward.

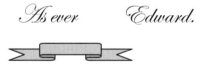

Fair Oaks Station Va.
June 16th, 1862

$\mathscr{D}$ear $\mathscr{M}$other

---

[40] A defensive obstacle formed by felled trees with sharpened points placed facing the enemy.

Your letter of the 8th inst. has been received in 7 days from the day it was mailed in Faribault which is quick time. It found me well and enjoying myself as well as usual. I am sorry to hear that you are not well for although I am far away I know just how you look and seem to feel. I am afraid that you are working to hard this summer trying to make the garden look so nice & other work that I know that I ought to be there doing myself and trying to lighten the burden of the work that both Father & you are now doing alone. But I trust the time is not far distant that the wars will be over and I hope to be able to return to you & try & repay you for numberless kindnesses that I have received when unworthy the least of favors. I hope you will not get very sick for how could I bear the thought of your being sick and suffering while I am away off here where I cannot render you the slightest assistance. You must not worry about me every little bit of news that you get from the seat of war for there are any number of false reports gain credit by the time they reach you. But you have undoubtedly received letters from me that were written since the battle. It is true such terrible conflicts are to be deplored and I earnestly hope there will be no more such bloody strife but a bloodless war was never known in all the history of nations and we certainly cannot expect such a one in this age of progression when there are as many thousands of devices for the destruction of life.

There has been a detachment of our Sharpshooters out scouting in the outposts today. They did not fire a single shot. The rebels have got heartily tired of picket shooting & sent a flag of truce to have it stoped which was willingly complied with by our men. The Sharpshooters exchanged the NY. Papers for Richmond papers but the exchange did not obtain any important news for us I believe & they are not much wiser I guess unless it should happen that there is a little good sense and manliness should happen to dawn upon their sun burnt & benighted pates by seeing for themselves that we are not a set of savages and barbarians as they mostly believe. The government is certainly treating them better than they deserve & when they come to find out that they are in reality fighting against the same old flag that they used to fight for there are many of them that would gladly throw down their arms and return to the Union.

June 17<u>th</u>

As I did not have time to finish my letter last night I will try and do it this morning. It is a beautiful morn cool and pleasant but it will be very hot by noon. Things are as quiet as usual. We are not doing picket duty now.

I received another letter form H.W. Donaldson yesterday. They were camped at Murfreesboro, Tenn. He writes that the health of the 3<u>rd</u> is very good. He said that he was going to Nashville in a few days and would get an order from Captain Rice for George's things and box them up neatly & express them to Hastings where you can get them. I have written to him that if he would do so I will forward him the necessary amount & pay him well for his trouble. He also states that George was in a good Hospital and well taken care of while sick. The rebels have been trying to carry out their threats of taking Nashville and driving the federals out but I guess they will be apt to be quiet now since Memphis has fallen and they have no foothold in the state.

How does Elford's Colt get along. How many cows have you got this summer? Are the folks diging any ginseng there this summer?

I would like to have Father write me a few lines once in a while if he can find time. But I know he must be very busy with only Elford to help him.

My love to all the family

Edward

CHAPTER 13
💣 SEVEN DAYS BATTLES BEFORE RICHMOND

Following the costly struggle at Fair Oaks, General Lee expected McClellan to move immediately with his entire 110,000–man army. President Jeff Davis and the citizens were greatly alarmed. The Virginia Legislature was in session and voted $200,000 to aid the fleeing residents who had been urged to take refuge in other cities. The frenzied clamor of church bells extolled the terror that fell over the Confederate Capital. Needing information about the strength and disposition of McClellan's forces, General Lee sent Jeb Stuart and his 1200-man cavalry to cross to the north or east side of the Chickahominy River. Stuart was to determine if a flank attack on General Porter's forces could be successful. The now famous "Stuart's Ride" around the entire Federal army illustrated the brilliance of this cavalry commander. Once across the river, he soon discovered he could not return the way he had come and decided to continue his ride all around McClellan. At one point, Stuart was even within sight of McClellan's Headquarters tent.

By the time Stuart had reported back to Lee, he had raised havoc behind the Union lines, destroyed supplies, wagons and even three transports on the river. He was hotly pursued by Union cavalry and narrowly escaped after burning a bridge he had hastily built from a barn his men tore down. The bridge allowed him to cross with his men and cannons and to swim the horses across. Just as his pursuers arrived and began shooting at him from the far side, his men set the bridge afire.

Stuart confirmed General Lee's hopes that the Union right flank and rear were weakly defended. Lee immediately ordered Stonewall Jackson recalled from the Shenandoah Valley. Jackson was sent with a force of 63,100 men to attack and destroy or capture General Porter's 28,100 men who had been left on the north side of the river to protect the Union rear. General Fitz John Porter, however, proved to be a tough adversary. Though outnumbered by more than 2-to-1, Porter launched a minor probing attack at Oak Grove on June 25. He fought Lee to a draw at Mechanicsville on the 26th and inflicted heavy losses at Gaines' Mill on the 27th of June. All the activity only seemed to heighten McClellan's fear that he was facing vastly superior numbers. On the 28th, he ordered Porter across the Chickahominy and, once again united his force. McClellan was convinced that Richmond was no longer in his grasp and to remain where he was, meant defeat or annihilation. He began the long, arduous withdrawal across the peninsula to the James River and Harrison's Landing where he had established another base of operations. McClellan chose to blame Washington for his situation and, upon issuing the order to retreat, rode off to the James River without appointing anyone as Second in Command in his place, thus leaving the army without the benefit of his organizational skills. The retreat was hurriedly begun and resulted in the destruction of huge amounts of supplies and equipment that could not be carried along. Recently rebuilt bridges were burned. Whole trains were run off railroad bridges as they were blown up. Mountains of materials of every description were set afire and at night the red glow in the sky could be seen for many miles.

The numerous battles and skirmishes that resulted as Lee continually tried to mold events that would allow him to deliver a fatal blow to the Army of The Potomac are referred to as the "Seven Days Battles before Richmond." The First Minnesota was heavily involved in some, but not all, of these actions. Its well established reputation as a unit that could be counted on when things got rough, led to its placement as one of the rear guard. In that position, its job was to defend the rear of the miles-long mass of retreating men and vehicles.

The job meant a good deal of fighting. The weather continued to alternate between hot sunny days and heavy rains, which kept the roads in a nearly impassible condition. The rear guard had to struggle through the mud after the columns had passed–often marching at double-quick time, nearly running, to keep in contact with the army.

Envelope from letter of June 27, 1862

The first two pages of this letter are missing.

Friday eve June 27th, As I did not get my letter finished in time to send it off today I thought I would write a few more lines.

Fighting has been rageing furiously all day on our right across the Chichahominy River & there is heavy cannonading to be heard in that direction now. General Porter is in command there I believe subject of course to McClellan. It is reported that Porter fell back during the day some 5 miles but as he advanced some ways yesterday PM. I do not immagine that he has been driven back or pursued as close as many think. It is stated that he is driving the enemy now in turn. But whatever has been done I am slow to believe that McClellan has been very badly beaten you will see the official report before you get this and you may laugh at me for writing such stuff but I am only giving you the summary of the evening talk & whether we are any where near correct you can tell when you see a full account. The contest has been fierce on both sides & the enemy undoubtedly thinks that they are fighting to hold the last ditch. The enemy made an attempt to shell some of the batteries & camps both to the right & left of Gorman's Brigade but their pieces which were planted in a wheat field about ½ a mile distant were subject to a heavy cross fire besides a number of guns in front & they retired after fireing something near 200 shots without killing a man.

Sat. morning June 28th. We were kept under arms all night last night. The rebels made an attack on our pickets right in front of where we are camped but they were driven back by our heavy reserves & these batteries which threw shell and grape among them. It was most likely done to try to keep us from reinforcing any other point. The troops that went to assist Porter yesterday have returned last night & this morning. They say that we are all right and the rebels have been defeated.

The rebels can be heard cheering this morning & their band is playing Dixie & other tunes appropriate to their section of the country. Such cheering it sounds like an army of infants their voices are so light. What will be done today we can't tell but I hope the work being commenced will not be allowed to lay nor do I believe it will. The boys are as well as usual this morning. Batt Soule, Chas. Parker, Wm. Coen, Jonathan Goodrich, Wm. Brown & all the boys from that vicinity are well as also Captain Messick. You all seem to think that the military hospitals are the most dreary & lonesome place that ever was & that the patients all despair & give up all hopes of recovery. But you are certainly mistaken in your idea for you will often meet with some unfortunate who has a leg broken or something worse who will talk & joke as did a fellow the other day that was wounded in a skirmish off to our left. He was riding along in an ambulance when he saw some soldiers passing he put his head out at a window & in a joking way said "the rebels have broke my leg but what of that. I will be back to pay them for it sometime." It is true there is a great deal of suffering but as the men enlist with the calculation of not being beaten nor discouraged as long as there is any hope they bear their sufferings better than they otherwise could. You also speak of my getting some one to write for me in case I should be disabled. Now I wish to assure you that you will hear from me just as often as you could wish if the mails go right along.

Now I wish you could all write and write all the news giveing the detail of all the proceedings in the neighborhood. I expect we will get payed off before long, part of the brigade have got their pay now. I will try & send home a little money if I can get some safe conveyance.

It is nearly 8 o'clock now & all quiet along the lines.

Please excuse me for this time & also excuse this long nonsensical letter. And believe me as ever yours with kindest regard hopeing that you may have health & all other blessings.

Edward Co. G

Minn 14th

1862

☄ BATTLE OF ALLEN'S FARM
June 29, 1862

During the retreat, Edward understandably did not write home with his usual frequency. His regiment was marching or fighting nearly continuously, getting very little opportunity to rest or even to eat. As Edward mentions above, they had been ordered to pack all their belongings which were sent away on June 27th and 28th. Remaining in camp at Fair Oaks all night, laying on their arms and without shelter, they kept the fires going to make it appear as though the entire army was still in camp. At 4 AM on the morning of June 29th, the regiment and the other remaining troops at Fair Oaks marched out with General Burns' brigade as the rear guard. About 9 AM, after reaching Allen's Farm, some two miles east of Fair Oaks, they halted for a brief period. The road was clogged with all manner equipment and men, guns and wagon trains. The sounds of close pursuit by the enemy could be heard in the rear. As General Burns' brigade was heavily engaged with enemy infantry and artillery, the First Minnesota was called up and placed on his left, near the peach orchard on Allen's farm to support the Rhode Island Artillery battery. The enemy attacked in force and, though the Minnesota First was exposed to a continuous and heavy artillery fire, it was not directly engaged. The fighting lasted until about noon on this very hot day. Having repulsed the enemy, the march toward Savage Station was resumed.

During this and following days, General Gorman, being very ill with malaria, often relinquished command of the brigade to Colonel Alfred Sully. As the march continued, the Regimental Chaplain, Chaplain Neil, felt depressed by what he saw:

> *"The saddest sight that day was sick soldiers, exhausted by the march, lying with closed eyes in the shade of trees, or tottering along with the aid of sticks."*

The decision was made to take a stand at Savage Station to give the main body of the column time to cross White Oak Swamp. It became apparent the massive stocks of supplies and ammunition there could not be taken along and would have to be destroyed. That work had begun earlier in the day and the conflagration of fires and explosions produced a billowing plume of colored smoke and a cacophony of sound. Doctor Hand wrote:

"The 29 th was one of the hottest days of the season, and when we reached the station, about five o'clock, many of the men were exhausted and fell down with sunstroke. While we were dragging them into the shade and pouring cold water over them an order came to form in line of battle."

☀ BATTLE OF SAVAGE STATION
June 29, 1862

Lieutenant William Lochren describes the battle that ensued when the rebels once again launched a determined, violent artillery and infantry attack on the army's rear.

"About 4 o'clock the Confederates ran down the railroad a heavy gun mounted on a flat-car, and protected by railroad iron, and opened fire on our troops. This was followed closely by infantry and other artillery. The First Minnesota and Gen. Burns' Brigade of our division were ordered to the point of attack, and soon drove off the enemy. But Confederate infantry at once appeared on another road farther to the left, and we were sent to that point, being joined by the other regiments of our brigade, the First Minnesota here forming the extreme left of the line, and resisting the heaviest brunt of the attack, which was made with artillery at canister range, and with infantry extending beyond our left flank which was in great danger of being turned. The fighting here was most persistent and severe, and as we got the enemy's fire diagonally from its extended right, as well as from the front, our loss was considerable. We held the position, however, without yielding and inch and about sunset the Vermont Brigade, which had been recalled from its route to

*White Oak swamp, came in on our left, and, joining in a
last counter attack, the enemy was driven back. The First
Minnesota lost forty-eight killed and wounded in this
battle. Gathering our wounded into the field hospital, as
there were no facilities for removing them, they were left,
with a sufficient number of attendants after their wounds
had been dressed, to the care of the enemy, and we
pushed on after night, still in rear of the army, across
White Oak swamp, bivouacking near morning for a brief
time soon after crossing the bridge."*

This battle could have been another disaster if not for the
extraordinary courage and dedication to duty exhibited by the
First Minnesota and General Burns' regiments. Two weak
points in the Union line were exploited by McGruder's
charging Confederates before Burns' request for two
additional regiments could be answered. The rebels broke
through to a rail fence, thus cutting the Union line in two. The
Minnesota and Pennsylvania men knew full well the risk of
staying there, but men such as these did not cower in the face
of danger. They stood their ground where others might have
turned and run. They fought with the calm coolness that had
defined them as being among the best in the army. As the
musketry and canister tore through their ranks they stood
loading and firing—tearing open the paper cartridges with
their teeth, pouring powder and bullets into the hot barrels of
their rifles, ramming the shot home with their ramrods,
fumbling with shaking fingers for a percussion cap in their
cap box, placing the tiny cap on the nipple and firing again
and again. Shortly, General Sumner, that courageous, old
war horse, charged onto the scene, hat in hand, waving
forward two fresh regiments to turn the tide. At Sumner's
order, the Irishmen of the 88th New York and the 5th New
Hampshire men, with bayonets at the ready and voices raised
in a fearsome yell, charged the enemy line. Confronted by so
determined an adversary, the rebels turned and ran from the
field and through the woods behind.

Of the day's action, Lieutennant Colonel Stephen Miller reports:

> *"That gallant officer, General Burns, said to me on the next day, "Your regiment did nobly, sir," and I heartily concur in the sentiment."*

General Burns was shot in the face that day, but showing the same unfathomable courage as the men he commanded, he never left his post or duty.

Battle of Savage Station – Sketch from Harper's Weekly - July 26, 1862

●❋ BATTLE OF NELSON'S FARM
June 30, 1862

About 10 o'clock on the night of the 29th, the regiment was ordered out of its position to again take up the march. This time, still serving as rear guard, they were to cross the White Oak Bridge. Having gone without rest most of the night before and marching or fighting all day, the men were very fatigued. They crossed the bridge and marched all night through the swamp on a narrow muddy trail without incident. The column bivouacked briefly on June 30th. They had rested with the huddled mass of the rest of the army for but a short while when the rebels opened fire with 31 cannons from across the swamp. Jackson was doing his best to cut the Federal army in two and destroy at least one half of it. Early in the morning the Minnesota boys, with the exception of Edward Bassett, were formed up and had marched out about 2 miles when ordered to countermarch back to the bridge where General Franklin was under artillery attack. Bassett had been left behind to help a wounded comrade get to an ambulance and was not re-united with the regiment until July 3rd. The regiment was sent to Brackett's Ford, two miles upstream from White Oak Bridge, where Munford's Virginia Cavalry was making an attempt to cross the very swollen creek. Observing the movements of the Federal troops through field glasses, Munford decided that any attempt to cross the creek would be a costly failure and withdrew after a minor exchange of fire.

Field Hospital at Savage Station June 27, 1862, Brady Photo
Barely visible in this photo, the field behind this scene was filled with tents equipped with 20 cots each, all of which were occupied by sick or wounded soldiers. 2500 were left to be cared for by the enemy.

☙ BATTLE OF GLENDALE, (WHITE OAK SWAMP)

June 30, 1862

All afternoon, the regiment could hear the ever increasing din of cannon and musket fire about 2 miles ahead at Glendale. About 5 PM, they were marched at the double-quick to Glendale, where the heaviest attack by the Confederates was under way. The men, totally exhausted, were placed in support of other troops long enough to catch their breaths. They lay close to the ground as a storm of lead wizzed like angry hornets above their heads. Shortly thereafter, they were put into the front line to relieve another regiment that was "hard pressed". General Sumner personally ordered the men into line saying, *"Boys, I shall not see many of you again, but I know you will hold that line."* (Lochren).

The report of Lieutennant Colonel William Miller, in command of the regiment that day, comments:

". . . and finally, under direction of General Dana, about sunset, the men threw away their knapsacks, blankets, etc. and charged upon the foe at a point in the edge of the wood which had just been abandoned by another Union regiment. We took the ground and occupied the front of the line, under a heavy and continuous fire. Here we were attacked upon my right about dark, by - as we learned from wounded prisoners – the Sixteenth North Carolina Regiment, but a few well directed rounds from my line in that vicinity caused the enemy to hastily retire, with considerable loss. At midnight, in obedience to instructions, I withdrew."

Knapsack Photo
Courtesy of
C. & D. Jarnagin Co.

When the men returned to pick up their knapsacks from

the pile where they had been discarded to ease their load, they were angered to find them gone, probably taken by looters or stragglers.

As their knapsacks carried many personal articles and necessities, they were sorely missed.

At the end of the battle, the First Minnesota had lost one man killed and five wounded. Among the wounded was Captain William Colvill of Company F. He was struck in the left breast by a Minnie ball. William Lochren showed his admiration for Colvill when in his "Narrative of the First Minnesota Regiment," he related it thus:

". . . who, after dark, was desperately wounded by a shot in the left breast. But, with that imperturbability for which he was distinguished he gave no sign of being hurt and turned over his command to his lieutenant as if for a few minutes' absence and no one knew that he was hurt until the next morning, when he was heard from as having walked to the field hospital at Malvern Hill".

The regiment held their position in the line until the next morning when they marched to Malvern Hill.

Mathew Marvin[41] wrote of the fatigue and deprivation the men faced during this time. He expressed it well, though simply:

"We were completely fagged out haveing no sleep for 3 nights and fore days & but little poor watter. Each man seemed to think that he could not live 15 minutes from the burning of the sun that was shineing and not a sign of any wind and doublequicking for nearly a half a mile." Charley Goddard also commented on the conditions: "Fighting day times and marching night almost killed the men. Getting no sleep nor time to make a cup of coffee will naturely ware a man out."

---

[41] Mathew Marvin was a Corporal in Company K of the First Minnesota He was promoted to Sergeant and then First Sergeant during his enlistment and was wounded at Bull Run, Harrison's Landing and Gettysburg.

☙ THE BATTLE OF MALVERN HILL
July 1, 1862

The battle of Malvern Hill was a decisive Union Victory. The Union held a perfect position atop the only hill in the area. Surrounded by open flatlands it offered an excellent defensive command of the countryside. Robert E. Lee was now convinced that McClellan and all his troops were resigned to defeat and their morale would make them an easy opponent to beat. His plan of a frontal attack on the Federal position proved to be a bad mistake. The Union artillery was massed on the hill and the army was far from beaten. In fact, most were very unhappy with the continual retreat. The First Minnesota was a reserve unit in this battle. Though they were subject to a good deal of artillery fire passing over their heads all day, they did not play an active part in the hard-fought battle that raged all day until evening. Rebel infantry attacked again and again and was blown to pieces by the cannons, and cut down and chewed up by the massed musket fire. Lee made the same mistake on this field as he would later at Gettysburg. He failed to commit all of his forces to the battle and, instead fed them to the slaughter piece-by-piece. At the end of the day, 6,000 of his men had been killed or wounded and the Federal losses numbered approximately 1,700.

According to the following letter, some of the wounded, perhaps those that could walk or be helped along by their comrades were able to escape capture and, upon reaching the James River, were placed on hospital boats.

Camped on the James River, Va.
On Harrisons Landing
July 4, 1862

Dear Parents,

As it is Independence day and I have no very handy way of doing anything in particular to celebrate the

218

occasion I thought I would write you a letter. You will most likely have heard of the recent movements of the Potomac Army in front of Richmond before you receive this. It was entirely unlooked for on our part for we expected every day to hear the command Forward to Richmond, but it seems from what we hear and have seen that the retreat was one of those mysterious moves in which such men as our worthy Commander in Chief Genl George B. McClellan indulge in to the great annoyance of the masses.

We are all confident of success and that soon. We left our camp at Fair Oaks Station on Sunday morn and marched down the R.R. a little way where the enemy made an attack upon our rear and were repulsed and we fell back to Savage Station a distance of some 7 miles from our camp. Here the enemy made another attack upon our rear and the Minnesota 1 st was brought into the action a little before sundown. The enemy came down in force upon our rear and the way the shells flew for a minute was a caution to beholders.

Drawing of the Battle of Malvern Hill – Harper's Weekly, July 26,1862

We went into the fight a little before sundown and remained on the field until about 9 o'clock in the evening. Henry Wells[42] and John McKinstry[43] of our Co. were severely wounded that night but they are now on the Hospital boats in the river and both expected to recover. Our flag bearer was killed also several others in the Regt. but the enemy were repulsed and we started about 10 o'clock and marched 5 or 6 miles further and crossed the White Oaks swamp and laid until morning and again started on the retreat but the enemy followed us closely and long before noon the booming of cannon told us that they were again at our rear but they were not quite as successful as they expected to be for I think they have not captured anything of great value besides being repulsed with loss each time giving our men a chance to retreat which was done in the best order. Our regt. arrived at the landing about night Wednesday and camped in a newly plowed field and as it was raining all the time besides the heavy rain that fell at noon the mud was soon as deep as we could get through. Many of the boys had neither blankets nor tents having been ordered to throw them away on the march. The first night was rather hard but last night we had mostly got some kind of a shelter and got some rest. This morning we left our camp and marched back into a field farther from the river and out of the mud. The rebels followed us very closely but they were met at all points by a full front. We have taken many prisoners and some guns. And I expect we have also lost some. Things look bright ahead now I think Genl Pope is here with part of Fremont's and Shields' command. They came up on the boats and have gone to the front. What the operations will be within the next few weeks we can only guess but we are all hopeful.

Genl McClellan rode through our camp at noon and

---

[42] Henry Wells was discharged for disability due to his wound on Nov. 28, 1862.

[43] John McKinstry returned to duty but was later killed at Gettysburg.

there was a salute fired from the batteries besides a grand display of red white and blue from all the masts of the river craft. At present the boys are very much fatigued and some are sick but a little quiet and rest will bring many of them all right. The two that I have mentioned were the only ones of our Company that were hurt and no prisoners. I don't know what the loss of the whole Regt. is but you will see by the papers soon. Johny Goodrich and myself had a fine dinner today we thought as it was the 4th we would have a little spree. The dinner consisted of a hard cracker and a cup of tea. Captain is well and stands the rough first rate. Both our Colonel and General Gorman are unwell and have been some time. Lieutennant Colonel Miller commands the regt. The Galena and several other gun boats are here and ready to play their part. This is a fine country here the wheat is nice but most of it has not been cut. I never saw larger fields. The corn also looks well and I have had two or three meals of new potatoes. The white population have mostly gone to Richmond leaving their negroes to take care of their farms &c. I hope to have good news to write soon and will try to write again as soon as I get rested a little.

With best wishes for your safety and health I remain your unworthy son.

E. H. Bassett, Co. G

Saturday Morn July 5th, 1862

Hot and clear. All quiet but sleepy as usual. I wish I was in Morristown this morning but I will have to be Patient, two years more will tell the story at most.

Edward

Edward's letter of July 10th and 11th in Chapter 14 gives more information on the Seven Days battles. Of note is his statement that they had no sleep from June 27th until July 3rd. On that night, they slept in a pouring rain in the mud without tents or blankets.

McClellan continued to retreat even though he won every battle in which his forces were engaged while moving across the peninsula to the James River. His field commanders never understood why they were not allowed to take advantage of their victories. At Malvern Hill, Lee could not believe his ears when it was reported the next day that the Federals had pulled out and were moving toward Harrison's Landing, leaving their dead and wounded on the field.

The Seven Days before Richmond was over. The First Minnesota Regiment had a loss of 6 killed, 47 wounded and 28 missing. The Union Army counted its loss at nearly 11,000 killed, wounded and missing; the Confederates lost 20,000. After all this struggle, and all the loss of men and material, nothing had been accomplished. McClellan withdrew to a fortified camp where he had a good supply line and Lee continued the struggle unabated.

The Civil War has often been referred to as turning brother against brother and father against son. The histories of the war are replete with stories of the tragedies of these events of human conflict. Such a tragedy was recorded at Malvern Hill. Captain D. P. Conyngham of the Irish Brigade, which had made a heroic charge that day, wrote:

" I had a Sergeant Driscoll, a brave man, and one of the best shots in the Brigade. When charging at Malvern Hill, a company was posted in a clump of trees, who kept up a fierce fire on us, and actually charged out on our advance. Their officer seemed to be a daring, reckless boy, and I said to Driscoll, 'If that officer is not taken down, many of us will fall before we pass that clump.

'Leave that to me,' said Driscoll; so he raised his rifle, and the moment the officer exposed himself again bang went Driscoll, and over went the officer, his company at once breaking away.

As we passed the place I said 'Driscoll see if that officer is dead, he was a brave fellow.

I stood looking on. Driscoll turned him over on his back. He opened his eyes for a moment, and faintly murmured 'Father,' and closed them forever.

I will forever recollect the frantic grief of Driscoll; it was harrowing to witness. He was his son, who had gone South before the war.

And what became of Driscoll afterwards? Well, we were ordered to charge, and I left him there; but, as we were closing in on the enemy, he rushed up, with his coat off, and, clutching his musket, charged right up at the enemy calling on the men to follow. He soon fell, but jumped up again. We knew he was wounded. On he dashed, but he soon rolled over like a top. When we came up he was dead, riddled with bullets."[44]

---

[44] "Battlefield Tragedy, 1862" EyeWitness to History,www.eyewitnesstohistory.com (1999).

CHAPTER 14
HARRISON'S LANDING

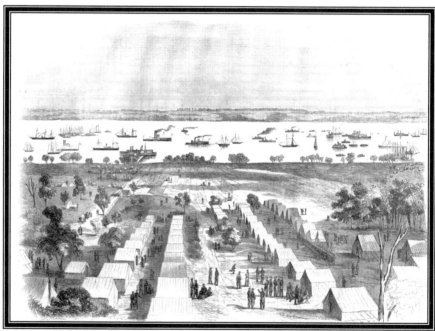

Army of the Potomac Camp at Harrison's Landing
Drawing by: A. R. Waud, Harper's Weekly, Aug. 23, 1862

The army withdrew from Malvern Hill during the night of July 1st and the following morning took up a new position at

Harrison's Landing. The First Minnesota continued to serve as part of the rear guard. During the night, the heavens opened as if echoing the thunderous fusillade of cannon fire that had reverberated across the land hours before. A deluge of cleansing rain tried to wash the gore of battle from the fields and the descent down the bluffs of Malvern Hill was dangerous on the rain soaked ground. Marching in the now well churned mud of the roads, the regiment covered the 7 miles by noon.

Usually Harrison's Landing was a sight pleasing to behold. The view across the broad plains and the James River was idyllic. Berkley mansion, which still stood there, was the ancestral home of the Harrison family. The estate had been the home of Benjamin Harrison, who had signed the Declaration of Independence and whose son, William Henry Harrison, had become President. The rain continued to pour down in sheets as the mass of men spread out onto a huge wheat field to make camp. Shelter tents were set up and wheat taken from stacks of the previous year's harvest was used as bedding. Within an hour the once handsome field was trampled into a sea of dark mud. The men awoke to find themselves under their collapsed tents, lying in pools of water, and their bedding submerged in the mud.

The morning of July 3rd was eventful for more reasons than the poor condition of the camp. Around 8 AM, as many of the men were trying to come up with something to eat for breakfast and others were still lying in their wet beds, artillery shells began whistling overhead. Jeb Stuart's Confederate cavalry had moved a gun into the woods across Westover Creek, a short way from camp. They lobbed shell after shell until about 2 PM when the ammunition was exhausted and they withdrew. They fired around 200 shells with no real damage being done. McClellan sent a force to cut down the trees in the area to avoid any further surprises.

After a couple of days the army moved about 1 mile inland and camped. During this 4 day time period Edward had been separated from the regiment, as he mentions in his diary:

"June 30th very hot. Started early on the road to James River. I was left to help one of the wounded to an

Ambulance. The Regiment left and I could not find it again all day. July 1ˢᵗ still hot. Heavy fireing in the rear, the Rebs are following us closely. July 2ⁿᵈ I went down river five miles, but not finding the Regt. I returned to the Landing.⁴⁵ July 3ʳᵈ Rainy. The regt. came down towards evening and camped in a corn field. It was very muddy. July 4ᵗʰ we moved out into the country about a mile and camped in a corn field near a creek."

Matthew Marvin, Company K, gives further insight into the exhausting pace the regiment had endured in his diary on July 4, 1862:

"I took off my shoes last night to sleep for the first time in 33 days."

Sabbath eve In Camp near
Harrison's Landing, James River Va.
July 6ᵗʰ, 1862.

Beloved Parents:

I received your letter of the 22ⁿᵈ & 23ʳᵈ instant by this days mail. I assure you that it was gladly perused by me. I am glad to hear that your crops and everything else are doing so well this summer, also that you are haveing health to enjoy yourselves during the sultry days of July & August. But how I wish that the war was ended & I back there so as to help do the work that must be done and I know it must come hard on you to have all the work to do alone. Then again when I think of poor brother George I almost think that I would rather not return for it would be so lonesome there without him. I would miss him every moment. I

---

⁴⁵ The camps of the army usually covered many miles. With often more than 100,000 men and all the related equipment and supplies and horses, they actually became fairly large temporary cities.

have often thought since he enlisted that we would have such a good time when the war was over if we could both meet at home once more. (Alas how often are our fondest hopes blighted in a moment all that we hold dear is lost & we are left to mourn). I also received a letter from Mr. Donaldson today. The regt. (3rd Minnesota Volunteer Infantry) was at Murfreesborro, Tenn on the 29. He writes that they have had some heavy marches lately but the health of the regt. was generaly good. He did not go to Nashville & therefore did not send those things as he expected but he says that he will the very first opportunity. We hear that the 2nd Minnesota is in Baltimore & is comeing here soon. I hope it is so for we would be glad to see any of the Minnesota boys.

We are camped in a small cornfield right in a bend of a creek that runs close by. There is a very nice farm house with saw & grist mill near by & things on the farm look as if the owner had lived at his ease as he most likely did. The house is ocupied by Genls Sumner & Sedgwick for their head quarters. This is a wealthy country. They raise good wheat & their corn & other grains look fine besides the fruit. The river at the landing is a little less than ½ a mile in width with good beach & heavy current. We are some few miles below City Point which is on the west side of the river. It has been a very hot day but the soldiers take the advantage of the creek & bathe very often. I don't fully understand the cause of the sudden move that brought us from within 5 miles of Richmond away down here but we are all willing to leave the result in the hands of little Mac & we consider that success awaits us at the proper time & it may come sooner than we now expect. It has been very quiet since we came here and it is said that reinforcements are landing every day. It is 9 o'clock & time to retire & I will have to finish this letter tomorrow so Good night to all.

E. H. B.

Monday morning 7th. It is quite cool & comfortable this morn & I hope it will remain so all day. There are several of the boys that are not very well, among then are J. Goodrich and B.K. Soule from Morristown. Cal Jackson is well & hearty. There is some talk that the Minnesota 2 & 4th are at the landing now. I only hope they are. Genl Sedgwick has just issued an order for two hours drill each day, one in the morning and one in the P.M. We have just had Genl McClellan's speech of the 4th read to us. He compliments the troops very highly for their bravery & coolness in the recent moves and says that each may be proud to say that he belongs to the army of the Potomac. He also declares that the army shall enter the capitol of the so called confederacy.

I see by the Republican that you are going to have a county fair in Sept. What will you have to take to it. I wish that I was there to go to the fairs & I think perhaps I could find several ways to amuse myself for a few weeks if I was only in Minnesota I guess you will think that I am sick of the service & want to get out but I am just about as well contented now as I ever was in Virginia. I was hopeing that the war should end before this time but it bids fair to last some time yet. One thing is certain the rebels have concentrated their forces to defeat us at Richmond & we have got to concentrate ours to fight & whip them & the operations in the future are to be in a diferent direction & manner than heretofore. The way the army is laying now along the James river they can be fed & supplied cheaper than before & we are under the protection of our gun boats. I remain as ever

Your undutiful Son   *Edward*

1st Minnesota Camped near Harrisons Landing
on James River July 10th, A.D. 1862

Dear Father & Mother

Your kind letter of the 29th June came to hand by this days mail. I am very glad to hear from you & also to rec. Dear brother's mineature, which came through safe. It looks quite natural although it is badly shaded. I think he looks considerable as he used to & it does not seem possible that he is gone & I cannot see him again as I used to when we were at home.

We being some distance from the outposts everything is very quiet. The weather is very hot and every one is seeking some shady retreat. At present there are but few of us that can stand the skorching rays of the sun any length of time & there are a large number under the Doctors care.

Pres. Lincoln visits McClellan at Harrison's Landing,
July 9, 1862. Brady Photo

There is but one of Co. G. confined to his bed & his fever is broken & he will be up again soon.[46]

---

[46] During the weeks spent at Harrison's Landing, sickness took a tremendous toll on the army. Over 6,000 were evacuated on transports and sent north to hospitals and another 12,000 were sickened with malaria and other fevers. The Minnesota First was exceptional for the few men that were stricken.

President A. Lincoln visited the camps on the 8th inst. He was saluted in the usual manner & as he passed the lines he waved his hat & seemed well pleased.

I wish I was there in Minnesota to get some of those nice strawberries. I had one little taste of them in May. Fruits of all kinds sell very high here. Oranges & Lemmons cost $1.00 per Doz. Corn, peaches, berries &c. sell for from 75 cts. to $1.50 apiece. Apples are all gone. When we first came down here I found a Mulberry tree that was full & I got what I wanted to eat once. There are so many camps here now that forageing does not pay, in fact what little there was has been used up. The timber here consists of oaks, pine, cedar, gums, beech, sycamore, holly, hickory, black walnut & now & then a chesnut & some two or three kinds that I cannot name. Fish are very plenty in their season judgeing from the nets &c. used in taking them. I saw several fine black bass & suckers caught in the creek that runs by our camp. There is a grist & saw mill on the creek just above tide water. The mills are run occasionaly by the soldiers but the water is geting very low for the want of rain which has not fallen since the 3d. of July. Colonel Sully is in command of the brigade. I believe the whole brigade think just as much of him as they can of any officer. He is universaly liked by all who know him in the army. It is now nearly sundown & cool. We have had a fine shower & the air feels better, still it will not compare with Minnesota atmosphere. There are but few men in the regt. that would be willing to live in this country if they could possibly get west. But there are many in the army that know nothing of the wild west of the Miss. river & some think that Michigan is the farthest point west that has a white population. You may not think it possible but it is true that we have been asked what regt. we were by men in some of the N.Y. regts. & when they were told that we were the 1 st Minnesota they have asked what part of York state that was. There are a great many people in the states that have but a very limited idea of our beloved little state Minnesota

Friday morning July 11th.

It is cool & comfortable & looks considerable like rain. We all feel better for the air is not so hot & oppresive as it has been for the past 6 or 7 days. Jonathan Goodrich & Caleb Jackson are unfit for duty but they are arround & will likely be well again in a few days. To tell the truth there are but very few of us that feel perfectly well & when you know what we have had to do since the 1st of June I don't think you will wonder at it. When we were at Fair Oaks there was from one half to two thirds of the companies out at work on the fortifications falling timber or unloading trains of cars & we were allways routed out at three o'clock in the morning & most every night there was some disturbance among the pickets which were within gun shot of our camp & we got but very little rest for several nights in succesion. On Friday the 27 of June we were under fire most of the time from the rebel batteries but they did but little damage. That night we were not permitted to lay in our tents but had to lay on the ground close to our works with our muskets by our sides & accouterments on ready for a fight at any moment. Sat. I was out with a working party & we got beyond our lines & right in range of a rebel battery not more than 80 rods distant in an open field. They opened upon us with shell but strange to say they did not hurt one of us although we had to march about 100 rods in plain view. There was several shell passed through the ranks & the pieces from those that burst to our right flew thick as hail. As soon as Genl Sedgwick found what had been done he called us back to camp & dismissed us. We were ordered to be ready to march that P.M. all but strikeing our tents which were kept up to keep up appearances. Sunday morning we were all ready to move haveing completed our arangements at night & by light we began to move. We went down as far as the R. Road where we halted & made preparations

231

to resist any attac that the enemy might make. We were scarcely ready before skirmishing commenced & the fireing soon became heavy but the enemy were finaly beaten & we then availed ourselves of the opportunity to retreat, which we all knew was what we were about to do. We fell back to Savage Station where we had another fight of which you have likely heard the particulars. From the station we fell back across White Oak Swamp & we had scarcely laid down to sleep before it was sunrise & we had to start again & another tedious days march was performed & no rest that night. Tuesday July 1st we were on the move again. The enemy tried hard to get some advantage but they were met by our forces on all sides, the 2nd was about the same & in the P.M. of the 3rd the whole division camped in a corn field at Harrison's Landing. The rain had been pouring in torents all the P.M. & as we had mostly lost our tents & many of us our blankets & everything else except our guns & accoutrements we were not very pleasantly situated but as it was the first night since the 27th of June that we had a chance to sleep it was improved in the best way that circumstances would permit. On the morning of the 4th it was clear & hot & we marched up here where we are now camped.   We will remain here for some time, I expect as soon as the boys have got rested I think they will be ready for another jaunt in Ole Virginia.   I think the prospect is good for great & important victories over the traitors. My paper is full & I must close. Captain Messick is well & ready as usual.
My love to Ellford, Ella & Anna & all the rest.

As ever your son

Edward H. Bassett

Co. G. 1st Minnesota

Chaplain has resigned & gone home. We will not miss him.

Dear Parents:

I have just received your kind letter of the 11th inst. & as I have a good chance I will try to answer it & have another one on the road to you. I am glad to hear that you are enjoying good health and I hope you may continue to enjoy it as long as life lasts. The weather is quite cool & comfortable this morning. We have our tents raised from the ground & a pole floor under them that looks considerable like the floor of a Minnesota corn crib but by picking boughs & spreading upon them we have a bed quite comfortable & being about 20 inches from the ground if is considerable cleaner & cooler than it would otherwise be. The first appearance of our camp to one unused to the camp of the soldier would think that the ground was wet & we were forced to raise our heads to keep dry. There are bushes cut & stuck up arround nearly every tent & it looks considerable like a low swampy place. The rays of the sun is so direct & hot that it is almost impossible to withstand it for any length of time in the middle of the day but as we are encamped in a small field surrounded on all sides by woods we miss a great many breezes that would otherwise visit us. I see by the extracts taken from the Richmond papers that the rebels are not at all pleased with the way that Little Mac has placed his command & his new line of defense. They have been beaten in all their games trying to trap the Yankees & we are now out of their way in a safe & healthy position where supplies & reinforcements can be easily got & we can take our time for future operations. They challenge Genl McClellan's operations in moveing his army so sudenly & with such success, admireing his generalship & they acknowledg their critical position at this moment. It is the opinion of many of us that there will not be any important moves made now before September but we don't know to be sure. We may be called out any day & when we do start there is no telling where we will stop. I never thought we would be away down here on James River but we are here & have got to do the best we can where we are. We all have great confidence in Genl McClellan. Active operations may commence immediately. Certainly no opportunity will be allowed to pass that will insure success.

You say that Mr. Carter has purchased the south half (or 80 acres) of Mont. Pool's farm & is going to move on it to live. Now I would like to know where he is going to build his house & where will he find any land that he can cultivate. He must be crazy I should think, but the duck & turtle business may pay to say nothing of the frogs & snakes. My opinion is that Betsy will find rather hard times there if they live there long. I don't think it compares well with the 80 that lays north of Bucks west 80. What do you think? [47]

We have not rec. our pay yet & there is over 4 months due now. I hope we have got to wait but a short time for the boys have nearly all run short. We have drawn new clothing since we came here & are very well off now. Most of the boys lost their knapsacks in the retreat. They were ordered by the Genl just before going to an engagement to throw them off & when they came back other regts that had lost theirs had picked them up but I suppose it will not be long before we will be fully equiped again. Jonathan Goodrich had his gun spoiled by a shot hiting it while in his hand. The stock was shattered & the barrel bent so as to ruin it. He soon found another gun & has it yet. The ball struck another soldier that was standing behind him but as the force had been checked & the ball completely flattened it did no harm. They picked it up & have it now.

Health is gradualy improving in the regt. Yesterday I attended divine services at 4 P.M. We had the chaplain

---

[47] Perhaps some newly wed youngster of Edward's acquaintance has purchased a parcel of swampy land that has little to offer for farming, and he suggests some alternative uses.

of the N.Y. 34 to preach. He was liked very well. It was the first time that I have heard a sermon for a long time. Our former chaplain never spoke to anyone except the officers & although we think he may be a good man he never was thought much of by the soldiers. I don't think he has preached once since we came down here. He spoke a short time on fast day & that is the last that I remember of his performances.

Captain Messick is quite well. Cal Jackson, B. Soule, Wm. Ramsey, C.C.Parker, Wm. Coen, Sam'l Lilly, Johathan Goodrich, A.Johnson & all the rest (if any) that you are acquainted with are about as usual. I don't feel quite as tough as I did last summer but I guess I will stand it well enough. There is but one from Co. G. in the Hospital. He is one of the recruits that joined us at Yorktown.

George's likeness looks more & more natural every time I look at it. If you have not sent another before you receive this you need not for I don't think we will be out more than until spring & if I had a good picture it would get spoiled.

How does the pie plant do this summer? Don't you think that it could be made to pay to raise it & market it at St. Paul early in the season? Are the mellons & vines doing well this summer. I would like to be there to help eat some of them this summer.(Out again). Excuse mistakes &c. Remember you all have my best wishes & I hope to see you all ere long.

As ever   Yours with respect

Edward H. Bassett.

I don't know about your showing my letters to the D.D's & exposeing my ignorance & they might not have any better opinion of me. Besides I have never once thought of any one criticiseing my writing. I don't take any pains & they are miserably spelled in most cases.

E.H.B.

Encamped at HarrisonsLanding Virginia
July 16th, 1862.

Dear brother Elford,

It is because I want to remind you that I have not forgotten you that I now write you a few lines. I am in the enjoyment of usual health and if I was in Minnesota I don't think it would be long before I would feel considerably as I used to. You know very well what kind of a time we would have if we could only meet at home. I think of you very often & wonder how you look, as you must have grown to quite a boy since I last saw you.

One year ago this morning the 1st Minnesota left Camp Minnesota at Alexandria & started on the road for Fairfax & from there we went to Centreville on Sunday July 21st 1861 the army of the Union started for Mannassas. Then I did not expect that the war would last as long as it has but it has not ended yet. I suppose that your colt must be growing very fast & I would like to see it very much.

Now you must remember me & every time that the folks write you must send a word for I like to hear from you at any time.

Please excuse me this time for I am geting tired & it is geting very hot.

Remember Father & Mother for me.

While I remain as ever your brother for the Union

E. H. Bissett

Co. G. 1st Minnesota

Encamped at Harrison's Landing
Virginia July 16th, 1862.

Dear Sisters:

I think I am indebted to each of you for a letter and I thought as it is cool this morning and I have no duties to perform this A.M. I would try to pay you. Now I would much rather be where I could see you face to face and then I could tell you a great many things that I cannot write.

Yesterday was about as hot a day as I ever remember of seeing although we have good shades to lay under & there was quite a breeze. We would sweat when laying perfectly still in the shade. It is said that this is the hotest part of Virginia and I don't know but it is being in the valley of the James River. We are deprived of the benefit of the sea breezes which in this country are so desireable during the summer months and which are enjoyed by those liveing on the higher lands in the eastern part of the state. To tell the truth Va. is better addapted to the raising of Negros & all the institutions of slavery than to the wants of the more industrious and enterprising people of the northern states. It was once a very rich and well cultivated state as you would judge from the looks of many of the old fields that are now grown up with forest trees & I have seen several fine looking apple & peach trees where once had been an orchard but now the only traces of civilization that you will see are the ridges where the corn last grew. But as you are studying Geography & history you are undoubtedly more familiar with the early history & settlement of the state than I am for I have no books & what little I ever did learn when I had & was going to school I have nearly forgotten. I think if you will take that history that I left at home you will find a very good description of Va. as well as many other very interesting & useful things. How I would like to be there & study with you. I never before felt the need of an education until since I have been in the army, not that it would be of any very great use to me while I am in the army but if I should ever be so lucky as to be free once more as I expect to before many months I think it would be worth more than money to me. If I was young as you are now & could only have a good chance to study and improve I think I would do better than I have.

As it is so hot there is not much going on although there was some 22 men from each company went out yesterday morning to work on the works in front. I think they are nearly finished & things appear as if we were going to remain here some time. I heard this morning that we were going to get soft bread in the place of the hard crackers which we have been liveing on ever since the 25th of February. It will be a great treat to us although it will not be much like the bread that you have at home as it will be heavy & in many instances sour judging from the kind we got last summer. It may be better, I hope it will. Such bread as you have would sell for 15 & 20 cts. per slice here & we would be glad to get it at that rate. We have to pay one cent a piece for common soda crackers & small ones at that. Cheese is 40 cts. per lb. butter 20, eggs 50cts. per doz. & other things in proportion. I don't know as these things will interest you & I will try to think of something else. As I said before I wish I could see you face to face for I would like to tell you a great many things that I cannot now. Everything must look beautiful at home now. The little trees must make quite a shade this summer and your flowers last though not least must be beautiful. Those moss roses which make such a complete carpet on the surface of the earth & innumerable other little things that serve to make home cheerful and pleasant although we don't notice them so much when surrounded by them & see them every day we get so used to them that we do not as much as think that we would miss them. But I find that many little things that I scarcely noticed when at home often come to my mind & I can see where I have often felt lonely when surrounded with enough to make me happy if I only knew how to enjoy it. I think that if I were in Minnesota situated as I was once I could enjoy myself much better than I used to. I wish I could draw. I would like to sketch our camp and send it to you but you know as well as I do that I am no artist & there is not much danger of my ever becoming one.

There is an account in the paper of a fight in Murfreesborro, Tenn. in which the 3d. Minnesota was engaged & they have nobly acquited themselves but as the enemy were in superior force they were forced to fall back when they shelled the town and at last accounts they were still fighting. I hope they will be successful. There was a report that the Minnesota 2nd , 3rd, & 4th were comeing here but it was a false report I think.

Please give my respects to all the folks & I hope to see you all before long.

So Good by.   As ever your brother

E. H. Bassett

Co. G. 1st Minnesota

Ella & Anna Bassett.

I sent Elford some apple seeds and I wish I could give him some of the apples. The Suttler brought up a few barrel from Alexandria. They sell for 5cts. here in the army. Good woolen shirts are $10.00 per pair. He has no boots yet but I expect they will be from 8 to 15 dollars per pair.

Edward

On July 22, 1862, General McClellan reviewed the troops of the 2nd Corps, and singled out the First Minnesota and the Nineteenth Massachusetts as being the best regiments in the army.

Matthew Marvin exhibited his boastful pride in his unit when he wrote:

"They was several hed (heard) McClellan say to

Sumner that Sully had the best regt. in Army. We do put on Stile & no mistake. You can see your face in the Leather after blacking. The Brass shine like Silver & the guns are brite as ever. No matter how lazy the man he must be clean or go to the guard house. Why is it . . . that when we have camped rite along side of another Regt when they would die like sheep & in our Regt their would be but 2 or 3 in the hospital & as many more in each company would go to sick call & get Pills or powder & go on duty. I believe We have not had more than 5 die from and desese in the regt since we have been in the service (most 18 months). Some regt have lost hundreds by desease aloan."

Encamped at Harrison's LandingVirginia
Sunday July 27th, 1862

Dear Parents,

I was delighted this morning when the mail came in to find that it brought me two letters from my dear home in Minnesota. I was eating my breakfast of baked beans & pork & a sprinkling of hard bread and coffee when one of the boys came in and handed me two letters. I saw at a glance that they were from home & in another minute I was I thought conversing with the folks at home. I soon found out my mistake but I can assure you that they were the most welcome visitors that could have at the moment appeared in this land of secessionists & traitors.

This is a beautiful morning very clear and will most likely be a very hot day. There was a nice rain fell last night and the air seems considerable clearer. This is the cleanest camp that we have ever had in Va. No matter how much rain falls we have no mud here. The soil is sandy and water is got by diging 5 or 6 feet. I am well and feel first rate and am gaining every day. The boys are all as well as usual & we are all enjoying ourselves well generally. We are all anxious about the movements in contemplation by those in command. We have all the news from every quarter in one day after it is received in New York City. What will be done next is more than any of us can tell but one thing is certain, there is going to be more men called into the field than there has ever been before and I hope that there will be a settlement of all the dificulties before spring. Genl Pope seems to be playing some good tricks on the rebels and all are expecting great things from a man so active and successful. The recent changes in the commands of the army are looked upon with fondest hopes of success. We have the encampments in the best of order now & things are going on in military order. There is a brigade guard mount in front of our camp every morning and everything is going on as well as could be expected.

How I would like to be at home & spend the day with you. Everything here is so monotinous & dull when we think it all over every day brings the same duties & there is so little change when we are in camp that we can scarcely tell what to do to amuse ourselves. All books & papers are read through in short notice and as we cannot carry many books arround with us we are idle much of the time. Our rations are very good now. We got some flour last week & yesterday I made some biscuit which we had for dinner. It was the first soft bread that I have tasted since we left Camp Stone. Now you may think that they must be great biscuit that I would make & you perhaps would like to know how I can make good light biscuit and how I baked them. Well I will tell you after assureing you that they were a tip top article and I am proud to say they were the first that I ever made. I took about one pound & one half of flour & two spoonsfull of salt 3 of yeast powders & 3 of fat & mixed with cold water. Put it on my plate & it was ready to bake which is easily done simply take a common pan, one of your milk pans would do. Put some coals on the ground, set the bread on them, turn the pan over it & cover with fire & hot ashes & in 30 minutes you can take out just as nice bread as I would wish to eat. The oven is one of John Goodrich's inventions. It works to a charm and he makes the best bread. [48]

I am glad to hear that your crops look so fine and I wish I could help you to harvest them. How is it about help this summer. How are the wages. Is there to be a great scarcity of help to do the work. How have the men that you rented part of your land to got along. Are they doing the fair thing. About how much grain will you have, provided it is all saved and does as well as it looks. And what do you think about farming; can you make it pay if I should get back in the course of the next year and one half if we should be in luck. What seems to be the natural tendency now of the farming community, is it to raise grain exclusively or are they going into the stock business more. How have the sheep done this summer. Are you useing your pasture as it was when I came away. How does the grass in the meadow look this summer. What changes have been made in the roads. What have you done with the old oxen. Have you got them yet or have you sold them. How are the steers geting along. I understand that you sold the younger ones. What were your taxes last year.

I hope some day to return to Minnesota and I feel interested in every little improvement. I want to know what is going on what improvements have been made and are being made and how things are prospering in general. Now I want to ask you what 80 acres of good improved prairie land is worth. What can a few head of sheep be bought for this next fall and how do you think it would pay to buy a few to start with. Have you timber enough or rather lumber to build a house. When the war will end is a question that nearly every one has asked now. There are none that can answer that is the poorer for all. I have no hopes now of a very speedy settlement although there may be something

---

[48] Edward's inventive and resourceful nature is demonstrated as is his sense of humor. His mother must have gotten a good laugh from his mock bravado in relating his culinary expertise.

turn up that will cause a more speedy settlement than any of us have ever thought of. I am sure that I have no objections. If it prolonged for any great length of time it is going to come very hard on the new states. I heard that they have called for the seventh regiment of infantry from Minnesota but I hope they will not be needed there are some few that I would like to hear of being drafted into the service.

As ever Your Unworthy son

Edward

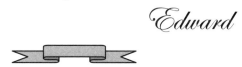

In the above letter, Edward refers to General Pope who had been recalled from the west by President Lincoln and placed in command of the newly formed Army of Virginia. Historians have debated long the series of events that unfolded here. Following the Battle of Malvern Hill, General McClellan had told Lincoln:

"I need 50,000 more men, and with them I will retrieve our fortunes". Lincoln, who was desperate for a decisive victory, responded: " Maintain your ground if you can, but save the army at all events, even if you fall back to Fort Monroe."

The President had for some time been reading about military tactics. Though he was aware that his crash course by no means made him an expert, he none-the-less began making military decisions and ordering their implementation. Realizing that calling for more troops could start a public uproar, he sent Seward to confer with16 governors explaining that additional troops were needed to "follow up recent successes of the Federal arms". The governors then signed a document requesting Lincoln to put out a call for 300,000 more volunteers. Of Course, he immediately complied with their wishes. By pulling together existing units he formed the Army of Virginia with 56,000 men and assigned them to General Pope. General Halleck and Secretary of War Stanton were by no means fans of McClellan. They, with Lincoln, had devised a strategy to launch a second movement on the Rebel Capital from the north. The plan was for McClellan to move toward Richmond from the peninsula in the south. Pope's new army would move from the north and, the two armies would crush the enemy and take the capital. With no unified central command of all Union forces, these bits of intrigue were frequent and rarely beneficial to the war effort. With the only available trained forces now assigned to Pope, there were none to send McClellan. Halleck was assigned to be General in Chief and soon conducted a review of McClellan's situation at Harrison's Landing and reported back to Washington that McClellan had not done anything and was not intent on doing anything in front of Richmond.

Encamped at Harrison's Landing, Va.
July 30th, A.D. 1862.

Dear Parents:

Your kind letter of the 20th inst. was received on the 28th or in just 7 days after it was mailed in Morristown. We have just received orders to be ready to march at short notice with three days rations & a full compliment of cartridges but where we will go we can only guess. Some say we are going back by the way of Washington arround up into the valley of the Shenandoah River. Some think we will not move at all (I share the latter opinion). There is most likely something going on somewhere & we are held ready in case that we should be needed. I hope there will he something done soon and we are all ready to go wherever we are wanted.

I rather guess that General Pope has been playing thunder with the rebs & there has got to be something done that will hurt the secessionists & their sacred cause. I hope there will for I think we have waited about long enough. It is very hot this afternoon and we will have some hard times most likely if we get to moveing arround this summer.

The boys are all in tolerable health and feel first rate. Captain Messick is quite well. I am glad to hear that things are going on so finely in Morristown. I am also much obliged to you for the general news & the details of your last. They all interested me a great deal. The letter written by Anna I will endeavor to answer as soon as convenient. I am very thankful for such a nice letter & I hope she will write just as many such as she can. Any word from home is very thankfully received. If there is anything that I want it is to see this war brought to an end & return to my friends.

The duties of the day commence with geting up & attending roll call a little before sunrise, after which we have an hours drill then breakfast, sweep up the streets and policeing (cleaning up)the camp generaly. The guard mount at 9 A.M. then next comes three hours for our own amusement which is used in writing letters, reading &c. then dinner at 12 N (Noon) and we usualy have all the P.M. to ourselves haveing dress parade just before sundown and roll call, then comes supper and roll call again at nine o'clock, after which we retire and everything is quiet until morning when we commence again and go through about the routine of duties. Speaking plainly and understandingly we are haveing very easy times.

It is rather dull but we have had our share of the rough since we came down here and we know what it is just as well as the best of them and if we start on a tramp now you may bet we know how to get along.

Tell Elford that I remember him. My love to you all.

As ever your unworthy Edward

Encamped Harrison's Landing Virginia
August 3d. A.D. 1862

Dear Father & Mother:

I am very glad to hear that you are well & geting along so well on the farm. I only wish that the war would end and I could be there to help you.

In my last I wrote you that we were under marching orders but it turned out about as I thought it would. The rebels came down one night and shelled our transports that were laying in the river at the landing but they were driven back by the gun boats which had anticipated their comeing & were prepared for them. The fireing commenced about midnight & lasted some time but they were finaly silenced and the next day in the P.M. there was a detachment sent across the James & burned all the buildings &c. that were near the river in which the grey Coats had been in the habit of occupying & watching our movements. The damage done the transports was trifling I believe although they were very close.

Last night about 9 o'clock we got orders to be ready to march in light marching order with two days cooked rations & 60 rounds of cartridges by 2 o'clock this morning. Well this came rather suden but we have heard such orders before & we were soon ready & laid down to get some rest for there was no time to be wasted & if we should get on the road once there is no telling when we would have another chance to rest. Well two o'clock soon came & we turned out after eating a good hearty meal of baked beans. We were just in ranks when the order was countermanded and we were told to go to bed if we chose. This was good enough for us, although we would like to have gone out into the country & had a little fun but we don't fancy the idea of getting up at midnight & then not starting until after sunrise the way we have done several times. What the intentions were or why they were given up is only guess work with us but the general impression is that we were intended to support a

246

reconoisance towards Malvern Hill which had gone out during the PM. This morning found us in camp as usual with the exception of a little sleep which we had lost, feeling just the same as if nothing had happened. We have an inspection of arms and accoutrements by Captain Messick and the duties of the day were attended to as usual & I thought I would improve the PM by writing a letter.

I am rather inclined to believe that the 3d. Minnesota if parolled will not be apt to return to Minnesota but they will most likely be exchanged & enter the field again where I hope they may be more successful.[49] It has certainly been a bad piece of business for them but I suppose they done the best they could. I see by the papers that the states are paying large bounties for Volunteers to fill up the old regiments. Now this may do but I think that if there was some fixed policy for conducting the war & instead of being so easy with the traitors we were to mete out justice alike to the rich & poor, high & low & make them to feel the effects of the war and take all of their property to pay the expense of the war & fight them in earnest, injureing them in every possible manner, destroying both property & lives with the greatest posible speed, there would be plenty of men to fill the ranks of the old regiments that would volunteer without a bounty. As it is the sooner we resort to drafting and a thorough & active war-fare the sooner we will have peace & tranquility restored to the people. At present everything is quiet here. There has been some fireing heard on the river but I guess there has not been any serious damage done. The health of the army is improveing all the time. I think that if we stay here through this month that we will be all right for any move that may be made. The weather is quite warm. Captain Messick is well.

---

[49] The 3rd Minnesota Regiment had been disgracefully surrendered by its officers without firing a shot in Tennessee and would soon be "paroled" meaning released or traded for rebel prisoners.

Cal Jackson is very anxious to hear from his folks but I guess he will get a letter before long. He is well & tough as ever.

Edward

Co. G 1st Minn

My respects to Elford.   You too.

A telegram to Gen. McClellan on August 3rd from Gen. Halleck brought new orders. *"It is determined to withdraw your army from the Peninsula to Acquia Creek. You will take immediate measures to effect this, covering the movement the best you can."* McClellan, like Grant and Sherman, was not enamored with Halleck. These new orders certainly rankled McClellan and though he knew they must be obeyed, he would take his time in doing so.

☀ SECOND BATTLE OF MALVERN HILL

On August 5, 1862, McClellan ordered a reconnaissance in force to determine whether the rebels were still present in Richmond in strength, or if they had moved out to meet General Cadimus Pope in the north. The two armies met once again on the same battlefield. The engagement proved to be primarily an engagement of artillery, though several sharp skirmishes by the infantry also occurred. In his "Narrative of the First Minnesota Regiment", William Lochren describes the action:

"On August 4th our division and some other infantry, with cavalry and artillery, moved by a circuitous route to the rear of Malvern Hill, and bivouacked on that part of the battlefield where the severest fighting between Porter's and Magruder's forces had taken place. The pits

where the dead had been buried in cords had sunk and bones were protruding. We now hoped that this movement was the beginning of a new advance along the James upon Richmond."

Mathew Marvin also described the gruesome scene in a letter to his brother:

"The Old Battle ground looked natural as life but the rebells buried our dead miserably. their wer in several graves Arms & Legs & eavon heads above ground."

As usual the men grew restless from the dull existence of camp life and any diversion was welcome. Ed Bassett noted the event in his diary:

"Aug. 5th. We started at 6 PM with two days rations, and marched all night. On the 6th we lay in front of the Malvern House and slept there all night. There was some fighting there the next morning, but the Rebs fled, leaving their camps and everything. Four companies of the Minnesota 1st went forward as skirmishers and pickets. Considerable fireing, but no one hurt on our side. We moved back to our camp at Harrison's Landing."

The day after their skirmish with the enemy the hazards of camp life became very personal for Mathew Marvin. While sitting in his tent after a rest he was wounded, as he says:

". . when a Minie ball of 57 cal (caliber) struck my thigh near the groin came out on the inside coming very close to the Ardery but without injury to it or the bone. It was done by some careless scallawag in the 5th N H regt whose camp is about 800 yards from here. . . the ball passed through 4 tents in our Regt."

He would spend the next month in the hospital nursing his wound.

Harrison Landing Va.
August 9th, 1862.

Dear Father & Mother,

The weather is very hot. We were out on the recent reconoisance to Malvern hill and White Oak swamp. We were gone 3 nights and two days and a good time. I will give you some of the particulars and tell you what I saw some time when I have time and feel like it.

Yours of the 28th was received on the 7th of August. Brother's likeness came through safe. It looks very natural and I think everything of it. Oh how I wish I could see him once more.

The boys are as well as usual. Three are to be sent north soon. Captain is well as well as the rest that you are acquainted with. Sergt. C.E. Davison is one going north, being sick.

Those that were taken prisoners from our Regt. on the retreat have been exchanged and have joined their regiments. They give a doleful account of affairs in Dixie. I am as well as usual and I hope you are all the same.

As ever   *Edward Co. G.*
                1st Minnesota Volunteers.

Harrison's Landing Virginia
August 13th, 1862.

Dear Parents,

We are under orders to march and have been since 2 PM on the 11th but as yet we are in our old camp liable to start at any hour and I shall not be very particular in writing. We are not aware as to where our destination is but the general opinion is that we are going to leave the peninsula to the rebels. We heard last night that there has been a severe fight between Genls. Pope, McDowel, Geary & Banks and that the two armies were occupying their old ground skirmishing & re-inforceing as fast as possible. There has not been anything of importance done here except we mention the shelling of our transports &c. in the James river yesterday but the gun boats drove them back, shelled the woods for some 10 or 12 miles, burnt City Point when they quit, I suppose because there was nothing else to destroy that was worth the while. The general impression is that we will march to some convenient & safe place and take the transports for the upper Rhappahanoc. The weather here is what would make good harvest weather in Minnesota hot and dry but we have not got the pure bracing air of Minnesota and I long to get back there where I can breath and feel free once more.

The boys are all well as usual. Captain was around this morning and wanted to know if I got a letter from home & inquired about you. We packed our knapsacks and sent them forward & most of my writing material is in mine so you see that I may not be able to write as often until I get it.

You speak of your nice vegetables, green corn &c. there. I am very glad if you are haveing a good supply but, you would tremble for them if I should get at them, for I am perfectly disgusted with anything else and the way I would lay into them would be a caution if I was there. We have been geting a tolerable good supply of such things lately but they are not fresh and nice like those that you have. I believe my last letter was a short poorly written thing but I did not feel very well and would not have written if I had not been waiting for several days to get a chance. I thought I would scribble a few lines at a venture.

As ever   Edward

Co. G. Minnesota 1st.

Sundown and we are in camp with prospects about the same. How I wish I could be at home this evening but the 3 years will soon be up at the rate time is passing now.

Edward H. Bassett.

This letter was written some time ago & was not mailed by some oversight.

Please excuse.   *E. H. B.*

CHAPTER 15
WITHDRAWAL FROM THE PENINSULA

Events during July had put Robert E. Lee in a difficult situation. Union General Pope, with his new army, left Washington crossed the Rappahannock River and moved into the area of Manassas. He was now becoming a real threat to the confederate supply line between the Shenandoah Valley and Richmond. Lee was informed on July 12th, that Pope and his new Army of Virginia had taken Culpeper, situated on the Orange and Alexandria Railroad. That railroad connected at Gordonsville, only thirty miles to the south, to the Virginia Central Line. The Virginia Central Railroad led westward to Charlottesville. If Pope gained control of this crucial link he would deny Lee the wealth of desperately needed crops of wheat and corn now ripening in the fertile Shenandoah. Lee did what he was so adept at doing, he split his forces. Keeping 70,000 on the peninsula, to prevent McClellan from making another attempt on Richmond, he sent Stonewall Jackson with two divisions to stop Pope. It took eighteen trains of fifteen cars each to move Jackson's 10,000 troops and his artillery from Hanover Junction to Louisa Courthouse, about fifteen miles below Gordonsville. His cavalry and wagon train moved by road.

General Lee despised Pope and wanted not only to stop him, but to destroy him! His contempt was the result of a series of bombastic orders Pope had issued upon taking command of his new troops. The orders instructed his army to live off the country. To take whatever they needed, without compensation, from anyone that could not prove their Union loyalty. Anyone behind the lines that would not take an oath of loyalty was to be expelled and if caught returning was to be treated as a spy. Talking or writing to the enemy was to be likewise treated as spying, and subject to the death penalty. All these orders flew in the face of Lee's code of honor and his sense of gentlemanly conduct. Non-combatants should be treated with respect. In Lee's own words:

"The miscreant Pope ought to be suppressed if possible."

Jackson informed Lee on July 19th, that he had beaten Pope to Gordonsville. Pope was still at Culpeper but with too large a force to be attacked without reinforcements. Weakening the defenses around Richmond would be taking a big chance, but Lee decided the prize was worth the risk. He ordered 20,000 of his troops to move immediately to assist Jackson. If Richmond was attacked, Jackson was to break off any engagement he was in and return with haste. Lee's hope was to defeat Pope's army while preventing McClellan from moving on Richmond, then to re-unite his forces to protect the capital and, should McClellan withdraw, to attack him as well. Lee was much relieved when on August 16th he discovered McClellan had abandoned his fortified positions and was withdrawing toward Williamsburg.

McClellan's army was to move back to Washington to quickly support Pope who was now becoming hotly engaged by the enemy. On August 20th, the Army of the Potomac, in spite of McClellan's exuberant protest to the orders, began its withdrawal across the peninsula and onto the road to Williamsburg. The movement continued to Yorktown then to Newport News, boarded transports and sailed past Fortress Monroe, headed for Alexandria. Bassett's company, Company G, actually left on August 15th as guard to the Brigade wagon trains. The remainder of The First Minnesota, in Sumner's Second Corp, began on the 20th, once again taking the position of rear guard.

Edward Bassett's diary records:

"Started in the PM and marched all night. We continued the next day, crossing the Chickahominy River on a pontoon bridge, and camped near River. Started for Williamsburg at sunrise, and continued to move. On the 19th we passed thru Hampton and camped near the wagon train. I went down and bathed in the sea. The Regt. moved to Newport News on the 22nd. They marched in the rain. Here on Aug. 25th I was on detail to load our things on the boat. The Regt. boarded about noon." (The boat was the steamer Mississippi)

The spectacle of McClellan's army on the march across and down the peninsula must have been something to behold. In many long stretches there was only a single road. The column was escorted by an advance guard followed by a wagon train 26 miles in length. Coming next were the miles of ambulances, miles of artillery and the endless column of soldiers. In all, this grand parade of the magnificent army stretched out for over 80 miles. The movement was accomplished in exemplary form and as rapidly as an exercise of such magnitude could be accomplished. If any wagon or other vehicle broke down it was to be moved aside so as not to impede the movement of the rest and left with an escort to attend to it. All the thousands of horses were well fed and watered before starting each day, as no stopping would be allowed once on the move. For those in the rear this was anything but a frolic in a parade. The tramping of hundreds of thousands of feet, hooves and wheels once again turned the dry dirt roads into powder and swirling clouds of dust. Throats burned and canteens soon emptied. Faces and all exposed flesh became caked with the grit. Dust saturated their wool uniforms and filled their shoes. All they could do was endure and plod on. Walking long distances was a common occurrence for men from the frontier of the time and 30 or more miles was considered "within walking distance". Marching in a military column was quite another matter. The accordion effect caused by interruptions miles ahead eventually caused long pauses while the men stood in line in the hot sun or pounding rain under the weight of their full loads. When they started to move again the order to 'Close-up the Ranks' would echo down the line and that meant nearly running to take up the slack. Five miles under such conditions was enough to fatigue even veteran soldiers. When the march continued day and night, as now, some of the weary men even went to sleep while marching. The caring hand of a compatriot clenching their sleeve kept them from wandering out of line or gently tugged them into consciousness when they began to stumble or lag behind. Food and water were often limited to the hardtack in their haversacks and what ever water they could find to fill their canteens. Sometimes getting a drink meant scooping your tin cup in the muddy water that filled a wagon track. When a halt was called it was often for a mere two or three hour break with barely time enough to make some coffee and catch a brief nap along the road. For the Rear Guard, as was often the case for the First Minnesota Regiment, the march was further complicated by the periodic skirmishes with the rebels that persistently dogged the rear of the column.

Encamped at NewPort News, Va.
August 23rd 1862.

Dear Parents,

Co. G. left the camp at Harrisons Landing on the 15th inst. We were detailed to go with the Brigade train as guards. We traveled all day & night and crossed the Chickahominy River on a pontoon about 5 PM on the 16th & camped until morning when we started for Williamsburg which we passed about noon & went on about 3 miles & camped near a Baptist church. The next morning we started for Yorktown which we passed about noon, after a march of 12 miles that PM we marched to Big Bethel and laid over until morn and the next day we went down to Hampton & camped between the town & Fortress Monroe & laid there until yesterday when we started on a tramp up here where it is expected we will take the transports for some new field of operations. We had a fine time on our way down making the Apples, Pears, Peaches, Plums, Mellons, green corn, Pigs, chickens, ducks, geese &c.&c. pay tribute to our apetites. On arriveing here yesterday and joining the regt. I rec. your very interesting letter of the 10th. I assure you that I was glad to get such a long letter from home just after comeing off a long hard march & I am sorry that I cannot write you a decent letter but I am doing the very best I can for I have no way of carrying paper only in my memoranda.

The boys are in good spirits. Where we are going we can only guess but we hope to be sent somewhere where we can do something to bring this war to an end. Our forces still hold Yorktown I believe but how long they will remains to be seen. The sick have all been sent to the general hospitals. We are camped right on the beach and when the tide is out the water for miles is full of soldiers out catching oysters which are quite plenty. I have not had any yet but think some of trying my luck this PM. The weather is quite comfortable but it has been very dry. I hope & trust that the war will end before next summer. Tell Ella that I thank her very much for her letter but it is impossible for me to answer it now.

Excuse for the present in haste as you know.

My regards to all.   *Edward.*

Captain is well.

Army of the Potomac landing at Yorktown
Sketch from Harper's Weekly, Sept. 7, 1862

After numerous battles and skirmishes, on August 30th, Pope's army fought the major battle of Second Bull Run, (Second Manassas). The battle was hard fought with heavy losses on both sides but at the end it was a complete rout of the Federal army. Pope was "outgeneraled" by Jackson and Longstreet and outflanked by the enemy. In short, he was badly beaten. His army began a helter-skelter retreat towards Washington in hopes of meeting with units of the Army of the Potomac and averting a further disaster.

Pope had misjudged his adversary. His army outnumbered that of Jackson, but it was spread out piecemeal over a wide area. That was all the opportunity Stonewall Jackson needed. Once reinforced, he attacked again and again with disastrous results. Further, the newly promoted General-In-Chief Halleck was in over his head as well. His indecision and inability had delayed two full corps. of troops in Washington, instead of immediately sending them to Pope's support.

CHAPTER 16
♦*BATTLES OF VIENNA AND FLINT HILL

As the units from the Army of the Potomac arrived in the Washington area, Halleck's shortcomings as General-In-Chief of the armies became apparent. Troops withdrawn from the peninsula to save Pope, were met with no preparations and no orders. Days passed with two full corps of the army being marched and countermarched to changing orders or resting in camp without orders. They should have been sent immediately to the front to relieve Pope and McDowell. The First Minnesota was a perfect example. The Regiment reached Alexandria, Virginia on the morning of August 28th. After landing onshore, their brigade was kept standing in the streets of Alexandria awaiting orders. They had no food or wagons, but were able to get hold of a couple of New York newspapers. Therein, they found an article about the Indian Outbreak on the frontiers of Minnesota. You can imagine the concern this news struck in the hearts of all these frontier lads for the welfare of their families. After several hours, the regiment marched to the edge of the city and, once again, stood waiting for orders and rations. The orders finally arrived and a march toward Farifax Court House began. About 3 miles down the road, a courier galloped up with orders for the column to halt and wait for supply wagons that were on their way. The hungry men cheered as the quartermaster with his wagons topped the crest of the hill at a full gallop and rolled down into the valley where they waited. Food was soon distributed. In no time, the valley was dotted with campfires and the aroma of fresh coffee and frying fat pork was everywhere. As the men devoured their suppers and dusk settled into the valley, a staff officer arrived with orders to wait in the valley for further orders.

While waiting here, bands of stragglers from Pope's army passed on their way to Washington, telling tales of terrific fighting and defeat. Since this was usually the tale told by stragglers, it was paid but little attention. This time it proved to be true. As darkess fell and no further orders arrived, the men stacked their arms and lay on the ground to rest. Aroused during the night, they were ordered to march back from whece they had come. They arrived in Alexandria at daylight on August 29th. They continued up the Potomac some eight miles to Long Bridge, where they again halted while a cadre of aides and officers scampered back and forth trying to decide where to send them. When a decision was finally reached, the First Minnesota Regiment moved out to relieve Pope's army near Manassas. The column resumed the march along the Virginia side of the Potomac, passing numerous small heavy artillery forts that were built as part of the Washington defenses. With each such passing, a good deal of banter ensued as the men from the forts came out to ask who they were and where they were going. When stopping for a brief rest at one of the forts, the men were greeted with wild cheers and an armada of men came out with kettles of hot coffee and loads of fresh soft bread. Every man received a loaf of bread and thankfully filled his cup and canteen with the hot brew. To men who had subsisted largely on hard crackers for months, this benevolent gesture would be long remembered. The march continued, halting after midnight a short way beyond the Chain Bridge–to rest.

The next day, August 30th, they continued through Alexandria to 6 miles east of Farifax Courthouse. The heat was nearly unbearable, but even worse was the thirst. Dust soon covered the men from head-to-foot and they took on the color of the dirt. Sunday morning, August 31st, reveille came early. Rain had started during the night and continued much of the day. As supply wagons had arrived while the men slept, the men drew two days' rations of hardtack and salt pork. Breakfasts were cooked over smoky fires of wet wood by the side of the now muddy road. Common fare on such a morning amounted to a culinary concoction called "skillygallee," prepared by frying crumbled hard crackers with salt pork. It was a favorite among the soldiers. A hot meal must have been greatly appreciated by the weary men that had marched 63 miles in a 64 hour time period. Captain John G. B. Adams of the Nineteenth Mass. Regiment, a sister unit to the First Minnesota, described the march:

"It was the hardest march we had made, twenty-four hours of the time it rained torrents. The shoes of the men were in bad condition; many marched bare-footed, and it was impossible for them to keep in the ranks. We did not have a hundred men in the ranks when we reached the line of battle."

The First Minnesota numbered about 300 after those men who were unfit for duty were sent back with the retreating army.

During this stop, many stragglers from Pope's army, that were too exhausted to keep up with the retreating column, passed by. A number of the regiment's absent, sick and wounded, who were left behind at Harrison's Landing, also rejoined the regiment. Captain Colvill, not fully recovered from his earlier wound, returned and the men were very happy to see him.

💣 FLINT HILL

September 1st found the regiment at Centerville. Everything was in mass confusion. Pope's army, in full retreat, clogged the muddy roads with troops, wagons, wounded, artillery and all the other materials of war. The First

Minnesota, with two Rhode Island artillery pieces, was deployed as extreme rear guard. As all the other forces moved off, they were left entirely on their own to protect the rear of the dispirited army on the move toward Vienna. The rebel cavalry was soon upon them and their gradual withdrawal was continually under artillery and musket fire. Near sunset the pickets were driven in by a growing rebel presence. A large body of rebel cavalry, ready to charge, formed a line of battle facing the Minnesota men. A full battery of reb artillery came into position and opened fire from close range, raking them with grape and canister shot.

The stalwart men stood their ground while Colonel Sully ordered the two Rohde Island guns to retreat and take up a position ½-mile down the road near Flint Hill. With this accomplished, he ordered the regiment to break ranks and "double-quick" to the guns. Here they took up positions on either side of the road in the woods. By this time, it was completely dark. The Minnesota men formed in a **V** with the artillery pieces centered at the point. William Lochren said:

> *"Silently we waited, but not long, for the rebel cavalry and artillery, finding the road clear, hurried on in pursuit, not discovering us until the advance was nearly at the muzzles of our guns. Sully's challenge, "Who comes there?" and the surprised response, "Who the devil are you?" and a pistol shot from the rebel leader directed at Sully, brought a volley of canister from the two pieces and musketry from the First Minnesota, which must have done fearful execution, judging from the cries, groans, curses and commands, as those who were able dashed madly to the rear, hastened by a second volley from the guns and regiment."*

Edward Bassett also describes this incident in his letter of September 2nd.

> *The rebels did not bother them again that night. Having fallen far behind the main column, the rear guard had to move fast to catch up before it was cut off and captured.*

☀ VIENNA

After loading their wounded on the gun carriages, they set off as quickly as possible. Marching on the starlit night required care, especially when the road passed through a wood. Just finding the way was difficult enough, but they also had to be watchful for the enemy. Nearing the little village of Vienna, they met an aide who was sent to determine their situation. The firing had been heard at the rear of the column and there was concern for their safety. Colonel Sully was informed that the 19th Massachusetts had turned around and was marching to their assistance. Sully reported that he and his regiment were alright and would not require assistance. The moon was now shining brightly and the column moved along at a faster pace. They were unaware that the Massachusetts regiment was only a couple-hundred yards to their front. Suddenly, from a hill off to the right, a flash like lightning followed by a streak across the sky, announced the coming of a shell that exploded in the woods to their front. Immediately, flashes of light and the sound of gunfire came from just around the curve in the road ahead. The shadows of men and horses appeared in the flashes and the instinctive reaction of trained soldiers took over. When charged by cavalry, they split to the sides and fired as the horsemen passed, and when fired on from ahead, they returned the fire with effect. This was done until the body of mounted men had swept past shooting and yelling. A storm of whistling 'minnies,' came ripping through the air from the men ahead on the road. It was then discovered that all involved were friendly troops. The cavalry unit was the 9th New York. This was one of those tragic episodes of war in the dark of night.

Losses to the First Minnesota regiment at Flint Hill and Vienna were four killed and five wounded, and one killed and seven wounded respectively.[50] The 19th Mass. and 9th New York lost several killed and about 20 wounded.

The following letters were actually Edward's writing

---

[50] Lochren, Minnesota in the Civil and Indian Wars, page 25.

endeavors while on the extended and exhausting march, without the benefit of his knapsack, which contained his writing materials. Still, he diligently continued to write even when he had no way to send out mail. These were finally mailed with the full letter that he wrote on September 4th.

His reference to General McDowell in this letter "as a traitor" reflects the general opinion of the troops after his defeat at Manassas. McDowell ordered his men to advance across an open area, bordered by thick woods on the left. The order was questioned by one of his officers who told him that the woods were full of rebel infantry and artillery and, they would be the target of a deadly enfilading fire if they advanced. The order stood even after a nearby soldier remarked, within earshot of the general, *"Don't the damned fool see that the Jonnies will flank us?"* The rebs turned loose a volley of fire that tore through the men with devastating effect, leaving the ground littered with wounded and dead. According to General McClellan, McDowell and his aides dared not even walk through the camp for fear of being shot. These veterans had come to believe they were intentionally betrayed and that the General was a southern sympathizer. That feeling quickly spread throughout the camp. The men commanded by General Pope so distrusted him, that if he appeared in camp, the men turned their backs to him and a grumble, not a cheer, met his ears.

In the final analysis, the Union defeat at Second Bull Run primarily resulted from a failure of officers to set aside their petty jealousies and rivalries. They failed to utilize their abilities and forces to serve the greater best interest of their country. The debate over who was to blame has raged for over a century and shall not be further treated here.

Once again, Lincoln placed McClellan in charge of the armies on September 2nd. He realized that McClellan was the only man available that could reorganize and unify the army at the time. The fragmented, exhausted and dispirited men would not follow Pope, McDowell or any other officer.

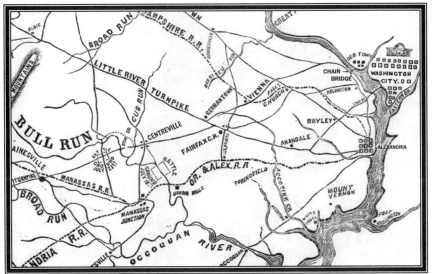

Segment of Map of area from Washington to Bull Run.
Frank Leslie's Illustrated.

I rec. an Advocate yesterday for
which I am much obliged
Staying at Centreville Va.
Sept. 1st, 1862

Dear Parents,

Thinking that you would like to hear from the army again I will try and write you a few lines although I don't know how soon I can mail it. My last was written while at New Port News where we embarked on board a steam ship for Aquilla Creek on the 25th inst. but we came up to Alexandria instead of stoping there. We camped near Alexandria on the PM of the 28th on the 29th about 4 o clock we started for Chain Bridge some 15 or 20 miles distant after marching all night resting only about 3 hours. We breakfasted near Chain Bridge on the morning of the 30th. About 2 PM we were ordered to Fairfax and we were again on the march and marching was the order until about N (noon) yesterday

265

when we found ourselves here at Centreville where we will remember of being some 13 months ago. Last night we got a very good nights rest the best since we left the peninsula. This morning we were out on reconaisance to our right but we saw no enemy. There is a very large army here now. Gen. Pope, (McDowell, a traitor), Banks and all the rest are here of the Va. Army officers also McClellan, Sumner, Sedgewick and the Potomac army officers so you see we have all the wise heads. There has been more fighting on the old battlefield at Bull Run but what the results of the whole battle are I don't know. There is something ahead and I only hope for the best. I am badly fatigued now but shall soon be all right again. The weather is cool and I feel as well as ever after a hard march. We hear horrible rumors about the Indians in Minnesota but I hope they will be settled. Captain Messick is sick at Washington. Well it is night and I will wait and finish this when there is a chance to send it.

Good night to all

Edward

September 2

On the night of the 23rd everything seemed quiet & we thought that by morning that there would be a bridge across the river made of Canal boats & other craft. We fixed up some brush to keep the wind from us & laid down to rest a little after sundown. We slept until about eleven when we were routed out of our nests by the officers & told to fall in which we done in a short time. The wind was blowing & it was quite cool. We did not know where we were going nor did we care. We were sure we could go where any white man could & we did not fear the blacks. Some said that we had got to go on picket on the outposts, some that we were going out to skirmish &c. I thought that we were going to relieve the picket before light but as it always is we could not find where we were going untill it was over with. We were marched upon a hill that overlooked the country for some distance where we scattered out single file. The three companies A. B. & G. extended about 1/2 mile. We had just got deployed when I heard the harnesses rattle arround the artilery & looking arround I saw one of the canon going down the hill & I knew well enough what was up then & my suspisions were confirmed that we were only trying to draw the enemy here to give a chance for an attac at some other point. Looking arround I saw that the army had nearly all crossed back over the river. We did not care for that. The Minnesota Reg. was the first accross the river & we were glad to have the chance to stay & be the last back & we were. We watched all the time with all the eyes we had but we could not see one Secesh to save ourselves we kept up appearances. The camp fires were kept up & we did not hear nor see anything. The last man crossed just before daylight & we returned to camp after paying another visit to the sacred soil of old Virginia. After all we did nothing more than to draw their forces from Mannassas & we are expecting to hear of some grand movement in the direction of Fairfax & Mannassas. We wait the next movement. There was not such luck in store for all our men as we had. The brigade that crossed 12 miles above here at what is called Conrad's Ferry were badly cut up & their General killed, Genl Baker. The Mass. 17th was cut up badly but on the whole I guess we have got the better of them. Time will tell.

As I told you in my last that we were about to make a move I thought that I would give you a kind of detailed account of what we done. General Gorman executed his movements in the best of style & it has inspired the men with confidence in his capacity to command. We are all so well pleased with our new Colonel. We are as well officered as any Regt. in the service I believe. Genl McClellan was up here & has got a telegraph communication with Washington. He has put it up within three days. The power of the

Government can begin to be seen. We hear that Freemont has cleared MO. & we feel like congratulating him for his success. I should go with Freemont every time. Success to him.

E. H. B.

Laying near Fairfax,Va. Sept. 2nd.

We marched at sundown for this place which we passed at sunrise after marching all night to get some eight miles. The roads are horrible on account of a heavy rain which fell just at night. There was a fight yesterday P.M. between here and Centreville. The loss on our side was considerable. One Gen. killed named Stephans. There was none of Sumners Corps engaged. I can't tell where we will fetch up but I hope the Potomac will stop us. This is what is called strategy very fine but we have not had but two nights sleep since we landed from the peninsula. I stand it well have not given up yet and don't expect to.

We have fearful stories about the Injuns but have nothing reliable as yet. We got our mail this morning but there is no way to send any letters off yet.

Encamped near Tennally Town, Md. Sept. 4th.

Well we landed safely in Md. after a active campaign of some 5 months in Va. with various success but ending in a total defeat of the Federal Army (I think), time will tell. We started from where we were laying on the PM of the 2nd, a little before sundown on the Vienna road the Rebs were on our heels and soon began to shell us. Gorman's brigade covered the retreat. Our Regt. with a section of the R.I. battery came on the main road. Colonel Sully in Command. We had come about 2 miles when we were halted to repel an expected cavalry charge from the Rebs. We had the battery planted in the road with the Regt. thrown out on either side to support it and had just got position when they came riding along Colonel Sully halted them and asked them who they were but they could not tell wanting him to come and see, be ready boys, said the Col, as they came slowly on for they did not seem to know how we were situated. Soon one of them fired at the Col with his pistol but missed him and we were ordered to fire. When there was just as handsome a volley of musketry from our Regt poured into them. The battery firing at the same time. Such a screeching and howling as followed among the Rebs told that some one was hurt and they left without further talk. We came on and camped towards morning within our lines near Washington. I can only guess what is to be done next.   I expect to get my knapsack today then I will try and write again. I have not heard from Captain but expect he is doing well.

Good by for the present,   *Edward*

Chain Bridge at Washington DC. – Brady Photo

Encamped near Tennally Town, Md.
Thursday PM. Sept. 4th, 1862.

Dear Parents:

I have just received two letters from home, I wish I was there so that I could go out & help drive the Indians back. I also have the Central Republican of the 27th. As I have not written home since we left our camp at NewPort News, Va. You will not hear so often as before from me but I tell you we have had some of the hardest times yet since we left Harrisons Landing. It has been impossible to write but we have got our knapsacks and things now and I will write often if I can. I am well but somewhat fatigued. We are getting soft bread now & plenty of meat, coffee & sugar. We expect to get 4 months pay on the 15th. There has been some fireing heard in the distance today but I have no fears of the Secesh crossing the Potomac. All the Morristown boys stood the marching well. C.B.Jackson, Bault Soule, Chas Parker & all the rest are all up & ready for the next time. If I was only in Minnesota now I would shoulder my rifle and go off to the wars on the frontier. There would be some fun. I hope the Indians will be made to suffer but they will likely be left as soon as they are driven beyond the settlements. However, I am glad they have not gone any further. Since war is the order of the times I hope Gov. Ramsey will exterminate those bands that have been commiting depredations. What use is there in playing war with the Indians or Secesh. This we have found out to our sorrow. We are all proud of our state (Minnesota) for the way the people have turned out for the war. They have certainly done well for a new state.

Friday morning 5th. Quiet as usual but I expect that our forces have evacuated Leesburg, Winchester and we will yet be sent up the Potomac. I am very glad that you are going to get George's things. I will forward the money to pay the charges as soon as I can get it. Please write & let me know what that is. The weather is very fine here, cold nights.

There was some frost on the night of the 3d.

Affectionately yours

Edward.

Encamped near Tennally Town, Md.
Sabath eve Sept. 7th A.D. 1862.

Dear Parents,

We left our camp at Harrisons Landing on the 15th of August and have been on a continual move ever since so that I have not had a chance to write but twice in all the time and then it was very difficult. We landed at Alexandria on the morn of the 28th of Aug. From there we went up to Chain Bridge then back to within two miles of Alexandria & took the Fairfax road which we passed on the morn of the 31st on out to Centreville where we met McDowells Corps in full retreat as we thought at that time and which has since proved to be the case. Yes, there was already another masterly retreat commencing & McClellans army had been marched out to cover the retreat of the whiped forces of McDowell, Pope & Banks. Well we must make the best of things that we can and accordingly we were held in readiness to move at any moment. On the morn of the 1st of Sept. Sumner's Corps was marched out on a reconoisance but we saw nothing of the enemy but that P.M. there was a fight between Centreville & Fairfax in which we lost two Genls - Genl Stephens & Kearney both killed. At night we started for Fairfax. The roads being very wet from a very heavy rain that had just fallen, we marched all night in the rain dark, crowded, wet, sleepy, hungry and with all thinking of our nights march on the same road on the night of the 21st of July 1861. Well we passed through Fairfax about sunrise. From there we took the Vienna road. We stoped and breakfasted out a few miles. There we laid until nearly sundown when we started on for the Potomac. We had only got fairly started when the rebs commenced shelling us. Colonel Sully was in command of the 1st Minnesota with a battery of two guns from a R.I. (Rhode Island) battery. They evidently thought that we were too badly scared to fight so they pressed on closely after us but Colonel Sully was wide awake & we prefered to have our time for marching that night. So after we had run something more than one mile we stoped in the edge of a strip of woods that the road run through. We planted the two cannon in the road & the regiment was placed on either side of the road opposite the guns. We were scarcely in position when Colonel Sully challenged a squad of rebel Cavalry. They tried to get the Colonel to come down to them but this was too good a thing for us and we were not to be fooled out of it. The rebs fired a few shots at the Colonel but missed him, when the Colonel ordered the boys to fire & we poured into them a voley similar to the one that we got at Bull Run. This was too much for them & they left for that night & we made our way through to Chain Bridge where we arrived a little before light. After breakfast we marched across the Potomac & camped near Tennally Town Md. Our loss on the night of the retreat from FairFax was 2 killed & some 7 or 8 badly wounded. There was none of our Co. (Company) hurt.

We left Tennally Town in the PM of the 4th & started for Poolsville as we supposed. The rebels were reported to be crossing the Potomac & we were calculating to have some fun but we were halted here yesterday PM some 17 miles from Poolsville. It is true that the rebs have crossed the river in considerable force above here. Winchester has been evacuated & the Union army is resting on the loyal side of the Potomac. Our 2nd Lieut. Mr. Spencer who is detailed as one of the signal officers in Genl Brink's Corps was out some 20 miles yesterday and saw the enemy on Sugar Loaf Mountain. They were displaying a large flag. We are laying still now but I expect that we will be on the move soon. Genl McClellan is the chief commander of the Union forces (so says rumor). The boys are in better health than could be expected after such hard marches. There are only 3 of Co. G. in the hospital beside the Captain I don't know how he is geting along. It is geting dark & how I would like to be at home this evening but alas I must wait until some other time, if ever. One good thing, I have good health and I will try to feel contented with a good night to you all. I must wait until morning to finish my letter.

Monday Morning   Sept.8th

It is a very pleasant morning. We are still in line of battle but I don't suppose the enemy are anywhere near. How I would like to be at home this week to help you on the farm. I suppose the farmers will soon commence their fall work.

I send you a sample of wheat that was grown up on the Chickahominy River also some few apple seeds to Elford. I wish you could have some of the apples & peaches that are plenty here. I manage to get all I want and I would be glad to trade some for some of your nice potatoes. I will try and write as soon as I can. At present it is not very handy but I hope we will get into a good camp soon.

Hopeing that the war will soon end and the people once more enjoy the rights of a people liveing in a free country, I will close.

As ever your son in the army

Edward

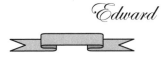

Immediately following the battle at Flint Hill and the unfortunate episode near Vienna, the regiment was preparing to continue their march as rear guard, when a situation arose that cemented the strong bond of respect the men held for Colonel Sully.

In his memoirs, James Wright of Company F, records the tale:

"We gathered up our dead and wounded, and – having no ambulances – a party was sent back to Vienna to secure some sort of transportation for them. It was here that the grim old regular, Colonel Sully, showed that he had a kind heart beneath his rough exterior and, by his action on this occasion, formed a new tie of attachment between himself and the men of the First Regiment whom he had so ably commanded on several occasions.

There was a delay in finding transportation, and orders came to move on, but he delayed the movement and asked for transportation. None could be furnished and the order was repeated to continue the march as the moon was now up and there was increased danger of an attack. He again declined to go without his wounded and again demanded transportation for them. He declared that he never had abandoned dead or helpless comrades except when actually forced to do so, and that he would not do it now. When the order was repeated, he grew wrathy, used a few of his strongest cuss words, and declared that there would be more dead and wounded to keep them company before he left them behind. Soon after, the detail returned with some conveyance in which the wounded were quickly placed, and the march resumed."

Although the chronological dates of the previous letters relate the movement of the army back to Washington and supersede the events they describe, they are included here for continuity of the story they tell.

Next, the movement of the army back to Washington and into Maryland in pursuit of General Lee's army into the North will be explored.

It was nearly 3 AM when the weary soldiers reached the camp of their division, near Chain Bridge, and stacked their arms. Without food, tents or any other convenience, they lay down on the closest piece of ground they could find and, within minutes, put the events of the day behind them as they slept.

CHAPTER 17
THE MARYLAND
CAMPAIGN

The morning of September 3, 1862, found the men awakened after sunup and preparing morning coffee. Just after finishing a hurried cup, they were ordered to fall in behind the long column of troops, already on the move toward Maryland. They crossed the Chain Bridge and moved into Maryland and, late in the afternoon, the column halted about 3 miles before reaching Tennallytown. The long march took a toll and many of the worn out men dropped out along the wayside—too exhausted to go on. By the time the halt was called, the regiment numbered less than 500 men fit for duty. As they put down their rubber ground and tent cloths to rest, some supply wagons appeared and they were issued two-day's rations, including some fresh meat. How they must have relished having a decent meal! Exhausted, dirty and ragged, they lay down to the first full night's sleep in over two weeks. Edward's friend, Charley Goddard, wrote in a letter home:

"We have been without clean shirts for 4 weeks and had not time to wash those we have on. You may bet we are used up soldiers."

The reveille bugles sounded at daybreak next morning, September 4th. The men rolled out expecting to continue the march, but such was not the case. They spent a day of leisurely rest. The mail arrived and everyone was engaged in reading mail and newspapers and catching up on writing letters home. Missing their treasured knapsacks and all the necessities of camp life they contained, they enquired of the Quartermaster. But, alas, the missing knapsacks containing their writing materials, extra clothing, cooking utensils and other desired contents could not be located.

General McClellan anticipated that Lee's next move would take his Confederate army across the Potomac. He was right. Between September 4th and 7th, Lee crossed his army into Maryland. The Confederacy was convinced only the oppressive military might of the North had kept Maryland from joining their cause. With his army in rags and in dire need of every manner of supplies and equipage, Lee reasoned that the people would respond in overwhelming gratitude when he marched into Frederick, the State Capitol. By moving into Maryland, he expected to recruit thousands of new volunteers to his army, as well as to avail himself of the wealth of food, forage and other supplies he needed. His invasion into the northern realm might even influence European powers to recognize the Confederacy and come to their aid—especially if, with his new found strength, he was able to capture Washington. Lee also calculated that the move would force the withdrawal of all Federal troops from Virginia and leave him the bountiful crops now nearly ready for harvest in the Shenandoah Valley. As the rebel army marched into Maryland, Lee issued a proclamation informing the inhabitants that he was there to *"restore their lost liberties"* and independence. He assured the populace that they would endure no harm or hardship and would be compensated in Confederate notes for any supplies they provided. Apparently, Lee was more concerned about their lost liberties than they were. The welcoming open arms he anticipated turned out to be cold shoulders. The wealth of supplies he expected to pour forth with jubilation had to be extracted with compensation. Upon entering Frederick, Lee's army found the streets hung with Union Flags, not crowded with wagon loads of supplies. He responded by sending out foraging parties to collect whatever they could from the barns, stables, granaries, hog pens, smoke houses and anywhere else supplies could be found. On September 10th, threatened by the advance of McClellan, Lee gave up his efforts as a liberator and marched to Hagerstown, where he split his army and sent Stonewall Jackson to take Harper's Ferry and Longstreet and D.H. Hill across South Mountain to Boonsborough.

While all this was going on, McClellan had been busy as well. Once again the head of the army, the result of Lincoln's direct order, he had brought it back into solidarity and restored its morale. In just a few days, he had completely reorganized the defense of Washington and completed the construction of defensive works. He quickly moved out of the environs of Washington toward Maryland taking care to keep his army positioned to prevent an attack on the Capitol. At all times, he had sufficient forces for defense within a 40-mile radius of the city. McClellan realized that Harper's Ferry was indefensible from attack. He sent a telegram to General-in-Chief Halleck, urging him to immediately withdraw the 9,000 men garrisoned there under Colonel Miles and the 2,500 men at Martinsburg under General White and to combine those forces with the Army of the Potomac. Halleck had been the source of a continual stream of telegrams to McClellan berating him for his all too rapid movement away from Washington. Upon receipt of McClellan's message, he restated that concern and further refused to withdraw the forces from Harper's Ferry. As usual, Halleck seemed more influenced by political pressure and his preoccupation with a possible attack on Washington, than by sound military judgment.

The march resumed following an inspection of arms and clothing before noon on the 5th of September, and bivouacked for the night about 3 miles from Rockville. The next morning, Saturday, they started early with the First Minnesota in the lead as the advance regiment. The supply wagons had not caught up and they were still without supplies of any kind. On Sunday, they stayed bivouacked all day in line-of-battle. The First Minnesota and 15 th Massachusetts were posted as guard on the Gaithersburg road, with their pickets posted far out in front. It was rumored that rebel forces were in the area. Monday, September 8th, some of their supply wagons came up and the men were issued three days' rations.

Edward Bassett's diary records the movement of the next few days to Fredrick City:

> *"On Sept. 8th we started about noon, and took the Frederick road. Encamped at night near a creek. The 10th I wasent (wasn't) well and rode in an ambulance. We started early on the 11th with Companies G and K as skirmishers. We had some fighting on the main roads. (We were) On picket at night. The next day the Rebs retreated towards Hagerstown, and we followed closely. The people all seem glad to see us. On the 14th we started early in the morning. There is heavy cannonadeing over the Mountains."*

Fighting on the main roads occurred about a mile from Hyattstown, where the rebels blocked the way in a show of force. A skirmish developed, but ended quickly when artillery was brought up. A few rounds of canister shells discouraged them and they retired. The First Minnesota and 71st Pennsylvania Regiments moved forward and occupied the town.

The First Minnesota entered Frederick on Friday, Sept. 12th, to find the rebels had retreated. They met only by a small cavalry unit which put up stiff resistance until artillery was brought forward and they were repelled. Returning with reinforcements of cavalry and infantry, the rebels attacked again and after a short fight withdrew. The townspeople welcomed the army with exuberance; women and children lined the streets cheering them on. Union flags hung from nearly every window and rooftop. When General McClellan rode into town, he was nearly completely covered with flowers and tumultuous cheers rang down the streets.

THE BATTLE OF SOUTH MOUNTAIN
SEPTEMBER 14, 1862

McClellan was still unsure of the position of the enemy forces. He was cautious about weakening his left flank along the Potomac to relieve Harper's Ferry, as Halleck was continually suggesting. An incredible piece of shear luck came McClellan's way on Saturday the 13th, when a soldier found a piece of paper wrapped around three cigars lying in a field on the Best family farm, located on the edge of Frederick. The importance of the find was immediately recognized and rushed to McClellan. The paper was a copy Lee's General Order #191—his complete action plan, including all troop movements and strategy. McClellan now knew everything he could hope for about his adversary's intentions. He immediately ordered General Franklin, with his 6th Corps, to move through the passes at South Mountain; cut off and destroy General McLaws' confederate force and relieve Harper's Ferry. Franklin reached the base of the South Mountain range about 8 AM on Sept. 14th and found the rebels had already occupied the mountain passes. Instead of immediately moving up the slopes, he delayed for four hours while developing a battle plan.

The South Mountain range, an extension of the Blue Ridge into Maryland, is a long line of steep-sided mountains, breeched only at a few places by high passes, commonly referred to as 'gaps'. The mountains rise to a height of 1,000 ft. Very good, but winding, roads approached the passes at a height of 800 ft. The rocky slopes are covered with crevices and deep wooded gulleys. The battle was actually two battles fought on the South Mountain range the same day. The fight at Turner's Gap to the north started early in the morning. At Crampton's Gap, in the south, Franklin did not become engaged until around noon. The battles raged all day with charges and counter charges. By night, the Federals had succeeded in turning the flanks of Lee's army and taking possession of the passes. Lee was forced to withdraw.

Drawing of the Battle of South Mountain by A. R. Waud
Harper's Weekly, October 25, 1862

The First Minnesota began the march to South Mountain at daylight on Sunday, September 14th, a beautiful sunny morning. Tramping through the idyllic green-robed countryside in the fresh mountain air was a delight compared to the infested tidewater swamps of Virginia. They passed through Middleburg to Catoctin Mountain, reaching the crest about noon. Somewhat worn out by the arduous climb and 12-mile march, they halted for a two-hour rest while they ate lunch. The view of the fertile Catoctin Valley below rolled out before them like a great painting. Dotted with fine farms, glittering streams, woodlands and a pattern of rich fields, crisscrossed by well-kept roads—lay a sight to remember. The peaceful tranquility was soon interrupted by the sounds of battle now raging at Crampton's Pass in the distance. The regiment, being near the rear, having covered a distance of 17 miles, reached the battlefield after the glowing sun had set behind the mountain. By now, the heights had been taken. In the dark, the men struggled up the rocky mountainside to relieve the

"Iron Brigade,"[51] which had been in the thick of the battle all day and had taken considerable losses. The regiment was pushed to the front and laid down to rest among the dead that littered the mountain side. They choose to ignore the occasional shell fired in their direction and the sporadic rifle fire, still coming from behind a stone wall, patches of woods and rocky clefts. Throughout the night, they held the line, taking turns on watch. Arising at first light, they discovered that the rebels had left and the regiment was soon assembled and marching in pursuit.

At 8 AM this same day, all the Union troops at Harper's Ferry and Martinsburg, completely surrounded, were surrendered after only token resistance. Since Colonel Miles had made virtually no provisions for defense and had no appreciable force in place to secure the Bolivar Heights, the Confederate forces of Jackson and McLaws had little trouble getting guns on the high ground, thereby making any kind of resistance fruitless. The only Union casualty was the man in charge, Colonel Miles, who fell mortally wounded by an accidental discharge as he was carrying the white flag out to surrender his men. Perhaps it was a kindness of fate for it is doubtful he could ever have lived down this action. The men of the Army of the Potomac thought the surrender of Harpers Ferry by Colonel Miles, a career officer with a record of gallantry, was an act of treachery, if not treason. The state of Maryland, Colonel Miles' homeland, was known to have a sizeable contingent of Southern sympathizers. Coupled with the fact that he had been found guilty of being drunk and unfit for duty at Bull Run, provided the rationale for such thoughts. The investigation into the surrender found that *"Miles' incapacity, amounting to almost imbecility, led to the shameful surrender of this important post."* The battle at South Mountain is often overlooked, overshadowed by Antietam which occurred 3 days later. It was, however, of great significance because Lee's first invasion of northern territory was stopped there. Though McClellan had not acted quickly enough to destroy or subdue

---

[51] The famous Iron Brigade, commanded by Gen. John Gibbons, consisted of the 2nd, 6th & 7th Wisconsin Regiments, also the 19th Indiana and 24th Michigan.

either half of Lee's divided army, he succeeded in denying them the supplies they sought. This forced Lee to go on the defensive and destroyed any Confederate hopes of taking Washington. After the fall of Harper's Ferry, Stonewall Jackson, in an incredible feat, marched day and night to rejoin Lee en route to Sharpsburg. Lee knew he was going to have to fight and decided to do so from a defensive position of his own choosing, along the banks of Antietam Creek.

South Mountain was costly for both sides, but Lee lost strength he could not replace. His only gain was measured in 13,500 stands of arms, 73 canons, and a huge quantity of supplies and stores. He also destroyed a crucial railroad bridge and canals at Harper's Ferry. The casualty count for the North was 2,340 in killed, wounded and missing; the South counted 2,900 killed and wounded. A total of 36,000 Union and 13,000 Confederate troops were involved, though not all Union forces were engaged. The casualties were roughly the same as at First Bull Run.

THE BATTLE OF ANTIETAM
SEPTEMBER 17, 1862

The full story of this great battle has been related by many authors in numerous volumes. The purpose of this volume is to relate the events of this historic day only as they pertain to the First Minnesota Regiment and, of necessity, leave the telling of the entire tale to others.

Hot pursuit of Lee's army on the morning of September15th proceeded down the west side of the mountain with the 8th Illinois Cavalry and flying artillery in the lead and followed by the First and Second Corps. infantry. The way was strewn with the castoff knapsacks and clothing of the retreating rebels. At Boonsborough, the cavalry and some of the leading infantry engaged the rebel rear guard in a lively skirmish. Turning southwest on the Sharpsburg and Boonsborough Turnpike, the column bivouacked for the night near Shepardstown. Early in the morning, they marched through the village of Keedysville and, a few miles farther, bivouacked on the eastern side of a strip of high ground that runs parallel to Antietam Creek. General Sedgwick's entire Division, including the First Minnesota, was camped on Pry's Farm, located on Antietam Creek in the far northeastern corner of the battlefield. During the day, a good deal of artillery fire and skirmishing occurred as the armies on both sides of the creek positioned themselves for the battle to come. The men of Gorman's Brigade were sheltered behind the crest of a low ridge, from which they could observe all the activity for a couple miles.

Antietam – Harper's Weekly Oct. 4. 1862

The Battle of Antietam began very early in the morning and raged on until around 9 o'clock in the evening. Both sides fought with unrivaled ferocity. The fields of battle were a scene of death and suffering of a magnitude never before witnessed. As numerous charges and counter charges ensued, ground was gained and lost, the lines of battle often brought the men to within 50 yards of one another as they blazed away as fast as they could reload. Artillery loaded with double loads of canister tore men to pieces. Shells exploded shattering trees into kindling. Shell fragments ripped through bodies of men and horses like sweeping scythes of doom. Rifle barrels became so hot they were rendered useless. Screaming and whistling projectiles ripped the air as the tranquil scene of early morning turned into one of destruction, agony and gore.

An insight into the nature of the conflict can be gained by an incident that occurred on the extreme right of the Union side at sunrise. Union General Hooker had moved across Antietam

Creek on the afternoon of September16th. At dawn he attacked. His objective was the little square white Dunker Church 1,000 yards to his front. With his three divisions spread out, line abreast, they moved forward forcing the rebels back, both sides took heavy losses. Pushing through the East Woods and nearing a forty-acre cornfield, the glint of bayonets was observed coming from the tall ripe corn. Six Batteries, 36 guns, of Hooker's artillery were brought forward and swung into line. With a thundering scream of death that shook the ground, they opened fire on Stonewall Jackson's rebel infantry occupying the corn field across the road east of Dunker Church. General Hooker reported:

"In the time I am writing, every stalk of corn in the northern and greater part of the field was cut as closely as could have been done with a knife, and the slain lay in rows precisely as they had stood in their ranks a few moments before."

The First Minnesota, in Gorman's Brigade, awoke at 2 AM on the morning of September 17th. Preparations for the day's action started with making coffee and something to eat, and the issuance of 80 rounds of ammunition. At 4 AM, the regiment was called up with orders to be ready to move at a moments notice and knapsacks were packed to leave camp. From their vantage point, the men could overlook much of the battlefield. James Wright commented about the nervous anticipation as the men waited to go into battle:

"The 'fires of battle' flashed up against gray, overhanging clouds and reflected back to waiting watchers do not start the same thoughts or stir the same feelings as a moonlit scene beside a quiet river. The Angry roar of cannon, echoed back from the hills, and the snarls and growls of an intermittent rifle fire rolling through the valley at the break of day – is not so cheerful a greeting as the pleasant "good morning" of a friend. Picture the scene, add to it the fact that you are under orders to 'go in,' and remember that we were still human, and you may fairly judge of our feelings..." [52]

---

[52] James A. Wright, "No More Gallant a Deed", page 199

As a small consolation, the men appreciated the cloudy sky—glad that, at least they would not have to fight under a broiling sun.

By 7 AM, General Hooker had cleared the Confederates from the East Woods and the fields of D. R. Miller's farm, east of Hagerstown Turnpike. The decimated rebel ranks took cover in the West Woods behind trees, boulders, rock ledges and in washes and gullies, as they sought protection from the murderous artillery fire. Hooker continued his advance until 9:15 AM, when the rebels were reinforced by three brigades of fresh troops and artillery, which resulted in a rout of Hooker's men, who retreated northward along the Hagerstown Pike. Other troops moved in to replace Hooker's troops, over half of which had now "skedaddled or straggled" to the rear. The new troops, led by Generals Crawford and Green fought hard and held their ground. Then onto the field came more rebel reinforcements and, after suffering heavy losses, they too, began to break and withdraw under the withering fire from the reinforced rebel line.

At 7:20 AM, the call came for Sedgwick's Division to move up. They moved out in three lines, each line formed by a brigade. Gorman's Brigade formed the first line, with the First Minnesota at the head of that brigade. They marched rapidly some ¾-mile to the northwest when Gorman's brigade turned and continued directly west. The artillery was supposed to go further upstream to a crossing without such steep banks and then return. However, it was not to be seen again that day, though its support was desperately needed. They marched in column-of-fours with about 50 yards between the lead and each of the two following brigades.

Antietam – Harper's Weekly Oct. 4. 1862

Encamped on the field near Keytsville, Md.
Sept. 17th, 1862.

Dear Parents

I have but a few moments to write you a line to let you know that I am well. We are chaseing the enemy out of Md. The guns are roaring now within 80 rods & the rebs skedadleing. Our Regt. has not been in a fight yet but we are anxious to get at them. Captain is with. He gets along well. The boys are all well. It has been over one month now since we have stoped 48 hours in one camp so you see I have but poor chances to write. My love to you all

In haste

Edward

Wading across Antietam Creek, soaking wet to their waists, they crawled up the brushy, steep bank. All the while, they were receiving artillery fire and, as they came into view of the enemy gunners and turned to the west, the firing intensified. Passing through the East Woods they were greeted by the sight of dead and wounded under every tree. They marched into what earlier had been a stately field of corn and now resembled a plowed field where a gory harvest of dead and wounded men lay piled in rows staring at the sky or moaning for water and help. The three lines of battle marched on, perfectly formed and spaced and without faltering, into the jaws of death. Twice they halted briefly to climb the rail fences that lined each side of the Hagerstown pike. As they entered the West Woods, their gallant flag bearer, Sam Bloomer of Company F, fell when a minnie ball shattered his leg. Tearing the flag from its staff, he stuffed the sacred pennant into his shirt to prevent its capture by the enemy. Fifty yards from where they formed into line, they were met by fire from Jeb Stuart's rebel batteries but they pressed on into the woods, where none of their comrades had been and faced the same troops they fought at Fair Oaks. Coolly, they advanced into the fusillade of grape and canister from the rebel guns. Sumner, riding in front of the regiment and noticing the U.S. flag was still in its sheath, yelled, *"In God's name, what are you fighting for? Unfurl those colors!"* Loading and firing as they advanced through this stately grove of regal oak trees, the men were led on by General Sumner himself— leading the charge, riding to and fro at the head of Gorman's Brigade waving his hat, His gray hair blowing in the wind. In his haste to get his men onto the field where he knew the situation was becoming desperate, Sumner kept his division in marching formation instead of reforming into line-of-battle. This would prove a costly oversight because the men remained packed together, this made them easy targets and hindered their ability to maneuver and fight. Upon clearing the woods, the men were astonished that there were no rebel troops to be seen. Within moments that all changed! The brief lull was replaced by a large commotion on the left.

Confederate Generals McLaws and Anderson had arrived from Harper's Ferry and came onto the field, just as Sumner had gotten into action. McLaws moved to Sumner's left and Anderson to Sumner's right. The left of Sumner's line was supposed to connect with General French, but French was not yet in position. This left a large gap in the Union line that was immediately noticed by the rebel General. Sumner now faced ten confederate brigades that nearly surrounded him on three sides and had artillery support on the high ground as well. He had marched into an ambush. The firing all along the front grew to a thunderous crescendo as the fresh rebel troops poured into line. The next twenty minutes saw some of the most furious fighting of the war. The Lines were only about 100 yards apart—the Union being mostly in the open fields, the Confederate mostly under cover among the brush, farm buildings, rock walls and fences. The Union left, still in tight formation, was being cut to ribbons by the enfilading fire. General Sumner had ridden along the rear of the line to the left. Upon reaching the Fifteenth Mass., he discovered that the enemy had turned their flank and was advancing on the rear. *"My God! We must get out of this"*, Sumner said, and rode off in a desperate attempt to reposition his troops to meet the threat. It was too late. Turning an entire brigade in a few minutes would be difficult on an open parade ground; in battle it was impossible. Soon, the domino effect began as regiment after regiment was forced to fall back to keep from being surrounded. While Gorman's Brigade, including the First Minnesota, was still fighting in the front, General Dana endeavored to hold the left. Dana, though badly wounded, repositioned the 42nd New York and 7th Michigan. They were immediately met by a storm of fire and lead that Dana called *"the most terrific"* he had ever seen. Within minutes, the two gallant regiments had lost half their number and were forced to retire.

The First Minnesota now was entirely on its own. Heavy, 12 pound Napoleon cannons from Stuarts Battery were brought up and began pounding its right. With both flanks having crumbled and under heavy attack from three sides, they fought on. Then, orders came directly from General

Sedgwick to withdraw. Colonel Sully, with his usual cool head, guided the orderly retreat, and on his command, they turned and fired. At one point, the 82nd New York and 19th Mass. took positions on their right and left and they stood their ground. The massed fire of this band of brothers is all that prevented their capture. By now, they had reached the Nicodemus farm, where they made another stand amidst the wheat stacks, buildings, and the many crazed and wounded cattle. About 100 yards back and to their left on a slight rise, they formed behind a stone wall and, again, poured a volley into their pursuers. For the first time, they were supported by artillery that opened fire on the confederates, who soon retired—out of range.

The fighting of Sedgwick's Division ended around 10 PM and they remained near the stone wall until relieved by Franklin's Corps. None suffered greater losses that day than the Second Division of the Second Corps and its splendid discipline and spirit saved it from complete destruction and capture. Sedgwick's Division of the Second Corps suffered most with a total loss of 2,255, of whom 355 were killed—from a division that entered the battle with just under 5,000 men less than two hours earlier.

Encamped on the field
Sept. 21st, 1862

Dear Parents:

Hopeing that you will excuse my long letter of the 17th. I will try now & see if I cannot do better. When I wrote last on the 17th I did not have but a few moments. We were expecting to march every moment. The battle had commenced & we had to be ready to move quick but I thought that a few words would be better than nothing so I scribbled a few lines & sent. We were soon called out & in an hour were where the bullets were flying arround in rather close proximity to our heads to sound very pleasant. Genl Sumner's corps was ordered to relieve General Sedgwick. We went onto the field in high spirits and were confident of success. Sedgwick's division was badly cut up by the rebel battery & infantry. The 82 N.Y., 42 & 15 Mass. & the 3 left companies of the Minnesota First were under very heavy fire & lost heavyly but the rebel ranks were also terribly thined. The Minnesota Sharpshooters took a rebel battle flag with 52 ball holes through it. It was about 2 ½ feet square. B. F. Soule had his forefinger on his left hand shot off. George Kenney was wounded in the face but not dangerously. These are all the casualties to Co. G. The Captain of Co. K. was killed. I stood within two feet of him when he was shot. There are hundreds of dead rebels laying on the field but they are burying them as fast as possible. I have seen some of the worst sights that I ever saw. They lay piled up against each other in some places. They fought desperate as also did our troops. The Irish brigade made several charges & drove everything before them. Genl Gorman was not wounded nor hurt although the horses of all his staff were wounded, his was not hit. Genl McClellan was on the field. It is said that the rebels have all crossed the Potomac & are makeing the best of their way for Richmond. They are very poorly clothed. All their dead that had good shoes on were striped of them & left barefoot (this seems hard but it is so). They had nothing to eat except corn & apples. Many of their sick were left in Fredrick & throughout all the country. The wounded are all taken good care of. There are hundreds of citizens from Pennsylvania here doing all they can for the wounded. You will most likely see an official account of the battle before you receive this. I don't believe that there will be another battle like the recent one very soon. It has been a terrible battle & the losses are very heavy on both sides. Our regt. lost something over 100 men. I see by the Faribault paper that the Indian troubles are not over & I wish I was there too. I think that the Minnesota 1st ought to have a chance to stand by their own homes when they are in danger as now from savages.

My only hopes are that the rebel army will be destroyed & the wars ended soon.

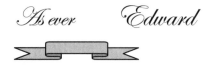

As ever   Edward

That night, after giving aid to the wounded wherever it could be rendered and having gone without food for 24 hours, the men ate pork and crackers from their haversacks and drank lots of hot coffee as they talked of the day's gruesome work. Having refilled their cartridge boxes and laying with their guns at hand, they covered themselves with whatever was available and sought the solitude of sleep. The next four days were spent gathering and burying the dead and caring for wounded, as well as dragging the hundreds of dead horses into piles to be burned. All present would long remember the horrors they saw and the terrible stench of what they would ever thereafter call "The Stinking Fields." Union losses on this day amounted to 2,010 killed, 9,416 wounded, 1,043 missing; Confederate losses are, in part, estimates but appear to have been over 3,500 killed, 10,500 wounded or missing.

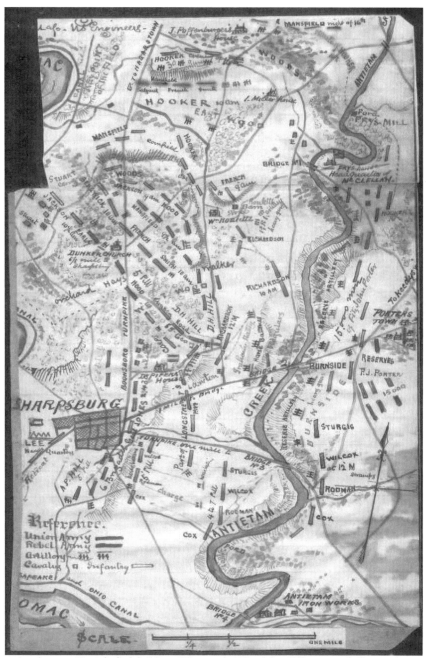

Antietam Battlefield–Map,Harper's Weekly, Library of Congress

293

The first page of the following letter no longer exists. The letter refers to the Maryland Campaign, the Battle of Antietam and the surrender of Harpers Ferry by Colonel D. S. Miles. It was written on September 22, 1862. Arriving at Harper's Ferry in the afternoon, following the march from Antietam, the men made haste to wash their filthy clothes and bathe in the river. Edward wrote to his parents while his regiment was encamped on Bolivar Heights.

The letter:

. . . . have lost all their stock. There is one of the prettiest valleys between the Blue Ridge & what is called the Bull Run range in Maryland that I ever saw. It looks as you stand up on the side of the mountain & look down the valley some 30 miles over the farms which are all well cultivated like a map. The fields are of different colors & it certainly is the hansomest place that I ever saw (except in Minnesota).

You have most likely heard of the surrender of the Union forces under Colonel Miles at this place. They were 11,000 strong & surrendered without fireing a musket. The citizens are many of them very indignant and say that we could expect nothing better as long as we have traitors among us. The rebels burned the Railroad bridge across the Potomac beside completeing the destruction of the few remaining government buildings. This makes three bridges that have been destroyed on the same piers within less than two years but I suppose there will soon be another & the cars will soon be bringing supplies into western Va. The Chesapeak & Ohio canal is also badly damaged all the way up from Seneca up as far as Hagerstown. The Union forces came in here again the day before yesterday I believe but yesterday rebel scouts were seen out between here & Charlestown and I suppose they are in force at Winchester & perhaps this side of that place.

We are encamped in a very pleasant situation and I am in hopes that we will get a few days rest but there is no telling where we will be in a week. These are stiring times & I hope there will be something done that will bring the war to an end. It is rumored that the gun boats have reduced Fort Darling but I do not credit the report. We also have a report that there has been a treaty formed with the Indians in Minnesota Although I no more than half believe it still I hope it is not so. What use is there in treating with them. I also heard that the troops that surrendered here have been parolled & will be sent to Minnesota to protect the frontier. Bishop Whipple was in our camp Sunday P.M. He made a short speech & a prayer & then talked about the Indians & home affairs.

We expect our pay soon as we stop long enough in one place to get it. It has been due some time & we are getting anxious to see the paymaster. Captain Messick is well & in fine spirits. He was cool as a cucumber in the fight. We have a new Lieutennant His name is Shepley. We like him very well. I have not heard from Boult Soule since he was wounded but he is undoubtedly doing well. His forefinger on his left hand was shot off close up to the hand. George Kenney, the other man that was wounded in Co. G, I heard was at Hagerstown & doing well. He was wounded in the cheek. I am well although I feel pretty tired from the marching & loss of sleep. We marched some 15 miles yesterday over a mountainous road carrying our knapsacks & from 40 to 80 rounds of ammunition. My whole load will weigh near 50 lbs. I have been doing my washing today. It is the first chance that we have had since we left the peninsula. It would surprise you to see what a change the Shenandoah water and soap makes on our fine linen when applied monthly.

Since August 14, when their knapsacks were sent away, the men had no soap, clean clothes or even a change of socks. Actually most had not had clean clothes for a week or two before that. When they arrived at the Potomac on September 22nd, the pontoon bridge was in use and it would be hours before they could cross. Rather than keep the men standing in the hot sun, General Sumner ordered them to ford the chest deep water.

James Wright tells about what happened next:

"We were very agreeably surprised to find that some of the wagons had already arrived, and, as soon as arms were stacked, rations were drawn and coffee was made. Very soon after, more of the brigade train came in, and we were able to get some camp kettles and soap for the first time (when we had time to use them) since leaving Harrison's Landing.

This was an opportunity not to be lost, and we hastened to the bank of the Shenandoah to wash our over-soiled clothing and indulge in a bath in the clear-running water of that beautiful mountain river. It was something we had been longing for ever since we had left the Peninsula. Fires were made; water heated; clothes washed and boiled and hung on the bushes to dry; and then our efforts were made more personal. However much they may have needed it, the individuals could not be boiled, but they were subjected to a series of applications of soap, water and scrubbing until the natural color of the skin was developed – to a degree that satisfied us of our own identity. Then we rinsed off with a plunge in the river, rubbed some, and wrapped a blanket around us, and lay on the bank to wait for our clothes to dry, for we had no 'changes of raiment.' Thousands of soldiers were engaged as we were as far as we could see up or down the river, but I do not recall that I ever saw a picture of it in the papers.

After dressing, we returned to the bivouac realizing that we were hungry, a sensation that the most of us had not really felt for several days. The seventy-odd hours' contact with the loathsome sight of discolored

296

and swollen corpse, misery, wreck, ruin, and general destruction of life and property was depressing to the extreme and took away desire for both food and drink. To get where we could breathe untainted air and find water to drink that we could feel was not contaminated by the dead was a relief that was in itself almost exhilarating. We returned to the camping place – with a satisfaction we had not felt for many days –cooked our suppers, ate them with relish, and prepared to lie down for the night".

On this day President Lincoln issued his Emancipation Proclamation. The following day, the men rested in camp and, for the first time in weeks, received a ration of fresh beef. The mail came and brought letters from home as well a liberal supply of newspapers. They read with interest the accounts of the Battle of Antietam. For the first time, they discovered the full magnitude of the day-long battle and read the particulars of Lincoln's proclamation freeing the slaves. Most of the men felt that the war could not end without the end of slavery.

Bolivar Va.
Sept. 25th 1862

Dear Sisters Ella and Anna

Since we came from the peninsula we have seen some of the hardest times that we ever have since I have been in the army we have marched several nights without getting any sleep nor could we sleep in the day time for the marching.

Hard marching has not been all we have seen we have been through some of the finest country that I ever saw. The farms were beautiful & plenty of fruit & green corn with now and then a chicken we have lived pretty well & enjoyed ourselves on the 14th we crossed over the mountain from Fredrick to another small town that I cannot name now. The roads were very dry but there was some very steep hills we could hear some very heavy cannonading & knew that our men were fighting the rebs on the other side. About noon we got to where we could see the smoke of the canon. It being Sunday the people were all dressed in their best clothes & stood at the gates to see us pass. Just before sundown we marched onto the battlefield and were on picket that night. The field was where the 5 & 6th Wis. Regts. & an Indianna Regt. had met the enemy in the open field. There was several dead & wounded lay on the field all night but early next morning they were taken care of. As we passed one of our canon that had been fired that evening I put my hand on it & found that although it had not been fired for over an hour it was almost blistering hot. The battlefield was on a steep mountain side up which ran the turnpike to Boonsborough, a very pretty town on the west side of the Blue Ridge Mountains. On the morning of the 15th we marched on & camped on what is called Antietam creek where we layed until the morning of the 17th when we crossed the creek & were engaged with the enemy for the second time since we came from the peninsula. That morning I did not think that there would be a general engagement that day although the shelling commenced early that morning & we were ordered to be ready to march and were furnished with 80 rounds of ammunition while we were waiting. I found that the mail was going out that day & as I had not written home for sometime I scribled a few lines with my pencil & sent it home just to let you know that I was well & alive.

The fighting that day was terible & the roar of the canon would almost deafen you. We all went in good spirits & if it had not been for the falling back of some forces on our left General Gorman would have driven the rebels before him but when them regiments fell back they let the rebs in behind our brigade & we were ordered back. The rebels came on cheering & fireing & seemed to be certain of success but we would rally every little ways & meet them with a voley. At one time they were but a few rods off & I stood on a little ridge where I could get a fair shot at them & I done my best. While I was loading & firening there the captain of the company that is next to us on the left was shot down within a few feet of where I stood. The ball passed in on his right side killing him in a short time. We soon fell back onto another ridge & the rebels give up the chase for our batteries were pouring in the shot rather thick. Since then we have not been under any musketry fireing but during the PM the rebels threw lots of shot & shell among us. Some went through the ranks but there was no one hurt by them in our regiment & we slept on the field that night everything settling down quiet & all the wounded were cared for as far as possible. During the PM General McClellan came riding up to the front & the boys cheered him. He took off his hat & bowed smiling very pleasantly. In a few moments, before he was 10 rods past our reg't., the rebels opened a battery opposite to us & the shot & shell flew arround the General like hail. There was several horses of his body guards were killed but he was not hurt. The next three days were spent in burrying the dead & careing for the wounded. I went nearly all over the battlefield & saw hundreds of the enemy laying dead where they had fallen. They had also burried what they could before they crossed the Potomac into Va. (McClellan estimated 500 had been buried by the confederates)

The sights I saw on that field I can never forget & hope I may never see another such a sight it was too horrible to contemplate!

We left the battlefield on the morning of the 22nd & came to Harpers Ferry where we forded the Potomac & camped very near where we were just 7 months ago the day that we crossed this time. We are having the easiest times just now that we have had for some 6 weeks. We drill one hour in the AM and one in the PM but the rest of the time we have to ourselves.

Yesterday I got a letter from home. I was very glad to hear that you are all well & that the Indians have not come down there & I hope they may never be seen in them parts again. I would like to go & fight them. I think it would make me feel good to shoot the rascals. (Indians)

How I would like to spend the winter quietly at home with my dear parents & brothers & sisters but I can only hope the wars will soon end & then we will all meet that are spared to see that happy time. But when I think of poor George I can hardly think it possible that I will not meet him if I should return to Minnesota I have a beautiful verse that I will send you that makes me think of him every time I see a piece of poetry.

> *"No Father near to guide me now*
> *No Mother's tears to sooth my brow*
> *No Brother's voice falls on my ear*
> *No Sister's voice to give me cheer"*

Good night to you all..

Your brother Edward

Friday morning 26th

It is a very pleasant morning but very cool. Early there was quite a frost & things begin to look dry. Corn is almost ripe. There was a frost on the 3rd of Sept. that killed the leaves on the locust trees.

We are all about as well as usual.

As ever your brother

E. H. Bassett

Co. G 1st Minnesota

The First Minnesota had entered the battle with only 435 men—one company being assigned to other duty. When the fighting ended, they had losses of 15 killed, 79 wounded and 21 missing.

The battle raged on all over the extensive battlefield until after dark. In the end, it was considered a draw; however, it was actually a Union victory in that, on the morning of September 19th, Lee's army had withdrawn. His badly decimated force crossed the Potomac and was retreating into Virginia, thus ending his foray into the North. Great Britain, thereafter, reconsidered recognition of the Confederate government and the South lost any chance of being recognized as a sovereign state.

This horrific engagement was the bloodiest single day during the war. Total losses at the battle were estimated at 23,100. The public perception that this was great Union victory, gave Lincoln the opportunity he needed to issue the Emancipation Proclamation.

Confederate dead in Bloody Lane – Antietam (M. Brady Photo)

On September 26, Colonel Alfred Sully of the First Minnesota Regiment was promoted to Brigadier General and assigned command of Gorman's Brigade. General Gorman had just been re-assigned to an important command in the west. Lieutenant Colonel George N. Morgan was promoted to Colonel and replaced Sully. Major William Colvill then became Lieutenant Colonel Colvill in his stead.

CHAPTER 18
A QUIET BETWEEN STORMS

Following the battle of Antietam, McClellan failed to pursue the confederates as Lee re-crossed the Potomac and withdrew into the Shenandoah Valley. This failure gave Lee time to re-supply from the riches of the valley and give his exhausted, ragged army a leisurely rest. Through an ambitious recruitment campaign and assistance from Richmond, Lee was able to replace his losses and bring his army up to strength in October. McClellan moved forces into the Harper's Ferry area where he placed two brigades on the heights and built extensive fortifications. Meanwhile, General-in-Chief Halleck continued his exchange of antagonistic telegraph messages with McClellan. Halleck had vociferously berated McClellan for moving away from Washington too quickly to engage Lee at South Mountain and Antietam. Now, he was all too eager to condemn him for having moved too slow. He sent a telegram demanding to know why he had not pursued the enemy instead of pausing to bury the dead. McClellan replied that his men were totally exhausted from the continuous marches and battles and were in no condition to pursue the enemy. The men under his command took exception to these comments; most eagerly wanted the chance to catch Lee and destroy him. Pinkerton, McClellan's civilian intelligence chief, had informed him that Lee's army had numbered 140,000 before Antietam, and still greatly outnumbered his forces. In truth, McClellan had roughly twice as many men as Lee. He reported 133,433 ready for duty and another 26,427 present. Lee' army actually totaled roughly 70,000 by mid-October and, perhaps less than 50,000 following Antietam. The real question on the minds of the President, the Cabinet and politicians was; *"Would McClellan move to crush Lee before winter set in?"*

On October 1st, President Lincoln made an unannounced three-day visit, although McClellan had received word that he was coming. They visited the fields of the last two great battles and reviewed the troops. More importantly, Lincoln made it clear that the army must move. McClellan said that was his intention, but he needed a little more time to get everything ready and, he doubted he would get that time. He directly stated that he believed the President, in response to the pressures in Washington would, remove him from command. President Lincoln replied, "General, I pledge myself to stand between you and harm."

Encamped at Bolivar Virginia
October 1st, 1862.

Dear Father & Mother,

The weather is quite warm and pleasant and very dry. We have not had any rain to amount to anything for a long time. Both the Potomac & Shenandoah rivers are very low and can be easily forded. I don't think the enemy has any large forces between here and Winchester although our pickets are only out a few miles. I suppose their cavalry are scouting through the country & make out to pick up a living among the people for the farmers are all secesionists. The cars run up as far as Sandy Hook from Baltimore but the bridge across the Potomac is destroyed & our provisions have to be brought across in wagons, the river being so low

304

that they cannot lay the pontoon bridge. The ford is very rough & stoney. There is a rumor that the Confederate authorities have sent commissioners to Washington under a flag of truce proposeing a settlement of the difficulties but what their terms are I don't know. I hope it is so & that they have come to the conclusion that it is time to end the war and come back into the union. President Lincoln's proclamation of freedom to all the Slaves found in the states bearing arms against the Union after Jan. 1st, 1863 will be apt to shorten the war I think and if the confederates don't gain their independence before that time I don't see how they can hope to afterwards. The papers say that there are two columns advanceing on Richmond, one by the way of Petersburg, which if successful, will cut off the supplies of the rebs and raise the prices in Richmond above what they already are. Now one thing is sure, the rebels have fought desperately in the late battles and their loss has been very heavy. They are short of provisions and clothes for they have left nothing of the kind in their camps & I have seen where they have taken the clothes from their dead on the field. By their conscription policy they have swelled their ranks to their utmost and they cannot fill up their decimated ranks again to oppose the Union army. It is a critical time with them and as they have failed to invade the northern states as Jackson proposed the best thing they can do is to quit & settle up as soon as possible. I believe they are about played out & heartily sick of the war but they may try with what they have got and risk another battle. They are fools if they don't at Richmond. The north has an army yet that has not been called out & although the old regiments number scarcely one half their original numbers they are most likely as good as the rebels old troops and they risk more in every battle than we do. Taking everything into consideration I think if we have not got too many traitors in our own ranks we will have peace by spring if not before and I hope it will come this fall.

The latest news we have of the Indian troubles is dated Sept. 26 stateing that Colonel Sibley had an engagement with them near Yellow Medicine & killed some 30 when they fell back & Sibley followed them. I hope he will round them up & keep them out of the state this winter. But if the winter is as cold as it is sometimes they will have rather cool fun. I suppose you all feel safe now as far as the Indians are concerned and I think you may. They will never penetrate as far down the country as there. I wish I was up there mounted on a good horse. I would like to hunt the black D---ls this fall and I would have a fine chance to see the country besides.

I don't anticipate that we will have any more fighting arround here during this war but there is no telling how soon we will be rolling on towards the enemy. I hope we won't winter here at least. I don't think it would be a very pleasant place. Our Colonel has received an appointment as Brigadier General. This makes the 3d. Colonel that they have made a brigadier of from our regiments. We are sorry to loose Colonel Sully but I suppose he deserves promotion & we will have to submit to the powers that be. Maj. Morgan has lately been made Lieutennant Colonel in the place of Lieutennant Colonel Miller who has been appointed Colonel of the 7th Minnesota Now I expect Lieutennant Colonel Morgan will be appointed Colonel of the Regt. & the thing will be straight.

We are expecting our pay every week & have been for the last 3 or 4 weeks and it will be apt to come before long. I expect we will get 4 months pay when it comes. The boys are all geting along about as usual. Johnny Goodrich is sick and in the hospital. He has looked very bad for several weeks & when I asked him what the matter was he would answer nothing. He kept up just as long as he could and I would not be sur-prised if he had a pretty hard time of it. Boult Soule is at Camp Curtain Harrisburg Pennsylvania. I have not felt first rate for a few days but this morning I begin to feel a little like I used to. The Dr. gave me some of his pills and powders but I don't know whether there was any virtue in them or not for I did not take them. As near as I can figure out them that take the most of the poisons get poisoned the worst and therefore I use none and get well first. Quinine and Opium are the principle drugs now used.

All that ails me now is I am worn out by hard marching & exposure. I have lost some 40 or 50 lbs. in weight this last summer. When we left Camp Stone last Spring I weighed nearly 160. The heavyest that I ever did weigh was 162. I will feel all right again if I can get a week or so to rest in.

Oct. 2nd,

The crops must be very fine, the frosts have held off so long. Captain Messick is well. President Lincoln was here to see us yesterday P.M.

As ever yours in the army

Edward H. Bassett.

About this time, the brigade was joined by a new regiment, the 19th Maine, which like 21 other new regiments, had responded to Lincoln's call for 300,000 new troops. All the new regiments were raw recruits sent to rebuild McClellan's army after Antietam. The 900 new members of the Maine regiment were a welcome addition and were anxious to learn all they could from the veterans. Of course, they became the beneficiaries of a great deal of sound advice, which was liberally laced with tall tales and good natured humor meant to bolster the stature of their benefactors. Though the new men would prove to be fine soldiers in time, they were totally unfamiliar with drill, soldiering and the fine points of camp life. Their ignorance nearly proved fatal for some on October 4, 1862. There were many artillery percussion shells 8-to-10 inches in length and 3-or-4 inches in diameter, lying around the camp, left there after Miles' surrender at Harper's Ferry. In need of supports for their cooking pots, the new recruits found that, when placed around their fires, the shells made perfect legs for the large pots. With supper simmering in the pots, they responded to the call for evening dress parade. The event was soon interrupted by numerous loud hissing sounds, flashes and explosions that sent clouds of boiling water, steam, ashes and flying metal into the evening sky. At first, it was thought an attack had been mounted, but further investigation revealed the cause of the maelstrom. Fortunately, the men were not crowded around the cooking fires and no one was killed or seriously wounded. The newcomers bore the brunt of a good deal of joking about learning to cook with less violent and dangerous means than loaded shells.

Distributing Rations in Camp: Frank Leslie 1896
Note: The hardtack crackers in this sketch are obviously
generous portions. They actually measured about 3"by 3 ½".

The tone of the following letter regarding both the Indians in Minneosta and the Blacks in Virginia is not at all typical of

Edward. It is here apparent, that the hard marching and conditions have taken a toll on his morale. He is both exhausted and quite ill, his regiment has just suffered considerable losses and his negativism is a reflection of his condition.

Encamped on Bolivar Heights.Va.
Sunday October 5th, 1862.

Dear Father & Mother,

The weather is beautiful & it makes me think of the pleasant fall weather of Minnesota. How I would like to be there this fall with nothing to do but roam arround on the prairies & in the woods with the old shot gun hunting chickens & ducks & geese. Everything is very quiet here in fact there is nothing doing in camp except turning out three times each day for roll call & two hours drill each day except Saturday & Sunday. The rest of the time is spent in eating, drinking, sleeping, talking, reading & writing. Time wears away wearily. Every paper & book is looked over and over again until we get entirely sick of them. As for books we have but a very few for they are very heavy to carry and we could never have carried more than just barely our clothing on the recent marches over the mountains in Maryland. I very often wish I could have my old school books with me for I believe that I have forgotten what little I once did know. In writing I spell many of the words wrong & if I stop to think I cannot get one half of them right. To tell the truth a soldier's life is not very pleasant unless they can enjoy things that I never can. If we were quartered at some Fort or some place where we could stay several months we would soon have things diferent but here we cannot tell what moment we may be called upon to pack up & march although things don't look much like a move. Although we have no guards to keep us inside the camp it won't pay to go out for if we go down into Bolivar or Harpers Ferry we will be picked up by the Provost guard & set to work on the mountains cutting timber or shoveling on the earthworks & if we go back into the country we would be sure to run onto the patrol & get arrested & turned over to the Provost. So you see we are in close confinement on a large scale. I don't object to it for my part. I am glad it is so for there is no use in an army unless there is some way to govern them and there are so many that would not be of any use at all to the service if they were allowed to run as they would if there were not very stringent orders. I only look for the end of the war to set me and my spirit free on old Minnesota soil.

The papers say the rebel congress have decided to raise the black flag[53] & fight under it from now on out, giveing no quarters to prisoners but destroying everything they cannot use that they take from us. I only hope they have. If they don't lower it by the time the James River gets up high enough for the gun boats to get up to Richmond if their black flag don't come down it will be strange. I don't believe they will ever dare to raise the pirate flag over Richmond and if they do it on the field I guess it will be taken care of. They are in a rage about Lincoln's proclamation. I wish Lincoln or Davis had every negro in America & were forced to dispose of them in some way so there would not be another one seen on the continent as long as it stands. If they are all turned out loose & free in the United States then I am for another war if necessary to capture the whole race & send them to Africa or some of the islands where they can live by themselves or die out as they like. I have seen enough of them & although there are a few among them that might be tolerated, the majority of them are miserable creatures. They are the cause of this war although not to blame for it. To think of carying on a war like this just for the

---

[53] Give no quarter, meaning take no prisoners.

310

sake of freeing the slaves - it would be one of the most cruel things that could be done. I wish you could see some of these little villages in Va. where the people are all slave owners & traders. Of all the border states I believe that Va. is the one that ought to support the war and I have always been glad that it was stoped on this side of the Potomac. Boasting Va. has been pretty well tramped down by the armies & it will bear the marks for years to come. The Potomac & Shenandoah rivers are both about as low as they can get but I expect we will have rain this fall that will raise them to raging torrents. The Railroad bridge at Harpers Ferry is nearly complete & I expect the cars will soon cross. There is some talk about our staying here this coming winter but I know nothing definite about it. It will be an easy place to get supplies and after we get our camp fixed up we could live quite comfortable. If we stay here this winter we will be pretty sure to have very comfortable quarters & I hope it may be the last winter that I shall be compelled to stay in these parts. The town of Bolivar used to be a very pleasant place. The houses are mostly of brick and surrounded by shade trees. The gardens are full of peach trees but the fences arround them & the outbuildings are nearly all miserable shaby whitewashed concerns. It is about one mile from Harpers Ferry and on a good road which runs up to Hall Town & Charles Town thence on to Winchester. We have not got our pay yet but they say we will get it this week. I see by the St. Paul Press that there has been a treaty formed with the Chippewas of Minnesota & they seem to desire peace but there is no news from the Sioux tribe. I would not like to have any more trouble among the people & Indians on the frontier than possible but I would like to have the Indians give Sibley a trial just to see what he would do. You will most likely have a very cold winter up there this winter but I would much rather stand the cold, up there than wade in the mud that we have here in the winter.

Oct. 6th.

The boys are about as usual. Johnny Goodrich is geting along very well. I feel the best that I have for three weeks. All I needed was rest and I knew it. I used none of the Dr's poisons and I don't intend to. Winter is coming & we can feel its breath.

The 19th Maine regt. has been appointed to our brigade. They are a new regiment and a fine looking set of fellows.

Oct. 7th,

Pleasant this morning and all quiet as far as I know. I feel first rate. Captain Messick says that he got a letter from his wife last night. They were all well. He looks first rate & seems to stand soldiering well. He is the only commissioned officer that we have with us. The Lieutennant is sick & off east.

Please write in your next how many bushels of small grain was raised on the place this year. I suppose the 240 bushels of wheat was what father sowed himself. You are certainly lucky in geting the grain all in, in such good order. I hope to be there to help you next fall. Remember me to all the friends & excuse this long letter.

As ever yours in the U.S.A.

E. H. Bassett Co. G

Once again, Lincoln was besieged by the political hacks and radicals in Washington, all demanding that he remove McClellan. Naming a replacement was not simple matter. Who was qualified to be put in his place? Senator Benjamin Wade, who hated McClellan, said "Oh just put anybody." The President replied, *"Wade, anybody will do for you, but I must have somebody!"*

A couple of days after returning to Washington, October 6th, Lincoln sent a peremptory order through Halleck, in part it read:

"The President directs that you cross the Potomac and give battle to the enemy or drive him south. Your army must move now while the roads are good. If you cross the river between the enemy and Washington, and cover the latter by our line of operations, you can be reinforced with 30,000 men. If you move up the valley of the Shenandoah, not more than 12,000 or 15,000 can be sent you. The President advises the interior line between Washington and the enemy, but he does not order it. He is very desirous that your army move as soon as possible."

Almost any other General would have considered such an order from the Commander-In-Chief to be immediately obeyed, but McClellan simply chose to ignore it. He replied only by a wire to Halleck that his men could not march without shoes. Within a week he received 95,000 pairs of shoes and still did not follow the order.

On October 10th, Jeb Stuart moved with 1,800 hard-riding confederate cavalry troopers on a daring raid into Pennsylvania. Like a whirlwind, he, once again, rode completely around McClellan's army and back into Virginia. His path was left marked by the destruction of any Union military stores he found. He captured a number of prisoners and rode away with 1,200 very fine fresh horses, including a number of high-bred draft horses, complete with harnesses. Though pursued by three Union Cavalry leaders, the dashing cavalier was not to be taken.

Camped at Bolivar Va.
Oct. 11th, 1862.

Dear Parents:

It is a cloudy day and rains a little. We have had some very hot days lately and it seems like August weather and we have not had any frost for some two weeks. It has been so very dry this fall that I expect that the rainy season will soon commence and perhaps last all winter. We need rain very badly. Everything remains quiet as usual. Some think we will soon commence fixing up for winter. Three of our boys have returned from the hospital. They look well. One is Henry Wells that was wounded at the Battle of Savage Station. Three of our Co. have died in the Hospital since we left the peninsula. One is Sergt. Charles E. Davison of Faribault, S. J. Pearl of the same place & Theodore Williams. Davis died at Crany Island Va. Williams at Alexandria. There are two more that will not be apt to recover. Jonathan Goodrich is well or nearly so. He is about all the time. The rest of the boys are tough as ever, also Captain Messick. He never looked better & he feels first rate.

We were payed off on the 8th - 4 months wages -52 dollars. I had 6 dollars stopages on the 1st years clothing account but after paying it and squaring up all arround I find that I come out with the 52 dollars and out of debt. Now I am going to send you $45 & if you think it will pay I want you to buy as many good sheep with $15.00 of it as you can & give the best one to Elford and keep the rest for me & I will see that you are well paid for the trouble when I get out of the army and if I should not, you may have them all. I think they will pay as big interest as anything that I could get. The one I give to Elford & I want him to have all the increase, wool & all. The other $30 I want you to take and use it for your own benefit this winter to buy clothes or anything else that you need for your comfort this winter. We will have another payment due this month and I will try & send you something more if I can. I would send the money by Express if I could do so handyly but I will have to trust the mail again. I received a letter from Mother yesterday. I am very glad to hear from home so often & I hope it may not be long before we will meet there. The news in the papers is exciting. A small force of the grey backs have got into Pennsylvania. We also have accounts of a desperate battle at Corinth, Miss. I am going to send Elford a paper and some songs with the music. Tell him that I want to see him very much. I would like to help him eat some of them nice turkeys next New Years day.

We are going out on picket tomorrow and I expect to have a good time if it don't rain. Yesterday's mail brought the Faribault paper of the 1st. I see that the Indians are still troublesome but hope to hear of diferent times soon. We can get good bread for 10 & 20 cts. per loaf. Butter is 35 cts. per lb. chickens from 20 to 30 cts. apiece, Apples 4 for 5 cts. Potatoes 35 cts per peck and other things in proportion. So you see it costs to live here if you have to buy your provisions. Uncle Sam is very liberal yet. Genl Gorman says that we are the best fed army in the world. We are also geting new winter clothing. A good pair of boots such as I used to get at Oberons for $5.00 costs here from 4 to $5.50 per pair according to the kind of a tradesman you trade with. Jews are plenty & as mean as ever.

I will close remaining as ever

Yours in the Army

E. H. Bassett Co. G

1st Minnesota Volunteers.

Direct to Washington D.C.

ARMED RECONNAISSANCE

Sunday October 12, was a dark, dreary day and blankets

of fog lay in the valleys. Once again, the regiment was sent out on picket duty and, several times, noted they were being observed by the enemy from the hills. From the Maryland side of the river, they heard sporadic cannon fire during the afternoon—the sound resulted from Jeb Stuart's daring foray into the north. After being relieved the next morning, the men faced a cold, driving rain as they marched back to camp. That afternoon, the first brigade drill in some time was conducted. On Tuesday, the sun returned and morning drill was followed by an inspection of arms, ammunition and supplies and then an afternoon regimental drill. All this activity indicated that a movement would follow. As anticipated, at 8 PM orders came to be ready to march at dawn.

Before the sun brightened the Eastern sky, the men were up and preparing their breakfasts and rolling their blankets in light marching order. Shortly after setting out on the road toward Charlestown, ten miles west of Harper's Ferry where John Brown had met his end in a hangman's noose—they learned they were on a special assignment with six other regiments. The First Minnesota was placed at the front, as skirmishers, behind a small cavalry force. Near Halltown, enemy cavalry was encountered but withdrew. As the column topped a rise neared Charlestown, the enemy appeared in force with the apparent intent of making a stand. Artillery was rushed forward and the skirmishers dropped to the ground in front. An enemy gun, hidden in some brush, responded to their first shot and immediately received the full attention of the union gunners. Others joined the fray and a lively artillery duel at long range followed for nearly two hours, with many shells falling near the men. The wounding of a horse was the only apparent result of the exchange. The skirmishers were then sent quickly forward as the rebels made an equally hasty withdrawal.

It was early afternoon when the First Minnesota reached Charlestown. They found all the fences knocked down and three enemy cavalry units drawn up, ready to charge. After a brief halt, the advance continued and the confronting cavalry decided to charge to the rear instead of facing the threat before them. The Minnesota boys moved forward to capture the town and continued the pursuit of the enemy about four miles beyond. The night was now pitch-black and a heavy rain was coming down when the rebels withdrew, the decision was made to return to Charlestown. In the dark, the guides became confused and a miserable night was spent stumbling about in the pouring rain. Just before daylight, they found their way into town. The rain ended about noon as the march began back to camp at Harper's Ferry. General Hancock had determined that Lee's army was still in the valley and encamped about ten miles to the west, along Opequan Creek. All that had been gained was the capture of a large quantity of wheat and hay and the position of the enemy was learned.

Segment of period map from Frank Leslies' Illustrated
By: W.A. Lane

Encamped on Bolivar Heights, Va.
October 20th, 1862.

My Dear Parents:

Once more I seat myself with pen in hand to seek an interview with those that are dear to me but far away. How glad would I be if I could see you face to face & tell you what I would write if I knew how. But as we always have to be governed by surrounding circumstances it becomes us to submit to the ruleing powers gracefuly & try to be as contented as possible (or appear so at least). And accordingly I will have to submit to the power Military and be thankful for the privelege of writing to my friends.

Things are being taken care of about as usual without any visible change in the outside appearance of our lives although we feel that we are growing old in the service and we still cherish the hope of seeing peace restored to the people on the old footing with some slight alterations.

We went out on a reconoisance last week beyond Charlestown. We left camp early on the morning of the 17th & shoved out on the main pike. There was some fireing from the batteries on both sides & the shells fell at one time right in the midst of our Co. & several men in the regiment came very near being hit by the shot as they came rolling along in the open field, tearing through fences & everything else that opposed. No one was hurt however and the rebels were driven back. We advanced in fine order through Charlestown & soon had our pickets posted some two miles beyond. We held the town all night & until PM the next day when we fell back into our camp in just about 36 hours after leaving it. The boys are very well pleased with the trip, although it rained hard all one night and we were without shelter.

We took 1500 bushels of wheat at Charlestown that was intended for the rebel army besides over 100 prisoners that were sick in town. I heard this morning that Captain Pell of Co. I of the Minnesota 1st was taken prisoner by the enemy out there. He was Provost Marshall of Harpers Ferry & I suppose he was out with some prisoners to exchange. Genl Gorman has command of the division now, Genl Howard haveing gone home to recruit his health. Captain Messick is well & tough as ever. We cannot tell yet where we are going to stay this winter but Genl Gorman said this morning that there was no prospect of our leaving here soon. We have large bake ovens built and will soon have soft bread issued in the place of crackers. We can get butter for 35 cts, & cheese for 25 cts. per pound now.

I was on guard last night & I don't feel much like writing as you may judge from the looks of this letter. The last letter I wrote to you I think was dated Oct. 11th. If it goes through all right you will find some $45 in the green backs that I have made out to save. I hope to be able to send a little more the next time we are payed. I wish I was at home this fall I believe that I could make good wages there. But I suppose all the talk is about the wars & those that have not enlisted are thinking about defending themselves in case the Indians should come down upon them this winter. I hope you may be spared the trouble of any more Indian raids in future. If the Indians are not checked before they reach the settlements there will be a dreadful tale to relate for they will be met & fought by each man at his own door.

Hopeing to hear from you soon & also to see you, I will close this letter & try to write again when I feel more like it.

Yours as ever in the U. S. A. of the Potomac.

Edward H. Bassett,

Encamped on Bolivar Heights, Va.
October 23, 1862

My Dear Sisters,

We were out on picket all day yesterday and all night last night. We could see but a few of the enemy and there were some two miles distant riding around on horses. The weather was pleasant although the wind blew very hard. I am in excellent health now and feel as well as I ever did. We have not got the large tents yet, but I expect we will soon and be fixing up for winter.

I was down town the other day and how I wished that I could step on the train of cars that stood there on the track, just ready to start, and off to Minnesota but I know that I must wait. We have not got the rebels whipped yet. We must try once more at least 18 months more then if I am alive and well shall start for Minnesota I hope the war will end before that time. Some of the boys are talking of enlisting in the 2nd U.S. Cavalry but I shall stick to the Minnesota 1st sometime yet altho I would like very such to have a horse to ride instead of trudgeing around on foot.

Sunday PM Oct. 26th

An unfinished letter and A cold rainy day but still I hope for a change sometime. I am going to try and finish this letter and you will be glad perhaps to get three days later news from the Army.

It has been raining all day. We are now curled up in my little tent trying to finish this poor letter and thinking of the folks at home.

As ever your brother,

Edward

To Ella and Anna Bassett

Bolivar Heights, Va.
October 26, 1862

Dear Father,

As I was writing to Ella and Anna I thought I would also send you a few lines. It is a cold rainy day and is not very pleasant out but we have plenty of good warm clothes and blankets and make out to keep comfortable. We are laying still in our camp expecting every day to get orders to move or fix up for winter where we are. There is a chance for any of us that wish it to enlist in the regular Service and quite a number have already joined the 1st and 6 th U. S. Cavalry for the remaining 18 months of their enlistment, for my part I shall stay where I am although if I was sure we would have to serve our three years out I would like to get into the cavalry but poor as the prospect is I am going to risk it and if we are discharged in 6 months I will certainly save 12 months. I have just been reading the Central Republican of the 15th. I see that Genl Pope and Sibley have finally got the Indians quieted and it has turned out about as I thought it would.

It is reported here that the rebs are falling back from the Potomac and taking up winter quarters at Gordonsville. Our picket lines extend but about two miles from here now. I cannot see any prospect of the war ending this next winter but still I hope it may. I want to get back and help you on the farm. I mailed a letter to you on the 15th inst containing two twenty dollar treasury notes and one 5. I requested you to spend part of it in the purchase of some sheep if you thought it would pay and the balance you may have to use as you think best. I would be glad to have you write to me as soon as you can if you can find time but I know you must be very busy this fall and perhaps cannot find time to write much but please find time to write a short letter anyhow. We are all as well as usual. Capt Messick sends his respects.

Good by this time.

Your son,

Edward H. Bassett.

P.S. Genl Gorman has been appointed Military Governor of Harpers Ferry.

How are the prairie fires raging this fall? I hope you may not have any trouble from them.

E. H. Bassett

Co. G Minnesota 1st

Tuesday Morn 28th, all well just come from picket.

CHAPTER 19
BATTLE OF
FREDERICKSBURG

The six weeks during which the army was encamped on Bolivar Heights at Harper's Ferry were primarily consumed by building fortifications on the heights. The decision was finally made to fortify and defend this important transportation center. Between fighting, marching, poor rations and exposure, the men had been pretty well used up. After the railroad bridges at the ferry were rebuilt, supplies again began to arrive and worn out clothing was replaced, rations improved and life became bearable again.

At this time, the regular army forces were authorized to recruit members from the volunteer units for service in the Cavalry and Artillery. A strange decision it would seem. The regular military was apparently having difficulty filling its ranks with men of quality. The veteran ranks of the volunteer regiments were 'a plum to tempting to resist picking.' There were substantial inducements to consider enlisting in the regular army. The prospect of riding a horse instead of tramping in the heat or mud, while carrying a heavily loaded knapsack was an appealing thought. Service in a heavy artillery unit meant garrison duty in one location for long periods with decent quarters and food. Furthermore, it did not involve the rigors or dangers of infantry battles or long periods on the march. The downside was that if a soldier enlisted in a regular unit, his enlistment was extended to the end of the war. Too many, the loss of the camaraderie of their long time brothers-in-arms was too high a price to pay and they declined the tempting offer. Realizing the impact this pirating of manpower was having on his brigade, General Gorman placed a double guard around the camp and forbade the issuance of passes. Registering to enlist in a regular unit required leaving camp, crossing the river and going to the enlistment office. Anyone caught out of camp by the Provost Guard without a pass faced extended duty on work details. Some daring souls took the risk and bribed a guard before making the clandestine crossing. About 100 men of the First Minnesota thus left the regiment.

On October 30th, the peaceful interlude came to an end and, once again, the army was on the march. Under continual pressure from Washington to go after Lee, McClellan finally felt his army was ready. He began the move without even notifying Halleck or Lincoln of his plans. Tired of the continual haggling, he simply did not bother. This action might have been "the straw that broke the camel's back" and led to his dismissal a few days later.

The morning was spent packing up and getting ready for the march. After all the other brigades, wagons and materials started moving out on October 26th, the Minnesota regiment brought up the rear. The bugle sounded assembly at noon and the men shouldered their gear and rifles and set off. It was a beautiful, though rather warm, autumn afternoon as they marched down from the heights and crossed over the Shenandoah River on the last remaining pontoon bridge. As they moved into the Loudoun Valley beneath the Blue Ridge Mountains, the day grew oppressively hot. The new 19th Maine, immediately in front of the Minnesota men, had yet to become toughened to the rigors of the march. Like so many new regiments, they had left home supplied with everything that could be imagined. Their knapsacks were stuffed and blankets, bedrolls and overcoats were neatly rolled and strapped on top. By mid-afternoon the well intentioned abundance became a loathsome burden. As anticipated, the Minnesota boys were soon marching through all manner of castoffs. Experience had already taught them the advantage of traveling light. As they marched along, the only decision they had to contemplate was whether they would be most pleased with a new overcoat or blanket. Sure enough, the first things to go were the new overcoats and heavy blankets on top, because they were the easiest to remove while marching along in the column. By late afternoon the First was well supplied for the winter that would soon arrive.

It was after dark when they halted and camped in a scenic wood on a hillside overlooking the Loudon Valley to the west. The forest floor was covered with a thick carpet of leaves that provided a welcome mattress for the weary soldiers. Twinkling camp fires dotted the valley for miles; the hillside soon glowed with the light of a thousand more, as the men made coffee and supper. Pickets were placed on the crest and the valley soon took on the stillness of the night, interrupted only by the sound of 100,000 sleeping men.

Camped near Snickersville, Virginia [54]
Nov. 1st, 1862

Dear Father & Mother

We left our camp on Bolivar Heights day before yesterday in the PM and crossed the Shenandoah River on a pontoon right at the mouth. Taking the road down the Potomac we marched down some 2 or three miles,

---

[54] Snickersville was a small hamlet of about 150 people 18 miles south of Harper's Ferry. Paris was just east of Ashby Gap, 28 miles from Harper's Ferry with a population of 168.

then took back into the country in a valley that extends up between the Blue Ridge & what is called the Bull Run range. The roads are very dry & good although the country looks rather rough to me. The inhabitants are mostly farmers but necesarily on a small scale. Genl Burnside crossed over the Potomac several days before we moved & has pushed out into the country without much trouble. I guess we have not heard anything particular from him. Genl Lee has fallen back towards Richmond and I suppose our Genls are trying to take advantage of it & I hope there will be something done this fall & winter that will bring the rebels to terms for it seems to me that there has been enough men gathered into the field now to round the warriors of the Confederacy up in Richmond so that they can't get out. Some have an idea that they will sue for peace this winter but I have no such hopes.

The boys from Morristown are all well. There is one or two cases of ague in the Company but otherwise the health of the Co. is good. I feel first rate & think I can stand 18 months more soldiering easyer than I have the last 18 months. We have just 50 men on duty now & one half of our time has passed. The remaining 50 are tough you may bet. There has 5 of our Comp. enlisted in the Regular Cavalry, three in the 6th, one in the 2nd, one in the 1st, Joseph Bemis of Faribault is in the 6th Co. F. They enlisted for the remaining 18 months of their first 3 years or during and will have to stay if the war ends today. We are camped in a fine grove of Chestnut & Hickory but it does not seem one half as pleasant as the grove up arround the lake back of Mr. Sprague's. (in Minnesota) We have the Faribault Paper of the 22 Oct. We have a new Chaplain. He is a Methodist free and easy as ever. The boys like him so far very well. He has been with the 4th Regt. & was also in the Indian war in Minnesota We had a large bakery built where we were camped at Bolivar but we left without getting any benefit from it. Our luck, but we have plenty of hard bread & coffee & sugar, so I guess we will not starve.

As you have good crops & they are bringing good prices I hope you will try and be as well contented as possible & although you are in debt some for the farm, I think that will all come out straight in a short time. I will try and help you a little by saving what I can of my wages and I hope that by the time the war is over the whole thing will be squared up & then I think that in a year or so we can get a good comfortable house built and you would certainly then have a very pleasant home in a good country & happiness will certainly attend those that have a good home if they are contented. I certainly think you will be contented when you have the farm fixed up & the country gets settled and society formed. [55]

As morning dawned, the men were already building fires, cooking breakfast and making coffee in preparation for the day's march. Learning that, once again, they would be waiting for the rest of the army to move out in advance, they assembled for their ninth bimonthly muster, which marked the end of the first 18 months of their 36-month enlistment. The assembly brought home the impact of the losses that were incurred during the marching and fighting over those arduous months. The treks from Washington to Bull Run, Ball's Bluff, the many battles on the peninsula, Vienna, Flint Hill, South Mountain and Antietam had taken a great toll. The men paused to wonder as they surveyed their ranks—where now only about one third of the numbers that stood in line just months before, were assembled. They puzzled over what was accomplished by all the brave lives that were forfeited for the cause in which they still so strongly believed. As they waited through the day they talked of times past and

---

[55] This letter was apparently not completed due to the regiment being on the march. In all probability, it was simply included with the following letter when Edward had a chance to send them out.

wondered aloud if their time would soon come to join their lost comrades.

The day passed as unit after unit marched out into the beautiful valley. Masses of cavalry, infantry and wagons moved into the distance, followed by a huge herd of cattle brought from Maryland. By mid-afternoon, a blanket of cold air settled upon the valley and gave warning of the winter soon to come. The sound of the bugle awakened the men early the next morning, Saturday, November 1st, as they rolled out of their warm blankets to find a low-hanging, grey sky above and the ground covered with white frost. Hot coffee and breakfast were soon prepared and, after a short delay, they joined the march. Their path carried them up the Loudon Valley on the eastern slopes of the Blue Ridge Mountains, with the Bull Run range bordering the valley further east. The men enjoyed the panoramic view of the fertile valley dotted with its many small farms and villages, each outlined by neat rail fences. The people were all strong secessionists but were willing to sell their produce for high prices. At this time, the men had quantities of counterfeit Confederate currency, supplied to the army by an enterprising printing house in Philadelphia and were happy to pay the prices asked without argument. Though foraging was strictly forbidden, the bounty of crops, fruit and plump livestock was a temptation too great to resist and provided many a fine meal.

Camped for the night at Paris near
Ashby's Gap Loudon Co. Va.
November 4th, 1862

Dear Parents,

We have been on the march all day. This place was left by the rebs this morning. They have passed through the gap & our troops are in close pursuit. As yet we have not got a chance at them. I am well & tough as ever. The roads remain good & things indicate the rebs are to be tried once more. We may fetch up in front of Richmond soon. Genl McClellan was up with our front this PM. He looks well & we still have confidence in him. We are feasting on secesh fowls, Mutton & beef, which we take where-ever we can find it (the boys are now picking two nice young Turkeys that they captured this evening. The inhabitants are all secesh & prefer confederate scrip (made in Philadelphia) to Uncle Sam's green backs.

Genl Sully commands Gorman's Brigade & Gorman commands Sedgwicks Division. You speak of C. E. Davison. I don't know but I was mistaken about his being dead. We had such a report & it was generaly believed in camp but I have since heard that it is not so. One of our boys that has been in Minnesota on a furlough since last June returned last eve. He looks well. Minnesota is certainly a good place for invalids. I am glad that money went safe. I had some fears that it was lost. Several of the boys have lost some. I would like to be there to kill some of them wild geese that you speak of & if I ever get there I will give them a trial. Captain is well. He got a picture last night of his little boy.

Excuse my pencil for the lead is very soft. I will try & find ink next time.

Good by this time.

Edward

Co. G. Minnesota 1st.

Period Map – Frank Leslie's Illustrated by W. A. Lane

During the succeeding days, the army advanced to the few gaps in the Blue Ridge Mountains where they were challenged by units of Jeb Stuart's Cavalry. Numerous skirmishes developed, though none of consequence. The Minnesotans were involved at Snickers' and Ashby's gaps. A few rounds of artillery fire and a large column of advancing infantry convinced the rebels to withdraw.

Mathew Marvin had returned to the regiment after nursing the accidental wound to his leg at Harrison's Landing. The rigors of marching soon made it clear his wound was not yet well healed. The resolve of these men is seen in a letter he wrote:

"My game leg is sorer than ever & the blisters nearly cover my feet but they are not as bad as my leg. Would give a Kingdom for a horse or a World for a mule or my life for an Ox. I want to rid(e) anyway but I wont ask for . . .sick leave as long as I can stand up. I will keep up or bust a trying."

As morning broke on November 7th, the weather had become quite cold, with temperatures below freezing and a strong wind was blowing. By mid-morning, it was snowing and General Sully had the camp relocated to a nearby wood to provide some cover. Some cattle were brought up and slaughtered, thus offering a hearty meal. The tallow was rubbed on shoes for waterproofing.

Saturday morning, November 8th, the forest floor was covered with four inches of snow and beyond the woods, it was deeper and drifted. The men crawled out of their bed rolls, tied their shoes and put on their belts. The strong wind had abated, though the air was very cold. Warmth from the morning cook fires and numerous cups of hot coffee drove the chill from their bones and they were soon ready to march. The sun came out, causing the snow on the frozen ground to thaw just enough so that balls of frozen mud stuck to the bottoms of their shoes. The regiment was guard for the wagon train and marched all day on the frozen clods of earth left behind by the wagon mules. The poor beasts struggled with mud frozen under their hoofs and toiled greatly to pull their loads up even slight grades. Wagon wheels became encrusted with the mud balls making them even harder to pull, some sliding and overturning on the hills. It was dark when Rectortown was reached; it had been a hard day's march. Everyone's feet were soaked and their bodies ached from carrying their loads on the uneven ground. On they marched, as the temperature dropped. It was 2 AM when they finally halted, after 20 hours on their feet. With no tents, they looked for a place to lie down. However, the ground everywhere was covered with snow. Kicking and scraping with their wet shoes, they cleared away the white carpet as best they could, rolled up in their blankets and were asleep. Morning found them soon enough. Stiff, sore and shivering in the cold, they built roaring fires and ate their breakfast of coffee, salt pork and crackers.

Warrenton, Faquier Co. Va.
Nov. 9th, 1862.

Dear Parents:

As we have stoped once more I will try & write a few lines. I am well although rather tired for we have been marching most of the time for the last twenty four hours without much to eat or anything else to make marching comfortable without it in our Knapsacks, which we find are quite handy when we stop these cold nights without any tents. We had about one inch of snow fall the PM of the 7th & that night it seemed quite like winter. It has mostly disappeared now but the weather is quite cool. We have not encountered the rebs yet on this trip but once & then they were flying as fast as possible from before our cavalry & horse artilery. I think that we will march from here in the direction of Culpeper and we ere long will be on the Rhapahannoc or (perhaps in Richmond). The Genls are concentrating their commands & I hope there will be some good done by the move.

I often think of home & you when I am marching along nights & when I come to fix my bed on the cold damp ground to try to take a little sleep. I think of the many times that I used to go to the cupboard & steal a cake or crust of bread as I passed up stairs and I remember that you used to say that I would not allways have it to run to. I begin to realize what it was to have everything nice right at hand. I hope that I may get to see that again.

It is rumored that Genl McClellan has been superseded by Burnside but as to the truth of it, I cannot say. I am not quite discouraged or ready to say quit but I would like to have the war end and I hope for an honerable settlement of the troubles. I sent you a letter when we were laying at Paris, or Ashby's Gap. We left there on the morning of the 6th and the rebs soon had their scouts in the town but they have not come in there in any large force yet. The boys are generaly in good spirits & tough as ever. Warrenton has been quite a fine town but looks some like a whipped chicken now. Rather mean. The roads are good. We have had no rain for a long time. I suppose you are now haveing a foretaste of a Minnesota Winter.

Rest assured that I remember you all as I roam.

Edward

McClellan relieved by Burnside
Drawing by: A.R. Waud, Harper's Weekly

Rumors that General McClellan was being removed surfaced on the November 8th and were confirmed the next day while the army was near Warrenton. Lincoln had ordered General Ambrose Burnside to immediately replace McClellan. The entire army was shocked by this latest change of command. Lochren wrote:

"Officers and men were exasperated almost to the point of mutiny, but this feeling was repressed by the bearing and counsels of McClellan himself. Burnside was personally liked and respected, and the more that it was known that he was a warm friend of McClellan. But his ability for leadership was doubted, and the army felt hopeless, under the conviction that, whoever was nominally put in command, Stanton and Halleck would direct all movements, and they were as cordially detested and distrusted as McClellan was beloved and confided in. Deepest sorrow and despondency prevailed on November 10th, when the army was drawn up to take leave of McClellan. Strong men shed tears. A majority of the line officers of the First Minnesota sent in their resignations, but, on the representation of Gen. Sully that such an act, in the face of the enemy, might subject them to disgraceful imputation, the resignations were recalled."

Monday Nov. 10th.

It is a very pleasant day. We are laying in camp and taking a little rest.

General McClellan left this morning at eight o'clock. The troops were all drawn up in line by the road & cheered him as he passed. There was also a salute fired by the batteries. We all hate to have him leave & feel as if we had lost one of our best friends. It is rumored that he is to be the commander-in-chief & that Halleck is going west but you will most likely know more about it by the time this will reach you than I do now. We all had confidence in him & were sorry to see him leave. I only hope for the best & shall be glad when the war is ended & we are once more enjoying peace & liberty.

Edward

General McClellan's Farewell, Harpers Weekly Nov. 29, 1862

General Burnside was a very likable, loyal patriot—a close friend of McClellan and a fine figure of an officer. He had taken his new assignment under vigorous protest and told President Lincoln that McClellan was the best man for the job. Burnside's tardy presence on the field of Antietam cast doubts in the ranks as to his qualifications. As the battle raged, he had thrown brigade after brigade onto the stone bridge in the face of withering fire, only to be cut down like sheep. His refusal to consider crossing the stream at the numerous fords, both up and downstream from the bridge, had cost many lives. The delay in getting his men across likely changed the day from a great victory into a stalemate. To his own credit, he was the first to admit that his new job would have been better served by someone else. Still, when ordered to do so, he undertook the task the best way he knew how and gave it all he had. As quickly as the reorganization of his staff could be accomplished, Burnside reorganized the army into three Grand Divisions and reassembled the scattered units of the army at Warrenton. This process consumed ten days. The right Grand Division was led by General Sumner, the Second Corps, including the First Minnesota, which was a part of this division, was commanded by General Couch,

President Lincoln and General Halleck strongly urged Burnside to mount an attack on the enemy before winter set in. He submitted a plan on November 9th, which, after some deliberation, was approved for immediate implementation. The plan was to concentrate the army at Warrenton and feign movements against Culpeper Court House, Orange Court House and Gordonsville as diversions. He would then rapidly shift the army southeast and cross the Rappahannock on pontoon bridges at Fredericksburg. This location would provide a valuable base of operations since supplies could be brought up the Potomac to Aquia Creek Landing and, then, shipped by rail to Fredericksburg. The high ground to the west of Fredericksburg would afford a commanding base that could be easily defended. From this base, a movement on Richmond, 48 miles due south, could be launched before Lee could unify his forces and determine what Burnside's intentions were. Success depended on haste, perfect timing and the assumption that Robert E. Lee would be slow to act because he was fooled by the feined movements. Because Burnside had no pontoon bridge equipment with the army, Halleck was to arrange for its arrival just ahead of the main force at Fredericksburg. Why Burnside did not cross the Rappahannock at any of the numerous fords available just north of Fredericksburg instead of depending on the pontoons remains a mystery.

The army began marching to Fredericksburg on November 15th. The lead elements arrived at Falmouth, a small village on the east bank of the river and about 1 mile north, on November 17th. The plan began to unravel almost immediately when it became apparent that Halleck had failed to deliver the pontoon bridges. Messages were immediately sent to

Washington urgently requesting the bridges be delivered without delay. General Sumner arrived on the scene to discover the enemy presence in Fredericksburg was only a token force of 500 cavalry and infantry. He urged an immediate crossing of the river to expel the rebels from the town and to take command of the heights to the west. Burnside's failure at this point would later prove very costly. He allowed fear of making a mistake to cloud his judgment. Worried that the autumn rains might swell the river and make the fords unusable, leaving Sumner cut off and subject to destruction, he chose to wait for the bridges.

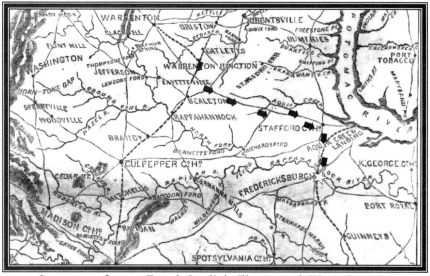

Segment of map–Frank Leslie's Illustrated–W. A. Lane
Arrows indicate line of march.

Encamped near Fredricksburg, Va.
November 19th, 1862

Dear Parents,

We are encamped some three or four miles from the river in a grove of oak & hickory. We camped here in the PM of the 17th. The rebels were then in possession of the town & had a battery planted so as to command the road but our battery gave them a shower of shell and shot that made Secesh Skedadle & our forces are now fixing the fords to cross. We were three days marching from Warrenton to this place. Our Brigade marched in the fields by the side of the road. The country is not very thickly settled but you will find once in a few miles an old farmer with a fine house and perhaps a dozen little buildings about 12 feet square all whitewashed which were the (stables) or Negro houses. The soil is rather poor & there are a great many old fields that have grown up to Pine but there is a good supply of Oak & Hickory. The few inhabitants that remain on their farms are Secesionists and own it. Many of them make no professions of loyalty to the U.S.

I am in excellent health & I don't remember the time that I ever felt better since I left home. The boys are all quite well & I guess will stand this winter's campaign very well. I hope we will see something done this winter that will tell towards ending the difficulties. Brigadier Genl Howard is in command of Sedgwick's Division. He is an old Methodist preacher as also is his Adjutant Genl & one or two other of his staff Officers. Genl Sully has command of the Brigade. The weather is very mild. There has not been any freezing this fall yet to amount to anything.

We have not had any rain for a long time & the roads are dry. It looks some like rain now & I expect we will have some mud before long in the place of snow. Captain is well & got a letter from home lately. We have small tents yet but make out quite comfortable but we make the fences suffer wherever we camp.

Please remember me to all inquireing friends.

 As ever

Edward   Co. "G"

The first of the pontoon bridges did not arrive until November 25th. By this time Confederate General Longstreet's Corps and Stonewall Jackson's Corps had both arrived and Lee was no longer to be fooled by anything. He moved into Fredericksburg with 90,000 men and 275 pieces of artillery and began building earthworks and rifle pits along the west bank of the river. He also built several lines of defense on the hillside behind the town. He placed most of his guns on Marye's Heights, about 1 ½ miles back from the river, and now enjoyed a nearly unassailable position.

General Burnside had a force of 312 guns and over 120,000 men, mostly laying in camps around Falmouth and building fortifications on their side of the river. Finally, on November 27th, most of the necessary pontoons had arrived. He mounted 147 of his guns on Stafford Heights just north and east of the town to prevent any confederate counter attack. Why he delayed two more weeks to put the long awaited bridges to use can only be surmised. Wait he did, building works and preparing for what looked like a siege, rather than an assault. This further delay gave Lee even more opportunity to dig in and acquire more supplies.

Falmouth, Virginia.
Sunday Dec.7th, 1862.

Dear Parents,

I don't know but you will think that I have forgotten home entirely if I don't write more often but I can assure you that I still remember you & there is not a day that I do not think of home.

We encamped on the 17th of Nov. on the banks of the Rappahannoc & have moved our camp three times since & still are within one half mile of the place where we first camped. The enemy was then laying in camp on the oposite side of the river. As the troops came in they were camped arround on the surrounding hills & in a few days there was an army of several thousands laying oposite Fredricksburg & the next thing was to throw up fortifications & if we have not got a second Yorktown we have got something equaly as big. The rebels are laying in camp in and arround the city (Fredericksburg) throwing up earthworks & mounting guns. We also have men at work day & night building breastworks & cutting trenches. Our pickets & those of the enemy are stationed on the bank of the river which is very narrow & shallow here so that they can talk with each other without speaking above the common tone of voice. They could easily shoot each other but for the convenience of all concerned they content themselves by cursing each other & general conversation about the war and soldiering. There is one Regt. from our Brigade detailed to build roads &c. which are geting bad. I heard yesterday that we have 130,000 men at this place.

There was some 4 inches of snow fell on the PM of the 5th & it is quite cold now. Our tents consist of a piece of common cotton about four feet square and we are surely haveing fine times these cold days. (The officers have large tents.) The boys are cutting logs and trying to build houses but as they do not know how long we are going to stay we don't know what to do. Rations are scarce & poor but the health of the boys is remarkable good & none doubt the good intentions of our praying Generals. Our Chaplain thinks it is a hard place to serve the Lord but still takes courage when he thinks of the Paymaster & the green backs that are forthcomeing. He gave us a lecture on Geology one night this week. He seems to be well informed but he cannot tell it in a very nice way. Still he is a fine old fellow.

I have received several letters from home every week. I got one from Ella yesterday but I cannot write much until the weather moderates which will not be long I hope. The boys are all well & tough as ever. There has been one death in our Co. since we left

Bolivar. I will have to close for it is cold & the wind is blowing.

I remain as ever yours in the U.S. A.

Edward

On Wednesday afternoon, December 10th, Burnside called a meeting of his commanders to review orders and asked what they thought of the battle plan. Brigadier General Rush Hawkins summed up their opinions when he answered:

"If you make the attack as contemplated it will be the greatest slaughter of the war; there isn't infantry enough in our whole army to carry those heights if they are well defended."

True to his now apparent incompetence, Burnside had made his plans and was determined they be carried out.

Finally, on the morning of December 11th, the engineers began assembling 6 bridges across the Rappahannock. It was 3 o'clock in the morning, a blanket of heavy fog lay in the valley and the ground was covered with snow. Assisted by infantry, they hauled out the heavy boats, slid them into the river and begin laying the beams and planks. By daylight they were within 100 yards of the far shore. As the fog thinned, the men working on the bridges came under intense fire from rebel sharpshooters in the trenches on the opposite side of the river and hidden in houses. They were forced back dragging their dead and wounded comrades with them. Determined to do their duty, nine times these stalwart lads faced the hissing hail of rebel lead, only to be cut down. Hundreds would lie dead or wounded before the deed was done. An artillery bombardment was ordered. Thunder from the guns on the hill rolled down the valley until more than 5000 shells pounded the beautiful little town. The cannons fell silent, and the rebel sharpshooters took up new positions among the ruins. Finally, Burnside's subordinates convinced him to send infantry across in boats to clear the sharpshooters out of the town. The 7th Michigan and 19th Massachusetts, totaling about 400 men, crossed under a devastating barrage of musketry fire. Though many were killed or wounded, they fought doggedly house by house and established a beachhead. More men followed and, by nightfall, the bridges were in place and the town was in Union hands.

The First Minnesota received orders to be ready to move at dark on December 10th, a time later changed to daylight on the next morning. They drew the usual extra 60 rounds of ammunition, prepared three days of cooked rations, wrote letters home and wrote their names and addresses on slips of paper that they pinned inside their clothing. Everyone knew full well the nature of the battle to come and the price in death, suffering and blood that would be extracted. Standing under an overcast sky; shivering in the strong cold wind and watching snow flakes fall at evening roll call, they were informed that they would be called in time to prepare breakfast before moving out in the morning.

"Take only overcoats, woolen and rubber blankets and fill canteens with hot coffee," they were told before retiring to the comparative shelter of their tiny tents to sleep. Blaring bugles shattered the frozen winter air at 2 AM. Crawling from their shelters to find the ground covered with six inches of snow, the men struggled to get fires going. The stillness suited the anticipation in the thoughts of these men as they waited to march into the valley of death. Breakfasts were prepared in the darkness and eaten in the tents. Canteens were filled, knapsacks packed with four-day's rations and extra ammunition, bed rolls strapped on, trouser legs tucked tightly inside the top of a second pair of socks and all was ready as they marched out of camp at sun-up.

Bombardment of Fredericksburg Dec. 11, 1862
Drawing from Harper's Weekly Dec. 27, 1862
(Federal Guns are firing from hills in right background)

They halted in the heavy morning fog two miles downstream along the north bank of the Rappahannock River, only to find the bridges they were to cross were not ready. Always watching out for his men, General Sully placed them behind the ridge of the hill along the river, safe from the bullets zipping freely about. The artillery batteries on the right drew continuous enemy fire. Waiting for something to happen soon become tiresome and, as the fog lifted, small groups broke away to peek over the crest to see what was happening. Any head poked above the hilltop for long was certain to get the interest of a rebel sharpshooter. It was sundown by the time the bridge was ready and General Couch's Second Corp, including the First Minnesota in General Sully's First Brigade, moved across and into the streets of Fredericksburg.

Fredericksburg, VA.; Feb. 1863 from east Bank of
Rappahannock River–Photo by Timothy O'Sullivan

The troops formed on the river bank and moved directly
into the town. Fighting ensued until nearly midnight as they
drove the rebels from the houses and their places of
concealment. The men took the houses as fair spoils of war
since the confederates had occupied them as cover for their
sharpshooters that had killed and wounded so many. They
freely helped themselves to whatever they wanted. Soon wine,
liquor, tobacco and food were found in abundance and fine
stuffed furniture filled the streets as many joined in a raucous
celebration. December 12th, the rest of the army crossed the
river and positioned itself for the battle to come. Sniper and
shellfire continuously raked the streets. Outhouses and picket
fences were relegated to duty as cooking fires. Soon after
dark, the First Minnesota was moved to the front on picket
duty where they spent a cold, unsheltered night. The next
morning, their division under General Howard, moved to the
right of the army. During the whole forenoon, they were under
heavy artillery fire.

The Confederates were positioned to the west of town
where an open plain ended at the foot of a range of steep,
broken hills. Running along the base of the hills was a long
stone wall and, behind it was an old stage road worn down by

long use and commonly referred to as 'the sunken road.' This was a formidable obstacle, especially since it sheltered veteran rebel infantry, four rows deep, able to deliver a wall of deadly fire. Marye's Heights rose behind and was now terraced by rows of entrenchments manned by more Confederate veterans commanded by General Lonsgstreet. Each row was elevated to allow fire over the heads of the men in front. Added to this formidable array of firepower were hundreds of cannons, able to target nearly any point below.

At noon, the dying began in earnest. Here, Burnside made the same mistake he had made at Antietam. He committed his forces in a piecemeal fashion in a frontal attack on a heavily defended position. Instead of exploiting his superior numbers and moving to flank the enemy on the weak left side, he fed his men into a maelstrom of enemy lead as they charged across the open ground. Brigade after brigade and division after division charged forward only to be mowed down like wheat before the scythe. On and on the butchery went. By late afternoon, thousands lay dead or dying on the field. The First Minnesota and the other regiments of the brigade[56] watched the slaughter from a place of *'comparative safety'* and knew full well what awaited them now. Placed on an elevated ridge on the extreme right in support of Kirby's artillery, the regiment spent most of the afternoon exposed to a tremendous cannonade directed at Kirby's battery. The call came for General Sully to send out the First Brigade, the only brigade remaining of the entire Second Corps. Sully, realizing the utter futility of another attempt, either refused to obey the order or it was countermanded. In any event, the brigade did not charge. As the day and battle drew to a close, fourteen charges had been made against the stone wall and no man had gotten within 25 yards of it. For all the death and suffering, nothing had been gained.

---

[56] The other regiments were the 34th New York, 82nd New York, 16th Massachusetts and 19th Maine.

Union forces massed on the plain below attack Marye's Heights.
Illustrated London News Jan. 31, 1863

Encamped near Falmouth, Va.
December 18th, 1862.

Dear Parents,

As there has been another terrible battle I know that you will be anxious to hear from me. I should have written sooner but for the cold. The Army of the Potomac has been repulsed with a terrible loss & the enemy are still in posession of their first lines & our army has gone into their old camps which they occupied before the battle. We left our camp on the 11th & marched down oposite the City of Fredricksburg where we lay all day. There was heavy cannonading commenced before sunrise that morning & about noon all our batteries that could opened on the city and bombarded it about one hour. Part of the city was burnt & there is not a single house that escaped without from one to 50 canon shot through & through them so that many of them are completely ruined. The first of our troops that crossed the river was the 7th Mich. They crossed about sundown on the 11th on a pontoon which had been laid during the day under a continuous fire from the enemy. The Mich. boys had a brisk skirmish with the rebs but they forced the rebs back driving them out of the street so we followed soon after the Mich, boys & the bullets were flying the whole length of the bridge when we crossed, but they soon fell back and our men had possession of the city before 10 o'clock that night. The next morning our pickets were stationed outside the city & the rebs threw a few shell during the day. Our regt. was on picket on the night of the 12th but were relieved early in the morning. On the 13th the great fight came off. Our Genls done the ordering and the soldiers charged up the hill and tried to force the rebs from their position but it was of no use. They were shot down by the hundreds. The fight raged until it was dark and we had nothing gained. There was some of the hardest fighting done that day that has been done during the war. Our regt. was ordered to charge but they were finally countermanded so we did not get into the hardest part of the fight but the shell burst all arround. On the 14th we lay in one of the principle streets all day. Our regiment went on picket again at night where we remained until about 10 o'clock on the night of the 15th when we were relieved & came back onto this side of the river. The last day that we were on picket the rebel sharpshooters kept us low all day. We had dug rifle pits during the night & we had to lay in them all day for every man that showed his head got a bullet after him. The rebs tried to shell us out of our pits but it was of no use although they threw the shell on all sides but not a man moved. The 127th Penn. regt. which was on our right run away & behaved disgracefully so that our flank was open to the enemy if they had wished to make an attack. It left us in a very dangerous situation and it would have been easy for the enemy to have killed nearly all of us if they had dared to try it. Genl Howard conplimented us very highly for our good conduct on that day after we came back onto this side of the river. We came right back into our old camp where I expect we will stay some time unless the rebs drive us out. Our loss has been very heavy but that of the rebels has been but light. (I don't pretend to say that McClellan would have whiped the rebels here. But I ask, has Burnside.) Who shall be the next one to try them.

The people of the city had all left before the bombardment commenced but their houses were full of nice furinture & everything that they had. I saw some splendid libraries and got some few small books to read but I could not carry many. We also got plenty of fresh pork & beef, chickens, also flour, meal, preserves, honey wines, tobacco besides any amount of other stuff that was left. Some of the boys got things that were quite valueable such as watches, rings & silver cups.

(The balance of this letter no longer exists.)

Fighting in the streets of Fredericksburg. Harpers Weekly

After dark the brigade was withdrawn and placed on picket duty at the edge of town and, in the morning, moved back to Princess Ann Street, where they remained there all day under occasional artillery fire. The enemy guns were trained to fire down the streets and any time a group of soldiers appeared, they were the immediate object of the rebel gunners.

The night of the 14th the Minnesota Regiment, and four others, were sent out to relieve General Sykes' Division. From their position, where the most intense fighting had taken place, they could hear enemy picks and shovels at work on their trenches. Upon realizing how untenable the Union situation was, they sent for tools and by daylight had completed a respectable entrenchment. The next afternoon the enemy had moved a cannon to a high ridge along the river and subjected the line to heavy enfilading fire from the right. The shells rained down exploding overhead and bounding along the line. Three regiments on the right broke and withdrew in disorder under the barrage, leaving the right flank of the First Minnesota exposed. True to their reputation, they stood firm and held the rest of the line intact. General Howard observed with alarm as the three regiments broke and ran. When the Minnesota men stood their ground, he turned to Sully and exclaimed: *"Sully, your First Minnesota doesn't run!"*

Sully calmly replied: *"General, the First Minnesota never runs!"*

The night of December 15th, they withdrew and crossed the bridge, returning to their old camp, this fight was over.

The men were very disheartened by their continual poor leadership. The sacrifice of so many good young men, they felt, should at least produce some positive results. The only apparent result before them was the ghastly toll of death and suffering. The Battle of Fredericksburg had cost the Union 12,153 killed, wounded and missing; while the Confederates had lost 5,377.

CHAPTER 20
WINTER CAMP
AT FALMOUTH, VA.

At this time, the morale of the army reached a low ebb. The defeat at Fredericksburg and the tremendous losses incurred, preyed on the minds of officers and men alike. Hopes for a successful winter campaign against Richmond had been dashed. It was a melancholy march back to their old camps where they would spend nearly five months. Here they were confronted by the folly of their exuberance of only a few days ago—the huts they had built for winter and then burned to the ground when they marched off "to defeat Lee and capture Richmond". The officers and men in the ranks blamed Burnside wholly for the fiasco. The unheeded call for the return of McClellan was common in camp. A few days after the battle, a grand review of the Second Corps was held in camp with Generals Burnside and Sumner present. As the troops marched by Burnside, the usual rousing cheers were replaced by a deafening silence. In an effort to relieve the embarrassing situation, General Sumner ordered General Couch to call for three cheers for General Burnside. The Corps and Division Commanders rode up and down the line waving their hats and swords to little avail. The men felt betrayed by a poor commanding officer; only a few half hearted cheers could be heard.

Intent upon snatching victory from the jaws of defeat, Burnside began immediately to make plans for another winter campaign to destroy Lee. Though no orders were issued to go into winter quarters here, the men reasoned that no one would be foolish enough to order a major move in the middle of the winter. They needed better shelter and decided to build it.

The building began spontaneously and, then, spread like wildfire. Equipped with thousands of axes from the supply wagons, the men spread out over the land like a swarm of leaf cutter ants. For miles up and down the Rappahannock,-the hills and ravines were laid bare and naked. The working swarm felled the trees, cut them into logs and dragged every useable piece back to its nest. A good deal of time and labor was expended building shelters suitable for the cold and snow to come. Winter quarters for the men usually amounted to a small rectangular hut roughly 12 feet-by-6 feet or 7 feet by 9 feet in size and housed four men that "buddied up" to build the hut. The walls, built of logs, stood 3-to-4 feet high with a raised ridge pole running down the center. The hut was covered with four shelter tent halves of canvas buttoned together to form a roof. Gaps between the logs were chinked up with mud. The open-peaked ends were enclosed with whatever could be found— boards, rubber ground cloths, more tent halves or any other manner of material that could be scrounged up. Most of the huts had a fireplace of one form or another. They were usually constructed of logs or sticks lined with mud and a chimney made of a barrel or two. The floor was covered with leaves or the pine boughs stripped from the logs. To provide a more comfortable ceiling height, the floor might be dug down a few feet into the ground. All manner of contrivance was conjured up to lend some small measure of comfort. Two double-wide bunks usually ran across the far wall. Experience had shown that two men sleeping together in a bunk and doubling up their blankets could keep much warmer than sleeping alone. In extreme cold, all four occupants might be found rolled in their blankets and sleeping nested tightly together to conserve warmth. Some of the more inventive lads dug a trench and covered it with packing crate boards and earth to construct a heat-circulating tunnel under the floor. The smoke from the fire was drawn though the trench and out a taller-than-normal chimney at the other end of the shelter. If everything worked as planned, this system kept the whole

351

place warm and the bedding on the floor nice and dry. When it did not work as planned, the boards in the tunnel could catch fire and the whole thing could go up in smoke in minutes. Chimney fires were a constant threat.

By early January, the hills and valleys for miles were covered by a neatly organized shanty town. Straight lines of huts, set in rows, formed streets along company and regimental lines. Open, cleared fields of hard-packed earth served as drilling grounds for the brigades of soldiers and, in some instances, even street signs were erected. Life settled into a repetitive, boring routine of making meals, drilling, picket duty, guard duty and making meals.

Sketch from Frank Leslie's Illustrated Weekly
"SOLDIERS AT THEIR CAMPFIRES" BY: A. McCallum

Encamped near Falmouth, Va.
Dec. 26th, 1862.

Dear Parents,

As I know of nothing to write about except the army

& what I am every day associating with. I cannot write to interest you unless you are interested in the worship of army commanders and government officials at Washington.

The recent battle goes to show that there is a deficiency somewhere but as Genl Burnside shoulders the blame & makes a public confession I suppose it will be overlooked & we will move on blindly as before and we will likely soon see the war ended. You will most likely see Burnside's letter to Halleck also the official reports of the diferent generals that were engaged in the late battle. Our world renowned ironclad fleets are all working wonders in the way of crushing the rebelion & will likely continue to as long as they remain in N.Y. harbor experimenting with new & useless inventions instead of going up James river or to Charleston or Savannah & there make their experiments where it will do some good. But that won't do. They might scare the Richmond people if they should knock Fort Darling down & go on up & knock at their doors in the city & demand its surrender. I would like to have Charleston served as Sumner served Fredricksburg.

We have fixed up very comfortable winter quarters here & are now liveing very well. Yesterday they say was Christmas but I rather guess there was a mistake somewhere for I did not see any chickens, turkeys.

You ask about Genl Gorman & Captain McCallum. Gorman has gone west. McCallum was on Genl Sully's staff and got shot through the foot. It is quite a bad wound. Genl Sully was bruised on the leg by a piece of shell which tore off the top of his boot. There was but two or three of our regt. that got hurt but there were several that got some close calls. I was hit for the first time by a piece of shell but it did not hurt me. The shell burst in front of where our Co. was seting on the ground behind a tight board fence. There was several pieces passed through the fence & one piece struck me on the bottom of my foot but it had lost its speed & did no damage. Captain is all safe although he got shot at several times. We had very fine weather while we were over there but it is quite cold now. I don't know what to think of the war. It seems to me that we are geting the worst of it but it may take a turn soon. I hope it will.

The boys are all as well as usual. I have excellent health. I see that you have got quite a snow. I wish I was there to enjoy it but you know how it is.

My best respect to all the friends

Edward.

Encamped near Falmouth Va.
Dec. 30th A.D. 1862

Dear Father:

1862 is nearly gone & the rebels are the strongest they were ever. I see by the late papers that the army in the west is falling back & the rebs are threatening to invade Ohio haveing already overrun Kentucky. Island No. 10 has also been evacuated by our forces & the guns spiked, ere (before) this reaches you there is no telling what will happen. If the enemy is not checked there will be quite an addition to the C.S.A. as for the Army of the Potomac, they are laying quiet on the Rappahannoc shore feasting on hard bread and salt horse.[57] We have two or three lions among us but they are quite harmless. Lion Burnside has been badly whipped. Sumner shot Fredericksburg all to pieces but dare not hold it & is now liveing in grand style at his head quarters on this side of Jordan in a splendid brick mansion of some fine Southern gentleman. Franklin fought bravely but Jackson the invincible Chief of Jeff Davis & Co. was too much for him & he was forced to save himself in the way that Noah Webster's lion did that fought with the Mastiff (Webster's Elementary spelling book). Franc Siegle,

---

[57] A common reference among the soldiers to Salt Pork.

the flying dutchman, lays up to our right but I suppose he thinks that prudence is the better part of valor and contents himself with his (Lager beer).

I was down to Falmouth yesterday. The town lays about 1/2 of a mile above Fredricksburg on this side of the river. There used to be a Bridge across the river but there is nothing but the ruins to be seen now. The bed of the river above the bridge is the roughest place I ever saw. As far as you can see there is nothing but large rocks from the size of a house down to a pebble. The rebs have their pickets posted on their side of the river & we on our side in easy shooting distance. There is a move about to be made and I expect we will soon be nicely quartered in Washington. I expect New Years day will pass away about the same but I don't care for that. If the war ever ends I hope to have a better time.

We have just received the Faribault paper of the 17th. You speak of the St. Paul Press. If it would not be too much trouble you may send me one once in a while if you don't wish to keep them.

Remember me to Elford and all the rest.

Edward H. Bassett

Happy New Year to all.   Edward.

Encamped Near Falmouth, Va.
Jan. 4th, 1863

Dear Parents

Once more I would assure you that long absence from loved ones at home does not make them forgotten.

I once had hoped to have seen you before this time but as affairs get no better I now expect that there will be no chance until my full term of enlistment has expired although some think there will be a settlement sooner. (I hope there may)

One year ago we were picketing on the Potomac at Edwards Ferry. I think that taking all things into consideration the enemy are stronger in Virginia than they were one year ago.

I received your letter of the 21st on New Years morning. I was very glad to hear that you were well and having such a mild winter. The weather here is also very mild it is not cold enough half the time so as to freeze nights and the days are very warm and pleasant. We have not had any rain for a long time & the roads are in excellent order. It would be a fine time for a move. There has been some talk of our moving but so far there has been nothing but a few reconnoitering parties sent out up the Rappahannoc.

It is thought that Lee is moving up the river but I guess it is only an extension of his lines for better protection.

There is some encouraging news from the west General Rosencrans has driven Bragg out of Murfreesboro & was pursuing him at last accounts, he is a good officer and has some good officers under him.

General Blunt has also been successful in Arkansas and at last accounts was shelling the rebel camp. We also hear of the sailing of four of our iron clad ships from Fortress Monroe & I hope soon to hear of their knocking at the doors of Charleston and Savannah and the capture of those cities. I don't think the war will last more than one year. The time of a great many of the troops will be out between now and next fall & some sooner and they are not going to reenlist right away. They will want to go home first at any rate and there cannot be another army raised as easy as the present one has been and I think things will be hurried up next Spring and there will be some way found to settle the difficulties. The slavery question is the leader now. I suppose that the much talked of proclamation of President Lincoln has been issued at last.

Now I wish he would issue another one to the effect that every Negro in the United States should be colonized in South Carolina, Georgia, Mississippi, Alabama, Florida, North Carolina and Louisiana and not have one running at large in the north.

The boys are all well as usual; in fact health was never better with us. I feel first rate & weigh 152 ½ pounds. How I would like to be home this year when I think of it, it seems as if I could wate no longer but there is no use. There are men being discharged from our regiment every little while. They have been worn out and will not be of any use if kept here until hot weather. Our old Bull Run prisoners have joined us but some of them will be discharged on account of wounds received in battle, as we receive no recruits our regt.[58] is getting quite small but what few there are left can be depended on every time. Our first Lieutennant has not been with us since the battle of Antietam. We were certainly very fortunate in not loosing more men at Antietam also at Fredricksburg. It was not because we were not in range of the enemies shots for they flew arround as thick as hail. We have seen some hard times within the last 12 months but I believe our regiment has stood it all as well as any in the service. As we were the first 3 years regt. in the service we will be the first three years regt. discharged if it is done right;

New Years was very dull with us there was nothing exciting, the weather was cool. At night just as we were about retireing there came an order to go on picket and we were soon out some three miles from camp in the woods. We soon found that we were to act as reserves & support the 19th Maine which was on the outposts. I don't suppose there was a reb within three miles but such is military life and we only wondered that is was not raining so as to make it more comfortable. We built

---

[58] This reference is to men from the regiment taken prisoner at the battle of Bull Run and now being "paroled" and returned to their unit.

up some good fires and those that had brought their blankets tried to sleep. We had a good time & in the morning we were relieved & went home to our camp well pleased with our commencement of the New Year. I am glad to hear of the execution of the Sioux Indians that have been murdering innocent settlers on the frontier. I would like to have been there & saw them hung. I hope the people of Minnesota will keep the matter in their own hands & not ask Old Abe's advice. I hope we will get our pay soon but there can be no dependence placed on the rumors about paymasters as yet money is scarce and everything eatable high. We receive our rations very regularly now. Pork from Indianna and Pilot Bread from N.Y. City also some fresh beef once in a great while. Rice and Coffee are supplied in abundance also a good supply of sugar & plenty of salt.

We drill between the hours of 9 & 10 AM and 3 & 4 PM each pleasant day. I am tenting with C. C. Parker our Second Lieutennant, Albert Johnson, and one other. We have a very good tent and live easy.

As ever Your Son

Edward

P.S.

Maj. General Sedgwick has recovered from his wounds received at Antietam & is in command of the 2nd Corps, he was in command of a division at Antietam. He is an excellent officer. He refused to be taken from the field when he was wounded until he saw his command safe.

Encamped Near Falmouth, Va.

Jan. 7, 1863.

Dear Parents,

I am very glad to hear that you were all well also

that you were all haveing such a mild winter. It must seem strange to have such warm weather at this time of the year up in that cold frosty country. I think the weather is warmer here than it was last winter. I am glad to hear of the execution of those Indians. I should like to have been there and witnessed it myself. I hope that if the Indians are troublesome next summer that our regt. will be called back there to protect the frontier. (I will save them the trouble of hanging what few come within reach of my musket if they do.)

You wish me to give you the particulars of the battle of Fredricksburg. I have written you three letters since the battle and in all of them I have given you a few of the principle details but you will understand it better by reading the accounts in the papers. I hope I may never see another such a battle. We are very anxious to hear from the army of the southwest. The last accounts we got were of a very uncertain kind. I expect we will get more definite accounts by todays paper. The little Hero Monitor that whipped the rebel Merimac has met with a sad fate. It was sunk off Hatteras inlet in a storm. If the rest of the iron clads do as well as the little Monitor has done we will soon have no need of a blockade on the coast because we can occupy the coast with our armies and then we will certainly have the rebs in a tight place. I don't think there will be another battle here soon although there may be.

You wish to know how many men there are fit for duty in our Regt. I cannot tell exactly our Co. is one of the largest in the Regt. and we draw rations for 51 men. There are eleven Companies in the regt. counting Co. L the 2nd Minnesota Sharpshooters which has been with us since last summer but some of the companies number but little more than one half what we do. There are a great many of the men in the hospitals north that have been sent off from time to time. I don't think we have more than 330 men in the whole regiment fit for duty all the time. If it were possible I would get a furlough next month and go and see you but there would be no use in trying besides it would cost considerable. A private soldier cannot get a furlough in this regt. and there is no use in talking about it.

(The balance of this letter no longer exists.)

****

Burnside's army was generally dispirited and no longer had any confidence in him. The men followed orders and would march off to battle when commanded but no longer manifested the air of jubilation that once marked such an event. Sickness and disease began to take a toll and had a further demoralizing effect. Junior regiments, not hardened to living with exposure to the elements, seemed most affected. As Edward mentions, many are gone to the hospitals.

Since the return to camp, weather conditions had been rather pleasant, with mostly mild, sunny days and the roads were in excellent condition. General Burnside had taken full responsibility for the demoralizing defeat that his army suffered at Fredericksburg and had offered his resignation to President Lincoln. However, he was still in command of the Army of the Potomac and, once again, he was subjected to pressure from Washington to somehow give the nation a victory against Lee. Burnside had been developing a plan to do just that and was now nearing the time when he would make a move. At this time in history, the axioms of war made it clear that engaging an army in a major movement during the winter was at the very least foolish, and at worst an invitation to disaster. Moving 100,000 men and all the heavy wagons and guns across a land with few dirt roads was always risky. Added to the risk was the fact that in mid-winter heavy rains and snows, driven by Northeast winds, might last for days and quickly turn the clay/sand soil into a bottomless quagmire.

Encamped near Falmouth, Va.
January 15th, 1863.

I received two letters from home this morning, one written by Mother and one by Sister Anna. I am sorry to hear in them that you are haveing the measles in the family for I know it is a very disagreeable disease although I know it will not be dangerous with you to doctor it. I know I wished that you could doctor me when I had it last winter. I can't understand why my letters are so long in reaching you. I wrote to you as soon as I could after the battle at Fredericksburg for I knew that you would get all sorts of stories about it and would not feel easy until you had got a word direct from me.

I am siting this evening in my tent right on the ground with a candle stuck in a bayonet for a candlestick trying to write you a letter. Mr. Parker is reading the paper with the latest news which is rather meager. The wind is blowing very hard but it is quite warm so that we need no fire in our tents.

I wish I could spend a few evenings with you so I could talk with you. I would then be able to tell you things that I cannot do by writing.

You will not be surprised to hear that all is quiet on the Rappahannoc and that we are still in our camps picketing on all sides. Things look rather dark. Our forces have been repulsed at Vicksburg and although Rosencrans succeeded in routing Bragg, he is now falling back towards Nashville. There is a great deal of talk about peace but as was said on a former occasion (there is no peace). I can only hope for the best and if peace does come I know it will be hailed with as much joy by me as any one. I think he who finds a way of settlement will be entitled to the thanks of the world.

I am well as ever and in good fighting trim as ever if there is any chance. Not that I want to fight but I would fight rather than run many miles to save myself now. I hear that Genl Sully has command of our brigade again. I hope he has. We will not get our pay this month & some say not before the 15th of next month. We are drawing new clothing of all kinds that we want. There is to be a review tomorrow if it is pleasant. Health is generaly good. Captain Messick looks a great deal more healthy than he used to when in Minnesota I will try to answer Anna's letter soon. Please remember me to John Russell and all the boys that inquire. Tell them to write to me for it is rather lonely here this winter.

As ever you son,

Edward Bassett Co. G

On picket five miles South East
From Brandy Station Virginia
Jan. 16th, 1863

Dear Mother,

Your kind letters have been received by me every week since I left home and I know of nothing that does me more good or cheers me more when I feel tired and lonely than they do. I often think that I would not know what to do without them but I fear I have paid you but poorly lately for so many long letters. It seems to me lately that I cannot write a letter and I believe I have failed every time that I have made an attempt although I have scribbled a few lines and sent you occasionaly.

To tell the truth it is a very dull time with us this winter and there is nothing that I can write that would be of any interest.[59] Today is the third day since I left

---

[59] Judging by the tone of this letter and its immediate predecessor, disenchantment due to the late pay and concern over Indian uprisings back home, Edward was feeling the winter doldrums. With little to do and no action taking place, boredom with camp life often became a reality.

camp and came out on picket. I have had a very pleasant time and enjoyed myself full as well as I could have done in camp. It will be some 15 or 20 days before I will be on picket again. Tomorrow we will be relieved. The weather is quite cool but the snow has now all melted. My health is good. There is no sickness in the company. I received a letter from Anna the other night and I think I answered it. Those socks came through all right. They are very nice and I think a great deal of them.

Sunday P.M. Jan 17th

I have just got back from picket.

I hope this will find you all well.

My love to all.

Your Son *Edward H. Bassett*

Co. G. 1st Minnesota Vols.

Encamped Near Falmouth, Va.
Sunday Jan. 18th, 1863

Dear Sisters,

It is quite a cold morning but the sun shines and there is no snow the roads are dry and if I was not a soldier I would have a fine time.

We had a grand review yesterday. There was several thousand soldiers all drawn up in line with their guns as bright as a dollar (in gold) while General Burnside and his staff with several other Generals rode along in front of the lines while the bands played beautiful music. The Generals present were General Burnside commanding The Army of the Potomac, Maj. General Sumner, General Couch, General Sedgwick, General Howard, Genl, French, General Sully besides several others that I don't know. We had a very pleasant time although it was quite cold. I wish you could have been where you could see the soldiers when they were all drawn up in line they looked grand.

We have but very little to do now and are living very easy but I want the war to end so that I can go home but I guess I can stand it through until the 29th of April 1864 when my time will be out & I can then leave the army.

I hope Ella has got well & that you are all enjoying good health.

Oh yes there is Elford, I came near forgetting him however please excuse me.

Well good morning, Sir (Toad) [60] how are you getting along this winter have you had any sleigh rides with the girls this winter? How is it Anna, does he go up to see Ella Storer very often or has he given it up. I'll bet he thinks just as much of her as ever but he won't own it he would like to make us think that he went to see Charles. Well Elford how do your sheep and colt get along this winter. You will soon have a fine horse to ride won't you. What would you say to my buying a mate to it then we can have a team between us and have grand times. I hope we will soon see each other and then we will have fine times indeed. Now I want you to get the girls to write a letter for you to me. Tell me all abut the farm, the sheep, calves, pigs, chickens, turkeys, ducks, horses, cows and everything that you can think of for it will all be interesting to me.

As ever your Brother   *Edward*

---

[60] This is a pet name for Elford, Edwards youngest brother, that is found more often used in early letters.

"The Mud March"

On January 20, 1863, General Burnside made his long-awaited move. He announced, in his general order to the troops, *"The auspicious moment seems to have arrived to strike a great and mortal blow to the rebellion, and to gain that decisive victory which is due our country."* This was one of those times when the good judgment of sensible men was trampled into oblivion for the sake of giving the public an emotional uplift. From a military standpoint, Burnside's plan was a very good one. He was acutely aware of the folly of a direct frontal attack at Fredericksburg. He planned to move up the Rappahannock River and install five pontoon bridges, across which he would move his entire army and attack Lee on his left flank. After defeating Lee, he would move quickly on to Richmond. The political hacks of Washington gave little heed to the fact that such a movement in mid-winter had a poor chance of success. They were so insistent on action that Burnside had no alternative. The struggle that ensued is worthy of the telling as it illustrates the hardship and exposure faced by soldiers on both sides when the shifting conditions of weather and war met and an army became entangled in the elements of nature. The 2nd Corps, including the First Minnesota, was to be the last to leave camp since they were nearest the river and, therefore, most easily observed by the enemy. As the rest of the army moved out, they were to carry on as usual, giving the enemy the impression that the entire army was still in camp. They were, however, under marching orders and supplied with the usual 60 rounds of extra ammunition and three-day's rations.

The bugles and drums sounded early, breakfasts were hastily eaten, tents struck and all things packed and loaded into the regimental wagons. The call of "assembly" echoed across the land as brigade-after-brigade formed in line-of-march. Flags waved in the gentle breeze and scattered clouds drifted across the blue heavens. The Army of the Potomac was on the move!

The army made a good start that pleasant morning as the

great, long supply wagon train and artillery left camp and moved upriver. By noon the sky filled with ominous grey clouds and drizzle driven by a brisk breeze, began to fall. The "good start" soon went bad. Once again, headquarters had forgotten to notify the engineers that their pontoon boats were needed. So, instead of the ponderous wagons heavily laden with the boats leading the column, they were far back. As the day wore on, the cold drizzle became a torrential deluge, driven by gale force icy winds. The roads and land were soon stirred into a tenacious pudding of sticky mud, miring down the pontoon wagons. As night fell, the men moved off among the scrub brush farther back from the river and pitched their shelter tents anywhere they could that might afford some shelter. Somehow, the men got fires, or rather smudge pots, going. Clouds of acrid smoke from the wet wood hung in the heavy air and the fires were useless to warm chilled bones or cook food. The smoke became so heavy that the men were forced to lie flat on the soaked ground to breathe. All night, the storm howled and the rains fell. By morning, the mud was worse than ever. The bottom seemed to have fallen out of the ground. All day the struggle worsened! Wagons sank to their axles and, then, to the wagon box. Men sank to their waist in the inextricable goo.

A dozen mules and 150 men pulling on ropes could move the mired wagons only inches at a time. Cannons sank until only the muzzles of the barrels were visible. Moving a 12 pounder defied the efforts of as many as 24 mules and 200 men. Horses and mules dropped dead from exhaustion and, sometimes, sank so deep that only their ears could be seen. Cut out of the harness, they were abandoned to be tramped into the sticky morass.

The morning of the January 23rd, the storm had abated and only a light drizzle was falling. The men's haversacks, in which they carried their food, were completely soaked, their hardtack reduced to dirty mush and the only food left to eat was uncooked salt pork. Initially, Burnside insisted that the effort continue but, by noon, he had to admit the task was insurmountable and ordered a return to camp, an effort that required a few more days of intensive effort.

The despondency that hung over the returning exhausted men worsened when they straggled into camp, only to realize that they were without even a decent place to rest. The sight of the winter huts they had built and then, once again, burned before marching out was nearly too much to bear. They had to make what shelters they could and sleep on the soggy ground.

The toll from this debacle will never be known for certain. Hundreds of horses and mules died. Huge quantities of stores and supplies were lost or destroyed. Most tragic was the toll of the lives of young men that simply dropped dead from exhaustion and exposure. Hundreds were just too exhausted to make it back to camp. They simply fell down on the marshy ground and died. Thousands died afterward from pneumonia and disease. All in all, most likely as many men died in this "Mud March" as in many regular battles. At his own request, General Burnside was removed as commander of the Army of the Potomac on January 25, 1863, and replaced by General Joseph Hooker by order of President Lincoln.

The Army of the Potomac interrupted in its progress by its old enemy,
Virginia Mud
Sketch by Frank Leslie, Leslie's Illustrated Weekly

Falmouth, Va.
Jan. 22, 1863.

Dear Parents,

The army is moveing up the Rappahannoc, I expect with the intention of crossing over. The papers state that the enemy have drawn 10,000 of their forces from here & it is thought that they are about to evacuate. It has been raining for about 48 hours & I expect that it is very bad on the roads. We are under orders to march with three days rations & 60 rounds of cartridges. Times are very dull and I guess there will be no change soon. There was a large fire over in the City last night. It must have been accidental for the rebs would not be foolish enough to burn the houses now after they have been all shot up in the way they have. I tell you it was a hard looking sight when we left it. I wish we could serve Richmond the same.

There was a review the other day of the right grand division of the Potomac Army, commanded by Maj. General Sumner (or Old Bull as we call him). I don't think that General Burnside found the troops quite as enthusiastic as he had hoped they don't seem to have much confidence in him. There was several regiments refused to cheer him after being requested to by their officers. Our regiment was one. General Howard asked the Colonel to give Burnside three cheers as he rode past but when the colonel called on the men there was not more than 20 or 25 that would say a word. For my part, I think that Burnside is an honest man and will do the best he can but I don't think he will ever be very successful while in command of this army. Some regiments have threatened to throw down their arms and some say that they won't go into another fight. I hope they will be pacified without any serious trouble but there are fears that there will be serious trouble if it is not checked soon. I don't think there will be any trouble with our regiment. They will be very well contented if the Indians don't commence their depredations again in the spring. But if the Indians do break out again it will be hard for us to sit idle here and allow our friends and everything that we have be destroyed. It matters but little how much we may think of the old flag & the Union. Our homes in Minnesota claim our protection from Savages and when the government fails to protect the frontier but allows those roveing savages to destroy our homes and murder our families I ask what hope can we have even after the Union is restored. We have been out long enough to have the South conquered and the Union restored if things had been conducted right on the part of the Federal government. We came out early and have endeavored to do our duty in every respect all the time, trusting and hopeing in a speedy settlement but what has been accomplished. The Confederate is stronger today than they ever have been since the war broke out. It is a critical period with us now. There are some 600,000 of our army whose time expires between now and the 1st of July at the farthest and if there is not something accomplished soon when can we do anything towards crushing the rebellion. I still have some hope but I scarcely know why. We are yet to be disgraced with foreign mediation in our affairs and simply because we cannot agree among ourselves. It certainly cannot be for the want of means to carry out any plan to conquer if we could only agree. I would not be surprised if the war was settled in the course of the next two months and we will then go home ashamed of ourselves.[61]

I hope the Governor will take some steps towards the protection of the frontier and take no more Indian

---

[61] Edward's concern was that France and England would recognize the Confederacy as a sovereign nation, broker a truce and the army would be sent home leaving the country divided. The men would be burdened forever with the shameful knowledge of their failure to keep their beloved homeland united.

prisoners to feed. If I was free I would soon shoulder my rifle & go out & kill every Indian I could see on the frontier and ask no odds of Gov. Ramsey or President Lincoln.

Please write often to me. Write all the news for I like to hear about home if I cannot be there. I will write again and let you know something about the move if the rain don't stop it. Captain is well I believe. There are a great many geting discharged on account of disability. Lieutennant Shepley of our Co. has got his, also Captain McCallum.

As ever your son,

Edward Bassett [62]

23rd.   It is fogy and damp. The Army is moving down the river straggling through the mud which is very deep (We have certainly been lucky we have not left our tents). There has not been any engagement yet and I guess the expedition is at an end. The troops are going back to their old camps. I received a package of papers from you this morning. They are very interesting. I expect to hear of some very important changes in this department soon (Burnside has played out). I am sorry to say that he is a good officer but every one don't see it. I will try to write again Sunday if I can. I think that if the rain had held off a few days longer we would have been marching to Richmond driving the enemy before us. I don't know what will be the next move but I rather guess there will be another long rest unless the enemy evacuate. We hear that Jackson is marching down the Shenandoah Valley, another one of his tricks. Our troops hold Winchester I think. Good by this time.

Edward

---

[62] This letter was badly stained as though it had been soaked with some liquid during delivery or perhaps fallen in the mud.

SOLDIERS' GRAVES AT FALMOUTH, VA.

Soldiers' Graves at Falmouth, VA.
Sketch from Leslie's Illustrated Weekly

Ecamped Near Falmouth, Virginia
Sunday Jan. 29th, 1863

Dear Father

I have just received your letter of the 18th. I also
have a letter from Uncle Charles dated Jan. 20th.

Uncle says that they are getting sick of the war and
begin to fear as to the result and the ability of the
north to conquer the south.

Wheat is worth $1.12½ in Milwaukee, Oats .50, Pork $4.50 to $5.00 per hundred. He writes that his taxes last year were $6.50 this year they are $16.50. Still he thinks the farmers can live if they can get the present prices for produce. Walworth Co. raised their quota of troops last summer consequently there was no drafting. 47 have died in the 22nd Wisc. which was raised there last August and went into Kentucky.

There has been another change in the command of the Potomac army. Maj. General Hooker has taken Burnsides place... Porter has been dismissed from the service so I suppose we have got rid of one more traitor.

We have been having some very bad weather lately. It snowed all day yesterday and this morning there was full six inches of snow on the ground but it is very wet and the mud is very deep. It would be impossible to move now but I guess there is no danger of our trying it very soon.

The paymaster came around this morning and payed us two months wages. There was four months due & we did expect to get it all but there are so many negroes to be paid that soldiers have got to take their turn with them in the future. I should have sent you some money if we had been paid four months in the place of two. There is three months pay due us now & we may get another payment soon. You speak of our holding Fredricksburg for winter quarters. I think that the rebs would object to that for my part I think we were very lucky getting out as cheap as we did. I don't think that the citizens have all returned to their homes in the city yet.

You ask how the Negros like their freedom. They are all for the union and seem to understand the cause of the war just as well as anyone but Negro like when they have their freedom they turn right arround and strike for higher wages and say they won't work for 10 dollars per month but they find a soldier once in a while that settles them.[63]

Health remains good we have very good quarters for pleasant weather but when it storms it is not quite so nice but we make out very well. I send you one dollar which I wish you would get me some letter stamps with please send me 25 one cent stamps & the rest in three cent ones and I will send you some papers. The boys are all well as usual.

I hope that the war will soon end and I suppose that you all wish the same.

As soon as the snow melts there will be a perfect sea of mud all over Va. How I long to leave (Ole Virginia). I am tired of this infernal clay and pine. We are burning green pitch pine for wood. It is mean stuff.[64]

Well I have written a long letter & must close it so as to send it off by this days mail.

Excuse my rough hand.

---

[63] As more and more slaves gained their freedom and had no place to go it was only natural that they would hold onto the sense of security provided by the army. Thus, the horde of camp followers continually grew and many were employed by the army or officers to work in the camp. These "contrabands", as they were referred to, received pay for their services for the first time in their lives and often adopted an inflated attitude of self importance. They were paid by the Paymaster of the army before the soldiers received their pay and when there was not enough to go around, the soldiers came out on the short end of the stick. This practice irritated the men who had risked their lives over and over for the slaves. When the blacks became so ungrateful as to demand equal pay with the soldiers, a strong resentment developed among the troops. The sympathy that was so broadly felt before began to wane.

[64] With thousands of men encamped and all needing fires for warmth and cooking the problem of having to use green wood was a serious one as the choking smoke became very dense and consistently hung over the camp like a thick cloud.

My love to you all

As ever your son

E.H. Bassett

Co. G. 1ˢᵗ Minnesota Vols.

In this letter, Edward mentions receiving his pay in the form of 'greenbacks.' These were promissory notes from the government that at the time were worth less than 50-cents-on-the-dollar compared to gold. The difference was solely determined by the fact that the general public did not trust the paper money. The demands on the treasury were such that, for the first time, the government began issuing paper money during the Civil War. In another letter Edward, cautions his parents not to accept anything less than full face value for the currency.

Gen. Joseph Hooker

James Wright of Company K wrote; *"There was always rejoicing when the paymaster visited us. The majority of the boys sent their money home, under the "allotment system"; some spent it at the sutlers; and some risked it at poker and chuck-a-luck, and the majority were broke within a fortnight after the paymaster was gone."*

Major General Joseph Hooker implemented many changes after taking command. He was a "dashing officer" and became known as "Fighting Joe." He disliked the name because he said *"It sounds as if I were a pirate"*. He was a genial man who made friends easily although he was known to have a quick temper. Always eager to fight the Confederates, he nonetheless insisted on a respect for private property. He issued a general order reminding his soldiers that, *"this is a war between fellow citizens of a common country and should be conducted accordingly. It will end in the triumph of the Union cause and then our present foes will be our warm friends."* Hooker reorganized the army, doing away with Burnside's "Grand Divisions" and instituting a Corps organization. The First Minnesota was in the Second Corps under the command of General Couch. Hooker worked hard to rebuild the morale of his army. He put them back on the drill fields twice a day and had full-dress reviews every evening. He reorganized the cavalry into one cohesive fighting unit instead of many small units individually assigned to brigades. Perhaps one of the most enduring achievements and

2nd Corps Badge

one that did the most to build an *"espirit de corps"* was the creation of distinctive badges assigned to each corps. The men were proud of their badges and they greatly aided in identifying friends and directing troops in battle. The badges took numerous shapes like hearts, diamonds, and crescents. The Second Corps' badge was the trefoil, three leaf clover or "white club" as the rebels called it. The confederates developed such a respect for the men wearing it that they knew when they were confronted by it they were in for a real fight. Supplies, and more importantly mail, were now brought up regularly from Acquia Creek on the trains. Visitors also came on occasion and life was quite bearable.

On January 27th, President and Mrs. Lincoln came to visit the camp. They stayed a few days and were entertained by General Hooker with a dinner at the Lacy House. A Grand Review of the troops was held and Lincoln visited the camp of the Second Corp.

Camp of the First Regiment Minnesota Volunteers
Falmouth Va.
February 8th, A.D. 1863

Dear Sister Ella:

It is a very pleasant day and seems like spring in Minnesota. There was about two inches of snow fell on the 6th inst. but it has rained since and the ground is bare now. I have seen more snow this winter than last. The roads are now very good, being frozen. The mail this morning brought the Faribault paper of the 28th. We were payed two months wages on the 23rd of Jan. so that we have plenty of money for the present. Captain Messick has gone to Minnesota on a furlough I am told. I don't know when he started but I presume he will be there some time before this reaches you.

There has been quite a number of furloughs granted to officers since Genl Hooker took command of the army but I have not heard of any privates getting one as yet. If I could get a furlough I would be in Minnesota as quick as I could get there. If I could settle the war & restore peace to the country I would do that but it is impossible. I could do one as easy as the other. There is no telling what laws may be enacted to secure an army by that time. You ask if I can leave the army after the three years are up if the war is not ended. This is a hard question to answer but I will explain it to you the best I can. According to the understanding when I enlisted I shall be free at the expiration of the three years whether the war is ended or not unless it becomes a military necesity to hold me longer, when they can hold us 30 days longer. After that they will have fun if they don't let us go. The army is a good place for me as far as health is concerned but fighting is poor business even if it is well followed. We are looking for exciteing news from the army in the west, also from our fleet on the Atlantic coast. I hope we may hear of the capture of Charleston, S.C. soon. The rebs have made a bold dash lately on our vesels there & I hope to hear of their being paid for it.

I don't think there is any prospect for another move here.

My love to all

Your brother   *Edward H. Bassett*

Co, G 1st Minnesota Vol.

To Ella P. Bassett.

Camp of the First Regiment Minnesota Vols.
Near Falmouth, Va.
Feb. 10th, 1863.

Dear Parents:

There are various rumors afloat about our regt. going west. The last I heard was that we were going to St. Louis but unless this army is broken up I think we will remain in this department. I would as soon stay here as to go into Ky. or Tenn. for my part. I hope if we leave we will be sent on the frontier under the command of Genl Sully. I think that by the 1st of March we will be on the move somewhere. I expect Captain Messick is in Minnesota before this time. I think he left here on the 30th of Jan.

There has been considerable excitement about the late dash of the rebel rams off Charleston & the rebs have proclaimed the port open to the trade of the world but I got a paper last night that gave a true account of the affair. They did not sink a single ship and failed to recapture the prize Princess Royal. It was merely a skirmish they will find when the trial comes.

We are expecting every day to hear of another battle at Vicksburg, Miss. There will be a big fight there when it does come off & I believe our side will be victorious.

You speak of catching fish and selling them at 3 cts. per pound. They would fetch 25¢ here and you could sell 25,000 pounds in one day ($625.00).

I don't think we will lay still much longer & when we get on the move once more we will feel better.

Please write often.

Yours as ever,

Edward

I send you Genl Heintzelman's account of the battle of Seven Pines or Fair Oaks. I think it is about correct. The 1st Minnesota was the first regt. that arrived on the field from Sedgwick's division. I saw Genl Abercrombie when we first got there. He had lost his hat in the fray & had just come from the thickest of the fight. He was covered with mud from head to foot and his grey hair hung in all shapes over his head & he was a frightful sight. If we had been 20 minutes later his command would have been overrun by the masses of the enemy. As it was they tried hard to get arround on his right but we punished them well for it and they were forced to stop. They came up in a point of timber that afforded them protection for a while but they soon found that we were prepared to receive them. Some of them fell within six or 8 rods of where our men were posted. The only way that they succeeded in geting up that near was by dodging from tree to tree & when they got up so close they could not move without meeting a bullet. They fought desperately as they most allways do but they were deceived & they will find it so sometime. The fighting the next day was harder but they did not try the woods again. They were whipped there as bad as we were here at Fredericksburg.

Edward.

Dear Mother:

We went out on picket last Wednesday & had a very fine time. The enemy are continualy strengthening their position on the other side of the Rappahannoc. They have thrown up several works since we were over there but they are mostly on the flat & would be rather warm to stay in if our batteries should open up on them.

The weather is very mild yet & the roads will soon be in excelent order if there is no more rains.

Wm. Potter of our Co. that was wounded at the battle of Bull Run & taken prisoner has been discharged & will leave in a few days. There are also some two or three others of our Co. that will be discharged soon. We have 73 enlisted men in the Co. now but nearly one half of them are off to the hospitals & detailed arround at different places. We have 32 men for daily duty.

I am sorry to hear of so much sickness with you this winter. Nearly all the neighbors will be so changed by the time that I get back that it will not seem like the same place. I am glad to hear that John Russell is geting better. I wrote him a letter the other day. As for honor in the army I cannot see it. The bigest rascals & them that can drink the most whiskey are usualy the ones that get honored by being connected with the army. I have seen it and know for myself. I never want to be honored for anything done in the army. As to trials in the army by Court Martial I never knew justice done. There is no justice about it. The courts are composed of commissioned officers entirely. When a private is tried it is like being judged by their worst enemies. When it is an officer (which is not very often) it is as good as being tried by sworn friends & they are most honorably acquited. But if military law was carried out to the letter there would be a great change. There are just as many ways to avoid the law as there are to avoid civil laws. But let them go. There is one consolation for me. I have but a little over one year to serve and I have got along two years nearly without any trouble and I am sure I ought to stand it one more. I hope however to be out of the army before my time is up. I have just read a long letter from A.G.Ward written to one of the boys. He seems to be having a very good time this winter.

You speak of the Indians. I hope that they will not trouble the frontier this next summer but if they do I wish we could be there to try our hand at them.

I sent you one dollar for some stamps but if you have not already sent them you need not, but keep the money & use it as you see fit. I bought a supply this morning.

As ever your son in the army,

Edward H. Bassett.

Tell Father that I would like to have him write to me as often as he finds time. His letters are very interesting to me.

Falmouth, Va.
Feb. 21st, 1863

Dear Parents,

All is quiet on the Rappahannoc and I thought I would write to you so that you can have it in due time. We are within sight of the City of Fredericksburg. We had a fall of about 6 inches of snow last Tuesday but it melted off by Wednesday and the water was breaking over the banks of the Rappahannoc and Potomac rivers. If it had not turned warm there would have been 12 inches of snow now but there were some of those unaccountable changes in the weather here that I did not know were experienced in the sunny south.

We received the Columbian Republican by this mornings mail. I see an account of the arrival of Captain Messick in Faribault also an account of the death of one of the discharged members of Co. G, another sacrifice to the freaks of (Commissioned Surgeons).

I hear that Ben Buck is home on a furlough if you see him tell him to remember some of his old comrades when he finds time. I am well and lazy as ever. We just received a supply of reading & will have something to amuse ourselves with for a few days. There are four of us in one tent and we each have a paper & with what is sent by friends at home we find considerable reading matter. I rec'd. the Columbian Republican this morning from Washington it is a McClellan sheet and got up in good style.

I see that you have got some sleighing at last, well we might have if the snow had only stayed on until we could sent up north for our sleighs but also for us we can't even dream of a sleigh ride without having it be spoiled by waking & looking out upon the bleak hills of 'Ole Virginia'. I am looking for a letter from you every day & it will most likely come tomorrow.

The roads are drying up very fast but they will not be likely to get very good before there will be another storm. We are getting some soft bread now in place of hard tack. Meal sells for $2.00 per bushel at the mill at Falmouth, flour $20.00 per barrel & Molasses at $4.00 per gallon. $1.00 worth of ginger wheat would hardly make a meal for a hearty Minnesotan and I could eat $1.00 worth of pies at any time if they were eatable, but such pies are not known north! General Hooker has ordered all unauthorized traders to leave the army & there was a scattering of Jews to the four winds. If I could have the privilege of pedling in the army I could make my fortune in a few months it is paying business. As ever

E. H. Bassett

The cards to Elford

Edward refers to "unauthorized traders" who were being expelled from camp. The Commanding General placed strict regulations on those allowed in camp to sell their wares to the soldiers. The purpose was primarily to keep whiskey out of the hands of the men. Approved traders were called Sutlers. Most of the men avoided the high cost of purchasing from these traders except for items not available from the army.

When a Sutler arrived with his wagon loads of goodies and every manner of wares and clothing, he would set up his tent and open for business. This usually brought on a rush from the camp to get there and buy some of the rare treats, such as pies. When the shelves were empty, he packed up and returned as soon as he could replenish his stores. On some occasions, when the men felt they were being cheated, they mobbed the offender and stripped his store clean.

SOLDIERS IN CAMP VISITING THE SUTLERS STORE
Sketch from Leslie's New Monthly Magazine

Falmouth, Virginia
Feb. 27th, 1863.

Dear Parents,

I rec. yours of the 15th & 9th this morning and will

now attempt to answer them. There was some news that I did not expect to hear in those letters. I was glad to hear of the safe arrival of Captain at his home and I hope he may have a good time while he stays. There are several of our boys going off on furlough as soon as things are arranged to suit. I hope it will not be long before we will be on the move again. I am tired of laying here. One year ago we were in Harper's Ferry where will we be one year from today and where will we go during the summer. We have had the deepest snow that I ever saw in Va. It snowed all day on the 22nd. There was about 8 inches fell & it was quite cold for a day or two. We went on picket on the 24th & had a very good time. On the morning of the 25th the rebel army made a dash on the picket lines & drove in our cavalry and came into the camp of the 82nd N.Y. which is a little over one mile from here. I believe they killed a Lieutennant of our Cavalry & took some prisoners but after all I guess the rebs did not make much afterwards for they were forced to hurry their boots to get off. It rained all day yesterday and is very warm today. You may bet that the roads are nice. Now would be a fine time for the authorities at Washington to order an advance! I don't think the roads will get very good before the first of April.

The news in the papers is unimportant except the reported capture of the Queen of the West. The rebs are making some important additions to their fleet & if they give us so much trouble with one or two insignificant crafts like those that they have, what will they do with a whole fleet of better boats.

I am enjoying excellent health as usual but I never feel easy for one moment in my mind. I want this rebellion crushed and the government to establish its authority, disband all the volunteer army, rid themselves of all the negros and then see if we cannot be a happy people. There are a party north that will have Fred Douglas in the White House if Mr. Lincoln does not beat them in some way. We are now on an equal footing with the Negro and it would be nothing strange if we were ruled by them in the course of time at the rate things are going now.

The Indian troubles that are threatening you on the frontier is talked of every day by the soldiers but I don't expect that we will be allowed to defend our homes if the whole Indian nation should make war with the white.

I sent you the January & February Nos. of Harpers New Monthly yesterday. I have sent for the Phrenological Journal & Life Illustrated for one year and if you would like them I will send them to you after I have read them. Those Harpers Magazines were quite interesting I thought. There are some good stories in them. If Captain Messick had let me know that he was going home I would have sent you some money but I did not know anything about it until he had been gone nearly one week. The mails are not safe for they have been robbed several times between here and Washington. Those stamps are just what I wanted after all. The boys sent to Washington several times for stamps but they don't come.

Edward H. Bassett.

With the rebel camps stretching for about eight miles on one side of the river and the Union camps on the other, it was only a matter of time before some interaction and discourse took place. At first, animosity reigned but, as time passed and pickets from both sides became familiar with one another, many conversational friendships developed. Although strictly forbidden, with little to break the routine of the camps, this was a welcome diversion that started with teasing and verbal jibes shouted across the water. Soon, men were crossing the river to sit and talk a spell or trade food and tobacco. When officers put a stop to this activity the ever-resourceful troops devised a means of sailing small, hand made boats back and forth. Cargos of coffee, sugar & tea were traded for fresh Virginia tobacco and perhaps a Richmond newspaper. A lively trade developed; although many cargos and craft were lost to the whims of wind and waves. If the sails were not set just right, an anxious trader could only stand on the river bank and watch as his much-anticipated treasure disappeared down the river or sank into the depths.

Falmouth, Va.
March 6th, 1863

Dear Parents,

Captain Messick has just returned safe and sound. He called in at my tent this evening and left that fine box of butter which you sent. He seems to be in good spirits although he must be fatigued by the way he has been flying arround since he left Camp. He spoke of seeing many of our friends while in the state and says that it is a free passport in the states to be a member of the 1st Minnesota (quite a compliment). As he has been in camp but a short time I have not had a chance to talk with him but a few moments. I will see him again and get all the news after he gets rested.

The weather has been rather cool for the past two or three days with high winds. Everything remains quiet on the front I believe. We will go on picket tomorrow to remain 24 hours and we will undoubtedly have a good time as usual. You speak of Maple sugar. If I was there I think I would like to try the old camp once more.

What did Mr.Clark want to pay for the farm? I fear you would not be able to make yourselves any better off while the war lasts if you did sell out. I suppose that business seems rather dull there now but Captain says that he found things in a more prosperous condition in Faribault than he had expected to & there seems to be a good supply of money & all seem to be cool & determined & look to the success of the cause of the

Union as certain in the end. You speak of our being permited to return to Minnesota in the spring. There is an effort being made now for that purpose but whether it will be successful or not we have only to hope & wait. There are some of the best men of the state at work at it now and we will be likely to know in a few days. If we are allowed to go to garrison the forts on the frontier & help to repulse the Indians in case of any trouble with them I think we would be doing a good service and I am sure we would be glad of a chance to recruit our ranks for if we are put in the field here with what few we have now & many of them nearly worn out we will not be asking many favors of any one by next fall if we have as rough times as we did last summer. However if we have to remain here we will try to sustain our reputation as the remnant of a first class Regt.

We were out this PM on a Division drill under Brigadier Genl Owen of Philadelphia. He is a dashing blade & a true son of Erin. There was also a grand review yesterday by Maj. Genl Hooker. Everything passed off pleasantly I believe. I was not out, being on guard at camp.

That butter is splendid and a great treat I assure you. It is an article that is not to be had every day in this country.

We have some rather exciting news from the west but it is not of a definite character. I hope that there will be a death blow dealt to the rebelious states before long. There has been two Corps of this army drawn away since the resignation of Burnside & I understand they have gone to Fortress Monroe. I think this whole line will be given up before long. There may be an advance made from the Pamunkey & York Rivers but I don't look for another general move in front of Fredericksburg. We are all expecting that there will be serious trouble with the Indians as soon as spring opens but I think they will be badly beaten off before fall and will not want to war with Uncle Sam after this next summer.

I have sworn vengeance on them if I ever have a chance. I don't think that Christianized warfare will work with the Sioux any better than it does with the Secesh. We will have to break over some of the silly rules of warfare & make our enemies feel the effects of war. The famous (John Pope) is not such a fool as some would believe. He knows how to treat his enemies & punish traitors. I long for peace and hope that there may be a speedy & honorable settlement of the great question.

Edward H. Bassett

Vol. 1st Minnesota Co. G

Falmouth, Virginia
March 12th, 1863.

Dear Father & Mother,

I think my last was written on the eve of the 6th. Captain Messick had just come back and we were ordered to be ready to go on picket at 8 o'clock the next morning to stay three days and as I had not written for some time and there would be no chance for three days. The weather is rather cool but we will soon have warm and perhaps hot weather. There has been some excitement in camp today about the enemy crossing the river above but I guess they have not crossed. (I wish they would). We were ordered to pack up and be ready to march immediately & each man got his sixty rounds of the needful & we are now fully prepared for them if they show themselves on our side of the Rappahannoc. I heard tonight that they were seen in force above here but had not crossed. I hope they will try us. I am geting tired of laying around. I would like to see Genl Hooker have a chance to pay the rebels up for the way they used us over in Fredericksburg. I think they will have something to do when old fighting Joe gets after them. I think we have lain still long enough now to go to work and we will be apt to as soon as the roads get dried up a little better. I don't think that this army has been used as well as it might although it has done some hard fighting, it seems as if we have got it all to do over again. Richmond would be in our hands if the army of the Potomac & Virginia had not been fettered by the continual howling of the northern traitors about the Genls of the army. There are no better Genls than McClellan & Pope if they can be supported by the authorities and allowed to use their own judgement in the field. If Richmond had been in Mexico or South America it would have been taken ere this. It is to near Washington & New York. I hope we may have better luck this time than we did last. Charleston & Savannah will be about the first then will come Richmond and then the rebelion will be about crushed and we may begin to sue for peace. I see by the papers that gold is worth $3.50 of confederate scrip in Richmond now and is still riseing.

I am glad to hear that Boultice Soule has got home for it is too much for him in the army. He was a good faithful fellow but it is not the kind of business for him.

You speak of the 1st returning to Minnesota. There was some talk of it and a great many thought that we would go but I guess there is no chance. There is work here that needs attention first. No one would be more pleased than I would if we could go but I shall make the best of it here if we stay. It won't be long before we can go and we can have just as good times as we could now and perhaps if we stay we may yet see Richmond taken and the old flag floating proudly o'er her and Jeff an exile. Perhaps you will think that I am dreaming but I am not. I think there is hope yet. I am going to hope about 12 months longer and then I intend to have a little rest for a time at least.

I will write again soon if we move.

My love to you all

Edward H. Bassett
Co G 1st Minnesota Vols.

That dried fruit was excellent. I thank you for it
hope to have a chance to see you all soon.

13th All quiet – snow squalls.

Falmouth Va.
March 26th, 1863

Dear Father & Mother,

Everything remains about the same. It rains every
day & the weather is quite mild. We will move as soon
as the weather will permit I expect & I hope it will be
soon for I am tired of laying here in camp. We have got
the best rations since Genl Hooker took command of
the army that we ever had. We have all the bread that
we want with a good supply of fresh beef & Potatoes &
Onions. Hooker has gained the entire confidence of the
army and I think he will do well when the fight comes.

I was sorry to hear of so many deaths in
Morristown. It must be very sickly there. Samuel Lilly
got word last night that his sister was dead. He feels
very bad about it but has a Christian's hope left I
suppose. Saml is one of the few religious ones that
enlisted that has stuck to his religion and has not
forgotten his pledge. Captain is well I think (except
being home sick). I want to see you all but I shall never
get a furlough for 15 days to go to Minnesota as long as
I am well.

Please excuse me this time.

Edward H. Bassett
1st Minnesota Vols.

Falmouth Virginia
April 1st, 1863.

Dear Father,

Thinking that you would like to hear what we are doing down here in Dixie I will write you a few lines. The weather is windy & blustering and there is some snow on the ground. There was about five inches of snow fell on the night of the 30th. It is just one Year since we landed at Hampton near Fortress Monroe, Va. The Peach trees were all in blossom there then and the grass growing so that it seemed quite pleasant. There has been rain or snow fell nearly every day for the past week but I hope that we will have warm weather soon.

We remain in our old camp near Falmouth and in full view of the City of Fredericksburg. Everything remains quiet as far as I know, although the picket lines have been strengthened lately so that it takes nearly again as many men to picket as it did in the fore part of winter. We are under Marching orders to start at a moment's notice but as near as I can learn there is no prospect of our moving right away. We were ordered to pack up this morning about 3 o'clock and some of the boys say that they have heard fireing on the outposts but my opinion is that it is an April fool got up by the (shoulder strap gentry). I wish the weather would get mild so that we could move. I had much rather be on the move than laying in camp. We expect Colonel Morgan & Gov. Ramsey in camp today, also the paymaster.

Everything is very dear here. We have to pay from 7 to 10 dollars for boots that we could get for 4 & 5 in Minnesota in 1860. Apples sell at 5 cts. each & everything accordingly. Health is excelent. There is no sickness in our Regt. The army is in good fighting trim and I think will give Lee a hard fight when the time comes. The army was never in better order than now. We are having the best rations that we ever had. I heard today that General Howard has taken command of the 9th Army Corps and General Sully takes command of the Division. I see by the papers that General E. V. Sumner is dead. I was sorry to hear it for the country needs such men as him. It will not be many days before the army will be doing something & I hope we will be able to take Richmond before fall.

I suppose you are expecting warm times with the Indians next summer but I hope they will be kept back but if they do come down on the frontier I would like very much to be there to fight them. I would like to kill one & get a good shot gun (& scalp). I wish that I could get a furlough for about 60 days to go to Minnesota but 15 days is the longest granted and then none but officers and their waiters have ever got furloughs in our Regt. There was an order to stop them until this morning there was another come allowing two to every hundred men. Are you going to crop all your land this summer. I suppose help is scarce and will be more so by harvest. What is wheat worth this spring? Do you think that you can make it pay farming this summer? Is there any one working the old sugar camp this spring I wish I was there in it.

I will close hopeing to see you all soon. Also that you may be prospered & have good health.

As ever your son in the 1st Minnesota Vol. Co. G.

Edward H. Bassett

Major General Edwin Vose Sumner was a career army officer who had served his country well. He was the first officer nominated by Lincoln and was appointed as the first new Union General created by the secession crisis on March 14, 1861. He became commander of the Second Corps of the Army of the Potomac under McClellan and was the oldest general in that army. His initiative during the Battle of Seven Pines prevented a Union disaster. He was wounded in the arm and hand at the Battle of Glendale and was commander of the Right Grand Division at the Battle of Fredericksburg where his 2nd Corps suffered heavy casualties. Soon after Hooker's appointment to replace Burnside, he was relieved of command at his own request. While waiting to take his next assignment as commander of the Department of the Missouri he traveled to visit his daughter in Syracuse, New York where he died of a

General Edwin Vose Sumner

heart attack on March 21, 1863. He was highly regarded by the soldiers of his command as attested to by Edward Bassett in the previous letter, *"the army needs such men as him."*

Falmouth, Virginia
April, 10th, 1863

Dear Father & Mother

You will no doubt be surprised to hear that we are still in our winter quarters on the Rappahannoc I thought we should be at work before this time & the only way that I can account for the delay is that it is not intended for this army to move until we see how the Charleston & Mississippi expeditions succeed. The enemy remain in their old camps in our front. Their tents can be seen for some 8 miles along the river. Yesterday we could see regiments drilling just back of Fredericksburg.

On the 8th the army was reviewed by the President

and General Hooker it was a very fine day and everything passed off pleasantly. There was 15 men in our company including Captain Messick.[65] Gov. Ramsey has been to see us & presented us with a state flag on the 3 rd inst. he made a few remarks which you will be apt to see in the St. Paul papers. I was on picket on the 4 th inst. the day was very pleasant except windy but about sundown it commenced snowing & snowed hard all night. In the morning there was some six inches of snow on the ground. I think it was the worst night that I was ever out since I have been in the army. The weather is beautiful now and the roads must be drying very fast. How I would like to be at work in the sugar camps.

My health is excellent this spring & I feel first rate. I received a letter last night from Mother and Anna. I wish I could mannage to go & see you all this spring but I cannot & shall have to be contented here.

There is nothing very interesting to write about & I fear you will find this a rather dull letter. I sent you the April No. of the Phrenological Journal [66] the other day. I will mail you the March and April No's. of Harpers new monthly to day. The pay master has not come but we expect him as soon as he gets the money. Captain is well.

Please excuse this short letter for there is not much to write about.

As ever your son, Edward H. Bassett

---

[65] This is an interesting number though it does not reflect the actual size of the company at this time. The company included 116 enlisted men and nine officers when mustered in on May 23, 1861, likely some of the company was assigned other duty on this day as its losses to this point in time would not account for the difference.

[66] A publication dealing with the then very popular interest in phrenology, the study of the conformation of the skull, based on the belief that it is indicative of mental faculties.

Falmouth Virginia
April 15th, 1863

Dear Sisters Ella and Anna,

I suppose you would like to hear once more from the army and Anna would like to have an answer to her last letter.

Well it is a rainy day & I am going to write you just as long a letter as I can & tell you every thing that I think of that will interest you. I was out on picket the day before yesterday and had a very good time the weather was very warm and pleasant. I saw a few rebels but they were across the river. Yesterday morning when I came back to camp I found a letter here for me from Cousin Ellen. She says that the folks were all well and wished me to remember her to you when I wrote. I expect we will move in a day or two. Part of the army has moved now and we have orders to be ready to go soon. Yesterday we packed all our blankets and extra clothing that we could not carry with us in boxes & it is to be taken care of for us so that we can get it next fall if we want it. Last summer we had to throw away our clothes that we could not carry. I lost about 15 dollars worth last summer. The weather has been beautiful for the last 7 or 8 days the roads are getting in a good condition but it is raining to day and I guess there will be mud enough now for a few days. The grass has begun to grow a little and I saw a few flowers in the woods when I was out there, there are also some birds such as Robins, Bluebirds, Wrens and I saw some little red birds about the size of a Wren. There are no Ducks nor Geese nor Loons nor Prairie hens. I heard a Rooster Crow yesterday morning but he was on the other side of the river. If he had been on this side I'll bet he would have lost his head before now. He must have kept still all winter for I have not heard one crow before since last summer.

I would like to be there in Minnesota this spring to hunt some ducks and spear some fish. I heard that there was some fresh fish comeing up from the depot but I guess they must have got back into the river. I saw one of the officers have a fresh Shad the other day but I don't know where he got it. The army was reviewed by The President and General Hooker on the 7th, 8th and 9th. We were out on the 8th. President Lincoln looked rather pale and careworn to what he did on the 4th of July last when he reviewed the army at Harrison's Bar on the James river.

One year ago today we were inspected by Maj. Davis of the 4th U.S. Infantry in our camp in front of Yorktown. Two years ago I was at Morristown. I hope that we will be able to take Richmond this Summer and I think we will if we are handled right. We were near enough to send a shell into the city last summer but had to fall back. General Hooker has issued some good orders to arrest stragglers & shoot Cowards. I expect that we would have heard the cannon at work early this morning if it had not rained. But now I would not wonder if there was a delay of a week or more.

We are expecting the pay master along every day, he is now paying some of the other Regiments.

I enjoy excellent health and think there will be no trouble about my standing the Campaign as well as I did last summer at least. I want to have both of you write to me very often this summer and tell me all about the farm garden and anything that you think of to write about. If you go to school I want you to write about it what you are studying &c. &c. Please remember me to Elford tell him to plant some Tomatoes, Potatoes, Mellons & sweet corn for me so if I come to see him next summer we can have a good time. Good by to you all this time.

As ever your brother

Edward

Falmouth, Virginia
April 15th, 1863

Dear Father,

I was just writing a letter to Ella and Anna & I thought I would write you a few lines also. We are having a very bad storm it commenced raining last night and has rained all the time since & it is now about 2 o'clock P.M. General Hooker commenced moving the army up from the left on the 12th & 13th the roads were in excellent condition & it would have been very easy for the army to move if the weather had continued good. (As it is I fear it will turn out similar to Burnsides move of the 20th of Jan.) We have had a few days of as fine weather as I ever saw & if it had continued I believe there would have been a fight by tomorrow if not sooner. The army is in first best trim and we have packed all our extra baggage and are as light as possible so that when the time comes I believe the rebels will have to give back. I hear that Hooker says he is going to make the cavalry pitch in. There are plenty of siege guns ready and I feel confident that there will be a victory to record before many days that will make all loyal people rejoice unless the rain continues.

The boys are all well. For my part I never felt better and I long to have the weather settled for it is time to commence our work if we intend to do anything this summer & I am sure I don't wish to lay here idle all summer. I want to see Richmond taken and if I have a hand in it I shall do my best. There has been considerable talk about our being sent to Minnesota & one of the full regiments taking our place but I guess there is no hope now of anything of the kind. For my part I don't care if we move and have good honest commanders so that we can whip the Rebels. I will enjoy myself about as well here as anywhere if I have got to be a Soldier.

I will write again in a few days.

Your Son, Edward H. Bassett

It is raining hard.

Thursday morning 16th: It has cleared off & the hard rain is over. I see no signs of a move to day as it is quiet. We have full particulars of the fight in Charleston Harbor. The ironclads were inside harbor the 7th inst. The Keokuck sunk from being riddled with shot. All is quiet here this morning.

E. H. Bassett

The Battle of Charlestown Harbor

Nine Union ironclads under the command of Samuel DuPont attacked Fort Sumter in an unsuccessful attempt to close Charleston Harbor. The guns of Forts Sumter and Moultrie were brought into action and launched a fusillade so intense that the ships were quickly so disabled as to prevent their returning effective fire and they were forced to withdraw. The Keokuck sunk the next day.

Period Drawing

CHAPTER 21
THE CHANCELLORSVILLE
CAMPAIGN

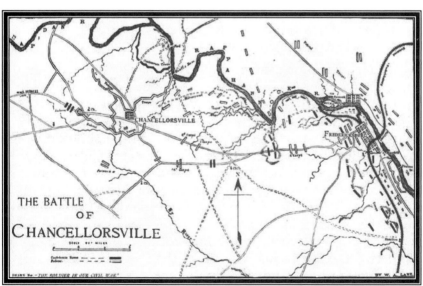

Map from Leslie's Illustrated Weekly drawn by W. A. Lane

During the time spent in winter camp, General Hooker made great strides in restoring the army's morale and reorganized it into well equipped fighting force of 125,000 men. By mid April the men were in good spirits and most were anxious to *"go to work,"* all seeking to gain a victory and finish the war. Mail was brought up almost daily. Supplies had been plentiful and the availability of better food and fresh vegetables along with better sanitary regulations had cut sickness and disease by half—from more than 10% to 5%. Comfortable huts had been re-built and tents repaired, making life in camp fairly comfortable. Daily drilling kept the men in shape and sharpened their skills. Best of all, after a long wait, the men finally received their pay which always raised their spirits.

Falmouth Virginia
April 20th 1863.

Dear Father & Mother,

When I wrote to you last it was raining and we were under marching orders. Well it is raining now & we are under the same orders. It has not been raining all the time since. We have had one or two April showers also some very pleasant weather. Yesterday was just as nice a day to be out as I ever saw. I thought we should be out after the rebs before this time but it is hard to tell when the army will move. We are ready at any time now and may start any day. Everything remains quiet and about the same as usual. I would not be surprised if we remained here until June and perhaps all summer. I hear that there has been quite a hard fight between our cavalry and the rebels up the Rappahannoc. Our side was victorious with a loss of about 400. The rebels loss was as heavy and we captured quite a number of Prisoners. I saw six rebel soldiers this morning that deserted and came within our lines. They are hard looking fellows and no doubt sick of Jeff D. We hear of a great deal of suffering among the rebs. They appear to be short of rations and there has been several bread riots in Richmond, Petersburg and several other cities in the Confederacy. The women turn out and take anything in the way of eatables that they find regardless of both public and private property. I expect some of these have been in a starving condition nearly all winter. Their pickets along the Rappahannoc are quite friendly and ask us to come over and see them. They also send over a Richmond paper once in a while. Since the fish have commenced running in the river they are continually fishing. They have neither coffee nor sugar and salt is scarce but I expect they have plenty of flour & meal and a tolerable supply of fresh meat. They seem to stick to it well & no doubt some of them think they will whip us yet. When we got orders to march we were to take eight days rations with us and the rebs ask us now since we don't seem to move when Joe Hooker is comeing with his eight days rations to see them. They seem to have found out in some way what we were intending to do.

Time is passing off rather lonely to me. I find but little to read that interests me and I am at a loss to know what to do to amuse myself a great deal of the time. I got a pass today thinking that I would go down to the Wisconsin Brigade and see some of the boys there but it has been raining all day & I have to stay in camp.

There are none sick in our Co. now. I rec. the St. Paul Press of Mar. 26th & Apr. 2nd last night. They were mailed on the 10th. We are having regular April weather here. It rains from 5 to 20 minutes & then slacks up and almost clears off, then rains again. Our old Parson gave us a lecture yesterday. I went out to hear him. It was the first sermon that I have heard this last 8 months. It made me think of old times. The paymaster does not seem to come. I don't know what the reason is. We have been expecting him for some time.

My love to you all. Please excuse mistakes &c.

As ever your son

Edward Bassett

Co. G – 1st Minnesota Vol.

Falmouth Virginia
Sunday April 26th, AD

Dear Father:

Again I have seated myself in my tent to write you a few lines. You will no doubt be somewhat surprised to hear that we are still in our old camp with no prospect of any move. Everything remains quiet as usual. I can see the rebel camps on the heights back of Fredericksburg very plain from where I am siting. They appear to be in heavy force.

The 7th New York Regt. of 8 months men started for home at 6 o'clock this morning. They have had quite easy times and have lost but very few men. It is a German Regt.

I was on guard last night and feel too sleepy to write much today. The weather is very pleasant except the wind which has blown very hard for two or three days. I have no doubt but that the weather is warmer in Minnesota now than it is here. The grass is growing a little on the hills but I cannot see that the buds on the trees have grown any yet.

The Paymaster has finaly come after keeping us waiting for a long time, we were payed four months wages yesterday. I have sent you by Adams Express forty-five dollars. It will likely go as far as Faribault and you can get it there. I thought it would be better to send it by express for then it will be perfectly safe. I have heard of the mails being robbed several times lately and large sums of money taken from Army mail bags. There will be two months more wages due us on the 2ᵗʰ of this month but we will not be apt to get it before June.

Health remains good with us. There has not been a death in our regt. except at the General Hospitals at Washington, New York, Baltimore and other places since we left the Peninsula (except those killed at Antietam). I don't think that is the case with many Regts. that have been out in the field the way we have. I would like very well to be working on a farm somewhere in the west this spring, but I guess I will find pretty steady employment in the army for another year and perhaps longer. Still I hope to have the war ended sooner.

I remain as ever your Affectionate son

Edward H. Bassett

Co. G 1st M.Vol. U.S.A.

General Hooker had been making plans to attack Lee, whose forces were only about 61,800 men, with part of his army sent south to forage for supplies. The moment to attack was now at hand. Having learned from Burnside's failure, he knew the folly of mounting another frontal attack against the well-entrenched enemy at Fredericksburg. Hooker decided to split his army, taking three corps, some 70,000 men, up river 25 miles to launch a major turning attack against Lee's weak left flank.

The Army of General Hooker on the march to the battlefield of Chancellorsville, Leslie's Illustrated Weekly, from a sketch by Edwin Forbes

To cover his movement, he left three corps of troops, about 27,000, led by Gen. Sedgwick, to cross the river below Fredericksburg and attack Lee's right flank after his turning force was well underway. Because this would force Lee to pull back from the city, Sedgwick was then to mount a direct attack across the river and force the confederates from their positions on Marye's Heights located behind Fredericksburg. Hooker would then cut the rebel supply lines and destroy their supply depots near Chancellorsville. The two powerful forces would then move toward each other, catching the confederates between them to be destroyed or forced to retreat toward Richmond. The first phase of the plan, Hooker's movement from camp to Chancellorsville and Sedgwick's flanking movement, has been praised as brilliant in its planning and execution.

Chancellorsville was actually just a single, fine, two-story brick house owned by a farmer named Chancellor. Its location at the crossroads of a first-rate macadamized[67] turnpike to Fredericksburg gave it strategic importance. It was also positioned on a good road running north to U.S. Ford over the Rappahannock. The house was surrounded at some distance

---

[67] A Macadamized road was constructed by compacting a layer of broken or crushed stone combined with a binder such as asphalt or cement on a well drained and crowned roadbed. Essentially a paved road.

by dense scrub brush. To the south and west lay the nearly impenetrable jungle of scrub-oaks and jack-pines locally known as *"The Wilderness."*

Period Sketch from Frank Leslie's Illustrated Weekly

The Battle of Chancellorsville, which encompassed a large area, took place from April 27 through May 6. The distance between Fredericksburg and Chancellorsville was ten miles, with forces spread over an even greater distance. This battle was not just a single engagement but many battles and skirmishes. Commanders on both sides were splitting their armies and maneuvering large numbers of men in thrust and counter thrust moves.

The principal events were:
- April 29: Skirmishes at Germanna Ford and Crook's Run
- April 29-May 2: Operations at Franklin's Crossing and Pollock's Mill Creek near Fredericksburg
- April 30: Skirmishes at and near Fredericksburg
- May 1-3: Battle at Chancellorsville
- May 2: Skirmish at Ely's Ford
- May 3-4: 2nd Battle of Fredericksburg (also called Marye's Heights) and the Battle of Salem Church near Bank's Ford
- May 4-6: Numerous skirmishes along the lines

Attention will be focused on the participation of the First Minnesota Regiment and limited to its action, commonly referred to as *"The Second Battle of Fredericksburg,"* while under the command of General Sedgwick.

On April 27th and 28th, General Hooker left camp with his 5th, 11th, and 12th corps—the "turning movement" mentioned earlier—marching 25 miles up the Rappahannock. These 70,000 troops marched with all their equipment and supplies along different routes, starting at different times, and crossed 2 rivers at separate locations. All the troops arrived at Chancellorsville on the evening of the 30th. The entire movement was accomplished without the enemy's knowledge and, was a masterpiece of execution.

As planned, General Sedgwick's diversionary movement to the enemy's right flank took place simultaneously. The 6th, 3rd, and 1st corps left camp during the night of the April 28th marching downstream three miles below Fredericksburg to Franklin's Crossing and Pollock's Mill. The morning of April 29th, two pontoon bridges were erected at these two locations. These positions held while under intense fire from rebel sharp-shooters. Also on April 28th, the 1st and 3rd Divisions of the 2nd Corps marched four miles up-stream from Falmouth to Banks' Ford then on to United States Ford, where a pontoon bridge was erected. The corps then marched to Chancellorsville, reaching that place at the same time as all the other units.

Meanwhile, the Second Division—Gibbon's of the Second Corps, including the First Minnesota—remained in camp. This division's camp bordered the river and was readily visible to the enemy. Their purpose was to mislead the rebels into thinking nothing unusual was happening in the Union camp. With only a fraction of the army left in camp, they were kept busy guarding the massive stockpile of stores, serving picket duty, drilling and generally trying to look like the whole army. The men found themselves almost continually on duty.

Dear Sisters Ella & Anna,

We are in our old camps yet although most of the army has moved. I expect we will start in a few days. Our men crossed the river this morning about three miles below Fredericksburg; they put pontoon bridges across last night.

I went on picket night before last about 8 o'clock in the evening and got back to camp last night about 11 o'clock. I saw a great many rebels in Fredericksburg some of them were drilling, some playing ball, some fishing; they all felt well and were singing talking and laughing all night. They asked us to come over and see them assuring us that we should have good quarters.[68] They sent over a little sail boat with a Richmond paper in it of the 27th, our men sent the boat back with a cargo of coffee. We were not allowed to talk to them at all. They waved their flags from the windows and if there had not been strict orders about fireing I should have tried to make them take their flags out of sight and range of my musket. I could kill a man at every shot across the river with my gun but it would be of no use and it is strictly forbidden to shoot unless they commence or try to come across the river. They appear to have very poor clothes and one of their soldiers that deserted and came over to us this morning says that they are very short of rations.

I think we will have posession of Fredericksburg this week and without fighting too. We have a large army both above and below that is crossing and as soon as they get across and drive the rebs back we will cross here. There are only three brigades left here and we will not be apt to have a hand in the fight if there is one.

I am well, and pleased with the prospect of moveing

---

[68] The "good quarters" referred to here are prison camps.

soon we have lain here since last November and I think it is high time for us to be moveing if we intend to do anything this summer. It is just two years since I was sworn into the service of the United States one more year and I will be free again. You don't know how bad I want to see you all but there is no use of wishing or freting about it. I am going to try and enjoy myself the most I can while I am in the army and if I ever get out alive and we whip the rebels I think I can enjoy myself much beter than I could if I had not enlisted. I am glad that I enlisted when I did.

The weather is very mild the grass and clover is growing and some fields look quite green. There are a great many fruit trees in blossom over in the city. I was looking at the city to day through Captain Messick's spy glass I can see very plain where the shell went through the church spire. I don't think there are but few families living in town now. I guess they don't like to risk the Yankee shells.

I got my likeness taken the other day to send to Elford. I did not try to get a good picture but it looks just like me every day in camp. Tell Toad that I would like to have his picture if he can send it to me. I send mine in this letter to him. Don't tell him who it is and see if he will know me. Well I have written a long letter and told you all about the rebs for I did not know what to write about & happen to think perhaps you would like to hear about them. Give my love to all the family and write soon and often.

I remain as ever your Affectionate brother

Edward H. Bassett

Ella F. Basset

Anna E, Basset

Co. G 1st Mn. V.

U. S. A.

Photo of the pontoon bridge mentioned in this letter.
Library of Congress
****

💣 2ND BATTLE OF FREDERICKSBURG

When Sedgwick's movement on the rebel left flank failed to develop into a general assault, Lee guessed it was a feint. He immediately pulled all but about 10,800 of his men out of the works at Fredericksburg and sent them to fight Hooker at Chancellorsville. The First Minnesota men spent the day in camp in a drizzling rain, marking the second anniversary in the service. The relative quiet of camp was punctuated by the muffled rumble of cannon fire far away on their right and the sharper boom of artillery down river on their left. Reports were sketchy as to the outcome of these engagements, leaving the men filled with speculation. The ever-present morning fog lifted earlier than usual on the April 30th and those who were not on duty anxiously went up on the heights at Falmouth to view events across the river. They observed a considerable force of Sedgwick's column that had crossed the river. The heard the sounds of cannon and musketry fire coming from both above and below their vantage point. The day grew very long as anxiety mounted and orders came to be ready to move. Everything in camp was packed except the tents. Sounds of battle were often heard from afar. Dawn the next morning found the men ready to get into the action, but again, they could only wait for orders. The resounding thud of artillery was again heard both up and down the river. It lasted until well after dark. The high arc of exploding shells created an interesting fireworks display in the night sky. As the men lay down in their tents, they could hear the muffled thunder of the guns and actually feel the ground tremble.

Looking toward Fredericksburg from Stafford Heights behind Falmouth
Sketch from Harper's Weekly by A. R. Waud

Although Hooker's force far outnumbered Lee's, he held about half of it in reserve and now had lost his initiative. Stonewall Jackson had done the unthinkable. Making a daring night march and a surprise attack, he nearly destroyed the Eleventh Corp on Hooker's right flank. With his right flank now attacked and crushed, Hooker lost his nerve. Over the objections of his field commanders, Hooker ordered his army to withdraw from the plains beyond the wilderness and to fall back to Chancellorsville. His splendid plan for victory now became a harbinger of utter defeat.

On Saturday night, May 2, 1863, General Hooker ordered Sedgwick to cross the river, occupy the town of Fredericksburg and then, to route the enemy from their defensive works on Marye's Heights, behind the town. With that accomplished, he was to move out on the turnpike road toward Chancellorsville and attack the confederates from the rear at daylight. The task was insurmountable. Sedgwick got the order at 11 P.M. He was already across the river in force but was still expected to take the town, defeat the rebels and, then, undertake a night march of 14 miles to mount an attack. General Sedgwick set his column in motion. They were continually confronted by rebel skirmishers. By daylight, they had covered the four miles to Fredericksburg. Including the soldiers in Gibbon's Second Division, who were still in camp, Sedgwick had a total of nearly 27,000 men and 54 pieces of artillery. The First Minnesota and the other units of Gibbons Division had retired to their tents that night without knowing Hooker was now in dire peril at Chancellorsville. Ordered to sleep in their clothes, the men knew that tomorrow there would be fighting to be done. They were aroused at midnight, hurriedly folded and packed their tent cloths and blankets in their knapsacks and strapped on their gear. Each man carried a full eight-day's rations and 140 rounds of ammunition as they stood to roll call and were ready to march. They soon learned their brigade was to take the lead, cross the river at the exact spot they had on December 11th, directly in front of Fredericksburg, and take the city. One can only wonder what thoughts went through their minds as they marched to the Lacy House and waited for the pontoon bridge to be erected. How

Sketch from Harper's Weekly 12/27/1862

could a single division really be expected to accomplish what half the army could not just four months ago? At the river, orders came for each of the four regiments in the brigade[69] to send 25 volunteers to act as sharpshooters to protect the bridge builders. They were also ordered, if necessary, to cross the river in the pontoon boats and drive the enemy from the shore. Although the men were well aware that on two previous occasions, hundreds were killed and wounded at this duty, they stepped forward without hesitation. In fact, so many volunteered only one in fifteen could be accepted. It was by grand good fortune that no fire was encountered and none were lost. As dawn broke and the thick fog that blanketed the river began to lift, the division crossed and entered the town. Unbelievably they marched through the streets to the far side of town without a shot being fired. The rebels had withdrawn to their trenches and rifle pits on Marye's Heights. At this time, General Sedgwick, with the 6th Corps, was heavily engaged with the enemy on the left and the Second Division was moved to the right. The move was interrupted while a bridge, which ran through town crossing a deep canal, was repaired. Marching a full mile while under heavy artillery fire, they moved along the base of the hills to the river bank and stopped almost directly across the river from Falmouth. On the hills in front of them the men could see confederates in a line of rifle pits across the hillside and another line of troops further up the slope. Colonel Colvill, temporarily in command of the Minnesota 1st, soon noticed an enemy battery being placed that would put the entire regiment under enfilading fire[70]. Always concerned for his men, Colvill moved them to occupy the abandoned rebel entrenchments along the river just as the rebel guns roared into life and the screaming ordnance rent the air. Thanks to Colvill's quick action, the barrage of exploding iron proved ineffective and soon ceased.

---

[69] The 19th Maine was away on duty guarding telegraph lines.

[70] Enfilading fire is fire that comes either from the right or left of a line of troops. Such fire can be exceptionally devastating since it travels down the line in parallel. A single cannon shot properly aimed, could travel down the line killing and wounding dozens of soldiers.

Skirmishers were sent forward up a road that ran back from the river, where they encountered rebel pickets. These were Alabama men under the command of General Wilcox—an ominous meeting perhaps; as these were the same men they would meet two months later in a hand-to-hand struggle of life and death at Gettysburg.

The brigade rested there for a time, all the while under constant fire, until being ordered away. The purpose of their move to the right had been to draw some of the rebels away from the point where Sedgwick's 6th Corp, led by the 100 volunteers, was charging the heights. Gibbon's men were now needed to support Sedgwick's forces. The determined Union soldiers charged the hill twice only to be met with murderous volleys of rifle and artillery fire and forced back to regroup. A third charge was ordered with fixed bayonets. As the men charged over their fallen comrades, faced with the wall of screaming men in blue and their glistening cold steel bayonets, the rebels broke and ran. A triumphant cheer, carrying the message of their success, echoed across the land.

James Wright wrote:

"The enemy had almost ceased to fire on us, and we were considering our whole movement a feint, when orders came to return into town. We started at once by the left flank at the double-quick. We were scarcely moving before we heard a crashing roar of artillery and roaring crashes of musketry, followed by continuous discharges. These might have continued for ten minutes, maybe more, when we heard the cheering, and recognized it as a Union cheer and knew that it meant that matters were going favorable to our side."

Sedgwick's now-unified army, pursued the fleeing rebels for some miles, collecting many prisoners and passing dead and wounded on the road. After covering about three miles, Gibbon's division was no longer needed. They were ordered to return to the north side of the river through Fredericksburg to guard the lower bridges, railway station, supply wagon trains, telegraph lines and supply depot at Aquia Creek. The brigade marched at quick-time back to town where they halted briefly to rest and retrieve their knapsacks which were left there under guard during the fighting. Passing through town, they crossed on the single pontoon bridge they had used earlier and went onto the heights near Lacy House. The First Minnesota was then ordered to march down river and guard the two lower pontoon bridges Sedgwick had used to cross the 6th Corps. Exhausted by the day's hot sun and marching, the men were pleasantly refreshed by a brief shower as they marched to the bridges. At sundown, a long line of dead and wounded, brought from the battlefields, crossed the bridges. Pickets and guards were stationed along the river and at the bridges. Men hastened to make coffee and prepare places to rest. They would have no shelters this night. After 20 hours on their feet and marching over 20 miles, they were tired enough to sleep anywhere. The showers that fell during the night went unnoticed.

The next day, May 4th, Hooker's army stayed in defensive positions at Chancellorsville. Lee, meanwhile, concluded that Hooker was not planning to renew his attack. After making detailed preparations, he left part of his forces to keep Hooker in check and moved with the balance of his men to attack Sedgwick on three sides. Sedgwick was now in a real predicament. With his army under attack on both flanks and in the center, he had no choice but to abandon all hopes of joining up with Hooker. Sedgewick withdrew toward the river. As darkness approached, a heavy fog again settled in; he was relieved to reach the Rappahannock and cross on the still-intact pontoon bridges.

Hooker called a council of war with his generals that night and, although some wanted to stay and renew the fight, others voted to withdraw. The meeting was actually a waste of time as Hooker had already decided on the latter course. The next day, his army fell back behind the Rappahannock, leaving all the dead and wounded behind on the field. He also abandoned 14 cannons, 20,000 small arms and a huge amount of other equipment and supplies. Lee thus gained a real treasure trove of desperately needed material and another great plan ended in disaster. With their hopes of victory thwarted once again, Hooker's dispirited army returned to its old positions, having accomplished nothing and taken considerable losses.

Camped at Falmouth, Va.
Thursday May 7th, 1863

Dear Father & Mother,

I improve the first opportunity to write to you for I know that you will be anxious to hear from me after the late battle of Fredericksburg. There has been fighting for the last 9 or 10 days and I suppose that we have been totaly defeated and the army has been forced to fall back to this side of the river. We left our camp on the night of the 2nd about 12 o'clock and marched down to the river where we lay until about five o'clock, when we crossed the river on a pontoon in the same place that we did last December, the enemy did not oppose our crossing. By eleven o'clock we had taken the first & second line of works on the heights back of the City. There had been hard fighting up the river for several days and we heard that Hooker was driving the enemy. General Sedgwick crossed with the 6th Corps below the city & was making his way up through to join Hooker, which I think he done on the 3d. There was but four men killed in taking the heights but there was some heavy fighting with Genl Hooker further to the right & I expect a heavy loss. Our Division is the 2nd Div. of the 2nd Corps. We are under command of Genl Gibbon & were left at Fredericksburg while the other Divisions of the Corps went above with General Hooker so we did not get into the thickest fight and have not lost many men from our Division. Our Regt. came back across the river on the night of the 3rd and went on duty below the City. The enemy raised reinforcements during the night. On the morning of the 4th they forced our men back & there was some hard fighting. On the 5th we were on picket on this side of the river below the City. The rebs came down about 8 o'clock AM and took posession of the City and the rifle pits along the bank of the river. Our men all crossed the night of the 4th & took out the bridge. It commenced raining about 4 o'clock PM of the 5th & I think we had the heavyest rain that I have seen since the war broke out. We got wet through and had a hard time of it that night.[71] We were laying on the bank of the river within 40 rods of Fredericksburg and the rebs were prowling through the streets hunting for knapsacks &c. that our men had lost. During the day we heard that General Hooker's army had been whipped and had fell back across the river. It seems hard but it is so & can't be helped now. We hear that Banks has taken Port Hudson and that we have also taken Vicksburg. I think the rebs have massed their forces against Hooker to defeat him. Our Surgeon (Dr. Morton) says that the rebs lost two to our one. They charged our batteries and were slaughtered by the hundreds. Some of our troops behaved badly I hear. We captured some guns from the rebs but they got more from us if reports are true. Albert Johnson was wounded by a bullet from a shell through the calf of the leg. He is doing well. Corporal Edwd. Phillips from Owatonna was wounded through the left arm below the elbow with a piece of shell. Walter Reed from Elysian had his thigh bruised by a piece of shell but will be able to do duty again in a few days. There were no more hurt in our Co. Two others were wounded by the same shell in Co. K. There were 11 wounded in our Regt. I believe but none killed. The boys are all well and feel like trying the rebs again soon if needed.

I have just rec. a letter from Father dated April 26th. I am glad to hear that the Indians are not going

---

[71] The torrential downpour lasted most of the night and caused the river to rise rapidly. Without shelters, the men could only lie on the sodden ground with their soaked blankets and clothes and try to rest in the mud.

to trouble the frontier this summer. I hope that there will be something done to end the war before another year. I would like to know who will be the next General to try to take Richmond. I believe that Hooker has done his best, although there will no doubt be any amount of charges prefered against him. I ask if McClellan's failure was worse than Burnside's or Hooker's. If we take Richmond I think it would be easier to do so from the peninsula or from most any point rather than this. There are more families in Fredericksburg than I thought there were. The women are nearly all Secesh and look poison. One old woman said that she hoped she would die before we should conquer the south, when our Lieut, said-he hoped she would. One old lady has five sons in the Union army and wants to see the rebels whipped. You will most likely get the particulars of the battle before you get this letter. I hope it may not be as bad for us as we hear it is. We are in the 1st Brigade & 2nd Division of the 2nd Corps.

Those pictures of the girls look very natural I think, although they have grown old fast within the last two years. Anna has got the same smile that she used to have and I should judge is just as full of fun as ever. I hope to see you all before another year. I shall improve the first oportunity whether I am in the army or not.

I hope you may yet hear of this army gaining a victory. I expect we will try them again soon. If we do I hope we may have better luck. I still hope for the best. Good Bye for this time.

Your Affectionate Son

E. H. Bassett.

Camped opposite Fredericksburg, Va.
Sat. eve May 9th, 1863

Dear Parents,

I suppose you are anxious to hear from these parts since the battle and you will very likely hear a great many terrible rumors before you get a true statement. I sent you a letter written on the 7th but as I had heard but little from the right wing of the army then I scarcely knew whether they had all got back to this side of the river. We even had rumors in camp that a large portion of the army was in great danger of being captured. It seems now that Genl Hooker found the enemy in very strong force and although he might have beaten them he saw fit to draw back to this side of the Rappahannoc and the different Corps and Divisions have many of them gone back to their old camps. Our Cavalry went around the enemy and some of them within two miles of Richmond they destroyed the Rail Road bridges across the Pamunkey and Chickahominy rivers. In the fight we have killed nearly two to their one and we have taken a great many prisoners and although we have not accomplished what we set out to do we have met the enemy and injured them more than they have us. Our army is not whipped for they fell back before they got whipped. Stonewall Jackson is wounded seriously and their army has been badly cut up and their supplies cut off for a time while our army is in good spirits and bountifully supplied with everything. Our division (the 2nd Div. of the 2nd Corps) which consists of three brigades; Sully's 1st, Danas 2nd, and Burnes' 3rd were left here opposite the city and when Genl Sedgwick's Corps (the 6th) tried to cut their way through to Hooker we crossed the river and operated with him as far as we were able. When the Heights were taken in the rear of the city on Sunday I thought that we had certainly gained a great victory and I did think that the enemy would be driven back to Richmond if not captured but Monday morning they had heavy reinforcements and soon drove our men back and took possession of the city and their rifle pits on the bank of the river below the city. They don't say much about the fight but some of them asked what we left our overcoats over there for. I saw a great many of them dressed in our uniforms yesterday when I was down on picket. They (the rebels) have brought all our wounded to Fredericksburg and sent over a flag of truce and requested us to come over and get them for they have no means of taking care of them. This morning our men sent over some pontoon boats and I expect have got all of our wounded on their way north where they can be cared for. It is said that our division is going to stay here to guard the supply depot and it is expected that the army will commence offensive operations soon. If we stay here we will get rid of some of the hard marches although we will be apt to have plenty of duty. The 1st Minnesota is encamped, about 3 miles from the old camp and right on the RR within less than 1/2 a mile from Fredericksburg the boys are all well and in good spirits those that were wounded have been sent north and will get good care. I received a letter from Father on the 7th and one from Anna to night. It has cleared off and today the sun has been quiet hot. The grass is growing and the fields look quite green. Everything has been quiet along the line since the battle. We got the papers today for the first time since the army moved. I see that Porter is still at work on the Mississippi and it is said that we have an army advancing on Petersburg below Richmond. I received a St. Paul Press and an Advocate the night before we marched. How I would like to see you all. Capt is well. I never was in better health.

Sunday Morning May 10th

It is very pleasant and will be a hot day. I did not have time to finish my letter before it got dark last night. We are encamped in a beautiful place there are plenty of nice creeks all arround. How I would like to be in Minnesota this morning. It is just one week this morning since we crossed the river and were in Fredericksburg. One year ago we were encamped at

Dovers Landing on the Pamunkey. Wm Ramsey is well and the same as ever. I have Harpers monthly for May and the Journal to read. I will send the Harpers to you when I have read it. I sent you the May No (number) of the Phrenological Journal. I have sent you the Jan. Feb. and Apr. Nos (numbers) of Harpers have you ever received them. I remain as ever your son,

Edward H. Bassett

Co. G 1st Minn Vols. 1863

P.S. I sent you 45 dollars by express after pay day and I expect it must be there before this time.

BATTLE OF CHANCELLORSVILLE, SUNDAY, MAY 3d, 1863.—GENERAL HOOKER REPULSING THE ATTACK OF THE CONFEDERATES.

Sketch by Edwin Forbes in Harper's Weekly showing the Battle of Chancellorsville May 3, 1863
****

The final tally in Union losses was 12,197 killed or wounded and 5,000 missing or captured. The First Minnesota had only nine men wounded, mostly by shell fragments, and none killed.

The Confederate losses were also heavy, with 10,266 killed or wounded and 2,733 missing or captured. Though Lee lost fewer in numbers, the impact was significant because his losses were irreplaceable.

Perhaps the greatest single loss that befell General Lee during the seven days of battle occurred on the night of May 2nd. General Stonewall Jackson had marched his army all day to make an attack on Hooker's right flank, which he accomplished with total surprise. His army came out of the tangle of the wilderness and swept through a Union camp, catching the men eating their suppers. By 7:15 PM, he had reunited his force with Lee and pushed the Federals back to Chancellorsville. The fighting stopped as darkness came and both sides paused to regroup and reorganize. With full intentions of renewing the attack before dawn, Jackson rode out in the night with his staff to reconnoiter the enemy lines and plan his next move. As he and the approximately 20 mounted officers returned in the pitch darkness, they were mistaken by their own pickets for a Union Cavalry unit. They were cut down in a hail of lead. Jackson was hit three times, a minie ball striking his right hand and two others shattered his left arm while knocking him from his horse. When the mistake was realized and the firing ceased, two of his aides were dead and several others were wounded. Jackson was rushed to the field hospital at Wilderness Tavern where his left arm was amputated. He seemed to be recovering, but then developed pneumonia and died on May 10th. The loss of this treasured friend and valued commander was a devastating blow to General Lee.

During the month after the battle, both armies paused to rest and an unofficial truce seemed to prevail. Soldiers, who just days before had been earnestly engaged in fighting to the death, now visited with each other across the river. The water had receded and was now fordable nearly everywhere. The confederates had made themselves a seine and were actively engaged in catching some of the abundant crop of fish. On occasion, some Union soldiers crossed over and helped with the seine in exchange for some of the catch. A lively illicit trade of newspapers and other goods was carried on by two mortal enemies only a stone's throw apart. The usual camp routine with its drilling and picket duty along with catching up on the news and writing letters home became the norm.

Hooker's failure became the subject of a great deal of "Monday morning generalship." The hindsight consensus was that Hooker had made several grievous errors. He should not have sent his cavalry away to attack the rebel supply line because it left him blind to the movements of the enemy. He should not have withdrawn into the wilderness and yielded the offensive to Lee. His greatest asset was his strength yet he left over half of his force out of the battle. He used his artillery very poorly and could have changed the outcome of the entire affair if had he been more astute. All in all, Hooker had simply been outgeneraled.

Falmouth Station oposite Fredericksburg, Va.
May 13, A. D. 1863

Dear Mother,

We are encamped in a beautiful place about 30 rods from the city of Fredericksburg. The general depot for the Army of the Potomac is just back of our camp about 40 rods. There are a large amount of stores here now for the army and they are continuously coming up from Acquia creek on the cars there is no prospect of the army evacuating this place unless the rebs whip us out and there is little danger of their doing that. Our camp is in full view of the city and we can see the rebel soldiers drilling and running around the city all the day. The rebels don't boast much over their victory. Genl Hooker went in for killing them and they have lost heavily. Stonewall Jackson is dead and the papers say he died from the effects of the amputation of his arm and pneumonia. He was one of the best Genls that the rebs had but there are a great many of the rebel soldiers that did not like him very well because he was so hard on them. Whatever he done he done with all his might and he would march some of his men to death. There are a great many of the 9 month men going home now. The 127th and 135th Penn. Vols left to day they have not lost any men in battle since they came out. The 127th was on picket last Dec. with us across the river and when the rebs commenced shelling us they up and run back into the city and tried to hide. They were on our right and if it had not been for our batteries the rebs would have used our regt up in a very short time. They run again the other day when we were across the river as soon as the rebs threw a few shell among them they scattered like sheep. I think it must be the fault of their officers for there certainly must be brave men among them. If they were only organized right and had good leaders. As they left the Depot this morning on their way home they were hooted (booed). There are but few regts in the army that have not behaved well but when there is one that runs away at the first fire they are despised ever after by all true soldiers. It is said that if it had not been for the bad conduct of the 11th corps Genl Hooker would have beaten the rebels. They are mostly Germans and done well when under General Siegle but they dont like Genl Howard and say they "wont fight mit him." There is one of the best regiments of our brigade going to leave us next month they enlisted for two years and their time will soon be out. They are the 34th N.Y. Vols. It has been very quiet here since the battle. We have had some very warm days but today it is raining and it is more comfortable. I have a very comfortable tent with a good table and seats. I don't care if we stay here all summer if we are not needed more elsewhere. I saw down to the depot today a 100 pounder rifled parrot canon that has been sent from Washington and I hear that there are more coming and they are going to be mounted around here to take part in the next fight. We had a battery of 20 pds. (20 pounders) and one of 32 before and now if we get a few 100 pds. I guess the rebs will think we are going to work in earnest. They say that two 32 pound shells thrown from one of our guns on this side of the river killed and wounded 100 of their men. I saw them scatter when the shell fell among them. The rebel works here are not near as heavy as I thought they were when we first fought them but they are hard to get at and they have got the side hill filled with rifle pits. I think we will have Fredericksburg and their works in our possession before July. Our Col. has resigned on account of his ill health. Lt. Col. Colvill will now be Col and Maj Adams will be Lieut Col and I expect that Capt Messick will be Major. We will be sorry to lose Capt from the Co. but he will get a better position and our loss will be his gain (as the old saying is) he is the coolest and bravest officer in the regiment in a fight. Genl Sully has gone to Minn and I hear that he is going to have a command on the frontier. The mail has just come we have the Central Republican of the 6th. Brown seems to be down on the Copperheads. The boys like the paper much better than they used to.

I would like to have Father write to me as often as he can. My love to you all. Good by this time.

As ever your affectionate son,

Edward Bassett

Edward refers to the transfer of General Sully to Minnesota where he took charge of the fight against the Indians. His service with the Minnesota First had endeared him to his men as perhaps no other commander they had. William Lochren wrote in his "Narrative of the First Regiment":

"On May 10th Gen. Sully left us for a command in Minnesota and Dakota, against the Indians. Brave and most capable in action, yet always careful to guard against any foolish or heedless sacrifice of his men; blunt, yet kind, in manner; humorous and playful as a

boy; always manifesting implicit confidence in the honor and good conduct of his men, and relying on that as the only restraint, while never relaxing any necessary discipline, he was perhaps more generally beloved by all than any other of our regimental commanders. The regiment parted with him with most sincere regret, having but a short time before manifested their regard by presenting him with a magnificent dress sword costing $1,000."

Falmouth, Station, Va.
May 13th, 1863.

Dear Sisters,

We are now encamped at Falmouth station, oposite Fredericksburg. It is a very nice camp. We have a fine view of the city of Fredericksburg and the rebel forts on the other side of the river. It is not more than one fourth of a mile to the rebel pickets but the river is between us. Everything is very quiet along the lines and has been ever since the battle. I have been up to Falmouth this forenoon and just got back. I found it rather unpleasant traveling arround to day. The sun was shineing very hot and there are few shades for the trees were all cut down last winter for fuel. I don't think we will move again very soon for we have been fixing up a nice camp as if we were going to stay here all summer. I am well as ever. We have heard from the boys of our Company that were wounded. They are all doing well. Albert Johnson is at Lincoln hospital Washington D.C. I see by the papers that there has been some more trouble with the Indians up north but I hope they will get driven back before they have a chance to do any harm to the settlers. General Sully has left us & I hear that he is going to take command in Minnesota. He said he was going to St. Paul. We are all sorry to part with him but if he is going to leave us we are glad to have him in Minnesota to punish the Indians. We are about two miles from the camp where we stayed last winter. My love to all the family.

Your brother

Edward.

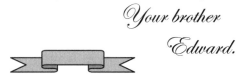

Falmouth Station, Virginia
May 20, 1863.

Dear Father,

I received your letter in due time and was glad to hear that you were well and geting your crops in. I would like to be farming myself this summer and if the war ends and I get out safe I shall try farming. This is a farming country but the farms are all growing up to grass and vines. The only place that I have noticed even a garden being cultivated was over in Fredericksburg and there they were not doing much. I would like to go up north where things are not all destroyed by the army.

It has been very quiet here since the last battle and judging from appearances I should not think the army would move again for a long time. There are a great many troops going home between now & next July and if the army was too small this last time to whip the rebels I don't see how they are going to operate successfully now since so many have gone home. There are from one to two regiments going home now every day. They have been out from nine months to two years and are from six to nine hundred strong. I think there was 37 two-years regiments from the state of New York and their time is out between now and the 18th of July.[72] Some of them have re-enlisted but they

---

[72] During the time Edward mentions some 30,000 men left the army as their enlistments expired.

have a furlough for 30 days and it will be one month at least before they will get back into the field so I don't think this army will do much for the next two months. The old troops are fixing their camps for hot weather. There are no indications of an early move. There are improvements being made at the depot for storeing and secureing supplies. General Gibbon our Division Commander is off on a furlough. Our Brigade is commanded by Colonel Morehead of the 106 P.V. (Pennsylvania Volunteers). There is a detail of about 120 men from the Brigade each day for picket directly oposite Fredericksburg. We picket about one half a mile on the bank of the river. The rebels were fishing with a seine the day that I was on and some of them swam half way across. They catch a few small fish. Shad are worth $1.00 apiece with them. We have to pay from 60 to 70 cts. but they are geting poor now. I wish I could get some bass from some of the Minnesota lakes. We draw soft bread every three days, it is baked at Acquia Creek and sent up on the cars. Eggs sell for 50 cts. per doz., Butter 75 cts per lb. small apples 6 for 25 cts. Oranges and Lemons 5 cts. apiece and other things in proportion. A hat that used to cost $1.25 & $1.75 in Faribault sells for 4 & 5 dollars here. I suppose you have to pay more for such things there now than you used to. Dried apples are worth 25 cts. per lb. here. I wish this army could gain one victory over the enemy but it seems as if there is no such luck in store for us. We have had several chances and fought some hard battles but the victory is never complete. We have been very lucky in withdrawing when we were likely to be cut to pieces by a superior force. Ever since the organization of the army of the Potomac under Maj. Genl McClellan we have been expecting Richmond to fall and I believe if there had been but the one purpose in view among the officers commanding the army we should have had our efforts rewarded by the possession of the confederate Capitol and their army would have been driven South and we in the place of pursueing them in the mountains of Va. & driving them from the valleys of Maryland, would be driving them out of North & South Carolina and ere this we could had Charleston or at least we could have been ready to operate on Charleston this summer in the place of being here on the Rappahannoc with a superior force in our front. When the army was at Harrison's Bar on James River they were in a much better place to operate against Richmond than they are likely to get this summer and if it had not been for Porter's bad conduct McClellan could have been reinforced and marched on Richmond last fall. I have confidence in our army and if our Generals could handle their 100 and 150 thousand men as well as they have 5 & 10 thousand they would soon whip the rebels. I believe they (the rebs) out General us in nearly every battle. Longstreet was here last winter when Burnside moved but as soon as he found that this army had got to be re-organized Longstreet was sent with his command to re-inforce Bragg in Tenn. and they came very near whiping Rosencranzs. They saw that he would remain quiet for some time and Hooker was in command here and they supposed he would commence an early campaign and Longstreet was called back to Richmond and lay arround Petersburg and Richmond ready to march to meet either Hooker, Peck or Keys whenever they should attempt to make a move. Hooker moved across the river, took up his position and could hold it until after Sedgwick was driven back for it seems that Sedgwick never formed a junction with Hooker but was forced to retire across the river and then the rebs could mass their forces against Hooker's army and although he might have whiped them it would have cost more than it would have been worth and so he retreated across the river and took up his old position. I wish there had been about 5000 Infantry mounted and sent arround with Genl Stoneman and took Richmond and if they could not hold it destroy every bit of rebel property and left.

They could have done it then and it would have been a severe blow on the rebs. I almost wish I belonged to some good Cavalry Regt. We have just got the account of the raid of our Cavalry through Mississippi and La. I would like to go on such an expedition a few such raids will do them more damage than we can inflict in any other way and it would be the best way to use up their guerrillas. We could capture all their horses where we went and destroy government stores. I believe the north will finaly be victorious but it seems as if we might hurry the matter considerable. The resources of the north will hold out for years but we hear continual howlings from the South about the scarcity of provisions and they have not the farming lands to raise provisions for an army as large as they have got to keep in the field. The Richmond papers say that the north will carry the war on for years before they will consent to a division of the old Union and I think they are about right. I would hate to have a war last 8 or 10 years but I would rather have it than to have the Confederacy acknowledged and the country divided in that way. I suppose there will be some howling among the Copperheads about the conscription act but I hope to see some of them bleed to pay for their acts.

The boys are all well and feel in good spirits. We drill twice each day. Yesterday we had a division Drill. My love to the whole family.

Your son,   E. H. Bassett
                                   Co. G. 1st. Minnesota V.

Falmouth Station, Va.
May 24th, 1863.

My Dear Mother,

The weather has been very hot for a few days. We have not had any rain since the 5th. We drill two hours each day and come on guard duty about twice every week now. The boys are all well. I have not been excused from duty once since last November on account of sickness. There is some excitement about the news from General Grant. Yesterday's paper stated that he was still advancing and he would make the rebs leave Vicksburg. The rebel pickets here said yesterday that Grant had got Vicksburg. There was one of their soldiers deserted yesterday right in their face & eyes. They were fishing in the river & he swam over without being shot at all. He said that he was tired of the war and longed for peace. They are rather short of provisions but get along very well.

You say that the school has commenced in Morristown. Who teaches it? I would like to be in Minnesota this summer. It must be delightful in the woods there this spring. Well, I have got but a short time to serve now & then I hope to enjoy a few summers in Minnesota I suppose wages will be very high in harvest there this summer. I see by the papers that the crops are very promising in Rebeldom but if our Cavalry commits such depredations among the farmers as they have lately they will be apt to benefit the Union Army as well as the rebel. I expect to hear of another attack on the forts around Charleston by our Iron clad vessels again soon and I think they will be successful the next time and perhaps Charleston will be captured this summer. Everything remains quiet here & I hear that our Corps Commander (Genl Couch) has planted quite a garden. I expect we will stay here all summer.

I am glad to hear that the money I sent got through safe. I wanted to save two hundred dollars out of my wages in the three years but I guess I shall not be able to do it. I have forgotten how much I have sent but I think it is $120. I see in yesterday's paper that the Army is going to be paid up to the 1st of March as soon as the money can be issued. We will most likely get two month's wages some time in June. I think I can send you $10 if we do. I will try. It is very still and hot today. I hope we will have rain soon.

Newspaper Vendor & cart in camp. Library of Congress
Period Photo by Alexander Gardner, 1863

I saw one of the boys that used to belong to my Co. but joined the 6th U.S. Cavalry the other day. He was out with Genl Stoneman. He said they had fine times among the farmers. The inhabitants are all Union but rather sour. They have plenty to eat & crops look fine. They went into one old fellow's house that had been left and found several hundred hams and barrels of sugar. He was a contractor for the rebel government. The citizens said it was private property but the negroes said it was intended for the rebel army. Our boys took what they wanted & left.

I remain as ever your affectionate son.

E. H. Bassett

Co. "G" 1st M.V.

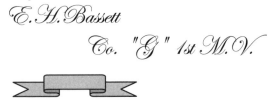

Falmouth Station, Va.
Sunday May 31st, 1863.

Dear Mother,

The weather is very pleasant here now. I was down on picket on Friday and had a very good time. The rebels were fishing in the river from early in the morning until in the PM when the tide came in and the water was too deep. Falmouth is at the head of the tide water on the Rappahannoc. There are ripples (rapids) there that prevent it from getting back any further. At the lower end of Fredericksburg the tide rises some four feet. There are the wrecks of several steamboats beside sailboats, barges and canal boats laying in the river below the City. They were destroyed when our Army advanced a little over one year ago. It is thought that the rebel army is moveing up the river and Lee says that he will invade Maryland again. Part of our army, I understand, is about to move but we have received no orders and everything has been very quiet with us until this morning when we were called out a little earlier than usual and remained under arms for an hour or so, when we returned to our quarters. There was considerable noise among the rebels in the City last night and they were stirring very early this morning which would account for our being called out. We are very close to the picket lines and I suppose it will stand us in hand to be on our guard against surprise. I only wish the rebs would try to cross & surprise us here. I would be glad to meet them on this side of the river. There was a large number of deserters from the rebels last week came into our lines and they have been sent north. They all tell the old story about poor rations &c &c. There is no sickness in the Regiment to speak of. Health is excellent.

We have very neat and healthy quarters now & good water. There is a prayer meeting at the Lacy house about 80 rods from our camp nearly every evening and preaching regular on Sunday. The boys go over every day and last night there was but about one third of the Co. here at roll call. They went down to the Depot to a Negro meeting. We will get our pay tomorrow two-months wages which square us up to the 1st of May. We signed the rolls yesterday and were to receive the money in the PM but there has been a delay for some reason and we will have to wait now until Monday.

We have nothing definite from Grant's Army before Vicksburg. The last we heard the work was progressing & he felt confident of success. The enemy were within their last line of defense and they have most likely surrendered before this time or Johnson may after being reinforced, attack Grant in his rear. We all believe Grant will compel Pemberton to surrender. It is one year today since the battle commenced at Fair Oaks. I shall never forget that day & the next.

Please accept this with My love to you all,

Your affectionate son

Edward Bassett.

I sent the May No. of Harper's to Father the other day.

CHAPTER 22
MARCHING TOWARD ETERNITY

The early days of June found the First Minnesota still encamped on Stafford Heights. The camps of all six corps of the army spread out for several miles. The weather was pleasant, supplies plentiful but everyone knew this peaceful tranquility would not last. Rumors of marching orders were numerous and speculation about where the army would fight Lee next occupied much of the conversation.

On the Confederate side of the river, General Lee began what would become his march to Gettysburg. On June 4th, Union pickets and balloon observers reported seeing dust clouds rising behind Fredericksburg and other signs of movement. On June 5th, General Hooker sent a request to Secretary of War Stanton and President Lincoln to approve a movement against the enemy's rear if their movement proved to be toward the North. His strategy was to cut Lee's line of supply and communication with Richmond. Stanton and Lincoln refused the request, once again insisting that the army be kept in a position that would protect Washington and Baltimore should the enemy move in that direction. On the same day, Hooker sent a force across the Rappahannock to determine the enemy strength at Fredericksburg. A lively exchange of artillery and infantry fire ensued. Exchanges between Hooker and his superiors continued until June10th. During this time, he broke up his encampments and prepared his army for a move.

Balloon Ascention–Library of Congress

Falmouth Station, Va.
June 6th, 1863.

Dear Parents,

There have been some demonstrations made by our

men down the river. It was thought that the rebels were throwing their forces up the river and sending some of them away to reinforce other points. Yesterday the pontoon train was taken down to the bank of the river near where Sedgwick crossed before and about 5 o'clock yesterday PM our batteries opened on the rebs oposite where the bridge was to be put across and there was heavy canonading for an hour or so but our men succeeded in laying the bridge and the 2nd Division of the 6th Corps soon crossed and drove the rebs out of their pits and captured quite a lot of prisoners. Our pickets were soon stationed and everything was quiet during the night except an occasional shot by some of the pickets and the rumble of the rebel trains as they came in with reinforcements. We had just come in from the PM drill when the fireing commenced and we were ordered to get ready to move immediately which we did. We were to march this morning but the order was countermanded and we slept this morning until after sunrise. Our men ocupy about the same ground that they did last night and there has been but little skirmishing during the day but our heavy guns have fired every little while all day without receiving any answer. The rebs won't fight us until they get us where they want us and although our siege guns annoy them continualy by droping a 20 or 32 pound shot in their midst whenever they see fit. They do not open on us with their guns. There has been a few more troops sent over today but there has not enough crossed to do much as long as the rebs are so numerous. I think the General has accomplished his object & perhaps will fall back to this side of the river before morning. I feel confident that it is not the intention to bring on a general engagement here. We have no orders now and things are going on as usual.

I received two St. Paul papers this evening. The 34th N.Y. which belongs to our brigade, leave next week. They have been out two years and have done their duty well. A great many of them declare that they will re-enlist in a short time. They want to see the war ended by fighting. I see by the papers that General Dix's Department is to be added to that of General Hooker's and Hooker to command. We are looking every day for the news of the fall of Vicksburg. The last accounts we have are up to the 2nd inst. when the work was progressing finely. I think if our armies do as well as is anticipated the war will be closed by fall. We are going to try Charleston by a regular siege and if it is rightly conducted it will succeed with the aid of the Iron Clads. The news is cheering from most every quarter (but it may change tomorrow). Hope not.

We had a fine rain this evening and it is quite pleasant. The weather has been very hot and dry. There can be no bad roads for an excuse now. You ask why Seigle resigned. I expect it was because he did not like Burnside. I understand now that he is anxious to take a command.

Period Photo of the Lacy House, named Chatam
Where Edward refers to their worship services being held.

Sunday morning 7th.

All quiet this morning. The weather is very pleasant. I have got to go on guard this morning or I would go over to the Lacy House to (Church) meeting. They have been having meetings there every evening for two weeks. I have been over twice and the house was crowded both times. I send you ten dollars we were payed on the 1st inst. up to May 1st. and I expect we will have to wait now until August before we will get payed again.

Please accept this with love to all.

Edward Bassett

Co. G. 1st Regt. Minnesota Vols.

Washington D. C.

On June 9th, Hooker ordered General Pleasanton and his cavalry to probe the enemy on his right. At Kelly's Ford, the largest all cavalry engagement ever fought on the continent developed. The attack on Confederate General Stuart's position came as a surprise and resulted in the capture of Stuart's personal baggage, including his letters and orders to move north. With this information in hand, Hooker knew he must move his army north to prevent his right flank from being exposed and to protect Washington. Lee began moving north on June 10th and Hooker followed on the June12th. Thus the winds of destiny began to blow the opposing armies inexorably toward the peaceful little Pennsylvania town called Gettysburg.

Lee's intention in invading the north was not to conquer and hold territory. He believed another move into Union territory would insight such a furor the Federals would have little choice but to mount an attack against him. His strategy was to accept such a battle on ground that favored him with a strong defensive position. He was confident that, under these conditions, he would win.

As he explained to General D. H. Hill[73], he hoped to *"turn back the tide of war that is now pressing the South"*. Virginia was being stripped bare by both armies. If he stayed in Virginia, the Union would likely amass its forces and deal him a crushing blow, if not defeat, or take Richmond. Unable to resupply his army or replace his losses with new enlistments, Lee reasoned that he needed to keep the Federals off balance and take the fight into their land. The rich farms and towns of Maryland and Pennsylvania would provide a great bounty of arms, food, forage, cattle, horses, clothing, desperately needed shoes and other supplies, and hopefully, more men. Harrisburg, the state capitol and Lee's destination, was the regions largest supply depot, stocked with mountains of every imaginable kind of war material. Staying in Virginia would gain him little, but, winning a great victory in the north or capturing Baltimore—even for a short while—could change the tide of war.

Falmouth Station, Va.
June 11th, 1863.

Dear Father and Mother,

Your kind letter of the 1st was recieved and read by me last night and according to your request I am answering it as soon as possible. Health remains about the same with us. The days are quite warm but the nights are cool. We drill one hour in the AM and one in the PM. We have a new brigade commander. His name is Harrow. He is a brigadier Genl from the army of the Cumberland. He was serenaded last night and came out and made a few remarks and the boys gave three hearty cheers for him. I think we shall like him. Our men still hold their position across the river. The pickets are skirmishing most all the time but they occupy the same ground that they did after the first

---

[73] Note: This is Confederate General D. H. Hill, not to be confused with Confederate General A. P. Hill.

night. There is no prospect of a general engagement unless they try to evacuate. I hear that there was quite a cavalry fight up the river on Tuesday. The ground is very dry and the roads excellent.

I am glad to hear that your crops are looking so fine. I would like to see a field of wheat or corn or in fact any kind of a crop growing.

We are anxiously waiting to hear of the fall of Vicksburg & Fort Hudson. It is rumored that Genl Butler is going to take the place of Genl Halleck. If he does I look for a change in things in general.

The 34th N.Y. Vols. started for home on the morning of the 9th. They were a two year regiment and one of the best that ever left the state. When the train started the band struck up Auld Lang Syne and the 1st Minnesota & 2nd N.Y. gave them three rouseing cheers. They have lost a great many men in the battles and quite a number by sickness. We have 30 men in our Co. now for duty. I believe there is but about 35 in the largest Co. in the Regt. I hope that I may see you all in one year at least but I don't think I shall much before. Please accept this with much love to you all.

Your son

Edward Bassett

Co. "G" 1st Minnesota Vols.

Hooker began moving his army in earnest; camps were packed up, horses and cattle taken from the stockades and columns of wagons, artillery and infantry began the march north. All the supplies that could be, were taken from Aquia Creek were packed and the thousands of tons that remained were put to the torch. The First Minnesota, part of the Second Division of the Second Corps, was again the last to leave camp on June 14th.

When dawn broke, it was already very warm and the air

heavy laden with moisture. Orders came to pack everything and hold themselves in readiness, prepared to march. The veterans immediately surmised that they would be taking the position of rear guard. Fires were built, coffee made, breakfasts cooked, tents struck and, by noon most of the army had left camp. Men not on duty stood in clusters discussing what it all meant. Many of them walked up on Stafford's Heights to take a last look across the river at the now–decimated town of Fredericksburg. The scene of desolation reflected the destruction of war. Hills once covered with green canopies now lay bare. Streets once filled with the bustle of busy people were now dirty alleys littered with the debris torn from houses by exploding iron balls of death. Hillsides scarred with trenches and holes, where the lush green carpet had been replaced by the lifeless blue clad forms of so many brave young men, were now bare and foreboding.

The day dragged on as division-after-division took up the march. By noon, only the First Brigade of the Second Division remained. As the sun neared the horizon, fires were started and coffee and food cooked. An aide rode up to the headquarters tent and word was passed down the chain of command, *"assemble the men."* Bugles spoke aloud and the notes of "Assembly" echoed across the valley. The companies formed, took their place in the Regimental line and then joined the Brigade. Darkness enshrouded the heavens, which glittered with a million stars as the First Minnesota marched out at the rear of the column, leaving the camp deserted and still. Though rather warm, it was a pleasant night to march. A contemplative quiet fell on the column and they made good time. Five miles down the road they came to a halt when they caught up to the rest of the division that had stopped to wait for them. Every veteran knew the value of resting at every opportunity while on the march. They soon joined the 4000 men already lying along the road. Before long, they were again called into line-of-march, only to be ordered to turn around and march back to the river. The reason was apparent; they had no cavalry behind them and thus had no warning should a rebel attack be mounted on their rear. They marched five miles back to where they had started, arriving about midnight. After pickets were sent out and guards placed the few remaining lucky ones laid down to sleep. None would ever know what confusion of command caused the unnecessary 10-mile march. Before dawn, they marched off again to catch up to the division. A quick pace was set and they met the division at Stafford Court House. The air was heavy and the day already promised to be incredibly hot. A rest was called and the men, not having eaten earlier, hurried to make their breakfast and dinner all in one meal. The blistering sun was directly overhead when the march resumed. The clear, blue sky offered no shelter from the searing heat and choking dust that billowed from the thousands of tramping feet. As the day wore on, excess baggage littered the road, soon joined by litter of another kind. Men who were overcome by the heat and dust fell by the way in ever increasing numbers. Some dropped dead in their tracks while marching as though shot through the heart. Having endured 28 miles of torment, when they halted in late afternoon, about a mile after crossing Aquia Creek, 70 had died and fully 1,200 were incapacitated along the way.

Sketch of the village of Dumfries from Harper' Weekly Aug. 29, 1863

When blaring bugles aroused the men at 3 AM on Tuesday, June 16th, they immediately fell into line and the march began. After passing the village of Dumfries and continuing on to Quantico Creek, a halt was called about 8 AM and breakfast was prepared. Then on they went in the heat until crossing the Occoquan River and going into bivouac about 7 PM, having tramped another 16 miles. As soon as possible the men threw off their gear and dashed into the cool, fresh water and washed the heat and dust from their tired bodies.

At this time, President Lincoln had issued a call for 100,000 more men from the militias of Pennsylvania, Maryland, Ohio and West Virginia. They were needed immediately to help fend off the rebel invasion. The Governors of New York and New Jersey also responded and soon every available railroad was ferrying men to the region. Perhaps their greatest accomplishment was the complete destruction of the bridge over the Susquehanna River just as rebel cavalry arrived, thus denying Lee access to Harrisburg and all it had to offer.

The march resumed after breakfast on Wednesday, June 17th–another day of blistering heat preyed heavily on man and beast alike. Rumors circulated along the column that Lee had crossed from Maryland into Pennsylvania. After covering about seven miles, the 2nd Division turned off to the left. About 3 PM, they halted near Sangster's Station, the first railroad station south of Fairfax, where they rested overnight and remained all the next day.

Encamped About 4 Miles
From Centerville, Va.
June 18, 1863.

Dear Father and Mother,

We left our camp on the Rappahannoc before Fredrickburg last Sunday (June 14th) about sundown and marched all night and the next day camping about 5 miles from Dumfrees. We passed Stafford Court House. Tuesday morn we started at 3 o'clock (AM) and camped on Occoquan Creek where we stopped until 8 o'clock Wednesday. Then we came and camped here where we have had quite a rest. The weather was very hot and there were a great many men droped down and died on the road. There was two or three died out of our Reg't. Company G is all here now but one and he is all right somewhere. I don't know what the move was made for but we hear that Lee has crossed and invaded Penn. and burned Chambersburg but I don't believe he has any very large force there. The stores were all burned at Acquia Creek and the road from here to Falmouth is strewn with blankets, knapsacks, canteens, coats, shirts, pants, socks and in fact everything that a soldier uses.[74] There was lots of wagons burned and any amount of powder and shells blown up. There has been wholesale destruction of army stores of all kinds. It is reported that Lee has over 90,000 men. You will be able to hear what damage has been done by him in Penn. as soon as we will. I hear that the Militia had all turned out. I am glad that we have got away from that slaughter pen of Fredricksburg. How I want Hooker to prove himself better than McClellan or else take back what he has said. If there was ever a disgracefull retreat from a position I think this has been one. The rebels did not trouble our rear much nor do I believe they had many men to do it with. I believe the 1st can yet stand as hard a march as any regt. in the service. I am well but somewhat tired. We are camped near where we were two years ago just before the Bull Run defeat. Please excuse this hasty letter and accept it with my love to all.

Edward Bassett,

1st. Minnesota Vols. 1st. Brig. 2nd Div.

2nd. Corps, Army of the Potomac

---

[74] Castoffs from the men in new regiments that had little marching experience and were now learning the value of carrying only the essentials.

Mail and newspapers, the first in a week, arrived on Friday, June 19, filled with stories of rebel raids in Maryland and Pennsylvania. The weather had changed—the oppressive heat was replaced by mild temperatures. About noon, the men were called to fall into line-of-march. The brief rest and cooler temperatures took the struggle out of the march and the column made very good time. The men cheered as they climbed the heights to Centerville, where they had camped the previous August. It had been a short day's march and at 6 PM they began to set up camp for the night.

Saturday morning dawned to find the men talking and listening to the distant thunder of artillery while awaiting orders to "fall in." Many felt ill-used by a sutler who was in camp selling to an artillery battery. With the arrival of the infantrymen, he immediately doubled his prices. Upon reflection and discussion, it became apparent the matter needed attention. Before long, a lively group had gathered near the offender's tent and soon the guards were disarmed and a cry went forth to "Rally on the Sutler." In less time than it takes to tell the tale, a mob of blue clad vigilantes descended on the scene and just as quickly dispersed. Like a swarm of locusts on a wheat field, they left little of use or value behind.

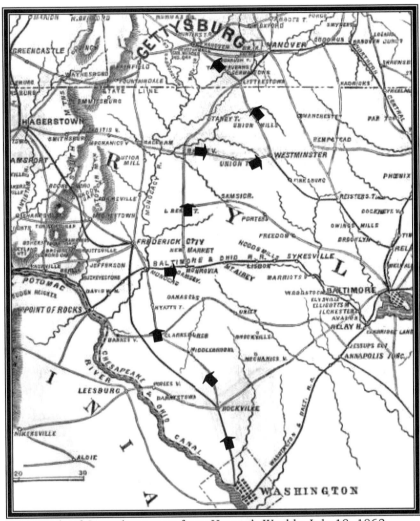

Battle of Gettysburg map from Harper's Weekly July 18, 1863
Arrows indicate line of march of the Army of the Potomac

Encamped near Thorofare Gap
Prince Williams County Va.
June 24th, 1863.

Dear Father & Mother,

My last was written when we were laying near Centreville & dated 18th. The next PM we marched to Centreville and camped near where we did last fall. Centreville is strongly fortified. There are some 8 or 10 thousand troops encamped there, where they have been ever since last Nov. The 111 regt. N.Y. Vols. that were surrendered at Harpers Ferry last fall is there. They were sent to Minnesota to protect the frontier but were sent back after they got to Chicago. They are one of the fancy pets regiments that are kept in the forts out of danger, to look at and talk about. If they had ever got to Minnesota the Indians would most likely give up. It makes me mad to think of the way things have been conducted. What sense is there in sending a regiment of city chaps onto the frontier to fight Indians when the state troops could be sent in their place without any additional expense. Besides they know the Indians and every foot of the ground that they are on and there would not be ten men in a thousand of the New York troops that could find their way across a Minnesota prairie or through the big woods. It shows how much the men that have command care & know about the settlers on the frontier. If there had been an honest man at the head of affairs this regiment would now be in Minnesota on the frontier & in the place of General Sibley's great wild goose chase to the Missouri river the frontier would be protected by Mounted men that were acquainted with the country and the Indians would be driven out of the state.

We camped at Centreville about sundown of the 19th. The next day about 3 PM we started out on the old Bull Run road we knew the ground and saw considerable to remind us of that fatal field. We marched that night untill about 12 o'clock through the rain and mud and camped a few hours near Gainsville on the R.R. Our regt. was rear guard for the Div. train. The next morning we marched passing through a small place called Hay Market. It has been burned but there were one or two old huts near by there. That day, Sunday the 21st, we camped here.[75] We heard heavy fireing over in the Loudoun valley which we have since learned was General Pleasanton's Cavalry fighting General Stuart's rebel Cavalry. Stuart was badly beaten and driven back. The rebs lost two pieces of artillery and many prisoners. The rebels have gained a big victory at Winchester capturing everything except a few men that made their escape at night. The country is full of rebel cavalry. We had to furnish an escort for the supply train yesterday to go about 6 miles to Gainsville for supplies. There was a sutler captured in the morning that started before the (supply) train. The rebs took one pair of mules and had to leave the rest for fear of our troops that were on the road. I don't know how long we will stop here but I expect not long. I hear that the 6th Corps is just over the mountains. There may be a battle somewhere this week but there are no indications of one here. The boys are well although rations have been rather short. The weather is very pleasant, the country beautiful, as nice as I have seen in Va. There are but few of the inhabitants remaining and they are mostly Secesh. It is only about 9 miles to the Old Bull Run battlefield. Our Colonel was out there yesterday. I would like to go out there but I can't. We have not had our mail very regular since we left Falmouth. I have not. rec. any mail for near two weeks. I hope to hear of something being done soon but the prospect is not very promising. I hear that the mail will be in tonight.

Good by for the present. As ever your son

E. H. Bassett.

---

[75] The regiment camped at Thoroughfare Gap for 4 days guarding the pass and doing guard duty for supply trains.

Since leaving Falmouth, Virginia, the regiment had marched nearly 130 miles. Some days, they marched in intense heat and other days in rain and mud—all under forced march conditions. Many men were completely exhausted. The number of stragglers increased daily and thousands were left behind to catch up as soon as they were able. The toll on new regiments, unaccustomed to the rigors of such continuous marching, was considerable. On June 29th, the First Minnesota Regiment marched 33 miles. Many marched with badly blistered feet as a result of the pompous ego of the 2nd Corps Inspector General, Colonel Charles Morgan. Morgan rode along the line of marching soldiers always calling out to *"close the ranks"* or *"lengthen the stride"* and generally trying to impress them with his undeserved rank. As the regiment came to a broad knee-deep creek, he ordered Colvill to march his men directly through the water and not to cross on the flat hewn log foot bridges. Some of the men ignored the direction and used the logs anyway—a direct confrontation to the Colonel's false pride. Morgan placed Colvill under arrest for failure to maintain discipline. The ignominious colonel on horseback obviously had never marched all day in water soaked shoes or suffered the resulting scalded and blistered feet.

The skirmish with the enemy cavalry at the little village of Haymarket would have great consequences in coming days. The rebel cavalry was led by none other than Jeb Stuart. As General Hancock's 2nd Corps, turned north through Haymarket, Stuart's cavalry came in contact with its skirmishers and observed the massive supply trains it was guarding. Desperately needing supplies for Lee, Stuart brought his skirmishers and horse artillery foreward and opened a heavy barrage on the Union force. He also captured General Hancock's escort, including Captain Johnson and some aides, carrying dispatches ordering General Zook to move up and join the Corps. The orders also defined the route he was to take, valuable information to the enemy. Stuart was under orders to determine the locations and strength of the Union forces around Bull Run and rejoin Lee in Pennsylvania after crossing the Potomac River above Edward's Ferry. His delay at Haymarket allowed the Union forces to reach the ferry before him, making necessary his lengthy ride around the Union army to cross the Potomac farther downstream. This "second ride around the enemy army," brought some degree of notoriety and fame and, allowed Stuart to capture 125 wagons loaded with supplies only a few miles from Washington. However, it proved to be a disaster for his commander, General Lee, who was thus left without his "eyes" as both sides moved inexorably toward Gettysburg.

Frederick Co., Md.
June 30th, 1863

Dear Parents,

I have a letter that I wrote to send to you some time ago but I have had no chance & I will try and write a few more lines and send with it if I have a chance. We left Thorofare Gap on the 25th and have been marching all the time since. That morning the rebel cavalry attacked our pickets but were driven off. We were shelled at Hay Market but no one hurt except one of the 19 Maine who was killed by an accident. Our Col's. horse was wounded so as to be left.[76]

We crossed the Potomac at Edwards Ferry on the night of the 26th and camped near our old camp from there we marched to Fredrick City where we lay night before last. Yesterday we marched 30 miles and today I expect we will go into Penn. There has been some rebels about 7 miles from here. The citizens are mostly Union people and we passed through three Union towns yesterday. One was called Liberty, one Union Bridge and Union Town where we lay now. It is a beautiful place and when we came through there last night the women brought out bread, milk, cakes and

---

[76] Colonel Colvill's horse was hit in the hind legs by a cannon shot and had to be destroyed.

pies and gave to the soldiers. There are but a few of them that will sell anything but they give freely. Many of their men are in the army.

They were very much surprised to see us yesterday. They had no warning of our approach and you can judge how they felt when they saw our column app- roach instead of the rebels which was expected by tomorrow. The crops look splendid. Wheat is ready to cut and some have commenced. There is a great deal of wheat raised in this part of Maryland. I heard that the rebels were fighting at Harrisburg but I don't believe it. We also hear that Hooker has been superceded by McClellan but I doubt that also but I can assure you that Mac. is the man for this army. I believe there is a large majority for McClellan in our regt. if not in the Corps.

I have stood all the marches first rate. My health never was better. There has but two left the company on any account since we left Falmouth. All the boys from Morristown are well. I suppose that Lee is this side of the Potomac with a large force and if our army is handled right he will be whipped and his army mostly captured. There are a great many rumors and you will most likely hear many that are untrue before you get the truth. I think he will be forced to fight or run this week. Our forces have left Centerville and Fairfax. We have had but one mail since we left Falmouth and I cannot tell when we will get one. I hope it will not be long, I will write you a line at every opportunity. I don't know when I can send this but will improve the first chance.

You must not think it strange if you don't get a letter very often for I expect that the mails will be a secondary matter until Lee is attended to.

Your Son,

Edward Henry Bassett.

During this time, the command of the Army of the Potomac would once again change hands. Frustrated by continual interference from Washington and the refusal of his request to withdraw the 11,000 men from Harper's Ferry, where they were no longer needed, Hooker sent his resignation to Lincoln. He was replaced by General Meade on June 30th. Was it wise to make such a change in command on what was now obviously the eve of a defining battle?

ONLY TIME WOULD TELL!

CHAPTER 23
BATTLE OF GETTYSBURG
JULY 1, 2, & 3, 1863

Accounts bearing facts, figures, reports and personal correspondence that relate the events of this great battle fill the shelves of numerous libraries. Museums full of artifacts, drawings and pictures reveal the great suffering and heroism manifest in this desperate struggle. The reverent stillness that, enshrouds these now peaceful fields, belies the violence and suffering that for three days heralded the combat of men. It is as though the souls of the young men that died there amid a storm of whistling bullets and exploding shells still inhabit the now tranquil rolling knolls. A tally revealing the numbers of men involved in the battle and the losses incurred can give us but a glimpse of its magnitude. Here, tens-of-thousands of brave men met, ready to die for opposing causes in which they so firmly believed. Here, these young warriors tested their mettle and determination on this now hallowed twenty-five square mile patch of earth known as the "Battlefield of Gettysburg."

This battle that, occurred not by design but by circumstance, was the largest battle fought and, marked the turning point of the war. It is perhaps the most chronicled event in American history. Over 170,000[77] men were actively engaged in the three days of unrelenting fighting. At least 51,000[78] men were killed, wounded or captured. Over 600 cannons belched fire, smoke and death as charges and counter charges left the land covered with the bodies of nearly 10,000 dead soldiers and 5,000 horses and mules. The Union line stretched across three-to-five miles on the high ground south of Gettysburg known as Cemetery Ridge; Lee's Confederate line extended six-to-seven miles along Seminary Ridge. A strip of farmland, about ¾ mile wide, with a small dry stream bed called Plum Run running down the center, separated the two lines. The fighting raged for three days and included many separate hard-fought battles and skirmishes.

The organization of the Union and Confederate armies was very similar, though the Confederate Army of Northern Virginia had fewer Corps, their Corps were larger in size. The Army of the Potomac included:

- <u>7 Infantry and 1 Cavalry Corps:</u>
  Comprised of 3 divisions each, but could be from 2 to 5.
- <u>19 Divisions:</u>
  Comprised of 3 or 4 Brigades each. At full strength a Division was 12,000 men.
- <u>37 Brigades:</u>
  Comprised of 4 to 6 Regiments each. At full strength a brigade was 4,000 men.
- <u>Regiments:</u> Numbers varied.
  Comprised of 10 Companies each. At full strength, a Company was 100 men.

---

[77] Exact numbers are difficult to assess, this number seems commonly accepted.
[78] Counts of casualties vary among historians. Some state as many as 60,000 were killed, wounded or captured. The total size of the armies was approximately 90,000 Confederate and 150,000 Union including wagoners, engineers and other non combatants.

At Gettysburg, many of the units on both sides were only at half strength due to the losses incurred in earlier battles and from disease.

Southern General Lee gathered his forces. All the roads, twelve in number, led to Gettysburg. On June 30th, General A. P. Hill's Corps was camped six miles west of town and General Ewell's Corps was about eight miles to the north. His cavalry, under the command of Jeb Stuart, was still nowhere to be seen. Lee desperately needed him to determine the location of the Yankee army.

On the Union side, General Meade was also moving quickly toward the town. General John Buford's cavalry division had been serving as a screening force to the left of the Army of the Potomac and, as ordered, occupied Gettysburg on June 30th. The forward units of the Union column were also nearby. General Reynolds' First Corps was only four miles south of town and under orders to move into town in the morning. Howard's Eleventh Corps was ten miles away at Emmittsburg; Sickles' Third Corps and Slocum's Twelfth Corps were also nearing the town. Sedgwick's Sixth Corps and Hancock's Second Corps were still at least a day's march away.

This volume will focus on the activities of the First Minnesota Regiment in the battle and will expand into a broader scope only as needed to give the reader an understanding of events related to that regiment. Edward Bassett's letters following the battle were written while on the march as they pursued the retreating Confederate army. With little time to write, he was most concerned with letting his family know he was well and his general whereabouts. As opportunity presented itself, he related more of the situation surrounding the battle. He was always careful not to expound on details that could cause his family to worry.

☀ *THE FIRST DAY – JULY 1ST*

On July 1st, while the First Minnesota was still 20 miles to the south, the Battle of Gettysburg began in earnest. John Buford's Union cavalry and the First Corps of the Union Army, led by General John Reynolds numbering 10,000 men and 28 guns were reinforced about noon by the Eleventh Corps under General Howard with another 10,000 men. Lee's forces at Gettysburg accumulated throughout the day to an overwhelming 40,000 men and 92 guns. Buford knew the importance of holding the "high ground." He was a fine officer, capable of adjusting to meet the situation. Well aware that the cavalry alone could not hold against massed infantry, he had his men dismount and fight on the ground. With their faster-loading carbines, they took a heavy toll as the rebels advanced three-lines deep. Putting his artillery to work, he fought them to a standstill. Hearing the firing from south of town, Reynolds hurried his men to Buford's aid on Cemetery Ridge and Seminary Ridge. As he was surveying the situation a Southern sharpshooter, hidden in a stone barn, took aim and fired. Reynolds fell, instantly killed. The event raised the ire of the Wisconsin boys in his Iron Brigade. They charged into the advancing rebels with savage fury, pushing them back to a railway cut. In determined pursuit, they attacked from the end of the cut catching the rebs in enfilading fire. After vicious hand-to-hand fighting, the Federals called for them to *"throw down your arms,"* and took hundreds of prisoners.

The hard-fought duel of artillery, infantry and cavalry lasted all day with heavy losses on both sides. As more confederate troops arrived, the early Union successes were reversed. Outnumbered four-to-one, Buford took to the defensive, determined to hold the high ground at all costs. The Eleventh Corps arrived on the scene and the rebel advance was again fought to a standstill. For once, Buford thought, *"we shall hold the advantage of position in the battle."*

By evening, conditions changed and the Federals were forced back to Cemetery Ridge. Losses had been horrendous. The First Corps now numbered only about 2,400 compared to the nearly 10,000 that came on the field in the morning. The revered Iron Brigade lost two-thirds of its number, never again to regain its strength. Early that evening, General Meade sent General Hancock to take command at Gettysburg and to assertain the situation. Positions were shifted and preparations made for the next attack of the Confederates; inexplicably, it never came. Had Lee seen fit to follow up on his afternoon success before more Union troops arrived, the entire Army of the Potomac would have had to retreat and Lee would likely have gained another great victory. Both sides were exhausted and, as darkness descended and the smoke cleared, everyone knew that tomorrow would bring a battle like no other. Throughout the rainy night, more units arrived and officers rode back and forth as plans were made for the carnage that would come with the dawn.

Early in the morning of July 1st, the First Minnesota resumed its march to destiny from its overnight bivouac two miles north of Union Town. The morning was damp with a light rain falling. Aroused at 3 AM, the men boiled coffee and prepared to move out but were kept standing in the rain while a lost set of marching orders was replaced. Finally, after a four-hour wait, the orders came and the regiment marched two miles back to Union Town and, turned right onto the road to Taneytown, Maryland. Some thought they could hear the faint sound of firing to the north and the march was kept at a brisk pace. At Taneytown, the men took a short rest to eat lunch and resumed the march at 1 PM with orders to march at quick-time and close-up the ranks.[79]

In mid-afternoon, about halfway between Taneytown and Gettysburg, a brief halt was called and the men filled their canteens from a small stream. The day had turned very hot with only a few puffy clouds to offer shade from the broiling sun. Upon crossing a high ridge around 4 PM, the thunder of distant battle became plain and seemed to increase with every stride. They soon met the always-present horde of fleeing camp followers, skedaddlers and just plain cowards running

---

[79] Quick-time meant marching at the rate of 110 paces per minute with each pace being 28 inches.

in terror from the scene of action. The fleeing throng passed with the usual litany of tales about total and utter defeat and chaos. The veterans of the First Minnesota greeted all such accounts with the contempt due the source. To an experienced ear, the volume of sound of battle belied the credability of such reports. The moon glowed in the dark night sky, as the column halted about three miles from Gettysburg. It was 9 PM, 18 hours and 22 miles had passed since dawn. Fires were kindled and strong coffee was made and quickly consumed. The foot-sore, dust-covered, exhausted men dropped to the ground, rolled up in their blankets and slept.

Settling in for the night may not have been quite as simple as previously stated. Soldier's letters and diaries offer differing accounts of this night. Some confusion arose as to whether the 2nd Corps would stop here for the night or be ordered to move on to Gettysburg. Sergeant Matthew Marvin, of Company K, wrote in his diary:

> "Three times we got permission to have fires and twice they were put out; four times we made coffee and three times we threw it away and packed up & fell in. At last the order came to build breastworks, that we should stay all night."

The weary men must have been very frustrated at the very least, most saw little need for the breastworks and it was far too dark to work on them anyway. The order was largely ignored.

THE SECOND DAY – JULY 2ND

The rest was brief. Shortly after 1 AM,[80] with but a few hours sleep, the men were aroused with some difficulty. told to prepare to march immediately and, to do so with as little noise as possible. There was no time to eat or make coffee as they fell into line for roll call and then moved on to the

---

[80] Time according to James A. Wright, Orderly Sergeant of Company F; "No More Gallant A Deed" pp 291.
Isaac Taylor records the time as 3 AM; "The Last Full Measure" by Richard Moe; pp 261

Taneytown road to join the brigade. The usual delays ensued before they finally began to move about 3 AM. The air was heavy with a mist or ground fog; droplets of water glistened on the grass and leaves in the moonlight. Marching along, the silence was punctuated only by the dull *"tramp, tramp, tramp"* of feet on the road and an occasional grumble about the lack of morning coffee. Men wondered in whispers about the results of yesterday's battle heard from afar and what the day, now dawning, held in store for the army and their regiment. Occasional brief halts were made and dawn awakened as the sun peeked above the eastern horizon to herald a beautiful summer morning. The sharp report of firing sporadically pierced the still air as though sounding the alarm of what lay ahead.

It was 5:45 AM when the First Minnesota Regiment reached the battlefield area. About 100-yards south of the little unpretentious, two-room, whitewashed house of Mrs. Lydia Leister, the column turned left and moved up the back side of Cemetery Hill. Here, the men deployed just to the left of the center of the Union line.

Widow Lydia Leister's house after the battle – note dead horses.
Mathew Brady Photo

The little white house was the approximate center and was being used by General Meade, Commander of the Army of the Potomac, as his headquarters. Colonel Colvill later recalled the position as:

"*just behind the crest of the ridge, to the left of the cemetery; a few rods to the left, and in front of a small white building near the Baltimore Pike, having the appearance of a summer house.*"

By this time, all but one Corps of the Army was at Gettysburg. As the units came on the scene, they were placed along Cemetery Ridge in a line over three-miles in length that followed the high ridge from Culp's Hill on the right over to the rocky knob called Little Round Top on the left. The line is commonly referred to as being in the form of a giant fish hook. The right flank, the pointed end of the hook, was anchored on Culp's Hill swinging north and west just to the south of the town. The arc then continued to the west, finally turning south and extended in that direction until reaching Little Round Top, which formed the eye end of the hook at the extreme left flank. Round Top, a much higher hill, lay only a few hundred-yards further south.

The Confederate forces were stretched out about one mile distant to the north and west in a line replicating the form of the Federal position. Lee's line encompassed nearly six miles. It began beyond the east side of Culp's Hill, sweeping north and west through Gettysburg and occupying the length of Seminary Ridge as it extended south. The majority of Lee's force arrived on July 1st and was well positioned.

The broad expanse between these two ridges was cropland, as was much of the high ground on Cemetery Ridge. As that ridge approaches Little Round Top, it descends to form a broad saddleback and then swoops up again to meet the slope. Starting at Gettysburg, the Emmittsburg Road runs southwest along a low rise that roughly-divides the valley between the two ridges. At the point opposite the saddleback, the Emmittsburg road is actually the higher ground. The sloping plain in front of this saddleback and Little Round Top––about 500 yards in width—featured a peach orchard and a broad wheat field.

BATTLE OF GETTYSBURG, July 2nd, 1863.
As seen from Rocky Hill on Meade's Left, from a drawing by Edwin Forbes

A tiny stream called Plum Run meanders through the center of the shallow valley between Cemetery Ridge and the Emmittsburg Road. Its course forms a muddy wash, only a couple feet in depth, lined in places with scrub brush, large rocks and bushes. In summer, as now, the creek was often dry.

By day's end, this pastoral panorama was transformed into a scene of pain, death and destruction. The orchards were reduced to shattered stumps by canon fire and littered with fallen warriors. The wheat field fell at the hands of the grim reaper. The entire 20-acre expanse of ripe wheat would be littered with the wounded or dead bodies of 4,000 men whose bravery and gallantry now covered the ground in a crimson cloak.

As the events of the day began to unfold, the 2nd Corps had marched onto the field. All its regiments were put into the line, except the First Minnesota which was placed in reserve

461

in support of artillery on the back side of the ridge. The position would prove to be a hazardous one. About this time, Company L (sharpshooters) was sent to support Kirby's Battery near the cemetery and Company C was placed on provost guard duty. As both sides moved to position themselves during the morning hours, the infantry did little serious fighting. The artillery, on the other hand, was very active. Rebel artillery firing from behind Culp's Hill, from Gettysburg and from the low plain in front of Round Top, sent shells screaming over the slight hollow that the Minnesota boys occupied. An occasional solid shot fell short and bounded across the ground where they lay or exploded in the sky above, spraying them with jagged iron fragments. After a few hours, word came that the Third Corps was going in on their left. Orders were given to be ready to move to their aid, should the need arise.

The Third Corps, under the command of General Sickles, was ordered to take up a position below the base of Little Round Top. Having reached that point, Sickles decided he liked the looks of the ground several hundred yards further ahead. Shortly after noon, without orders, he moved his entire 3rd Corps to a position near the Emmittsburg road, which placed him far out in front of the Union line and without support on either of his flanks. He was now in jeopardy of being attacked from three sides.

Lee had concluded he must fight here and laid out his plan of attack. Since Jeb Stuart had still not returned with the cavalry, Lee was effectively blind, with no way to reconnoiter or probe the Union line for weakness. Small patrols, sent out to gather what intelligence they could, were his only source of information. He concluded that the Union line was weak on its left flank near Round Top and, ordered General Longstreet to move there with an all out attack as quickly as possible. Longstreet did not like the idea and was slow in getting all his units into position to launch the attack. It was 4 PM before the attack began.

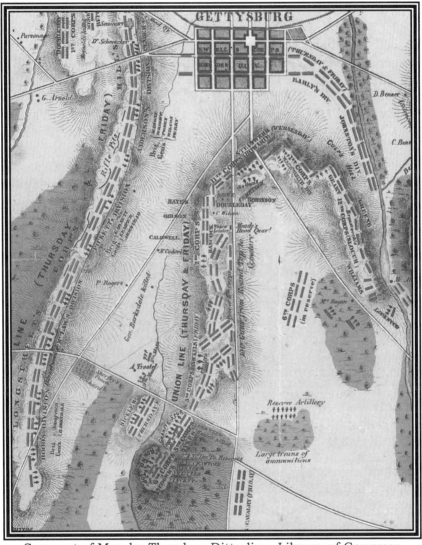

Segment of Map by Theodore Ditterline, Library of Congress

While Longstreet was making preparations to attack, General Meade became aware that Sickles was well out in front of the Union line and rode immediately to investigate. Sickles explained that his orders left him with full discretion to take a position as he thought best. Meade very firmly stated that his orders gave no such authority. Sickles was just in the act of offering to withdraw his troops to his assigned position when Longstreet began his attack. Informing Sickles that he no longer had the option to withdraw and would have to hold the position he had chosen, Meade rode off telling him he would send what reinforcements he could.

By 4:30 PM, the battle was in full swing. The frontal attack of the Confederate brigades of Wilcox, Barksdale and Perry, started on the Union left flank and gradually progressed across the entire front and met the Union right flank where Confederate General A. P. Hill had launched an attack upon Culp's Hill.

Sickles was soon in dire straights in the area of the wheat field and the peach orchard and, there was grave danger that the rebels could capture both of the Round Tops. The Union Fifth Corps was sent to Sickles aid and became cannon fodder. The quick thinking of General Warren, a signal officer, brought aid to Little Round Top and saved that critical position when he sent Vincent's Brigade of troops and Hazlett's artillery battery from the Fifth Corps. These men performed an incredible feat by dragging the 3,000-pound guns and their ammunition caissons up the hill by hand! By 5PM, attack-after-attack had struck the now badly thinned Federal line. Many units had broken under the pressure and fell back in disorder. Brigadier General John Caldwell was ordered to move his 1st Division of the 2nd Corps in to support Sickles. At double-quick time, they ran into the maelstrom of death in the wheat field. Charge-after-charge and repulse-after-repulse ensued as the toll continued to rise.

In an attempt to plug the hole in the Union line left where Caldwell had been, General Gibbon ordered the First Minnesota Regiment out of its position in reserve and they rushed to their left to fill the gap.

One small, undermanned regiment must now fill the space that, moments before, was being held by an entire division of about 6,000 men[81]. After taking their position to the left of Captain Evan Thomas' Battery C of the 4th Regular Artillery, Colonel Colvill realized the danger they were in from enemy fire directed at the guns. He moved the men slightly down the west slope of Cemetery Ridge. This position was midway between Cemetery Hill on the north and Little Round Top on the south. The ground sloped on a shallow grade, down through a pasture about 200 yards westward to the dry Plum Run creek bed. As they laid there on the ground, they watched Sickles' men struggle with the overwhelming enemy force in Mr. Sherfy's Peach Orchard and on Abraham Trostle's farm just to the east.

The grey tide struck the protruding salient of Sickles' corps like a rogue wave. Through the veil of heavy smoke, the Minnesotans watched with mounting apprehension as the Union line trembled from the shock. Gradually the force of numbers began to tell and the blue line staggered and began to falter. The 46 rebel cannons and brigade-after-brigade hurled everything they had at the protruding angle of Sickles' position. As more Union regiments were fed into the fray, notably the 82nd New York and 15th Massachusetts, who fought so desperately, the tide shifted back in their favor. Artillery and musketry cut down entire lines of men and more rushed in to meet the hail of death. The Peach Orchard changed hands six times before the Union line broke and units began to fall back. They rallied, at intervals, turning to pour a volley into their yelling pursuers.

At about 6 PM, the role of the Minnesota men began to change from spectator to combatant. Musket balls kicked up puffs of dust and whistled overhead as the men began to take fire from the left where rebel sharpshooters had gained a position among some rocks and fences a few hundred yards

---

[81] A Division with a full complement of officers and men would number about 12,000 men. In this instance, with the numbers reduced by over 2 years of fighting, actual strength was likely around 6,000.

away. Colvill ordered Company F, under the command of Captain John Ball, to skirmish in that direction and silence the menace. Sadly, Company F would not see many of its brothers-in-arms again.

Harper's Weekly Aug. 8, 1863-Longstreet's Attack on the left of center – Drawing by A. R. Waud

More units were rushed in to shore up the now decimated 3rd Corps. Caldwell's division of the 2nd Corps had already lost half its strength. The salient[82] collapsed under the weight of the onslaught. What had started as an orderly retreat with regiments falling back in good order and continuously halting to return fire soon degenerated into an all-out rush to the rear. Artillery pieces, their horses lying dead in the harness, were left only to be turned around and used by the enemy. Officers valiantly tried to rally the retreating mass only to be shot from their saddles.

General Sickles was severely wounded as a cannon ball

---

[82] Salient: an outward projecting part of a fortification, trench system or line of defense.

struck him in the leg at the knee while on his horse. He fell to the ground with the limb hanging by threads and was carried from the field. Meade then placed General Hancock in charge of the 3rd Corps in addition to his own 2nd Corps.

From their vantage point, the First Minnesota men watched as the sweeping grey line descended down the slope from Seminary Ridge, over the Emmittsburg road and across the sloping plain toward Plum Run. It was a very hot, humid day with little, if any, breeze to waft away the smoke. It seemed as if atmospheric conditions had conjured up a strange spell and cast it on the pall of smoke, which hung in sheets like huge draperies suspended from the puffy clouds. The interplay of smoke, light and shadow created a strange illusion that caused the contestants in the battle being waged below to appear very tall. The effect was that of watching a battle between giants on a distant hillside.

The scene became one of retreat and desperation as "Sergeant," an anonymous correspondent from the regiment, wrote:[83]

> "*The second line met the attack gallantly and turned the enemy back. They charged again and for a while the contest was sharp and desperate - at this critical moment a fresh division of the enemy charged down – the Third Corps gave way and came to the rear in squads carrying back men, flags and wounded and running over our ranks in spite of all our attempts to rally them. The enemy's artillery poured grape and shrapnel into the retreating groups, and in return our Battery "A" opened upon the rebel infantry, who were advancing with loud cheers and pouring volley after volley into the broken lines of the Third. This turned their attention to the battery, and soon a dozen of their crimson battle flags, followed by as many regiments, were advancing towards it, its only support being our eight companies of the First Minnesota.*"

---

[83] Letter from "Sergeant" to the St. Paul Pioneer dated August 9, 1863.

William Lochren also describes the scene and events:

"No other troops were then near us, and we stood by this battery, in full view of Sickles' battle in the peach orchard half a mile to the front, and witnessed with eager anxiety the varying fortunes of that sanguinary (bloody) *conflict, until at length, with gravest apprehension, we saw Sickles' men give way before the heavier forces of Longstreet and Hill, and come back, slowly, at first, and rallying at short intervals, but at length broken and in utter disorder, rushing down the slope, by the Trostle House, across the low ground, up the slope on our side, and past our position to the rear, followed by a strong force—the large brigades of Wilcox and Barksdale—in regular lines, moving steadily in the flush of victory, and firing on the fugitives. They had reached the low ground, and in a few minutes would be at our position, on the rear of the left flank of our line, which they could roll up, as Jackson did the Eleventh Corps at Chancellorsville."*

Conditions had now reached a critical state on the battlefield with the entire left flank in jeopardy of being overwhelmed. As the Minnesota men looked on, an entire Rebel brigade under the command of General Cadmus Wilcox, of General Longstreet's Corps, moved out of the smoky haze along the line of woods on Seminary Ridge. The sight was grand but alarming as the of men from the 10th, 11th and 14th Alabama regiments formed into two lines of battle and began to march in perfect order across the sloping plain. The 11th Alabama was in the lead, the 14th slightly back and to their left and the 10th back and to their right, all forming a spearhead. As they advanced, cannons to their right and rear roared to life hurling a curtain of cast-iron death before them. The rebel line swept over the rise along the Emmittsburg Pike, their artillery advancing as they came. One hundred Federal guns on the crest of Cemetery Ridge opened in reply. Shells from two sides concentrated their fire on the enemy's guns, killing and maiming the crews. Guns tumbled from shattered carriages, horses screamed in agony as solid shot tore through their bodies and ammunition caissons exploded in

468

thunderous roars. On came the two relentless, unwavering lines! The ranks shifted to fill gaping holes left by exploding shells. The onlookers knew that if this threat was not met and repulsed, the day was lost. Indeed, if the enemy gained the heights of the Round Tops and broke through in the saddle near Little Round Top, they could bring enfilading fire to bear on the entire line.

In his Narrative of the First Minnesota, Lieutenant William Lochren relates the steadfast nature of his regiment:

> *"Most soldiers, in the face of the near advance of such an overpowering force, which had just defeated a considerable portion of an army corps, would have caught the panic and joined the retreating masses. But the First Minnesota had never yet deserted any post, had never retired without orders, and desperate as the situation seemed and as it was, the regiment stood firm against whatever might come."*

General Hancock, seemingly always present at the point of greatest danger, arrived to survey the situation, having, only moments before, narrowly escaped being killed or captured when he rode out with an aide into a rebel unit of skirmishers. He tried to help Colonel Colvill and his dismounted officers rally the retreating remnants of the 3rd Corps and Caldwell's Division as they ran in a headlong dash to the rear. Hancock had already ordered reinforcements from the right to plug the gap in the Union line but, even at a dead run, they would not be able to cover the half mile distance in time. Hancock hastily surveyed the area as he realized that the only force nearby was the small contingent led by the Colonel who had been trying to stem the flight of the retreating throng. As Colvill looked on, Hancock surveyed the 262 men before him and rhetorically exclaimed, *"My God! Are these all the men we have here?"* He then turned to Colvill and asked, *"What regiment is this?"* Colvill's instant reply, *"First Minnesota,"* must have brought some small hope to Hancock who knew they were the regiment that *Never Runs*.

Motioning toward the closing enemy, Hancock issued the order, *"Charge those lines."* [84]

Every man knew instantly what the order meant—a charge across open ground against a force more than five times their number and, into a screaming, whistling, screeching hail of artillery and musket fire, would likely leave them all dead or dying on the field, as their lifeblood drained into the dry earth. Still not a man hesitated. The countless hours of training and drilling took effect and the men formed into line of double-ranks by company. In order of the seniority of their Captains, from left to right companies D, I, E, A, B, K, H, & G formed a line 250 feet wide. It must have seemed of Lilliputian scale compared to the rebel line of 1,600 men spanning across the field.

Now 350 yards away, the Confederate line marched bravely forward. Every piece of artillery and musket spewed deadly missiles among them. Canister tore wide gaps in their line and, like the veterans they were about to meet, they closed their ranks and marched unfalteringly toward Plum Run, firing as they came.

All eyes of the First Minnesota were on their Colonel waiting for his order, willing to do what they knew must be done. At the command, *"Attention!"* the men shouldered arms and dressed the line on their flag. Private Charles Muller of Company A remembered Colonel Colvill stepping before the regiment and asking *"Will we go along?"* to which all the men emphatically replied *"YES!"* The order rang with finality. *"Forward, double-quick![85] March!"*

Colonel Colvill later recalled the moment:

> *"I noticed as the regiment started, the swinging of*

---

[84] This according to Lochren's narrative. As is often the case in such adrenalin and emotion charged events, the recollections of Hancock, Lochren and Colvill differ slightly. Hancock remembered asking, *"Colonel, do you see those colors?"* And after receiving a reply saying, *"Then take them."* Colvill recalled the order as *"Minnesota Forward."*

[85] Double Quick cadence was 165 and sometimes 185 paces per minute, each pace being 33 inches.

the gleaming muskets, as the right shoulder shift was made in one time and two motions corresponding to the steps of the advance & seemed to emphasize the unity of the start: the gleam of the muskets you can imagine. It was grand."

In the red glow of sunset, they moved down the slope in perfect disciplined order. Their stride gradually quickened as hearts began to pound. Enemy guns hastily swung to meet this new threat, hurling their deadly salvos into the charging line. They swept through the pasture and into the stubble of the wheat field—no time to stop to aid the comrade who had just fallen. Men dropped all along the line in pain and agony though not one cried out. Wounded men struggled to rise and rejoined their brothers only to be struck down a second time. Sergeant Alfred Carpenter of Company K remembered:

"Bullets whistled past us, shells screeched over us; canister and grape fell about us; comrade after comrade dropped from the ranks; but on the line went."

"Faster, we must move faster," they thought, if they were to survive the hailstorm and meet the foe. Closer and closer they drew to the swale and the enemy. Their magnificent line now thinned with every step, still they held their fire. The smoke-enshrouded, thicketed swale was only 15 yards farther. *"Charge!"* Colvill commanded and in unison the rifles swung from shoulders to *"charge bayonets"*. Thoughts whirled through their minds as they now ran with all speed. *"Don't fire yet, can't reload. Use your bayonet when you hit em. Club with your rifle. Stop them! Stop them!"*

With orders to "keep the pressure on and the movement forward," the four rebel brigades had advanced across the 600 yards from the Emmittsburg Pike toward Plum Run. Their lines became somewhat jumbled by their long charge under artillery fire and, in considerable disorder, they neared the rock-strewn, brushy, low ground along the run. Officers were separated from their men and the confusion slowed the advance as they drew close to the oncoming men in blue.

The anonymous correspondent 'Sergeant' was at the rear of the Minnesota line acting as file closer to stop any stragglers.

". . . *every faculty was absorbed in the one thought of whipping the enemy in front. I know we reached the brink of the little run and gave them one volley which swept them from the earth; but a new line rises from the bed of the run at our feet, and a brigade advances down the hollow on our right; both open fire and our men fall, many pierced by balls, both from the right side and front, which crossed each other in their courses through the body. We fire away three, four, five irregular volleys, and but little ammunition is wasted when the muzzles of opposing guns almost meet. The enemy seemed to sink into the ground. They are checked and staggered.*"

Running for all they were worth, the men vented their building anxiety, fear, anger and determined exuberance in a tremendous roaring yell as they heard Colvill's order to fire. The sight of those leveled bayonets approaching at break-neck speed and the salvo of lead that tore into their ranks broke the rebel line into complete confusion. In wild disorder, the first line turned and fled back into and through the second line and third lines. Lieutenant Martin Maginnis of Company H, to the immediate left of the Company G, described the wild melee that ensued:

"*But little ammunition was wasted at the volley. A perfect swath of men sink to the ground, and the living recoil back on their second and third lines. Their supporting lines, confused and excited, wildly commenced firing through the mass in front, slaughtering their own men by the hundreds and throwing the whole column into confusion, while their artillery from the rear fired on friend and foe alike.*"[86]

Three times, the men saw their flag fall as its bearer was shot down, and three times, it rose again in the hands of

---

[86] Newspaper Article "The First Minnesota: The Most Gallant Charge of the War" appeared in a paper called "Gouverneur", New York 1881?

another gallant comrade. More than 100 of their number already lay dead or wounded on the slope behind.

"We kept running as fast as we could so as not to give the enemy a chance to reload their rifles again", said Charley Muller of Company A. *"And we got there before they had loaded; we run up on to them to within 4 yards when we begin to fire our first shot, and then we went at them with our bayonets."*

As the men fought at Plum Run and took cover behind the scattered rocks, boulders, bushes and in the shallow gully. Colonel Colvill fell badly wounded, as he later recounted:

"I saw a number of our men lying as they had fallen. Then came a shock like a sledge hammer on my backbone between my shoulders. It turned me partly around and made me 'see stars.' I suppose it was a piece of shell. Just then I perceived Captain Coates who said: "Colonel, are you badly hurt." I said, I don't know. Take care of the men.' Just then I was putting my foot on the ground; there was a smart pang through it; it gave way and falling to the ground I saw just beside me a gully not more than two feet wide and less in depth."

"As I struck the ground I rolled over into it and listened among other things to the bullets zipping along the ground and thought how fortunate for me was the fact of the gully."

Colvill was indeed badly hurt! A Minnie ball had struck near the top of his right shoulder, traveled across his body just in front of his right shoulder blade, tore a piece from a vertebrae in his spine and finally lodged itself under his left shoulder blade. The second wound shattered his right ankle.

As evening came and the light waned, the much longer rebel line began to wrap around the regiment's right and left flanks, subjecting them to heavy fire from both the front and right. The enfilading fire from hundreds of muskets and cannons ripped through the remaining men as they fired at will. Their trembling hands grappled with their cartridge boxes and tiny percussion caps. White teeth showing from powder-blackened faces tore at the paper cartridges. Powder and Minnie balls were rammed down the searing hot barrels of their rifles as they loaded and fired at a fever pitch. Companies H and G swung to meet the flanking fire; meanwhile, the remaining clusters of men fired furiously into the enemy at their front. The situation was now becoming desperate. Cannon shells, grape and canister shot tore through bodies with a sickening 'thwack' from all directions. Every man knew he had no choice but to withstand the galling fire and give back better than he got, but very few were left to return the fire. The minutes seemed like hours in the twilight. Where were the reinforcements? Second in command, Lt. Colonel Charles P. Adams had been hit five times when a sixth ball pierced his chest, punctured his lungs and exited his back. Command fell to Captain Messick of Company G when the third and fourth officers in the chain of command were also wounded. Colvill realized the position was no longer tenable, and as he lay bleeding, ordered Captain Messick to take command and order the men to withdraw. The order to *"Fall Back"* was passed down the line. The order was repeated several times but the men would not budge. Finally, as the color bearer turned and began to slowly walk up the slope, the men followed. Each man dreaded the thought of the long upward slope of open ground behind them over which they would, once again, have to run the gauntlet of enemy fire. The Confederates had nearly surrounded them and, looking to their rear, they discovered an opening only 50-yards wide remained. As they began to pull back, their sister regiment, the 82nd New York, came to their rescue on the right. The 3rd Corps units, which had regrouped after their headlong retreat, and the recently arrived 6th Corps stormed to their support on the left. Only 15 minutes had passed since they had reached Plum Run but it seemed like an eternity.

All the while, Confederate General Wilcox tried to get reinforcements. None came, and though he was sure he could have broken through the Union line with reinforcements, he ordered his men to withdraw.

The storm of bullets continued while the Minnesota boys pulled back, leaving their dead, helping the wounded that could walk and still turning to fire as they left the field. Sergeant Henry Taylor, finding himself now in charge of

Company E, described the withdrawal:

Every other officer and sergeant in the company was either dead or wounded. The dead, of course, had to be left behind, and the wounded who were unable to walk had to fend for themselves. Some crawled back toward the ridge while others sought shelter behind boulders and small trees to avoid flying bullets as well as capture."

Henry was unaware during the withdrawal, that his brother Isaac had been killed.

"I help our colonel off the field but fail to find my brother who, I suppose, is killed. I rejoin the regiment and lie down in the moonlight, rather sorrowful. Where is Isaac?"

He found his beloved brother the next morning and wrote a letter on July 6th, to tell his parents that Isaac was killed. An artillery shell exploded directly above him and the jagged fragments struck him, taking off the back of his head, then sliced through his body severing his waist belt and nearly tearing him in two.

As the men gathered around the tattered remnants of their flag on the crest of Cemetery Ridge, the full impact of the fight struck home. Of the 262 who so gallantly charged the rebel onslaught, only 47 were left fit for duty and 215 lay dead or wounded on the field. Not even the 47 men escaped unscathed. Their regimental Quarter Master observed:

"Every man, without exception, had his clothing riddled–some of them all to rags."[87]

The regiment had accomplished the task that was asked of it—they prevented the rebel breakthrough and gained General Hancock the five minute's time he asked for plus nearly 10 more for good measure. They stood their ground against astounding odds leaving the field under orders and still in the possession of their flag. Their loss of 82% of their men in this brief, but costly, engagement is without equal in the annals of warfare. Even the much-heralded "Charge of the Light Brigade" pales by comparison.

---

[87] From letter by Francis Bassen to St. Paul Pioneer, July 18, 1863.

The charge of the First Minnesota at Gettysburg, Don Trioani,
Minnesota Historical Society

In a later reflection on the famed charge, General Winfield
Scott Hancock said:

*"There is no more gallant deed recorded in history. I
ordered these men in there because I saw I must gain five
minutes time. Reinforcements were coming on the run, but
I knew that before they could reach the threatened point
the Confederate, unless checked, would seize the position.
I would have ordered that regiment in if I had known that
every man would be killed. It had to be done, and I was
glad to find such a gallant body of men at hand willing to
make the terrible sacrifice that the occasion demanded."*

In the dark of the night, some survivors of the regiment
ventured back across the hallowed ground that was now
littered with the lifeless remains and suffering forms of their
fallen friends. Alfred Carpenter of Company K wrote:

*"The ground was strewed with dead and dying, whose
groans and prayers and cries for help and water rent the*

air. The sun had gone down and in the darkness we hurried, stumbled over the field in search or our fallen companions."

With only moonlight to guide them, they searched for the wounded. Though exhausted in the extreme by the events of the day, they rose again, called by the bond of brotherhood to their duty. Their beloved Colonel and other wounded were tended to before they dropped to the ground to rest among the dead men, dead horses, and all the other debris of war.

☙ *THE THIRD DAY – JULY 3ᴿᴰ*

In anticipating of new attacks, the troops were aroused from their rest well before dawn. Initially there was nearly complete stillness all along the opposing lines, yet every man present knew that this was just the precursor to another terrific battle soon to be joined. As a bright, red sunrise appeared in the eastern sky, the sounds of battle once again shattered the still morning air. Shortly after 3:30 AM, artillery fire was heard from the left near the Round Tops and the right on the backside of Culp's Hill, where Union troops were pushing back the rebel gains still held from the previous day. The fighting soon abated and silence returned along the entire line.

Captain Ball of Company F, which had suffered the loss of 3 men seriously wounded and one missing while fighting in support of Sickle's right flank, had long been awake. He hastened his men to make ready to rejoin the remaining men of the First Minnesota. Their regiment had suffered unimaginable losses and they were anxious about their friends. Sergeant Hamlin returned and reported he could only find a few men left. Upon finding the remnants of their unit at the place where they had left them, they greeted one another with both exuberance and deep-felt sorrow. The addition of the 20 men who remained of Company F now swelled the regiment's number to 67. At some point during this time, the regiment moved to the right and took its usual position in the brigade on the line. It was slightly to the left and forward of Meade's headquarters, about

400-feet to the south of a small cluster of trees.[88] It has been said they were put in this position of 'relative safety' in the center of the Union line in deference to the losses they had suffered. Facing the enemy, the men took their place in line just behind a slight rise that ran across the face of the hill. They hastily threw up a low breastwork of any material they could find. Fence rails, tree branches, stones and sticks were piled up. Using their tin plates, cups and bayonets, they dug dirt and threw it on top. Their knapsacks and even their blankets were filled with earth and added to the meager barricade, even then, it was only some 18-inches in height. The work completed, they checked their weapons and ammunition, sent details out for fresh water, built small fires, made some much appreciated hot coffee and ate a few hardtack crackers. James Wright of Company F wrote:

> "No man can fully and rightly appreciate the value of a cup of coffee until he has partaken of one under some similar circumstance."[89]

At 11 AM, enemy artillery opened fire and a brief, but lively, duel ensued as Hancock's artillery replied. Then, all was again quiet and the men lay down behind their shelters and slept, paying little attention to the occasional shell or bullet that struck the ground to their front.

To this point Robert E. Lee had concentrated his attacks against the Union's right and left flanks and believed that he now had weakened and nearly broken the Union forces. He felt certain he could successfully mount a decisive attack upon the center and gain the victory he had come north to achieve. He also believed that he still faced the same dispirited Army of the Potomac that he had whipped on the Rappahannock. The preceeding night, General Meade, in speaking to General Gibbon, who commanded the Second Corps, said that since Lee was unsuccessful in his attacks on both flanks, he would likely make an all-out effort the next day against the Union center, where the Second Corps was positioned. His presumption

---

[88] This according to Richard Moe, Last Full Measure, 278; This copse of trees, became the focal point of Lee's attack.
[89] Wright, No More Gallant a Deed, 303

478

proved to be correct. After the early morning fighting, silence again covered the battlefield although tension permeated the air. To the veterans, the silence was an omen they knew well. It meant the enemy was positioning his artillery to begin a bombardment that would precede a massive attack. As the morning wore on, the sun rose and now shown brightly; the day became very hot. The scorching rays made things quite uncomfortable for the men lying behind their crude shelters in their wool uniforms.

In the distance across the valley, the movements of the enemy could be observed as battery-after-battery of artillery moved into place. Robert E. Lee had now placed 83 guns in battery near the peach orchard and another 89 along the crest of Seminary Ridge—a mass of 172 guns.[90] Their intention to mount a major attack was now a certainty. Confederate General Longstreet, whom Lee referred to as 'my old war horse,' was not in favor of mounting the attack against such a well-entrenched Federal line. Several times, he asked Lee to change his plans and mount a flanking attack. In "Battles and Leaders of the Civil War," page 342, he reveals his conversation with General Lee about noon.

> "I want you to take Pickett's Division and make the attack. I will re-enforce you with two divisions, Heth's and Pender's, of the Third Corps," Lee said. "That will give me 15,000 men," I replied. Then I continued: "I have been a soldier, I may say from the ranks up to the position I now hold. I have been in pretty much all kinds of skirmishes, from those of two or three soldiers up to those of an Army Corps, and I think I can safely say there never was a body of 15,000 men who could make that attack successfully."
> "The General seemed a little impatient at my remarks, so I said nothing more. As he showed no indication of changing his plan, I went to work at once to arrange the troops for the attack."

---

[90] Wright, No More Gallant a Deed, 305; Richard Wheeler, "Witness to Gettysburg" Page-231, numbers the rebel guns at 237.

On Cemetery Ridge, men, horses and guns were rapidly shifted into position. Caissons were resupplied with ammunition and brought up. Eighty guns were placed in battery along the crest of the ridge, located a short distance back from the line of ragged, dirty faced, determined, blue-clad troops. The cemetery on the north end of the ridge harbored six more batteries and another five batteries were positioned on the ridge to the south of the cemetery. Still more were in the rear in the artillery reserve. Around 12:30 PM, General Gibbon ordered Captain Wilson Farrell to return Company C, which had been on provost guard duty at Division Headquarters, to the regiment. It was now apparent that every man and rifle would be needed to hold the hill.

At Gibbon's headquarters, the mess wagon pulled up and the mess chest was lifted down. It was 1 PM. The General had invited his staff and General Hancock to join him for lunch. His stewards had somehow acquired some old roosters and prepared a hearty dinner. As the bread was served, the orderly bringing the butter was cut in two by a shell that came screaming from Seminary Ridge. A second shell followed, as the two signal guns of the rebel command spoke the order to open fire. Instantly the air was filled with shrieking, tearing, exploding shells as every gun fired in unison and a sheet of flame and billowing smoke enshrouded their entire line. Union officers scrambled for cover or their horses in a mad dash to get back to their men.

The greatest artillery duel that ever occured in America had now begun. Shells, case shot and cannon balls, tore through the air at the rate of three-per-second or more. Immediately General Hunt's mass of guns on Cemetery Ridge replied immediately, belching a storm of missiles from their muzzles amidst angry tongues of orange flame and billowing smoke. No less than 300 guns[91] now spoke with a voice so loud it shook the ground; the muffled sound of the conflict was reportedly heard 150 miles away. The rebel gunners soon

---

[91] This figure is based solely on the accounts of men that participated in the battle. The true actual figure is a matter of continuing dispute among historians.

got the range and shells began to fall among the Union troops as they hugged the ground and clutched their rifles. The incoming hailstorm of death and destruction seemed to come from every direction and focus to the left of the center of the Union line. Most of the shells passed over the Minnesota men, although some struck the ground to their front and bounced over just above their heads. They were so close that one man had his knapsack torn from his back as he lay there. The anonymous 'Sergeant' of the First Minnesota wrote:

> "The roar was terrific and deafening, and cannon balls, bursting shells, grape, canister, shrapnel, railroad iron and Whitworth bolts from England, and even sledges, caisson bolts and spikes – iron in every imaginable shape, was tearing up the ground and flying with horrible screeches as of invisible demons through the air. An ammunition caisson would explode, scattering fragments of timber, wheels, clothing and bodies high into the air."

Widow Leister's tiny white house with the picket fence, being used by General Meade for his headquarters, was the subject of attention of many rebel gunners. Cannon balls tore holes in the walls, knocked down the front porch posts and killed 16 horses belonging to his staff. Some horses were killed outright by exploding shells while others were disemboweled or torn apart by solid shot. The yard was plowed by cannon balls on all sides and sections of the picket fence were blown to bits. Meade and his staff hastily relocated to safer ground. General Hancock, joined by his staff, now engaged in one of the most heroic and dangerous acts of the war. With his staff trailing behind and the 2nd Corps Flag proudly flying, he rode his horse in his usual stately manner slowly along the crest of the ridge from right to extreme left, calming and assuring his men, while exhibiting the bravery and fearlessness he felt his duty required. With shells flying as thick as hail and men dying all around him, he rode among them like a gallant knight.

Trees shattered and sent jagged sharp splinters flying in every direction. Caissons exploded, killing entire gun crews.

Two-thousand-pound canon barrels were blown from their carriages. Guns were abandoned when no men were left to serve them or they became so hot that shells exploded while being rammed down the barrels. A thick wall of acrid smoke soon enshrouded the entire battlefield with only the flash of cannon fire to mark the targeted enemy guns. For two hours, the nearly unbearable bombardment continued, raining wholesale death and destruction on both sides. About 3 PM, the Union artillery fire gradually slackened and finally ceased. Shortly thereafter, the Confederate barrage also ended. Both sides had consumed much of their ammunition; Meade wanted to conserve enough to meet the attack that he knew would soon follow. He also hoped the enemy would think their intensive fire had silenced the Federal guns. In fact, most of the rebel fire was aimed to high and passed over its intended targets. The shells fell to the rear wreaking havoc among many of the wounded sheltered under the trees near the field hospitals. A relatively brief silence returned to the scene. During this interval, the rebel troops of the divisions of Pickett, Pettigrew, Trimble and Wilcox's brigade, which the 1st Minnesota had fought the day before, formed into line-of-battle in the woods on Seminary Ridge.

A good deal of activity also occurred along the Union line. Disabled artillery was hurriedly replaced with fresh units from the reserve. Ammunition was replaced from the same reserve and the artillerists repositioned and re-sighted their pieces for the attack. Relieved to be no longer relegated to just lie and embrace mother earth while praying not to be blown to bits, the infantry soldiers stood up.

"They're coming!" "Here they come!" was excitedly echoed all along the line as the confederates, three-ranks deep and a mile wide, emerged from the shadowed woods into the sunlight. The sight was magnificent, even awe inspiring. Three-quarters-of-a-mile distant, 16,500[92] courageous Confederate soldiers with rifles at right shoulder shift and their bayonets glistening like a jeweled garland above their heads, moved forward at double-quick time in perfect formation. James Wright relates how the

---

[92] According to Confederate authorities.

482

Minnesota volunteers readied to meet the oncoming charge:

"The tense inaction of hours was ended, and we hastily made preparations to meet this avalanche of bayonets that was being projected against us. The line was adjusted, advancing it a few paces for better position. Then, front rank kneeling, we awaited their coming and the order to fire. Command was given not to fire until ordered – and then to fire at their feet. This was to correct, as far as possible, the tendency to overshoot."

Almost immediately, the Union guns opened with deadly effect. Nearly 200 pieces roared into action, hurling round after round of case shot into the grand lines of advancing rebels.[93] In seconds, the entire ridge was once again engulfed in a cloud of choking smoke. On they came! Unfaltering, these brave, determined soldiers marched headlong into the storm of death toward their foe and a date with eternity. Screeching, screaming shells exploded directly over their heads; wide gaps appeared in the magnificent formation. Gallant lads stepped over the dead to fill the holes. Hundreds fell before the oncoming wall of death to join the lifeless forms of their comrades, who still littered the valley from the day before. Inexorably forward they moved, down the slope of Seminary Ridge, across the Emmittsburg Road, down to the shallow ravine at Plum Run, across the broad valley and, now, up the grade toward the massed Union infantry on Cemetery Ridge. All the while, they held their formation in the face of unbelievable destruction. Pickett's Division, swinging to direct its course toward the copse of trees on the ridge, was now exposed to enfilading fire from above. The entire rebel line closed upon its center and seemed drawn by some unseen force to converge at that shattered little clump of trees. General Hancock knew an opportunity when he saw one. He immediately ordered the

---

[93] Case shot is a thin walled cast iron projectile invented by Henry Shrapnel of Britain. It contained a black powder bursting charge and lead or iron balls. The bursting charge was triggered by a timed fuse with the shell set to explode in the air above its target, spreading "shrapnel" in every direction. Primarily an anti-personnel weapon.

13th and 16th Vermont regiments to move forward and swing into a flanking movement on the left, while other regiments of the Second Corps on the right performed a similar movement. About this time, Hancock took a Minnie ball through the groin. Though badly wounded, he refused to be taken from the field until the outcome of the battle was known. General Gibbon was also hit as he directed the 19th Maine to make a flank attack. A bullet struck his left shoulder, nicking his shoulder blade and passing out through his back. With blood running down his arm and dripping from his left hand, he realized he could not continue and turned his command over to General Harrow as he was taken to an ambulance. When a surgeon later informed him he would be dead if the ball had passed a quarter-inch further to the left, he said, *"Ah, the quarter-inches are in the hands of God."*

The First Minnesota men and the entire Union line watched while nearly 200 guns spewed out their deadly fire. Double loads of canister and grape shot now whistled through the air, mowing down hundreds of enemy soldiers at every salvo. Battle flags fell everywhere, only to be snatched from lifeless hands and, once again, hoisted aloft. As the range closed to 300 yards, the order to fire rang forth along the Union line and tens-of-thousands of muskets rose from behind their makeshift shelters and erupted in a wall flame. The fusillade struck the rebel line with terrible effect.

Alfred Carpenter wrote:

> *"They are now within musket range and our infantry open fire; men stagger from their ranks by the scores, hundreds, thousands, but on they come like an inrolling wave of the sea. They have gained a part of our line; the rest of their line is within a few rods of us; but torn, bleeding, decimated, they halt, plant their colors, and wait for their reserve to come up."*

James Wright described the desperate fight:

> *"It was not until after that we got the order and sent a rolling fire to the right oblique,[94] directed at their feet,*

---

[94] At an angle

which was about all we could see of them at the time – as all above their knees was covered with the smoke from their own guns. Then every man fired as rapidly as he could handle cartridges and adjust caps."

Every man in the three Union ranks loaded and fired as fast as humanly possible. As rifles became too hot to handle, they were dropped to the ground and quickly replaced with others taken from the wounded. Cartridge boxes ran empty and men scrambled among the dead for more. As the distance closed to mere yards, the entire remaining rebel force shifted to their left, focusing on the clump of trees. They struck the 71st Pennsylvania which could not hold and was forced back from the stone wall as Cushing's Battery was overrun. It was here that Confederate General Lewis Armistead, waving with his hat on the point of his drawn sword over his head, fell mortally wounded, while leading his men in a charge against the remainder of Cushing's guns. In spite of the premonition of his death he had the night before, Armistead stood to his duty with unfaltering bravery.

Captain Farrell with Company C of the First Minnesota rejoined the regiment as the order was given to leave their position and move to the right and charge the enemy flank.[95] More likely, the charge was actually a spontaneous rush due to an overwhelming drive to get at the enemy in the thick of the fight. The last able-bodied member of the Color Guard, Corporal John Dehn, dropped the regiment's battle flag as a bullet tore through his hand. Instantly, Henry O'Brien of Company E grabbed it up, held it high and raced toward the rebels. This reckless, impulsive act caused all the Minnesotans to charge and all the others to follow. A wild screaming melee ensued as

---

[95] The number of men added to the fighting line of the regiment with the return of Company C was likely 27. The muster rolls of June 28th show the company strength of 62 officers and men. Private Rufus M. Eastman of Company C wrote the strength was only 50 of which only 27 joined the fight. Presumably the rest were unofficially assigned to Provost Guard duty to handle the prisoners that were being sent to the rear.

they tore into the enemy with bayonets and clubbed rifles in a hand-to-hand fight to the death. Lieutenant William Harmon of Company C described the frenzy:

"If men ever become devils, that was one of the times. We were crazy with the excitement of the fight. We just rushed in like wild beasts. Men swore and cursed and struggled and fought, grappled in hand-to-hand fight, threw stones, clubbed their muskets, kicked, yelled and hurrahed. But it was over in no time."

Rifles fired through every opening that occurred. The men to the rear picked up stones that lay all around on the ground and hurled them over the heads of their comrades at the besieged rebels. As Company G, of the First Minnesota, rushed forward, their beloved Captain Nathan Messick fell when a piece of shell tore through his brain. Captain Farrell of Company C was also mortally wounded here. As the adversaries fired at one another from point-blank range, it was apparent that neither side could long endure such losses.

Almost as quickly as it had started it was over. *"We surrender,"* came the cry, as rebel soldiers dropped their rifles and raised their hands. Motioning the defeated men to the rear, the regiment rushed on to where the stone wall had been breached and, in minutes, all the rebels there were killed or captured. This point of the rebel advance has since come to be known as the 'High Water Mark', marking the highest point the Confederates reached in their charge and the point at which the fortunes of the Confederacy were reversed. When the smoke cleared, the enemy, under the cover of their artillery fire, could be seen running toward Seminary Ridge. The bodies of thousands of dead and wounded marked the path of the attack. One General said the ground was so covered with dead and wounded that he could not ride his horse across the battlefield. Torn and mangled men crawled and dragged themselves to whatever shelter they could find from the fire of their retreating comrades and their own artillery. While the rebels retreated and the indescribable roar of battle diminished, prisoners by the hundreds were gathered and sent to the rear.[96] No aid could be

---

[96] The First Minnesota was credited with taking over 500 prisoners.

given to the wounded lying everywhere; the line had to reform in case of another attack. But no further attack came. Robert E. Lee's army was now but a tattered remnant of the glorious line that had swept across the valley less than an hour before. Both sides had shed enough blood and were too exhausted to fight more. James Wright tells of the exhaustion:

"Now that the critical part of the struggle was apparently over, the intense feelings that had carried us through it subsided rapidly. And the usual relaxation following such high-pressure emotions followed. For about 65 hours we had been under almost constant physical or mental strain or both and had pretty nearly reached the limit of both. As soon as the need for further exercise of muscles or will ceased to be imperative, most of the men realized that they were bordering upon a condition of collapse."

Three days of all-out combat took a toll beyond comprehension that could not be counted for days to come. Surely the chorus of mournful wailing that reached into every corner of the land must have been far greater than the thundering cacophony of the battle just ended. This day, the First Minnesota lost another 17 men, either killed or wounded, but none were reported missing.[97]

The carnage was beyond belief. Everywhere, the field was covered with rifles, destroyed or damaged cannons, caissons, horses and every manner of equipment, as well as dead and wounded heroes too numerous to count. The Quartermaster Corps gathered over 24,000 rifles from the field. Thousands of these had numerous rounds jammed down the barrels, attesting to the noise and confusion that was so great during the fighting. Men nearly deafened by the noise could not tell if their rifle fired, in the excitement they often forgot to put a percussion cap on before trying to shoot. One rifle, now in the National Civil War Museum in Harrisburg, Pennsylvania, contains 24 unspent cartridges packed into the barrel.

---

[97] James Wright recorded the loss as 32 men killed and wounded, "No More Gallant a Deed", page 309.

Confederate Dead at Gettysburg, Mathew Brady Photo

A list accompanying the monthly report of August 31, reported the First Minnesota's losses for the two days it was actively engaged as follows:

- Seven officers and 88 enlisted men killed
- Nine officers and 141 men wounded but not mortally
- No men were missing or captured
- The losses totaled 245 of the 330 engaged

Some of the wounded later returned to active duty. The average loss to the Corps involved was 25%, although the Second Corps, which included the First Minnesota Regiment, had losses of 40%.

About 6 PM, the clouds gathered and a brief, but heavy, shower brought a cooling respite. Intermittent drizzle and showers marked the night and were the prelude to three weeks of heavy rains. So often did heavy rains follow a major engagement that the men became convinced that the roar of the guns and the heavy pall of smoke had upset the heavens and produced some type of meteorological condition that caused the rain.

Darkness cloaked the field of gore from sight and a comparative stillness again fell over the battlefield. It was not quiet; the calls and moans of the wounded came piteously from everywhere out in the darkness. As it became apparent that no further attack was forthcoming, the soldiers left the line and helped with the wounded. Though desperately in need of sleep, many of the exhausted survivors searched for wounded and brought them water and aid. About 10 PM, their flickering campfires joined the thousands of others where friend and foe alike were making some much-relished coffee and something to eat. Exhausted, they lay down to sleep under a clear sky and bright moon amid the dead that lay everywhere.

For the first time, the Field Medical Service was now well equipped and manned and did an admirable job of caring for the wounded. Dr. Jonathan Letterman had completely reorganized the Ambulance Corps and, at Gettysburg had 3,000 drivers and stretcher bearers, 1,000 ambulance wagons and 650 medical officers available. All night long, the glow of lanterns twinkled hither and yon as stretcher bearers and medical aides worked to relieve the suffering of wounded Union and Confederate soldiers alike.

Well before dawn on the morning of July 4th, the Federal soldiers were aroused and, as soon as roll call was taken, were again under arms in line-of-battle, at-the –ready should Lee launch another attack. Sunrise was not apparent as the sky was now enshrouded in a heavy overcast of clouds and the air was very warm and heavy. James Wright gives us an insight into the condition of the men after their long ordeal:

"Unwashed and uncombed since we had left Uniontown, we had gathered the usual defilements of the road and the bivouac. To these ordinary accumulations of grime–which come to those who labor and sweat over dusty or muddy roads and sleep by the wayside where night or necessity dictates–had been added the uncompromising black of gunpowder. As it was our custom to tear the paper cartridges with our

teeth, many loose grains of powder had adhered to our sweating faces and hands and been smeared over them, until a question as to the original Caucasian color might consistently have been raised. Also, the color of our uniforms might have been questioned, for the 'army blue' was less prominent than the chocolate and mahogany mud stains they had gathered crossing Maryland and Virginia. We were generally as soiled as pigs that had been rooting in the fields and sleeping in the fence corners. Every man's face showed anxiety and physical suffering, and the eyes were swollen or inflamed."

While waiting for orders to come, fires were built and a breakfast of coffee and hardtack was prepared. The men sat about on the ground, talking little, and many slept. Before noon, the sky darkened ominously and, soon, a light rain began to fall. The cool, refreshing rain was a blessing to the many thirsty, wounded men still lying on the battlefield. Some skirmishing and artillery fire occurred during the day but no major action developed. Lee had actually already sent his supply trains off toward the Potomac and, by late in the afternoon units of his army were also moving out. The light rain had changed to a heavy rain and men woke to find themselves lying in pools of water. Some paired up and buttoned their two shelter tent halves together and affected a small shelter. In his book, "History of the First Regiment Minnesota Volunteer Infantry," Return I. Holcombe described the Conditions:

"Toward morning came on a terrible rain storm, another instance where rain followed a battle. In this case the downpour was proportioned to the tremendous cannonade of the previous afternoon. Only a very few of the troops were in tents and the soldiers were drenched in an instant. Sudden torrents swept over the hills and poured down the hillsides. The field hospital of Hays' Division was in a valley on a level with Rock Creek. It was flooded in a few minutes. Hundreds of Confederate wounded had been collected there, and some of them

were really saved from drowning by being hastily carried
to higher ground.
Out on the battlefield lay hundreds of the dead, the
downpour washing their bloody wounds and stark faces,
as if preparing them for sepulture."[98]

Captain Messick was given a proper burial beneath a big tree and a wooden marker was made to mark his resting place. Union troops spent their Independence Day caring for the wounded and going onto the field to gather muskets and accoutrements. Holcombe states:

"The bayonets were fixed on the muskets and then
stuck in the ground, and in a little time there were acres of
muskets thick as young trees in a nursery. The First
Minnesota, Fifteenth Massachusetts and Nineteenth
Maine gathered up 1,740 muskets and 600 sets of
accoutrements, according to General Harrow's report."

On July 5th, it was soon determined that the confederates were gone. Lee was marching his decimated army back to Virginia. The regiment's survivors were called out on burial duty and buried those of their unit who had given their "last full measure" during their charge on the 2nd. Graves were marked with crude markers made from boards salvaged from ammunition and hardtack crates and inscribed with pencil. Late in the afternoon, they marched out four miles and made camp in a new location away from the stench of the battlefield. For the next two weeks they marched on a course parallel to that of the retreating Confederate army toward the Potomac River.

In the events that make history, it is inevitable that some, who were not directly involved, will call into question the decisions of those in command. Their motives, competency and, even their patriotism, will be questioned again and again by many self-appointed jurors of time. Latter-day experts, without the burden of responsibility or authority, will set themselves up to judge the actions of the leaders and officers

---

[98] Sepulture – A place of burial.

in charge at the time. Gettysburg was no different. General Meade failed to pursue Lee's defeated force with a counter attack, failed to follow him immediately as he retreated with his army toward the Potomac, did not attack and destroy the enemy when it was stopped by the swollen Potomac River and, in total, moved with too much caution to suit his detractors. To assume such a mantle is little more than pompous presumption for anyone not present, not exhausted by the demands of the battle and not bearing responsibility for it. In fact, it is a great credit to General Meade that he assumed command of the entire army only three days before this great battle and that he moved with determination to deal his adversary the stunning blow that none before him could. Taking into account the weeks of strenuous marching and skirmishing his men had endured to get to Gettysburg, the fact that most had been without sleep, had eaten very little food and fought the most intense battle of the war, Meade was likely wise in his cautious approach. His great victory could have been his great defeat if he had decided to immediately charge the rebel lines on Seminary Ridge after Picket's repulse. Lee's army was repulsed, not destroyed. General Longstreet actually hoped such an attack on the rebel line would come. He was confident he still had enough strength to stop anyone who tried to take his fortified position, and deal them great losses for their effort. James Wright was there and commented afterward:

"*Those who have not had the experience cannot easily understand how the intense energies necessary to carry men through days of action and excitement – and worked to their utmost in such struggle–use up the vital forces. But most who have 'been there' do not need to be shown.*

I have frequently been asked why our army did not make immediate pursuit of their broken lines and destroy them? It was not then certain that their lines were 'broken, and we know now they were not. Only their assault had failed. Gen Meade decided that in his judgment it was best not to take the risk. So far as our division or corps was concerned (and we presume it was

*a fair sample of the others except the Sixth), it is much
like asking why an engine does not continue on its way
when it has exhausted its supply of fuel or water and
the track ahead is obstructed."*

Battle of Gettysburg, Friday July 3rd, 1863
Sketch by Edwin Forbes from Harper's Weekly

The following two letters written by Edward Bassett to his family after the Gettysburg Campaign, describe his involvement in the battles and the pursuit of the rebels in the days that followed. The letter of July 12th is somewhat fragmented as it is a compilation of writings over a period of days while the regiment was continually on the march.

Stopping Near Sharpsburg, Md.
July 10th A D, 1863
10 O'clock AM

Dear Father and Mother,

Knowing that you will be anxious to hear from me during these times I will try and scribble a few lines. After we whipped the rebels at Gettysburg we marched back down to Frederick and are now laying between a small town called Rohersville & Sharpsburg. We can hear fireing up towards Williamsport where it is said the rebels are trying to re-cross the Potomac. Our army is in full pursuit will trouble them some in crossing. We marched about 23 miles yesterday the weather was quite cool. I would have written before if it had been possible but we have been very busy marching. We lost 4 killed & 18 wounded in Co. G in the fight. The wounded are being taken good care of and will mostly recover. Vicksburg is ours and I expect Port Hudson has fallen before this time. We have not stopped long enough since we left the Rappahannoc in one place for me to get rested so as to write letters and you will have to excuse me. I will endeavor to write as soon as we stop. I expect that Lee's army will be badly cut to pieces before it reaches Richmond. The Potomac is very high and will be difficult to cross. There were two spies hung in Frederick lately one of them was a man that sold songs in our camp last fall.

4 PM: We are now about 6½ miles from Williamsport. There is some fireing in that direction now. Our men have drove the rebs about 6 miles to day and I expect we have taken a great many prisoners. We passed over the Antietam battle field today. The rebs did not make a stand there as expected. I think we will be in old Va. before August. We will follow the enemy towards Richmond.

I think now is the time to use the musket and if we succeed in destroying Lee's army I have hopes of a settlement of the difficulties. The rebels are sick and tired of the war and most all of them that I have talked with say that they want the war ended as soon as possible. There was a great many of them threw down their arms at Gettysburg and came over to our side and there was one man that wanted to take a musket and go into our ranks, but some of them fight to the bitter end.

The farmers sowed a great deal of wheat in this state last fall and it is a splendid crop. I think it will average as good as any I ever saw. There are not near enough men in the country to harvest the crops and the wheat is mostly dead ripe and if it is not cut soon it will be lost. Corn does not look very well it does not stand well and is small although some pieces look very well. There is a good supply of fruit such as apples, pears, peaches, cherries and blackberries. Potatoes look quite well for this country there are some large enough to use. [99]

The roads are good although there has been considerable rain lately.

I don't know when I can send this but I will send it as soon as possible and you must take it as it is for I am tired besides we are laying in the field and liable to march at any moment so good by this time and I will endeavor to find a spare moment sometime to write a few lines. There is a great deal that I would like to tell you but I cannot write it now so good by again.

Your son

Edward H. Bassett

Co. G. 1ˢᵗ Minnesota Vols.

Sunday 12th..all well about 5 miles from Hagerstown. (The Morristown boys are all well that are here, I have not heard from the wounded)

I don't think we will have any more fighting to do very soon. (that is our Brigade)

---

[99] Foraging for something different than the normal bland fare to eat was common. At one point the men had all been suffering from dysentery and during a march had broken ranks to collect wild blackberries from a patch by the road. The officers told them they would only worsen their problems but the men ate the berries anyway. To everyone's surprise the dysentery cleared up right away. Thereafter the men looked for blackberries at every opportunity.

Captain Henry Coates relates the impact of the losses to the First Minnesota at Gettysburg:

"Our loss of so many brave men is heartrending, and will carry mourning into all parts of the state. But they have fallen in a holy cause, and their memory will not soon perish. Our loss is 4 commissioned officers and 47 men killed; 13 Officers and 162 men wounded, and 6 men missing, – total 232 – out of less than 330 men and officers engaged."[100]

Stopping 4 ½ miles from Hagerstown, Md.
July 12th A D 1863

Dear Father and Mother,

As we have stoped for a few hours I will try & write you a few lines and tell you what we have been about since we crossed the Potomac into this state. We crossed the Potomac at Edwards ferry on the night of the 26th of June and camped about 2 miles from the ferry where we lay until morning when we packed up and marched through Poolsville and camped that night the 27th east of Sugar Loaf mountain. The next morning we marched at light and that day we made about 33 miles. We passed through four towns that day. They were called Liberty, Johnsville, Union Bridge and Uniontown. The citizens along the road were mostly good union people and gave everything they had to eat to the soldiers. Tuesday 30th we lay in camp about two miles from Uniontown. The rebel pickets were out about 8 miles and there was some skirmishing

---

[100] The six men Captain Coates lists as missing were in fact not missing at all. They were discovered among the bushes and rocks on the field, wounded and unconscious or sleeping, to weak to join their brothers without aid. These figures of losses were preliminary and reported to the Governor of Minnesota on July 5th.

with them during the day. The boys went out into the country that day & bought all the bread, pies, cakes, butter milk & etc. that they could get. Wednesday, July 1st we marched early towards Gettysburg stoping for dinner at Taneytown. We stoped that night about 3 miles from Gettysburg. There had been some fighting there most all day and we were told that the rebs had rather beaten us. General Reynolds was killed and our forces were driven back about one mile. The next day the 2nd of July we marched to the front where we lay quiet all the AM and until most dark when the rebels drove our men back in the center and we were sent to their support. We charged down across a stubble field about 30 rods and stoped in a ravine lined with brush & trees but the rebels were three to our one & had gotten the first fire on us when the General ordered us to retire which we did loosing some over 200 killed & wounded in about 15 minutes. We rallied what were left on the same ground that we started from & were ready for another fight but a battery to our right had opened with grape and cannister on the rebs and driven them back. Captain Messick was now in command of the reg't. he being the senior officer that was not disabled for our Colonel, Lieutenant Colonel & Major were all badly wounded. As soon as we were rallied and we saw that the rebs had been repulsed by the battery Wm. Ramsey, Cal Jackson and myself went down onto the field to do what we could for the wounded and as soon as the stretchers & ambulances could be got they were borne from the field to the hospitals. After we had done what we could for the wounded we joined our reg't. & lay on our arms until morning.

The next day there was continued skirmishing along the lines and about noon the rebs opened upon us with their artillery and I believe the shot and shell flew the thickest that I ever saw them. They passed over our heads like hail some bursting directly over us but we lay flat on the ground and no one was hurt by them in our reg't.

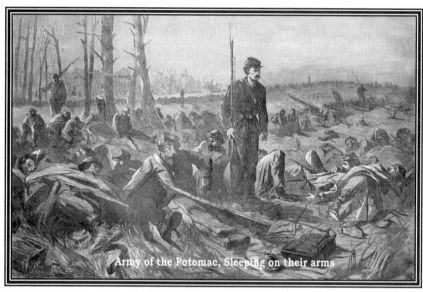

Army of the Potomac, Sleeping on their arms

Sketch from Harper's Weekly

It is said the rebs had over 100 guns fireing along the line at one time and it lasted over an hour. Our batteries replied briskly at first but were ordered to cease fireing when the rebels also ceased and immediately advanced their infantry with an idea that we had been scared away by their shelling. Lee told his men that it was Militia that were opposed to them & he rightly supposed that they could be shelled out but it was the old Potomac Army that he was trying to shell out and he found his mistake during the PM. As soon as we saw them advancing across the field we prepared to meet them and as soon as they came in range of our guns we sent them our compliments in the shape of one ounce bullets. They came determined to drive us back but when they were one half shot down they commenced to retreat and we chased them and took many prisoners. The loss in our reg't. was not so heavy as on the previous day although the fireing lasted about one hour. Captain Messick was killed and Corpl. Jones & one private wounded in our company. I passed the Captain Just before he fell but I did not know that he was killed until after the fight. He was killed instantly being shot through the head. After the fight was over I went & helped carry him off the field and one of the boys that has been cooking for him and taking care of his things said that he would see that he was burried. July 4th was rather dull to us. There was some shooting all the A.M. and in the P.M. there was a heavy rain it continued to rain most all night & the rebels took advantage of it and left. July 5th we were in posession of the battlefield & in the A.M. I was put on detail to bury the dead. About 3 P.M. we started and marched out about 4 miles and camped in an old field where we lay until the morning of the 7th when we started again and marched to Taneytown & camped where we stayed until

Capt. Nathan Messick

5 o'clock in the morning of the 8th when we started in the rain for Frederick. We marched about 20 miles through an awful road & camped on the Monocacy river about 5 miles from Frederick.

July 9th. I was sick but the regt. marched early and I followed the best I could. We marched about 23 miles that day and I made out to get up to camp about one hour after they camped. We passed through Frederick, Jefferson & Barkitsville. The next day I was not very well but I made out to keep up. We passed that day through Rohersville & Keedysville two small towns, crossed the Antietam creek and part of the old battlefield and camped about 6 miles from Williamsport.

Yesterday morning July 11th we left camp at light

and marched about 4 miles where advance cavalry found the rebel pickets and had a little skirmishing with them. We lay quiet during the PM in a wheat field and at night we fixed for a good night's rest & I was taking the best rest that I have had for a month when we were ordered out at 12 o'clock to march. We went about 2 miles and lay down on the stones in the road and slept until after sunrise, then we got up and made a cup of coffee & ate a few hard tack & were ready for our days work. We have marched about one mile from where we were when I commenced this letter & are now laying in an old pasture lot. I sent you a letter this morning & as I had a chance I thought I would scrible another. There was some fireing towards Hagerstown & Williamsport yesterday & there is some fireing to be heard today up the Potomac. It is said that the rebels are crossing the river as fast as possible and some of them have drowned & are floating down the river straped to their horses. I don't think there will be much of a fight this side of the Potomac but of course can't tell. The army is about tired out, although there are not many down sick. We are up most every morning long before light and very often march until 10 & 12 o'clock at night. The weather has generaly been very cool but it is very still & hot today. We are on reserve and if there is a battle we will not be the first engaged. I hope to see this campaign ended soon although now is the time to rush if ever. I think we will have rain before long.

There is a great deal of wheat going to waste in this state. There is no one to harvest it. The crop is splendid and well filled. Our Chaplain has just come from the hospital where our wounded are. He says they are all getting along finely.

Chas. Parker, Wm. Ramsey, Cal Jackson and myself are all the Morristown boys there are here now.

Well I have given you an account of most of the doings of the regt. since we crossed the Potomac. We are now ready to follow the rebels into Va. and I think we will be in Va. before next Saturday. I rather guess Lee is tired of invading Northern soil. I don't think he will be apt to try it again soon. Please excuse mistakes for I have written this in a hurry.

My love to all.　　　As ever your son

E. H. Bassett

Co. G. 1st Minnesota Vol.

A matter that Edward fails to relate to his family about the Charge of the First Minnesota at Gettysburg is that, although he escaped without wounds, his wardrobe took a beating. After the battle, he discovered that he had a bullet hole in his hat, a bullet hole in his blouse, a bullet had torn off his knapsack and a bullet had torn the heel off of his right shoe. In the scheme of the day's events, this might seem like an insignificant matter but, it most likely made quite an impression on Edward. Of further interest is the strange curiosity that occurred 35 years later when Edward's son, Elmer, was involved in a charge by the Thirteenth Minnesota Volunteers during the Spanish American War in the Battle of Manila in the Philippines. In a letter home he reported that he had received "*a bullet through my hat, a bullet through my blouse, a bullet had torn away my knapsack and a bullet had destroyed the heel on my right shoe.*"

During the dedication of the monument honoring the heroes of the First Minnesota Volunteer Infantry Regiment at Gettysburg on July 2, 1897, the following speech was given by Colonel Martin Maginnis, a former member of Company H in the regiment. The speech was sent by special telegram to *The Minneapolis Tribune* where it appeared in the next edition as part of an article reporting on the festivities at the commemoration. Following a brief speech by Colonel William Colvill, which brought rousing cheers from the crowd of veterans who were gathered there, Colonel Maginnis was introduced and gave *"the most effective speech of the occasion."*

His speech as reported:

INTO THE JAWS OF DEATH.
A Story of Heroism as told by:
Colonel Martin Maginnis
"Special telegram to the Tribune:"

GETTYSBURG, Pa., July 2.–Hon. Martin Maginnis, formerly a delegate to congress from the territory of Montana and a member of the First Minnesota regiment, tells the story of the invaluable service rendered by this handful of men more than a third of a century ago. The charge to almost certain death in the face of vastly superior forces was absolutely necessary at the time, and was one link in the chain by which the battle was won and the nation saved.

Colonel Maginnis said:"

"The Second Corps occupied the central part of the line. From it the regiment to which I belonged was detached and sent over to support some guns down there on the ridge, from which Sickles, line had been advanced. There in the rear of the fighting we were quite easy, we chuckled over getting a safe position. Obliged to keep low and not expose ourselves to the cannon balls, shells and bullets, which coming over the heads of the troops in front, we beheld a grand sight. All the way from Little Round Top to the Peach Orchard, and from there as far as we could see in the direction of the village, the battle joined and fiercely raged. We could see all the movements of the troops engaged except where hidden in the woods, and there the walls of smoke marked out the lines of battle.

We watched the movements of the combatants with the anxiety of spectators so deeply interested in the result. Little of this anxiety could be seen in the faces of our men long accustomed to the vicissitudes of battle. Emotions were concealed beneath masks of indifference, and the fighting of friend and foe was criticized with great impartiality and apparent indifference. As the sun declined the view became more obscured. The air was damp and the smoke hung heavily over the fight; sometimes in rolled cloudy masses, and again like well defined walls, conforming to the lines of battle, rising high in the air. Through this could be seen the charging battalions, the darkened forms wildly tossing to and fro above the struggling masses and looming gigantically in the maze between us and the setting sun. Again the sulphurous face would hide everything from view, but the air would be dark enough to show fire instead of smoke, and the flashes gleaming readily through the darkness revealed the new positions of the batteries and the changing lines of the musketry fire. At these times we would intently listen, endeavoring to tell from the yelling and cheering that came up from the chaotic turmoil to which side the advantage leaned. Then the breeze would roll up the smoky curtain and the most stoic could not repress a shout of joy to see that our men were crowding the fight and every heart felt the expressive words of our national anthem, "Our flag is still there."

Lee's entire line was in attack now everywhere. The advanced angle of Sickles' line crumbled before the enfilading fire. Pushing their attack, the enemy forced its crumbling brigades from one position to another. Fresh regiments and brigades could scarce get into position before they would be outflanked and forced backward. Caldwell's division went in behind Sickles' left and stiffened up the line in front of and to the right of Little Round Top; we witnessed the dreadful conflict of the Wheat Field. The troops directly in our front were gallantly endeavoring to sustain themselves and to check the momentum of the enemy. Every once in a while some reserve regiment came up and made the advancing foe halt and waver. The contest was sharp and heavy and success trembled in the balance.

Fresh lines of confederates came up, and pouring through the gap in the center outflanked the lines to the right and left and forced our boys back from their untenable positions. General Sickles was wounded about the time his center broke and his people came back carrying their colors and slightly wounded, and rallying in groups to empty again their guns at their pursuers. Humphrey's division slowly changed front backwards as its flanks were exposed by the break to his left, and meantime it kept up a spirited fight to the front.

It was evident that all effective, organized, concerted action on the part of the Third corps was at an end. The enemy's batteries advancing poured grape and canister into the retreating groups and their infantry, advancing with triumphant yells, threw rapid volleys of leaden hail into the broken ranks, which were reeling and staggering back, but still turned to make a fight like some enfeebled but spirited giant beneath the blows of a young and vigorous opponent.

So our battery and our battalion in our safe place to the rear had nothing in front of it.

The guns we were supporting opened on the advancing foe as soon as our front was clear of the retreating troops. The enemy answered this new defiance with new yells and soon a half dozen crimson southern flags were advancing towards us. Just then General Hancock rode up and cried: "Is this all the men we have here?" He looked to the right, from which Alpheus Williams was hurrying a division to patch up the broken line. The reinforcements were still five minutes distant. Not 200 yards behind the crest was the road crowded with wagons and behind that our hospitals. Once in there the confederates would be in the rear of the larger portion of our line. If Hancock could only stop that advancing mass, whose fighting force must be nearly expended, for fine minutes! A hope lit up his face and pointing to the smoke colored flags of the advancing foe he cried: "Colonel, advance and take those colors!"

It is easy enough to charge when the enemy is retreating and the battle going well, but it requires steady troops to even hold a position when columns are crumbling and lines are flying. It seemed a strange order to a small battalion to charge the advancing mass, which had just carried one of our best divisions off its feet. But the men looked as Nolen might have looked at the Russian cannon at Balaklava,[101] with some

---

[101] Referring to the famed, "Charge of the Light Brigade," during the Crimean War.

disposition to unquestioning obedience. "Forward!" and as one man the battalion steps down the slope. The batteries open on this new force and the more deadly Enfield rifle centered on the audacious advance. At every step a man falls, but no one wavers; every gap is closed up, and bringing down the bayonets, elbow touches elbow, and without noise or excitement or cheer, with silent, desperate determination, the line moves forward. Five color bearers are shot down and not a shot at the enemy. "CHARGE!" ran the order along the line and with a cheer we ran at them. They recoil before the impact of our motion. But their extended mass swept round our flanks. "FIRE!" and the guns are emptied in their very faces. Not much ammunition was wasted in that scorching volley. A swath of men sink on the ground and the mass which had lost order and alignment in the fight with and pursuit of Sickles' men, recoils. The rear lines, confused in the excitement, fire through their own ranks and kill their own men. Their batteries, to stop us, fire from their rear into the general mass on friend and foe. The officers try to restore order and reform the crowd.

And in another moment, it looks as if the mass would recover itself and sweep from the earth the obstacle which had checked its momentum. But the precious moments have been won. A battery from Round Top plays on the disorganized victors. Another, nearer, opens from our left. The fresh troops are running into line behind us on the crest; a movement from the flank sweeps the confederates back and before we have recovered from the shock we find ourselves amid groups of prisoners; and our bewildered senses take in the fact that our enemy has left our front, all but the wounded and dead; and over their prostrate bodies ring the hearty cheers of our reinforcing troops as they re-establish the line.

I got so much interested in this business that I did not know much about the rest of the field just them. I had no time to take observations. Indeed, I have been told something of this scene by those who were lookers on. For who that was an actor there can give the order or detail the changes of the eventful and exciting moments following that word "Forward!" When we heard neither ball nor shell nor saw our comrades fall; when blood rushed like fire through the distended veins, and every faculty was absorbed in the one desire to conquer or to die?. No! Not to die. Thoughts of the icy king of terrors chill the heart of the bravest when the battle is beginning or the lines being silently set, but every thought of that grim dweller on the threshold of eternity is lost in the glorious enthusiasm of action.

The lines were re-established, but of the 250 men who had moved down that slope only 47 gathered round the torn and shattered colors. But the rest were all there, under them. Two hundred and five within a few hundred square yards of the crimson sward, [102] killed, wounded and none missing–all present and accounted for. Over there you will find as many graves from that one regiment as some entire states have left on the field. Of my own company of 34, 17 were killed, and 13 wounded. Five of us buried them on the night of the 3rd, and made a sketch of their names and order in the shallow pit. But it must have been lost for I see that company is represented only by nameless stones. But they are known to that God who keeps the living and the dead, and their nameless graves and sorrowful but glorious story will tell their countrymen that not to the most vaunted fields of the old world need they go for instances of devoted courage and records of heroic daring."

---

[102] Sward: A grass covered area of ground. In this case, a blood stained grassy field.

CHAPTER 24
THE PURSUIT OF LEE

Perhaps General Meade can be forgiven for his laconic pursuit of Lee during the first couple of days following the battle at Gettysburg, his sloth-like movement thereafter, however, would challenge the forgiveness of nearly everyone. Meade was a man of impeccable integrity. He refused to become a part of the always-present cliques, intrigues and jealousies that permeated the army. During his earlier military service, with the topographical engineers along the eastern coast, he was known for his unequaled skill in building lighthouses. Although seriously wounded in the Battle of White Oak Swamp during the Peninsula Campaign, he quickly returned to duty at the Battle of Antietam before he had fully recovered. His brigade served outstandingly at First Fredericksburg on Dec. 13, 1862, and nearly broke through Lee's heavily fortified line. Just two months before Gettysburg, he was greatly angered by General Hookers desire to retreat from Chancellorsville. Meade was among the few who had voted to stay and fight. General George McClellan spoke of Meade as *"an excellent officer, cool, brave and intelligent."*

Meade failed to realize that his army, now invigorated by their victory, had the energy and perseverance to endure the demands of a spirited pursuit. The product of an affluent family and a well-educated, regular army veteran, he doubted the dependability and endurance of his volunteer force. Additional fresh troops were on their way and, since his main supply depots were near, he could resupply while on the march and, the railways could deliver mountains of material to him. Meade, however, seemed to manifest the traits of his former commander and friend George McClellan, when, he chose to err on the side of caution rather than throw caution to the wind and move with swiftness and determination.

General Lee was in a very precarious situation. He was desperately short of supplies; he had sustained losses that he could not replace and had no resources of any kind available until he got back into Virginia. Lee and Longstreet both admitted they were in great jeopardy, especially if their long, poorly-guarded wagon trains containing all the supplies they possessed were cut off from them. Without question, catching Lee and cutting his column by flanking movements would have required great effort, but the prize was worthy of the attempt. It is likely, that Lee's Army of Northern Virginia could have been captured or destroyed as a fighting force and, the war brought to a much earlier conclusion. But alas, it was not to be.

Meade's cautious pursuit of Lee was also likely influenced by his orders to protect Washington. To do so, he needed to keep his army between the Capitol and the enemy while pursuing him along a parallel route. His command structure was badly decimated by the loss of so many key officers. The 1st and 3rd Corps had incurred such losses that they would later be transferred into Hancock's 2nd Corps. Meade was not afraid to attack Lee, but he always sought the counsel of his corps commanders. On the night of July 4th, he called a council of war and questioned his officers asking their preferences on the course of action to be taken. Should they attack Lee immediately or take a defensive posture? Most answered they were against an offensive until Lee's intentions were known. Meade anticipated that Lee would retreat from Gettysburg to the Potomac River at Williamsport, Maryland; and there cross into Virginia. He asked if he should pursue Lee directly on his line of retreat or follow on a parallel course east of the Blue Ridge mountains. His generals advised the latter course and that was the course he followed, although it is uncertain if their response influenced his decision. Another event of great significance occurred on July 4th. A squadron of the 14th Pennsylvania Cavalry, led by Major Shadrack Foley, burned the pontoon bridge built by the Confederates when they crossed the Potomac on their way to Gettysburg and, captured part of their guard detail. When the retreating rebel column reached Falling Water, a short way downstream from Williamsport, they had no way to cross. The river was very swollen by the recent rains and too deep to ford. The only other conveyance was a small ferry boat—hardly adequate to transport an entire army across.

Meade waited to be sure that the Confederates were actually retreating from Gettysburg and not attempting to trick him into a premature movement where he could be easily attacked. Lee moved immediately to get his wounded gathered and loaded into wagons. He ordered Brigadier General John D. Imboden to take the 17-mile-long wagon train bearing the wounded and supply wagons to Williamsport. The wagons left Gettysburg in the torrential rain that turned the roads into mud holes and washed the soft top dirt away exposing the rocks everywhere. For the wounded lying in the freight wagons with no springs and not even straw bedding on the floor, the ensuing ordeal was excruciating. The jarring, pounding ride on wood-plank wagon bottoms would have been difficult for healthy men to endure. For these men with torn, missing and broken limbs; still-hemorrhaging from wounds and enduring great pain, it was unbearable. Adding to their discomfort, most of them had not eaten for more than 36 hours and had very little water to drink. Plaintive cries asking to be put off the wagons and left to die, or to be shot to stop the pain and calls to God for mercy could be heard all along the train. Dying men begged for someone to take their last words to their loved ones. Yet the wagons rolled on; there could be no stopping for any reason until they reached Williamsport.

The First Minnesota, which marched out on the afternoon of July 5th, was among the first units of the army to leave Gettysburg. They traveled only about four miles and bivouacked at 'Two Taverns.' On July 7th, the regiment set out for Taneytown, Maryland, marching 15 miles. The men found the march quite fatiguing.

James Wright wrote:

"Though the march had not been long, we were both tired and hungry. Practically, we had been living on coffee, crackers, and salt pork for nearly a month, frequently enduring the extremes of exercise and exposure and other hardships incidental to active campaigning, and were in no condition for hard marching."

Leaving camp at 5 AM the next morning, they marched 20 miles[103] in heavy rain and deep mud and camped near Frederick. On July 9th, they marched through the South Mountains to the small towns of Rohrersville and Keedysville near Antietam. The next day, they continued on to the tiny hamlet of Tighlmanton, located very near Williamsport where Lee's army had been busy building breastworks and digging lines of rifle pits. They had constructed a strong defensive position, well covered with artillery. Lee had not intended to stop here but when it was discovered the pontoon bridge was destroyed, he had to wait while a new one was built.

On the 12th, more of the Union army arrived and Meade made plans to launch an assault on the Confederate position. The next day was spent getting everything in order for the attack and, on the morning of the July 14th, skirmishers were sent out and reported back that the rebels were gone. Lee had made his escape and cut the pontoon bridge loose behind him.

The 2nd Corps then marched through Sharpsburg and the Antietam battlefield, crossing the Antietam Creek, on what has come to be known as "Burnsides Bridge", and bivouacked at Sandy Hook near Harper's Ferry.

---

[103] Holcombe, in the "History of the First Regiment, Minnesota Volunteer Infantry" page 281, counts the distance as 24 miles.

Burnside Bridge at Antietam–Period Photo

The march continued the next day going 5 miles and passing through Sandy Hook and into Pleasant Valley. This was old familiar ground to the men, and here, they enjoyed two-days of rest and a chance to bathe for the first time in weeks. Supply wagons arrived and some of the men were able to draw new clothing to replace their battle worn rags. New high top shoes were issued and with fresh supplies and clothing they began to feel alive again.

According to James Wright:

"I was called before it was fairly light and directed to make out requisitions for such shoes and clothing as was urgently needed – and three days' extra rations. We were obliged to wait some time, and then got three days' field rations, a partial supply of shoes, but no clothing."

Lee was also getting resupplied as his men rested in the Shenandoah Valley, their land of milk and honey. Food stores were replenished and ammunition trains brought much-needed supplies and equipment, as well as a number of new conscripts to swell his depleted ranks.

On July 18th, the Minnesota Regiment crossed the Potomac on a pontoon bridge at Harper's Ferry and immediately crossed the Shenandoah on a new wire (cable) bridge. They then continued marching eight miles up the Loudon Valley. The next day, they marched eight more miles stopping near Wood Grove for the night. At daybreak they continued on twelve more miles to Snickers' Gap, where they again rested for two days. This place was well remembered by the men for its bountiful supply of blackberries, which were enjoyed immensely, sprinkled with their government-issued brown sugar. Wednesday morning July 22nd, found them on the road again, marching toward Ashby's Gap, which they reached after sundown. On Thursday, the pace was quickened in anticipation of meeting the enemy after moving through Manassas Gap to near Front Royal. Friday, July 24th, the 2nd Corps followed in support of two other corps that advanced up the Shenandoah Valley to Front Royal only to find the rebels had already left; once again, Lee had made a safe retreat. During the next few days, the First Regiment marched five miles back from the gap to Markham Station, then 20 miles to White Plains and another 20 miles to Warrenton. They remained there in camp until July 30th. On the Thirty-First, the 2nd Corps left its camp on Elk Run near Warrenton and marched 18 miles south to Morrisville, a point about 20 miles northeast of Fredericksburg. Here they remained camped in a wooded area until August 15th.

Camped Near Warrenton Junction, Va.
Monday July 27th ,1863

Dear Father & Mother,

I still keep my health altho we have been making some hard marches. We marched 23 miles yesterday & some say more. We crossed the Potomac & Shenandoah at Harpers Ferry on the 18th and followed up on the southwest side of the Blue Ridge to Mannassas Gap where we found the rebels but they were driven through the pass at Front Royal on the 24th. We marched down this way & I expect we will soon be at Falmouth or some other point on the Rappahannock. Our boys are standing the march well considering. The weather has been cool most of the time but there has been no chance to rest.

We find all the blackberrys that we want.(I have had two quarts today).

I think this campaign will end before the middle of August. There has been men sent on for the conscripts[104] from most of the old Regiments. We have about 100 men in our Reg't. for duty now.

We have not had any mail since we crossed the Potomac last. The mail goes out this P.M. at 4 o'clock for the first time since we crossed the river on the 18th. We have not had a paper and know nothing about the world out of our line of march. I hope we will hear something being done when we get out of this wilderness.

I am looking forward to next summer when if I am alive & well I hope to enjoy myself in Minnesota.

There can not be any large rebel force very near us but the country is full of Guerrillas. They have captured a few stragglers from our column, but they usually get punished before they get away.

I was on Picket last night & did not get into camp until late this morning.

Please accept this with my love to you all,

Edward

Camped on the road between Warrenton Junction and Kelley's Ford, Va. August 1st, 1863

---

[104] Conscripts were men brought into the service by the 'Draft'.

Dear Father & Mother,

I believe we will remain here long enough for me to write you a letter. Since we left Falmouth Station I have only scribbled a few lines as we stopped to rest but as we have got almost back to our old Home at Falmouth I begin to think perhaps the army will stop to rest and reorganize. The general opinion now is that we are going to act on the defensive for a time but it is uncertain as yet which river will form our line. I hope our forces will hold Fredericksburg so as to have one less strong position in the hands of Lee.

The weather is very hot but not quite as bad as it was last summer at Harrisons Bar (sand bar) on James River. We lay in camp near the Junction from Sat. Eve until Thursday PM at 4 o'clock we packed up and marched until about midnight making about 8 miles. The Brigade was detailed for train guard and we were delayed several hours on that account. Yesterday we started about 11AM and marched about 8 miles and stopped in a grove of Oaks and Pines where we are now camped. We have finally reached a point where the mails can reach us and for the last three or four days we have got the daily papers. Yesterday I rec'd. the Phrenological Journal for August (The July No. got lost) I will send you the August one as soon as I read it. I see that Genl Howard is going to take command of the 2nd Corps. That will suit us very well for we consider him as one of our best Generals. I should be glad if we could have a few weeks rest but if Meade says go I suppose we will have to go as long as there is life enough to move. If part of Lee's Army has gone to Charlestown as reported I think the rebel army will be drawn back near Richmond and as our army will be filled up by the draft there may be some lively times next fall but not much before in this department. We rec'd the Central Republican of the 22nd. Last night I read it through and think that Brown is about right about the Indian expedition and the conduct of the Indian War.

The boys are mostly well although rather tired from the continual marching since we have been on this campaign.

Eve. of 1st Aug. I was forced to defer finishing my letter for we had to move our camp. We have a fine location now and the officers say we may stop here two weeks or more but they don't know anything certain. There has been fighting somewhere today for we have heard heavy cannonading most all day. I expect it is the cavalry banging away at Lee's rear guard. The mail has just come in. You ask me to tell you how the boys are that are wounded. If I knew I would make out a list of all the wounded of the regiment and send it to you but you will be apt to see a more correct account in some of the Papers than I can give you for I have not seen but a few of the boys since they were wounded. One of our boys that was shot in the hand has recovered and came back to us the other day from Chestnut Hill Hospital Philadelphia where several of our boys are he says they were all doing well when he left except Geo. Hopkins. He had chills and fever. His wound is not dangerous. William Coen is in a hospital in Rhode Island. He was doing well when he wrote. He wrote Sam Lilly was in the 6th Corps Hospital near Gettysburg when we heard from him. He was hit near the back bone, the ball passing through and coming out on his right side it was a severe wound but the worst was over. I have not heard from John Goodrich yet. Al Johnson has not recovered from his wound rec'd at Fredericksburg. After laying in the Lincoln Hospital Washington for 90 odd days he has been granted a furlough. He will have nice times among his friends in Ohio and Indiana.

I fear that you worry yourselves about me more than you need to for I always come out all right. So far I have not got even a scratch.

Sunday Morning August 2nd. It is going to be a very hot day but we are camped in a fine grove of Oaks, Pines, and Cedars, and it will be quite comfortable. J. J. McCallum has been in camp for a few days but he starts for Washington this morning where his family is living. I believe he has got his discharge. Co. G is commanded now by Lieut M. Shepard. He is a fine man. He used to belong to Co. B. The boys all like him. He treats a private soldier with respect and has not forgotten that he is only a man although he wears an officers Uniform. I am glad to hear that your crops are doing so well. What do you think of the Sugar Cane. Will it ripen so as to make good molasses. I have not seen a stalk of cane in all our travels through Va. Md. and Penn. There has been more attentions paid to raising wheat than anything else. I saw one field of Buckwheat in Md. but no Barley. The corn was generally very poor and Potatoes the same. I did not see any nice gardens anywhere. I think you must have new vegetables fully as early there in Minnesota as they did here this spring. If the boys of this Regt were in Minnesota now I bet the Indians would have to keep scarce. I have heard nearly every one say that they would hunt them out and kill every one they came across and now since there is a bounty offered I will bet there would be none allowed to escape. I should think they are getting rather bold from the way they steal horses and all, through the country. I hope they will not be allowed to live in peace away from their own land and reservations. The papers report that Little Crow has been routed and has retreated across the Missouri river. I hope they will be kept there.

There is a great deal of good grass in Va. this year that has not been cut. Some of the meadows were very nice but there would be no use in the farmers cutting their grass for they would be liable to have it stolen by either army when they make their raids through the country. Virginia has been pretty well run over by both armies. There has a great many of the citizens left the state some going south and some north but there are a few that chose to stay and run the risk. Most all the fences have been destroyed where the army has been and many of the houses have been burned and destroyed in other ways. I would like to have been in Morristown when they were having their rejoicings over the Union Victories. I would like to see the old Barn illuminated with tallow candles. I think it must have shone like the New Jerusalem that Russ Morris used to tell about unless they have battoned some of the cracks in the walls. Please write as often as you find it convenient. Tell me all about the crops and the farm what the prospects for making farming pay in Minnesota. Is there much of a rush to get onto the Winnebago reservation. Are the lands going to be sold very cheap. My love to you all,

As ever your son, Edward H. Bassett

Co. G 1st Minn Regt

Camp of the 1st Minnesota Vols. In Virginia
August 2nd, 1863

Dear Sister Anna:

I received your kind letter of the 23rd last night with two from Mother, one dated July 19th and one 23rd. You think right when you think I would like to get a letter from home. I am glad to hear that you have such nice weather and that your flowers are doing so fine and I assure you I would be glad to be there with you to enjoy the nice weather and flowers and above all the company of my Dear friends. I suppose the trees that were growing all arround the house when I left make quite a nice shade by this time. I am glad you have got a little bird and I will try and get you a mate for him next summer if I get back there. You also speak of the Sunday School and the weekday school which I suppose you enjoy very much. I am glad to hear that Elford is learning so fast and how I would like to see

517

him and I guess I will next summer. You speak of having nice Beans & Peas and new Potatoes there. I have not seen any this summer yet but I expect there are a few in the country but they are hard to find. We have had plenty of Blackberries and they were very nice.

My love to you all.

Brother Edward

Encamped near Morrisville, Va.
Wednesday August 5th, 1863

Dear Mother,

I wrote a letter a few days ago but we have since moved our camp about two miles. We are now camped in an old stuble field that has grown up for the last two years to grass & weeds. The 2nd Corps is all camped near here and the prevailing opinion is that we will remain here for some time. I expect that we will remain here until those regts. that are to be filled up with conscripts have been drilled and reorganized which will take until the middle of September. Our Depot for supplies will be Bealton Station which is about five miles distant on the Orange and Allexandria Railroad. We are about 68 miles from Richmond, 16 miles from Fredericksburg, 45 miles from Alexandria, 53 from Washington and about 8 miles from Rappahannoc Station where the Railroad crosses the North Fork of the Rappahannoc River. I think it must be three or four miles to the river in a direct line. We have a fine place for a camp there is a fine brook close by and there is plenty of timber handy so we can get plenty of timber to fix up our tents & shades. I have got my tent fixed up off the ground so that it will be cool and comfortable.

Co. G numbers 17 men in all now in the field. There was one came from the hospital today. We heard that Jerome Farnsworth of our Co. died in the Garvis Hospital in Baltimore lately, he was from Elysian. I saw him when he was on the field that night that we charged & helped him part way off the field. He was shot through both thighs. I thought that he would recover but there has a great many died from very slight wounds. 5 have died besides the Captain from that fight out of our Company and there are several wounded so that they will never be fit for service again. Lieutenant Delaney [105] is recovering slowly he is going north in a few days on a furlough to New York. I see by the papers that the soldiers in General Grant's army are getting furloughs to go home and visit their friends.

The weather has been very hot for a few days. I think it has been quite as hot as it was last Summer. Thursday Morning Aug 6th 63

We received our pay yesterday, two months wages. I think I shall send some home when it is a little safer between here & Washington. The rebel cavalry show themselves at times along the road now but I think they will be drove away in a few days. We have a fine view of the Bull Run Mountains which extend along the west side of the Rappahannoc River. One year ago today we lay on Malvern Hill. We were then out with General Hooker on a reconnaissance towards Richmond.

I am surprised to hear that crops are so promising in Minnesota this summer. I have heard all along that there was not going to be any good crops there this season. You speak of Oats & wheat being ripe there about the 26th of July & corn being out in silk. I assure you the corn & oats are far ahead of any that I have

---

[105] This name is not listed in the muster rolls for any company of the regiment in "Minnesota in the Civil and Indian Wars" and he was perhaps a replacement officer or transferred from another unit.

seen here. I have not seen any corn out in the silk yet and I know of plenty of corn that was not knee high at that time here.

P.M. 6th

I have not heard a word from Jonathan Goodrich yet. I don't know why he don't write.

We are going to draw three days rations of soft bread now every week it is baked in Alexandria or Washington and sent up on the cars. I went out this A.M. & picked a lot of grapes and Elder berries and stewed them for dinner. The grapes are about four times as large as the Minnesota Wild grape.[106] We draw rations now every day keeping three days on hand all the time. We have plenty of music most all the time there are four brass bands in the Division & they all camp near by, some of them are playing most of the time.

My love to Father, Mother, Brother and Sisters

Edward

Camp of the first Minnesota Vols
Near Morrisville, Virginia.
August 9th, 1863.

Dear Father,

I suppose you are very busy now harvesting your grain and I wish I could be there to help you. The weather has been very hot here lately but health is generally good. The conscripts have commenced to arrive but I have not seen any of them yet. Some of the boys that have, say that they are a gay looking set of

---

[106] This seems to be typical of Edwards creative nature. His earlier comment about raising his tent off the ground and other documented events make it clear that he was inclined to make the best of any situation and invent as needed for his comfort.

fellows with their pockets full of Green backs. Our pickets capture a rebel or two every few days. They are mostly straglers from the rebel army and men that have been home on furloughs. Their homes being within our lines. The road between here and Alexandria is infested by Guerrillas and they have captured quite a number of sutlers. They rob the men and take everything that they think they can get away with.

We draw rations for 17 men in Co. G now. We heard of the death of one of the boys that was wounded at Gettysburg last night. He died in Fort Schuyler, N.Y. his name is Anthony W. Ernst, he enlisted in Owatonna he is the third one that has died in the Hospitals from wounds rec'd at Gettysburg from our Co. It seems rather lonely in our camp there are so many of the boys gone. I believe I feel just as tired at night after laying arround in camp all day as I would if I had done a moderate days work in the harvest field.

Our Sutler came up last night and the boys have had a treat. He brought up two four horse wagon loads at sundown last night and has sold out clean now (exactly 24 hours) for it is just sundown now. I feel confident that this army will now move before September. I will send you ten dollars in this letter. We have been paid up to July 1st now.

As ever your son,

Edward H. Bassett.

Alexandria, Va.
Aug 16th 1863

Dear Father and Mother,

You will see that we have got back to Alexandria. We got orders yesterday morning about 8 o'clock to report immediately at this place. The order included the 1st Minnesota and 7 Mich. out of the 2nd Div. and the 8th Ohio from the 3rd Div. We were to receive transportation by rail to this place where we are to wait for further orders. We got onto the cars last night at sundown and arrived here at 12 o clock. It is reported that we are going to New York but we cannot tell yet. I would not be much surprised if we were to go to some of the Northern cities to secure peace and quiet during the completion of the draft. One thing is sure we are relieved from duty in the field for a time and it is doubtful about our ever being sent into the field with the Army of the Potomac again. The conscripts have begun to come in and the old regts are getting their ranks filled quite fast.

I see by this mornings paper that Genl Sibley has had a fight with Little Crow and his warriors and whipped him and Genl Sully is after the Indians with his command of cavalry and following them up. Well I have written about all I can today it is so hot. I will write again as soon as we find out where we are going. Your affectionate son,

Edward H. Bassett

The boys are all well. The regts that came with us are very small having lost very heavy in all the battles. I think that we will be put to some duty around Washington.

Our Col. is away north and I don't expect we will see him again soon. His health is poor this is the second time he has gone north to recruit himself. I hope the war will play out soon.

Give my respects to all the folks,

As ever your Son in

Co. G" 1st Minnesota Volunteers
of the U. S. Army

Edward H. Bassett

The regular monthly muster of July 31, 1863, reported the Regiment's strength at 14 officers and 130 men "present and equipped for duty." Company L, the company of sharpshooters attached to the regiment, numbered 2 officers and 22 men. The total strength at this point then numbered 168.

Some men wounded at Gettysburg later rejoined the regiment, still led by Captain Coates.

CHAPTER 25
THE NEW YORK ADVENTURE

The last day of July found the regiment about four miles north of Kelly's Ford, on the Rappahannock River. Their new camp was located in a pleasant area with plenty of trees and a fresh, cool stream. It was a perfect place for a well- earned rest after all the fighting and marching.

With the losses suffered by both armies during the last several months, they were in desperate need of new volunteers. Unfortunately very few were forthcoming. The situation in the Union Army of the Potomac was made worse as regiments that enlisted for nine months or two years left when their enlistments expired. With only 556,000 officers and men present for duty and more than 100,000 deserted or absent-without-leave at the end of 1862, something had to be done. The Confederates instituted a Conscription Act in the early spring of 1862. This 'Draft Law' allowed them to refill their depleted ranks on a regular basis. The Union had depended entirely on volunteers but, by early spring of 1863, this proved insufficient. Aware of all the defeats and casualties, men grew reluctant to volunteer. President Lincoln signed the 'Draft Act' into law on March 3, 1863. This law would be exercised as soon as offices could be established and personnel trained. In early summer, the system was finally in operation.

In most states, the people accepted the necessity of the draft. In New York and Boston, however, there was great resistance. The big eastern cities had large populations of immigrants that had no feeling of patriotic fervor, lived in lower-class slum neighborhoods and, generally held menial labor jobs. A large percentage of these immigrants were Irishmen who fled Ireland to seek a better life in America but found their lot to be a very hard one. Many were also members of Fire Companies, which were little more than organized gangs. They feared an influx of large numbers of freed slaves who would work for lower wages and take their jobs. Out of this fear grew a hatred for the blacks. They vowed to fight rather than succumb to the draft and be sent off to fight and die in any 'Nigger War'. On Saturday, July 11th, the first drawing of names in New York was held. The wheel was spun and cards bearing the names of hundreds of eligible men were pulled by a blindfolded clerk. The event went off smoothly and without incident. On Sunday, the names appeared in the local newspapers and the reality of the matter struck close to home. Those men not selected now realized they could be next. By Monday, their resentment had been whipped into wild rage and lawless gangs spilled into the streets in lower Manhattan and began moving uptown. Reaching the draft office on the corner of Third Avenue and 46th Street, they forced their way in, broke out windows, smashed furniture and set the building ablaze. The mob turned their anger on Superintendant Kennedy and beat him almost to death. Only the presence of a small group of militia, hastily reinforced by a detachment of veterans from the invalid corps, prevented the crazed mob from taking the 2nd Avenue Armory where cannons were placed to fire down the streets. Buildings and homes were set ablaze everywhere and any blacks found on the streets were beaten and some were killed. Any business or building owned by, or catering to, the black population was a target for destruction. That night, the Colored Orphan Asylum was looted and burned while the mob took everything they could carry away. Were it not for the actions of a brave Irishman, the 237 children housed there would likely have been murdered. He took the children out of harm's way to the police precinct station where they were taken to a boat anchored in the middle of the East River and safety.

Orphan Asylum in flames
Leslie's Illustrated Weekly

With the police and small contingent of militia and soldiers so greatly outnumbered and powerless to control the mob, New York Mayor Opdyke telegraphed Secretary of War Stanton requesting troops be sent immediately. Realizing that if the draft could not be enforced in New York, it would soon be unenforceable anywhere, Stanton moved with unusual swiftness. Troops began arriving on July 15th after three days of rioting. Six Thousand veteran soldiers spread out into the streets with bayonets fixed and rifles loaded and, without hesitation, opened fire on any group that refused orders to disperse. When some small cadres of diehards chose to make a stand, cannons were wheeled into position in the street and the hail of grapeshot did much to dampen their resolve. By Thursday evening, the streets were quiet once again. The rioting accomplished nothing and left nearly 150 people dead[107] and two-and-one-half-million dollars worth of property destroyed. Ashbury estimates the casualties at 2,000 killed and 8,000 wounded.[108] It seems likely the latter figures are more realistic considering the scale of the unrest and that troops and cannons were employed in quelling the riots.

As Edward relates in the following letters, the orders sending the First Minnesota and several of its sister regiments to New York were somewhat of a surprise.

On August 15th, the morning started as usual, with duties assigned and details being sent out. Shortly thereafter, orders came from headquarters to get the companies ready to march. The camp was abuzz with speculation as to where they were going, some said New York while others believed they were going to help with the attack on Fort Sumter in Charleston. Word spread

Sketch of Bealeton Station by Edwin Forbes, Harper's

that they would be joined by the 7th Michigan and 8th Ohio regiments. Friends from all over camp came to ask questions and express their regrets at loosing their brothers, with whom they had shared so much hardship and the fortunes of war. When marching orders came in early afternoon, the regiment was ready with their tents, trappings and equipage all packed. The entire division lined their way as they marched out of camp. Ringing cheers and the 7th Pennsylvania Regiment band *"played them out of camp"* to the strains of "Bully for

---

[107] McPherson, James M Ordeal by Fire: The Civil War and Reconstruction P. 399

[108] Asbury, Herbert (1928). *The Gangs of New York.* Alfred A. Knopf., p 169

You." Tears filled the eyes of many strong men at their parting. The march was met with mixed emotions, sadness at leaving the men they had shared both life and death with for two years and a spirit of adventure at the prospects of some new duty.

Dusk found them at Bealeton Station on the Orange and Alexandria Railroad where they rested while waiting for their train. It was growing dark when the train, puffing, screeching and clanking, backed onto a siding and the men were ordered to "Pile on." The conveyance provided for the 60-mile trip was by no means luxurious. The train consisted of ordinary flat cars with rough plank floors and no provisions of any kind for passengers. The men sat in rows on their knapsacks and those around the sides sat with their feet dangling over the edges. About all that could be said for the ride was that it was better than walking. As the train rumbled and jolted along through the cool night air, the clatter of the wheels told the tale of the many times the tracks had been torn up by raiders and hastily repaired with little attention paid to perfection. The trip was far from restful; the choking clouds of smoke and cinders from the engine swirled back and engulfed the men. When a little after midnight, they pulled into the outskirts of Alexandria, they were covered with soot and ash. Exhausted from the march and six hours of bumping and swaying, the men hastily disembarked and were soon asleep on the ground. The First and accompanying regiments would lay-over here awaiting transport ships until August 20th, the day the drafts resumed in New York.

By the time they arrived in New York Harbor on August 23rd, other troops had already put down the insurrection and order was restored. Instead of being faced with the prospects of having to shoot fellow citizens, the soldiers enjoyed a well-earned and much welcomed respite from the ardors of marching and fighting. Captain Coates, then the Regimental Commander, was very liberal with granting passes so the men could go out of camp and see the city. For Edward, it was a chance to visit his Uncle Eber Lines, his mother's brother, whom he likely had not seen since he was a very young boy. True to his inquisitive nature, Edward took every opportunity to explore the city and visit points of interest. The local citizenry welcomed the men and showed their appreciation for their service with many sumptuous banquets.

Governor's Island, New York Harbor
August 24th, 1863.

Dear Father and Mother,

You will be surprised to hear that the 1st has finaly left the front and is now quartered on Governor's Island, New York Harbor. We left Alexandria on the 21st inst. on board the steamship Atlantic. There has been a new brigade formed consisting of the 8th Ohio, 4th Ohio, 14th Ind. 7th Mich. & 1st Minnesota. They

Steamship Atlantic

number about 1500 men and are commanded by Colonel Carroll of the 8th Ohio. We arrived here yesterday about noon. We had a very pleasant time on the way except being crowded. The sea was very smooth. There is several thousand troops here from the army of the Potomac. I hear that we are to garrison the forts and do duty in the City. We started for N.Y. City last evening but were ordered back as soon as we got onto the ferry. Everything is quiet in N.Y. now I believe but I suppose it is owing to the military force at hand. The Irish are very mad about the draft and there would be trouble right away if the soldiers were taken away.

The boys are very well. We have not got settled yet but I expect we will get tents and fix camp today. We may go to N.Y. or Brooklyn after a while. The Harbor defenses have not been garrisoned for some time and there has been considerable complaint about it. I expect the Government is going to put the oldest regts. that have been used up in the last two year's campaign in the forts and fill up the army with the conscripts.

It was rumored yesterday through rebel sources that Charleston has been taken by General Gilmore. There is large quantities of shot & shell laying on the dock here for shipment to Morris Island. This is a beautiful place to live. The Island is strongly fortified. It covers about 80 acres.

Well I wish I knew what the Army of the Potomac is about this morning. I expect they are drilling their conscripts and watching Lee in Va. Our Regt. numbers about 190 men now. All the men on detached service have been returned to the regt. Well I have written about all I know now so I will close hoping this will find you all alive & well. Direct your letters to Co. "G" 1st Minnesota Vols. Carroll's Brigade, Governor's Island, N.Y. I will write again soon after we get more settled. I hope we will stay here all winter.

Good By this time,

Edward.

Sketches of the New York Draft Riots
from Leslie's Illustrated Weekly

First Regiment of Minnesota Volunteer Infantry
Camped on Governor's Island New York Harbor.
August 26th A. D. 1863.

Dear Father and Mother,

I suppose you would like to know what we are doing here and very likely you will be as much surprised to hear that we have been sent here after two years of active duty in Virginia as I was when we got the order to come here. It seems that it had become necesary to send a military force to this place in consequence of the attempt of the Copperheads to resist the draft and there was a selection of old troops from the army of the Potomac sent & in place of sending New York State troops and Pennsylvania troops they sent Ohio, Ind., Mich., Vermont, Wisconsin & Minnesota troops thinking I suppose that they would have less sympathy with the mob. I heard yesterday that there was not a night that the mob-ites did not stick up notices & threats against the Police and military forces. I think it is a sign that they are a rather cowardly set and they will not be apt to do much as long as there are any soldiers arround. The Herald of today says that the draft went on yesterday without any trouble and I don't think there is any disturbance there today. We left Alexandria Va. on the 21st on board the Steamship Atlantic and arrived off Sandy hook before light on the 23rd but we did not cross the bar until light and landed in the PM. It is a very pleasant place although the Island is small. It is an old military post and I should think there was about 100 guns in all mounted but they are most all old fashioned 42 Pdrs. Some of them are being removed and larger & better guns mounted in their places. As we have not been here but a short time we have not got fixed up any yet. There is a twelve hour pass allowed to two men in each Company every day to go to the City if they wish. The Steam Ship Great Eastern is anchored off the bar. If she comes into the harbor I shall try to get a sight of the Monster.

Loading the Steamship Atlantic, Sketch from Harper's Weekly

Today's paper says that Genl. Gilmore has driven the rebels out of Fort Sumpter and has shelled the city of Charleston. (I hope he will burn the city to the ground). It seems rather hard after all our fighting for the last two years to have to turn our attention to the Great Empire state of the North to put down a rebelion there but I hope there will be no more trouble here and you may be assured that if we ever get to fighting a mob in New York City that some one has got to die. I don't think we will be apt to fire many blank cartridges at them. I expect there is somewhere near 30,000 troops in and arround the City now. I heard today that as soon as the draft is over & the conscripts sent away we will resume our old place in the army of the Potomac. We will not be apt to leave here before October or November I don't think, and we may posibly stay here all winter. We have been formed in a Brigade with the Michigan troops now so we will be in General Hugers Brigade instead of Colonel Carroll's as I wrote to you before. The weather is very comfortable. The nights are cool and there is a constant breeze from the sea. We go down and have a swim most every night and today when the tide went out some of the boys went out and dug a mess of clams but they are poor things. It would take about 1000 to make a meal for a hungry Minnesotan if he liked them. Fruit is plenty but very high and mostly of the poorest quality. Eggs sell at 30 cts. per doz, Butter 40 cts. per lb. and so on but I expect if a fellow could run arround and knew where to go things could be got much cheaper. I saw one of the Monitor boats laying near Staten Island when we came in. It has one turret and mounts two guns, I wish we could stay here until our time is out but I suppose we will have another chance to see Va. before we give up soldiering.

It is time for roll call and I will have to close so Good Night.

Your son,

Edward Bassett

Governor's Island, New York Harbor
August 26th, 1863

Dear Sisters Ella & Anna,

I thought I would try to answer your very interesting and welcome letters. We have had some good times since we left the old Army of the Potomac. We lay at Alexandria several days waiting for the vessel that was to take us to New York. While we were there the boys run all through the city and had a good time. I went to the Theatre twice while we were there and tried to enjoy myself all the time that we were waiting for the boat. It finally came & we went on board about 4 o'clock PM on the 20th & the next morning at daylight we started down the Potomac River.

Steamship Baltic – Period Drawing - Unattributed

About noon we passed a large ocean steamer called the Baltic that had grounded near the mouth of the Potomac. We soon passed out into the Chesapeake Bay then we had room enough to sail in. We passed out of the bay during the night and at light the next day we were out on the Atlantic Ocean out of the sight of land. Some of the men were very seasick although the ship was very steady, I went up on the upper deck and set there most all day watching the fish and thinking of you and home. I think some of going over to the City tomorrow on a pass but I don't expect I will enjoy it much for everything will be perfectly strange to me. There is about 100 little boys on this Island that have been picked up in New York and they are being clothed and fed and learned to drum and fife for the Army. They are taken good care of and if they like it they can enlist and get pay. They are from 10 to 15 years old. It makes me think of Elford every time I see them for some of them are about the size he was when I left but I expect that he has grown so much that I would scarcely know him.

As ever your brother *Edward*

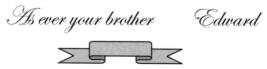

Camped on Fort Green Brooklyn
Aug 30th, 1863

Dear Mother,

Knowing that you are always anxious to hear from me I will improve a few moments in writing this evening. Uncle Eber was down to our camp this morning to see me, he heard that the regiment was somewhere around & he hunted us up. He wanted me to get a pass and go up home with him but I could not get one he stayed and talked until late this PM. He is working in a rubber factory in Harlem and wants me to get a pass and go up there this week if possible. I promised him that I would and if I can get a pass from camp for 24 hours I intend to do so & go up there.

We came over here from Governors Island on Friday last and are camped on the Green. It is a fine place to camp and I would not mind soldering here for the next 8 months. The draft commences here tomorrow and the Irish promise us some fun.[109]

Uncle says that there was some 20 men drafted in the factory but (his number was blank) he was missed this time. The camp has been full of visitors all day there is a great many of the boys meeting their friends here and they are having a good time.

I don't think we will have any trouble here the draft will commence tomorrow but there will be no call for the Military. I was over in New York last Thursday from 9 AM to 8 PM but I could not see much in so short a time. I went into several of the Picture galleries on Broadway, was at Fowler and Wells No. 308 Broadway and spent about two hours in at Barnum's Museum when my pass was out and I had to go back to camp. I intend to see more of the city if I can. I will be on guard tomorrow & next day. If I can I intend to go over & make Uncle a call. I intend to improve every

---

[109] The draft lasted 10 days and following the riots of the first draft there was no further disturbance.

opportunity I have while I am in the army to see and learn all I can and although I am green [110] I don't mean to give up on that account. The people seem to take a great interest in the welfare of the soldier and there are thousands of visitors in camp all the time from sunrise till dark. They bring lots of fruit and all sorts of delicacies to their friends and I assure you we are having good times now. Well I must close for it is getting late so good night to all.

Your son

Edward Bassett

Camped on Fort Green, Brooklyn
September 5, 1863.

Dear Father and Mother,

We are enjoying ourselves as well as we could wish. The citizens of the City of Brooklyn have tried in every way to make us comfortable and happy. Last night they had a supper for the whole command and I don't think I ever saw a richer table or a more friendly gathering of citizens and soldiers. There is not a night passes that there is not some of the boys invited out to tea & to spend the evening with some of the most wealthy and influential men of the City. I never saw citizens and soldiers so friendly. I expect we will have to go out and have another feast tonight. The one given last night was by the Methodists and now I expect the other churches will show their good will. I was over to see Uncle Eber last Tuesday. I got up there about 3 P.M. and stayed all night and got back to camp about 10 A.M. on the 2nd. I had a very pleasant time. It had

---

[110] Edward must have found the big city very interesting and obviously relished the new experience.

been over two years since I had set down to a table to eat but I made out very well after all. He has got a very pretty little boy (and if I did not have some fun with him). He works in a rubber factory and as business was pressing he thought he could not go. He is coming down here to see me again tomorrow if I don't go up there but I want to go up there so I can go and see the Central Park. He said he would take me around & show me the sights. I will try to get a pass for two or three days & then I can have a good time. There has not been any trouble in Brooklyn about the draft nor do I think there will be.

The weather is quite cool but we have plenty of everything to keep warm. We don't get many letters from Minnesota now but I guess they will come around some time. I think we will stay here some time yet. The boys are well and enjoying themselves tip top. I will try to go up to New Haven if we stay here this fall. It will take about 6 hours to go on the cars. Write often, love to all.

Affectionately your son,

Edward H. Bassett.

On August 28th, Shortly before leaving New York, the First Minnesota joined the other army units in a march and parade through Brooklyn. A woman that had seen the Regiment two years earlier as they left Fort Snelling to go off to war, observed this tattered, proud segment of the once–grand body of young men now so reduced—but not broken—by the ravages of war. Deeply moved by the scene, she wrote the following account to the St. Paul Press:

"As I saw this little fragment of the once splendid Minnesota First march by me, carrying their stained and tattered flag, scarcely a shred of which is left, except the design close by the staff, and take their places in line of battle just as they stood on that bright morning more

538

than two years ago at Fort Snelling, when so many of us were there and heard General Gorman's last directions and Mr. Neil's prayer previous to their breaking camp and embarking for the war, and their glorious destiny. I absolutely shivered with emotion. There the brave fellows stood, a grand shadow of the regiment which Fort Snelling knew. Their bronzed faces looked so composed and serious. There was a history written on every one of them. I never felt so much like falling down and doing reverence to any living men. The music of the band, as the men went steadily through the changes of the drill was very sweet, but it seemed to me all the while like a dirge for the fallen."

****

Steamship Empire City-Period Drawing-Unattributed

On Board the Empire City
about 20 hours out from N.Y.
Sept.7th, 1863.

Dear Father & Mother,

When I wrote you last I did not think we would leave Brooklyn so soon. I wrote on the 5th in the AM and at 8 PM we got orders to strike tents and pack up to go to Alexandria immediately but as usual we had to lay arround a few hours before we could get off. I was intending to have a good time and if we had not got marching orders I should have gone up to Uncle Ebers on Saturday PM and Sunday. He was going with me down to the Central Park and arround to the most interesting places but as it is in the army we don't know ten minutes beforehand what we are going to do.

I had made arrangements to meet Uncle & was just going to start when the orders came. He said if he did not hear from me he would come down to our camp and I was calculating if he did to go out to Greenwood Cemetery but everything worked against me. He got to camp about one hour before we started and we went down & crossed the river into N.Y. and was on board the boat in less than two hours after he came to camp. I never saw the boys feel so bad to leave a place as they did to leave Brooklyn. If we had stayed there one week longer I should have gone up to New Haven.[111] It would take only 4 hours to go up on the cars and I should certainly have gone if we had stayed this week. We are now going back to the Army of the Potomac & take our old place in the same Brigade. They are encamped on the Rappahannoc near where they were last winter. We are glad that we are to take our old place in the army for it will be much more pleasant than to go into any other command. I expect we will have to help them through one more campaign and I hope it may be a successful one.[112] I would not wonder if we had a very bad winter for active operations in Va. this winter. It has been so dry all summer and now the ground is quite dry.

Tuesday A.M. Sept. 6th.

We are now running up the Potomac and will arrive at Alexandria about 4 PM if we have good luck. I will mail this letter in Alexandria. The boys are all well and

---

[111] The Bassett family had lived in New Haven, Connecticut before homesteading in Minnesota.

[112] Edward had guessed right, upon returning to the 2nd Corps they would embark on the Bristoe Station Campaign.

in very good spirits although they had hoped to spend the rest of their time out of Va. We know what it is and I guess we can stand it 8 months longer. I wish it was possible for me to spend the winter with you this winter but as we have so nearly served our time out I shall be quite contented. We will be apt to get payed off again soon. I was sorry to hear of the failure of John Russell's health again. I was in hopes that he would recover. If you see him tell him for me that I send him my best wishes for his recovery & still hope to see him as well as ever. I hope we will he able to get some duty that will be some easier than being right in the field in the way we have, but we may not. If we had as many men as we had last winter I would not expect to see a moment's rest but it seems as if we might be granted some favors after so long a time on the front.

My love to you all.

Edward H. Bassett

Direct to Washington D. C.

CHAPTER 26
THE BRISTOE CAMPAIGN

THE BATTLE OF BRISTOE STATION

While the First Minnesota was away from the army on its assignment to New York, there was a great deal of maneuvering and positioning done by both the northern and southern armies in Virginia. Continual marching and counter marching occurred on both sides yet no major engagements developed. During the almost three months that passed since the costly battles at Gettysburg, the depleted ranks of both armies were slowly being replenished by conscripts from the draft.

In Tennessee, the fortunes of the Confederate army under the command of General Braxton Bragg were anything but promising. He was forced to hole-up in Chattanooga while the remainder of the state was effectively under the control of the Union Army, commanded by General Rosecrans. Confederate President Jefferson Davis instructed General Lee to send his 1st Corps, commanded by General James Longstreet, to reinforce Bragg. As the troops moved out on September 7th, the loss of so many veteran soldiers and his most trusted commander must have been severely felt by Lee. Union General Meade soon heard of the transfer of Longstreet's Corps and was not long in planning an attack on Lee's weakened army. September 13th, Meade mounted a very strong reconnaissance in force to determine Lee's strength and position. To his surprise, they met little resistance and the rebel cavalry withdrew after only minor skirmishing. On the 14th, his column had reached the banks of the Rapidan River, a branch of the Rappahannock, after capturing the town of Culpeper, Virginia—General Lee's stronghold since the battle of Gettysburg. The War Department in Washington once again interfered with the field commander, insisting on more decisive action. Lincoln, desperately hoping to bring the war to an end, instructed General-in-Chief Halleck that Meade *"should move upon Lee at once in a manner of general attack".*

On September 16th, Meade moved his whole army across the Rappahannock River in pursuit of Lee. It was here, after returning from New York, that the First Minnesota Regiment rejoined the army on the south side of the Rappahannock. For the next five days, Meade continued to cautiously push forward, looking for the right opportunity to mount a successful attack. Meade's cavalry continuously clashed with the Confederates all along the front of his line.

Army of the Potomac Second Corps artillery, repelling rebel attack at
Bristoe Station Oct. 14, 1863
Drawing by A. R. Waud, Harper's Weekly

Segment of Period Map–Civil War Battles in Virginia–Library of Congress
White dots trace route of 1st Minnesota Sept. 16 –Oct. 16, 1863

Encamped at Culpeper, Virginia
Sept.16th, 1863.

Dear Father and Mother,

As we have finaly got back to our old position in the first Brigade, 2nd Div., 2nd Corps after an absence of just one month. I will write you a few lines to let you know what is going on here now. We landed at Alexandria on the 8th and lay there until the 12th waiting for the balance of the Brigade. On the morning of the 12th we packed up and started for the front. That night we camped at Fairfax. The next day we marched to Bristoe Station on the Orange & Alexandria R.R.

On the 14th we did not start until about 11 o'clock on account of rain. We camped about 3 miles from Warrenton Junction. On the 15th we started early and camped about 2 miles from Brandy Station crossing

544

the north fork of the Rappahannoc about 1/2 a mile below the R.R. Bridge. We marched four days and made as good as 20 miles each day. Water was very scarce and we had to use some as bad as any that we got on the retreat from Bull Run. This morning we started from camp early and got to Culpeper about 10 o'clock. The second Corps left camp before we left Alexandria on a reconaisance. The Cavalry is on the advance and fighting every day. The rebs are falling back and I hear today that they are across the Rapidan. There has been canonading all day in that direction. I don't think it is the intention of our Genls to bring on a general engagement if the rebels try to stand. I would not be surprised if we fell back across the river this week. The boys are all well and will make a good fight if they are called on.

We have not got any mail since we left Brooklyn except once and then I only got one letter which was from Amplias Ward. I expect there is a lot of letters somewhere for us. I like the country up arround here very well. Culpeper has been quite a nice town once but it shows the marks of the war now. Some of the houses have been riddled with shell. The cars come up here with supplies for us. I wish I could see you all but I cant for the present.

Respectfuly your son,

Edward H. Bassett.

Saturday Sept. 19th.

I did not have a chance to send my letter off so I will scribble a few more lines this morning. We are now camped on the Rapidan about 8 miles from Culpeper. The rebels are about one mile off and have kept skirmishing with our pickets for the last two or three days. We were out but come out all right. Everything is quiet now. We are all well. I will try to write again soon.

In Tennessee, meanwhile, the Confederacy resigned itself to the inevitable loss of Chattanooga. Union General Rosecrans succeeded in forcing the rebels out of the city; a major battle was on the horizon. Confederate General Longstreet had arrived with his corps to reinforce Bragg's beleaguered rebel force. The Confederates now launched an attack on Rosecrans' spread-out army, and the three-day battle of Chickamauga resulted in a disastrous Union defeat. Rosecrans now became the one surrounded in Chattanooga.

Washington perceived Meade's cautious movement as a reluctance to attack the enemy. When the news of the great defeat at Chickamauga reached the War Department in Washington, they realized the urgency of sending reinforcements south to stop the enemy advance. The feeling was, that if Meade would not use his army they would send some of it to Chattanooga. Meade was summoned to Washington for a consultation where he, once again, offered his resignation. Lincoln declined the resignation, assuring Meade that he had the utmost confidence in him. On September 24th, orders were sent to Meade for his 11th and 12th Corps to be detached to Chattanooga. Thus, 18,000 troops were to leave the Army of the Potomac for the south.

Upon hearing the news, Lee recognized the opportunity to disrupt this movement. He immediately began to make plans to advance with all the forces at his disposal against the Army of the Potomac. On October 8th, Lee embarked on a move to the north intent on catching Meade off guard and attacking the Union right flank.

On October 10th, Meade sent General Buford's cavalry up the Rapidan River to secure the upper fords. He planned to hold his 1st and 6th Corps at Culpeper and send his remaining forces to cross at the upper fords and attack Lee's rear. At the same time, his troops at Culpeper would force a crossing and attack the enemy's front. Buford, however, reported that Lee had already passed the fords and was moving north with the apparent intention of attacking and turning the Union's right flank. Meade now began a masterful withdrawal of his entire army toward his fortified base at Centerville. Of course, he must get there before Lee and try to entice the Confederate

Commander into attacking. Meade did a brilliant job of moving his entire army rapidly north and at all times being prepared to meet the enemy should they attack him before he reached Centerville. His whole endeavor was complicated by false information. After crossing the Rappahannock, Meade received a report that Lee had once again occupied Culpeper. Meade took his 2nd, 5th and 6th Corps, turned around, re-crossed the river and marched back to Brandy Station—within 15 miles of Culpeper—to attack Lee, only to find the Confederates were no longer there. Hastily he reversed his course and force-marched back toward Centerville.

Meade's ability is best appreciated by examining how Lee, his adversary, perceived him. At one point, Lee told General Longstreet and his staff:

"General Meade is the most troublesome Federal commander we have yet met. He is not only a general of courage, intelligence, and ability, but conscientious and careful. He is not afraid to fight upon an equal chance, and is constantly looking for an opportunity. If we make any mistake in his front, he will be certain to take advantage of it."

Camped on the Rapidan
about eight miles from Culpeper Va.
Sunday, Sept. 20th, 1863.

Dear Mother:

We got our back mail last night so I got eight letters yesterday, four of them were from you, one from Anna, one from Uncle Eber, one from cousin Libbie and one from B.F. Buck of the 8th Minnesota Vols.

I need not tell you that I was very much pleased with all the letters. There is nothing does me more good than to get a good lot of letters from my friends. I am very much pleased with Elford's picture. I think he has changed a great deal in his looks. He would make quite a soldier now if he had the uniform.

We were ordered to lay under arms last night and it was expected that the rebels were comeing out. They have got a good position and I guess they will be slow to leave it to meet us on our own grounds. It was very quiet all night and I have not heard any fireing this morning. We will have to go on picket this PM I expect but that is just what I like. I had much rather be on picket than to be where we are. I am counting the moments from now until the 29th of April next. There was one of the substitutes deserted to the enemy Friday night from the 19th Maine. He is supposed to have had a great deal of information for the rebels. I hope we will get him back sometime and shoot him. There was two deserters shot in the 3rd Division on Friday. I have no sympathy for them and I am glad they are being punished. We ought to get paid off again but there seems to be no signs of its comeing at present. I wish I was in Minnesota this morning. It seems a long time to me since I left there. You wished me to send you some choice seeds from the fruit that we got in Brooklyn. I am sorry that I did not think of it before we left there but it is too late now. I did not see any melons nor tomatoes as nice as you raise in the garden. Minnesota can beat all their vegetables and part of their fruit. Well you know that I think more of Minnesota than any other place in the world but when you come to ask me how I like Brooklyn compared with the southern towns I say that I would rather have Brooklyn for a home than any southern city I was ever in. From what I saw of the place while we were there I think that I would like to live there as well as I would in any city. I could never live in a city any way. There would not be anything for me to do and I would get lonely and desert. We may make our winter quarters here yet. The cars run up from Alexandria. I have not heard from Goodrich.

Please excuse me for the present. Love to all.

Your affectionate son

Edward Bassett.

P.S. Everything remains quiet. The Co. has most all gone on picket. I was on Brigade guard but am relieved now and will have a few hours rest. You don't know how I want to see you all.

Camp of the 1st Minnesota Vols.
on the Rapidan near Raccoon Ford, Va.
Sept. 30th, 1863.

Dear Father & Mother,

There has been but little chance for me to write since we came here for I have been on picket every day untill today.

The weather is beautiful and I think of the many happy days that I have spent at this time of the year in Minnesota. Health is excellent, in fact, there is no sickness at all in the army of the Potomac. There is no prospect of a move here right away, although we have eight days rations on hand. I hear that there has been two Corps of this army sent away, perhaps they have gone to help General Rosencrantz. He seems to have had a hard time of it but I suppose he is safe by this time. There is one of the substitutes from some of the Regts deserts to the enemy most every night.[113] One went over the night before last taking his gun and everything else with him. He was on picket. One of the rebels came over last night to us. He belongs to a

---

[113] One new draft law provision that inflamed much of the violence was that which allowed anyone with $300 to pay a substitute to take his place. Some, "substitutes", made a habit of deserting and going back to substitute again and collect another $300". Shooting those captured for committing this offense did much to discourage it.

Georgia Regt. He says that his wife is on her way north and he promised to meet her in N.Y. There was some 20 of his comrades comeing over with him but they were too closely watched to get away. The rebels don't feel so joyful over their victory in the West as they did at first. I guess it cost them too many men.

I suppose you are very busy now gathering the fall crops and preparing for winter. How is your corn this year. Is it hurt by the frost. I hear that corn has been ruined by early frosts this fall. I hope it is not the case. If I was in Minnesota this fall I believe I would try trapping for a while. Fur seems to bear a good price.

It is now about 8 o'clock in the evening and I will finish my letter so as to send it out tomorrow. I will wait patiently. I have not heard from any of the wounded boys. I believe Goodrich is in Baltimore. Albert Johnson and Saml Lilly have come back to the camp. Albert is a little lame yet but I guess he will get over it in time. Wm. Coen wants to get back to the Regt. and will as soon as he can. I am as uneasy as most when I have nothing to do. There is nothing to read that is worth reading unless we send for books and that will hardly pay now for we would have to throw them away if we moved. I hope to be able to get some good books next summer if I live.

My love to all the family. Please excuse pencil marks for I can't write with a pen.

Affectionately your son

Edward H. Bassett

Co. G 1st Minnesota Vols.

Oct. 1st all quiet.

Culpeper, Virginia
Oct. 7th, 1863

Dear Father & Mother,

We left our camp on the Rapidan yesterday morning being relieved by the 6th Army Corps. It was reported that we were going to Tenn. but I heard today that the order was countermanded and we are to stay with the Army of the Potomac. We have been doing rather hard picket duty ever since we camped on the Rapidan being on picket every day. I hope we will have an easier time now for a while. We are about ½ a mile from town where the whole 2nd Corps is camped in a large field. I would not be surprised if the army went into winter quarters out here. Genl Meads Hd. Quarters are at Culpeper. The rebels are digging rifle pits all along the Rapidan and they have a very strong position. It is raining tonight and I would not be surprised if we had considerable bad weather this month. Maj. Downie has come back and is in command of the reg't. now. Lieutenant Jas. DeGray returned today from Minnesota he says he was at Faribault and called on Mrs. Messick, he looks well. The officers are trying to have us reenlist for three years longer under the recent orders issued from the War Dept. & a large bounty and a promise of 30 days furlough. Maj. was over to Genl Meads Hd. Quarters to day to see if we could not reenlist as mounted infantry provided there would be half of the men enlist. If they will be accepted in that way I think there will about 150 men enlist and the regt. will go home to the state to recruit. The bounty offered is $402 and might be quite an inducement for some men but I shall not try it. I never enlisted for money and I don't think I ever will. I will try a few months in Minnesota if I live before I enlist again and if I ever enlist again. I have a letter from Uncle Eber dated Oct. 2nd he was well, things are going on there about as usual. There is a great demand for substitutes to relieve the Firemen and Police. He writes that Coz. Ellen Scott is very sick and they don't think she will get well he says that he thinks she has the consumption.[114]

The weather has been very fine here for some time. (Indian Summer) Oct. 8 A.M. It rained so hard last night that I had to put away my writing until this morning. It is raining some now and looks like being rainy all day I expect we will have some bad weather now.

The boys are as well as usual and if we should go into winter quarters we will have jolly times this winter. It is rather early for that but I don't believe there can be anything accomplished here this fall. How I would like to be in old Minnesota this next winter.[115]

Burning the Rappahannock Railway Bridge–October 13, 1863
Sketch by A. R. Waud–Harper's Weekly

---

[114] The term used during that era to refer to tuberculosis.
[115] The remainder of this letter is missing.

The next several days were marked by numerous skirmishes as Union Cavalry and rear guard units turned to intercept repeated Confederate attempts to overrun segments of Meade's retreating Army. The most substantive of these clashes occurred on October 14th, near the village of Bristow, more specifically at a railroad station on the Orange and Alexandria Railroad. The name of the station itself was spelled 'Bristoe.'[116] At this time, the 2nd Corps was temporarily under the command of General Gouverneur K. Warren while General Hancock was recuperating from the wounds he received at Gettysburg. Warren had distinguished himself at Little Round Top by promptly recognizing the critical situation that was developing there and moving quickly to stop a rebel breakthrough.

Meade did an incredible job of out-marching the enemy. He got ahead of the Lee and destroyed huge piles of stores at Warrenton and burned railroad bridges and stores at other locations along the Orange and Alexandria Railroad. On October 14th, the advanced units of his army reached Centerville, only 20 miles from Washington. The army was stretched out over a distance of 35 miles with the 1st Corps in the lead and farthest north followed by the 3rd, 6th and 5th Corps. The 2nd Corps was at the rear where it had again been serving as rear guard and the First Minnesota was at the extreme rear, fanned out to the right and left acting as flankers and supported by cavalry. Through a misunderstanding, a gap had occurred between the 5th Corps and the 2nd Corps. Meade's orders of that morning were written without him being aware that heavy skirmishing and cavalry action were already taking place in the rear on the Union left. General Sykes' 5th Corps was ordered to wait until

---

[116] Note the difference in the two spellings. During the time of the Civil War the village was spelled Bristow while the station was spelled Bristoe. Over time either spelling has been accepted as correct.

making contact with the lead elements of the 2nd Corps before crossing Broad Run at Bristoe Station. However, Sykes became anxious and moved out prematurely, as chance would have it this was exactly at the time that Confederate General A. P. Hill came on the scene. Lee had ordered Hill to move forward and cut the Union column in two. Observing a few stragglers making coffee near Broad Run creek and the rear of Sykes 5th Corps marching off about a mile away to the east, he concluded he had arrived too late. Hill was anxious to strike a crippling blow to Meade's army and even the score for Gettysburg. He saw what he thought was the 2nd Corps marching off in the distance and believed he had missed his opportunity to split Meade's army by breaking through its center while it was strung out and vulnerable. He ordered up his artillery and immediately opened fire upon the disappearing column, which accomplished little but to hurry them along. A.P. Hill sent three brigades under General Heth to attack the rear of the disappearing Union column and hold them while he moved around to the left and mounted an attack on their center. His haste in deploying his infantry, and mounting an attack against the apparently small number of troops at Bristoe Station proved to be a mistake. Little did he realize that, just then, the entire Union 2nd Corps was marching onto the field.

The Minnesota men heard the cannon fire from Hill's guns while they were still a mile-and-a-half from Bristoe. Though very tired from the nearly continuous, hard marching of the last few days and with little rest, carrying heavier than normal loads and having had no cooked rations, they resolutely quickened the pace. The enemy shells arched across the sky from the left, over their line-of-march and exploded on the hills beyond Bristoe Station. Being the lead regiment of the 2nd Corps, The First Minnesota was ordered to fan out to the left of the railway as flankers and skirmishers where a dense thicket of scrub pine might conceal rebel troops. The brush was so dense that it took a determined effort to penetrate it, and visibility was but a few yards at most. The First Minnesota was thus placed on the left of the railway grade while the remainder of the Corp was deployed along the right side—hidden from the enemies view. The First Minnesota was soon drawing fire from rebel infantry that was pushing through the brush on its left. After getting off a few rounds of return fire, they were ordered to fall back. Clearing the thicket, they hastily covered the 100 yards of open ground to the railroad and dropped down in a shallow ditch where they opened fire on the Confederates as they emerged from the brush. After continuing to fire for five minutes, they were ordered to fall back to the right side of the railway embankment.

Pursued by the screaming rebel line, the men ran up and over the embankment just as a fusillade of whistling lead zipped above their heads. They were indeed pleased to find their entire division in position along the bank and all rose in unison to pour a heavy volley of fire into the rebel throng crossing the open plain. The withering fire took an awful toll. The rebel line seemed to melt into the ground; those not killed or wounded fell to the ground to escape the storm and the crews of five Confederate guns, brought up to the right of the woods, abandoned their pieces without firing a shot. Union Artillery batteries soon galloped though behind the Union line, their horses dripping with sweat and covered with foam. Within moments, the guns were placed on the hills to the east and opened with effective fire, able to strike any point along the Confederate front.

The carnage was heartrending. Brave North Carolinians struggled to advance into the howling gale of rifle and artillery fire and refused to break before it. In front of the First Minnesota some men came within yards of the tracks and were soon met by a mass of Yankees who could wait no longer and burst forth from the embankment in a wild, headlong charge. Hand-to-hand fighting ensued, rebels unwilling to risk retreating in the withering fire raised their hands and yelled out *"We Surrender!"* The First Minnesota captured 322 unwounded prisoners and the five abandoned rebel cannons, which were hurriedly pulled from the field, as well as two stands of colors. Company G, to which Edward Bassett belonged retrieved two of the guns.

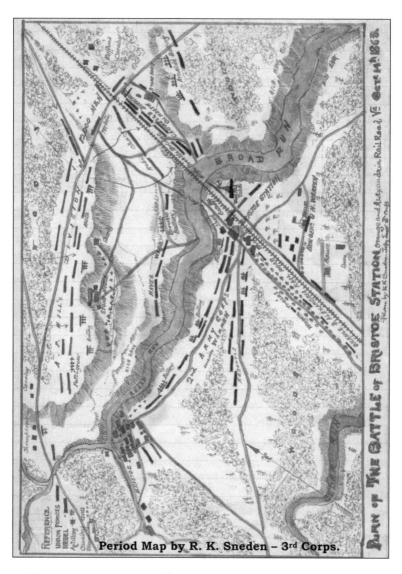

Period Map by R. K. Sneden – 3rd Corps.

The 450 prisoners were grouped into three companies and, still in possession of their arms, each company was escorted from the field by a single lieutenant to the custody of the Provost Guards. The adversaries on this field had met just three months earlier at Gettysburg, the rebels identified their foes by the white trefoil corps badge on their clothes and were heard to exclaim: *"Here's those damned white clubs again!"*

The battle lasted less than an hour and ended almost as quickly as it had begun as the defeated, but none the less courageous, North Carolinians withdrew. As darkness came on, General Warren ordered the burial of his 31 fallen soldiers and, for the 192 wounded who could be moved, to be cared for and put on wagons. The First Minnesota had lost one man killed and 16 wounded from its already-decimated ranks. After it was fully dark, the exhausted caravan moved with strictest silence across the front of the line of glowing rebel campfires, located just three-to-four hundred yards distant. Cautiously, they withdrew to rejoin the rest of the army at Bull Run.

After crossing Broad Run, Warren's 2nd Corps marched in the darkness across the once verdant but now desolate, plain between Bristoe Station and Manassas. It was nearing 4 AM when the footsore, exhausted men finally dropped to the ground near Bull Run battlefield at Blackburn's Ford and slept.

Holcombe relates conditions of the last few days:

"Of the 69 hours that had elapsed since they left Bealeton, on the 12th, they had been 60 hours either in column marching in the road, or in line of battle, or skirmishing with the enemy – only 9 hours for rest and sleep in three days. And when they marched, General Walker says, "they carried the heaviest loads I have ever known troops to carry on a campaign."

"The First Minnesota never forgot that march. But the men did not whine or whimper over it. They were proud of it."[117]

---

[117] Return I. Holcombe, History of the First Regiment Minnesota Volunteer Infantry, P. 409

Camp at Centerville, Virginia
Oct. 16th, 1863

Dear Father & Mother

Knowing you are ever anxious to hear from the seat of war (as the boys call Virginia), I thought I would

Sketch of Bealton Station–Leslie's Illustrated Weekly

write a few lines to send off at the first opportunity. We broke up camp at Culpeper on the 10th and marched out towards Gordonsville about 3 miles where we lay until the next morning at 2 o'clock when we started and marched to Bealton Station where we arrived about noon of the 11th and lay until noon of the 12th and then the whole Corps was marched back to Brandy Station about half way between the Rappahannoc River and Culpeper. Here we lay down for the night and were making arrangements for a nights sleep but about 11o'clock we were turned out and had to march until sunrise going back across the

Rappahannoc and beyond Bealton Station about 4 miles where we got our breakfast of Coffee & Hardtack and proceeded on our march to about 4 miles from Warrenton Junction where we camped for the night. On the morning of the 14th we started about sunrise, we had only started when there was skirmishing commenced in the front. The rebels had a battery in position and were trying to stop us from crossing the stream but we were not easily stoped. We drove them back and although the skirmishing was sharp for a time they did not delay the columns five minutes. There was none of the 2nd Corps engaged there but the 3rd Corps which was just in front of us lost a few killed. Our Regt. was deployed on the right of the brigade to act as flankers and skirmishers. Soon after we left camp and marched out as far as Catletts Station where the 2nd Div. of the 2nd Corps stoped to let the train pass. We then started on following the Rail Road untill we got within abut ½ mile of Bristoe Station where we found a large force of the enemy. Our Reg't. was sent out immediately as skirmishers in front of the Div. and had not advanced more than 40 rods when we saw about 300 rebels right in front. As soon as they saw us they went behind a thicket of pines. We advanced about half way through the thicket when they opened on us but most of their bullets went high over our heads. We did not fire but a few shots for the brush was so thick that we could not see them. Some of the boys got a shot or two at them but as I could not get sight of them I did not fire.

We were soon called back and followed on down by the side of the Rail Road about 80 rods where we found that the enemy were determined to fight us in a large field. Our regt. was soon opened on by their skirmishers and after we had returned a few shots our General ordered us to fall back across the R.R. and form our line behind the embankment.

Sketch of the Battle of Bristoe Station
By: J.A. Davis–Harpers Weekly

As soon as we began to fall back the rebels opened a tremendous volley on us wounding two or three slightly. We soon got behind the bank and then you may bet we let them have some of our best rations of Uncle Sam's manufacture of cold lead which taking effect in many a reb caused him to give up the Ghost then and there. Besides wounding a large number who will recover & I hope learn better than to fire on the old stars and stripes again. We were soon reinforced by the 111th N.Y. Vol's. and after about one half an hours fireing we drove the enemy back with a slight loss on our part but we killed about 500 rebs and took 450 prisoners besides about 100 that were left wounded on the field. We also took 5 pieces of rifled canon. There was another piece that our batteries had dismounted but we could not get it off. [118] We whipped them nicely. I never had a nicer chance to pay them up on the old

[118] Dismounted" here means that the barrel of the gun was knocked from its carriage by artillery fire. The barrel could weigh around 2000 lbs. and would be very difficult to lift without many men or equipment. Captured artillery was removed as soon as possible to keep it from falling back into enemy hands.

account and I done the best I could as did all the boys. The loss of the reg't. was one man killed in Co. F. and 13 wounded. Merill Benson of Co. G. got a bad though not dangerous wound in the side. Many of the boys narrowly escaped though that is getting to be an old thing. Lieutennant Jas DeGray was in command of our Co. and came out safe. The rebels fought desperately as they usually do. They belong to A. P. Hill's corps and were mostly North Carolina troops. We got prisoners from the 27th & 15th N.C. There was also two stands of rebel colors taken.[119] As we were the rear guard of the army we left the field about 11 o'clock at night and fell back across the Bull Run. Before morning all but a few cavalry were all safe across and in position on this side. So we are safe through one more bloody battle and the boys are in the best of spirits with plenty to eat. I don't believe the army was ever in better fighting trim. Besides they have great confidence in General Meade. So far we have not lost any of the trains except some few wagons that broke down. And the army is in a good position. Yesterday the enemy opened some batteries on us but their attention was soon called in another direction for two divisions of our cavalry were in their rear and on their right flank. Since about 2 PM yesterday we have not been disturbed. It is only about two miles to Centreville where we have good fortifications. There is no particular news to write about except our movements. General Mead has issued an order complimenting the 2nd Div. 2nd Corps for their success in the fight of the 14th inst. There was a deserter shot in the 1st Div. 2nd Corps this PM. There was quite a heavy rain today and it looks showery now. The roads have been in excellent order. I don't know what Lee's intentions are, whether he wishes to take Washington or drive us back so that he will have this part of Va. to winter in, whatever his intentions are I don't think he will make himself much better off.

---

[119] Colors–Regimental battle flags.

I rec. a letter from home a few days ago but as we have been marching both day and night I could not write. I will write again soon as I can get a good chance. Please accept this with my love to you all.

Affectionately your son,

Edward H. Bassett.

P.S. I forgot to tell you that I captured a rebel uniform except the jacket. I have a new pair of pants, shirt, draws & socks. I shall try to keep them. I expect you will see my name on the list of wounded. I have been told that it was there, but I told them not to put it there for I have not got anything worth mentioning. There was a ball struck me on the left side of my head passing through my hat but as soon as it hit my head it glanced off only bruising it so as to make it pretty sore. It did not break the skin although it made me dizzy for a while. I did not leave the field. There is four large holes in my hat but I think it was done by two bullets and I know there was not more than three. It was a close call but I paid them for it. There was one bullet hit my knapsack and tore a large hole in it. I told the boys not to give my name among the wounded but it was so close a call to a bad wound that is why it is there.[120] Good night.

Edward

---

[120] Though Edward made light of the wound to the side of his head, in later years its effects proved a good deal more serious. He developed Cataleptic seizures which eventually forced him to quit farming. It is likely that the impact of the bullet caused a skull fracture and a piece of skull bone put pressure on his brain causing the seizures. When a seizure occurred, every muscle in his entire body would go rigid and he could not move. When the seizure abated he had no recollection of it.

CHAPTER 27
THE MINE RUN CAMPAIGN

After Bristoe Station, both of the two opposing generals moved to withdraw. Meade withdrew his army during the night and counter-marched back along the same route they had traveled from Manassas Junction, destroying the railroad bridges along the way. Lee had started his move north with the hope of threatening Washington; nonetheless, he found no chance of providing subsistence for his army in this war ravaged region and decided to withdraw to the south of the Rappahannock River. As the Confederates pulled back, they systematically tore up the railroad tracks, burned the wooden ties and, in places, leveled out the grade. Lee thus denied Meade its use should he decide to mount an attack. With an eye toward renewing his northward thrust, Lee kept a pontoon bridge across to the north side at Rappahannock Station with a contingent of troops to protect it. He then occupied the old Union line on the south side of the river and built it into a formidable defensive position.

General Meade, however, acted first. Upon learning that several fords across the Rapidan River on Lee's right flank were unguarded, Meade developed an offensive plan. He would move south, cross the Rapidan at the unguarded fords and then swung to the west to attack Lee's rear. The Rapidan is a tributary that flows from the west into the Rappahannock near Chancellorsville. Above this point, the Rappahannock flows from the northwest. A large pie-shaped section of land bordered on the south by a region, commonly referred to as 'The Wilderness,' lies between the two rivers above their point of convergence.

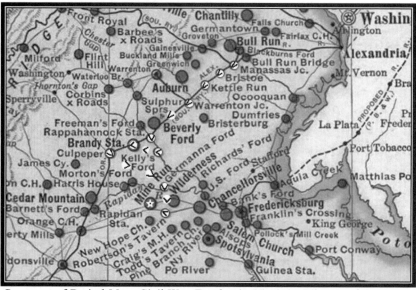

Segment of Period Map–Civil War Battles in Virginia–Library of Congress
White Dots with arrows trace route of 2nd Corps, Army of the Potomac

With his plans now made and approved by Halleck in Washington, Meade resumed his pursuit of Lee, albeit in a somewhat slow and cautious manner. Once again, the Army of the Potomac moved south along the same familiar trail.

Camped on Kettle Run, Va.
Thursday Oct. 22nd, 1863

Dear Mother,

Your letter of the 6th inst. was rec'd. last night and I

assure you that it was very welcome. It has been over one week since we have had our mail. I suppose you are hearing all sorts of rumors about the movements of this army now.

The 2nd Corps is now encamped near Warrenton Junction. Where the rest of the army is I cannot tell neither do I know where the rebel army is. (I don't believe they have a very large army in Va. now). I have not seen any rebels except a few prisoners since the 14th when we had a fight with them. We are under marching orders with 10 days rations and 60 rounds of ammunition but I don't believe we will go beyond the Rappahannoc. The weather is quite cool there has been several heavy frosts so the leaves have mostly fallen. Health is good and the boys are all in good spirits. We marched from our camp on Bull Run near Centerville last Monday and camped that night near Bristoe Station. Tuesday we marched up here fording Broad Run three times and Kettle Run once the water was about knee deep at each place. When we came here on the 20th we found some of our men laying on top of the ground that had been killed on the morning of the 14 th and had to be left, the rebels did not bury them. I guess they had enough of their own to take care of. They admit a loss of 2000 at Bristoe Station. They are now evidently falling back and will most likely take the Rappahannoc as their line. I still believe we will winter on that line. We have 11 privates in our Co. now for duty.[121] Al Johnson is so lame that he cannot do much. Charles Benson who was wounded on the 14th has gone to the hospital his wound is not a very dangerous one although it will lay him up some time.

You ask me some questions abut the death of Captain Messick. I have no reason to doubt that he did request that his body should be sent home if he was killed but he must have made the request before he

---

[121] A further reminder of the losses this unit suffered since their beginning with 116 enlisted men in the company.

was hit for he certainly did not live to make any such request after he was hit. I think he did make the request. I helped to carry his body from the field after the enemy had been driven from the field. Perhaps it was half an hour after he was killed that we took him back to the hospital where his cook took charge of him until an ambulance came up and he was taken back to the General Hospital. His sword and pocketbook were taken from him in fifteen minutes after he fell. Who took them I can't tell I have been told that he had but little money about him, some ($15) I think was all. There was a gold watch in one of his pockets that belonged to Lieutennant Colonel Adams who was wounded the day before that was not taken, they did not happen to see it so it was saved and returned to Colonel Adams to whom it belonged. I was not present when he was burried, my duty called me to the front and I returned immediately to my place. I don't think I was gone more than 25 minutes. The enemy were still shelling us from a battery of long ranged rifled guns that were some three miles off on the side of the mountain. After we had laid him down I was looking at him for the last time and thinking if there was anything that I could do that would do any good but there was nothing.

I asked Mr. Williams, his cook, to take off his shoulder straps and send them to his wife which he did. Lieutennant DeGray was then in the hospital suffering from a very dangerous wound in the head that he had received the day before. I was very sorry that we could not save his sword but in a battle like that there is a great many things that we would like to do that cannot be done. It is enough to know that he died at his post doing his duty. Thousands fell that day in the same way. Captain Messick died as he would wish to die, fighting for his country. He was a true Patriot and never was known to shrink from duty in any way. 1st Lieutennant Jas. DeGray enlisted in the company at the first and was appointed a Corporal which office he held untill we went onto the Peninsula in 1862 when he was promoted to Sergt. and about one year ago he was commissioned as 2nd Lieutennant and assigned to Co. G. immediately after he came back from Minnesota he received his commission as 1st Lieutennant He is a man of steady habits strictly <u>temperate</u> and <u>honest</u> he is a great favorite among the boys and I am sorry to hear that people should try to injure him. He is in command of our Co. now and I hope he will be our Captain. You all know very well why Capt's. body could not be removed last summer. It can be done now, or it can be burried on the field where he fell as it has been purchased for the purpose of making a burrying ground. [122]

Now I have written this because you spoke about it in your letter. I don't wish to write or say anything that would cause Mrs. Messick to feel bad or make anything seem mysterious about her husband's death. Everything was done that could be done under the circumstances. [123] Please give my respects to Mrs. Messick and tell her that we are trying to keep up the reputation of the 1st. Albert Johnson also sends his respects. His knee is quite lame yet. I don't believe he will ever get entirely over it.

I rec'd. a St. Paul paper & Advocate last night. I wish I had known that John Scott was in the 2nd Wis. I could have found him just as well as not. I think the Spencer boys are in that Regt. I have heard that Harry Lines Jr. was in a telegraph office somewhere in Ill. since I've enlisted. I wish Father would write to me if he can find time it has been a long time since he has

---

[122] Now Gettysburg National Cemetery.

[123] Lieutenant DeGray had just returned from a trip to Minnesota. It would appear that the folks back home for some reason thought he may be responsible for the fact that Captain Messick's body had not been returned home for burial. Edward wishes to correct that misconception to keep it from harming a fine officer.

written. Please ask him if he will not try to write a short letter at least although the longer the better.

I think of you all every day and long for the time to come when I shall see you all. For the present accept this with my love to all.

As ever you Affectionate Son

Edward H. Bassett

Co. G 1ˢᵗ Minn Vol.

Well I have filled two sheets & have not told you all I want to nor can I do it on this, and all the paper there is in my hand could not contain what I would like to say to you. I wish I was only there where I could see you all how I would like to spend the winter with you if the wars were only ended & the country once more in a prosperous condition but alas the prospects are dim at present. I hope they may brighten soon. There is a strong force here now but the exact number I don't know or whether there will be a move made from here into Winchester. One thing sure we have got a fine high country to work in if we do and unless the rebs run I don't see how we are going to get as much marching as of late.

It is sundown & I must get my supper of coffee & Hardees[124] as we call the crackers. Although we don't wish to compliment General Hardee yet we mention his name very often.

I will end this letter

As ever

Edward

I send a few apple & Damsen[125] seeds to Elford tell him that I remember him still & want to see him very much also the girls. I will write them soon if I can.

---

[124] Hardtack
[125] The Correct spelling is "Damson"; this is the common name for the Damascus Plum, a small bright purple fruit.

Camped near Warrenton, Va.
October 30th, 1863.

Dear Father & Mother,

My last letter was written while we were near Centreville about the 22nd I think. We are now encamped about 3 miles from Warrenton. We came here on the 23rd and went into camp. Since then we have been very busy building houses so now we have better quarters than we did last winter at Falmouth. The weather has been quite cool. There is a heavy frost most every night. There seems to be a good prospect of our stoping here for a few weeks and we thought we would fix ourselves up as comfortable as possible.

I rec. (received) a letter from Mother this morning dated October 18th. I am glad to hear that you are all well. I read those papers that you sent and I found them quite interesting. I have a journal that I will send you. I was out on picket last night. I don't believe there are any rebels within ten miles but their cavalry makes a raid through the country once in a while and we have to be on our guard. They destroyed the R.R. from Bristoe Station through to Bealton leveling down the grade in many places and blowing up every culvert. It is being rebuilt now but it will be some time before it is complete. I hope there will not be any more moves in this department this winter for we don't seem to accomplish anything when we do move. I think the rebels will fall back to their old line for the winter and perhaps we will stop here where we are. As we have got only six months more to serve I think we would enjoy ourselves here in our snug quarters very well. Health is as good as usual. How I would like to be at home in Minnesota this winter. I believe you will have a very cold winter but it won't be like the winters here. Do you take the Central Republican? We get about one doz. copies sent to the Co. every week. The boys have lots of fun over Brown's editorials and his corespondent with the Sibley expedition.

There has just been a man shot for desertion that belonged to the 15 Regt. Mass. Vols. He was a substitute. I did not go out to see him but most of the boys did. The Regt. was called out to witness the execution. He is the first one that has been executed in this Brigade. There is nothing going on in camp except fixing up our quarters and that is about over with now. Every four men have a nice snug building with a fireplace in it so if we should stop here this winter we are in time with our houses. They are about 9 feet long and 7 wide with a door in one end and the fire place at one side. The walls are from 3 to 5 feet high. For roofing we use our shelter tents. What did your wheat yield per acre. I saw some very nice wheat last summer when we were up in Maryland but it was all winter wheat. There might have been a good crop of corn raised in Va. this year if it had not been for the army.

Please excuse me this time. I am tired and sleepy. My love to all.

Your son   E. H. Bassett
                  Co. "G" 1st Minnesota

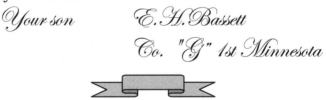

Winter Quarters – Camp of the Army of the Potomac, Brady Photo

Camp of the First Regiment Minnesota Vols.
Near Warrenton, Va.
November 2nd, 1863

Dear Sisters Ella & Anna,

    I have received several letters from you since I have written to you and I suppose you are getting tired waiting for me to write. I have been very busy for some time. We have been building houses and fixing our quarters up as comfortable as possible but we have got fixed up now so that I shall have more time to write and I will try and answer all letters immediately if we stay here. I received a letter from Ella this morning and I am very glad to hear that you were all well. You say that you hear that we have had another battle. I guess you got a pretty true statement of the loss of our Regt. I wrote to Father & Mother about the battle and you have most likely heard of our loss by the St. Paul papers by this time.

I have not seen a rebel soldier since that day except a few prisoners. I don't think we will have another fight very soon for the rebs have fell back across the river and destroyed everything that they could find that could be of any use to our army.

Our sutler came up last night with a load of goods but he sells everything at very high prices. It is hard to get any goods to the army now for the RailRoad is not in very good order. I will tell you the price of some of his things so you can compare them with prices in Minnesota now.

Butter is worth 50 cts. per pound, poor at that.

Cheese   "   "   "

Eggs are worth 50 cts. per dozen

Apples 5 cts. apiece

Cookies sell at 15 for 20 cts.

Onions are 25 cts. per pound

Potatoes about 12 ½ cts. per pound

And most other articles in the same proportion. It makes me think of the first two years we were in Minnesota. I hear that we are going to be furnished with some vegetables by the government as soon as the roads are finished. I hope so for we have not had many this summer.

Monday evening - - - - - - - - I was called out to go on drill before I could finish my letter so I will do it now. We have a very good time drilling. This is the first time that I have been out for drill for a long time for I have been on duty most every time there has been a drill. How I would like to be with you this evening. I hope to spend many pleasant evenings with you yet. I sent the Phrenological Journal and a Frank Leslie to you today. I have the November No. of the Journal that I will send as soon as I have read it.

Who is going to teach the select school in Morristown. I hope you will go to school if you want to and I know you do but I guess you will find it rather cold in the winter to go so far. You must excuse this large sheet of paper for it was all I could get. The sutler did not bring up any smaller and I was out. I will get some better soon. Tell Elford that I look at his picture most every day and how I would like to have an old fashioned scuffle with him. Please accept this with my love to you all.

Your Affectionate Brother,

Edward H. Bassett

Co. G. 1ˢᵗ Regt. Minnesota Vols.

To: Ella F. Bassett
    Anna E. Bassett

Camp near Brandy Station, Va.
Nov. 11ᵗʰ, 1863

Dear Father & Mother,

For some time there had been talk of our starting on another fall and winter campaign among some of the boys while others thought we would advance as far as Rappahannoc River and take up a position for the winter none seemed to believe we would remain in our quarters near Warrenton.

We were kept supplied with eight days rations and were ready to move whenever the Genls. said so. The railroad had been fixed so that trains came up as far as Warrenton Junction and to Warrenton. We were snugly quartered and did not much like the idea of leaving our houses but on the night of the 6ᵗʰ we were told that we would march early next morning so we made up our minds that we would enjoy the use of our shanties one more night and then bid farewell to winter quarters and take a little hunt for the rebels. We were called up at 4 o'clock and got our breakfast and by sunrise we were marching down the R.R. towards Warrenton Junction from there we went to Bealton Station and then we took a direct road to Kelly's Ford where we arrived at dark and camped for the night. There had been considerable cannonading during the PM and when we arrived at the ford there was some sharp skirmishing between some of the U.S. Sharpshooters and a party of rebels that were trying to prevent our crossing but our men finally charged through the river and took about 300 of the rebels prisoners. Sunday morning the 8th we crossed the river on a pontoon bridge and advanced that day about five miles but as we did not meet any large force of the enemy we did not have any fighting.

Bridge Pontoons on Wagons
M. Brady Photo

There was some considerable fireing up towards the R.R. and the rebels seemed to be trying to check us by planting batteries on the heights around Culpeper but about dark the fireing ceased and I expect the rebels did not make another stand this side of the Rapidan. I hear that General Sedgwick had quite a fight at Rappahannoc Station where he crossed with his command the 6th Corps. and took some 1,200 prisoners and 6 pieces of cannon. I think he must have lost rather heavy if he charged the works as I hear he did. The rebs seem to have been taken by surprise they had built nice winter quarters and seemed to be making calculations to stop all winter.

At Kelley's Ford the first they knew of our advance was when a 32 pound parrot opened on their camp. [126] They left in a hurry not taking time to gather up their things. They left lots of clothing wet that had just been washed and they did not have time to dry it. I expect we have taken some two to three thousand prisoners already. We lay in camp all day on the 9th and yesterday until about noon when we moved about two miles and are now stoping in a large rebel camp. They had been building some very good quarters and we thought we would occupy them while we stop here. The one that I am in has a fireplace and will do very well for four of us for a few weeks if we should stay that long. I think we will advance again as soon as the R.R. is finished up to Brandy Station. I don't know if they destroyed the road any farther than Rappahannoc Station but from there to Bristoe Station a distance of about 25 miles they destroyed every rail and they burnt every bridge and in some places leveled down the grading. I wish you could see the boys pitch into a farmhouse that stands about 80 rods from camp. It was a very good house and nicely finished inside yesterday when we came here but the boys wanted some boards and the house had to furnish them. The siding, doors, floors, caseings, stairs and even the window sash are all torn out and before night the roof will be off and then the frame will have to come down for the fun of seeing it fall if nothing more. I have seen several torn down this fall they are secesh and the owners have left them.

I have got a rebel paper that I will send you there is but little in it but perhaps you would like to see it. The

---

[126] To an unsuspecting camp engaged in relatively quiet camp chores, this would indeed have been quite an awakening! The average field artillery pieces were in the range of 8 to 14 pound guns, that being the weight of the shot they fired. The 32 pound Parrot was a fairly large gun with a rifled barrel, considerable range, accuracy and a very loud report.

weather is very cool the ground freezes nights. On the 9th there was a few flakes of snow fell and the top of the mountains are white with snow now. Health is good and duty light at present. The roads are in excellent order and the army can move fast if they wish.

I hear that there is considerable snow now in some of the northern states and I suppose you are having some cold weather in Minnesota now.

I send you the Phrenological Jounal to day. Did you rec'. the August and September Numbers?

The July No. I never got.[127] Excuse me this time and accept this with my love to all.

From your son

Edward H. Bassett
Co. G. 1st Minnesota Vols.

The rebel camp the men occupied afforded somewhat luxurious quarters in comparison to the usual. The huts were built of logs with roofs covered with hand split wooden shingles and most had a fireplace built of clay and baked hard so it would not crumble. To the men of the First Minnesota it was a welcome booty of war, especially after they had just been forced to leave the quarters they had built near Warrenton. The regiment remained in camp here through November 25th, mostly doing picket duty along the north bank of the Rapidan River, where Lee's Confederate Army of Northern Virginia was spread along the opposite bank.

---

[127] "Numbers" meaning issues.

Camp of the 1st Minnesota Vols.
In an old rebel camp
Near Brandy Station, Culpeper Co. Va.
November 17th, 1863.

Dear Father and Mother,

Your kind letter of the 5th was received in due time. I am glad to hear that you are well and geting along so finely. I expect you must have some snow and cold weather by this time up there as it is geting about the time of the year for such things in that latitude. The weather has been very pleasant here this fall and untill the rain which fell on the night of the 14th the roads have been in excelent order. The railroad is completed now so that the cars run to Culpeper I believe. I expect we will be on the move again in a few days and if the weather should be favorable I would not be surprised if we got some nearer Richmond by the time we stop again. It is just one year today since we arrived at Falmouth and drove the rear guard of the rebels across the river at that place. The pay master came up yesterday and payed us up to the 1st of Nov. If you would like any money to use this winter I can send you 15 or 20 dollars as well as not. Write and let me know in your next. I suppose it will hardly pay to sell your wheat at present prices. I expect we will be sent home next April but all rumors about our being sent away as soon as the army goes into winter quarters must be started in Minnesota for there is no such thing thought of here. I don't expect to see the Regt. sent home or discharged one moment before their time is out and there is no reason why they should be. There was an order from the Sec. of War requireing Corps Commanders to send in a list of those Regts. whose time expires next spring. I was told that our Regt. is the first three years Regt. to be discharged from the army of the Potomac. You ask how many of our Regt. will reenlist. There was a time when we were laying at Culpeper about the 7th of Oct. that there was 104 put their names down to go as a mounted Regt. provided they could be granted that privilege and they got a recommendation from General Mead to the Secty. of War to grant it and when the reports were called for Maj. Downie reported that there was none to reenlist. There are but very few that would reenlist in the Infantry service now. I decided two years ago to serve my three out and do the best I could but never to enlist in the Infantry again. I would prefer Cavalry or Artilery. The marching would not be as hard and wearing. I hope the war will end soon so there will be no more use for an army of Volunteers and it will if the people of the north stick to their avowed principles in the late Elections. The Confederates are loosing faith in their cause every day and they are certainly hard up for both men and means to prosecute the war. I sent you a Richmond paper today. It is a miserable dirty thing but as I could get no other I sent it thinking perhaps you would like to see one. It is printed on a half sheet as all their papers have been for the last year (it costs only $20 per year) and is a fair specimen of a first class southern daily.

We are now quartered in a rebel camp and are very comfortably situated. Health is good. There is some of the boys that were wounded at Gettysburg come back most every week. I see that General Mead in his official report of that battle estimates his loss in killed at 2,834, wounded 13,709, missing 6,643. Total loss in killed, wounded and missing 23,186 men. I have seen it estimated that the rebels lost over 40,000. They don't say much about it themselves except in a few of their papers where they claim a complete victory over the Federal army and one writer said they were amply paid for their loss in the stock and plunder they carried away with them. They will have another great victory to record when Charleston falls which I hope will be before spring. I hear some talk about General Mead being relieved from the command of the army. I hope it is only talk for I think there is but little to be gained by continual changeing of commanders. If he is relieved, I think General Sedgwick will be appointed to the command.

Well I have written a long letter and I will close biding you all good night.

Affectionately your Son

Edward H. Bassett

Co. G. 1st Regt. Minnesota Vols.

On November 26th, the First Minnesota Regiment once again joined the other regiments of the 2nd Corps and marched off to what would be its last engagement. This proud remnant of patriots that had endured hardships, battle, death, injury, and deprivation of every imaginable kind, once again answered the call to duty. Much had changed since that first battle at Bull Run. The Regiment was now under the command of Major Mark Downie; the 1st Brigade commanded by Colonel D. C. Baxter, the 2nd Division by Gen. Alex S. Webb and the 2nd Corps by General G. K. Warren. The regiments were forewarned of the upcoming march when, on November 24th, they were awakened at 3 AM, told to get their breakfasts, pack everything and await orders. It was 5 AM when they marched three or four miles to General Webb's headquarters in a cold drizzling rain. After standing for hours, they were finally ordered to return to camp. Apparently, the plans were not yet completed. The next day was more pleasant and the men laid around camp in anticipation of what would obviously be another major movement. Weapons were inspected, ammunition drawn and rations issued; everything was made ready for battle.

Stars still twinkled in the clear sky when the men were aroused at 4 AM on Thursday the 26th —Thanksgiving Day. They were ordered to get breakfast and be ready to move with all their belongings in an hour. Carrying 60 rounds of ammunition, shelter tents, extra clothing, including overcoats, for those that had them, and all the other essential paraphernalia, the men marched under heavy loads across the frozen ground. During the march to the Rapidan River, news came that General Grant had taken Chattanooga, Tennessee and the rebel army there was scattered and broken up.

Building a Pontoon Bridge across the Rappahannock
Sketch from Harper's Weekly

The river was found to be quite swollen from two days of heavy rain. Boats were sent across with troops to guard the opposite shore and the engineers began to assemble a pontoon bridge. It soon became evident that there were not enough pontoons available to bridge the widened river so trestles had to be built to complete the structure, thereby causing a delay. Meade's plan called for splitting his army into three columns, each one advancing on the enemy and crossing the Rapidan at different locations. For his coordinated attack to succeed, all three columns had to accomplish their task within 24 hours and be ready to mount the attack simultaneously. The plan began to unravel at the swollen river. General French's 3rd Corps was to lead but was late breaking camp. He had failed to reconnoiter his route and took a wrong road. This mistake forced him to countermarch and, consequently he was late in arriving at Jacob's Ford where he was to cross. To make matters worse, French didn't like the steep banks at the ford and decided to send his artillery to Germanna Ford. A tremendous traffic jam ensued when the artillery trains added confusion to the already great mass of men and wagons trying to cross at that point. French's bungling would later cost him his command but, at this time, it delayed the attack on Lee's spread-out army by one full day, giving Lee time to unify his force and further strengthen his fortifications. Meade's chance of success now was now reduced by half.

The First Minnesota had reached Germanna Ford about 10 AM but was unable to cross until nearly 4 PM when the bridge was finally completed. After marching another four miles, they went into bivouac at Flat Run for the night. French's Corps was still not in position to the right of the 2nd Corps, leaving their flank exposed.

After more than 16 hours on their feet, the men were exhausted and hungry. They wasted no time getting fires started. Aware that this was Thanksgiving Day, the men set about preparing a meal. As hungry as they were, a meal of coffee, hardtack and salt pork may have seemed like a feast. According to James Wright some had said they were hungry enough to *"eat a grindstone."* Talk of home and Thanksgiving dinner with turkey and pie and the wonderful aroma's of the holiday gave testimony to how much every man present yearned to return to his family. The night was very cold and sleeping on the ground, wrapped only in a blanket, and knowing that they would fight again tomorrow provided anything but a comfortable night's rest.

At 4 AM, on the morning of November 27th, they were awakened and told to get ready to march. Coffee and a hurried breakfast were consumed and, following a long practiced drill, they fell into line-of-march and set off through the scrub oaks, brush and swamps on the edge of 'The Wilderness.' The 3rd Division, under the command of Brigadier General Alexander Hays, took the lead followed by Webb's 2nd Division, including the First Minnesota. By noon, they reached Robertson's Tavern after skirmishing repeatedly with rebel cavalry during the morning and later with infantry. They had also taken control of the Orange and Fredericksburg Turnpike. Their situation was somewhat precarious because neither one of the units on their right and left flanks were in position. Cannon fire was heard occasionally from both directions, although apparently French's 3rd Corps, some distance away on the right, was most heavily engaged. Throughout the afternoon, skirmishes developed along the right of the Union line, although none were very severe. Well after dark, the men wrapped up in their blankets seeking shelter from the icy wind that was howling through the trees. The temperature was below freezing, yet after a long day of marching and skirmishing, sleep came quickly to the tired soldiers.

After but a few hours of uneasy rest, the men were again called at 4 AM, on Saturday morning, November 28th, as daylight dawned on this freezing cold gray morning, the men ate their meager breakfast and formed into line, rifles in hand, and took their position on the right of the division. Facing a stiff wind blowing through the trees, they marched out ahead as skirmishers. They soon came upon a row of logs that marked the line of the enemy the day before—only to find it deserted. After a brief halt, the line of skirmishers continued their slow advance through the tangle of brush and scrub oaks, with two lines of battle following in their rear. A few hours later, a steady rain began to fall as a dark storm gathered. They struggled through the increasing rain and continual shower of water from the trees and bushes. Soaked to the skin, they tried desperately to keep their cartridges and rations dry. By noon, they reached Mine Run where the enemy was discovered in strong force on the hills across the now swollen creek.

They waited in the pouring, freezing rain while a few skirmishers went ahead to reconnoiter. The 5th Corps came up on the left and the 6th and 3rd Corps joined the line to the right, bringing relief to the 2nd Corps which was sent back to the second line. The Army of the Potomac was again united.

By mid-afternoon, the storm had diminished, and the temperature dropped below freezing. After a careful survey, the Confederate forces were determined to be in strong force and well positioned in defensive works on the higher ground, with an abundance of artillery positioned for their support. The valley was now flooding as the rain continued to fall. The engineers and generals concluded that a successful attack would be impossible.

As darkness approached, the temperature continued to drop and the men began to search for shelter from the elements where they could get some desperately needed rest. Orders that no fires would be allowed did nothing to improve matters. James Wright wrote:

"Contrary to orders, men went, a few at a time, to a little ravine back of us, made small fires, and boiled coffee. One who has not had a cup of hot coffee under such circumstances does not know how to fully appreciate one."

The night was one long remembered. The soaked ground offered no place to lie down with any comfort. The men dared not simply go to sleep for fear of dying from exposure in their drenched uniforms. All they could do was doze awhile and then get up to slap their aching bodies with their arms in a vain attempt to get warm. It was later reported that some men actually succumbed to the cold.

The frightful night ended very early on Sunday morning, November 29th, when they were called to move quietly through the woods to the rear. Ice-covered twigs and leaves crunched underfoot at every step and any attempt at silence was hopeless. Shortly, they came to a road and clearing to find the entire 2nd Corps assembled there. A halt was called while they prepared a hasty breakfast, replaced their wet cartridges and drew three days fresh rations. Somewhat refreshed, they took up the march back to Robertson's Tavern.

BATTLE OF MINE RUN, VA.
POSITION of the ARMIES of LEE & MEADE, Dec. 1ST 1863
Etching from a sketch by Edwin Forbes, Leslies Illustrated

Camp Near Brandy Station, Va.
Dec. 4, 1863.

Dear Parents,

Knowing that you will be anxious to hear from me since the last move I scribble these few lines to ease your mind.

The 1st Minnesota is back in their old Camp all safe. We had a hard march but are all right now. There will be no other advance this winter. We may fall back to the north of Rappahannoc. I am well and will write to you as soon as I can and let you know what we have

584

been doing. We were out six days. I received two letters from you today. I am very glad to hear that you are well.

Please accept this with my love to all.

As Ever Your Son   Edward H. Bassett

Co. "G" 1st Min. Vols.

I will write again in a day or so if we don't fall back.

Here, once again the 2nd Corps benefited by the quality of leadership of its commanding officer. General Warren, realizing a frontal attack on the rebel position was likely to fail, suggested to General Meade that he take his corps around to the left to mount an attack on Lee's right flank. With no other option available, Meade consented and further strengthened Warren's force by adding a full division from the 6th Corps, thereby boosting his total strength to over 16,000 men. At Robertson's Tavern, they left the supply wagon train behind and, accompanied by four batteries of artillery, resumed the march headin west on the Orange Plank road. A cavalry unit they encountered warned them that the enemy was in considerable force to the front. The 1st Division was sent forward and lively skirmishing continued at the front all afternoon but the rebels were driven back nearly four miles across Mine Run. The advance of the Union troops by a circuitous route had covered nearly 18 miles, although they were now only five miles from their starting point. As darkness came on, they stopped in a wood where they made fires and boiled up some hot coffee. The weather was disagreeably cold and the weary men were anxious to get a night's rest, but it was not to be. Orders came to form up and move out. Silence was to be observed—no talking—and the army was to move quietly. The futility of such an order must have caused more than a few chuckles among the men. Asking 16,000 men to march through woods littered with ice coated leaves and branches without making any noise seemed foolhardy. The night was very dark and the going was quite slow. Orders could not silence the sound of thousands of feet crunching through the ice enshrouded wood. Everyone expected to be fired upon at any moment.

It was nearly midnight when the First Minnesota was sent to the front to a small stream, where they halted awaiting further orders while the rest of the Corps formed into three battle lines behind them. Then they moved cautiously to their left along the edge of the stream where they could hear the voices and see the reflections of the rebels' campfires on the far side. Their feet broke through the ice on the many small pools, making what seemed to be a great deal of noise. At every move, they expected to draw fire from the enemy pickets that they were certain were just across the stream.

After a brief halt along the the stream bank, they were ordered to cross over. The thin sheet of ice gave way under foot with a great crashing sound and the men were now wet to the knees. Still, for some unexplainable reason, they were undiscovered. Emerging from the stream into an open field, they advanced cautiously to a low ridge, behind which they could observe the enemy. They watched from about 300 yards away, as the shadowy forms of rebel lookouts on the hillside walked back and forth stamping their feet to keep warm.

The night had turned bitterly cold. Before long the wet trouser legs were frozen tight around the legs of the silent onlookers. From now until dawn, they would fight a battle of different kind. Without fires or cover and unable to move about for fear of being discovered, they could only lie there shivering and exhausted. To sleep was to invite death and to stop rubbing their ankles and tapping their feet together would likely lead to them freezing in the cold wind. The night was a cold version of hell.

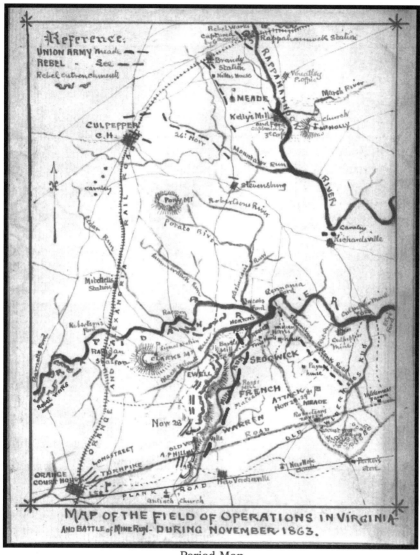

Period Map

As the moon broke through the thin clouds the enemy position could be seen with more clarity. The rebel lookouts on the hillside occupied a line of rifle pits. With the entire corps now massed behind them, the First Minnesota was ordered to lead the attack at daylight. The signal to advance would be the firing of five successive cannon shots. Upon hearing the signal, the regiment was to charge forward and bayonet the men in the rifle pits. They were then to take their place in the first line as it advanced up the hill and continue on to take the enemy breastworks. The thought of a straightforward, frontal attack on such a fortified position had a further chilling effect on the men. They would follow their orders and do their best but none believed he would live to see tomorrow.

Without flinching in the face of such likelihood, the men went about making ready. They pinned small pieces of paper bearing their names to the outside of their coats or blouses and exchanged last messages to be sent home to loved ones in the event of their death. Knapsacks were removed and piled up; rifles and ammunition were carefully checked. When all was ready, they crept up the slope to the top of the little rise to await their fate. Within pistol shot of the enemy skirmishers, they lay waiting in the freezing cold for the signal. Daylight came and no signal was heard. 8 AM came and still no signal. By this time, the skirmishers from both sides were stamping about to get warm, each apparently oblivious to the presence of the other. All the while, the nervous anticipation was building. Every man on either side wondered to himself whether he would see his loved ones again or be horribly wounded and left suffering on the field. Yet, not one faltered. Just after 8 AM, a couple of cannon shots were heard. Was that the signal? No! A few rifle shots rang out but the regimental signal gun has not fired. What could it mean? Must they wait yet longer? After what seemed an eternity, word came that General Warren believed the chances of success were too small to warrant the attack. The men were ordered to hold their positions and not engage the enemy skirmishers. An uneasy truce prevailed as both sides waited wondering what would be next.

As the hours ticked away, the tensions eased and men on both sides laid down their rifles and relaxed a little. Soon the Union men, realizing they were very hungry, built fires to make coffee and something to eat. By chance, they found a field of potatoes and turnips that had been dug and covered with straw and earth and were still in good condition. They were soon appropriated and handed down the line to be relished with the meal. Although a truce of sorts prevailed, no one moved far from his rifle as a single accidental pistol shot could set off a great battle. The day dragged on tension-filled and very cold, especially on open ground with no cover from the sharp wind. Sometime after dark, the order came to gather up their things and silently withdraw back across the creek. Apparently General Meade had listened to General Warren and decided the attack posed a greater chance of failure than success; thus, the attack was cancelled. Upon crossing the creek, they were greeted by the 19th Maine waiting to relieve them. After pausing awhile to make certain the enemy had not heard them withdraw and decided to pursue, they marched back together some three-fourths-of-a-mile to join the division in line of battle. Nearing midnight, the regiment took its rightful place in the line.

James Wright, who experienced the entire affair, gives his account of the end of the day and conclusion of the battle that did not happen:

"The strain of the last 24 hours had added considerable to that tired feeling the best of men get after three or four days of activity and exposure at the rate of 20 hours out of 24–and we lost no time in preparing to sleep. It was dark; we were in the thick woods; and we were required to remain in line of battle–so there was little room for choice of place or conditions. Men as weary as we were are not apt to be overly particular, and we disposed ourselves on the ground and inside of ten minutes were sleeping soundly–some in half that time."

Camp of the 1st Minnesota Vols.
on Mountain Creek Near Stevensburg,
Culpeper Co. Va.
Dec. 11th, 1863.

Dear Father & Mother:

I have received several letters from you since I have written & I don't know but you will think that I have forgotten you. But I assure you that I have not. There is not a day that I do not think of you all. We have been very busy for the past week and in fact two weeks past so that I could not write. We have moved our camp two or three times and have finaly stoped and built good comfortable quarters. The weather is quite cold but no snow yet. The whole army is going into winter quarters and they are granting furloughs. I will be on duty tomorrow and then I hope to have a little time to answer some letters if we stop here a few weeks. My health is good. I got a letter from you last night dated Dec. 1st. I am glad to hear that you are well. Well I hope to see you all next spring. I will write again in a few days but I must close for the present.

Please accept these few lines with my love to all.

As ever your Son

Edward H. Bassett
Co. "G" 1st Minnesota Vols.

Camp near Stevensburg,
Culpeper Co. Virginia
Dec. 14th, 1863.

Dear Parents,

I believe I have not written to you since about the 25th of Nov. except a line I sent the other day. On the 26th we left camp early in the morn and by sunrise we had got some 3 or 4 miles on our way to the Rapidan which we crossed in the P.M. at Germanna Ford.

Scene at Germanna Ford – Harper's Weekly

About sunrise Genl Webb commanding our Division read a dispatch from General Grant to us stating that he (Grant) had driven Bragg from Lookout Mountain and scattered the rebel army in every direction taking many prisoners &c &c. This was good news and we were glad to hear that our men had gained a victory in the S.W. if we did not gain one here in Va.(Virginia) As we were just starting on an expedition against the traitors it gave me hope that we would be more successful than we had been on some other occasions. On the 27th we marched to Robertson's Tavern on the Orange Court House pike where we found the enemy who skirmished all the P.M. with us. The 15th Mass, from our Brigade was sent forward as skirmishers and drove the rebs about 2 miles when they were driven back themselves by a large force of Rebel Infantry and some Cavalry. Their Lieutennant Colonel who was in command of the Regt. was wounded and supposed to be taken prisoner but has since been heard from at Washington. The 15th we lost several men wounded but none killed. Towards night our regt. was advanced to a piece of woods where the rebel skirmishers were but the rebs fell back about this time and about dark Genl Warren, our Corp commander, decided to advance the whole line and fight that night but as it grew dark it was found difficult to distinguish friends from foes in the thick woods through which we had to pass and the Genl had to give up his plans for a battle that night and we lay on our arms all night. Sat. Nov. 28th, we were up early and got our breakfast and as soon as it was light the troops were put in position and about 8 o'clock we started and marched in line of battle near three miles through thickets of pines and timber all the way. We passed over one line of rebel Breastworks which the rebs had built the day before.

We found the enemy strongly posted at Mine Run and there we stoped for the artillery to come up. It came up before noon but we did not advance that day.

Union Troops entering the village of Mine Run
Sketch by A. R. Waud – Harper's Weekly

Towards night our Regt. went on picket where we had some fun with the rebel pickets fireing at each other to see how near we could come at a range of about 800 yards. They did not hit any of our boys although they gave us some close calls. What damage we done to the rebels I can't tell. They wounded about 20 of the regt. that we relieved but we all came out safe. Here is the only place that I got a shot while we were out (five days).

Sunday Nov.29th – We were relieved by the 5th Corp in the morning and marched to the left flank of our line which rested near New Hope Church. It was rumored that we were going on a Stonewall Jackson flanking expedition but when we got up there we found the rebels were prepared for us and had got a fortified position. We lay in the woods from about 3 o'clock P.M. of the 29th until about 3 o'clock on the morning of the 30th. We were turned out and marched out to the front where the troops were all formed in line within about 30 rods of the rebel forts before it was light. We were to charge the works at 8 o'clock. The 1st Minnesota was deployed as skirmishers about five paces apart and were to drive in the pickets and go as far as they could when they were to stop and wait until the line of battle came up and then fall in with them to charge the main works. The morning was cold and frosty and while we lay there for some two hours before light we had to keep very quiet. We could see the rebels arround their fires and it did not seem possible that we could be where we were and they not open on us. As soon as it got light and they saw our army drawn up in line ready to move at any moment it created quite a stir among them and in a few minutes we could count some 12 pieces of cannon to our front. We also found the works stronger than was anticipated and it appeared that they had received more reinforcements so that it seemed doubtful whether we would be able to drive them back to our advantage. Just at light our skirmish line advanced a few rods and relieved our pickets who were within pistol shot of the rebel pickets. Right on our picket line where Co."G" was stationed stood the house of a secessionist by the name of Joseph Reynolds. He had left the day before and most of the household furniture remained. There was a loom in the house with about 25 yds. of home spun in it and there was large packages of cotton and woolen yarn in the house. Feather beds that would weigh 75 lbs and all kinds of nice bed clothes, two fine clocks and in fact most everything that white folks have in a house besides a good supply of slave furniture. There was a barrel of flour, one of meal, one of Beef that was divided in the Regt. besides about 20 bushels of Potatoes. The boys took everything they wanted and destroyed what was left. We found out about 9 o'clock in the A.M. that the idea of chargeing the works had been given up and we lay there all day expecting they would open on us but they did not and we were relieved at night and went to the rear so we got out of another bad place without loosing any men. If the charge had been made as first intended I don't believe there would be ten men of the 1st Minnesota Regt. came out alive. It was one of the worst places I ever saw and I hope I may never see another like it. I shall never forget the 30th of Nov. 1863. Dec. 1st we lay back to the rear about one mile. Everything was quiet. About 9 o'clock at night we started and marched all night in the direction of the Rapidan which we crossed at Culpepper Mine Ford and made our way back to our old camp. I see that Genl Mead reports that the loss of the army is about 1000 in the whole move. We had some bad weather while we were out and by the time the trains got back into their old camps the roads were almost impassable. We lay arround in our old camp a few days and then crossed over to this side of Mountain Creek where we have built new quarters and I hope we will stop here untill spring.

There has several of the boys came in from the hospital that were wounded last summer. Goodrich is among them. Colonel Adams has also come back. He is very lame and crippled for life. Caleb Jackson starts tomorrow on a fifteen day furlough to Indianna. I tried to get one but will have to give it up without a hearing. One good thing I have not long to stay.

December 15th. All well, a pleasant day and time is passing on. I want to see you all very much but I will have to wait until next spring. My love to you all and write often.

As ever your son,
Edward Bassett
Co. G. 1st. Minnesota

Alhough Edward Bassett mentions the march they began at 9 PM on December 1st, he failed to describe the long, arduous march they made toward Brandy Station. They marched all night, reaching the Rapidan River at Culpeper Mine Ford in the forenoon of December 2nd. They made a crossing and continued on to the camp they left near Brandy Station on November 26th. After marching for nearly 24 hours in rain and snow and slogging through deep mud the entire time, they were totally exhausted. All the while, they toiled onward with anticipation of reaching the comfortable winter quarters they had left behind at their old camp. The thought of having a warm, dry place to rest at the end of the day spurred them on. For a week, they had spent night-after miserable-night in wet clothes sleeping on the freezing ground. Upon arrival they were disgusted and angered to find their cozy huts all burned to the ground and covered with a blanket of snow. This destruction was the depraved work of the ever-present, no-good slackers, stragglers and scalawags who always trailed behind the army but disappeared whenever there was fighting to be done. The next day, after yet another very cold night in the rain and snow, sleeping on the freezing ground they, once again, started building new shelters.

CHAPTER 28
WINTER QUARTERS

All that was gained by the now-completed Mine Run Campaign was an intimate familiarity with the roads, streams and surrounding countryside. This information would prove to be of considerable value to General Meade when he launched a similar, but more successful, campaign the following spring. Efforts to rebuild winter quarters in their old camp soon halted when it became known that the army would be moving again in a matter of days.

The move began just after sunrise on Saturday, December 5th. After marching to within one mile of the tiny village of Stevensburg, they turned towards Brandy Station. Just short of reaching it, they turned off the road to bivouack for the night. The expected move the next day did not materialize and the men were anything but thrilled with their present location. The camp was located on a high ridge with a constant cold wind. The pine forest that bordered the camp promised a plentiful supply of firewood but, was found to be too green to burn. Every endeavor to build a fire failed or resulted in producing little more than a cloud of choking smoke. On Monday, they moved again, this time back toward Stevensburg to a point about 5 miles southeast of Culpeper Court House, only two to three miles from their old camp. Here they would stay. In no time, every man in camp was busily engaged in building new winter quarters. Picks, shovels, saws, axes and any other useful tools were put to use.

The huts were generally about 7-feet by 9-feet and housed four men and, were tall enough to stand up in. Though not spacious or luxurious, they provided a warm, dry place to sleep and take shelter from winter storms. Though available materials were always in short supply, there was no shortage of invention and innovation. Most huts were started by digging a hole of the appropriate size a couple feet deep. Small logs, boards or anything else deemed workable were used to build walls several feet in height. Then a simple wooden frame was erected to hold up the roof, which was usually made from shelter tent cloths. The dirt from the excavation was banked up along the walls to drain water away. With an entrance at one end and a fireplace at the other, this design served well. The fireplace might have been made of sticks and lined with clay or from whatever bricks or stones could be found. Chimneys were extended with wooden barrels when they could be appropriated. When the gaps between the logs were chinked up with clay, the floor covered with a rubber blanket, some rough bunks built and a fire blazing in the fireplace, the huts were quite comfortable, even in very cold weather. By Thursday, December 10th, most of the men were now enjoying the comfort of their new domiciles.

For the next two months this camp would be 'home, sweet home,' but the time spent there should not be misconstrued as leisure. Indeed, it was a time consumed with picket duty, guard duty, road building and cutting trees and hauling logs to corduroy the roads to make them passable in the spring. Building roads in the middle of the winter, with nothing but hand tools, was just plain hard work. Being on picket duty along the Rapidan, where the rebels were just on the other side, was a welcome break from the hard labor. All this work had a purpose. Meade was not pleased that he had failed to mount an attack on Lee at Mine Run and was building a base of operations to renew his effort in the spring.

Christmas came, although camp life didn't change much. Soldiers who came from the east might have received some packages from home with special holiday treats or a gift or two; but for the Minnesota boys, this was extremely rare. They all had a dinner of real beef soup, which was a treat since fresh beef was a rarity. New Years went mostly unnoticed except there was a fair supply of liquor in the camp.

Camp near Brandy Station, Va.
Sunday December 20th, 1863

Dear Father & Mother,

Last nights mail brought me your pictures and two letters all of which I prize very highly. I can't tell you how glad I am that you sent those pictures I have often wished that I had. They both look very natural. I think fathers looks a great deal older than he did when I saw him last. I now have all your pictures. The last one you sent to me of George got broken but I have the other. I am going to get a frame for Elford's and George's as soon as I have a chance. I have a nice double case for Ella's and Anna's.

I am glad to hear that you are well and having such fine weather but I am sorry that you worry so much about me.

There are a great many times that soldiers are enjoying themselves first best and their friends at home are worrying about them and wondering if they are not famishing in Libby Prison (which is acknowledged to be the worst place on earth). If our friends could see us sometimes when we are in front of the rebs I believe they would see that we are enjoying ourselves even there. The boys are as jolly as ever and even on the hardest marches there is most always something to make the time pass more pleasant than a great many suppose. We have learned to endure all the hardships of the Campaign much better than we used to. Every soldier seems to be perfectly at home as soon as there is a halt and I have seen them drinking a cup of hot coffee in less than fifteen minutes after we halted. For my part I have no fears of Libby prison for I calculate to keep out of it but I know I could stand it there as well as thousands have before if I should happen to be confined there.

I suppose you know ere this the reason of my not writing more often within the past two or three weeks. We have got very comfortably quartered now and I will try to write often. My health is excellent and now while most every one has a bad cold and cough I am perfectly free from both.

We have a good supply of clothes and can get all we want. We are also getting a better supply and quality of rations than we have drawn before since last Spring. I think we will stop here all winter although there is some talk of our moving back to the other side of the Rappahannoc River. We have got also a very good supply of reading matter now in the tent. We have Harpers Monthly, Phrenoligical Journal, Washington, New York and Faribault Papers of late date, Davies Arithmetic, Sketches from Life published by the American Tract Society and a number of pamphlets & papers on different subjects. We are also expecting some more books by mail soon so you see we have something to interest ourselves with stormy days and evenings.

O. Brown's Second book of St. Benjamin from the New Gospel of Peace makes lots of sport. We have had no snow yet and I guess we won't have many sleigh rides this winter but next winter look out if all goes right and I guess it will. [128] I think there are a few soldiers that will be free about that time.

Well I have written a long letter and will close. I send my love to you both also to Ella, Anna and Elford

Affectionately your Son

Edward H. Bassett

Co. G. 1ˢᵗ Minnesota Vols.

---

[128] Even though Edward is obviously trying hard in this letter to dispel his mother's concern about his well being, his desire to be home once again with his family shows through.

Camp near Brandy Station–Period Photo–Library of Congress

Camp Near Brandy Station, Va.
Dec. 31st, 1863.

Dear Father & Mother,

I have just come in from picket today. We were out three days and although it rained untill the mud is about 18 inches deep I enjoyed myself as well as I could in camp.

I am well and as hearty as ever. I received several letters from you lately but as I am on duty most every day I could not answer them as soon as I would like. I received a letter from Cuz. Andrew Jackson the other day. He was with the Regt. camped on Lookout Mountain near Chattanooga Tenn. He was well and thinks they will stop there all winter.

The roads are so awful muddy that we have got to build a corduroy everywhere that we wish to haul any loads and there is a large detail out every day to work on the roads. I will have to go out tomorrow at 6 o'clock.

The boys are all well and what live untill their time is out will try old Minnesota for a while before they can see the $402 and 30 days furlough. No re-enlisting in the 1st Minnesota. No temptation to us although it is to some.

There is no news to write about the army and you know that there is nothing else that I know anything about now. <u>Mud, mud, mud everywhere.</u> This year is ending about as it commenced with mud enough to lose any army in if they attempt to move before it dries up a little. I think I told you that I received those pictures. They look more natural than at first. I hope to see you all next spring.

Well I have written enough this time so good night and a happy New Year to you.

Affectionately your Son,

Edward H. Bassett

Co. "G" 1 Minnesota Vols.

The question is; is this the road to Richmond? Well I begin to think the war is about to end and I expect I will be home by the time the grass grows in the spring of 1864. I am well & weigh 152 1/2. There has three of our boys that were taken prisoners at Bull Run returned. Their names are Squires, Potter & Russel. They look well. Health is generaly good. I received a letter from A.G. Ward this morning. He says they are haveing fine times at Forest City with from 15 to 20 of the Company home on furlough. I wish we could get furloughs in our Regt. but it would be easier to go to Richmond for one of us. Christmas with us passed off quietly and I expect that New Years will be enjoyed & celebrated by us in a muster. I for my part expect to be on guard as it is going to be my turn. I hope you may all have a happy year and see the National dificulties settled in an honorable way. Hopeing that this may be the case although it looks rather dark now. I bring this letter to a close.

Your son as ever,

Edward H. Bassett

P.S.   The weather is beautiful being very mild. It does not freeze nights one half the time. We have four months pay due but I don't know when we will get it. I will send you some when I get it.

Camp Near Brandy Station, Va.
Jan. 3d. 1864.

Dear Father,

The army lays about the same as it has been since the retreat from Mine Run. The roads have been in an awful condition for some time but about 4 o'clock P.M. on New Year's Day it turned cold and commenced freezing so that now instead of mud we have frozen hubs & ice to get arround on. New Years was a very dull time with us. It rained until about noon and the mud was of unknown depth.

I see by the Faribault paper of the 23rd that you have snow and cold weather in Minnesota. It would seem that business is very brisk in Faribault by what Brown says. I guess the war does not injure business as much as I had supposed. I am glad to hear it and I hope the Rail Road will be built as soon as possible for it will help the State and secure a better market. There is a considerable talk among the boys about going west onto the frontier and taking claims under the Homestead law but I guess they will be apt to find poor picking there unless they go a great ways for I suppose that there has been plenty of home seekers marching west within the least two years. I hope the war will end soon and then I am sure there would be the most lively times in the west that have ever been known.

Since the army has gone into winter quarters there has been a great many re-enlisted as veteran volunteers. I hear that there is some 23,000 already. They are being furloughed as fast as possible and there is no furloughs allowed to any soldier who has less than one year to serve among those that don't re-enlist so you see there is no chance for the first 75,000 that came out to get a chance to see their friends untill their time is out unless they will enlist as veterans. I think I can wait a few months longer and then I will have something better than 30 days or $402 to boast of. There will not be a man re-enlist from the 1st as long as we remain in Va.

The rebel Cavalry have been making a raid from Fredericksburg arround in the rear of our army but they did little damage and it will not compare very well with General Averill's raid of the fore part of last month.

I expect the mails have been delayed on account of the snow in Wisconsin or Ill. The Luray Mountains which show very plainly from here are covered with snow now and there is a cold wind from that direction.

What kind of a prospect have you for farming next summer. Have you got any ploughing done. Did you save your Sugar Cane and did the seed ripen. Where do you get your wood. I suppose the University timber has played out long ago. There are a great many Questions that I would like to ask you but I will have to wait I guess.

I am well and since the army has settled down for the winter I have been counting the remaining days of my term of enlistment. There has a great many more re-enlisted than it was thought would and there is still going to be a large army after those whose term expires next summer have been discharged. Besides there will be over 50,000 Negroes to take the field. I feel confident that the war will end between now and Sept. next if our army is led by competent officers. Gold in Richmond is worth 2,000 of the confederate notes to the dollar and the Richmond Enquirer of the 23 contains an article recomending the government to call upon the people to turn in their Gold & Silver plates and jewelry to the treasury to restore its credit. In the N.Y. Herald of the 30th Gold is quoted at $1.52 &c &c. I must now close. Excuse mistakes and accept my love to the family.

As ever your Son,

Edward H. Bassett

Co. G. 1st Regt. Minnesota Vols.

Dear Mother P.S.

I had just folded this as the mail came in and I found that there was two letters for me from Mother. They are postmarked Dec. 25th. I am very glad to hear that you are all well and I hope you may still enjoy that Blessing for which Minnesota has been famous. I am pleased to hear that the girls & Elford had such nice times Christmas. I was thinking of them all day and wondering what they could be doing and if I could have done it I would liked to have sent them something. I must thank Anna for them nice socks. They will be very comfortable for this cold weather. Give my respects to John Russell if you should see him again. Also to Hugh Donaldson.

Excuse this P. M. and remember as ever your Son,

Edward

Camp near Brandy Station, Va.
Jan. 12th, 1864.

Dear Sisters Ella & Anna,

I received that nice pair of socks that you sent me by last nights mail, also a long and very interesting letter from Anna dated Dec. 31st. I thank you both for your kind remembrance of me and I hope to be able some day to repay you in some way. Those socks are the best I ever saw and I shall always think of my dear sisters when I see them.

An Advance of The Army of the Potomac – Drawing by A. R. Waud,
Harper's Weekly

I come on duty about one day in seven besides what
we have to do on the roads. The roads are now good so I
guess we won't have to work on them any more.

Times are very dull as it most always is in camp at
this season of the year. (I have made a mistake and
turned my paper over so you will see that I was not
paying much attention to my writing; in fact it is almost
impossible for me to write a letter lately. You must tear
this up immediately).

It has been rather cold so far this year and we had
some three or four inches of snow and several days
were so cold that it did not thaw during-the day. I
expect you have had some very cold weather in
Minnesota. I was out on Picket Friday, Sat. & Sunday
and although the weather was the coldest I have seen
since I left Minnesota I enjoyed myself well and kept
very comfortable arround the large fires that we built.
There was a line of Cavalry pickets in our front so there
would be but little danger if the rebels should try to
make a raid on the picket lines and outposts. I guess

the rebel army will not be apt to trouble us much this winter. I am well and if I was at home I could do a very good day's work or enjoy a sleigh ride.

Please write to me as often as convenient for your letters are always very interesting and although I cannot do justice to them in answer I will try to scribble a few lines in my miserable way. Good by this time.

Your Brother,

Edward H. Bassett

Camp Near Brandy Station, Va.
Jan. 18th, 1864.

Dear Sisters Ella & Anna,

Your kind letters have been received and it gave me much pleasure to read them and to think that I have such kind friends to write to me while I am away down here in old Va. I was very glad to get such long letters and I wish I could write one as long and interesting in return. I mailed a letter to Mother yesterday which you will be apt to get when you get this for I suppose the mails do not go as often this cold winter weather as they did last summer.

Today has been a dark and rainy day and I have been reading and thinking of you all day and talking about Minnesota and the war. I suppose you are haveing fine times at school this winter and I am glad to hear that you have such a fine school. I suppose you are both learning very fast. Anna wants to know if I don't think Mother looks diferent from what she did when I left. I can only judge by the picture and I think that looks very natural. She also speaks of Father wearing spectacles. It must look queer enough to see him with his spectacles on. I don't think I should know him at first. It seems to me that I have almost forgotton how Morristown looked when I left, but I suppose it looks much better now than it did when I left. I got a letter from Uncle Eber the other day and he sent me a Photograph of himself and aunt - - - his wife (Mary) and his little boy - - - I forget the names but Mother will know, to send to Mother. I think they all look very natural. I sent them to Mother in yesterday's mail. I had a very pleasant time when I was there last summer. Aunt got one of the best suppers and breakfasts for me that I have had since I enlisted. I believe she is one of the best hearted women in the world. The picture shows her to be so I think.

I see that you have some fears that I will re-enlist before I go to Minnesota. You need have no fears about my doing anything of the kind. I once thought that I would stay in the army untill the war was ended if it should last 10 years but for certain reasons I have changed my mind and it seems to be the prevailing feeling throughout this Regt. to do their duty faithfuly untill the 29th of April when we will be free and can go into any Regt. or branch of the service that we may choose. I will wait untill I have seen you before I enlist again and then if I think best to try another term of service and the war is not over, there will be as good chances as there are now for Volunteers. It is very dull in camp this winter and it seems a great task for me to write a letter.

I have not said a word to Elford and I thought I must remember him this time. Mother says I will have no little brother and sisters when I get back, they have grown up to be almost as large as I am. I suppose Elford is big enough to do a great deal of work on the farm. I will scarcely know him. I remember just how he looked and I am anxious to see him now and I guess I will next spring. It makes me feel better to get a letter from you than you think. I know that I don't write very long letters but I will try to write often. Remember me to Father & Mother and Elford.

As ever your Affectionate Brother

Edward H. Bassett

Co. G. 1st Minnesota Vols.

P.S. I sent some pictures for Elford a few weeks ago. Did he receive them? They were some that I captured across the Rapidan. *Edward.*

"A Soldier's Dream" – Drawing by A. R. Waud, Harper's Weekly

Camp Near Brandy Station, Va.
January 25th, 1864.

Dear Father & Mother,

I have been thinking of you all day and tonight I thought I would try and write you few lines. I expect it will take a long time for a letter to reach you up in that ice-bound region this winter. I saw a St. Paul paper of the 10th today and from the accounts I should think the weather was about as severe as it was the first winters we were in Minnesota How diferent it is here. Today has been very warm and I could hardly believe it was a midwinter day. I must say that I like this climate although I do not like the soil. If reports are correct we will not have to stay here much longer. The Regt. is to return to Minnesota to Recruit. It being the wish of the Officers to keep up the organization of the 1st Regt. they have used their influence to have us sent back thinking thereby to influence many of the men to reenlist which they will not do while they are here in Va. Some Minnesota men in Washington went to see the Sec. of War about it and he told them that we should go if General Meade was willing and Meade refered it to General Warren, our Corps Commander who signed the papers immediately and they are now at Washington for the final approval of the Sec. of War. I suppose they will get arround in due time and we will start sometime next month. This is the story in camp and I have the word of officers that ought to know for they are as anxious about it as any one. It seems hard for me to believe that we will leave so soon but I hope it may be our good fortune for once at least. However if we should not get off before the midle of Feb. I would not be surprised. I suppose there is a possibility of the whole thing falling through and we have to remain here until April 29th. Even that seems to me like a short time now. There being no prospect of a very early campaign in the spring and our time being out so soon I think the prospect is quite good for us. I expect we will all get furloughs (if we go) after we reach the state so I may posibly see you a few weeks sooner than I ever expected to. All the officers seem to be very confident that we are going. I hope we shall know for certain very soon for it is so unpleasant to be kept in suspense. The weather here for the last few days has been beautiful, mild and the sun shines out so warm about noon that it seems to me that it must be Sept. instead of January. I expect one good cold Minnesota day would freeze us up stiff. There does not seem to be much going on here now. The Christian Commission are haveing quite a revival and hold meetings most every evening. I believe that they are building a house to hold services in each Brigade of the 2nd Div. Our Chaplain is a very earnest man and seems to be thought as much of as any Chaplain that I know of and more than some. He is such a good man among the wounded and sick and he tries to accomodate the boys in every way that he can, being just as friendly and free with a private soldier as with the officers. Health is very good in the Regt. now there not being as many men with bad colds as there was. We have got the best camp in the Brig. the best houses I mean and our camp is kept as clean as any in the army. I will venture to say the commanders are very strict and that is one reason why health is so good I suppose. There is a grand display of Broad-cloth and Gold lace up arround General Webb's Hd.Qtrs. most every day. He was a Captain on Genl Hooker's staff at the battle of Chancelorsville and now he is a Brigadier Commanding the 2nd Div. of the 2nd Corps.

It will seem strange enough to me to leave the field and go among folks again. Although we have some very hard times here and there are many things that seem hard to endure, I cannot help feeling a strange kind of attachment to the life of a soldier, although I know I will enjoy my freedom and the society of my friends better than I ever did or can enjoy myself in the army.

Tuesday January 26th,

It is a warm and very pleasant morning. I think this is the most beautiful weather that I ever saw this time of the year. Our camp is in a very sightly position, being on a high ridge that extends across from Pony Mountain to the Luray Mountains. Culpeper is some six miles due west from us and when it is not smoky we can see the spires of the churches. We have a fine view of the Luray Mts. The snow is all gone from them now but they are often white with snow when we have had only rain here.

Well I don't know as I can write any more now so I will close. I hope we may see Minnesota again next month. It takes a great while to get things done here sometimes and we are not sure of anything untill after we get it. We live on hopeing and perhaps we will be rewarded sometime.

Please write to me as often as you find it convenient and accept this with my love.

As ever your Son   *Edward.*

You must not be disappointed if we do not return to the state before April. After all that has been told us there may be some deception and the Genl may not think we can be spared now for there are a great many men to go home that have re-enlisted and you know it would not do to allow the army to get too weak while they are in front of a large force of rebels. For my part I feel perfectly contented as long as we stay here if we are realy needed. It is but a short time to the 29th of

April.   *Edward.*

Camp Near Brandy Station, Virginia
Feb. 3d. 1864.

Dear Mother,

The weather is very good although for the last 24 hours the wind has blown very hard. I wrote to you some time ago that there was a tolerable prospect of our being sent home to recruit but that soon played out and we expect now to stay here. There were a lot of officers sent to the state to recruit but I suppose they will have hard work to find recruits for this Regt. I don't want to go to Minnesota now untill we can be discharged. I am well and as stout as ever since I enlisted. Health is good throughout the Regt. Tell Father not to forget to write for I would like very much to get a letter from him.

The President has made another call for troops and he seems to be determined to clean out the rebels next summer. I suppose now there will have to be a draft in Minnesota and some that have been waiting may find they are the ones that old Abe wants. They had better volunteer and get the bounty. Have Wm. or George Soule enlisted. I heard they had. Well time is wearing away and the three years are fast comeing to a close. Accept this with my love to all

Your Affectionate Son

Edward H. Bassett.

Co. G. 1st Minnesota Volunteers

Thursday 4th. All well and quiet this morning. It froze quite hard last night.

After a great deal of anticipation and speculation, the War Department ordered the First Minnesota to return to its state to be mustered out of service.

CHAPTER 29
HOME AGAIN!
HOME AGAIN!

On February 4, 1864, the wild rumors that were circulating through the camp were confirmed and jubilation turned these serious, young soldiers into giddy, joy-filled gadabouts. The Regiment would be leaving on Friday morning, February 5th. The prospect of returning home to their families and loved ones after nearly three years of war was almost too good to believe. Many a service-roughened hand reached up to brush tears from a weatherworn cheek. Hearts were filled with both joy and sadness at the same time, with the realization that returning home also meant leaving the brothers they had fought beside in so many life-and-death struggles. Perhaps the most difficult part was going through the camp to say goodbye to old friends, knowing they would never see them again. Everywhere, men gathered to wish them well and a safe journey home.

There was much to do to make ready. Personal belongings had to be packed, haversacks filled with rations for the trip, uniforms brushed and cleaned and all the other insignificant details that would help hurry the day along had to be attended to. With the exception of their guns, haversacks, canteens, knapsacks and accoutrements, all government property needed to be accounted for and turned-in to the Quartermaster. The last things to be returned before leaving camp were the tent cloths that covered the roofs of their shanties. The sound of excited chatter could be heard coming from many huts long after midnight.

On February 5, 1864, the unit left its camp near Stevensburg and Brandy Station for the last time and began their journey home. The men, who were up long before dawn, stood for roll call and then proceeded to make breakfast and tend to the last of their preparations. It was still dark when they were ordered to form in-line and proceed to General Webb's tent at Division Headquarters. Suddenly, from out of the dark, came the music of a brass band and they were surprised to discover the entire brigade was formed, under arms, to salute them. General Webb expressed his sincere regrets at loosing such an outstanding group of fighting men and congratulated them on their splendid service record. The band of the 82nd New York paraded them out of camp as flag bearers of their comrade regiments stood in salute at their passing. With throats choked with emotion and hearts pounding, they marched across the bridge over Mountain Creek and on toward Brandy Station. No one seemed to notice how cold the morning was except that the ground was frozen hard and they were not marching in mud. The glory of this new day and new beginning was soon heralded by the rising sun as it lifted the curtain of darkness to reveal a land cloaked in a mantle of glistening frost.

The men waited anxiously for the train in the crisp morning air at Brandy Station. When it finally arrived, it surely did not offer much more than a ride. The only thing good that could be said of the ride in the dirty, unheated, seat-less freight cars was that it was better than walking. Once again, they retraced a route over which they had so often marched and fought, the spectacle of the war-ravaged land offered little to help pass the time.

By late afternoon, the weary travelers had passed through Alexandria and were soon comfortably quartered at the Soldiers' Rest in Washington. The 200-plus men who left camp would here be joined by others of their regiment who were out on detail when the regiment left. In Washington, all the wounded from the regiment who could travel would also join the trek homeward, this would bring the number present to a little over 300 men. Soldiers' Rests, or Retreats as the men called them, were large complexes hastily erected or commandeered in major cities during the war to provide a place of shelter for troops in transit. They were clean and provided decent food and a comfortable place to sleep. The Soldiers' Rest in Washington was actually the U.S. Soldiers Home, which was commandeered by the government for the duration of the Civil War and converted into a sprawling, temporary housing facility for troops.

"Soldiers' Home Washington, D.C."
from a color lithograph by Charles Magnus – 1868
Library of Congress

In the morning, passes were issued and most of the men spent some time in the city. The afternoon was consumed with an inspection, drill and a dress parade, where it was announced that the senators and representatives from the state, along with numerous other notables, would present the regiment with a grand banquet. The event would take place at the National Hotel, one of the finest in Washington. It was an affair none would forget. The 309 men of the regiment entered the dining room to a sight they could not have imagined. Long

615

rows of tables stood heaped with every imaginable eatable. The hall was lavishly decorated with evergreens, flowers, flags and banners. A rousing cheer rang forth as Colonel Colvill, still suffering from the wounds he received at Gettysburg, was carried into the room. Fifty dignitaries, including the Vice President, were there to pay tribute to the survivors of 'The Senior Regiment' of the army. After devouring a sumptuous dinner, the regiment was showered with accolades as speaker-after-speaker came forward to honor them and their fallen brothers. It was an evening of celebration and revelry that could scarce be imagined by these plain fellows from the frontier. It was well into the early morning before the last toast was held high and the men returned to the 'Rest.' It was decided at the banquet that Colonel Colvill and all the wounded men who were able would return with the regiment to Minnesota. What a grand thing, to be coming home with all who could travel!

After only a few hours sleep, the boys had breakfast at the Soldier's Rest, packed their belongings and filled their canteens with fresh coffee. All was ready before the cars arrived and they waited anxiously to resume their homeward journey. Again, they were disappointed to find the cars provided were just boxcars with just a single coach car in the train. Rough boards had been installed across the cars to form rudimentary seats. Undaunted, the men climbed aboard and set off for Baltimore. They were jostled about in the cold cars onto railroad sidings and switches and waited for hours before they finally were underway. It was dark when they rolled into the yard in Baltimore where they were, once again, shunted from one track to another, spending the entire night in the cold cars fretfully trying to sleep. On Monday morning, February 7th, the train pulled out of Baltimore en route to Harrisburg, Pennsylvania.

The trip was anything but a comfortable in the cold, drafty box cars. The rations the men carried in their haversacks were nearly gone and no opportunity to replace them developed. Finally at Harrisburg, they boarded a train with heated coach cars and genuine seats, although no meals were available except from peddlers selling their wares. Still

616

hungry, but at least warm and comfortable, they rode on and arrived in Pittsburg just before dawn on Tuesday. An hour's stop allowed the men to stretch their legs and at last, to get breakfast.

Railway Station in Harrisburg, Pennsylvania. Library Of Congress

A telegram was sent ahead in hopes preparations could be made to feed the men and dinner was waiting for them to purchase in Alliance, Ohio. After passing through Fort Wayne, Indiana, where they ate supper, they arrived in Chicago at dark, here, they accepted the invitation from a committee that had boarded the train earlier, and spent the night as the first guests of the newly completed Soldiers' Rest. By the time they left the train, formed up and marched to the Soldiers' Rest it was 11 PM. The night was quite cold and a storm appeared eminent. After receiving a hardy welcome and enjoying a sumptuous meal served by ladies of the community, they retired in the early morning to get a few hours sleep. It was not yet light when they marched back to the railway station in a brisk wintry wind, blowing in off Lake Michigan. Due to some mix-up, there were no railcars, engine or train crew on hand to carry them on. After some delay, cars were arranged and the men left the depot in passenger cars attached to the rear of another train.

The storm that was threatening the previous evening had now become a reality. As the single engine struggled along with its greater burden, the snowfall became very heavy and drifts began to cover the tracks. The men's hopes of being in La Crosse by night were beginning to fade. The howling wind piled the ever increasing snowfall into deep drifts in every railway cut or sheltered spot and another engine was sent to help pull the train. At times, the train halted while the front engine was unhitched and plowed ahead to break a path through the drifts. By dark, the storm became a full-scale blizzard and progress was very slow. It was now intensely cold and a thick coating of ice covered the coach car windows in spite of the two large, wood-burning stoves in each car. Prospects began to look dim. It was now the sixth night of their journey and the men were all extremely tired but conditions did not accommodate sleep. They played cards, sang songs and generally did what they always did—they made the best of the circumstances they found themselves in.

☀ THE BATTLE OF LITTLE ROUNDHOUSE (OR... THE SKIRMISH AT PORTAGE STATION)

It is generally accepted that the last engagement in which the First Minnesota was involved was at Mine Run, but that is not entirely true. An account by James Wright revealed an encounter that was to become their "last battle."

Before morning was near, even the most optimistic among them realized that they were now at a standstill. With the wood supply for the stoves nearly exhausted, the cars were getting cold. Morning light brought with it another rude awakening. They were sitting on a railway siding near a tiny station at Portage, Wisconsin and the engines, trainmen and the train pulling them were all gone. They had been left behind when the going got too tough to pull the added load. This realization did not sit well with these homesick veterans, who simply did not take kindly to being dropped off like excess baggage without warning or notice. It was bitterly cold, the wood for the stoves was gone and there was little, if any, water or food left. If their commanding officer was informed that they were to be left behind, no one heard of it. Foraging parties, sent out to inspect their situation, discovered that the tiny station was in the middle of open prairie and was locked up. In the windblown snow, it was impossible to see for any distance. However, a large water tank and a woodpile were found, at least they could rekindle their fires and get a drink of water. Rummaging through their haversacks produced the makings for coffee and a meager breakfast with nothing left behind but crumbs and lint.

Late in the morning, the wind had died down some and the Stationmaster and telegraph operator arrived, opened the station and built a fire. The telegraph lines had been blown down somewhere and several hours passed before any communication could get through. The station keeper and telegraph operator seemed indifferent, and even resentful, of inquiries as to why the men were left in such a condition. Lieutenant Colonel Adams finally got through to the railroad officials but received the same standoffish response, *"They didn't know why the men had been delayed and if they had any means of moving on, they should do it."* Even this irritating response was only extracted by use of authority. The Army contract was not being honored and this irresponsible handling soon brought relations to a breaking point.

The officers talked things over and concluded that abandoning the soldiers without transport, food and adequate shelter, constituted the creation of a 'military necessity' under which they were granted full authority to seize whatever supplies and transportation they deemed necessary. The officers demanded of the stationmaster and operator to know what the condition of the rail line was and what was being done to provide transportation. The peevish reply was, *"All we know is that the regular train has left La Crosse and is headed this way bound for Chicago."* The decision was made that when the train arrived, it would be forced to turn around and convey the soldiers to La Crosse. To insure compliance, the men piled railroad ties across the track as a roadblock. This action seemed to rub the stationmaster against the grain, evoking his vehement protest. Well, he was probably just doing his duty as he saw it, but confronting a few-hundred armed, veteran soldiers who were being delayed on their first trip home in three years was an ill-advised move. He was promptly confronted by an armed guard, placed under arrest and 'jailed' atop of a huge snow pile near the station. When the telegrapher responded in like manner at further inquires, he was treated likewise. Not long thereafter, the sounds of the approaching train could be heard and, by the time the whistle sounded as it neared the station, all the men were out watching along the track.

The train rolled to a stop and the engineer was instructed to turn his engine around and hook up the soldiers' train and take them to La Crosse. When he refused, he was given the choice of complying with the orders and returning to La Crosse with his engine or joining the station men on the cold snow pile. Since his engine was going back to La Crosse either way, after brief consideration he wisely consented. Even a fool would realize that at warm engine is better than a cold snow pile. A guard joined him in the engine while it was taken to the nearby turntable and turned around. The 20 passengers in the cars that had just arrived from La Crosse did not think much of this situation. However, when their conductor informed them that another engine would be sent for, they decided to stay with their cars and wait at the station instead of going along with the soldiers. When all the men were back on the cars and the engine was hooked up, the prisoners were released with apologies for their rough treatment, though they did not fall on forgiving ears.

Things were looking much brighter now as they clattered along the tracks in the bright sunshine. Even though the temperature was still below zero outside and the frost on the windows prevented watching the snow covered landscape, home was getting closer with every chug of the engine.

It was dusk when the men reached La Crosse—some 30 hours later than planned. The train proceeded to the Mississippi River, about a mile west of town, where the soldiers were to board sleighs for the trip to St. Paul. Due to the very late arrival, the teams, drivers and sleighs had gone back to La Crosse and across the river to the village of LaCrescent to take shelter and await their passengers. Word was sent to summon the sleighs while the men stood waiting in the crisp winter air without the advantage of proper clothing. The sleighs had been arranged for by Captain Russell Blakely, superintendant of the Northwestern Transportation Company. He was a man of patriotism and insight who had anticipated the men's needs. In short order, a caravan of large bobsleds pulled by teams of stout horses arrived. These were freight sleighs with a wood box that had been filled with straw, planks placed across the box provided seating and piles of buffalo robes assured a warm ride. With 22 men in each sleigh, they set off across the mirror-smooth ice on the river. Forgetting the difficulties of the last few days, the boys laughed and sang as the ride became somewhat of a frolic. Within an hour, the joviality died out and the most of the exhausted men fell asleep huddled in the straw and warm robes. The horses moved swiftly along in the clear star-studded night, arriving at Winona in about three hours. The men awakened as they approached to see a huge bonfire out on the ice welcoming their arrival.

Stiff and cramped from the cold, the men hastily dismounted and were surprised to be surrounded by a very large crowd of people who were cheering them and welcoming them home. Somewhat overcome at this outpouring, they formed up and marched to a large warehouse along the river bank. The doors were flung open to reveal long rows of tables set with mountains of food of every imaginable kind. Little time was wasted on oratory. A few welcoming remarks were followed with prayer and, then, everyone was invited to eat. The nearly-starved men, while trying to be courteous to the ladies attending them, tore into the food with ravenous fervor. The banquet went on until nearly 3 AM when the men began

621

to make preparations to bed down on the floor but another surprise awaited! Arrangements had been made to house all the soldiers for the night in the local hotels and in the homes of the local citizens. A night's sleep in a real bed for the first time in nearly three years was a surprise beyond expectation! At this announcement, the men were given permission to go wherever they wished but they were to be ready to leave again at 9 AM.

The morning of February 13th was bitterly cold and very windy. The sleighs were late in arriving and the caravan was finally ready to leave at 10 AM. Orders had been given that Company K, the Winona Company, was granted a furlough and was to remain in their hometown. One can only imagine the cheering reception this news evoked.

Edward's diaries fill in the details of his trip home from Winona, as related in later years by his youngest son, Morton Bassett, in the small volume he wrote in 1961.[129]

"Part of the regt. started early the next day, but G Co. waited until after dinner. The drive to Minnieska took us until dark. Stayed at the hotel there at night.

A show in town and a dance afterwards kept us up until midnight. The next morn we drove to Wabasha, where we stopped to feed the teams, then to Lake City, where we got our supper. Then on to Red Wing. There at 11 PM. we filled again the inner man with a fine banquet. At the Methodist Church, we spread our blankets on the floor and slept for two hours. When we were ready to start the ladies again insisted that we eat some more. Leaving Red Wing at five in the morning, we drove to Hastings where we met the Regiment. After dinner we started for St. Paul arriving there at three PM.

---

[129] "From Bull Run to Bristow Station"

The citizens gave us a grand reception. Governor Miller, General Sibley and the Mayor welcomed us back, with some nice speeches."

The arrival at St. Paul on one of the coldest days of the winter was heralded by a grand ovation; thousands came out regardless of the cold to welcome 'their boys' home. After another huge banquet, the men marched to Fort Snelling where they were comfortably quartered. Furloughs were given so that they could all go home to their families before reuniting again to be mustered out of the service.

Edward's Diary records:

"The Company was furloughed as fast as possible. At three in the afternoon (Feb. 16th) we went to Hastings, and stayed at the Fremont House over night. The citizens payed our Hotel bills. We left in wagons, early in the morning, for Faribault. Dinner was served to us at Northfield, then on to Faribault, where we arrived about seven in the eve. Father and several of the neighbors were there to meet us. Stayed at the National Hotel, where the bills were again settled by the local folks.

Feb. 18th Left for Morristown about eight o'clock, in sleighs and reached home at noon. Hurried home to see mother, the girls and Elford. They have grown so much that I hardly knew them. I am tired, for it was a hard trip."

"Home again, home again ! *I slept in my old bed last night, and feel some better this morn. It looks dreary out doors. I wish the trees were growing and the flowers in bloom. I almost wish I was back in the old camp for a few hours.*

Feb. 21st I went to church in the afternoon, the first time that I have attended since 1860. There was a dance down town last night, but I dident go."

From February 18th until March 16th, Edward enjoyed getting reacquainted with his family and friends. Doubtless, he also spent some time tramping the woods that he so dearly loved and often mentioned in his letters home. The time must have passed quickly and it was soon time for him to leave again to rejoin his old comrades for the last time at Fort Snelling and await his last day in the service and be mustered out.

Diary entry:
"Left home on the 16th (of March) *and went to Faribault where the Company is to assemble. The ladies gave us a fine supper, then a dance in the hall until three in the morning."*

Ed Bassett wrote the following letters after rejoining the regiment following his long-awaited reunion with his family in Morristown. How good it must have felt to be "BACK HOME."

Fort Snelling, Minnesota
March 20th, 1864

Dear Sister Anna:

I suppose you remember that I promised to write you when I got up here and I hope you have remembered your promise to write to me. I find that there has been a great change in things here since I was here before. The day that I left home I only got as far as Faribault where the company met and took wagons for Snelling. The ladies of Faribault gave us a splendid supper in the evening after which there was toasts and speeches with some singing until about 11 o'clock. Then those that wished went over to the Hall

624

and danced untill 3 o'clock. I enjoyed myself first rate. At 9 o'clock the next AM we started on our way stopping at Northfield for dinner. We stopped at a place about 16 miles from St. Paul at night, called Rose Mounds. (Rosemount) The next day we reached St. Paul about noon and stoped at the Temperance Hotel for dinner. Then we drove on up to the Fort. The weather was very cold all the time but the roads were good. We have very good quarters now although we have not got things as good as they will be next week. There are a great many recruits here that are going away Monday and then we will have more room.

I am well and feel first rate although I will not have quite as good a dinner as I did last Sunday. (Turkeys are not very plenty). I don't know what will be done with us yet. There is some talk of furloughing us again soon but I guess it is all talk, although we may be furloughed. I will be back again as soon as I can get a furlough or discharge. The weather for the last few days has been so awful cold that I have almost wished that I was down in old Virginia. If it don't get warmer I want to have you say that I may reenlist as then I can go down where it is warmer. Please write soon and remember me to all.

Your Brother

Edward H. Bassett

Co. G. 1st Mn. Vols.

The time spent at Fort Snelling during the remainder of their enlistment required very light duty. Passes were freely issued allowing the men to relax, and perhaps visit with friends or go into the city to explore and look for entertainment. After all the hard duty and fighting they had seen, it was a well-deserved reward.

Fort Snelling, Minnesota
March 26th, 1864

Dear Father and Mother:

Thinking perhaps you would like to know what is going on up here I will try and write you a few lines. Soldiering up here is a different thing from soldiering down in old Virginia. I had no idea that I would be as contented here as I was down there.

There are a great many recruits here for the different Regts. but they are being sent off ever day and I expect that as soon as the Mississippi opens there will be a general cleaning out. It will not be long before the boats will be running at the rate the ice is going away now. Work is progressing on the R.R. finely. They are doing some very heavy grading around the Fort and up towards Minneapolis. The abutments for the bridge across the Minnesota River are built and I think very likely the cars (trains) will be running by next winter. Some of the boys of the Regt. have re-enlisted. There are some 60 of them in all I believe. Bounties and promises of commissions are plenty but some of the boys laugh at them. For my part, I have no more notion of re-enlisting now than I had when I was at home. I was down to St. Paul the other day and had some Photographs taken. I will get them next week and send you some. We have nothing to do but run around. I can get a pass most any day but it is rather dull business here. Our rations are plenty but of a rather poor quality, still they are good enough for a soldier. There was some talk of our being furloughed but there is no prospect of anything of the kind now. We will remain here until the 29th of April.

I think our mail is lost somewhere. The boys are all well & feel first rate. I will get a furlough if I can in April and be there to help you a few days but there is no telling for certain. We may be kept here all the time.

I heard that the smallpox was up in Rice Co. I hope it won't spread in Morristown.

Respectfully your son,

Edward Bassett.

Fort Snelling, Minnesota
Sunday, April 3d. 1864.

Dear Father and Mother,

Everything is quiet up here. The ice got out of the Mississippi yesterday so that the ferry commenced running. The boats have been running up as far as St. Paul for several days. Recruits continue to come in. There was about fifty Negroes brought up yesterday. I expect there will be a company of them formed here and sent to Dixie land. There was five of Co. G reenlisted but they have mostly been promised good positions. Charles Parker has gone in and he will he sure of a commission. If the boys felt sure that the war would not last more than one year longer they would every one reenlist for the bounties that are now given. I know I would not hesitate one minute. They get over $300 down including back pay on the old bounty of $100. For my part I think that the war is likely to end in one year. The 6th Regt. is going south this spring and I should not be surprised any day to hear that the 8th Regt. had orders to go. There is a report here now that the 1st is going up to establish a new military post up on Devils Lake. If they do go up there I believe they will stay in the state one year if not two. I hope the war will end before then.

You say the stock is all doing well. I am glad to hear it. I was thinking that feed would be rather scarce when it was so cold but I guess now that the grass will commence growing by the first of next month. I am glad to know that the Oxen are doing well. I always considered them cheap, although I knew nothing about what stock was worth. I suppose the sheep are all right although you say nothing about them. I think wool will be worth from .75 to 1.00 during the summer.

I was down to St. Paul the other day and got my pictures. They are rather dark but I will send you one. I think I will get some more in a few days. I am going up to Minnehaha Falls now so I will wait and finish this tonight.

Well I went up to the falls and have got back. The Ice is not quite all gone yet but the falls look quite pretty. I go out onto the prairie a mile or so most every day. It is so dull here in the fort. Some of the boys have taken their guns and gone up the river and shot some Geese & ducks. They are quite plenty and I long to get back home so I can have fun shooting a few of them. Wages are going to be very high this summer. They are paying two and three dollars per day now on the river.

My time is growing short in the service and I am glad of it. I believe I can enjoy one summer at home.

As ever your son,

Edward Bassett.

Sometime between April 3rd and 15th, Edward returned home to help on the farm before going back to Fort Snelling to be mustered out.

His diary records:

"I wrote out a furlough for myself and asked Colonel Adams to sign it, which he did without any delay. I am going home by stage to help father sow some wheat.

At home in Morristown this fine day, April 15th, I plowed all forenoon that day and finished up at dark on the 19th. The 20th I sowed ten acres of wheat and got done about dark. Left home on the 21st of April for Fort Snelling. Stayed at Farmington, eighteen miles from the Fort. I walked up to the Fort the next afternoon.

April 28, 1864. Cloudy and cold. At a review of the Regiment in the afternoon, Gov. Miller and Gen. Sibley made short speeches, and Colonel Adams bid us an affectionate farewell. He said that he had orders to disband the Regt. The Vets who reenlisted and recruits are to be formed into companies, officered and sent on to Washington for duty. Due to a mix-up somewhere, I reckon, we were not paid off and discharged until the afternoon of May 5th. It was late, so I stayed over at the old Fort and went home the next day."

On April 28th, the last review of the much heralded First Minnesota was held at Fort Snelling. Governor Stephen Miller, the first Lieutennant Colonel of the regiment, addressed the men followed by Lieutennant Colonel Charles P. Adams.

The following is an excerpt from the speech of the latter as included in Lochren's "Narrative of the First Minnesota Regiment."

"Officers and Men of the First Regiment: The time has arrived when the organization of this regiment must be broken up. Three years ago you rushed from the peace and tranquility of your firesides, at the call of the President, to meet the traitors whose hands had trailed our glorious flag in the dust at Sumter. You came from the hillside and valley, the city and the plain, with brave hearts and strong arm, to shed your blood in defense of your country's honor. You were the first three-years' regiment in the volunteer service. Then you were a thousand strong, but stronger in your love of country and devotion to its flag. The promise of your organization has been more than fulfilled in the glory of your achievements. Your deeds have a world-wide renown. The battle-scented breezes from Bull Run, Edwards' Ferry, Yorktown, West Point, Fair Oaks, Peach Orchard, Savage Station, White Oak Swamp, Glendale, Malvern Hill, Chantilly, South Mountain, Antietam, Charlestown, Fredericksburg, Marye's Heights, Bristow Station and the immortal field of Gettysburg have wafted them to the most distant climes. The seal of your blood was stamped upon all of the twenty odd battlefields emblazoned on your flag. The blood of more than seven hundred of your companions has crimsoned those heroic fields, and more than two hundred and fifty of them have passed from the smoke and clangor of battle strife to their eternal bivouac beyond the skies. Let the memories of these three years' associations, the common dangers and trials we have shared, be cemented in the mutual blood we have shed, and cherished with a true soldier's pride. Forget and cast into oblivion all the little piques incident to the service. Let these lie buried forever. Officers and soldiers of the First Minnesota Regiment – heroes of more than twenty battles! I now bid you an affectionate farewell. Never again will you all assemble until the reveille at the dawning of eternity's morning shall summon us from the slumber of the grave, to pass the review of our lives before the Commander-in Chief of the armies of the skies. May a merciful Providence direct you, and crown you here with earth's brightest honors. But however brilliant may be your future, you proudest boast will ever be, "I belonged to the First Minnesota".   Farewell."

The next day, April 29, 1864, all the men whose terms had expired were mustered out of the service and the story of this distinguished regiment was brought to a close.

Renowned for its unsurpassed valor in battle and unfaltering devotion to duty and country, the regiment shall always be remembered as an example unexcelled in the annals of American warfare. Certainly worthy to be called:

THE FIRST MINNESOTA, SECOND TO NONE!

Edward returned home to the family farm and spent the summer and winter helping his parents and engaging in some farming of his own. The years he spent in the service were difficult times on the frontier. Drought was the prevalent summer condition during the majority of that time. 1864 proved to be another year of the same. Weather conditions were peculiar during the spring and provided little rainfall and very warm temperatures followed by only small amounts of scattered rainfall. The temperatures went from one extreme to another. There was widespread concern that the state would not get enough of a crop to provide food for its inhabitants. Water levels on the Mississippi River were the lowest in recorded history, making commerce on that lifeline of the Midwest difficult. Prices were high on any supplies that were brought up the river. As the summer progressed, many areas saw the fields dry up and wither with little rainfall amid frequent periods of blistering hot sun. In other areas, sufficient rainfall to save the crops often came just in time. For many people in the western part of the state, the problem became catastrophic when the skies filled with huge swarms of grasshoppers that descended on their fields, ate every green thing in sight, and left only stubble behind. The Bassett family and their neighbors struggled just to make enough money to survive.

After all the excitement of fighting a war, living the rather-mundane life on the farm was a difficult adjustment for many returning young men to make. When it became nearly impossible to do anything to help the family, even with great physical exertion on the farm, many began to go back to the army. At least there, they could make some money to send home.

After nine months at home, Edward, like so many others, decided to re-enlist. His son, Morton, mentions his Father's decision.

"Dad was very uneasy and dissatisfied over the summer work on the farm. It was pretty tame after the strenuous campaigns and battles of the previous years. So he reenlisted in the First Minnesota Heavy Artillery this time. No more hoofing it for him. This is very evident by the following note taken from his diary:"

"What a fool I was to try and raise wheat, or do anything last summer. I came out $136.00 in cash and one year's labor behind. This besides some $30 that I owe. That after a hard summer's work, and the fall and winter spent for nothing. I am compelled to enlist in the Army, where I think that I had better stay."

At the age of 23, Edward H. Bassett, was once again off to war. On February 9, 1865, he enlisted and was mustered into Company L of the First Minnesota Heavy Artillery on February 21st and promoted to the rank of Sergeant on February 25th.

A new adventure begins. . . . . . .

CHAPTER 30
THE HEAVY ARTILLERY

The loss of his and his father's crops, after all the labor and cost that went into them, was a heavy blow to Edward and his family. He often mentioned in his letters about neighbors selling out while he was away in the army and now the reason is clear. After a long stretch of winters with a great deal of snow and intensely cold temperatures, a change in weather patterns brought mild winters in 1860, 61 and 63. For nearly five years, the spring and summer months brought drought-after-drought and with so many men gone to fight, labor costs were very high. To make matters worse, as the war began to wind down the government's demands for supplies diminished and the war-driven prices of agricultural products dropped rapidly. The falling prices of wheat, corn, wool, beef and all other farm products made it extremely hard to make a living on the small farms. Then, as men returned home at the end of their service, there was more labor available than jobs, and wages were poor.

Edward's decision to return to the army was likely due to financial necessity. Bonuses, in the form of bonds, were offered to entice volunteers. Many veterans of the old First Minnesota Regiment jumped at the chance when Colonel Colvill announced that he was forming a new volunteer regiment of heavy artillery. Colvill was highly regarded by the men he had commanded, so, when the word got out that he was looking for men to join a new unit that did not require all the marching, they came from all over the state to join up.

After signing the enlistment papers on February 9th, Edward spent the next week saying goodbye to friends and neighbors, and then set off again for Fort Snelling. He mentions these and following events in his diary:

"Spent the week running around and going to parties. The time passes very slowly for me since I got back last May. I hope I will not return again until times get better than now. We left Morristown for St. Paul on Feb.16th. Stopped overnight at Northfield. Then on to St. Paul where we were examined and given our uniforms. We were mustered in the next day, the 26th, at Snelling and started for Dixie. We went by sleigh and stopped overnight at Cannon Falls. In the morning we got an early start and arrived at Oronoco that night. (A small village about 10 miles north of Rochester) At two AM we drove on to Rochester by wagon. Then by rail to LaCrosse where we arrived at nine. We traveled about one hundred miles – twelve by wagon, fourty by sleigh and fifty by rail."

Edward's letters from this time on, with a few exceptions, reflect his writings in his diary and provide a fairly-thorough look into his daily life in the Heavy Artillery in the Deep South. The regiment consisted of 1,700 men formed into 12 companies of 140 men each, not including officers. This occurred at a critical time when Confederate General Hood had reorganized the armies of the South and Southwest and was believed to be preparing to move against Chattanooga, and then Knoxville, with intentions of joining forces with General Lee. The heavy concentration of artillery in the shadow of Lookout Mountain in the forts of Chattanooga had to be protected at all costs. If Hood were to gain these positions and the huge cache of supplies, the outcome of the war might be greatly delayed. Edward, now a Sergeant in Company L, found the duty too uneventful and dull to suit him. They were not engaged in any fighting while in Chattanooga and never got to fire the guns in their charge. The 87 men, who the regiment lost during its service, all died of disease, mostly fevers.

Some diary entries that offer other insights not found in Edward's letters to his family are included.

Diary entry:

"We lay in LaCrosse all day and boarded the night train for Milwaukee and Chicago. In Chicago we were quartered at the soldiers rest, where we had super and a chance to sleep. Next day after breakfast I got a pass and went to the Hospital to see Curtis Ward. He was so sick however that the doctors allowed no visitors. The next morn we rolled on to Indianapolis and stayed at the Soldiers Home. I started to look the city over but the mud was so deep I turned back."

LaCrosse, Wis.
March 1st, 1865.

Dear Father & Mother,

I am now on my way to Nashville and we are stoping over here one day. I and all the boys that enlisted with Parker have been assigned with Co. L. of the Heavy Artillery. We left the Fort on the 26th and arrived here last eve about 9 o'clock and were expecting to take the morning train but were disappointed and will now leave this eve at 8:30. I am well and think that I will get along first rate. I will send my Certificate of Muster with this and would like to have Father see that the Bonds are issued and taken care of.[130] When I write again I will know something

---

[130] These were bonds issued by Morristown to pay the bonuses offered the soldiers to enlist. They were to be payable at the end of the term of service.

about what we are going to do.

I will have some pictures in St.Paul, when I send the money for them & I will send you some.

Please excuse me for the present and I will write again when we get settled. With much respect I remain as ever your Son,

E. H. Bassett
Co. L. 1st Regt.
Minnesota Heavy Artillery.

Nashville, Tenn.
March 7th, 1865.

Dear Parents,

The Co. to which I belong arrived here last evening and are now quartered in the Zolicoffer House, the largest Hotel in the city. It is an unfinished brick and there are some 6,000 men quartered in it now. We left Louisville yesterday about 7 o'clock and had a very pleasant time comeing through. From here we will be sent to Chattanooga as soon as the R.R. bridge can be repaired, which have been swept away by the recent freshet. (Flood) The streams are very high and some houses have been swept off. We may have to remain here for a week or more. The City is crowded and we are not allowed to run arround much. The weather is quite warm today but there is a fine breeze. Most of the boys are well. C.D. Ward was left at Chicago very sick with the typhoid fever. He was crazy for several days most of the time. Wm. Adams was sent to the hospital here last eve and I hear that he has been sent to Wisconsin this morning to the General Hospital at Prairie du Cheine. When you write direct to Co. L. 1st Regt. Minnesota Heavy Artillery, Nashville Tenn.

I am enjoying myself well and am in a Co. of good fellows. There are 4 of the old Co. G. boys here.
As ever your son

E. H. Bassett.

Chattanooga, Tenn.
March 12th, 1865.

Dear Father & Mother,

As we have finaly come to a halt I will try & write you a few lines to let you know where I am. We arrived here about 9 o'clock on the evening of the 10th and are now camped about ½ a mile from the Chattanooga Depot & about 80 rods from the Tennessee River. The Regt. is all here now I believe and I think will stay here for some time. Co. L. is to have a small fort to garrison here and I expect we will take possession tomorrow. Co's. A. B. & C. have been here all winter and look well. I saw Dr. Coe yesterday. He looks first rate.

We were a long time comeing down here. We left Snelling February 26th and arrived here on the 10th of March. We lay one day at LaCrosse, one at Millwaukee, one at Chicago, one at Indianapolis, one at Louisville & four at Nashville. I like the place very well and I think it will be healthy. We have a fine view of Lookout Mountain and the Tennessee River. My health is good & I calculate it will keep so although we have had rather poor rations most of the time.
Please direct to Chattanooga.

As ever your son,   *E. H. Bassett.*

View of train depot at Chattanooga, looking toward Lookout Mountain with the Army camp in the background. Leslie's Illustrated Weekly

Chattanooga, Tennessee
March 27th, 1865.

Dear Sisters Anna & Ella:

Thinking that you might be pleased to receive a line or two from me I will endeavor to gratify you both by writing a short letter. It is now 2 o'clock in the morning and all the camp is sleeping, except the Guard. The weather is quite warm and there are strong indications of rain.

We have very comfortable quarters now. When we first came here we camped down in our shelter tents but it was not many days before most of the boys had lifted lumber enough to fix themselves up quite comfortable. There is quite a number of buildings being built arround here by the Government for the purpose of boarding the men that are working in the diferent mills and shops. Now the way we would get our lumber would be by going out at night and steal it from the buildings and then we had to be very sly for there is always plenty of guards watching every board. One night there was about 25 men went out and while one stepped up and talked with the guard the rest of them picked up a load of boards & walked off.[131]

It is very dull soldiering here I tell you, not much like the Army of the Potomac. I have wished several times that I was where there was more stir (action) than there is here. I hardly ever leave camp except on duty. There is nothing worth seeing in town and there is no chance to go out into the country if I wanted to. There is a Rolling mill about 20 rods from our camp where they make R.R. Iron. I go down there once in a while to see them work. I manage to kill time in some way and that is about all that I can do. We commenced drilling on the big guns last Sat. I think I would like it very well as soon as I understand it a little better. We received orders to turn over our fort to Co. A. today and the prospect is that we will move soon. I can't tell where we will go but I hope we will move out of here before long. We may go to Knoxville. I heard today that Richmond has been evacuated by Lee and Old Abe helped to hoist the Union flag over the City. I hope it is so. I feel confidant that the war will end this summer and I think that by the time that my year is out the country will become quite settled.

Your Affectionate Brother,

Ed. H. B.

Direct to Battery L. 1st Minnesota H.A.
Chattanooga, Tennessee.

---

[131] Lumber and supplies were not always made available from government stores on the basis of need. Graft and corruption played common part. These veterans had long ago learned the need to exercise the—"midnight requisition."

Photo of a Heavy Artillery Battery – Obviously a posed photo, the men are all dressed in full dress uniforms, note the white gloves. Though this is not in Chattanooga, it is included to give the reader a sense of what a heavy artillery battery looked like. Photo from the National Archives–Public Domain.

FROM UNITED STATES SANITARY COMMISSION

Chattanooga, Tenn. 1865
Monday Eve. April 3rd

Dear Parents,

Richmond has fallen – Petersburg is evacuated and the Union still exists–traitors are whipped and the war

640

is about to end. General Grant has routed Lee and will soon use what little there is left of him up. We received a telegraph dispatch here today to that effect and at sundown there was a salute fired from the forts around town and tonight the soldiers can be heard cheering in every direction.

The weather is getting quite warm and the trees have commenced to leaf out. Health is generally good and we are haveing very easy times. Lieutennant J.G. Parker joined the Co. on the first. inst. He reports 19 inches of snow in Minnesota when he left and the weather mild.

I am looking for some word from Minnesota every day. All the boys from Morristown are well. The Company is all split up now or will be soon. I leave tomorrow morning with 24 men for Kingston, a small town some 150 miles up the Tennessee River. We are going up to cut timber and logs for the use of this Post (Chattanooga). There are a great many Gov't. buildings going up here and the timber has to be cut & rafted down here, where it is sawed. I expect we will have a good time & I hope we will stay there all summer. I saw James Hand today. He looks well and says he is enjoying himself well. Dr. Coe is here and doctors all our boys when they want anything. The Paymaster is expected around among the old companies soon and then the boys will have some fun.

I never had such an easy time as I am haveing now. It is almost too easy for good health but I guess I can stand it. This is not much like soldiering with the Army of the Potomac. We belong to the Post Garrison and think we have a good thing for a time at least.

I don't know as I shall write very often after I get up in the woods but I will try to write one letter for every time the mail goes out, which will be once in ten days. I never enjoyed myself better than I have since we came down here. I wish that I had enlisted for three years in the place of one and gone into the Cavalry.

There are a few guerrillas around the country but they are not very strong and will play out if the war should end.

I believe I wrote to you about the death of William Adams. We have lost three men in all I believe since we left Minnesota. I will now close hopeing to hear from you before long. Remember me to Elford & Ella & Anna.

Respectfully you son

Edward H. Bassett

Battery L, 1ˢᵗ Minnesota H.A.

Chattanooga, Tenn.

You need not think I am out of paper because I use this. I thought I would show you what they were doing. The U.S. Sanitary Commission here gave away some 15 barrels of sour kraut today to the Soldiers besides quantities of other things. They are doing a great deal of good everywhere.

Diary entry:

"On the 17ᵗʰ (April) I took my mule and rode up to the mouth of the Emory River and back. Stopped at a southern mans home by the name of Centree and looked around his yard. Had a chat with his daughter, who seemed to be a fine Gal, except that she was strong Pro-Southern. She thought the Confederate cause was right and that slavery should be perpetuated for the benefit of the Negro. In the PM we crossed the Clinch River and called on a good Union man by the name of Clark. He has a fine place, as it is with every place that I have seen in Tennessee. Everything is about fifty years behind the times. They seem to think that if they get ten or twelve bushels of corn or wheat per acre, they are doing well.

I went up town in the eve and found that the rumor we had heard the day before was true. Lincoln and Secretary Seward had been murdered. Every one that I saw seemed sad. There is great excitement on the streets. On Tuesday, the 18th, I left about eight AM, I followed the London road about seven miles, and then turned out into the country. After traveling about three miles, I was in the Mountains. It was about as rough a road as I cared to travel on. However, I made out to get thru and reached Camp about two PM.

April 19th, 1865: Clear and pleasant. I helped finish up the Lieutenants shanty and built me a bunk. Still nice weather the next day. I took a walk down the river in the PM. On the 21st we finished hauling for the raft. We are going to float a raft of logs down to the dam. Lieutennant Daniels came up from Kingston with eight days rations, the balance for April. Lieutenant Hussey went down to Kingston. I enjoy looking the country over, so I roamed down river about four miles. April 24th was cold. The Lieutenant came back from Kingston about noon, and brought a lot of mail for Company L. I received four letters, the first I have received since I reenlisted. We sent a raft of 175 logs down to the Dam."

Big Bend, Tenn.
April 24, 1865

Dear Sisters,

Your letters of April 4th & 6th were received by me today. I am glad to hear that you are well &c. I am still in the wood & haveing a good time. The weather is very mild & pleasant. We have no chance to get any war news and consequently it seems very dull. I went down to Kingston one week ago today & stayed two days. I fairly hate this country it is so rough & the people are the poorest and most ignorant set of beings that I ever saw for whites. Most all that owned any property were rebels and if we find a good Union man he has been robbed of most everything since the war. I have a very easy time and any day when I choose I can go four or five miles into the country and visit the farmers.

All the young ladies take snuff & smoke & chew tobacco, dress in homespun & live (like every one else here) on corn bread & bacon. They are very handsome & would make a fine appearance up north.[132] I have not seen a cook stove in a single house in Tenn. yet & I have been in more than 100. More than 3/4 of the houses are miserable log huts and a shingled roof is as rare a sight here as a brick barn in Minnesota. As near as I can find out there is not a news paper in this settlement and you will never see any books in the houses except an old worn out Bible or a pack of cards. There was an old Baptist deacon comeing in here last week but I guess he got lost. There are two churches in Kingston but no preacher. One church is used for a cow yard and the other is laying idle. Kingston is one of the oldest towns in the state and was once the Capitol of the state. It is now a rather rusty looking place. There are a few Yankees in there now keeping store and they appear to be doing well. They sell goods much cheaper than they were sold in Minnesota last winter. It is reported here that the Indians have broke out in Minnesota again & that 6 Companies of the R.A. (Regular Army) are ordered to the State. I hope we will not be one of the 6. I would rather stay here all summer than not. You must have had a hard storm there from what I can hear. I received a letter today from Mother dated April 6th.

There is some talk about enlisting in the Regular service here and I guess there are quite a number of

---

[132] A comment obviously meant in jest.

the boys will go into it if there is a chance. They would most likely be sent onto the western frontier and would have a good chance of taking a homestead when their five years were up.[133] I guess your letters have not all come through yet. I was never enjoying myself better in the world than I do up here. Health is first rate up here but there is considerable sickness down at Chattanooga. I heard today that Curt Ward was dead but I guess it is not so. He has been very sick at Chicago. Write soon & remember me.

Your brother,

Ed. Bassett.

Roane Co. Tennessee
April 26, 1865

Dear Mother,

Your letter of the 6th was received on the 24th and I assure you I was glad to hear from you. I am well & enjoying myself as usual. We are encamped in the woods about 150 miles above Chattanooga on the Tenn. River.

I would much rather be up here than down with the Co. We have plenty to eat up here and but little to do. The country is miserable & rough and the people poor and ignorant. There were mostly Union when the War broke out and they were forced to go across the mountains to Kentucky where many of them joined the Tenn. & Kentucky regiments. I went down to Kingston the other day and had quite a good time for a couple of

---

133 Soldiers that enlisted in the Regular Army were given the opportunity to homestead land in the west. They gained clear title to the land after 5 years if they "proved up", meaning made improvements including a house, on the land. Their enlistment for 5 years would expire at about the same time they were granted their clear title.

days. There were a few of our boys left there for guards and I went all arround through the country. The town is small & old. I think that the first state legislature met there.

We hear no war news any sooner than you would in Minnesota, here. I have not had a chance to read the particulars of Grant's & Sherman's moves this spring and if peace should be declared you would know it sooner than we would up here. The boys are all very sad about the assassination of the President and would shoot any man down that would say that he was glad of it or rejoiced over it in any way. I hope that peace will be declared soon and it will be as soon as it can be obtained in the right way. I will enlist for life rather than give one inch to rebels.

You speak of it not being as healthy down here as in Virginia. I think that up here where I am now stationed it is just as healthy as in Minnesota or Virginia either but I would hate to have to stay in Nashville or Chattanooga this summer. I should think there was going to be a chance to raise something in Minnesota this summer if you have some rain but I suppose wheat is not worth more than 30 or 40 cts. per bushel now and it will be still lower if the war ends and peace is declared. I am glad to hear that them bonds are issued but it seems to me that they have not issued them as they agreed to, but I guess it will make no difference. They are rather poor things anyway. You may keep them for me if you will until I return and perhaps I may sell them sometime.

I shall be glad to hear from you all at any time and you must write often and I will write once in a while.

As ever ...Your Son,

E. H. Bassett

Battery L. 1st Minnesota H. A.

Chattanooga, Tenn.

Dear Sisters Ella & Anna:

I have received several letters from you within the last few days. Our back mail has finally reached us. I am glad to hear from you and that you have a prospect of summer for I know that you must be tired of the long dreary winter. We have not had any very warm weather here as yet but the trees are all fully leaved out & apples & Peaches are as large as hazelnuts. Most of the farmers have their corn planted. I suppose you have all heard of the capture & killing of J.W. Booth, the man that shot the President & the surrender of Johnston's Army. The prospect seems to be fair for the war to end before the 4th of July and the troops may all be sent home by next August. We have orders to quit logging and return to Chattanooga where the Regt. is stationed. I hear that Gov. Miller & Colonel Colvill have been there and there is some talk that the Regt. will be sent home for duty on the frontier. I hope they will. The war is about over and I feel anxious to get back north.

I was out to a party last eve. It was a dance and we had some fun. There were some 7 ladies there in all and I should judge that they would be between the ages of 25 and 50. They all chew & smoke Tobacco. They know nothing about dancing except a kind of old fashioned jig reel and were considerably amused at the way we conducted a dance. They think they have some great violin players here but when they hear one of our players they say he beats anything that they ever heard. They say that we-uns don't play as you-uns do & we-uns can't dance as you-uns do. They want to have us come up again some evening if we have time & I guess we will if we stay here long enough. I would not go two rods to go to such a party up north but you know that soldiers must try in some way to kill time and wherever they can spend a few hours and have a little excitement there they will go.

I was down to Kingston again last week and got quite a lot of mail from you. Before this reaches you I expect we will all be back to the Company at Chattanooga.

Please write often and remember me as ever your brother. . . *Ed.*

Chattanooga, Tenn.
May 10th, 1865.

Dear Sisters,

We were ordered down some time ago and are now camped in Chattanooga with the company. I had quite a pleasant time comeing down and enjoyed the trip very much. The Co. moved camp since I went away and they have a very-pleasant place now with comfortable quarters. All the talk here is about going home. Some think that we will start in a few days others think we will stay all summer. The war is ended now and we will be apt to be discharged as soon as they get arround to it.

There are lots of Rebel prisoners comeing in here every day. There were several hundred came in here today and the Military Prison downtown is stored full of them tonight. Most of them are willing to take the Oath & go to their homes acknowledging themselves a whipped community. The telegraph brings the news of the surrender of another Rebel General Dick Taylor and his men. It also states that Jeff (Jefferson Davis) and his few followers are closely followed and stand a slim chance for escapeing. I wish that I could have one shot at him. I think I could cure him of all his trouble in a short time.

Health is generaly good here I think if Soldiers will take care of themselves. I think I can go out West somewhere now and feel contented after I get my discharge and the <u>war is over.</u> Soldiering is about played out with me I think although I have had some idea of joining the regular army after I got out of this.

I am so sleepy that I can hardly write but I will have to stay up for a while because I am on guard. I have been making some rings that I will send to you in this letter. They are rather rough being the first and only ones that I ever made. Some of the boys make very nice rings but I am too poor a workman, that you all know. I want you both to write often and write all the news. Tom McClary the preacher from Morristown was here the other day. He is one of the Christian Commissions Chaps. I did not see him for he left the day before I came down.

I send three rings. The white is made of clam shell taken from the Tenn. River above Kingston and I send it to Ella. The black one is made of Guttapercha and the sets are the same as Ella's ring. The other is a laurel ring and was dug on the mountains of Tenn. I send it to Elford. Please write soon and often.

I remain as ever your Brother. . .   *Ed.*

The black ring is for Anna.

Diary Entry:
"May 13th.   I went up on Lookout Mountain and rambled around all day. The weather was fine and I had a good time. Sunday the 14th was very nice. I was on guard duty. We received the news of the capture of Jeff Davis and family. The next day, May 15th, very pleasant. The Rebels are still coming in every day."

Chattanooga, Tennessee
May 18, 1865

Dear Parents,

I am enjoying myself as usual although it keeps rather dull here now for me. There are a great many rebels comeing in every day. They are mostly from Johnston's Army and are on their way home on parole. They seem to he glad to get home although they hate to see their slaves free and soldiering for Uncle Sam.

There is considerable excitement here now about the Indians who have commenced murdering the inhabitants on the frontier. There are a Great many men in the Company that have families living out on the extreme frontier and they are very uneasy about them and would give anything to be back to Minnesota.

Period Photos: Views on Lookout Mountain: Courtesy of Library of Congress

I have a much better opinion of this place than I had before I went up the river. It is in fact a very pretty place for a town although it has been ruined by the army. It is all dug up and fortified so that it would take some fighting to carry it if well garrisoned. I went up on Lookout the other day and got a fine view of the surrounding country as far as the eye can reach and also the works of the rebels on the mountain. There are some large caves that extend a long distance under the mountain and I intend to visit them sometime.

We have not received any mail for several days. I don't know what the trouble is but I think that the high water is the cause.

Don't you think it is a rich joke on Jeff Davis the way he was captured? I wish he had been shot. There is nothing very exciteing going on except the talk among the boys about going home and the army being disbanded. They contend that the war is over and they are in a hurry to get back. Cal Jackson is as happy and jolly all the time as he can be and seems to enjoy himself most when he can be joking some of the homesick drones. I hope there will be something done to bring the Indians to punishment soon.

I will now close sending my best wishes to you all.

Edward.

Chattanooga, Tenn.
May 23, 1865

Dear Sisters,

There are lots of <u>rebel soldiers</u> passing through here every day. (Surrendered Confederates) They are mostly Kentucky and Tennessee troops and came from most all parts of the states. <u>I saw one fellow Saturday eve that was at Yorktown, West Point and Fair Oaks in 1862 and Gettysburg in '63.</u> He was right in our front at the three last named places. They acknowledge that they are badly beat and the Confederacy is done up and they are willing to go home and behave themselves. They say that they were deceived by their leader and as they are such an ignorant class of people I think they were.

The war is now ended and most of the Volunteer force will be sent home right away. There is a great deal of talk among the men already. There is some talk of enlisting in the regular army for five years. I don't know how many there are that will go in but I guess there are some in most every Co. I see an account of the death of Serg't. Pence of Co. B. 8th Minnesota Vols. in the Faribault paper. I have not heard from any of the boys of the 8th nor any other Regt. since I enlisted. I think they will most all get home during the summer.

There has been two rebel officers killed downtown within the last 4 days. The first one was killed by one of his own men, the other was stabbed by a Union soldier from Michigan. The rebel was boasting that he was not whipped yet nor could not be, he said that he would go in again to fight the North if he could get an opportunity. There happened to be a soldier standing by that has served some 18 months in the Libby prison at Richmond and he took his knife out and struck the reb. killing him instantly. There will be many a reb. drop if they don't keep quiet. I talked with one rebel officer that lives near Murfreesboro and had a hand in tearing up and destroying the R. R. between there and Nashville at the time of the last battle there, the time that the 8th Minnesota was there and Captain Petit was sent out to repair the road and guard a train through.

Well I have written all I can this time.

Your Brother,

Ed.

Diary Entry:

"May 20th, rained most all day. I went down town in the eve and had a long talk with a lot of Rebs that were on their way home. Most of them seemed willing to return to their homes and become peaceable, law abideing citizens. Saw seven that I had fought against in Virginia. One man in particular, was at Yorktown, West Point, Fair Oaks, Seven Pines and Gettysburg. There were between 1500 and 2500 rebels left town on their way home, during the day and night."

Chattanooga, Tenn.
May 27th, 1865.

Dear Parents,

I was glad to hear that you were not driven from the country by the Sioux. We have had all sorts of stories here about the depredations being committed in Minnesota by the Indians but I guess there is but little truth in the reports that we hear.

Times & things are about as usual here. I never had better health and I live entirely on government rations. The farmers bring in Butter & Eggs some and there is a tolerable supply of Onions, Radishes & Lettuce to be had by those that want such things and as soon as Apples & Peaches are ripe I think there will be an abundance of them to be had for money. There was a Brigade of Cavalry came in town yesterday. They were a part of General Wilson's Command and had been through from the western portion of this State down towards Mobile destroying any amount of rebel property & Captureing Jeff Davis & Co. They were a hard looking set and were about one third of them dressed in rebel grey and more than one half of them were mounted on mules, their horses haveing given out on the way. They were going on to Nashville where they expected to be mustered out & sent home.

I don't think there would be much trouble to get enough men for the regular Army if there was only a chance to enlist from present volunteer forces. I hear today that the Paymaster has arrived to pay off some of the troops. I don't know as we will get anything. I am sorry to hear that Mother is sick. I hope she will recover soon.

Edward

Chattanooga, Tenn.
June 3d. 1865.

Dear Sisters Ella & Anna,

There is nothing going on here to make soldiering very pleasant. There has been a lot more of General Wilson's Cavalry comeing in for the last two or three days. They are a rough and ready set of fellows and have seen some hard times. I was out on Mission Ridge the other day and saw where our troops charged the rebel works on the summit of the ridge and drove the rebel army into the valley beyond. I saw some places where there was some very hard fighting and many of the trees are badly scarred up from the effects of bullets fired from both sides. The ridge is very long and high and was a splendid place to post an army.

Now that the war is about over the talk is all about going home but I guess we will spend the summer down here. The weather is quite warm and it approaches the hot order some days along about noon. The farmers have commenced to fetch in vegetables and some fruit such as cherries, Blackberries and Squashes, which they sell for all they can get. Butter is worth 60 cts. per pound and such butter it is A-#1 and will last well. Eggs are scarce oweing to the hens haveing quit laying since the organization of the Southern Guerrilla bands but they have commenced again since Jeff and his army have been captured and they will soon be plenty & cheap no doubt. I hear that Gold & Silver is plenty but I have not seen any of it. I did hear something jingling like silver the other day as an old farmer drove past but I was unable to find out whether it was Silver or the chains on his gear which covered his mules except their ears. I think he must have had some silver for he would not stop where there were any soldiers. I guess he knew his "Bis". I think I would like to live here in this country after the war is over and things get fixed up as they were before the war. The climate is more mild and I can't see any reasons why it should not be healthy. I am sure of one thing and that is that it would be a fine country to ride down hill in the winter if there was as much snow as there surely is in Minnesota.

(The remainder of this letter is missing.)

Chattanooga, Tenn.
June 7th, 1865.

Dear Mother,

I am glad to hear that things are comeing on so finely in Minnesota this summer. You speak of hot weather there and we have had some days here that might be called warm, although no warmer than some I have seen in old Virginia when we were marching every day.

My health remains good and I find use for full rations of Uncle Sam's fodder every day. Last Sunday I went out into the country about six miles and went to a Negro meeting in the State of Georgia. Some crops look well out in the country. Wheat will be ripe in two or three weeks, some Corn is ten inches high and Potatoes have commenced to blossom. There is an abundance of fruit this year. Blackberries are very plenty and have commenced to ripen. I had all I wanted today. The farmers bring them in and sell them for 20 & 25 cts. per qt. Cherries and milk are the same price, Buttermilk sells for 15 to 20 cts. per qt. Most all the people in the county are very poor and just barely live.

Amaziah Eddy is very sick tonight and I am siting up with him. He has a severe attac of the Bilious fever but I think he will soon get over it now Dr. Coe has been prescribing for him. He will be sent to the Genl Hospital today where he can have better care. I don't think it is dangerous but you must not let any of his folks know that I said anything about him. He will have the best of care and there will be no reason in their worrying about him. All the other boys are well.

I would like to see you all this summer if it is convenient but I can't tell how it will be.

Write often.

Ed.

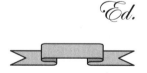

Hd. Qtrs. Battery L.
1st Minnesota H. Artillery
Chattanooga, Tenn.
June 10th, 1865.

Dear Parents,

Things are going on here about in the old way except that I have to record the death of two of the best men in the company. A. Eddy from Morristown and a man from Waseca Co. by the name of Gilbertson. Eddy died on the eve of the 8th.[134] He was taken to the Hospital the day before. He was very sick and was crazy all the time. The Doctor told me that he had no hopes of ever geting well although they done the best they could for him. He tried hard to drive the fever off and kept up and arround as long as he could before he would give up. He was burried yesterday with military honors. As we were going to the funeral yesterday we heard and saw a heavy explosion of ammunition down in the lower part of the City which proved to be a Govt. warehouse where there was a quantity of captured ammunition stored and although there was three fire engines there they could do but little and the buildings were burned down. Most of the Ammunition being fixed or charged, the pieces of shells fell thick and fast all arround killing some & wounding others. By sundown the fire was burned so low that there was nothing but smouldering ruins which were a great curiosity to many of the soldiers who gathered arround to see how shells and other combustibles looked after being burnt. Some of the men were careless enough to pick up Shot & shells that were nearly red hot. While many were stiring up the ashes and ruins just about sundown they happened to come onto a large pike that had not exploded but they were all charged and nearly red hot so that by stiring them up a little they commenced to burst and there soon followed two of the heavyest explosions of the day. As the curious soldiers were standing arround thick there was a good chance for some more broken heads than there had been before but luckyly there was but four or five killed as near as I can find out besides some that were wounded. The man of our Co. who was killed was struck in the head by a piece of shell that flew from a shell that he (or another man who was killed at the same time) were examining. He was burried today and I think it will be

---

[134] One day after Edward had set up all night with him.

a warning to some so they will not be quite so curious next time as to risk their lives in such a place. The fire is supposed to have started from sparks that flew from a locomotive that stood on the track. I have not been down to the fire but I expect it is a black looking place. I had no desire to be down among the things not considering a renewal of old acquaintance at all desireable since the war is over. It was mostly rebel ammunition that was captured here by Generals Thomas, Hooker & Sherman.

There has been some talk about our being sent to Minnesota this summer but we have gotten no orders that will touch any men in this Regt. except Companies A.B.C.& D. who have some men whose time expires between now and October next.

Blackberries are ripening fast and they have commenced to bring in some Whortleberries.

All the boys from Morristown are well now and getting along finely. The Dr. called Eddy's case Bilious Fever and I think they were about right although I think that it was inflamations in the bowels that carried him off so suddenly. I can assure his friends that they have the sympathies of the whole Company for he was liked by all and was one of our best soldiers. I heard from Wm. Soule yesterday. He was doing well now although he had been somewhat unwell for a few days.

Please excuse me this time.

Edward

Battery 'L' 1st Minnesota Heavy Artillery.
Chattanooga, Tenn.
June 19th, 1865.

Dear Sisters:

The weather here is very dry and hot but I stand it

first rate. I was out in the country yesterday thirteen miles which made some ten miles into the State of Georgia. Blackberries are plenty and I got all I could eat. I never saw better picking and they are very nice. Apples and Peaches will soon be ripe and they are very plenty.

There has been four Companies of the Regt. have been mustered out and started home. The companies are A.B. C. & D. All men whose time expires before October 1st are ordered to be mustered out immediately. You speak of there being an order issued to discharge the artillery. There has been no orders issued yet that will effect us. The 11th Regt. are on their way home now I expect. We are going to move our camp over to the place that Co. "A" has left. It will be better on some accounts than it is here where we are now but we will not have quite as good a chance to trade with the Farmers for vegetables and fruit.

Good bye for the present.
Your brother,
Edward.

Chattanooga, Tenn.
June 22nd, 1865.

Dear Mother,

We have been changing camp over into Co. "A" place. It is called Fort Mihaltzy, a rather queer name I think.

I don't think the ladies of Morristown had better give up their preparations for a good time on the 4th because the soldiers are not going to get arround in time. They had better go on and show their good will at least. Tell Cal's folks that he is well and all right but wants a letter every day and looks for one.

The paymaster is here and we will be paid off tomorrow and I will send for my Photographs. I suppose you must have heard of the death of Amaziah Eddy by this time. He was the fourth one out of the load that I started with from Snelling, a rather unlucky load I think.

Accept this with my love to you and Father.

Remaining as ever your Son,

Edward H. Bassett

Battery "L", 1st Minnesota H.A.

Chattanooga, Tenn.
Sunday P.M.
June 25th, 1865.

Dear Sister Anna,

We have moved our camp from Fort Phelps which is on the south side of town to Fort Mihalotzy, which is on the east side of town. We are now near where we camped when we first came down here. I like our present camp about as well as any camp I know of arround town. It lays well up and we can look right down onto town. The weather is very warm and we need rain very much.

You say that Mother wishes I was there to weed the garden. I think she would be sadly mistaken if she expected me to weed the garden if I was there for I am so lazy that it is all I can do to eat when I am hungry. The facts of the case are, I have given up the idea of ever working and there is no use of talking about it.[135] If I was going to cultivate the garden I would take a yoke of oxen and a Harrow. You say that Father's birds have nested in the grove. I don't know what birds you mean unless it is the Geese and if they have gone to nesting in trees I think they must be expecting a flood and you had better begin to pack up and make arrangements accordingly. You seem to think that you have some smart young ladies in Morristown. Now I have no doubt about that at all and besides being smart they are very handsome but there are few that can compare with some of the

---

[135] Edward's sense of humor is intact.

Southern Belles that I have seen and if it were not for the habit of chewing and smoking tobacco some of them here would be hard to beat anywhere, allowing me to judge to which I know you would have no objections as you cannot see the fairys here to judge for yourself, and a soldier's opinion on such subjects is about as good as his word which everyone knows the value of. I am very glad to hear that you are about to complete your education and I am happy to learn that you are improveing so fast, knowing that you are endeavoring for obvious reasons to be prepared to welcome home some young and gay volunteer Viz-a-vie, J e r i m i a h . (likely a reference to some young man of interest in the army) You have my best wishes for your success and I hope to be present at the happy meeting. I would like to have been there and went to the camp meeting. I expect you girls raised particular thunder with the Dutch. I will know when I get a paper.

Blackberries are very plenty yet and one of the boys in my mess has just brought in some three gallons of very nice ones. Whortleberries sell for 25 cts. per qt.

The army is being reduced very fast and I think most of the volunteers will be discharged during the summer. Most of the men in my Co. are very anxious to get home before harvest.

Excuse me this time and write often accepting this with my respects to all.

Your Brother

Edward H. Bassett

Batt. "L" 1st Minnesota H.A.
Chattanooga, Tenn.

Chattanooga, Tenn.
July 7, 1865

Dear Sister,

661

The weather is so very hot that it would be impossible to write in the daytime so I have to take the evening for it. The 4th was dull enough here with us. There was no public doings and about the only excitement I heard of was among the Negroes. They had a kind of Picknick during the day and at night they had a prayer meeting in town. There was an effort made to get up some fireworks but they did not amount to much on account of the danger there would be of starting a fire among some of the Govt. Store houses. At noon there was a National salute fired from the 100 Pdr. Parrots (100 Pounder Parrot Cannons) on Cameron Hill that was all the fireing I heard. I must say that it was about as dull a Fourth as I ever knew. I often thought during the day (which was one of the hottest) what times there must be in the north and when I look back it seems to have been my luck to have kept rather sober and quiet on the Fourth always, but I intend to make up for it all sometime.

I wish you would send me a copy of your composition on old maids. I would like to see if you have changed your mind from what it was last summer. Please send me a copy. I expect that the gals are having everything about their own way there this summer but it will be diferent soon for there are lots of soldiers going home soon and they will not find it so easy a matter to carry the day as it is now. You say that your teacher gave you some subjects. I should think she did. (Old maids), well they must be subjects sure enough and taken in connection with (Old Batches). I think you ought to have got up some matches. Well perhaps you did. You will let me know won't you? I am glad to know you have such a good school. You are improveing in writing very fast. I hope you will continue to practice and improve for it will be worth a great deal to you to be a good writer. I would give most anything to be a good writer. It would be worth money to me here in the Army.

Remembering me as ever

Your brother Edward.

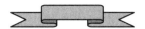

Diary Entries:
During this time Edward was the Acting Commissary Sgt. for Battery L. It was his responsibility to draw rations and keep records of them. These lists were copied in his diary:

Rations drawn for five days for Battery L, 1 st Minnesota Heavy Artillery, July 1, 1865.

Pork . . . . . . .188 lbs.	Candles 6		
Hard Bread . 100 lbs.	Soap	19 ½ lbs.
Fresh Bread .98 loaves	Salt . . . . 18 lbs.
Beans . . . . . . .36 lbs.	Pepper . . . . 3 papers
Rice . . . . . 24 ½ lbs.	Vinegar . . . . 5 gals.
Coffee . . . . . 38 ½ lbs.	Fresh Beef. . . . . . 306 lbs.
Sugar. . . . . . 73 ½ lbs.		

Turned over to the Commissary 292 lbs. of hard bread and got a receipt for same.

Edward H. Bassett

Acting Commissary Sgt. L Battery

Rations drawn for Battery L, 1 st Minnesota H. A. for ten days commencing July 6, 1865:

Pork . . . . 371 lbs.	Candles . . . . . 11 ½ lbs
Hard Bread . . 970 lb	Salt . . . . . . 38 ½ lbs
Beans . . . . . 74 ½ lbs.	Pepper . . . . . ½ lbs
Rice . . . . 49 ½ lbs.	Fresh Beef. 615 lbs
Coffee . . . . . . 79 ½ lbs.	No. of men 99
Vinegar . . . . 9 ½ gals.	No. of days 10
Soap . . . . . . 39 ½ lbs.	

E. H. Bassett
A. C. Batt. L

Chattanooga, Tenn.
July 10th, 1865.

Dear Mother,

I am glad to hear that you are geting along so well and have such a fair prospect for good crops.

The weather is very hot and dry here. I was out into the country some 8 miles yesterday. Blackberries are very plenty and apples are geting so that they will do to commence useing. We could buy all the vegetables and fruit we wanted if we had a little money but as it is we go out into the country and gather it ourselves. Peaches are very plenty and have about got their growth. Some have commenced to ripen. It is so dry and hot that corn leaves roll all up and I notice that the vines and plants in the gardens drop flat onto the ground toward the middle of the day. If there is not rain before long I don't think the corn will amount to much.

I can't enjoy soldiering now as well as I used to when we were moveing about the country continualy although I have a much easier time now than ever before in the army. William Soule has rejoined the Camp. He has been up the river on duty for some two months. The boys that were up there all look well and say they have had a very good time.

Respectfully your Son

Edward Bassett.

P.S.   In reference to those Town Bonds I would like to ask a few questions. What right had the Town to issue those bonds payable one year from Sept. 1865 when they should be due in one year from the 9th of February, 1865. I don't understand why they were issued in that way. If I remember right at the Town meeting they voted to give the bounty of $300.00 for each volunteer to fill their quota under the 1st call and for that purpose they issued Bonds not to exceed $300.00 for each payable in one year at twelve per cent interest. Now I hold that they had just as much right to date those bonds and make them payable one year from January 1st A.D. 1900 as to do the way their have done if I understand it right. I would like to have Father explain the matter to me if he can.

Chattanooga, Tennessee
July 14th,1865

Dear Mother,

    I was out into the country seven miles yesterday on a kind of foraging expedition. Two of us went out on mules and got all the Berries and Apples we could fetch in. I went up what is called the Chattanooga Valley. I saw some nice Apple and Peach orchards and some very good looking farms for this country. I saw Sugar Cane that was in the blossom and Corn silking but I don't believe it will average any better here than it does in Minnesota

    You don't seem to believe in my witching for water.[136] I knew there would be plenty of water there if we could only have rain enough to fill up that hole. I hear that land is on the rise in Minnesota and there is a prospect of lively times soon among the farmers. I think it must be fun to sell wheat for 50 and 60 cents per bushel now when it would readily brought $1.10 to $1.50 last fall and Winter.

    I am well as usual and so are all the boys from there.

As ever you Son   *Edward H. Bassett*

---

[136] A method for locating water sources under ground by using a willow or other flexible forked stick and holding it straight out in front of yourself then walking slowly forward, if you cross underground water the stick will begin to vibrate and the end will move downward toward the ground. This method has been used for centuries and is still practiced today.

Chattanooga, Tenn.
July 26th, 1865.

Dear Sister Anna,

Try and get as good an education as you can with your limited advantages and when you are older you will be glad of it and the better you are informed the better you can enjoy life. I think that the most pleasant time I ever saw was when I was about Elford's age and if I could have had a good chance then and improved it I should value it now more than anything else. You speak of not likeing Grammer, I would like to assist you if I could but I know as little about it as the Indians do. If you have a good teacher I should think it might be explained to you so that you could soon understand it. My opinion is that you are improveing very fast in all your studies and if you have half a chance you will have a good education and be fited to enjoy life. Hope for the best and enjoy the present as much as possible is my way of liveing.

You speak of soldiers camps and how they live and want to know if the camps look like a camp meeting. They might be made to resemble one by moveing them into some fine grove and introducing about a dozen long faced well dressed chaps and a few hundred hansome girls; the former to strut and talk and then the latter for company for the soldiers and to act as special police for the occasion to keep the soldiers from stealing the preachers' wine & whiskey. I wish it could be tried on our camp. I believe it would be quite a pleasant change for us just now.

Peaches and Watermellons are quite plenty. Peaches at 25cts. per doz. and Mellons from one to three dollars each.

From what you say I should think it must be a right smart place back thar in Morristown for schools if the

666

Gals has all got schools as you named. Thars a heap of schools down here but they are mostly colored ones and I tell yer theys larnin right fast. The darkeys are thick down here and they are free now and they know it.

I will send Father a Chattanooga paper. It has a couple of pretty fair jokes in it. One is a letter from P.V. Nasby and is a good one I think. The other is Poetry for Jefferson D.

As ever   *Ed*

View of Lookout Mountain and the Tennessee River
Frank Leslie's Illustrated Weekly

Chattanooga, Tenn.
August 2nd, 1865.

Dear Parents,

Our mail has been stoped for the last 8 or 10 days for some reason that we know nothing about and I have been waiting, thinking it would come and I would then answer all letters that I might get, but as there does not seem to be any prospect for a change I will send this. We are here doing the same duty that we have been since we came down here and although we are not organized with any of the Brigades that are to be kept in Tenn. I have not seen any orders for us to leave. We have been payed up to May 1st and the boys are haveing good times. Health is good and the weather some cooler than it was. I have to go on duty now and I will close.

Affectionately your Son

Ed. H. Bassett

Batt. "L" 1st Minnesota H.A.
Chattanooga, Tenn.

Chattanooga, Tenn.
August 12th, 1865

Dear Mother,

I am glad to hear that you are improving in health and I sincerely hope that you will continue to untill you are entirely well. Our mail seems to be a long time in coming through lately and for several days we have had scarcely any mail. The weather is very hot but my health remains excellent.

I suppose every farmer is very busy now in their fields saveing their grain which is reported to be an excellent crop. I am laying back in the shade this summer in the place of sweating in the Harvest field. I would like to be there and see the boys of the 8th as they come home but I am getting along finely here and will not complain. Our turn will come sometime and then I guess I shall feel free being that the war is over.

I am pleased to hear that Morristown is being built up so fast and I think I can see a glorious future in store for the favored City of Schools and Churches to say nothing about other things which abound in that land of wonders. I will be arround that way on a foraging expedition sometime between now and next year about this time and perhaps some sooner. I cannot tell you exactly when you may expect me but if I am favored I shall call arround sometime. I would like to get arround there before cold weather comes on but if not, I think I would rather not venture there before spring. I remember going up into those parts once alone in February and I don't care about experienceing another season exactly like that was.[137] I would prefer waiting until the weather gets warmer. How does Father get along with his work this summer. Does he think he can make his farm pay expenses this summer if it does it will do better than it did last summer. That I know by actual figureing.

As ever your Affectionate Son

Ed. H. Bassett

Batt. "L" 1st Minnesota H.A.

Chattanooga, Tenn.
August 17th, 1865.

Dear Sister Anna,

Everything jogs along here about as usual. Day succeeds night and night day in the way it always has. Soldiering is soldiering but I call this playing Soldier. The weather is very warm and rather dry but I think we will be apt to have some rain next month and if we should stop here all winter we will most likely have a chance to wade through mud to our hearts' content. I have not been out into the country for several days but I intend to go out again soon to see my <u>Ducky</u>[138]and

---

[137] An obvious reference to his trip home in February of 1864 when it was intensely cold.

[138] It would seem Edward has found a lady of interest.

eat some Peaches. I have been waiting for some time for the weather to get cooler but I shall have to go soon if I get roasted by the hot sun. Chattanooga is rather a dull place for amusements of all kinds. The Theatre is a miserable sham and most everything in and arround town is of the same stripe (Except Duckey. She lives in Georgia.)

There was one of my old comrades died in the Hospital this eve about 10 o'clock. I was there with him when he died. [139] He has been sick little more than one week with the Diarhea. He was a member of the old First Co. G. His name is W.M. Houser from Wilton Minnesota. The rest of the Company are well except one or two and they are mending very fast. I don't think this is as healthy a country as Minnesota but I should not be alarmed about my health here as long as I took good care of myself. Fruit is quite plenty but I eat scarcely any except Peaches.

Please write often and let me hear all the best news, good night.

Saturday eve - August 19th, 1865.

Nothing new. The mail does not appear to be very large but I guess it all comes through. Co. L gets from one to three letters per day from the north.

Your Affectionate Brother

Ed.

Chattanooga. Tennessee.
August 19th, 1865.

Dear Father and Mother,

We have the same dull round of camp life every day and many of the men are geting tired of it and long to return to their homes and friends.

The Company mourns the loss of another member - a young man by the name of W.M. Houser and an old member of "G" Co. 1st Minnesota Infantry. He died in Hospital No. 1 at this place on the 16th inst. of chronic diarhea after about ten days sickness. He was a young man of strict moral principles and a good soldier. He was burried on the 17th with military honors by the Company. His is the eleventh death in the company from disease and one man that was killed at the fire makes a loss of 12 men in a little over six months. Houser was our second Sergt. and the best drill master we had in the camp. He had the best of care from the surgeon in charge of the Hospital but it was of no use. He seemed to run right down and all that could be done was of no use.

I wish I could send you a few bushel of nice Peaches and Apples. They are very plenty here and if it was not so far I would send you some by express. Good peaches sell for 75 cts. & 1.00 per bushel. Apples about the same. Potatoes $2.00 and poor at that.

There has been quite an excitement of late among the military on account of some of the soldiers refuseing to mix and go on duty with the Negroes and this week this Regt. has made a strike for their rights and there are some 20 men of Co. "L" in the Guard House now for claiming their rights and the whole Regt. are ready to back them up. They have been required to do duty contrary to the rules and regulations governing the army and I think they will gain their point as soon as it is found that they are determined. I have heard it hinted that the Commander of this District is not quite what he should be but I cannot say now. Time will tell. I know one thing and will say it and that is that there is no good amount of Discipline in this portion of the army stationed in and arround Chattanooga. I think there will be trouble all over the U.S. about the Negro yet and there will have to be some provisions made for seperating them from among the whites before we can have perfect peace. What do the good people of Morristown think of allowing the negroes to vote? What do you think they would say if called upon to decide? This Regt. has appointed three delegates to attend the Union Convention at St. Paul so you may expect to hear from us next fall if good luck attends our efforts.

Remaining as ever your son,   *Ed.*

Chattanooga, Tenn.
August 24, 1865

Dear Mother,

I sometimes think that there is nothing that cheers a soldier more than letters from their friends. I write so little this summer that I scarcely know how to write a letter or anything else and every time I commence one I get discouraged before I have half finished it and think it is the last time I will try. There is nothing new or exciting and the dull rounds of Camp life are gone through with every day without creating any excitement worth mentioning. I am on guard every other day so I have but little time to run arround if I was inclined to do so, but as the weather is very hot and dusty I prefer staying in the shade during the day and it is dangerous to be caught out nights by the Negro Patrol that is moveing arround through town all night to pick up any unlucky fellow that may be caught out and send him to the Military Prison where he will be kept eight or ten days and worked on the roads under a Negro guard for the benefit of the riseing generations of Secesh and Negro. I would like to see the city of Chattanooga baptised with as pureifying an

672

element as some of the citys were that we read of and if Andy should try to pick out three men holding an official position in the place that were strictly honest to save it I fear he would give it up in despair before he had gone far in his investigations of their official character. Soldiers are misused here the worst that they ever have been in the volunteer army and while there remains a party like the present in power I fear there will be but a poor chance to get justice done. The District Commander owns about one half of the town and of course is somewhat interested in the improvements being made and especialy the roads and streets. The Post Commander is a Negro Colonel and most of the officers in the city are of that stripe. I guess I have said enough about it this time but I will tell you more if I see you.

I was over to see James Hand on Sunday. He looks well now and said that he felt well. He was sick for a long time but I think he has got cured now. I think there will be some of the Regt. kept here all winter and perhaps all of them.

Accept this with my love to all

Your Affectionate Son

Edward H. Bassett.

Chattanooga, Tennessee
Sept. 4th, 1865.

Dear Sister Anna,

We have had a little rain for the last two days which makes it quite comfortable to what it was. Peaches and Apples are very plenty and cheap so you may bet I have very good times. (What shall I do to make time pass away pleasantly is the question I ask myself most every morning). Camp life is so very dull here in this place. I would be glad if we would get orders to move most any where. I would care but little where it was.

We have Dress parade once every week and we are on guard one half of the time so time passes off quite briskly after all and it does not seem over two months since we left Minnesota and here the 7th month is passing away and I shall hardly miss the time before our One Year will be up and as the war is over there will not be much likelyhood of any re-enlisting. I am glad to hear that Father is geting along so finely with his harvesting. I had heard that the grain was most all blown down by the heavy winds in that part of Minnesota. I hope he will get all his grain saved in good condition for I know he has worked very hard to put in so much land and have such a large crop. There is a great deal of talk about our being mustered out soon but it takes orders to do that business and there has been no orders yet that will send us away from here that I know of. I would like to be back there a few weeks this fall to run arround and shoot Prairie Chickens & wild ducks. Well I must close hoping that I shall have a chance to talk with you before long. Please accept this with my love to all & remember to write again.

Your Brother

Edward H. Bassett

Batt. "L" 1st Minnesota H. A.

Enclosed: (newspaper clipping from the New York Mercury)

P O C A H O N T A S ,   (By J.L. Bowman)
  A remnant of a great and mighty tribe
  was gathered in a wood, beside a stream
  That watered many a fair and verdant vale
  In its meanderings, to meditate
  And act, with honest earnestness, upon
  The wrongs and dire injustice that had come
  From enemy in blood. Fierce, stalwart men;

But few in number, they had brought them there
For deeds of vengeance that were planned against
An adversary, whose unlucky stars
Had made him theirs. The warriors, tried in skill
And proud of many a hard-fought battle, won
From weaker fragments of their native race,
And wearing now the trophies of their wars.

Head Qtrs. Batt."L" 1st Minnesota Heavy Artillery
Chattanooga, Tenn.
Sept. 7th, 1865.

Dear Mother,

I am glad to hear that you keep well and that there is such a flattering prospect for good times in old Minnesota. From what you write I should judge that business was never better. The prospect for a good market for all kinds of farm produce must necessarily encourage the farmers. From what you say about Morristown I should think the people were going to build it up in spite of all the disadvantages arriseing from a mixed community and various other causes. I think Smith's project of enlargeing the school district will work like a charm now and it would seem strange too if it should not meet with some opposition from some source. Perhaps it will yet. That road has turned out about as I thought it would end now if the farmers on the prairie will try they can have a good road. (Did Walker ever build that bridge across the marsh that he was going to this summer?) From what you write I would think that Father was going to do well on his farm this summer. You say it would do me good to see the shocks of grain standing so thick in the field. It may be that it would but I am very well satisfied with my present vision of them which is quite a vivid one in imagination and when I come to think of the many hard days of work they have called for and still call for before they can be of any earthly benefit to any one I beg to be excused but perhaps I shall be forced to try some kind of an experiment at farming or something else next summer for it is quite certain that Uncle Sam is about done with us and it is doubted by some about his keeping us over the winter.

There is considerable excitement among some of the troops about the shooting of a white soldier by the colored Patrol on the streets of Chattanooga and his comrades have retaliated by killing some 12 or 15 Negros. The soldier that was shot belonged to a Missouri Cavalry Regt. and they are very much excited about it and threatened to clean out all the negroes at this Post. We were called out under arms about 9 o'clock Tuesday evening in anticipation of a fuss with the Cavalry but they did not appear as it was reported they had and seem to have only succeeded in scareing the authorities a little and killed quite a number of <u>Negroes</u>. There is not very good feelings generaly between the colored soldiers and the white and I don't think there ever will be as long as they are kept near each other. There are some five colored Regts. here now and it is reported that one of them are to relieve us this week. It is hoped so. My health continues first rate and I weigh about as much as I did last winter - vis 148. You speak of hot weather. I think we can beat you. It was so hot here one day that all the Thermometers melted down and since then we have been unable to tell exactly how hot it was. There was one week that we used no wood to do our cooking, the sun being sufficiently hot to heat our coffee. (Edward's sense of humor remains intact) It has been dryer here this summer than it was in Minnesota last but we are looking for rainy times this fall.

Please accept this with my love to all

As ever Your Son

Edward H. Bassett.

676

The war is over; it's time to go home!

With the war now ended, the regiment was anxious to join the hundreds-of-thousands of other soldiers finishing their duty, packing their belongings and returning to their homes and families. The following entries in Edward's diary describe this last page in the history of the First Minnesota Heavy Artillery.

Diary entries from September 9th through October 17th, 1865:

"Sept. 9th: We were relieved by Company B, 1st Colored Heavy Artillery, and are to move into the 44th Indiana Camp. The 10th was very warm. Had Dress Parade in the evening. I was sent over to the 44th Ind. camp with a squad to clean out the quarters for our Company. We moved over in the afternoon, and got quite comfortably fixed by dark. We fixed up the camp the next day, but the general belief is that we will remain but a few days."

"Sept. 13th: I was on camp guard. We had Regimental Guard Mount this morning. We have fifteen posts around the camp."

"Sept.14th: All quiet along the lines. Received orders to turn in all Quartermaster property. Dress Parade in the evening. We may leave Saturday next. "

"Sept. 15th: We had Battalion drill at 9 AM the first time that the Regiment has been out together on drill. Dress Parade in the eve. Orders are to break camp tomorrow at 11 o'clock in the morning. I turned in my gun today. By orders of the Colonel I am to carry the colors. The boys were released from prison today. They feel good and look well. [140]

---

[140] Edward was given a considerable honor by being selected to carry the Regimental Colors when they left camp. I believe the prisoners he refers to are all the men in the regiment that will no longer have to serve on garrison duty.

We left Chattanooga at two for Nashville. The Regiment was on two trains. Run very slowly all night. It was all the two engines could do to push the train up the mountain."

"Sept. 17th: We reached Murfreesboro about 10 AM and Nashville at 12. Lay there at the Depot until 4 PM, when we packed down to the Soldiers Home, where we took up our abode for the present."

"Soldiers Home at Nashville, Tenn.: It is quite rainy this morning. I went down to the New Theater in the evening."

"Sept. 19, 1865: They have made a commencement on our muster rolls today. I went down town in the afternoon and went all thru the Statehouse. Went to the Old Theater in the evening. On the 20th we had a heavy force at work on our muster rolls. I remained in camp all night. The next day I roamed all over town, and went to the New Theater in the eve."

"Sept. 27th: We were mustered out in the AM and might have started home if the transportation had been ready. I went to the New Theater in the eve and saw the "Hidden Hand" played. Will start for home sometime tomorrow."

"Sept. 28th: was a pleasant day. We started from Nashville and crossed the river and lay there near Edgeville until 4 PM when we started and run about fifty miles that night. On the road between Nashville and Louisville."

"Sept. 29, 1865: We reached Louisville about sundown, and crossed over to Jeffersonville, Ind. Crossed by ferry. Boarded the cars for Indianapolis, starting at 9 o'clock. Reached Indianapolis about 9 AM where we got some breakfast and started for Chicago. Changed cars at Kokomo, and run all night."

"Oct. 1st: We reached Chicago about 10 AM Changed cars again and run on to Prairie-du-Chien, Wisconsin, arriveing there about sunrise. We boarded the Steamer Key City here and started up river. We made it as far as Hastings, where we layed over all night. Left Hastings about 8 AM and run up to St. Paul where we arrived about noon. The people made plans to give us a grand reception. We marched up to the State Capitol, where the ladies had tables loaded with all kinds of eatables. We were invited to walk in and help ourselves, which we did. Everything was done to make the occasion one to be remembered. After dinner we marched down to the boat, boarded it, and steamed to Fort Snelling. We camped about two miles from the Fort."

"On Monday Oct. 11, 1865 : We were paid off and discharged. I went over to Mendota and stayed over night. The next day I took the ten o'clock train for Northfield and arrived there about 2 PM. Here I took the stage to Faribault and put up at the National House."

"Wed, Oct. 13th: I arrived at home about noon. There seems to be a good deal of business going on, but it is among those who have something to 'Do With'. I have no particular business and don't feel inclined to work hard, and it is pretty dull here. On the 16th I went to Faribault to try to find something I can do. The time drags heavily with me, as I feel no interest whatever in the business of the Country. I have decided to try for something better."

"Oct. 17th: It is raining and dreary. I have a notion to buy a lot of traps and go out trapping fur. It will be an independent business, and will pay off, if the fur prices stay up. There is considerable excitement on account of the railroad having been finished. The trains are running in daily. Everybody is making big calculations, and business appears to be on the increase. "

For Edward, like most soldiers who came home from the war, civilian life had changed while he was away. It took some time to adjust to the changes at home and in his personal life. Trying to fit in, making a new place for himself and

679

determining what he wanted to do with the rest of his life was a heavy burden. Eventually, he like so many of his comrades, would become very successful and a highly-regarded member of his community and county. His service to his country in a regiment of American Patriots was always a source of great pride.

EPILOGUE

After returning home from the war, Edward Bassett spent time with his family, working the farm, adjusting to the many changes that had taken place around Morristown and learning how to be a civilian again. The railroads, which now extended into southern Minnesota, brought an insurgence of new residents, all looking for new land or a new start. In November 1865, Edward traveled to Wisconsin by stage coach and train to visit relatives, a marked improvement in travel as compared to just five years earlier when he started off to war.

The next spring on May 14th, Ed and two friends took two yoke of oxen and two wagons loaded with supplies and headed off to the Minnesota River Valley in search of land on which to stake claims. Minnesota veterans were granted the right to a 160 acre parcel of land for their service. They found the land they wanted and set to work, staying there until July 17th. His youngest son, Morton, wrote:

"They each took a claim and built three log cabins. They also broke up a little sod and planted some corn and potatoes. They also mowed some hay with a scythe, and stacked it. Dad undoubtedly figured on going back sometime but he never did."

For the next few years, Edward was involved in a number of endeavors—whatever could be found to make a living. His father, Henry Bassett, sold his farm during the autumn of 1867. Ed and his brother Elford helped move their folks to Faribault on November 18th. There is no doubt that Edward knew how to work. He farmed and ran a sawmill in the summer and worked in the big woods cutting logs and hauling them to the mill in the winter. These were big logs—5 of them made a sleigh load, yet he would cut from 15-to-20 in a day. He made hand-split wooden shingles which sold for $3.00 per 600 and also sawed and sold lumber—a jack of all trades, During the summer and fall of 1870, Edward worked near Duluth on a government surveying project to establish section lines and township corner monuments and boundaries.

Edward H. Bassett married Hattie A. King on March 21, 1871. Together they faced the grasshopper plagues, the harsh winters and the hard work of homesteading and raising a large family on the Minnesota frontier.

Arthur Rose, in his Nobles County Illustrated History, stated:

"For a period extending from 1873 to 1879 the people of Nobles county, in common with those of all southwestern Minnesota, suffered as few pioneer settlers in any country ever suffered. Adversity followed adversity......The picture cannot be painted too dark."

Morton Bassett provided a look into the life of the family in his unpublished "Reminiscences." The following is an excerpt from that work:

"Edward first built a sod house in LeSuer Co. for them where they lived about a year. Looking for better land and a brighter future, in 1875 Edward took a soldiers homestead in Dewald Township north of Rushmore on 60 acres of land."

"He built a 16 x 20 frame building, boarded up & down w/ rough lumber, some boards were 2' wide. He covered it w/ tar paper w/ battens nailed over the cracks. It had 1 door & 2 windows. Inside it had a rough lumber floor. Edward & Hattie used prairie hay and buffalo chips for fuel to heat their home in the early years."

"The area was mostly prairie land & had very few trees & the few, that were there, had been cut for fuel & building homes. He & Hattie, both came from timber country in Rice County & they both loved trees, so the first thing they did was to plant a large grove of trees. They planted a lot of trees for windbreaks & for fruit."

"Later he bought an existing house & moved it to their property on a wagon. They dug a cellar for it to sit on. They had an outside cellar entry & an inside trap door in the kitchen to enter the basement."

"He broke new land & planted crops. The only tools Ed had to work the land in the early days were an old plow, &

a wooden frame spike toothed drag made in 3 sections. It was called a Boss Harrow. They were pulled by a team of oxen. He seeded the fields by carrying a partial bag of grain seed, on his shoulder and scattering it by hand w/ a sweeping swing of his arm. He then covered it by taking the drag over it. The corn he planted had to be planted by hand and covered with a hoe."

"There were many bad summer storms, prairie fires, sicknesses, accidents, & in 1876-1879, they suffered the grasshopper plagues. There were terrible winter storms (in which many lost their lives). Many winters the snow came in October & lasted until April or later. (In 1880, the snow came on October 15th, & did not melt until the next June!) The winters were harsh w/ very cold temperatures & the winds blew so across the prairie areas that they would often find snow on the interior floors of their homes. (In the winter, they kept a rope tied to the door knob of the house & tied the other end to the barn so they could find their way back & forth in the winter storms.)"

"July 4th gathering, 1890: 25 years after the Civil War, they held a 4th of July gathering for friends & neighbors. Ed fixed long tables under the trees & fixed the old wooden pump for drinking water. He stretched a rope high across the driveway & hung a large flag from it so everyone would drive under it. Midmorning 3 men came & as they drove under the flag, 1 man grabbed for the flag. He missed the 1st time, so they stopped the team & the man climbed up on the wagon seat & tore down the flag! There was almost a riot, they were going to hang the man! Cooler heads prevailed & the man was taken to jail at the county seat. The next day when the man sobered up, he was released." (Many of the early settlers of Nobles County, were Union army veterans)

Edward truly cared about education and gave land for and helped build, the Edison School (also called Bassett School) for District #9. It was also used as a church.

In 1886, Edward built a new house. A few years later he added other buildings

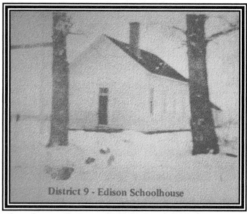

District 9 - Edison Schoolhouse

to the property. In 1890, he bought an additional 160 acres across the road from their property.

Author, Arthur Rose, said: "The Bassett home place is one of the finest improved farms in the county"

Morton remembers how his dad always kept his jackknife really sharp, how he always kept mutton tallow under the stove and how important it was to use it everyday on their boots. On Sundays and other special days, they were to rub a bit of soot from the stove on their boots & polish them with a rag & enough elbow grease until they had the proper shine!

Edward and Hattie had 11 children, Six boys & 5 girls. Three of his son's fought in the Spanish American War, one of them, Elmer H. Bassett, was the author's grandfather,.

Edward lived on his homestead in the Rushmore, MN area in Nobles County the rest of his life. He survived 34 Civil War Battles, the illnesses during the Civil War, homesteading 160 acres in SW Minnesota and another 160 acres he purchased to go with that. He suffered the rest of his life with Catelepsy, resulting from the head wound he sustained at Bristoe Station. Edward was a pillar of his community and highly regarded by his many friends and neighbors. A man of uncompromising principles and a dedication to improving his homeland, he lived the days granted him to their fullest.

Edward H. Bassett died on April 9, 1897 in Rushmore, MN. He was 56 years old

HIS LAST MUD MARCH!!

And then amid the lonely gloom
Beneath the tall old Chestnut trees
My silent marches I resume
And think of other times than these...

Funeral notes from Morton's, "Reminiscences":

"When Father was gone, he was buried in Worthington cemetery beside the grave of one of his sons who had died at the age of 4. Worthington was 12 miles from where they lived. "It was a dark, cold, gloomy day in mid April, 1897, that the caravan of buggies and wagons made the long trip through the mud to town. One man rode ahead of the procession on horseback to pick out the best route. At least he tried to guide them around the deepest mudholes."

His final resting place . . . .

Worhtington City
Cemetery

Worthington, MN

Photos by Carolyn Soper N.C.G. G.

So we come to the close of this brief Chronicle of Edward Bassett, who, like so many others, responded to his country's call. Men, who with an unfailing sense of <u>Duty</u>, endured unimaginable hardships and danger while they fought to preserve their beloved country.

APPENDIX

Chronology of the
Minnesota First Regiment Volunteer Infantry
In the American Civil War

1861:

- Sunday April 14, 1861:
  Tendered by Gov. Ramsey to Secretary Cameron of the War Department in Washington D. C.

- April 18:
  Call issued for volunteers for one regiment of infantry of 10 companies.

- April 29:
  Regiment mustered in at Fort Snelling, "drilling began at once and was carried on vigorously."[141]

- May 2:
  First dress parade took place with a large crowd present.

- May 9:
  Regiment furnished with black felt hats and black pantaloons with red flannel shirts as uniforms except Co. K which had neat gray uniforms given them by the people of Winona. (Note: Some of the shirts were a flowered print).

- May 10:
  Regiment re-mustered into service for three years.

- May 26:
  Regiment is presented with the Minnesota State Flag by the women of St. Paul which it carried throughout its service.

- May 28:
  Companies B and G were ordered to Fort Ridgely to relieve two companies of theU. S. 2nd Infantry.

- May 29:
  Company A marched to Fort Ripley.

---

[141] Minnesota in the Civil War and Indian War, St. Paul: Pioneer Press Co. 1889

- June 6:

  Company E moved to Fort Ripley.
- June 14:

  Gov. Ramsey received a dispatch ordering the Regiment to Washington by way of Harrisburg, Pa.
- June 18:

  Companies B and G leave Fort Ridgely for Washington, pass through Baltimore, Md. on the way.
- June 22 - 26:

  Regiment moving to Washington DC, intermediate stop at Harrisburg, PA.; arrived D.C. midnight on 26th.
- June 27:

  Moved a short distance East of Washington and went into camp. Resumed daily drills.
- July 3:

  Embarked on steamers at Navy Yard, landed at Alexandria Virginia, the little town was abandoned except for large groups of astonished Negroes standing on the corners. Made camp one mile west of town in a 20 acre field.
- July 4-15:

  Camped at `Camp Franklin, VA.; about 7 miles from Washington. Made several scouting forays looking for the enemy.
- July 16:

  Left camp near Fort Elsworth on the march to Bull Run in "Light Marching Order".
- July 17:

  Reached Fairfax Court House at 3 PM sixteen miles S.W. of Washington.
- July 18:

  Camped after sundown one mile from Centerville and six miles East of Bull Run.

☙ July 21: Battle of Bull Run

First Blood, after a day long battle that at first appeared it would be a Union Victory but then turned into a rout the First Minnesota lost 42 men killed, 108 wounded and 30 missing, the heaviest losses of any regiment on the field. The Minnesota regiment was one of the few that stood their ground and left the field in good order serving as rear guard. Camped on field.

- July 23:

  Camped again in Washington D.C. on same grounds as when they first arrived from Minnesota

- August 2:

  Began March to Edward's Ferry, stopped at Brightwood five miles from Washington.

- August 3:

  Marching to the Upper Potomac.

- August 5:

  Marched to Rockville – Montgomery County, Virginia; county seat, a small village.

- August 6:

  Montgomery County, Maryland; foraging for food while on the march.

- August 7:

  Resumed their march to Seneca Mills on Seneca Creek.

- August 8:

  Camped near Seneca Mills, about 30 miles from Washington, on the Potomac River, three miles from Darnstown.

- August 16:

  Moved to ˋCamp Stone', Maryland between Edward's Ferry & Poolsville.

- September 8:

  New replacement recruits arrive.

- September 21:

  Major Dike returned from Minnesota with a new regimental flag given to them by the citizens.

- September 25:

  Minnesota Governor Ramsey visited the regiment.

- October 19:
    On Picket duty near Edward's Ferry
- 💣 **October 21 - 22: Battle of Ball's Bluff**
    21st - The First made a crossing and was lightly engaged at Edward's Ferry, wasn't involved in heaviest fighting.
    22nd - Minnesota once again shows its steadiness under fire and maintains order manning the boats to withdraw troops across the Potomac and serves as rear guard.
- December 1:
    Rain and mud at Camp Stone.
- December 8:
    Picket duty at Conrad's Ferry.

1862:

- February 5:
    Camped at Harper's Ferry quartered in remains of the old armory buildings where John Brown was captured.
- February 26,
    On the move to camp at Harper's Ferry.
- March 4:
    Camped on Bolivar Heights, Maryland, having been on the march for 17 days.
- March 7 & 8:
    Left camp on Bolivar Heights, Maryland- marched eight miles to Charlestown and camped ½ mile from town.
- March 10:
    Marched 12 miles to capture the town of Berryville, first infantry to enter town, 10 miles from Winchester on Winchester and Leesburg turnpike, Slept in rain without tents or fires.
- March 11:
    Men published "First Minnesota" newspaper in Berryville.
- March 13:
    Marched out eight miles toward Winchester then countermarched back to Berryville. "Orders were wrong".

- March 14:

   Marched 12 miles back to old camp at Charlestown, Virginia.
- March 15:

   Marched all day in mud and rain, camped near old camp at Bolivar, rained all night.
- March 17:

   General McClellan begins moving the Army of The Potomac for the Peninsula Campaign.
- March 22:

   Marched to Sandy Hook, rode trains to Washington, quartered at Soldier's Rest.
- March 23:

   Camped on Capitol Hill
- March 26:

   Marched across the "Long Bridge" – took rail cars to Alexandria, marched to same camp as last July
- March 27:

   Camped in old camp near Alexandria and set up tents.
- March 29:

   Packed three days rations, laid around town until 2 PM, marched to docks and boarded transports N.E. Edmunds & Tacoma bound for Fortress Monroe.

☀ The Peninsula Campaign, April 1-5: Advance on Yorktown, Va.

- April 1:

   Anchored under the guns of Fort Monroe.
- April 2:

   Went up to Hampton, disembarked and camped in a field.
- April 3:

   Moved to Big Bethel.
- April 4:

   Marched to Yorktown.

☀ April 5 though May 4: Siege of Yorktown

   Extended period of skirmishes, road building and breastworks construction. Incessant rain without tents.

- April 16:
  Heavy skirmishing all night, cold and wet.
- April 26:
  Very heavy skirmishing all morning, rebels are driven back.
- May 4:
  (Sunday) Left camp, marched out three miles in rain and mud, worked on the Forts, out until 3 AM in rain.
- **May 5: Battle of Williamsburg**
  Heavy fighting between Federals and retreating rebels.
- May 6:
  Marched to wharf and boarded transport ship Long Branch at Yorktown.
- May 7:
  Sailed on transports up the York River.
- May 9:
  Marched up the Pamunky River two miles to Eltham, camped for a week.
- May 15:
  Left camp on Pamunky River at 9AM, marched all day in rain and mud, made camp in woods at sundown.
- May 17:
  Camped in woods between New Kent and Cumberland, Kent County, Virginia.
- May 18:
  Marched in rain and mud eight miles, camped on plantation of Dr. William Mayo, a surgeon in the Confederate Army. Remained three days.
- May 25:
  Set up camp near the Chickahominy River.
- May 27:
  The First Minnesota built the famed "Grapevine Bridge".
- **May 31- June 1: Battle of Fair Oaks**
  Fighting from 1 PM until dark.
- June 2:
  Went into camp near Fair Oaks (Camp Sully).
- **June 25 – July 1: Seven Days Battle before Richmond:**

♦ **June 25: Battle of Mechanicsville**
♦ **June 26: Battle of Gaines Mill**
♦ **June 29: Battle of Allen's Farm**
First Minnesota repulsed an hours' long attack by enemy infantry and artillery.
♦ **June 29: Battle of Savage Station**
Nearly on its own, the First spent a long day defending the Union left flank not leaving the field until 10 PM.
♦ **June 30: Battle of Nelson's Farm**
After dropping their blankets and knapsacks, the First charged and repelled the enemy and took the front of the line position all under heavy and sustained fire.
♦ **June 30: Battle of White Oak Swamp (Glendale)**
Crossed the White Oak Swamp in early morning, marched to Bracket's Ford an on to Glendale where they were engaged in fighting until midnight.
♦ **July 1: Battle of Malvern Hill**
• July 2 – August 15: Duty at Harrison's Landing
• July 9: President Lincoln visits and reviews troops.
• July 22: McClellan reviews 2nd Corp., Comments to Gen. Sumner that the "First Minnesota is the best regiment in the army."
♦ **August 6: Malvern Hill**
Under General Hooker - on reconnaissance.
• August 15 – 28: Movement to Centerville.
• August 15:
Left camp at Harrison's Landing guarding Brigade supply train wagons, marched all day and night.
• August 16:
Crossed Chickahominy River on pontoon bridge at 5 PM and camped for the night.
• August 17:
Started march for Williamsburg, passed it at noon and continued on three miles making camp by a Baptist Church.
• August 18:
Marched to Yorktown then another 12 miles to Big Bethel.

- August 19 - 21:
    Marched to Hampton, camped between town and Fortress Monroe.
- August 22:
    Marched to Newport News and camped right on the beach.

💣 **August 30: Second Battle of Bull Run**

- August 31:
    Counter marched to Fairfax Road near Alexandria then to Centerville to cover McDowel's Corps in full retreat. Marched 65 miles in four days, often under fire as they served as rear guard. Much of the marching was done in deep mud as the retreating army and heavy rains had turned the dirt roads into a quagmire.

💣 **September 1: Covering Pope's retreat to Washington**
    Marched out on reconnaissance, engaged in fight between Centerville and Fairfax. Generals Stephens and Kearney were killed. Marched all night in rain passing through Fairfax about sunrise.

💣 **September 2: Battle of Vienna**
    Took Vienna road, stopped three miles out for breakfast and rested till sundown then started for the Potomac. Shelled by rebels four miles out and skirmished with Jeb Stuart's cavalry.

💣 **September 2: Battle of Flint Hill**
    Withdrew in the dark and in silence from above mentioned and set up a successful ambush at Flint Hill, causing considerable losses to rebel cavalry.

💣 **September 6 – 22: The Maryland Campaign:**

💣 **September 14: Battles of South Mountain**

💣 **September 16 - 17: Battle of Antietam**
    In action on the extreme right during Sedgwick's charge, the regiment took heavy fire from both flanks loosing 147 killed & wounded and 21 missing. The First was one of few regiments retiring from the field in good order.

- September 18 – 21:
  Spent 4 days on the battlefield, "The Stinking Field", burying the dead.
- September 22:
  Left Sharpsburg Battlefield and marched to Harper's Ferry, forded the Potomac River and made camp on Bolivar Heights.
- October 1:
  President Lincoln visits camp on Bolivar Heights.
- **October 17, Armed Reconnaissance:**
  Left camp early in AM on reconnaissance toward Charlestown skirmishing with enemy.
- October 18:
  Captured Charlestown and held it until evening then returned to camp.
- October 30:
  Left camp on Bolivar Heights in PM, crossed Potomac on pontoon bridge. Camped at Snickersville, Va. in a valley between the Blue Ridge and Bull Run mountain ranges.
- November 4:
  Encamped at Paris, near Ashby's Gap in Loundon County, Virginia.
- November 6:
  Left camp at Ashby's Gap in the morning and marched to Warrenton, Va.
- November 17:
  Encamped near Fredericksburg, Va.
- November 23:
  Camped on opposite side of river from Fredericksburg, one mile from Falmouth, Va.
- December 7:
  Falmouth, Virginia, where 130,000 troops are gathered. First Minnesota has moved camp three times since Nov. 17 and is in camp in the winter with no tents or shelter.

- December 11:

  Left camp and marched down opposite Fredericksburg where they lay all day. When pontoon bridge is finished the First Minnesota crosses following a Michigan regiment.
- 💣 **December 12 – 15: Battle of Fredericksburg:**
  - December 12: Skirmishing at Fredericksburg.
  - 💣 **December 13: First Battle of Fredericksburg.**
  - 💣 December 14: Regiment lay on the streets of Fredericksburg all day.
  - December 15: On picket duty at Fredericksburg till 10 PM.
- December 26:

  Encamped near Falmouth, Virginia building winter quarters. Army of the Potomac spends nearly five months at this camp.

1863:

- January 20:

  Under command of General Burnside the infamous "Mud March" occurs.
- March 30:

  Six inches of snow falls. Rain or snow has fallen every day for the past week.
- April 1:

  Under marching orders, ordered to pack up at 3 AM.
- April 8:

  Army was reviewed by President Lincoln.
- April 15:

  All extra baggage is packed to be stored for the summer.
- April 29:

  Pontoon bridges put across the Rappahanoc to Fredericksburg.
- May 2:

  Left camp at noon and marched down to Rappahanoc River, lay their till 5 AM.

- 🎇 **May 3: 2nd Battle of Fredericksburg:**

  By 11 AM the first and second lines of defensive works before Fredericksburg have been taken, the regiment returns across river at night.

- May 5:

  Torrential rains fall all day.

- May 7:

  Camped ½ mile from Fredericksburg by the railroad at Falmouth Station until mid June.

- 🎇 **June 14 – July 5: The Gettysburg Campaign:**

  - June 14:

    Struck camp at sundown and marched all night, first about 5 miles towards Stafford Court House then were ordered back on picket duty at Sedgwick's Crossing, below Falmouth. So begins the movement to destiny at Gettysburg.

  - June 15:

    At 3 AM withdrawn from picket and resumed march serving as rear guard of the army, passed Stafford Court House, camped at Acquia creek near Dumfrees, covered twenty eight miles.

  - June 16:

    Picked up the march at 3 AM and marched sixteen miles to camp at Occoquan Creek.

  - June 17:

    Marched to Fairfax Station, within four miles of Centerville, Virginia. The weather is extremely hot and many died of heat stroke while on the march. Rumors circulate that General Robert E. Lee has crossed into Pennsylvania.

  - June 18:

    Encamped at Fairfax Station.

  - June 19:

    Moved to Centerville about sundown.

- June 20:
    Resumed march about 3 PM in very heavy rain and mud as rear guard to Division wagon train. Stopped at midnight near Gainesville on the railroad.
- June 21:
    Marched through burned out small town of Haymarket, shelled heavily by enemy, continued to near Thoroughfare Gap about 9 miles from old Bull Run battlefield. Served on picket duty until 25th.
- June 25:
    Took up the line of march for the Potomac. Marched twenty-two miles and reached Gum Spring that night.
- June 26:
    Crossed the Potomac River at Edward's Ferry at night and bivouacked near old camp.
- June 27:
    Marched through Poolesville and camped East of Sugar Loaf Mountain.
- June 28:
    Reached the Monocacy River and camped on the river bank three miles from Frederick City, Maryland.
- June 29:
    Began march at daylight passing through Liberty, Johnsville, Union Bridge and Uniontown to near the Pennsylvania state line. Covered 33 miles.
- June 30:
    Laid over in camp 2 miles from Uniontown.

Battle of Gettysburg: July 1, 2nd and 3rd; Wednesday, Thursday & Friday:

July 1:
    Began the march early, stopped at Taneytown for lunch break then continued to within three miles of Gettysburg.

💣 **July 2:**

About 3 AM regiment was ordered into position in the line of battle near the center. Lay on the field under heavy artillery fire until late afternoon when ordered to the left to support Battery C, Fourth U.S. Artillery. About 7 PM ordered by General Hancock to charge and stop the advance of approximately 1,600 Alabama troops threatening to break through the line. Suffered 82% losses, stopped the rebel advance.

💣 **July 3:**

After suffering incredible losses the previous day the regiment is moved to a "safer" position in the center of the Union line. Becomes heavily involved in repelling "Pickett's Charge." Loses 17 more men.

💣 July 4; Saturday:

Some sharpshooting all morning, heavy rain all afternoon and night, rebs retreated.

• July 5, Sunday:

Burying the dead at Gettysburg, Rebels gone; left battlefield about 3 PM and marched out four miles and camped in an old field.

• July 7; Tuesday:

Marched to Taneytown and camped for the night. Wagon Train caught up and rations issued.

• July 8, Wednesday:

Broke camp at 5 AM marched to Woodboro, caught turnpike and marched through Waterville to five miles from Fredrick, camped along Monocacy River.

• July 9:

Marched through Frederick, Jefferson and Barkitsville.

• July 10:

Passed over Antietam battlefield and camped six miles from Williamsport.

•

700

- July 11:

  Left camp at daylight, marched four miles and halted while cavalry skirmished with rebels. Slept in a wheat field and resumed march at midnight.
- July 12:

  Marched two miles and lay down on stones in the road to sleep. Aroused at sunrise and marched one mile and camped in an old pasture.
- July 18:

  Crossed the Potomac and Shenandoah at Harper's Ferry, marched along the Southwest side of the Blue Ridge Mountains to Manassas Gap.
- **July 24: Battle of Kelly's Farm at Manassas Gap.**
- July 26:

  Marched 23+ miles to near Warrenton Junction.
- July 30:

  Left camp at Warrenton Junction at 4 PM, marched till midnight-eight miles.
- July 31:

  Started march at 11 AM – traveled eight miles and camped in woods of oak and pine.
- August 1 & 2:

  Camped on the road between Warrenton Junction and Kelley's Ford.
- August 3:

  Moved two miles to near Morrisville, Virginia.
- August 15:

  Received orders to go to Alexandria, Virginia with the 7th Michigan and 8th Ohio regiments.
- August 20 & 21:

  Left camp at 4 PM and boarded Steamship Atlantic, sailed for New York on 21st.
- August 26:

  Camped at Governor's Island, New York.
- August 30 thru September 6:

  Camped at Fort Green, Brooklyn, New York.

701

- September 7:
  At 8 PM the regiment received orders to strike tents and prepare to return to Alexandria, Virginia.
- September 8:
  Aboard ship traveling up the Potomac River to Alexandria, Va.
- September 12:
  Started for the front, camped at night at Fairfax.
- September 13:
  Marched to Bristoe Station.
- September 14:
  Started march at 11 AM to within 3 miles of Warrenton Station.
- September 15:
  Started early and marched to within two miles of Brandy Station having marched 80 miles in last four days.
- September 16:
  Broke camp early and arrived at Culpeper about 10 AM.
- September 19:
  Camped on the Rapidan River 8 miles from Culpeper, having had skirmishes with enemy for the last 3 days.
- September 20:
  Camped on Rapidan eight miles from Culpeper.
- September 30:
  Camped on Rapidan near Raccoon Ford, Virginia.
- October 10:
  Broke camp at Culpeper and marched three miles to Gordonsville.
- October 11:
  Began march at 2 AM and arrived at Bealton Station at noon.
- October 12:
  Started at noon, the entire 2nd Corps marched back to Brandy Station. The men were preparing to rest at 11 PM when they were called out to resume the march.

- October 13:
  Marched until sunrise, re-crossed the Rappahannoc and proceeded to within four miles from Warrenton Junction and camped for the night.
- **October 14; Wednesday: Battle of Bristoe Station**
  Marching at sunrise, met resistance and repelled rebel attacks. Continued thru Catlett's Station to within ½ mile of Bristoe Station. Went into battle with large force & captured nearly 500 and three cannons.
- October 15:
  Camped on Bull Run near Centerville, Virginia.
- October 19:
  Left camp on Bull Run and marched to Bristoe Station.

- October 20:
  Marched to Kettle Run, Va. having crossed Broad Run three times and Kettle Run once en route.
- October 22:
  Camped on Kettle Run, Virginia.
- October 23:
  Marched and camped 3miles from Warrenton, Va., began building winter quarters.
- November 2:
  In camp near Warrenton, Virginia.
- November 6:
  Ordered to be prepared to march next morning.
- November 7:
  Called up at 4 AM, prepared breakfast and began march at sunrise. Marched to Warrenton Station, Bealton Station and arrived at Kelly's Ford at dark.
- November 8:
  Crossed Rapidan River on pontoon bridge advanced five miles and camped.
- November 10:
  Left camp and marched two miles and occupied abandoned rebel camp near Brandy Station.

♠ Mine Run Campaign:

- November 25:

    Marched to General Meade's headquarters at dawn, awaited orders then counter marched back to camp.

- November 26:

    Marched to Germanna Ford, waited in freezing cold till 2:30 PM while pontoon bridge was built then crossed and marched four miles to Flat Run.

- November 27:

    Marched to Robertson's Tavern on the Orange Court House Pike. Fought skirmishes all afternoon. Lay on their arms all night in thick woods.

- November 28:

    Marched in line of battle three miles through woods. Found enemy in strength at Mine Run. Waited for artillery. Went on picket duty at night.

- November 29:

    Relieved by 5th Corps and marched to front 500 feet from rebel forts. Advanced at dawn to within pistol range. Waited two hours in extreme cold. Attack was called off around 9 AM.

- December 1:

    Moved one mile to the rear. Took up march at 9 PM and marched all night in direction of Rapidan River.

- December 2:

    Crossed Rapidan River at Culpeper Ford, marched all day in cold rain and mud. Reached old camp at Brandy Station at evening.

- December 5:

    Broke camp and marched four miles, crossed Mountain Creek, stopped 1 mile north of the village of Stevensburg, population 75, built winter quarters. Spent months here building corduroy roads and other fatigue duty.

- February 5:

  Having received orders to return to Minnesota, the regiment left its camp near Stevensville, marched to Brandy Station and boarded cars of the Orange and Alexandria R.R. for Washington where it was quartered in the Soldiers Rest.

- February 6:

  The regiment was given a "Grand and Sumptuous" banquet and was showered with honors for its distinguished service.

- February 7:

  Took the train to Baltimore and laid over there until 3 AM.

- February 8:

  Passed through Little York and Harrisburg stopping at the larger town for lunch, changed trains at Pittsburg, passed through Lime, Ohio; Fort Wayne, Indiana; arrived Chicago at 11 PM and marched to Soldiers Rest where they were furnished a splendid reception and dinner.

- February 9:

  On the train through Janesville, Wisconsin and on to the end of the rail line at LaCrosse in the afternoon. Travel continued by sleigh up the frozen Mississippi River to Winona, Minnesota and another grand dinner then resumed and arrived at Minneiska at dark. Attended a "Show" in town and a dance until midnight then stayed at a hotel.

- February 10:

  Took the sleighs to Wabasha and Lake City where they had supper and traveled on to Red Wing arriving at 11 PM to enthusiastic reception and a large banquet.

- February 11:

  Started at 5 AM for Hastings, stopped for dinner, went on to St. Paul and a "Grand Reception".

- February 12:

  Men are given furloughs as quickly as possible and released to go home to see their families.

- April 28:

    Regiment is assembled at Fort Snelling for a final Grand Review.
- May 4, 5, 6:

    Regiment is paid off, discharged and mustered out of service.

BIBLIOGRAPHY

Ashbury, John, "The Gangs of New York"' , New York, 1928

Bassett, Morton H., *"From Bull Run to Bristow Station"* , St. Paul, MN., 1962

Board of Commissioners, *"Minnesota in the Civil & Indian Wars" Volumes 1 & 2*, St. Paul MN, 1890

Bowman, John S., *"The Civil War Day by Day"*, Greenwich, CT, 1989

Canton, Bruce, *"Army of the Potomac: A Stillness Appomattox", Garden City, New York, 1953*

Canton, Bruce, *"Army of the Potomac: Glory Road"*, Garden City, New York, 1952

Canton, Bruce, *"Army of the Potomac: Mr. Lincoln's Army"*, Garden City, New York, 1962

Canton, Bruce, *"Grant Takes Command"*, Boston, Toronto, 1969

Canton, Bruce, *"Picture History of the Civil War"*, Avenel, New Jersey, 1960

Carley, Kenneth, *"Minnesota in the Civil War"*, St. Paul, MN, 2000

Christianson, Theodore, *"History of Minnesota"*, Volumes 1-5. Chicago, IL & New York, NY. 1935

Commager, Henry Steele, *"The Blue and the Gray"* Volumes 1- 2, New York, NY, 1950

Dyer, John D. *"The Gallant Hood"*, New York, NY, 1950

Foote, Shelby, *"Fort Sumter to Perryville"*, New York, 1986

Foote, Shelby, *"Fredericksburg to Meridian"*, New York, 1986

Foote, Shelby, *"Red River to Appomattox"*, New York, 1974

Goff, Al, *" Nobles County History"*, St. Paul, MN.,1958

Hennessy, John J., *"Return to Bull Run"*, Oklahoma University Press, 1999

Holcombe, Return I, *"History of the First Regiment Minnesota Volunteer Infantry,* Stillwater, MN, 2006

Hunter, Alexander, *Johnny Reb & Billy Yank"*, New York, NY, 1904

Leehan, Brian, *"Pale Horse at Plum Run"*, St. Paul, MN, 2002

McPherson, "Ordeal By Fire", McGraw-Hill 2001

Mitchell, Reid, *"Civil War Soldiers"*, New York, NY, 1988

Norton, Oliver Willcox, *"The Attack & Defense of Little Round Top, Gettysburg, July 2, 1863"*, New York, NY, 1913

Pfanz, Harry W., *"Gettysburg the Second Day"*, University of North Carolina, 1987

Priest, John Michael, *"Antietam, The Soldier's Battle"*, Oxford University Press, 1989

Moe, Richard, *"The Last Full Measure"*, New York, NY, 1993

Nevins, Allan, *"The War for the Union"* Volumes 1-4, New York, NY, 1959

Robertson, James I., *"General A. P. Hill, The Story of a Confederate Warrior"*, New York, 1987

Robinson, Charles M., *"Shark of the Confederacy"*, Annapolis, MD., 1995

Robotham, Tom, *"The Civil War"*, Greenwich, CT, 1992

Rodenbough, Theo. F., *"The Bravest 500 of '61"*, New York, NY 1891

Sandburg, Carl, *"Abraham Lincoln"* New York, NY, 1954

Stackpole, Edward J., *"The Fredericksburg Campaign"*, Harrisburg, PA, 1957

Sully, Langdon, *"No Tears for the General"*, Palo Alto, CA, 1975

Wheeler, Richard, *"Witness to Gettysburg"*, Edison, NJ, 1994

Wiley, Bell Irvin, *"The life of Johnny Reb"*, Indianapolis, IN & New York, NY, 1943

Wiley, Bell Irvin, *"The Life of Billy Yank"*, Indianapolis, IN & New York, NY, 1952

Winik, Jay, *" April 1865, The Month That Saved America"*, New York, NY, 2001

Wright, James A., *"No More Gallant a Deed"*, St. Paul, MN, 2001

INDEX

Army of The Potomac
In Seven Days Battles, 207
Army of Virginia, 243, 253
Ashby's Gap, 328

B

B & O Railroad, 140
Baker, Colonel Edward, 97, 117
Killed at Ball's Bluff, 97
Ball, Capt. John-1st MN. Co. F, 466, 477
Bank's Ford, 405, 406
Banks, General Nathaniel, 140, 148, 266
Shenandoah Valley Campaign, 148
Barksdale, General William, 464
Barnum's Museum, 536
Bassett, Anna
Sister of Edward, 9, 55
Bassett, Edward H., 1, 14, 595
Account of Capt. Messick's death., 565
At Bull Run, 42
Mine Run Account., 590
Wounded at Bristoe Station, 562
Withdrawal from Peninsula, 256
Account of 2nd Fredericksburg, 415
Account of Battle of Fredericksburg, 346
Account of fight on Vienna Road, 268
At 2nd Malvern Hill, 249
At Bristoe Station, 555
Baking biscuits, 241
Gettysburg letters, 493
Grave site, 685
Married Hattie A. King, 682
Meets Rebels he fought at Seven Days and Gettysburg, 653
Move to Fredrick City, 279
Reenlists in 1st. MN. Heavy Artillery, 632
Sergeant– In 1st MN. Heavy Artillery, 634
Bassett, Elford
Brother of Edward, 9
Bassett, Elmer H., 684

Bassett, George, 106, 118
Brother to Edward, 11
Notice of his death, 178
Bassett, Morton, 622, 632, 682
Battle of Allen's Farm, 211
Battle of Antietam, 284
Battle of Ball's Bluff, 96
Battle of Chancellorsville, overview, 405
Battle of South Mountain, 279
Baxter
Col. D. C., 579
Bealeton Station, 528
Bealton Station, 558
Beauregard, General Piere G. T., 38
At Bull Run, 40
Benson, Charles Merill
Wounded at Bristoe, 561
Beophy, James, 13
Berryville, 149
Berryville Conservator, 149
Big Bend, Tenn., 643
Big Bethel, 162
Black Horse Cavalry, 42, 53
Blakely, Russell, 621
Bloomer, Samuel
Wounded at Antietam, 288
Blue Ridge Mountains, 328
Bolivar Heights, Virginia, 145, 304, 323
Boonsborough, 278, 283
Booth, John Wilkes
Death, 647
Brackett's Ford, 215
Bragg, General Braxton, 542
Brandy Station, 544, 547, 558, 614
Bristoe Campaign, 542
Bristoe Station, 544, 553
Rebel losses, 565
Broad Run, 553
Brooklyn, NY.–Fort Green, 536
Brown, W. W., 156
Buford, 455, 456, 546
At Gettysburg–holds the high ground, 456
Bull Run, 557
First Battle of, 37
Bull Run, Map, 40

717